Ready®
Common Core

2 Mathematics
INSTRUCTION
Teacher Resource Book

Teacher Advisors

Crystal Bailey, Math Impact Teacher, Eastern Guilford Middle School, Guilford County Schools, Gibsonville, NC

Max Brand, Reading Specialist, Indian Run Elementary, Dublin City School District, Dublin, OH

Helen Comba, Supervisor of Basic Skills & Language Arts, School District of the Chathams, Chatham, NJ

Cindy Dean, Classroom Teacher, Mt. Diablo Unified School District, Concord, CA

Randall E. Groth, Ph.D, Associate Professor of Mathematics Education, Salisbury University, Salisbury, MD

Bill Laraway, Classroom Teacher, Silver Oak Elementary, Evergreen School District, San Jose, CA

Jennifer Lerner, Classroom Teacher, PS 57, New York City Public Schools, New York, NY

Susie Legg, Elementary Curriculum Coordinator, Kansas City Public Schools, Kansas City, KS

Sarah Levine, Classroom Teacher, Springhurst Elementary School, Dobbs Ferry School District, Dobbs Ferry, NY

Nicole Peirce, Classroom Teacher, Eleanor Roosevelt Elementary, Pennsbury School District, Morrisville, PA

Donna Phillips, Classroom Teacher, Farmington R-7 School District, Farmington, MO

Maria Rosati, Classroom Teacher, Harwood Elementary School, Warren Consolidated Schools, Warren, MI

Kari Ross, Reading Specialist, MN

Sunita Sangari, Math Coach, PS/MS 29, New York City Public Schools, New York, NY

Eileen Seybuck, Classroom Teacher, PS 57, New York City Public Schools, New York, NY

Mark Hoover Thames, Research Scientist, University of Michigan, Ann Arbor, MI

Shannon Tsuruda, Classroom Teacher, Mt. Diablo Unified School District, Concord, CA

Acknowledgments

Vice President of Product Development: Adam Berkin
Editorial Director: Cindy Tripp
Executive Editor: Kathy Kellman
Supervising Editors: Pam Halloran, Lauren Van Wart

Project Manager: Grace Izzi
Cover Design: Matt Pollock
Cover Illustrator: O'Lamar Gibson
Book Design: Jeremy Spiegel

Table of Contents

Table of Contents

M = Lessons that have a major emphasis in the Common Core Standards
S/A = Lessons that have supporting/additional emphasis in the Common Core Standards
Standards in boldface are the focus standards that address major lesson content.

	Standards	Embedded SMPs	Emphasis

Mathematics Lessons, *continued*

Welcome to *Ready*® Mathematics

Ready Mathematics prepares students for mastery of the Common Core's rigorous standards through a balance of conceptual understanding, procedural skills, fluency, and application.

Ready's clear, thoughtful pedagogy and research-based instructional model supports a rich classroom environment in which mathematical reasoning, mathematical discourse, and a range of mathematical practices thrive.

Rigor that is reachable

- Uses real-world problem solving as instruction to develop deep conceptual understanding

- Presents multiple representations to make connections and show the conceptual meaning behind procedural fluency

- Connects new problems to prior knowledge, demonstrates multiple approaches, and provides multiple access points to learning

- Strengthens students' ability to use critical thinking and complex reasoning through questions that focus on higher DOK levels

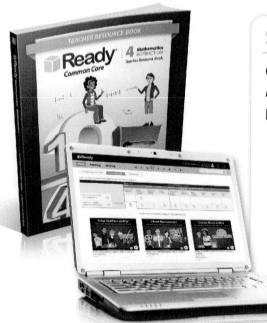

Support that simplifies

Offering step-by-step guidance and embedded teacher support, *Ready Mathematics'* teacher tools are simple to implement and support powerful, effective teaching

- A comprehensive Teacher Resource Book provides point-of-use strategies, tips, and mathematical discourse for teaching every step of every lesson

- A K–8 Online Teacher Toolbox offers a virtual filing cabinet of instructional resources to support teaching throughout the year

- A rich array of assessment tools helps monitor student progress and guide responsive instruction

Meet Our *Ready*® **Mathematics** Authors

Ready Mathematics was built to reflect the connection between the latest research and practical classroom application. Guidance from our program's authors continues to shape *Ready* to ensure that it is rigorous for students yet easy to implement for teachers.

Mark Ellis, Ph.D.

 Awards & Key Positions

- Board of Directors, Executive Committee, NCTM
- Department Chair and Professor, Education, CSU Fullerton
- National Board Certified Teacher

 Known for Research On

- Middle grades mathematics teaching and learning
- Equity, discourse, and technology in mathematics education
- Preparation of teachers of mathematics

Gladis Kersaint, Ph.D.

 Awards & Key Positions

- Board of Directors, Executive Committee, NCTM
- Board of Directors, Association of Mathematics Teacher Educators
- Dean of the Neag School of Education, University of Connecticut

 Known for Research On

- Equity and discourse in mathematics education
- Middle grades mathematics teaching and learning
- Preparation of teachers of mathematics

Program Components

Ready®

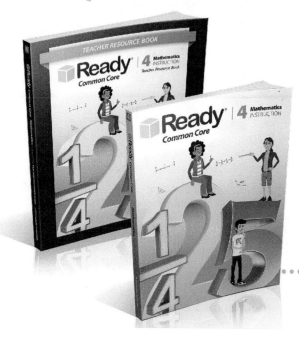

Instruction Books
- Addresses every Common Core State Standard with clear, thoughtful instruction
- Provides step-by-step guidance and point-of-use support on every page to support teachers

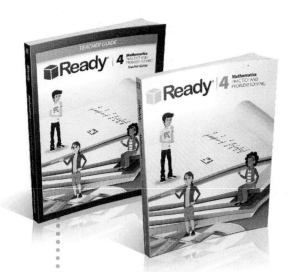

Practice and Problem Solving Books

For every lesson:
- Family Letter
- Practice for each section in *Ready* Instruction

For every unit:
- Unit Games
- Unit Practice
- Unit Performance Tasks
- Unit Vocabulary
- Fluency Practice Worksheets

Assessment Books
Three full-length benchmark assessments that match the latest consortia guidance

Ready® Instruction, *Practice and Problem Solving*, and *Assessments* are available on the Teacher Toolbox.

Online Teacher Toolbox
(Teacher-Toolbox.com)

The easy-to-use **Online Teacher Toolbox** is a virtual filing cabinet of instructional resources designed to address the needs of all learners and differentiate instruction.

Complete access to all K–8 content:

- Interactive Tutorials
- *Ready Instruction* Prerequisite Lesson PDFs
- Tools for Instruction PDFs
- Center Activities PDFs
- Lesson Quiz PDFs
- Mid-Unit and Unit Assessments

Ready Central

Online teacher portal with resources including:

- Training videos
- Planning tools
- Implementation tips
- Discourse support

i-Ready®
(i-Ready.com)

Online Assessment and Instruction
i-Ready integrates powerful assessments with engaging instruction to help all students grow and succeed.

*Spanish Diagnostic Available

Using *Ready*® with *i-Ready*®: Program Overview

Whether using the *i-Ready*®/*Ready*® blended program or *Ready* as a stand-alone program, you have the flexibility to meet all your instruction and assessment needs.

Diagnose and Monitor

Adaptive Diagnostic and Growth Monitoring
i-Ready® Diagnostic

45–60 minutes, 3 times a year

Adaptive diagnostic designed to collect a broad spectrum of information on student ability to identify where students are struggling, measure growth across a student's career, and plan instructional paths with a single measurement tool

Standards Mastery Monitoring
i-Ready® Standards Mastery

10-15 minutes per standard

Our new Standards Mastery tool provides targeted insight into student's mastery of individual, grade-level standards.

Alternatively, the following *Ready* assessment tools can be used instead of *i-Ready*. For pacing recommendations see pages A42–A45.

- **Growth Monitoring:**
  Ready Assessments
- **Standards Mastery Monitoring:**
  Ready Instruction Interim Assessments

Instruct

Whole Class Instruction
Ready® Books and
Online Teacher Toolbox

Small Group Differentiation
Ready® Online Teacher Toolbox

Personalized Learning
i-Ready® Instruction

Instruct
Ready® Instruction

**45–60 min per day,
1 lesson per week**

Teacher-led whole and small group instruction

Practice
Ready® Practice and Problem Solving

20–30 min per day

Practice that can be assigned after every section of the *Ready* lesson for use in class, after school, or at home

Assess
Lesson Quiz and Unit Assessment PDFs

**15–20 min per quiz,
30-45 min per assessment**

Lesson Quizzes and Unit Assessments assess students on lesson and unit content and identify the need for reteaching

Reteach
Ready® Instruction Prerequisite Lesson PDFs

45–90 min per lesson

Teacher-led in-depth instruction using *Ready* lessons from earlier grades to review prerequisite concepts or fill in gaps in student knowledge

Student-Led Activity
Math Center Activity PDFs

20–30 min per activity

Student-led games and activities available for each standard in three different versions for use with on-level, below level, and above level groups

Teacher-Led Activity
Tools for Instruction PDFs

20–30 min per activity

Teacher-led activities for use with small groups of students requiring additional instruction on a prerequisite or on-level skill

Online Instruction
i-Ready® Instruction

At least 45 min per week

Animated, interactive lessons that allow students to work independently on their personalized online instruction plan

Answering the Demands of the Common Core with *Ready*®

The Common Core State Standards have raised the rigor for mathematics instruction in several important ways. *Ready Mathematics* has been written to specifically address those shifts.

Demand: Focus

Ready Mathematics lessons reflect the same focus as the Common Core standards.

- The majority of the lessons in each grade directly address the major focus of the year.

- Each lesson was newly written specifically to address the Common Core Standards.

- There is at least one lesson for each standard and only lessons that address the Common Core Standards are included.

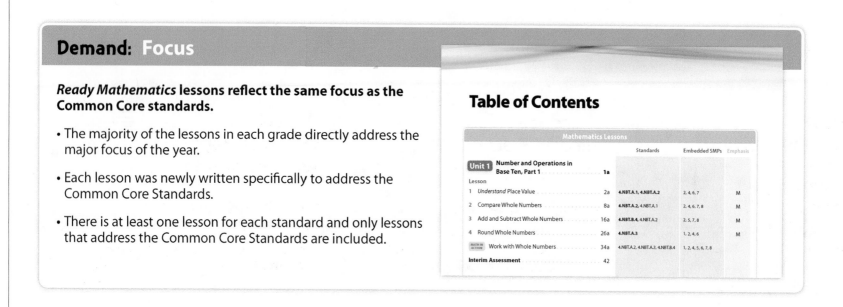

Demand: Rigor and Higher-Order Thinking

Ready Mathematics lessons balance conceptual understanding, skill and procedural fluency, and applications.

- Students are required to use different cognitive strategies as they respond to problem situations of varying difficulty levels.

- Students are asked higher-order thinking questions throughout the lessons as they discuss and interpret concepts, multiple representations, applications, and skills and strategies.

- Students must be able to explain their thinking, critique the reasoning of others, and generalize their results.

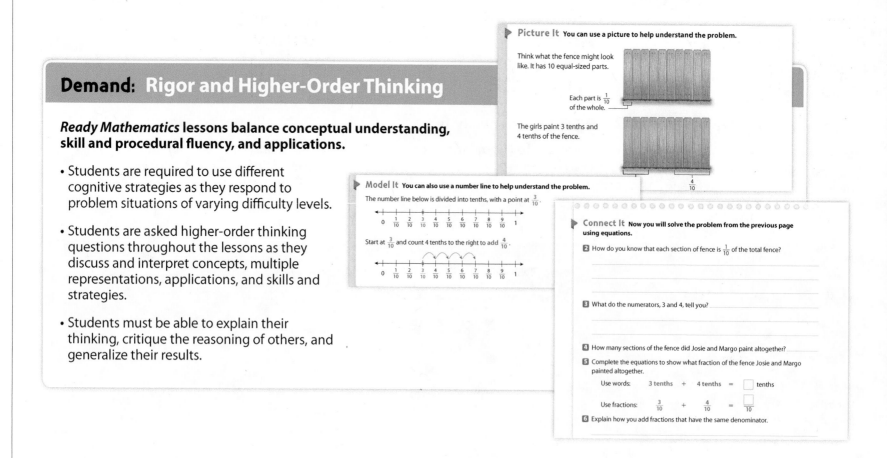

Demand: Mathematical Reasoning

Ready Mathematics **lessons build on problem solving as a main component of instruction.**

- Students analyze problems, determine effective strategies to solve them, and evaluate the reasonableness of their solutions.

- Students work through problems, discuss them, draw conclusions, and make generalizations.

- Guided Practice problems ask students to critique arguments presented by fictional characters and justify their own solutions.

18 Emily ate $\frac{1}{6}$ of a bag of carrots. Nick ate $\frac{2}{6}$ of the bag of carrots. What fraction of the bag of carrots did Emily and Nick eat altogether? Circle the letter of the correct answer.

A $\frac{1}{6}$

B $\frac{1}{3}$

C $\frac{3}{6}$

D $\frac{3}{12}$

Rob chose **D** as the correct answer. How did he get that answer?

_____

_____

To find the fraction of the bag Emily and Nick ate altogether, should you add or subtract?

Pair/Share
Does Rob's answer make sense?

Demand: Coherence

Ready Mathematics **lessons build on prior knowledge, making connections within and across clusters and domains, and within and across grade levels.**

- Each lesson starts by referencing prior knowledge and connecting to what students already know.

- These connections allow students to see math as more than just a set of rules and isolated procedures to develop a deeper knowledge of mathematics.

- Connections are highlighted in the Learning Progressions of the Teacher Resource Book so teachers can see at a glance how the lesson connects to previous and future learning.

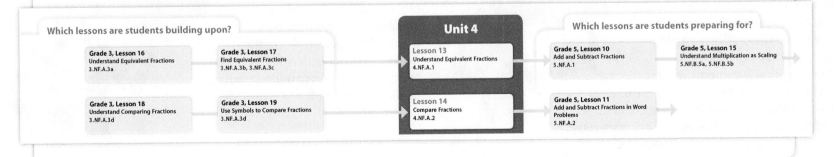

Which lessons are students building upon?

Grade 3, Lesson 16
Understand Equivalent Fractions
3.NF.A.3a

Grade 3, Lesson 17
Find Equivalent Fractions
3.NF.A.3b, 3.NF.A.3c

Grade 3, Lesson 18
Understand Comparing Fractions
3.NF.A.3d

Grade 3, Lesson 19
Use Symbols to Compare Fractions
3.NF.A.3d

Unit 4

Lesson 13
Understand Equivalent Fractions
4.NF.A.1

Lesson 14
Compare Fractions
4.NF.A.2

Which lessons are students preparing for?

Grade 5, Lesson 10
Add and Subtract Fractions
5.NF.A.1

Grade 5, Lesson 15
Understand Multiplication as Scaling
5.NF.B.5a, 5.NF.B.5b

Grade 5, Lesson 11
Add and Subtract Fractions in Word Problems
5.NF.A.2

The Standards for Mathematical Practice

The Standards for Mathematical Practice, which support the teaching of the content standards through intentional, appropriate use, are fully integrated throughout each lesson in the *Ready* Student Book. The Teacher Resource Book includes SMP Tips that provide more in-depth information for select practice standards addressed in the lessons.

1 Make sense of problems and persevere in solving them.

Try more than one approach, think strategically, and succeed in solving problems that seem very difficult.

Ready lessons lead students through new problems by using what they already know, demonstrate multiple approaches and access points, and give encouraging tips and opportunities for cooperative dialogue.

2 Reason abstractly and quantitatively.

Represent a word problem with an equation, or other symbols, solve the math, and then interpret the solution to answer the question posed.

Ready lessons lead students to see mathematical relationships connecting equations, visual representations, and problem situations. Each lesson challenges students to analyze the connection between an abstract representation and pictorial or real-world situations.

3 Construct viable arguments and critique the reasoning of others.

Discuss, communicate reasoning, create explanations, and critique the reasoning of others.

In *Ready* lessons, the teacher-led Mathematical Discourse feature guides students through collaborative reasoning and the exchange of ideas and mathematical arguments. *Ready* lessons also provide error-analysis exercises that ask students to examine a fictional student's wrong answer, as well as multiple opportunities to explain and communicate reasoning.

4 Model with mathematics.

Use math to solve actual problems.

In *Ready* lessons, students create a mathematical model using pictures, diagrams, tables, or equations to solve problems. In the Teacher Resource Book, the Real-World Connection feature adds another dimension to understanding application of a skill.

Use appropriate tools strategically.

Make choices about which tools, if any, to use to solve a problem.

Ready lessons model the use of a variety of tools, including diagrams, tables, or number lines. Guided Practice problems may be solved with a variety of strategies that involve the use of tools.

 Attend to precision.

Explain and argue, draw, label, and compute carefully and accurately.

Ready lessons guide students to focus on precision in both procedures and communication, including special error-analysis tasks and group discussion questions that motivate students to employ precise, convincing arguments.

Look for and make use of structure.

Build mathematical understanding by recognizing structures such as place value, decomposition of numbers, and the structure of fractions.

Ready lessons build understanding of new concepts by explicitly reviewing prior knowledge of mathematical structure.

 Look for and express regularity in repeated reasoning.

Recognize regularity in repeated reasoning and make generalizations or conjectures about other situations.

Ready lessons lead students to focus attention on patterns that reflect regularity. Where appropriate, students draw a conclusion or make a generalization and explain their reasoning by referencing the observed pattern.

Supporting Research

Ready® Mathematics is founded on research from a variety of federal initiatives, national mathematics organizations, and experts in mathematics. As a result, this program may be used in support of several instructional models.

Ready® Uses ...	Examples	Research Says ...
Scaffolded Instruction		
Scaffolded instruction is the gradual withdrawal of support through modeled, guided, and independent instruction.	*Ready* lessons follow the pattern of modeled and guided instruction, modeled and guided practice, and independent practice.	"*Successful teachers help to create independent learners ... Contingent scaffolded instruction ... is a powerful tool for achieving this goal.*" —Beed et al., 1991
Applying Prior Knowledge		
These are experiences and knowledge that a student brings with himself or herself to learn about a topic.	In each *Ready* lesson, **Use What You Know** introduces a new skill by guiding students to solve a new problem by applying prior knowledge.	"*What and how students are taught should reflect not only the topics that fall within a certain academic discipline, but also the key ideas that determine how knowledge is organized and generated within that discipline.*" —Schmidt, Houang, & Cogan, 2002
Collaborative Learning		
Students work together in pairs or small groups to attain their individual goals.	*Ready* lessons provide multiple opportunities for collaborative learning. • **Talk About It** leads students through discussions of key ideas. • **Pair/Share** prompts students to compare answers and reasoning to identify misconceptions.	"*Collaborative learning improves computational skills. Use of cooperative or collaborative learning has been advocated in various mathematics education reports and in state curricular frameworks, policies, and instructional guidelines.*" —National Mathematics Advisory Panel, 2008
Visual Representation		
Visual representation is using an image to help describe or define a mathematical problem or relationship, or to depict a real-life problem situation.	*Ready* routinely uses visual representations as part of instruction. • **Picture It** and other visual models such as number lines (**Model It**) illustrate mathematical concepts. • **Visual Support** in the Teacher Resource Books suggests additional visual representations.	"*Graphic representations of mathematical concepts and problems ... are crucial components of programs used in nations that perform well on international comparisons, such as Singapore, Korea, or the Netherlands.*" —NCTM, 2007

Ready® Uses ...	Examples	Research Says ...
Mathematical Discourse		
Mathematical Discourse in instruction uses questioning, listening, writing, and reflection to encourage conversation about mathematics.	*Ready* lessons include regular verbal exchange of ideas and sharing of understanding in whole group, small group, and pair settings. • **Talk About It** leads students through discussions of key ideas. • **Pair/Share** prompts students to compare answers and reasoning to identify misconceptions. • **Mathematical Discourse** in the Teacher Resource Book suggests thoughtful question prompts.	"*The process of encouraging students to verbalize their thinking—by talking, writing, or drawing the steps they used in solving a problem—was consistently effective.*" —NCTM, 2007)
Multiple Representations		
Multiple representations are the ways in which a teacher or student represents a math idea, including spoken, written, symbolic, and concrete formats.	*Ready* lessons routinely use multiple representations to illustrate mathematical concepts. • **Connect It** develops the symbolic representation. • **Hands-On Activities** and **Visual Support** in the Teacher Resource Book offer suggestions for additional representations.	"*The usefulness of numerical ideas is enhanced when students encounter and use multiple representations for the same concept.*" —National Research Council, 2001
Formative Assessment		
Formative assessment (or Progress Monitoring) is a strategy that involves frequent, in-classroom progress checks of students' understanding and mastery of math concepts and skills.	*Ready* lessons are structured so teachers can monitor understanding throughout. • **Solutions and Explanations** with **Error Alerts** in the Teacher Resource Books create ongoing formative assessment opportunities, with support for correcting misconceptions throughout each lesson. • **Assessment and Remediation** charts at the end of the lesson help the teacher assess mastery of the skill, identify specific misconceptions, and remediate on the spot as necessary.	"*Teachers' regular use of formative assessment improves their students' learning, especially if teachers have additional guidance on using the assessment to design and to individualize instruction.*" —National Mathematics Advisory Panel, 2008
Hands-On Activities		
Hands-On Activities are any activities in which the student is handling manipulatives used to explore mathematical quantities, relationships, or operations.	Hands-on Activities are found throughout the Teacher Resource Book, both at point-of-use during instruction, and at the end of the lesson.	"*The benefit of this [hands-on, manipulative] approach may be that its intensity and concreteness help students maintain a framework in their working memory for solving problems of this type.*" —NCTM, 2007

Supporting Research, *continued*

Ready® Uses ...	Examples	Research Says ...
Differentiated Instruction		
Differentiated Instruction is an approach to teaching that gives students multiple ways to access and make sense of mathematical ideas.	*Ready* lessons provide a full range of support for differentiating instruction. • *Ready* Student Books provide verbal, visual, and symbolic representations of each new skill and concept. • **Hands-On Activities, Visual Support, Concept Extension,** and **Challenge Activities** in the Teacher Resource Books provide additional differentiation options.	"*Many teachers and teacher educators have recently identified differentiated instruction as a method of helping more students in diverse classroom settings experience success.*" —Hall et al., 2003
Conceptual Understanding		
Conceptual understanding is the knowledge of why math processes and rules work.	All *Ready* lessons begin by laying a foundation of conceptual understanding of the mathematical principles underlying the skill being addressed. • **Understand** lessons put a special emphasis on these principles. • **Concept Extension** features in the Teacher Resource Book further support conceptual understanding.	"*To prepare students for Algebra, the curriculum must simultaneously develop conceptual understanding, computational fluency, and problem-solving skills.*" —National Mathematics Advisory Panel, 2008
Computational Fluency		
Computational fluency is having quick recall of number facts and knowledge and ability to apply multiple computational methods involving whole numbers, decimals, fractions, and other numbers as appropriate to the grade level.	*Ready* lessons all directly address computation skills, develop the conceptual understanding to support computation, or provide applications of computation skills.	"*Basic skills with numbers continue to be vitally important for a variety of everyday uses. They also provide a crucial foundation for the higher-level mathematics essential for success in the workplace, which must now also be part of a basic education.*" —Ball et al., 2005
Problem Solving (or Application)		
Problem solving (or Application) is the process of formulating a real-life problem as a mathematical problem, then performing the calculations necessary, and interpreting the result to find the solution to the problem.	Problem solving is at the heart of *Ready*. • *Ready* presents new math problems in real-world contexts and models finding the solution in **Use What You Know, Picture It, Model It, Connect It.** Students then practice with similar problems in **Try It.** • Independent Practice problems always include real-world problems.	"*... An important part of our conception of mathematical proficiency involves the ability to formulate and solve problems coming from daily life or other domains, including mathematics itself.*" —National Research Council, 2001

Meeting New Expectations &
Best Practices

What Ready Mathematics
Instruction Looks Like

How to Implement
Ready Mathematics

Ready® Uses …	Examples	Research Says …

Standards for Mathematical Practice

Standards for Mathematical Practice (SMP) identify habits of mind and everyday ways of approaching math that are hallmarks of successful math students.	The Standards for Mathematical Practice (SMP) are an integral part of *Ready* instruction. • The **Mathematical Practices Handbook** at the front of the Student Book serves as reference for students. • Throughout the *Ready* Student Book, SMPs are built into the instruction and problems. • Teacher Resource Books feature SMP Tips in every lesson to alert teachers to particular instances of each SMP.	"*These practices rest on important 'processes and proficiencies' with longstanding importance in mathematics education.*" —CCSS, 2010

ELL Support

ELL support provides teachers with the content knowledge and pedagogy to minimize obstacles to learning math due to language or cultural issues.	*Ready* lessons use many approaches to help teachers support ELL students. • The *Ready* Student Book uses pictorial and visual representations combined with direct simple text to clearly present concepts. • Point-of-use **ELL Support** tips for teachers are found throughout the Teacher Resource Book as appropriate. • Language Objectives are included in the Teacher Resource Book for all lessons.	"*Expanded opportunities should be available to English language learners (ELL students) who need them to develop mathematical understanding and proficiency.*" —NCTM, 2008

Answer Explanations for Students

As a part of scaffolded instruction, students receive immediate feedback on their answer choices and the reasoning behind correct and incorrect answers.	In the **Guided Instruction, Guided Practice, Independent Practice,** and **Interim Assessment** sections of the Teacher Resource Book, answer explanations are given for each question.	"*When students receive direct instruction about the reasons why an answer choice is correct or incorrect, they demonstrate long-term retention and understanding of newly learned content.*" —Pashler et al., 2007

Cognitive Rigor and *Ready*®

The following table combines the hierarchies of learning from both Webb and Bloom. For each level of hierarchy, descriptions of student behaviors that would fulfill expectations at each of the four DOK levels are given. For example, when students compare solution methods, there isn't a lower-rigor (DOK 1 or 2) way of truly assessing this skill.

Depth of Thinking (Webb) + Type of Thinking (Revised Bloom)	DOK Level 1 **Recall & Reproduction**	DOK Level 2 **Basic Skills & Concepts**	DOK Level 3 **Strategic Thinking & Reasoning**	DOK Level 4 **Extended Thinking**
Remember	• Recall conversations, terms, facts			
Understand	• Evaluate an expression • Locate points on a grid or number on number line • Solve a one-step problem • Represent math relationships in words, pictures, or symbols	• Specify, explain relationships • Make basic inferences or logical predictions from data/observations • Use models/diagrams to explain concepts • Make and explain estimates	• Use concepts to solve non-routine problems • Use supporting evidence to justify conjectures, generalize, or connect ideas • Explain reasoning when more than one response is possible	• Relate mathematical concepts to other content areas, other domains • Develop generalizations of the results obtained and the strategies used and apply them to new problem situations
Apply	• Follow simple procedures • Calculate, measure, apply a rule (e.g., rounding) • Apply algorithm or formula • Solve linear equations • Make conversions	• Select a procedure and perform it • Solve routine problem applying multiple concepts or decision points • Retrieve information to solve a problem • Translate between representations	• Design investigation for a specific purpose or research question • Use reasoning, planning, and supporting evidence • Translate between problem and symbolic notation when not a direct translation	• Initiate, design, and conduct a project that specifies a problem, identifies solution paths, solves the problem, and reports results
Analyze	• Retrieve information from a table or graph to answer a question • Identify a pattern/trend	• Categorize data, figures • Organize, order data • Select appropriate graph and organize and display data • Interpret data from a simple graph • Extend a pattern	• Compare information within or across data sets or texts • Analyze and draw conclusions from data, citing evidence • Generalize a pattern • Interpret data from complex graph	• Analyze multiple sources of evidence or data sets
Evaluate			• Cite evidence and develop a logical argument • Compare/contrast solution methods • Verify reasonableness	• Apply understanding in a novel way, provide argument or justification for the new application
Create	• Brainstorm ideas, concepts, problems, or perspectives related to a topic or concept	• Generate conjectures or hypotheses based on observations or prior knowledge and experience	• Develop an alternative solution • Synthesize information within one data set	• Synthesize information across multiple sources or data sets • Design a model to inform and solve a practical or abstract situation

The following table shows the *Ready*® lessons and sections with higher-complexity items, as measured by Webb's Depth of Knowledge index.

Depth of Knowledge Level 3 Items in *Ready Mathematics*

Lesson	Section	Item	Lesson	Section	Item
1	Guided Practice	12	14	Independent Practice	6
1	Guided Practice	14	15	Guided Practice	9
1	Independent Practice	15	15	Independent Practice	6
2	Guided Practice	15	Unit 2	Interim Assessment	6
2	Independent Practice	5	16	Guided Practice	16
2	Independent Practice	6	16	Independent Practice	17
3	Guided Practice	12	17	Guided Practice	16
3	Guided Practice	13	17	Independent Practice	6
3	Guided Practice	14	18	Guided Practice	12
3	Independent Practice	15	18	Guided Practice	13
4	Guided Practice	12	18	Guided Practice	14
4	Guided Practice	13	19	Guided Practice	13
4	Guided Practice	14	19	Guided Practice	14
4	Independent Practice	15	19	Guided Practice	15
5	Guided Practice	9	19	Independent Practice	16
5	Independent Practice	4	20	Guided Practice	15
5	Independent Practice	5	20	Independent Practice	5
6	Guided Practice	17	21	Guided Practice	15
6	Independent Practice	6	21	Independent Practice	6
Unit 1	Interim Assessment	5	22	Guided Practice	15
Unit 1	Interim Assessment	6	22	Guided Practice	16
7	Guided Practice	15	22	Independent Practice	17
7	Independent Practice	5	23	Guided Practice	15
7	Independent Practice	6	23	Independent Practice	5
8	Guided Practice	16	24	Guided Practice	9
8	Independent Practice	5	24	Independent Practice	6
8	Independent Practice	6	25	Guided Practice	15
9	Guided Practice	14	25	Independent Practice	6
9	Independent Practice	6	Unit 3	Interim Assessment	6
10	Guided Practice	11	26	Guided Practice	12
10	Guided Practice	12	26	Independent Practice	6
10	Independent Practice	14	27	Guided Practice	14
11	Guided Practice	9	27	Independent Practice	15
11	Independent Practice	4	28	Guided Practice	14
12	Guided Practice	15	28	Guided Practice	15
12	Independent Practice	5	28	Guided Practice	16
12	Independent Practice	6	28	Independent Practice	17
13	Guided Practice	14	Unit 4	Interim Assessment	5
13	Independent Practice	6	Unit 4	Interim Assessment	6
14	Guided Practice	14			

Built for Rigor and Engagement

The Common Core State Standards demand instruction that balances conceptual understanding, procedural skills and fluency, and application. **Ready Mathematics** achieves this balance with lessons that develop understanding and procedural fluency in tandem so students can easily apply what they have learned to new situations.

The **Mathematical Practices Handbook** helps students develop the habits of mind used by proficient mathematical thinkers. Presented in student-friendly language, it serves as a reference for students throughout the year.

Skills and Strategy lessons focus on helping students acquire and apply efficient procedures for calculation and symbolic representation. They teach a skill, procedure, or algorithm using models and multiple representations to connect to understanding.

Lessons that begin with **Understand** in the title focus on developing conceptual understanding. Occurring at critical points in the instruction sequence, these lessons help students connect new concepts to familiar ones as they learn new skills and strategies.

Math in Action lessons feature open-ended problems with many points of entry and more than one possible solution. Students interact with an exemplary response modeling the problem-solving process, then apply that thinking to solve complex problems that integrate multiple standards.

Table of Contents

Standards in boldface are the focus standards that address major lesson content.

Table of Contents **iii**

Student Instruction Book

Structure of a *Ready* Lesson*

Engaging **Ready** lessons develop mathematical reasoning through rigorous real-world problem solving as instruction. **Ready** provides ongoing opportunities for cooperative dialogue and mathematical discourse, strengthening students' ability to use higher-order thinking and complex reasoning.

Part of the Lesson	Teacher Actions	Student Actions
Introduction Activates prior knowledge, connecting what students already know with the new skills and concepts they will be learning in the lesson. **Modeled and Guided Instruction** Explores ways to solve problems using multiple representations and prompts students to reason and explain their thinking.	• Allows student think time • Supports effective partner communication • Facilitates whole class discourse of student discussions • Guides students to connect multiple strategies • Encourages effort • Recognizes mistakes as opportunities for learning	• Perseveres in thinking about problems and questions • Actively listens to partners and whole class conversations • Participates in small group and whole class conversations, politely critiquing the reasoning of others • Solves problems using multiple strategies or mathematical tools • Recognizes mistakes as opportunities to learn • Applies learning to new problems
Guided Practice Models self-questioning and mathematical habits of mind as students solve problems and discuss their solution strategies. **Independent Practice** Provides problems in a variety of assessment formats that integrate and extend concepts and skills.	• Observes student strategies • Asks questions to guide or correct understanding • Differentiates instruction as needed in stations or small groups	

* The majority of the lessons in *Ready Mathematics* follow the format shown above.

What does *Ready* Instruction Look Like?

The Think-Share-Compare instructional routine is the recommended framework for teaching most *Ready Mathematics* lessons. With this routine, teachers can easily and confidently engage students in discourse and the mathematical practices while using standards-aligned teaching practices.

Think-Share-Compare Routine

What Is It?

The *Ready* Think-Share-Compare Routine helps students achieve greater mathematical proficiency and rigor within a collaborative structure. Students develop greater understanding of mathematical models and strategies using think time, partner talk, individual writing, and whole class discourse.

When to Use It

Use the Think-Share-Compare Routine during the Introduction and Modeled and Guided Instruction sections of the *Ready* lessons.

Why It Matters

There are many ways to approach mathematical thinking and solutions to problems, but when only one way is presented, students may think they "didn't do it right," even when their solution process or thinking is accurate. Exposing students to a number of models and approaches helps them:

- Build mathematical confidence.
- Make connections between representations.
- Develop flexible thinking.
- Deepen and extend conceptual understanding.
- Construct viable arguments and politely critique the reasoning of others.
- Stay engaged, focused, and motivated.

Ready-made routine slides are available on the Teacher Toolbox for most lessons.

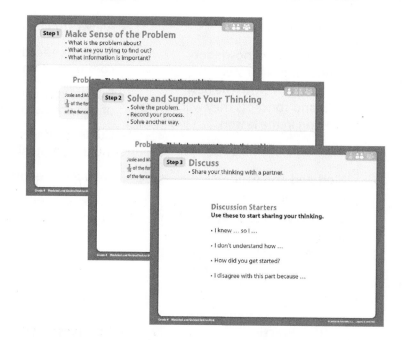

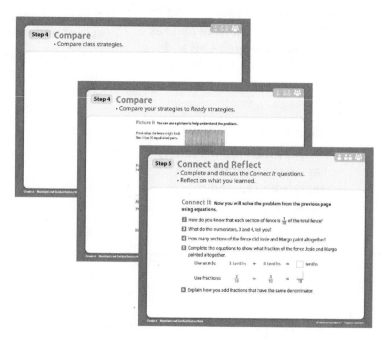

"Talking can help us better understand ways to solve a problem."

Think-Share-Compare Routine

1. Make Sense of the Problem
Read and understand the problem or question. Think about the key information.

Read the problem together as a class. Make sure students understand what they are being asked to do. Ask a few students to describe what the problem is about. Have several students explain what the problem is asking them to do and what information they know.

2. Solve and Support Your Thinking
Include pictures, models, and/or explanations in your solutions. If you have time, show another way to solve it.

Allow enough time for students to persevere as they think through their solutions. Make sure students are showing the models and strategies they use.

3. Discuss
Explain your thinking to a partner. Discuss how your strategies are alike and different.

Have partners discuss their strategies. Circulate to hear conversations and select and sequence solutions to discuss with the whole class.

4. Compare
Compare your strategies with the class, including the strategies in the *Ready* book.

Call on students to share their solution strategies with the class. Have students open their books and connect their strategies to other students' strategies as well as those in the book.

5. Connect and Reflect
Complete and discuss the *Connect It* questions.

Have students complete the *Connect It* questions or *Reflect* question from the *Ready* Instruction book. Choose key questions to discuss as a class.

6. Apply
Apply what you have learned to a new problem. Be sure to support your answer.

Use *Try It* questions or practice problems corresponding to the lesson in *Practice and Problem Solving*.

Teacher Resource Book: Lesson Overview

Use the information on these pages to plan whole class instruction, ongoing monitoring, and small group differentiation.

Standards Focus sets expectations for what students should understand and be able to do.

Prerequisite Skills can be used to monitor the understanding of students at different levels and to scaffold instruction for small group discussions.

Content Objectives identify the mathematical goals for the lesson, while **Language Objectives** identify how students demonstrate their understanding of those goals.

The **Learning Progressions** set a context for the standards of the lessons based on how the standard builds on prior knowledge, particularly from the previous grades, and how it leads to expectations for the next year.

LESSON OVERVIEW

Lesson 16
Add and Subtract Fractions

CCSS Focus

Domain
Number and Operations—Fractions

Cluster
B. Build fractions from unit fractions by applying and extending previous understandings of operations on whole numbers.

Standard
4.NF.B.3 Understand a fraction $\frac{a}{b}$ with $a > 1$ as a sum of fractions $\frac{1}{b}$.
a. Understand addition and subtraction of fractions as joining and separating parts referring to the same whole.
d. Solve word problems involving addition and subtraction of fractions referring to the same whole and having like denominators, e.g., by using visual fraction models and equations to represent the problem.

Standards for Mathematical Practice (SMP)
1 Make sense of problems and persevere in solving them.
2 Reason abstractly and quantitatively.
4 Model with mathematics.
5 Use appropriate tools strategically.
6 Attend to precision.
7 Look for and make use of structure.
8 Look for and express regularity in repeated reasoning.

Lesson Objectives

Content Objectives
• Add fractions with like denominators.
• Subtract fractions with like denominators.
• Use fraction models, number lines, and equations to represent word problems.

Language Objectives
• Draw pictures or diagrams to represent word problems involving fraction addition and subtraction.
• Use fraction vocabulary, including *numerator* and *denominator*, to explain how to add and subtract fractions with like denominators.
• Orally define and use the key mathematical terms *add, subtract, equal parts, fraction, numerator,* and *denominator* when reasoning and arguing about fraction addition and subtraction.
• Write and solve equations to represent word problems involving fraction addition or subtraction.

Prerequisite Skills

• Understand addition as joining parts.
• Understand subtraction as separating parts.
• Know addition and subtraction basic facts.
• Understand the meaning of fractions.
• Identify numerators and denominators.
• Write whole numbers as fractions.
• Compose and decompose fractions.

Lesson Vocabulary

There is no new vocabulary. Review the following key terms.
• **numerator** the top number in a fraction; it tells the number of equal parts that are being described
• **denominator** the bottom number in a fraction; it tells the total number of equal parts in the whole

Learning Progression

In the previous lesson students begin developing an understanding of adding and subtracting fractions with like denominators. They develop an understanding of adding fractions as combining parts referring to the same whole.

This lesson extends student's understanding of fraction addition and subtraction. Here students begin to deal with addition and subtraction in the abstract. Students use visual models to represent word problems involving the addition and subtraction of fractions with the same whole. Students also use equations to solve word problems.

In the next lesson students will add and subtract mixed numbers with like denominators. The focus in Grade 4 is on adding and subtracting fractions with like denominators. In Grade 5 students begin to add and subtract fractions with unlike denominators.

Meeting New Expectations &
Best Practices

What Ready® Mathematics
Instruction Looks Like

How to Implement
Ready® Mathematics

Lesson Pacing Guide

The day-by-day pacing guide can be used to plan whole class and small group instruction, for ongoing monitoring, and for individualized learning with *Ready* and *i-Ready* blended learning options.

Plan teacher-led **whole and small group instruction** following *Ready's* gradual release model. Practice can be assigned after every section of the lesson in class, after school, or at home with *Practice and Problem Solving*. Assess students' mastery of lesson content and identify the need for reteaching with lesson quizzes.

Plan **small group differentiation** using *Ready Instruction* prerequisite lessons for in-depth instruction from earlier grades to review prerequisite concepts or fill in gaps in student knowledge, student-led Math Center Activities for standards practice in three different levels, and teacher-led Tools for Instruction activities for small groups of students requiring additional instruction on a prerequisite or on-level skill.

Plan students' **personalized learning** using *i-Ready's* adaptive instruction to remediate and fill gaps.

Teacher Resource Book

Lesson 16

Lesson Pacing Guide

Whole Class Instruction

Day 1 *45–60 minutes*

Toolbox: Interactive Tutorial
Understand Adding and Subtracting Fractions—Level D

Introduction
• Use What You Know *10 min*
• Find Out More *15 min*
• Reflect *10 min*

Practice and Problem Solving
Assign pages 175–176.

Day 2 *45–60 minutes*

Modeled and Guided Instruction
Learn About Adding Fractions
• Picture It/Model It *20 min*
• Connect It *10 min*
• Try It *15 min*

Practice and Problem Solving
Assign pages 177–178.

Day 3 *45–60 minutes*

Modeled and Guided Instruction
Learn About Subtracting Fractions
• Picture It/Model It *10 min*
• Connect It *20 min*
• Try It *15 min*

Practice and Problem Solving
Assign pages 179–180.

Day 4 *45–60 minutes*

Guided Practice
Adding and Subtracting Fractions
• Example *5 min*
• Problems 16–18 *15 min*
• Pair/Share *15 min*
• Solutions *10 min*

Practice and Problem Solving
Assign pages 181–182.

Day 5 *45–60 minutes*

Independent Practice
Adding and Subtracting Fractions
• Problems 1–6 *20 min*
• Quick Check and Remediation *10 min*
• Hands-On or Challenge Activity *15 min*

Toolbox: Lesson Quiz
Lesson 16 Quiz

Small Group Differentiation

Teacher-Toolbox.com

Reteach
Ready Prerequisite Lessons *45–90 min*

Grade 3
• Lesson 14 *Understand* What a Fraction Is
• Lesson 15 *Understand* Fractions on a Number Line

Teacher-led Activities
Tools for Instruction *15–20 min*

Grade 3 *(Lessons 14 and 15)*
• Parts of a Whole
• Parts of a Set
• Fractions on a Number Line
• Place Fractions on a Number Line

Grade 4 *(Lessons 16)*
• Fractions as Sums

Student-led Activities
Math Center Activities *30–40 min*

Grade 3 *(Lessons 14 and 15)*
• 3.25 Write the Fraction
• 3.26 Show Fractions
• 3.27 Use Fraction Vocabulary
• 3.28 Identify Fractions on a Number Line

Grade 4 *(Lessons 16)*
• 4.31 Different Ways to Show Sums

Personalized Learning

i-Ready.com

Independent
i-Ready Lessons *10–20 min*

Grade 3 *(Lessons 14 and 15)*
• Understand What a Fraction Is
• Understand Fractions on a Number Line

Lesson 16 Add and Subtract Fractions **166b**

Student Book: Introduction

The Introduction presents a problem or poses a "big idea" question that connects what students already know to what they are about to learn.

Use What You Know *(whole class)*

Teacher's Role As students answer the questions on the page, ask them to explain their reasoning and help them see how they can use what they already know to solve the problem.

Use *Real World Connections* in the Teacher Resource Book (TRB) for active learning as students connect the math of the lesson to their own experiences. Encourage students from other cultures to share their experiences.

Student's Role Students who come to understand that they can apply what they have already learned to new problem situations develop a deeper understanding of mathematical relationships. This understanding allows them to see mathematics as interconnected concepts and skills rather than as separate, unrelated ideas.

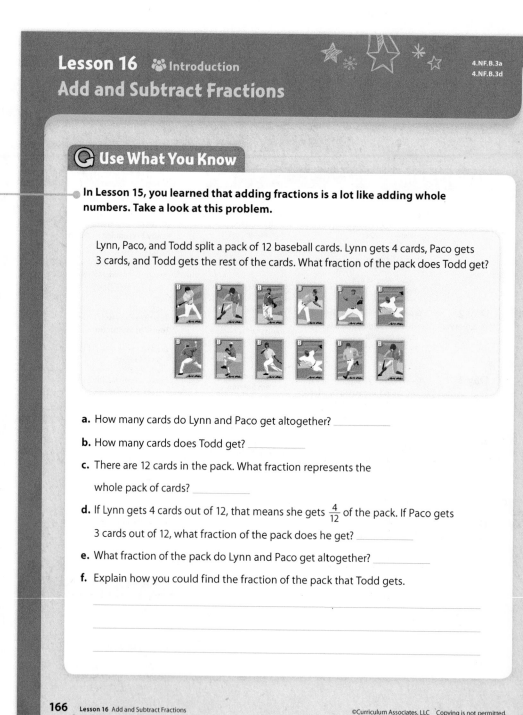

Lesson 16 🐾 Introduction
4.NF.B.3a
4.NF.B.3d

Add and Subtract Fractions

Ⓖ Use What You Know

In Lesson 15, you learned that adding fractions is a lot like adding whole numbers. Take a look at this problem.

Lynn, Paco, and Todd split a pack of 12 baseball cards. Lynn gets 4 cards, Paco gets 3 cards, and Todd gets the rest of the cards. What fraction of the pack does Todd get?

a. How many cards do Lynn and Paco get altogether? _____

b. How many cards does Todd get? _____

c. There are 12 cards in the pack. What fraction represents the whole pack of cards? _____

d. If Lynn gets 4 cards out of 12, that means she gets $\frac{4}{12}$ of the pack. If Paco gets 3 cards out of 12, what fraction of the pack does he get? _____

e. What fraction of the pack do Lynn and Paco get altogether? _____

f. Explain how you could find the fraction of the pack that Todd gets.

_____

_____

_____

166 Lesson 16 Add and Subtract Fractions

©Curriculum Associates, LLC Copying is not permitted.

⊳⊳ Find Out More

We often use **fractions** in real life. Fractions can describe something that has several equal parts, as in the baseball card problem. In that problem the "whole" is the pack of cards. Since there are 12 cards in the pack, each card represents $\frac{1}{12}$ of the whole.

$\frac{4}{12}$ $\frac{3}{12}$ $\frac{5}{12}$

Fractions in real life can also describe the equal parts of a single object, such as a pizza cut into 8 equal slices. The pizza is the "whole," and all the slices of pizza are equal parts of the same whole. Since there are 8 equal-sized slices, each slice is $\frac{1}{8}$ of the pizza. Even if a person takes away one or more slices, the "whole" is still the same 8 slices.

▶ Reflect

1 Give another example of a "whole" object with equal parts that can be described by fractions.

_____

_____

_____

_____

Lesson 16 Add and Subtract Fractions   **167**

Find Out More *(whole class)*

Teacher's Role Discuss as a class, guiding students to see how the questions they just answered and the formal mathematics presented are related. Use the suggestions in the Step By Step to help guide the discussion.

Use the *Hands-On Activities* in the TRB to reinforce a skill or concept through another, often concrete, approach. Hands-On Activities can help ELL and other students visualize concepts.

Student's Role As they engage intellectually with the content, students build foundational understanding of what they will be learning in the lesson.

Reflect *(small group)*

Student's Role By summarizing what they have learned in their own words, students are encouraged to look for and make use of structure.

Teacher's Role Have students read and discuss the *Reflect*, then write an answer in their own words. Observe responses to assess student's understanding.

Ready Mathematics
PRACTICE AND PROBLEM SOLVING

Teacher's Role Assign *Practice and Problem Solving* as independent work in class or at home for additional practice with key prerequisite skills of the lesson.

Meeting New Expectations &
Best Practices

What Ready® Mathematics
Instruction Looks Like

How to Implement
Ready® Mathematics

Student Book: Modeled and Guided Instruction

The Modeled and Guided Instruction supports students as they explore different ways of solving a real-world or mathematical problem.

Lesson 16 Modeled and Guided Instruction

Learn About Adding Fractions

Read the problem. Then explore different ways to understand adding fractions.

> Josie and Margo are painting a fence green. Josie starts at one end and paints $\frac{3}{10}$ of the fence. Margo starts at the other end and paints $\frac{4}{10}$ of it. What fraction of the fence do they paint?

Picture It/Model It *(whole class)*

Teacher's Role Read the problem at the top of the page, then work through the *Picture It* and *Model It* as a class. Pose the scaffolded questions to guide students' understanding of the approaches on the page.

Use *Mathematical Discourse* questions in the Teacher Resource Book (TRB) to promote thoughtful dialogue about the models and strategies. Encourage the exchange of ideas among students by having them suggest solution methods that differ from those shown. Have students share which solution strategy works best for them and explain why.

Student's Role As they discuss different ways of representing a given problem, students begin to understand there are multiple access points from which they can draw on prior knowledge.

Looking at other ways to solve the problem encourages students to think in ways they would not have otherwise, building flexibility in their ability to solve problems.

Picture It **You can use a picture to help understand the problem.**

Think what the fence might look like. It has 10 equal-sized parts.

Each part is $\frac{1}{10}$ of the whole.

The girls paint 3 tenths and 4 tenths of the fence.

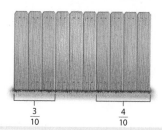

$\frac{3}{10}$ $\frac{4}{10}$

Model It **You can also use a number line to help understand the problem.**

The number line below is divided into tenths, with a point at $\frac{3}{10}$.

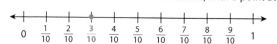

Start at $\frac{3}{10}$ and count 4 tenths to the right to **add** $\frac{4}{10}$.

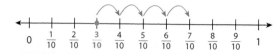

○ ○

▶ **Connect It** Now you will solve the problem from the previous page using equations.

2 How do you know that each section of fence is $\frac{1}{10}$ of the total fence?

_____

_____

_____

3 What do the numerators, 3 and 4, tell you? _____

_____

_____

4 How many sections of the fence did Josie and Margo paint altogether? _____

5 Complete the equations to show what fraction of the fence Josie and Margo painted altogether.

Use words:　　3 tenths　　+　　4 tenths　　=　□　tenths

Use fractions:　　$\frac{3}{10}$　　+　　$\frac{4}{10}$　　=　$\frac{\square}{10}$

6 Explain how you add fractions that have the same denominator.

_____

_____

▶ **Try It** Use what you just learned to solve these problems. Show your work on a separate sheet of paper.

7 Lita and Otis are helping their mom clean the house. Lita cleaned $\frac{1}{3}$ of the rooms. Otis cleaned $\frac{1}{3}$ of the rooms. What fraction of the rooms did Lita and Otis clean altogether? _____

8 Mark's string is $\frac{1}{5}$ of a meter long. Bob's string is $\frac{3}{5}$ of a meter long. How long are the two strings combined? _____ of a meter

©Curriculum Associates, LLC Copying is not permitted.　　**Lesson 16** Add and Subtract Fractions　**169**

Ready Mathematics
PRACTICE AND PROBLEM SOLVING

Teacher's Role Assign *Practice and Problem Solving* as independent work in class or at home for additional practice with the skills of the lesson.

Connect It *(whole class)*

Teacher's Role Discuss the *Connect It* as a class, guiding students to make the connection between the representations on the previous page and a more general symbolic representation of the problem and solution.

Use *SMP Tips* in the TRB to help students advance through the content, critically analyze information, and use complex cognitive thinking. This reflects the expectation that students are actively engaged in doing mathematics rather than passively receiving mathematics instruction.

Student's Role Students who engage with the symbolic representations by making and defending conjectures are able to apply what they have learned to solve similar problems. This helps them understand their own progress as they look for approaches that work best for them and find what they still need feedback on.

Try It *(small group)*

Student's Role Discussing how the responses to the *Connect It* relate to the problem they are about to solve adds to students' understanding as they apply the newly learned skill to a new situation.

Teacher's Role Have students read and discuss the Try It, then solve the problems on their own. Look for errors in student thinking and use the TRB *Error Alerts* to provide support.

Meeting New Expectations &
Best Practices

What Ready® Mathematics
Instruction Looks Like

How to Implement
Ready® Mathematics

Student Book: Guided Practice

The Guided Practice provides feedback to students as they share their thinking and find solutions to real-world problems.

Example (whole class)

Teacher's Role Have students work together in small groups to respond to the *Pair/Share* question. Encourage students to explore multiple approaches and use both linguistic and nonlinguistic representations.

Student's Role As students explain their solutions and strategies to their peers, they develop the understanding that there are many ways to formulate real-life situations as mathematical problems. Hearing other approaches guides them to look at each problem from multiple perspectives, enriching their understanding of the mathematics and helping them make connections.

Problems (small group)

Student's Role Students work individually to represent their mathematical solutions in concrete, symbolic, or written form as they solve real-world problems.

In the *Pair/Share* discussion, students explain their solution pathways to others and respond to clarifying questions. This encourages students to examine their premises and build logical arguments.

Teacher's Role Circulate and ask guiding questions that require students to elaborate on important information and summarize their thinking.

Lesson 16 👥 Guided Practice

Practice ▶ Adding and Subtracting Fractions

Study the example below. Then solve problems 16–18.

Example

Jessica hiked $\frac{2}{5}$ of a mile on a trail before she stopped to get a drink of water. After her drink, Jessica hiked another $\frac{2}{5}$ of a mile. How far did Jessica hike in all?

Look at how you could show your work using a number line.

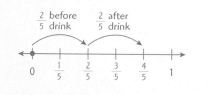

Solution _Jessica hiked $\frac{4}{5}$ of a mile._

> The student used labels and "jump" arrows to show each part of the hike on a number line. It is just like adding whole numbers!

> **Pair/Share**
> How else could you solve this problem?

---

16 Ruth made 1 fruit smoothie. She drank $\frac{1}{3}$ of it. What fraction of the fruit smoothie is left?

Show your work.

> What fraction represents the whole fruit smoothie?

> **Pair/Share**
> How did you and your partner decide what fraction to start with?

Solution _____

©Curriculum Associates, LLC   Copying is not permitted.

Meeting New Expectations &
Best Practices

What Ready® Mathematics
Instruction Looks Like

How to Implement
Ready® Mathematics

Student Instruction Book

17 Mr. Chang has a bunch of balloons. $\frac{3}{10}$ of the balloons are red. $\frac{2}{10}$ of the balloons are blue. What fraction of the balloons are neither red nor blue?

Show your work.

> I think that there are at least two different steps to solve this problem.

> **Pair/Share**
> How is this problem different from the others you've seen in this lesson?

Solution

18 Emily ate $\frac{1}{6}$ of a bag of carrots. Nick ate $\frac{2}{6}$ of the bag of carrots. What fraction of the bag of carrots did Emily and Nick eat altogether? Circle the letter of the correct answer.

A $\frac{1}{6}$

B $\frac{1}{3}$

C $\frac{3}{6}$

D $\frac{3}{12}$

> To find the fraction of the bag Emily and Nick ate altogether, should you add or subtract?

Rob chose **D** as the correct answer. How did he get that answer?

> **Pair/Share**
> Does Rob's answer make sense?

Lesson 16 Add and Subtract Fractions   **173**

Pair/Share *(small group)*

Student's Role Actively discussing their approaches after solving a problem on their own helps students identify what they are clear about and where they are confused. As they are challenged to justify their thinking, they gain experience in providing logical explanations.

Teacher's Role Continue to have students solve each problem individually, then *Pair/Share* to discuss the solution pathways they chose. Observe discussions, listening for indications that students are actively engaging with content to gain understanding.

Use the *Solutions* in the Teacher Resource Book as examples of one way to solve the problem. Encourage students to tell how their solutions are similar to or different from these solutions.

Ready Mathematics
PRACTICE AND PROBLEM SOLVING

Teacher's Role Assign *Practice and Problem Solving* as independent work in class or at home for additional practice with all the skills of the lesson.

Student Book: Independent Practice

The Independent Practice provides students with questions in a variety of assessment formats that integrate and extend concepts and skills.

Problem (independent)

Student's Role As students read each problem, they think about possible approaches, create a plan, and make decisions about how to represent the problem. Checking their work to be sure their answer makes sense prompts them to provide more complete responses.

Teacher's Role As students work on their own, walk around the room to maintain student engagement and to monitor their progress and understanding.

Open-ended questions are an opportunity for students to show multiple approaches, and when appropriate, more than one correct response.

Use the *Solution* and DOK level or the scoring rubrics in the Teacher Resource Book (TRB) as a guide to the level of complex thinking each item requires.

Lesson 16 👤 Independent Practice

Practice Adding and Subtracting Fractions

Solve the problems.

1. Liang bought some cloth. He used $\frac{5}{8}$ of a yard for a school project. He has $\frac{2}{8}$ of a yard left. How much cloth did Liang buy?

   A $\frac{3}{8}$ of a yard

   B $\frac{7}{16}$ of a yard

   C $\frac{7}{8}$ of a yard

   D $\frac{8}{8}$ of a yard

2. Carmela cut a cake into 12 equal-sized pieces. She ate $\frac{2}{12}$ of the cake, and her brother ate $\frac{3}{12}$ of the cake. What fraction of the cake is left?

   A $\frac{1}{12}$

   B $\frac{5}{12}$

   C $\frac{7}{12}$

   D $\frac{12}{12}$

3. Lee's muffin mix calls for $\frac{2}{3}$ cup of milk and $\frac{1}{3}$ cup of oil. How much more milk than oil does she need for the muffin mix?

4 Put It Together Lucy and Melody are painting a room. They divided the room into 8 equal sections. Lucy painted 2 sections and Melody painted 4 sections. Which model can be used to find the total fraction of the room they painted? Circle the letters of all that apply.

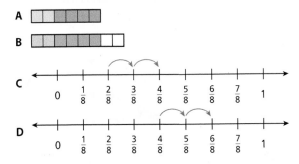

A

B

C

D

5 In all, Cole and Max picked $\frac{9}{10}$ of a bucket of blueberries. Cole picked $\frac{3}{10}$ of a bucket of blueberries. What fraction of a bucket of blueberries did Max pick?

Show your work.

Answer Max picked _____ of a bucket of blueberries.

6 A melon is cut into 8 equal slices. Together, Regan and Juanita will eat $\frac{5}{8}$ of the melon. What is one way the girls could eat that fraction of the melon?

Show your work. Write an equation to represent your answer.

Answer Regan could eat _____ of the melon, and

Juanita could eat _____ of the melon.

Equation _____

✓ **Self Check** Go back and see what you can check off on the Self Check on page 143.

Teacher Resource Book

Point-of-use professional development and step-by-step instructional ideas help teachers address even the most challenging standards effectively.

The **At A Glance** explains what students will be doing on each page.

The **Step By Step** organizes content into appropriate chunks for student learning, and provides guiding questions about the key points within each chunk.

SMP Tips highlight a particular Standard for Mathematical Practice within the lesson. This is an opportunity to have students refer to the Mathematical Practices Handbook at the front of their book and reflect on its use.

The **Mathematical Discourse** questions engage students and advance them through the content. They include answers as well as key ideas to listen for in student responses to facilitate further rich discussion.

Lesson 16 Add and Subtract Fractions

Modeled and Guided Instruction

At A Glance

Students use models and number lines to review adding fractions. Then students revisit this problem to learn how to add fractions using equations. Students continue to solve other addition word problems.

Step By Step

Read the problem at the top of the page as a class.

> **SMP TIP Look for Structure.**
> Help students generalize that adding fractions is like adding whole numbers. (SMP 7)

Picture It

- Have a volunteer name the denominator of the fraction in the problem. [10] Point out that each fence section is $\frac{1}{10}$ of the total number of length of the fence.
- Guide students to recognize that since Josie painted $\frac{3}{10}$ of the fence sections and Margo painted $\frac{4}{10}$, the picture is shaded to represent the total number of fence sections painted, 3 for Josie and 4 for Margo. Have students count aloud to find the sum.

Model It

- Direct students to look at the number line. Emphasize that the number line is divided into tenths to represent the total number of fence sections.
- ▶ **Mathematical Discourse 1 and 2**
- You may wish to draw the number line on the board and have a volunteer demonstrate 4 jumps to the right to add 4 tenths to $\frac{3}{10}$.
- ▶ **Concept Extension**

Lesson 16 Modeled and Guided Instruction

Learn About ▶ **Adding Fractions**

Read the problem. Then explore different ways to understand adding fractions.

Josie and Margo are painting a fence green. Josie starts at one end and paints $\frac{3}{10}$ of the fence. Margo starts at the other end and paints $\frac{4}{10}$ of it. What fraction of the fence do they paint?

▶ **Picture It** You can use a picture to help understand the problem.

Think what the fence might look like. It has 10 equal-sized parts.

Each part is $\frac{1}{10}$ of the whole.

The girls paint 3 tenths and 4 tenths of the fence.

$\frac{3}{10}$ $\frac{4}{10}$

▶ **Model It** You can also use a number line to help understand the problem.

The number line below is divided into tenths, with a point at $\frac{3}{10}$.

$$0 \quad \frac{1}{10} \quad \frac{2}{10} \quad \frac{3}{10} \quad \frac{4}{10} \quad \frac{5}{10} \quad \frac{6}{10} \quad \frac{7}{10} \quad \frac{8}{10} \quad \frac{9}{10} \quad 1$$

Start at $\frac{3}{10}$ and count 4 tenths to the right to add $\frac{4}{10}$.

$$0 \quad \frac{1}{10} \quad \frac{2}{10} \quad \frac{3}{10} \quad \frac{4}{10} \quad \frac{5}{10} \quad \frac{6}{10} \quad \frac{7}{10} \quad \frac{8}{10} \quad \frac{9}{10} \quad 1$$

168

▶ **Mathematical Discourse**

1 *How could you use fractions to label 0 and 1 on the number line?*

Students may suggest that you can write both as a number out of 10, so $\frac{0}{10}$ and $\frac{10}{10}$.

2 *What is another way you could solve the problem?*

Responses may mention using fraction strips. You could line up three $\frac{1}{10}$ strips and four $\frac{1}{10}$ strips in a single row. Then, you could count how many tenths you have altogether.

▶ **Concept Extension**

Illustrate the Commutative Property of Addition.

- Ask: *What if I drew the starting point at $\frac{4}{10}$ instead of $\frac{3}{10}$? Could I still solve the problem?*
- To emphasize the point, draw a number line on the board with a point at $\frac{4}{10}$. Then, have students explain how to count on from $\frac{4}{10}$ to find the answer. Encourage a volunteer to come to the board and demonstrate how to find the sum.

---

168   **Lesson 16** Add and Subtract Fractions

Teacher Resource Book

The image shows a reproduced student workbook page on the left:

Connect It Now you will solve the problem from the previous page using equations.

2 How do you know that each section of fence is $\frac{1}{10}$ of the total fence?
Possible answer: The denominator tells the total number of fence sections.
The numerator tells the number of fence sections that you are talking about.

3 What do the numerators, 3 and 4, tell you? 3 tells the number of fence sections that Josie painted. 4 tells the number of fence sections that Margo painted.

4 How many sections of the fence did Josie and Margo paint altogether? 7

5 Complete the equations to show what fraction of the fence Josie and Margo painted altogether.

Use words: 3 tenths + 4 tenths = 7 tenths

Use fractions: $\frac{3}{10}$ + $\frac{4}{10}$ = $\frac{7}{10}$

6 Explain how you add fractions that have the same denominator.
Add the numerators and leave the denominator as is.

Try It Use what you just learned to solve these problems. Show your work on a separate sheet of paper.

7 Lita and Otis are helping their mom clean the house. Lita cleaned $\frac{1}{3}$ of the rooms. Otis cleaned $\frac{1}{3}$ of the rooms. What fraction of the rooms did Lita and Otis clean altogether? $\frac{2}{3}$

8 Mark's string is $\frac{1}{5}$ of a meter long. Bob's string is $\frac{3}{5}$ of a meter long. How long are the two strings combined? $\frac{4}{5}$ of a meter

169

▶ English Language Learners

Write fraction words.

- Write the word *tenths* on the board. Circle the letters that spell *ten* in the word and write the number 10 below it.
- Repeat using the word *eighths*.
- Have students write *tenths* and *eighths* on a piece of paper. Next to the words, have them write fractions associated with the words.
- *If time allows, repeat with other fraction words.*

Lesson 16

Step By Step

Connect It

- Read **Connect It** as a class. Be sure to point out that the questions refer to the problem on the previous page.
- Review the meanings of *numerator* (the number of equal parts of a set you have) and *denominator* (the total number of equal parts the set is divided into).
- Ask: *If the fence Josie and Margo painted had only 8 sections, what fraction would represent 1 section of the fence?* $\left[\frac{1}{8}\right]$

▶ English Language Learners

Try It

7 **Solution**
$\frac{2}{3}$; Students may show $\frac{1}{3}$ on a number line divided into thirds and count 1 mark to the right. They also may write the equation $\frac{1}{3} + \frac{1}{3} = \frac{2}{3}$.

8 **Solution**
$\frac{4}{5}$; Students may show $\frac{1}{5}$ on a number line divided into fifths and count 3 marks to the right. They also may write the equation $\frac{1}{5} + \frac{3}{5} = \frac{4}{5}$.
Error Alert Students who wrote $\frac{4}{10}\left(\text{or }\frac{2}{5}\right)$ added both the numerators and the denominators.

Ready Mathematics
PRACTICE AND PROBLEM SOLVING

Assign *Practice and Problem Solving* **pages 177–178** after students have completed this section.

Lesson 16 Add and Subtract Fractions   **169**

Try It Solutions provide complete explanations and include multiple solutions to show different approaches.

TRB activities such as **Concept Extensions, ELL Support,** and **Visual Models** (not shown here) engage students and allow them to participate in activities that support varied abilities. A range of techniques encourages all students to contribute.

Teacher Resource Book

Point-of-use professional development and step-by-step instructional ideas help teachers address even the most challenging standards effectively.

Complete **Solutions** at point of use provide a correct response and model at least one way to solve the problem and include the DOK level of each question.

In the **Quick Check and Remediation**, an "exit" question is given to monitor understanding of the lesson content. A chart provides a list of incorrect answers based on common errors and gives specific remediation suggestions for each error.

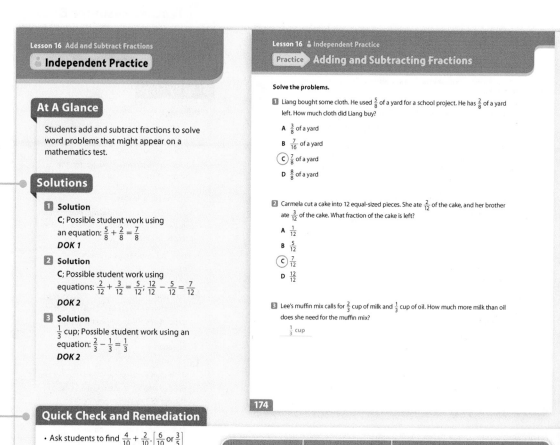

Teacher Resource Book

(Student page, left)

4 Lucy and Melody are painting a room. They divided the room into 8 equal sections. Lucy painted 2 sections and Melody painted 4 sections. Which model can be used to find the total fraction of the room they painted? Circle the letters of all that apply.

A ▢▢▢▢▢▢▢▢

B ▢▢▢▢▢▢▢▢

C

D

5 In all, Cole and Max picked $\frac{9}{10}$ of a bucket of blueberries. Cole picked $\frac{3}{10}$ of a bucket of blueberries. What fraction of a bucket of blueberries did Max pick?

Show your work.

Possible student work using a number line:

Answer Max picked $\frac{6}{10}$ of a bucket of blueberries.

6 A melon is cut into 8 equal slices. Together, Regan and Juanita will eat $\frac{5}{8}$ of the melon. What is one way the girls could eat that fraction of the melon?

Show your work. Write an equation to represent your answer.

Possible student work using a model:

Answer Regan could eat $\frac{2}{8}$ of the melon, and

Juanita could eat $\frac{3}{8}$ of the melon.

Equation Possible equation: $\frac{2}{8} + \frac{3}{8} = \frac{5}{8}$

✓ **Self Check** Go back and see what you can check off on the Self Check on page 143.

175

Lesson 16

Solutions

4 Solution

B; The model shows $\frac{2}{8}$ shaded in light blue for Lucy's sections and $\frac{4}{8}$ shaded in dark blue for Melody's sections. The total shaded sections represent the total fraction of the room they painted.

D; The number line starts at Melody's fraction $\left(\frac{4}{8}\right)$ and adds $\frac{2}{8}$ for Lucy's fraction, for a total of $\frac{6}{8}$.
DOK 2

5 Solution

$\frac{6}{10}$; Possible student work using an equation: $\frac{9}{10} - \frac{3}{10} = \frac{6}{10}$
DOK 2

6 Solution

Possible student work using equations:

$\frac{0}{8} + \frac{5}{8} = \frac{5}{8}, \frac{1}{8} + \frac{4}{8} = \frac{5}{8},$

$\frac{2}{8} + \frac{3}{8} = \frac{5}{8}, \frac{3}{8} + \frac{2}{8} = \frac{5}{8},$

$\frac{4}{8} + \frac{1}{8} = \frac{5}{8}, \frac{5}{8} + \frac{0}{8} = \frac{5}{8}$
DOK 2

▶ **Hands-On Activity**

Use fraction strips to add fractions.

Materials: strips of paper, markers

- Distribute paper and markers to each student.
- Direct students to fold a strip of paper in half, and then in half again in the same direction.
- Tell them to unfold the strips and use the marker to show the 4 equal sections.
- Tell students to color $\frac{1}{4}$ of the strip. Then have them color another $\frac{1}{4}$ of the strip. Write $\frac{1}{4} + \frac{1}{4}$ on the board.
- Challenge them to use their fraction strips to show that the sum is $\frac{2}{4}$, or $\frac{1}{2}$.
- If time allows, repeat for other denominators by folding another strip of paper three or four times.

▶ **Challenge Activity**

Write a problem for a given sum.

- Tell students that the sum of two fractions is $\frac{2}{5}$. However, the original fractions did not have denominators of 5.
- Challenge students to write a fraction addition problem that has a sum of $\frac{2}{5}$. $\left[\text{Possible answer: } \frac{3}{10} + \frac{1}{10}\right]$

A **Challenge Activity** gives students who have mastered the skills and concepts of the lesson an opportunity to apply their understanding to more sophisticated problem solving.

A **Hands-On Activity** extends the concepts and skills of the lesson using common classroom manipulatives and group collaboration.

Lesson 16 Add and Subtract Fractions **175**

Monitor Understanding in *Ready® Mathematics*

Ready Mathematics provides a comprehensive assessment system, as shown below and on pages A12–A13. This includes practical, easy-to-use progress monitoring tools embedded within instruction, highlighted on the table to the right.

Diagnose

Use *i-Ready Diagnostic* to **diagnose individual student skill levels** and identify instructional needs.

Monitor Understanding

Use the informal assessment opportunities in the *Ready* Student Book, Teacher Resource Book, and Teacher Toolbox to **inform ongoing instruction.**

Assess Mastery

Use *i-Ready Standards Mastery* or *Ready Unit Interim Assessments* to **evaluate student mastery of content** at the lesson and unit level.

Measure Growth

Use *i-Ready Diagnostic* or *Ready Assessments* to **track student progress towards end-of-year goals.**

Tool	What it does	How to use it
Student Book		
Try It, Connect It, and Reflect	Prompts students to explain their thinking	Observe student understanding and respond with specific strategies for additional instruction and to support individual needs
Pair/Share	Encourages students to collaborate as they justify their reasoning and critique the reasoning of others	
Independent Practice	Provides opportunities for students to demonstrate understanding as they apply lesson skills and concepts to solve problems	
Teacher Resource Book		
Mathematical Discourse and SMP Tips	Encourages classroom discussion so students share their thinking	Use the key topics provided to listen for student responses, provide immediate feedback to address misunderstandings, and support students with targeted remediation strategies and activities
Error Alerts	Explains a common computational error, the wrong answer it might produce, and explanations to help students avoid the error in the future	
Quick Check and Remediation	Poses an "exit" question to check student understanding	
Online Teacher Toolbox		
Lesson Quizzes	Assesses lesson concepts and skills in a variety of item types	Evaluate mastery of lesson content

Pacing for *Ready*® Mathematics

Ready Mathematics provides a full year of instruction. The Year-Long Pacing Guide below shows a recommended schedule for teaching when using *Ready* as a core program.

Year-Long Pacing	Grade 2	
Ready Instruction Lesson	**Days**	**Minutes/day**
i-Ready Diagnostic	3	60
Lesson 1 *Understand* Mental Math Strategies (Fact Families)	5	30–45
Lesson 2 Solve One-Step Word Problems	5	30–45
Lesson 3 *Understand* Mental Math Strategies (Make a Ten)	5	30–45
Lesson 4 *Understand* Even and Odd Numbers	5	30–45
Lesson 5 Add Using Arrays	4	30–45
Lesson 6 Solve Two-Step Word Problems	5	30–45
Math in Action	5	30–45
Unit 1 Interim Assessment or i-Ready Standards Mastery	**1**	**30–45**
Lesson 7 Add Two-Digit Numbers	5	30–45
Lesson 8 Subtract Two-Digit Numbers	5	30–45
Lesson 9 Solve One-Step Word Problems With Two-Digit Numbers	5	30–45
Lesson 10 *Understand* Three-Digit Numbers	5	30–45
Lesson 11 Read and Write Three-Digit Numbers	4	30–45
Lesson 12 Compare Three-Digit Numbers	5	30–45
Lesson 13 Add Three-Digit Numbers	5	30–45
Lesson 14 Subtract Three-Digit Numbers	5	30–45
Lesson 15 Add Several Two-Digit Numbers	4	30–45
Math in Action	5	30–45
Unit 2 Interim Assessment or i-Ready Standards Mastery	**1**	**30–45**
Practice Test 2 or i-Ready Diagnostic	3	60
Lesson 16 *Understand* Length and Measurement Tools	5	30–45
Lesson 17 Measure Length	5	30–45
Lesson 18 *Understand* Measurement With Different Units	5	30–45
Lesson 19 *Understand* Estimating Length	5	30–45
Lesson 20 Compare Lengths	5	30–45

Ready Instruction Lesson	Days	Minutes/day
Lesson 21 Add and Subtract Lengths	5	30–45
Lesson 22 *Understand* Reading and Making Line Plots	5	30–45
Lesson 23 Draw and Use Bar Graphs and Picture Graphs	5	30–45
Lesson 24 Tell and Write Time	4	30–45
Lesson 25 Solve Word Problems Involving Money	5	30–45
Math in Action	5	30–45
Unit 3 Interim Assessment or i-Ready Standards Mastery	**1**	**30–45**
Lesson 26 Recognize and Draw Shapes	5	30–45
Lesson 27 *Understand* Tiling in Rectangles	5	30–45
Lesson 28 *Understand* Halves, Thirds, and Fourths in Shapes	5	30–45
Math in Action	5	30–45
Unit 4 Interim Assessment or i-Ready Standards Mastery	**1**	**30–45**
Practice Test 3 or i-Ready Diagnostic	3	60

Ready Mathematics
PRACTICE AND PROBLEM SOLVING

Use the lesson practice and unit resources in *Practice and Problem Solving* throughout the year to extend classroom learning.

- Before each lesson, send **Family Letters** home separately or as part of a family communication package.

- After completing each lesson section, assign two pages of **rigorous lesson practice** as independent work in class or at home.

- After completing each unit, use Unit Games, Unit Performance Tasks, and Unit Vocabulary to **integrate skills and consolidate learning.**

- Throughout instruction, use **Fluency Skills Practice and Fluency Repeated Reasoning Practice** worksheets to reinforce procedural fluency.

Pacing for *Ready*® Mathematics, *continued*

Each *Ready Mathematics* lesson provides approximately one week of instruction.
A day of instruction assumes 45–60 minutes of mathematics instruction.

Monthly Pacing Guide

Month	Lessons
September	Lessons 1–3
October	Lessons 4–6 Unit 1 Math in Action
November	Lessons 7–10
December	Lessons 11–13
January	Lessons 14–15 Unit 2 Math in Action
February	Lessons 16–19
March	Lessons 20–23
April	Lessons 24–26 Unit 3 Math in Action
May	Lessons 27–28 Unit 4 Math in Action

Weekly Pacing Guide — Whole Class Instruction

Day 1
45–60 minutes

Toolbox: Interactive Tutorial
Subtracting Three-Digit Numbers

Introduction
• Opening Activity *20 min*
• Use What You Know *10 min*
• Find Out More *10 min*
• Reflect *5 min*

Practice and Problem Solving
Assign pages 139–140.

Day 2
45–60 minutes

Modeled and Guided Instruction
Learn About Subtracting Hundreds, Tens, and Ones
• Picture It/Model It *15 min*
• Connect It *15 min*
• Try It *15 min*

Practice and Problem Solving
Assign pages 141–142.

Day 3
45–60 minutes

Modeled and Guided Instruction
Learn About Regrouping to Subtract
• Picture It/Model It *15 min*
• Connect It *15 min*
• Try It *15 min*

Practice and Problem Solving
Assign pages 143–144.

Day 4
45–60 minutes

Guided Practice
Practice Subtracting Three-Digit Numbers
• Example *5 min*
• Problems 12–14 *15 min*
• Pair/Share *15 min*
• Solutions *10 min*

Practice and Problem Solving
Assign pages 145–146.

Day 5
45–60 minutes

Independent Practice
Practice Subtracting Three-Digit Numbers
• Problems 1–6 *20 min*
• Quick Check and Remediation *10 min*
• Hands-On or Challenge Activity *15 min*

Toolbox: Lesson Quiz
Lesson 14 Quiz

Instruction for each section of the lesson in the Student
Book follows a similar routine. The chart below shows the
structure and goals for one part of the lesson.

Daily Pacing   **~45 minutes**

Day 3   **Modeled and Guided Instruction**   **Learn About Regrouping to Subtract**

Picture It/Model It 15 minutes	Teacher guides via Student Instruction Book, promoting rich classroom discussion (Mathematical Discourse questions) and extending learning (Hands-On Activity) via the Teacher Resource Book
	Goal: To engage in mathematical discourse and deepen instruction in the Student Instruction Book
Connect It 15 minutes	Teacher facilitates via Student Instruction Book, focusing on a specific Standard for Mathematical Practice (SMP Tip) via the Teacher Resource Book
	Goal: To help students actively engage with the lesson content
Try It 15 minutes	Teacher circulates while students work
	Goal: To provide an opportunity for students to practice and apply skills to a new situation
Practice and Problem Solving	Students work independently at home extending learning
	Goal: To get additional practice with skills and concept of the lesson

Unit 1 Operations and Algebraic Thinking

Which lessons are students building upon?

Grade 1, Lesson 6
Doubles and Doubles Plus 1
1.OA.C.6

Grade 1, Lesson 9
Number Partners for 10
1.OA.C.6

Grade 1, Lesson 11
Facts I Know
1.OA.C.6

Grade 1, Lesson 3
Add and Subtract in Word Problems
1.OA.A.1

Grade 1, Lesson 5
Subtract to Compare in Word Problems
1.OA.A.1

Grade 1, Lesson 13
Understand Sums Greater than 10
1.OA.C.6

Grade 1, Lesson 15
Add Three Numbers
1.OA.A.2

Grade 1, Lesson 16
Make a 10 to Subtract
1.OA.C.6

Grade 1, Lesson 30
Compare Data
1.MD.C.4

Grade 1, Lesson 13
Understand Sums Greater than 10
1.OA.C.6

Grade 1, Lesson 15
Add Three Numbers
1.OA.A.2

Grade 1, Lesson 3
Add and Subtract in Word Problems
1.OA.A.1

Grade 1, Lesson 5
Subtract to Compare in Word Problems
1.OA.A.1

Unit 1

Which lessons are students preparing for?

Lesson 1
Understand Mental Math Strategies (Fact Families)
2.OA.B.2

→ **Grade 3, Lesson 9**
Use Place Value to Add and Subtract
3.NBT.A.2

→ **Grade 4, Lesson 3**
Add and Subtract Whole Numbers
4.NBT.B.4

Lesson 2
Solve One-Step Word Problems
2.OA.A.1

→ **Grade 3, Lesson 11**
Solve One-Step Word Problems Using Multiplication and Division
3.OA.A.3

→ **Grade 3, Lesson 12**
Model Two-Step Word Problems Using the Four Operations
3.OA.D.8

Lesson 3
Understand Mental Math Strategies (Make a Ten)
2.OA.B.2

→ **Grade 3, Lesson 9**
Use Place Value to Add and Subtract
3.NBT.A.2

→ **Grade 4, Lesson 3**
Add and Subtract Whole Numbers
4.NBT.B.4

Lesson 4
Understand Even and Odd Numbers
2.OA.C.3

→ **Grade 3, Lesson 7**
Understand Patterns
3.OA.D.9

Lesson 5
Add Using Arrays
2.OA.C.4, 2.NBT.A.2

→ **Grade 3, Lesson 1**
Understand the Meaning of Multiplication
3.OA.A.1

→ **Grade 3, Lesson 4**
Understand the Meaning of Division
3.OA.A.2

Lesson 6
Solve Two-Step Word Problems
2.OA.A.1

→ **Grade 3, Lesson 11**
Solve One-Step Word Problems Using Multiplication and Division
3.OA.A.3

→ **Grade 3, Lesson 12**
Model Two-Step Word Problems Using the Four Operations
3.OA.D.8

Unit 1
Operations and Algebraic Thinking

Unit 1
Operations and Algebraic Thinking

Let's learn some addition and subtraction strategies.

Real-World Connection Jenna has 8 girl cousins and 9 boy cousins. She likes to plan fun events with her cousins. To do this, Jenna has to answer a lot of questions. For example:

- How many cousins are there altogether?
- How many movie tickets do they need?
- Can she group her cousins into two even kickball teams?

In This Unit You will learn many ways to add and subtract. Then you will be able to solve problems like Jenna's.

✓ Self Check

Before starting this unit, check off the skills you know below.

I can:	Before this unit	After this unit
use fact families to add and subtract.	☐	☐
count on to add and subtract.	☐	☐
add two numbers by finding a sum of 10 first.	☐	☐
solve a one-step word problem.	☐	☐
find even and odd numbers.	☐	☐
use addition to find the total number of objects in an array.	☐	☐
use addition and subtraction to solve a problem with more than one step.	☐	☐

Ready Mathematics
PRACTICE AND PROBLEM SOLVING

Practice and Problem Solving Resources

Use the following resources from *Practice and Problem Solving* to engage students and their families and to extend student learning.

- **Family Letters** Send Family Letters home separately before each lesson or as part of a family communication package.

- **Unit Games** Use partner Unit Games at classroom centers and/or send them home for play with family members.

- **Unit Practice** Assign Unit Practice as homework, as independent or small group practice, or for whole class discussion.

- **Unit Performance Tasks** Have students solve real-world Unit Performance Tasks independently or in small groups.

- **Unit Vocabulary** Use Unit Vocabulary throughout the unit to personalize student's acquisition of mathematics vocabulary.

- **Fluency Practice** Assign Fluency Skills Practice and Fluency Repeated Reasoning Practice worksheets throughout the unit.

At A Glance

- This page introduces students to the general ideas behind adding and subtracting.

- The checklist allows them to see what skills they will be learning and take ownership of their progress.

Step By Step

- Explain to students that they are going to begin a new unit of lessons. Tell them that in all the lessons in this unit they will be learning about addition and subtraction strategies.

- Have the class read together the introduction to the unit in their books. Invite and respond to comments and questions, if any.

- Then take a few minutes to have each student independently read through the list of skills.

- Ask students to consider each skill and check the box if it is a skill they think they already have. Remind students that these skills are likely to all be new to them, but it's still possible some students have some of the skills.

- Engage students in a brief discussion about the skills. Invite students to comment on which ones they would most like to learn, or which ones seem similar or related to something they already know. Remind them that the goal is to be able to check off one skill at a time until they have them all checked.

Lesson 1
Understand Mental Math Strategies (Fact Families)

CCSS Focus

Domain
Operations and Algebraic Thinking

Cluster
B. Add and subtract within 20.

Standards
2.OA.B.2 Fluently add and subtract within 20 using mental strategies. By end of Grade 2, know from memory all sums of two one-digit numbers.

Standards for Mathematical Practice (SMP)

2 Reason abstractly and quantitatively.

3 Construct viable arguments and critique the reasoning of others.

4 Model with mathematics.

7 Look for and make use of structure.

8 Look for and express regularity in repeated reasoning.

Lesson Objectives

Content Objectives

- Identify the three related numbers that form number sentences as part of a fact family.

- Apply counting strategies to find an unknown addend or difference.

- Use inverse operations to find an unknown addend or difference.

Language Objectives

- Record addition and subtraction facts in number bonds.

- Draw an open number line to show addition and subtraction facts.

Prerequisite Skills

- Add numbers within 20.

- Count back from 20.

- Use counting strategies: counting on, making tens, and doubles plus one or two.

Lesson Vocabulary

- **sum** the result of addition

- **difference** the result of subtraction

Review the following key terms.

- **fact family** a group of related number sentences that use the same numbers, but in a different order

- **add** to combine or find the total of two or more quantities

- **addend** a number being added

- **subtract** to take away or separate one quantity from another, or to compare two quantities

Learning Progression

In Grade 1 students build on earlier experiences with addition and subtraction. They are introduced to mental strategies that help them remember basic addition facts within 20 and begin to explore addition with regrouping.

In Grade 2 students master facts within 20 and extend their understanding to two- and three-digit numbers. The ability to utilize mental strategies with understanding builds confidence and flexibility with numbers and operations.

In this lesson students focus on fact families and the relationship between addition and subtraction. They informally explore addition and subtraction as inverse operations, which reinforces the commutative nature of addition.

In Grade 3 students connect the concept of fact families to multiplication and division, recognizing the inverse quality of the two operations. This helps to solidify their understanding that addition and multiplication are commutative, while subtraction and division are not.

Lesson Pacing Guide

Whole Class Instruction

Day 1 45–60 minutes	Toolbox: Interactive Tutorial* *Relating Addition and Subtraction Facts* **Introduction** • Opening Activity *10 min* • Think It Through Question *5 min* • Think *10 min* • Think *10 min* • Reflect *5 min*	**Practice and Problem Solving** Assign pages 3–4.
Day 2 45–60 minutes	**Guided Instruction** **Think About Using Different Strategies to Subtract** • Let's Explore the Idea *20 min* • Let's Talk About It *15 min* • Try It Another Way *10 min*	**Practice and Problem Solving** Assign pages 5–6.
Day 3 45–60 minutes	**Guided Practice** **Connect Ideas About Subtraction Strategies** • Explain *15 min* • Analyze *15 min* • Identify *15 min*	**Practice and Problem Solving** Assign pages 7–8.
Day 4 45–60 minutes	**Independent Practice** **Apply Ideas About Subtraction Strategies** • Put It Together *30 min* • Pair/Share *15 min*	
Day 5 45–60 minutes	• On-Level, Intervention, or Challenge Activity *20 min* **Toolbox: Lesson Quiz** Lesson 1 Quiz	

Small Group Differentiation

Teacher-Toolbox.com

Reteach
Ready Prerequisite Lessons 45–90 min

Grade 1
• Lesson 6 Doubles and Doubles Plus 1
• Lesson 9 Number Partners for 10

Teacher-led Activities
Tools for Instruction 15–20 min

Grade 1 *(Lessons 6 and 9)*
• Doubles Addition Facts

Grade 2 *(Lesson 1)*
• Counting Back to Subtract
• Addition/Subtraction Fact Families

Student-led Activities
Math Center Activities 30–40 min

Grade 2 *(Lesson 1)*
• 2.5 Use Mental Math to Subtract

Personalized Learning

i-Ready.com

Independent
i-Ready Lessons* 10–20 min

Grade 1 *(Lessons 6 and 9)*
• Addition Facts: Doubles
• Addition Facts for 10

*We continually update the Interactive Tutorials. Check the Teacher Toolbox for the most up-to-date offerings for this lesson.

Opening Activity

Build Fact Families

Objective Identify the two addition and two subtraction facts in a fact family.

Time *15–20 minutes*

Materials for each student
- Activity Sheet 1 (Digit Cards):
  - three cards with the numbers in a fact family
  - three cards with the symbols +, −, and =
- paper and pencil

Overview

Students are challenged to build and record all possible addition and subtraction facts given cards with numbers and symbols to form a fact family. Students discover that there are four facts in each fact family: two addition and two subtraction.

Step By Step

1 Prepare and distribute cards.

- Prepare sets of number cards from Activity Sheet 1. The three numbers in each set should belong to a fact family. For example: 4, 5, 9 or 2, 6, 8.

- Prepare sets of symbol cards from Activity Sheet 1. Each set should have +, −, and =.

- Provide each student with a set of number cards and symbol cards.

2 Build facts.

- Instruct students to arrange their cards to form a fact and then record it on paper.

- Ask students to form as many facts as possible with their cards and record each one.

3 Compare facts.

- Have students compare the facts they wrote with a classmate. Alternatively, you may want to do the comparison as a whole-class activity.

- Ask: *How many facts were you able to form with your cards?* [four facts] *How many were addition and how many were subtraction?* [two addition and two subtraction]

- Tell students that this lesson will help them learn more about how the numbers in their facts are related.

Teacher Notes

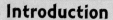

Introduction

At A Glance

Students explore the meaning of a fact family. They relate subtraction to a picture, relate fact families to a number bond, and complete facts. Then students rewrite a subtraction problem as an unknown addend problem and count on as a mental strategy for subtraction.

Step By Step

- Introduce the question at the top of the page. Emphasize that the picture shows removing a group of objects from a larger group.

▶ **Mathematical Discourse 1 and 2**

- Read the **Think** question together. Review the meaning of a fact family. Make sure students recognize that no more than three numbers belong to a fact family.

▶ **English Language Learners**

▶ **Mathematical Discourse 3**

- Draw students' attention to the number bond. Have students write the number that belongs in the empty box. Discuss what the position of each number means.

> **SMP TIP Look for Structure**
> Help students recognize the commutative property within the structure of the number bond. Point out that the numbers in the two bottom boxes can be switched. *(SMP 7)*

- Ask students to fill in the blanks to complete the facts. Help them recognize that the four facts are each part of the same fact family.

- Students may mistakenly think that the numbers in a fact family can be put in any place in an addition or subtraction problem. For example, they may think $12 + 3 = ?$ and $12 - 3 = ?$ are in the same fact family. Using number bonds helps students identify the greatest number in the fact family and avoid this type of misconception.

Think It Through

How can you use fact families and counting on to add and subtract in your head?

You know how to draw a picture to subtract.

$$\begin{array}{r} 12 \\ -3 \\ \hline 9 \end{array}$$

How can you subtract in your head?

Think I can use fact families.

Find the **difference**. $12 - 3 = ?$
Think of the problem as $3 + \boxed{?} = 12$.

Complete the number bond for this fact family.

Now you can write the four facts in this fact family.

$3 + \underline{9} = 12$ $12 - 3 = \underline{9}$

$\underline{9} + \underline{3} = 12$ $12 - \underline{9} = \underline{3}$

The **sum** of each addition fact is 12.

2

▶ **Mathematical Discourse**

1 *Why do 3 stars have Xs on them?*
That is how many stars are taken away.

2 *How do you subtract 3 from 12 in your head?*
Possible responses: I use my fingers; I count back; I count on.

3 *Can you think of a fact family that uses only 2 numbers? Explain.*
Listen for responses that include doubles. Emphasize that the two addends are the same number. Although the addend is used twice, it is still just one number that results in only 2 facts rather than 4 facts.

▶ **English Language Learners**

To reinforce the term *fact family*, use a student's native language for the word *family*. Discuss that the numbers in a fact *family* (native word) belong together in a special way, just as the members of a *family* (native word) belong together in a special way.

Think I can use counting on.

What is $11 - 8$?
Think of it as $8 + \boxed{?} = 11$.

What number do I add to 8 to get 11?

Circle 8 in the table. Mark each box you count to get to 11.

1	2	3	4	5	6	7	⑧	9 /	10 /
11 /	12	13	14	15	16	17	18	19	20

How many numbers did you count on? ___3___

Now you know four facts. Write the facts.

$8 + \underline{3} = 11$ $11 - 8 = \underline{3}$

$\underline{3} + \underline{8} = \underline{11}$ $\underline{11} - \underline{3} = \underline{8}$

▶ **Reflect** **Work with a partner.**

1 **Talk About It** You want to count on to find $2 + 6$. What number would you start with? Why?

Write About It Possible answer: I would start with 6 and count on 2.

This way is easier than starting with 2 and counting on 6.

3

▶ **Visual Model**

Show students how a fact family can be displayed in a triangle.

• Draw this model on the board.

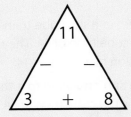

• Connect this model to a number bond model and to the commutative property of addition. Help students recognize that the numbers at the base of the triangle are the addends and can be added in any order. The top number is the sum. If you subtract either of the addends from the sum, the result is the other addend.

▶ **Mathematical Discourse**

4 *How could a number bond help you think about the numbers in this subtraction problem and addition problem?*

Listen for responses that indicate students recognize that each problem, when solved, uses the same three numbers and can be shown in a number bond. Therefore, the numbers are part of a fact family.

5 *What are some other things you could do to help you count on?*

Possible responses: I can tap out the counts; I can use my fingers to count on; I could use blocks to see how many to count on.

Step By Step

• Write the subtraction problem and addition problem from the top of the **Think** section on the board.

• Help students relate these numbers to a fact family.

▶ **Mathematical Discourse 4**

• On the board, draw a number bond or model like the one shown in the Visual Model activity to help students recognize they are trying to find the unknown number in a fact family.

▶ **Visual Model**

• Tell students that counting on is one way they can find the unknown number. Have students look at the table and describe how it shows counting on.

▶ **Mathematical Discourse 5**

• Have students fill in the unknown numbers to complete each equation.

• Read the **Reflect** question together. Ask students to discuss the question with a partner and then write their answer.

Ready Mathematics
PRACTICE AND PROBLEM SOLVING

Assign *Practice and Problem Solving* **pages 3–4** after students have completed this section.

Guided Instruction

At A Glance

Students connect subtraction to finding an unknown addend. Then students analyze strategies for subtracting mentally.

Step By Step

Let's Explore the Idea

- Work through the first problem together as a class. Make sure students recognize they are working within a fact family.

- Have students work individually on the remainder of the problems on this page and then share their responses in groups.

- As students work individually, circulate among them. This is an opportunity to assess student understanding and address misconceptions. Use the Hands-On Activity to help students who are struggling with the concept of a fact family.

▶ Hands-On Activity

- After students have completed the problems, encourage them to share their strategies with the class. Although this lesson focuses on number bonds and counting on, some students may have developed strategies that are mathematically accurate and perhaps more efficient for them.

- Listen for strategies such as: *I know that 14 is 4 away from 10, so I subtracted 4. Then I subtracted the extra 2 from 10 to get 8. I know that 12 minus 6 is 6. 14 is 2 more than 12. So the answer is 8, since 8 is 2 more than 6.* Be sure to validate all appropriate strategies.

> **SMP TIP Construct Arguments**
> Encouraging students to share strategies and then justify the mathematical accuracy of them not only validates the strategy but also develops number sense and builds mathematical confidence. (SMP 3)

Think About ▶ Using Different Strategies to Subtract

Let's Explore the Idea Use fact families and counting on.

2 Fill in the blanks in the equation.

$12 - 8 = \boxed{?}$ is the same as $\underline{\ 8\ } + \boxed{?} = \underline{\ 12\ }$.

3 Show how to find $12 - 8 = \boxed{?}$ by counting on.

Students' work may vary. Students may list numbers 8 through 12 or put the numbers in a table. Be sure students demonstrate starting with 8 and counting on 9, 10, 11, and 12.

4 Explain what you did in Problem 3.

Possible answer: I started with 8. Then I counted numbers

until I got to 12. I counted 4 numbers: 9, 10, 11, 12.

So $12 - 8 = 4$.

5 Fill in the blanks in the equation.

$14 - 6 = \boxed{?}$ is the same as $\underline{\ 6\ } + \boxed{?} = \underline{\ 14\ }$.

6 Fill in the number bond to find $14 - 6$.

7 Explain how picturing a number bond can help you find $14 - 6$ in your head.

Possible answer: The number bond helps me think about

the number that I add to 6 to get 14. I know $6 + 8 = 14$,

so $14 - 6 = 8$.

4

▶ Hands-On Activity

Use connecting cubes to understand fact families.

Materials: connecting cubes (a cube train of 6, a cube train of 8, and a cube train of 14, each in a different color) or paper strips (in lengths of 6, 8, and 14 units, each a different color)

- Have students start with the cube train of 6 and connect to it the cube train of 8. Ask them to compare the cube train they just made to the cube train of 14. They should notice that both are the same length. Record the addition fact $6 + 8 = 14$.

- Have students repeat, beginning with the 8-cube train and attaching to it the 6-cube train. Ask what they notice. [It is also the same length as the cube train of 14.] Record the addition fact $8 + 6 = 14$.

- Then have students remove a train of 6 cubes from the 14. Ask how many are left. [8] Record the subtraction fact $14 - 6 = 8$. Have students repeat, removing an 8-cube train from the 14.

- Relate the cube models to a number bond and fact family.

Let's Talk About It
Work with a partner.

8 Katie says she would not count on 9 from 2 to find 2 + 9. Do you agree? Why or why not?

Possible answer: I agree. Starting with 2 and counting

on 9 would take a long time. I would start with 9 and

count on 2.

9 How would you explain to a student who missed class what you can do to subtract in your head?

Possible answer: You can think of subtracting as an

addition problem. Then use addition facts or count on to

find the answer.

▶ **Try It Another Way** Use an open number line.

10 Dana is finding 13 − 7. She pictures this open number line in her head. What is Dana's answer?

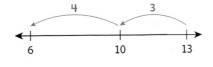

13 − 7 = ___6___

11 Draw an open number line you can picture in your head to find 15 − 7. What is your answer?

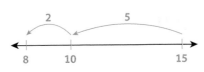

15 − 7 = ___8___

5

Step By Step

Let's Talk About It

- Organize students in groups to answer Problems 8 and 9. Walk around to each group. Listen to and join in on discussions at different points.
- If students respond to the first question by saying they don't agree, ask: *How would you keep track of counting on 9? Could you change the order and count on 2 from 9?* Explain why doing this makes sense.
- As students answer Problem 9, make sure they justify the strategy they would use. If they respond, "It's easier," ask them to explain what makes it easier.

Try It Another Way

- Direct each group's attention to **Try it Another Way**. Ask: *Why do you think Dana first subtracted 3? Why did she subtract 4 next?* Lead students to understand that it's easy to subtract 3 from 13 because it makes a ten. Since you have to subtract a total of 7, you need to subtract 4 more from 10.

▶ **Mathematical Discourse 1 and 2**

- Invite volunteers to come to the board and draw the open number line they used for Problem 11. Have them explain how the number line shows subtracting 7 from 15.
- Ask the class if anyone used different number lines than the ones the volunteers showed. Discuss the similarities and differences in students' strategies.

Note: Mental calculation involving the make-a-ten strategy is developed more completely in Lesson 3.

▶ **Concept Extension**

 Ready Mathematics
PRACTICE AND PROBLEM SOLVING

Assign *Practice and Problem Solving* **pages 5–6** after students have completed this section.

▶ **Concept Extension**

Connect fact-family relationships to place-value relationships.

- Start with multiples of 10, such as 50 + 40. Since 5 + 4 = 9, 50 + 40 = 90. Ask students to find 9 − 2 mentally. Then ask them to find 90 − 20 mentally. Have students describe the similarities and differences between these two problems.
- Make number bonds with other multiples of 10. Have students write addition and subtraction facts to show these fact families.
- For further extension, apply these strategies to other numbers. For example, 2 + 5 = 7, so 32 + 5 = 37. Or 8 − 5 = 3, so 28 − 5 = 23. Have students practice these pairs of problems using number bonds on paper. Then ask them to try to do the calculations in their head. Guide them to picture the number bond in their head to help them do the calculations.

▶ **Mathematical Discourse**

1 *Think about the way Dana used the open number line to solve this problem. How is it like adding to make a ten? Why is it helpful to subtract to make a ten?*

Students may answer that just like adding to make a ten, you can also subtract to make a ten. They may find this helpful if they know all the facts that include subtracting a number from 10.

2 *How can you use what is on the open number line to find the addition facts that belong in this fact family?*

Students should notice that the number they subtracted (subtrahend) added to the difference results in the sum. Reversing the order of the addends results in the same sum.

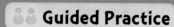

Guided Practice

At A Glance

Students demonstrate their understanding of fact families and counting on. Then students demonstrate their use of mental strategies by showing how to solve a subtraction problem and an addition problem in different ways. They explain reasons for choosing which strategies to use.

Step By Step

- Discuss each problem as a class using the discussion points outlined below:

Explain

- Ask students to explain the error Tia made. [She rearranged the 8 and 5 by subtracting 5 from 8, which equals 3, instead of subtracting 5 or 8 from 13.] *Why do you think she may have made this error?* [She doesn't know that there are only 3 numbers in any fact family.]
- Invite volunteers to come to the board and write the other facts that are in the same fact family as $5 + 8 = 13$, and the other facts that are in the same fact family as $8 - 5 = 3$.
- Emphasize that *two* of the same numbers are used in each fact family, but *all three* are not the same numbers.

Analyze

- For Problem 13, make sure students recognize that counting on by more than three or four is time consuming and can lead to errors. Ask: *What might happen if you tried to count on 8 times?* [I might lose track of my counts, so I'd have to start over; I might get mixed up and end up on the wrong number.]

Identify

- To help students make sense of the error that was made, have them draw a row of 11 squares (or any easy-to-draw shapes) on paper or individual whiteboards.
- Ask students what number they are counting on from. [7] Instruct students to circle this number of shapes. Explain that this is the number they start with; these shapes have already been counted.

Connect ▶ **Ideas About Fact Families**

Talk about these questions as a class. Then write your answers.

12 **Explain** Tia says that the equations below belong in the same fact family because they both have 5 and 8. Do you agree? Explain.

$$5 + 8 = 13 \qquad 8 - 5 = 3$$

Possible answer: I disagree; Possible explanation: The third numbers in

the equations are different, so the equations are in different fact

families.

13 **Analyze** Which problem would be faster to solve by counting on? Why?

$$7 + 8 = ? \qquad 7 + 2 = ?$$

7 + 2 is faster. Both start with 7, but it is faster to count on 2 than to

count on 8.

14 **Identify** Dan counted on to find $7 + 4 = \boxed{?}$. He showed how he counted on in this table.

What did he do wrong?

⑦	8	9	10	11
/	/	/	/	

Possible answer: Dan started counting numbers at 7. His first mark in the

table should be at 8.

6

- Have students locate the 7th shape. Ask: *Is it in the group that has already been counted or the group that still needs to be counted?* [already counted] *What number should I start counting at?* [8]

Apply ▶ **Ideas About Fact Families**

Put It Together   Use what you have learned to complete this task.

15 Look at these equations.

$$11 - 6 = ? \qquad 9 + 4 = ?$$

Part A   Show one way you could solve $11 - 6 = \boxed{?}$.

Possible answer:
$6 + ? = 11$
$6 + 5 = 11$

$$11 - 6 = \underline{\quad 5 \quad}$$

Part B   Why did you solve the problem this way?

Possible answer: I find it easier to add than to subtract, so I thought

of the problem as addition.

Part C   Show a way you could solve $9 + 4 = \boxed{?}$ that is different from what you did in Part A.   Possible answer:

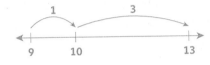

$$9 + 4 = \underline{\quad 13 \quad}$$

Part D   Which way do you think you will use most often to add numbers in your head? Why?

Possible answer: I think I will picture numbers in a number bond.

I can use it to add or subtract.

7

Step By Step

Put It Together

- Draw students' attention to the two facts they have to complete. Remind them to think about what strategies work best for them as they work though the page.

- Direct students to complete the **Put It Together** task on their own. Tell students that they are free to use the open space on the page to make drawings or models as they think about and solve each problem.

- As students work on their own, walk around to assess their progress and understanding, to answer their questions, and to give additional support, if needed.

- If time permits, have students share the strategies they used in completing this task.

📦 **Ready**   **Mathematics**   PRACTICE AND PROBLEM SOLVING

Assign *Practice and Problem Solving* **pages 7–8** after students have completed Guided Practice.

Scoring Rubrics

Parts A and B

Points	Expectations
2	The student correctly solves the subtraction problem using a mathematically sound strategy. The justification for strategy choice is reasonable.
1	The student correctly solves the subtraction problem, but the strategy demonstration or justification is incomplete or weak.
0	The student's answer to the subtraction problem and use of strategy are incorrect.

Parts C and D

Points	Expectations
2	The student correctly solves the addition problem using a different strategy than in Part A. The justification for the strategy choice is reasonable.
1	The student correctly solves the addition problem but uses the same strategy as in Part A or provides weak justification of the strategy choice.
0	The student was not able to accurately solve the addition problem and explain a strategy choice.

Differentiated Instruction

▶ Intervention Activity

Model a fact family.

Materials: paper plate with lines dividing it in thirds, counters, number bond cards with one unknown number that is written on the back

- Students place counters on the plate to model the numbers given in the number bond. If the top number of the bond is given, they place that number of counters in the top section. Students then move the number of counters that belong in one of the lower sections to model subtraction. What remains in the top section now belongs in the other bottom section and should be moved there.

- If both bottom numbers are showing, students place the counters in the two bottom sections and then combine them into the top section.

- Once students find the unknown number, they should write it in the number bond, check the answer, and then model and write all the facts belonging to that family.

▶ On-Level Activity

Show facts on a number line.

Materials: counters, unknown addend cards (for example, 3 + _____ = 12)

- Provide each student with an unknown addend card. Draw a number line that has labels from 0 to 20 on the board. Ask students to copy it on a sheet of paper or individual whiteboard.

- Students use counters to model their problem on the number line. They put counters on the given addend and sum, and then determine and place a counter on the jump (the missing addend). They record the fact below the number line.

- Students check with a partner to make sure the answer is correct. Then each student records the remaining addition and subtraction facts to complete the fact family.

▶ Challenge Activity

Write all the facts.

Materials: number cards and symbol cards +, =, −, and □ from Activity Sheet 1 (Digit Cards)

- Students randomly select two number cards. They arrange them with the symbol cards to make either an addition or a subtraction problem (9 and 6 could be 9 + 6 = □ or 9 − 6 = □). Students then write all the other facts that belong in that fact family.

- If students began with addition, they should rearrange the cards to show a subtraction problem and record the facts in that fact family. If they began with subtraction, they rearrange the cards to show an addition problem and record the facts in that fact family.

Optional: You may wish to have pairs of students play the following game. Each student picks two numbers and uses the symbol cards to make an addition or subtraction problem. The partner writes all the facts in that fact family. The student who is done first gets 1 point. Play several times. The player with the most points wins.

Teacher Notes

Teacher-Toolbox.com

Overview

Assign the Lesson 1 Quiz and have students work independently to complete it.

Use the results of the quiz to assess students' understanding of the content of the lesson and to identify areas for reteaching. See the Lesson Pacing Guide at the beginning of the lesson and the Differentiated Instruction activities that follow for suggested instructional resources.

Tested Skills

Assesses 2.OA.B.2

Problems on this assessment form require students to be able to identify and write number facts that belong to the same fact family using equations, number bonds, and other diagrams. Students will also need to be familiar with finding an unknown addend and adding and subtracting within 20.

Ready **Mathematics**

Lesson 1 Quiz

Solve the problems.

1 Which equations belong to the same fact family as $12 = 7 + 5$?
Circle all the correct answers.

A $7 - 5 = 2$

B $12 - 5 = 7$

C $12 = 5 + 7$

D $12 = 6 + 6$

E $12 - 7 = 5$

2 Emily has 6 goldfish. Her brother buys more goldfish. Now there are 11 goldfish in all. Emily wants to use this equation to find how many goldfish her brother bought.

$6 + \boxed{} = 11$

Emily writes a subtraction equation to help her find the answer. What equation can Emily write? Write your answer in the blanks.

_____ − 6 = _____

Lesson 1 Quiz continued

3 Decide if each statement is true about fact families.
Circle *Yes* or *No* for each statement.

a. The numbers 1, 5, and 6 can be used to make an addition and subtraction fact family. Yes No

b. The facts $7 + 7 = 14$ and $14 - 7 = 7$ make a complete fact family. Yes No

c. The facts $6 + 3 = 9$ and $9 - 3 = 6$ belong to the same fact family. Yes No

d. If a fact family has the numbers 4 and 6, then it has to have the number 2. Yes No

4 Do the equations below make a fact family?
Explain why or why not.

$6 + 7 = 13$

$7 + 6 = 13$

$7 - 6 = 1$

$13 - 6 = 7$

_____

_____

_____

_____

_____

Common Misconceptions and Errors

Errors may result if students:

• interpret fact families as any two addition and subtraction equations that have some numbers in common.

• overlook doubles facts and think all fact families must have two addition equations and two subtraction equations.

• count on from a given addend instead of the next number.

Ready® **Mathematics**

Lesson 1 Quiz Answer Key

1. B, C, E
DOK 1

2. 11, 5
DOK 2

3. a. Yes
b. Yes
c. Yes
d. No
DOK 3

4. The equations do not make a fact family. Possible explanation: Only one of the equations uses the number 1 and all four facts in a fact family should have the same three numbers.
DOK 3

Lesson 2
Solve One-Step Word Problems

CCSS Focus

Domain
Operations and Algebraic Thinking

Cluster
A. Represent and solve problems involving addition and subtraction.

Standards
2.OA.A.1 Use addition and subtraction within 100 to solve one- and two-step word problems involving situations of adding to, taking from, putting together, taking apart, and comparing, with unknowns in all positions, e.g., by using drawings and equations with a symbol for the unknown number to represent the problem.

Additional Standards
2.OA.B.2, 2.NBT.B.5 (see page B3 for full text.)

Standards for Mathematical Practice (SMP)

1 Make sense of problems and persevere in solving them.

2 Reason abstractly and quantitatively.

3 Construct viable arguments and critique the reasoning of others.

4 Model with mathematics.

5 Use appropriate tools strategically.

7 Look for and make use of structure.

Lesson Objectives

Content Objectives

• Analyze one-step problems and write equations that can be used to solve them.

• Apply the use of fact families as a strategy to solve one-step problems and build number sense.

• Interpret models that represent one-step problems.

Language Objectives

• Draw a tape diagram to represent and solve a word problem.

• Write an addition or subtraction fact to represent a word problem.

Prerequisite Skills

• Add and subtract within 20.

• Know fact families.

• Understand addition and subtraction situations involving adding to, taking from, putting together, taking apart, and comparing.

Lesson Vocabulary

• **equation** a mathematical sentence that uses an equal sign (=) to show that two expressions have the same value

Review the following key term.

• **equal sign (=)** a symbol used to compare numbers that have the same value

Learning Progression

In Grade 1 students solve word problems by connecting pictures and number sentences to a physical model that represents a problem situation.

In Grade 2 students represent a problem using pictures and abstract diagrams, and write a number sentence that models the situation.

In this lesson fact families become a vehicle for finding an unknown as students recognize the relationship between the difference in a subtraction sentence and an addend in an addition

sentence. By identifying the whole and the parts in visual models, students are preparing to solve problems involving two-digit numbers and two-step problems that come later in Grade 2.

In Grade 3 and beyond, students will use these skills to represent problems in varied ways. This will prepare students for the increasingly complex problems they will face in the future as well as enable them to apply these strategies to solve problems with multiplication and division.

Lesson Pacing Guide

Whole Class Instruction

Day 1
45–60 minutes

Toolbox: Interactive Tutorial*
Subtraction in Separation Situations

Introduction
• Opening Activity *15 min*
• Use What You Know *10 min*
• Find Out More *10 min*
• Reflect *10 min*

Practice and Problem Solving
Assign pages 11–12.

Day 2
45–60 minutes

Modeled and Guided Instruction

Learn About Solving Take-Apart Word Problems
• Model It/Understand It/Picture It *15 min*
• Connect It *20 min*
• Try It *10 min*

Practice and Problem Solving
Assign pages 13–14.

Day 3
45–60 minutes

Modeled and Guided Instruction

Learn About Solving Comparison Word Problems
• Understand It/Picture It *20 min*
• Connect It *15 min*
• Try It *10 min*

Practice and Problem Solving
Assign pages 15–16.

Day 4
45–60 minutes

Guided Practice

Practice Solving Different Kinds of Word Problems
• Example *5 min*
• Problems 13–15 *15 min*
• Pair/Share *15 min*
• Solutions *10 min*

Practice and Problem Solving
Assign pages 17–18.

Day 5
45–60 minutes

Independent Practice

Practice Solving Different Kinds of Word Problems
• Problems 1–6 *20 min*
• Quick Check and Remediation *10 min*
• Hands-On or Challenge Activity *15 min*

Toolbox: Lesson Quiz
Lesson 2 Quiz

Small Group Differentiation

Teacher-Toolbox.com

Reteach
Ready Prerequisite Lessons 45–90 min

Grade 1
• Lesson 3 Add and Subtract in Word Problems
• Lesson 5 Subtract to Compare in Word Problems

Teacher-led Activities
Tools for Instruction 15–20 min

Grade 2 *(Lesson 2)*
• Solve Subtraction Word Problems
• Solve Subtraction Comparison Problems

Student-led Activities
Math Center Activities 30–40 min

Grade 2 *(Lesson 2)*
• 2.2 Word Problem Equation Match

Personalized Learning

i-Ready.com

Independent
i-Ready Lessons* 10–20 min

Grade 1 *(Lessons 3 and 5)*
• Counting On to Solve Addition Problems
• Subtraction Concepts: Comparisons

*We continually update the Interactive Tutorials. Check the Teacher Toolbox for the most up-to-date offerings for this lesson.

Two Unknown Addends

Objective Solve a word problem involving a put-together situation in which both addends are unknown.

Time *15–20 minutes*

Materials for each student
- Counters in two different colors

Overview

Students are given a put-together addition word problem in which both addends are unknown. They discover that more than one answer is possible and make the connection between related equation solutions and fact families.

Step By Step

1 Pose the problem.

- Provide students with counters in two different colors.

- Pose this open-ended problem. *Dan has 14 stickers. Some are cars and the rest are trucks. How many car stickers does Dan have?*

2 Organize the counters.

- Encourage students to think about what they would do to decide how many car stickers Dan has. Ask them to organize their counters to solve the problem. Students should put together some combination of colored counters for a total of 14.

3 **Share ideas.**

- Invite students to share their thinking with the class. List the various combinations of 14 that they find.

- Ask questions such as: *How did you know to put 8 and 6 together? What did you do to find that there are 5 car stickers?* As students describe their thinking, record the following on the board: cars + trucks = 14; trucks + cars = 14; 14 − trucks = cars; 14 − cars = trucks

4 **Relate the problem situation to fact families.**

- Discuss how the equations on the board are like the fact families students studied in Lesson 1.

- Tell students that in this lesson, they will learn how to use different models and both addition and subtraction to solve word problems.

Teacher Notes

Introduction

At A Glance

Students explore one-step word problems by examining a bar model and an equation. Then students use varied models to represent a word problem and analyze the three possible positions of an unknown.

Step By Step

- Tell students that this page will help them understand one-step problems by providing a model they can use to organize the information from the problem.

- Have students read the problem at the top of the page. Ask a volunteer to review for the class the information given in the problem.

- Work through **Use What You Know** as a class. Make sure students understand that the top box in the bar model shows the whole, and the bottom boxes are the parts that make up the whole.

- Once students have filled in the model, ask: *What is the part shown by the 9?* [the number of grapes Seth ate]

- Have students complete Part c.

SMP TIP Reason Abstractly

Ask students to explain why the question mark is used to represent the unknown. You may want to examine other ways to show the unknown, such as using a box or a blank line. Using a symbol for an unknown helps prepare students for the concept of a variable. *(SMP 2)*

- After students complete Part d, ask Mathematical Discourse question 1 to make sure they understand that subtraction could also be used to solve the problem.

▶ **Mathematical Discourse 1**

▶ **Real-World Connection**

Use What You Know

Solve a one-step word problem.

Seth ate 9 grapes. Then his dad gave him more grapes, and he ate them. Seth ate 15 grapes in all. How many grapes did Seth's dad give him?

a. What is the total number of grapes Seth ate? Write this number in the top box.

b. How many grapes did Seth eat first? Write this number in the bottom left box.

15	
9	?

c. What does the ? stand for?

   The ? stands for the number of grapes Seth's dad

   gave him.

d. Write an equation using the numbers in the model.

   $\underline{9} + ? = \underline{15}$

e. How many grapes did Seth's dad give him?

   Seth's dad gave Seth 6 grapes.

8

▶ **Mathematical Discourse**

1 *Could you use subtraction to solve the problem? Why or why not?*
   Students' responses should indicate an understanding that any of the four equations in the fact family can be used.

▶ **Real-World Connection**

Have students look at the models on this page and the next page. Ask students to think of a real-life situation that could be answered using one of the models (like the problem about Seth's grapes). Do some examples together as a class. Then have students write a real-world problem that can be solved using one of the models. Students can work individually to write their problems. Then have students give their problem to a partner, who will draw a model for the problem. The pairs of students should then discuss the models with each other. Have a few students share their problem and have the partner share the model he or she used to represent the problem.

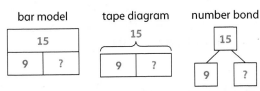
Find Out More

You can use models to show the problem on the previous page.

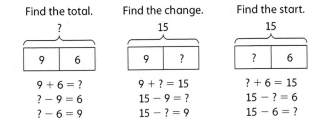

bar model   tape diagram   number bond

The ? can be in different places in the models and **equations**.

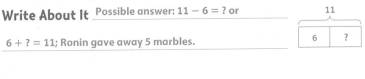

Find the total.

$9 + 6 = ?$
$? - 9 = 6$
$? - 6 = 9$

Find the change.

$9 + ? = 15$
$15 - 9 = ?$
$15 - ? = 9$

Find the start.

$? + 6 = 15$
$15 - ? = 6$
$15 - 6 = ?$

Reflect   Work with a partner.

1 Talk About It Ronin had 11 marbles. He gave some away. Now he has 6 left. How could you use a model and equation to find how many marbles Ronin gave away?

Write About It Possible answer: $11 - 6 = ?$ or

$6 + ? = 11$; Ronin gave away 5 marbles.

9

Hands-On Activity

Use physical models to understand visual models.

Materials: 3 rectangles (one 9″ × 3″, and two 4½″ × 3″) cut from construction paper for each student; 15 counters per student

- Place the two small rectangles below the large one to show the bar model. Remove the large rectangle to show the tape diagram. Fold the large rectangle in half and slightly separate all three rectangles to show the number bond.

- Use the counters to model each situation on the student page, moving them as needed to show or find the unknown.

Mathematical Discourse

2 *How are the models on this page alike? How are they different?*

Listen for responses such as: They are the same because the whole is at the top and the two parts are under it. They are different because some are put together next to each other and one is spread apart.

3 *How is finding the unknown part like using fact families?*

You can either add the parts to get the whole or subtract the known part from the whole to get the unknown part.

Step By Step

- Ask students to look at the models in **Find Out More**. Ask: *Where are the parts in each model?* [the two boxes at the bottom] *Where is the whole?* [the box or number at the top] Point out that the models can be used to show both addition and subtraction problems. Ask students to describe how each model shows addition and how it shows subtraction.

▶ **Mathematical Discourse 2 and 3**

- Read and discuss the possible positions for the question mark. You may want to use the Hands-On Activity to physically model each of these situations.

▶ **Hands-On Activity**

- Ask students to work in pairs and think of a simple problem for each position of the unknown. Encourage students to share their problems. Analyze each one as a class to ensure it is asking for the part stated.

- Have student pairs read and solve the **Reflect** problem. Discuss how this problem is the same and how it is different from the problem on the previous page.

Ready· Mathematics
PRACTICE AND PROBLEM SOLVING

Assign *Practice and Problem Solving* **pages 11–12** after students have completed this section.

Modeled and Guided Instruction

At A Glance

Students model a one-step problem in different ways and record what is known and not known. Then students revisit this problem by writing equations to represent what is shown in the models. They then solve the problem.

Step By Step

Model It

- Read the problem at the top of the page as a class and direct attention to **Model It**. Ask students to tell if this is a "find the total," "find the part," or "find the start" question and why. [find the part]

Understand It

- Read **Understand It**. Ask students to describe how the information here relates to the tape diagram above.

▶ **Mathematical Discourse**

Picture It

- Replicate the picture from **Picture It** on the board. Invite students to tell what the picture shows and how it relates to the tape diagram in **Model It**. Encourage them to describe the relationship between boys, girls, and players in the problem.

▶ **English Language Learners**

Learn About Solving Take-Apart Word Problems

Read the problem. Then you will explore different ways to solve word problems.

> There are 15 players on a team. There are 7 girls. The rest of the players are boys. How many boys are on the team?

▶ **Model It You can use words in a tape diagram.**

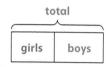

▶ **Understand It You can write what you know and don't know.**

Total players: 15

Number of girls: 7

Number of boys: ?

▶ **Picture It You can draw a picture.**

10

▶ **Mathematical Discourse**

How does writing what you know help you solve the problem?

Writing what you know helps you decide what are the parts and what is the whole. Then you know what you need to find to solve the problem.

▶ **English Language Learners**

Some students may struggle to comprehend the language used in a word problem. You may want to type or write the problem on a piece of paper so that each sentence is on a separate line. Cut out each sentence and have students match the sentence to the appropriate part of the model, then fill in the blanks:

_____ are on the team.

_____ are girls.

_____ are boys.

Connect It Use a model and equation to solve the problem.

2 What number is the total? What part do you know? Complete the model at the right.

15

3 Write two equations for the model.

$\underline{7} + ? = 15$ $\qquad$ $15 - \underline{7} = ?$

7	?

4 Explain what the equations show.

Possible explanation: 7 girls plus a number of boys equals 15 players.

15 players minus 7 girls equals the number of boys.

5 How many boys are on the team? Tell how you know.

8 boys; Possible explanation: I know 7 + 8 = 15.

6 **Talk About It** Why can you add or subtract to solve the problem on the previous page?

Write About It Possible answer: I know the whole and one part. I can

add on from the part to the whole. Or, I can subtract the part from the

whole to find the other part.

Try It Try another problem.

7 Jen has 12 pencils. 7 are blue and the rest are white. How many white pencils does she have? Write an equation to solve.

Jen has 5 white pencils. Possible answer: 7 + ? = 12; 7 + 5 = 12

11

Step By Step

Connect It

- Read **Connect It** as a class. Make sure students understand that the questions refer to the problem on the previous page.

- For Problem 3, make sure students understand that both of the equations are ways to show the problem on the previous page.

- As students complete Problem 4, allow them to refer back to the picture on the previous page, if necessary, to represent each part accurately.

Try It

- Tell students that they may use a picture or other model to help them solve the **Try It** problem. Have students explain the thinking they used in solving the problem.

SMP TIP Model with Mathematics
Record each response to Problem 7 on the board and connect students' equations to pictures or models they could have used to write them. Make sure both addition and subtraction equations are represented, as well as different types of models. Connecting an equation to a situation and a visual model prepares students to solve increasingly difficult problems and problems that may arise in their everyday lives. (SMP 4)

7 **Solution**
7; Students should write an equation showing the problem:
7 + ? = 12, ? + 7 = 12, or 12 − 7 = ?

Error Alert Students who wrote 12 + 7 = 19 added the numbers shown in the problem to find a whole rather than finding an unknown part.

Ready Mathematics
PRACTICE AND PROBLEM SOLVING

Assign *Practice and Problem Solving* **pages 13–14** after students have completed this section.

Modeled and Guided Instruction

At A Glance

Students solve a word problem using a picture model and analyze what is known and not known. Then students revisit this problem, writing an equation to model the situation.

Step By Step

Understand It

• Read the problem at the top of the page as a class. Help students connect the information in the problem to the abbreviated version in **Understand It**.

• Discuss that this is a comparison problem. The small and big bags are both wholes. Explain that students are not trying to find one of two parts of a single whole. Instead, they need to find how many balls are in the whole big bag. To do this, they need to find how many more balls are in the big bag than the small bag.

Picture It

• Examine and ask students to explain **Picture It**. Make sure students understand that in the picture, the 3 "fewer" circles shown are not soccer balls. These are only images (or your thinking) of the number that would need to be added to the small bag to make it equal to the number in the big bag.

▶ **Mathematical Discourse 1**

▶ **Visual Model**

Learn About ▶ **Solving Comparison Word Problems**

Read the problem. Then you will explore different ways to solve word problems.

> A small bag holds 3 fewer soccer balls than a big bag. The small bag holds 9 soccer balls. How many soccer balls does the big bag hold?

▶ **Understand It** **You can write what you know and don't know.**

Know: small bag = 9 balls
Know: small bag + 3 = big bag
Find: How many balls in the big bag?

▶ **Picture It** **You can draw a picture.**

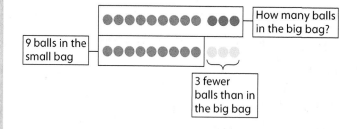

12

▶ **Mathematical Discourse**

1 *How does the picture help you compare the number of balls in the big and small bags?*

Students should recognize that the picture shows the 9 balls in the small bag lined up with 9 of the balls in the big bag and that "3 fewer" in the small bag means there are "3 more" in the big bag.

▶ **Visual Model**

Use a graph to model the concept of more and fewer.

• Replicate the graph below on the board, oriented either horizontally or vertically.

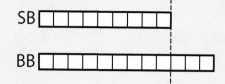

• Compare the number of balls in the small bag (SB) and big bag (BB) by asking questions that use the words *more* and *fewer*, such as: *How many more balls are in the BB than in the SB?* [3]

• Use a ruler to indicate where the SB and BB are equal as shown. Discuss that since they don't have the same amount, one must have *more* and one must have *fewer* balls.

▶ **Connect It** Write an equation to solve the problem.

8 The small bag holds ___3___ fewer balls than the big bag. So, the big bag holds ___3___ more balls than the small bag.

9 How many balls does the small bag hold? ___9___

10 Write an addition equation to solve the problem. What does the equation show?

9 + 3 = 12; Possible answer: It shows 9 balls in the small bag plus 3 more

balls equals the number of balls in the big bag.

11 **Talk About It** Can you write a subtraction equation to find the answer to this problem? Explain.

Write About It Yes; Possible answer: The number of balls in the big

bag minus 3 equals the number of balls in the small bag, so ? − 3 = 9.

▶ **Try It** Try another problem.

12 Ted has 8 white balloons and some red balloons. There are 2 fewer white balloons than red balloons. How many red balloons does Ted have?

Possible answer: 8 + 2 = 10. Ted has 10 red balloons.

13

▶ **Mathematical Discourse**

2 *Meg says there are 6 soccer balls in the big bag. What do you think she did wrong?*

Students should note that 9 − 3 = 6. They may suggest that because the word *fewer* is in the problem, Meg just subtracted the two numbers shown.

Step By Step

Connect It

- Tell students that **Connect It** will help them learn how to write an equation for the problem on the previous page.

- Help students understand the logic involved in Problem 8. You may wish to use a picture or physical model to emphasize how the words *fewer* and *more* are used in each sentence to describe the same model or situation.

- Use the Visual Model on the previous page to reinforce the concepts of *more* and *fewer*. Discuss that if the big bag had the same number as the small bag, they would each have 9 balls. So the big bag has *more* balls than the small bag.

- Then explain that if the small bag had the same number as the big bag, they would each have 12. So the small bag has *fewer* balls than the big bag.

- Have students discuss their answers to Problem 10. Make sure they connect the equation to the logic described in Problem 8.

▶ **Mathematical Discourse 2**

- Have students discuss *Talk About It* in pairs and then write an answer using their own words. Suggest that they think about how a fact family can help answer the question.

Try It

- Remind students that for the **Try It** problem, they can use a picture or physical model to help them make sense of the problem, but they should also write an equation and show their work.

12 **Solution**
The number of white balloons plus 2 equals the number of red balloons. 8 + 2 = 10.

Error Alert Students who answer 6 subtracted 2 from 8.

Ready· **Mathematics**
PRACTICE AND PROBLEM SOLVING

Assign *Practice and Problem Solving* **pages 15–16** after students have completed this section.

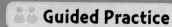 **Guided Practice**

At A Glance

Students model and solve one-step word problems involving addition and subtraction.

Step By Step

- Ask students to solve the problems individually and show all their work, including the equations they wrote. Encourage students to describe their thinking.

- **Pair/Share** When students have completed each problem, have them Pair/Share to discuss their solutions with a partner.

Solutions

Example A picture model and equation are used as examples for solving this problem. Students may also solve it by using counters.

13 Solution

There are 8 brown dogs at the park; Students may solve the problem by drawing a picture or using any other model. Students may also write a subtraction equation: $14 - 6 = 8$.

DOK 2

Practice **Solving Different Kinds of Word Problems**

Study the model below. Then solve Problems 13–15.

Example

Jen scored 6 more points than Sue. Jen scored 13 points. How many points did Sue score?

You can draw a picture.

Jen's points: • • • • • • • • • • • • •

Sue's points: • • • • • • •/ / / / / /

Jen's points − 6 = Sue's points.

$$13 - 6 = 7$$

Answer Sue scored 7 points.

---

13 There are 14 dogs at the dog park. There are 6 black dogs. The rest are brown. How many brown dogs are at the dog park?

Show your work.

Possible work:
6 black dogs + ? brown dogs = 14 dogs

$6 + 8 = 14$

What do you know? What are you trying to find out?

Answer There are 8 brown dogs at the dog park.

14

Teacher Notes

---

14 Kim had 12 stickers. She gave some to her sister. Now Kim has 6 stickers left. How many stickers did Kim give her sister?

Show your work.

Possible work: 12 − ? = 6

```
        12
       /  \
      6    ?
```

I know 6 + 6 = 12, so 12 − 6 = 6.

You can add or subtract to find the answer.

Answer _Kim gave her sister 6 stickers._

15 Kyle has 7 fish. He has 4 fewer fish than Ana. How many fish does Ana have?

A 3

B 4

(C) 11

D 12

Who has more fish?

Deb chose **A** as the answer. This answer is wrong. How did Deb get her answer?

Possible answer: Deb subtracted 7 − 4. She should have added 7 + 4.

15

Solutions

14 **Solution**
Kim gave her sister 6 stickers. See possible work on the student page. Students may also model the problem by drawing a picture.
DOK 2

15 **Solution**
C; Kyle has 4 fewer than Ana, so Ana has 4 more than Kyle. 7 + 4 = 11.
Explain to students why the other two choices are not correct:
B is not correct because 4 is how many more fish Ana has.
D is not correct because 7 + 4 = 11 not 12.
DOK 3

Ready Mathematics
PRACTICE AND PROBLEM SOLVING

Assign *Practice and Problem Solving* **pages 17–18** after students have completed this section.

Teacher Notes

Independent Practice

At A Glance

Students use addition and subtraction to solve one-step word problems that might appear on a mathematics test.

Solutions

1 Solution
A, **B**, and **D**; 13 is the total, so equations that show adding 9 and 4 or subtracting 9 or 4 from 13 can be used to solve the problem. *DOK 2*

2 Solution
D; Since there are 8 fewer cows in the barn than in the field, there are 8 more in the field. $8 + 5 = 13$. *DOK 2*

3 Solution
a. **Yes**; b. **No**; c. **No**; d. **Yes**; 9 is the total, so equations that show adding 5 and 4 or subtracting 5 or 4 from 9 can be used to solve the problem. *DOK 2*

Quick Check and Remediation

- There were 11 children riding bikes. Some children rode home. Now there are 7 children riding bikes. Ask students to find the number of children who rode home. [4]
- For students who are still struggling, use the chart to guide remediation.
- After providing remediation, check students' understanding using the following problem: Sue finds 13 socks under her bed. 5 socks are blue. The rest are black. How many black socks does she find? [8]

Practice ▶ **Solving Different Kinds of Word Problems**

Solve the problems.

1 Rick has 13 marbles. 4 marbles are blue. The rest are white. How many white marbles are there?

Fill in the blanks. Then circle the letter for all the equations that can be used to solve the problem.

(**A**) $13 - 4 = \underline{\quad 9 \quad}$ **C** $13 + 4 = \underline{\quad 17 \quad}$

(**B**) $13 - \underline{\quad 9 \quad} = 4$ (**D**) $4 + \underline{\quad 9 \quad} = 13$

2 There are 5 cows in the barn. There are 8 fewer cows in the barn than in the field. How many cows are in the field? Circle the correct answer.

A 3   **C** 12

B 8   (**D**) 13

3 Jin has 9 markers. He has 5 more markers than pencils. How many pencils does Jin have?

Circle *Yes* or *No* to tell if each equation can be used to solve the problem.

a. $9 - 5 = 4$ (Yes)   No

b. $9 + 5 = 14$ Yes   (No)

c. $14 - 5 = 9$ Yes   (No)

d. $5 + 4 = 9$ (Yes)   No

16

If the error is ...	Students may ...	To remediate ...
18	have added the given numbers.	Provide students with counters to act out the problem. Guide them to see that when some children go home, subtraction is involved.
5	have subtracted incorrectly.	Help students use a counting back strategy or fact families. Since $11 - \underline{\quad} = 7$, $7 + \underline{\quad} = 11$. Encourage students to think of making a ten to help solve mentally. ($7 + 3 = 10$ and one more is 11, so $7 + 4 = 11$.)
any other number	have subtracted incorrectly or misrepresented the problem.	As you read each sentence in the problem, have students describe what the sentence says and model it with counters or a picture. Write an equation for the problem and compare it with the equation the student wrote. Check for computational accuracy.

4 There were 4 children on a rug. More children joined them. Now there are 10 children on the rug. How many children joined the first 4 children? Circle the correct answer.

A 4   **C** 6

B 5   **D** 14

5 Write a problem that can be solved using the tape diagram at the right.

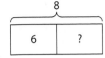

Answers will vary. Possible answer: I have 8 stuffed

toys. 6 are bears. The rest are dogs. How many stuffed

dogs do I have?

6 Show how to solve the problem you wrote in Problem 5. Then ask a partner to solve the problem a different way. Show how your partner solved it.

Answers will vary. Possible answer: I wrote the addition

problem 6 + ? = 8. So the answer is 2 stuffed dogs. My

partner counted on 2 from 6 to get to 8. So my partner

also got the answer 2 stuffed dogs.

✓ Self Check **Now you can solve one-step problems. Fill this in on the progress chart on page 1.**

17

Solutions

4 **Solution**
C; 4 children + more children = 10 children; 4 + 6 = 10.
DOK 2

5 **Solution**
See sample problem on Student Book page; Problem should reflect that 8 is the total, 6 is a known part, and there is an unknown part.
DOK 3

6 **Solution**
See sample solution on Student Book page.
DOK 3

▶ **Hands-On Activity**

Use counters to solve a one-step word problem.

Materials: counters

• Provide each student with 15 counters and pose this problem. Sarah bought some apples to make a pie. She used 8 apples for the pie. Now there are 5 apples left. How many apples did Sarah buy?

• Guide students to recognize that they are trying to find the total number of apples. Help them organize the counters in a group of 8 (apples that were used) and a group of 5 (apples left). Invite students to describe their thinking and solution. Encourage students to think about the problem as 8 + 5 = [13] or as [13] − 8 = 5.

▶ **Challenge Activity**

Write one-step word problems.

• Challenge students to write word problems from their daily lives that involve using one step to solve. Tell them to write at least one problem where the unknown is at the beginning, at least one where the unknown is the change or part, and at least one where the unknown is the result. Encourage them to write at least one problem involving a comparison.

• When completed, students can exchange and solve each other's problems.

Teacher-Toolbox.com

Overview

Assign the Lesson 2 Quiz and have students work independently to complete it.

Use the results of the quiz to assess students' understanding of the content of the lesson and to identify areas for reteaching. See the Lesson Pacing Guide at the beginning of the lesson for suggested instructional resources.

Tested Skills

Assesses 2.OA.A.1

Problems on this assessment form require students to be able to determine the operation (addition or subtraction) needed to solve a one-step problem, interpret models that represent a one-step problem, and solve one-step problems. Students will also need to be familiar with adding and subtracting within 100 and identifying situations that involve adding and subtracting.

Ready® Mathematics

Lesson 2 Quiz

Solve the problems.

1 Mrs. Diaz has 9 eggs. She cooks 5 eggs for breakfast. How many eggs are left?

Which model shows the problem?

Circle the correct answer.

A

C

B

D

2 Hana sees 3 birds in the morning. She sees some birds at night. Hana saw 12 birds in all.

How many birds did Hana see at night?

Show your work.

Answer: Hana saw _____ birds at night.

Lesson 2 Quiz continued

3 Some children visit a farm. 7 children go inside the barn. Then 8 more children go inside. How many children are inside the barn now?

Circle *Yes* or *No* to tell if each equation can be used to solve the problem.

a. $7 + 1 = 8$ Yes   No

b. $8 + 7 = 15$ Yes   No

c. $7 + 8 = 15$ Yes   No

d. $8 - 7 = 1$ Yes   No

4 There are 6 toy trucks in a box. There are some toy cars in the box. There are 11 toy trucks and cars in all. How many toy cars are in the box?

Part A

Complete the model. Choose a number from the box for each place in the model.

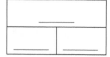

Part B

Write an equation that can be used to solve the problem.

Equation: _____

Common Misconceptions and Errors

Errors may result if students:

• interpret a start or change unknown problem as a result unknown problem.

• misidentify the operation needed to solve the problem.

• identify the parts and whole in a problem incorrectly.

• do not understand how to represent a word problem using a number bond or a tape diagram.

Ready® **Mathematics**

Lesson 2 Quiz Answer Key

1. B
DOK 1

2. 9
DOK 2

3. a. No
  b. Yes
  c. Yes
  d. No
  DOK 2

4. *Part A:*
  Students should write 11 in the top box and the numbers 6 and 5, in either order, in the bottom two boxes.
  DOK 2

  Part B:
  Answer choices: $11 - 6 = 5$, $6 + 5 = 11$, or $5 + 6 = 11$ (students may also use a box or ? in place of the 5)
  DOK 2

CCSS Focus

Domain
Operations and Algebraic Thinking

Cluster
B. Add and subtract within 20.

Standards
2.OA.B.2 Fluently add and subtract within 20 using mental strategies. By end of Grade 2, know from memory all sums of two one-digit numbers.

Standards for Mathematical Practice (SMP)

1 Make sense of problems and persevere in solving them.

3 Construct viable arguments and critique the reasoning of others.

4 Model with mathematics.

5 Use appropriate tools strategically.

7 Look for and make use of structure.

8 Look for and express regularity in repeated reasoning.

Lesson Objectives

Content Objectives

• Demonstrate the mental process involved in the make-a-ten strategy when adding and subtracting numbers within 20.

• Interpret models that represent the reasoning behind the make-a-ten strategy.

Language Objectives

• Draw an open number line to show the make-a-ten strategy.

• Record equations that show the steps used in the make-a-ten strategy.

• Listen to the ideas of others and compare their strategies.

Prerequisite Skills

• Compose and decompose tens and ones in two-digit numbers less than 20.

• Add numbers within 20.

• Break apart numbers into the sum of two other numbers.

• Understand how a model represents a numerical situation.

Lesson Vocabulary

There is no new vocabulary.

Learning Progression

In **Grade 1** students model the make-a-ten strategy using physical models such as connecting cubes and tiles.

In **Grade 2** students extend those models to more abstract visual representations, such as an open number line and a ladder model.

In **this lesson** students build on the foundations laid in Grade 1 for applying mental strategies to addition and subtraction within 20. Students refine their understanding of the commutative and associative properties. For example,

they realize that when solving 4 + 9, they can start with the 9 since it is closer to 10 and then add 4. This mental flexibility will assist students later in Grade 2 as they work with two- and three-digit numbers.

In **Grade 3** students gain fluency with addition and subtraction of numbers within 1,000. They use the make-a-ten strategy with number lines as a way to help attain this fluency. Students also apply what they have learned about the commutative property of addition to multiplication.

Lesson Pacing Guide

Whole Class Instruction

Day 1 *45–60 minutes*	**Toolbox: Interactive Tutorial*** *Addition Facts: Using Sums of 10* **Introduction** • Opening Activity *20 min* • Think It Through Question *5 min* • Think *10 min* • Think *10 min* • Reflect *5 min*	**Practice and Problem Solving** Assign pages 21–22.
Day 2 *45–60 minutes*	**Guided Instruction** **Think About the Strategy of Making a Ten** • Let's Explore the Idea *20 min* • Let's Talk About It *15 min* • Try It Another Way *10 min*	**Practice and Problem Solving** Assign pages 23–24.
Day 3 *45–60 minutes*	**Guided Practice** **Connect Ideas About Making a Ten** • Demonstrate *15 min* • Compare *15 min* • Analyze *15 min*	**Practice and Problem Solving** Assign pages 25–26.
Day 4 *45–60 minutes*	**Independent Practice** **Apply Ideas About Making a Ten** • Put It Together *30 min* • Pair/Share *15 min*	
Day 5 *45–60 minutes*	• On-Level, Intervention, or Challenge Activity *20 min* **Toolbox: Lesson Quiz** Lesson 3 Quiz	

Small Group Differentiation

Teacher-Toolbox.com

Reteach
Ready Prerequisite Lessons *45–90 min*

Grade 1
• Lesson 14 Make a Ten to Add
• Lesson 16 Make a Ten to Subtract

Teacher-led Activities
Tools for Instruction *15–20 min*

Grade 1 *(Lessons 14 and 16)*
• Find the Rule

Grade 2 *(Lesson 3)*
• Make a Ten to Add within 20

Student-led Activities
Math Center Activities *30–40 min*

Grade 2 *(Lesson 3)*
• 2.6 Make a Ten

Personalized Learning

i-Ready.com

Independent
i-Ready Lessons* *10–20 min*

Grade 1 *(Lessons 14 and 16)*
• Addition Facts for 10
• Addition and Subtraction Fact Families

*We continually update the Interactive Tutorials. Check the Teacher Toolbox for the most up-to-date offerings for this lesson.

Opening Activity

Partners of Ten

Objective Find all one-digit whole number pairs that have a sum of 10.

Time *20–30 minutes*

Materials for each student
• Pencil and paper or whiteboard and marker

Overview

Students record all possible number pairs that have a sum of 10. They organize equations to check that they have found all possible combinations and to discuss the patterns they see.

Step By Step

1 Write all the partners of ten.

• Ask students to write all the ways that two numbers can be combined to make 10.

2 Organize the equations.

• Invite volunteers to read aloud one or two of the equations they wrote. Record the equations on the board in the order shown below.

0 + 10 = 10	10 + 0 = 10
1 + 9 = 10	9 + 1 = 10
2 + 8 = 10	8 + 2 = 10
3 + 7 = 10	7 + 3 = 10
4 + 6 = 10	6 + 4 = 10
5 + 5 = 10	5 + 5 = 10

• Discuss how organizing the equations like this can help to check that all possible equations are included.

3 Talk about patterns.

- Talk about the patterns students see in the list of tens facts on the left. Ask: *How does the first addend change as you go down the list? How does the second addend change?* [Each first addend is 1 more than the one before it. Each second addend is 1 less than the one before it.]

- Now ask the same questions about the list on the right. [It's the opposite. Each first addend is 1 less than the one before it. Each second addend is 1 more than the one before it.]

- Ask: *How can finding a pattern help you remember the tens facts? Give an example.* [If you know that $5 + 5$ is 10, then just take 1 away from one 5 and add it to the other 5 to get $4 + 6$.]

- You may want students to use cubes to model this. They should notice that the total number of cubes does not change. No cubes are added or subtracted; they are just rearranged.

Teacher Notes

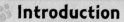
Introduction

At A Glance

Students explore breaking an addend apart in order to make a 10 to add. Then students explore the make-a-ten strategy as it applies to subtraction.

Step By Step

- Introduce the question at the top of the page. Allow students to generate ideas about the ways in which they mentally compute.
- Draw attention to the number bonds at the top of the page. Encourage students to describe what they know about number bonds.
- Read through the **Think** section together. Make sure to emphasize that the 10-frames show a way to organize $9 + 7$. Use the Hands-On Activity to help students solidify the concept.

  Note: The process shown here is an application of the associative property of addition. That property will be explored in more depth later in the lesson.

▶ **Hands-On Activity**

- Use Mathematical Discourse questions 1–3 to promote flexible thinking and the use of the commutative property of addition.

▶ **Mathematical Discourse 1–3**

Understand Mental Math Strategies (Make a Ten)

Think It Through

How can you make a 10 to add and subtract in your head?

You know how to break apart numbers into tens and ones.

You can break apart numbers to make a 10 when you add or subtract in your head.

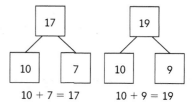

$$10 + 7 = 17 \qquad 10 + 9 = 19$$

Think You can make a 10 to add.

Add $9 + 7$.

Think of 9 red counters and 7 blue counters on two 10-frames.

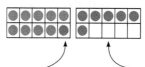

The first blue counter makes a full 10.

There are 6 more blue counters in the second 10-frame.

Add $9 + 7$.
Think of 7 as $1 + 6$.
Add 9 and 1 to make 10.

$$\begin{array}{c} 9 + 7 \\ 9 + 1 + 6 \\ 10 + 6 \end{array}$$

✎ Write the sums.

$$10 + 6 = \underline{16} \qquad 9 + 7 = \underline{16}$$

18

▶ **Mathematical Discourse**

1 *Why is it easy to add numbers when one of them is a ten?*

Students may respond that you can think of the number that is not the ten as part of a teen number, like $10 + 6 = six$teen. They might also find it easy to add 10 plus a one-digit number because they know how to break apart the numbers 11–19 into tens and ones.

2 *When adding $9 + 7$, why does it make sense to start with the 9 instead of the 7?*

Nine is closer to 10. You only have to add 1 to it to get 10.

3 *Could we start with the 7 first? Why? What might it look like?*

Yes, because the order of the addends does not change the sum; $7 + 3 + 6 = 16$.

▶ **Hands-On Activity**

Use connecting cubes to understand making a 10.

Materials: connecting cubes

- Distribute 20 cubes to each student. Ask students to make a train of 9 and a train of 7 cubes. Ask: *How can you make the 9 a 10?* [Add 1 cube.] *Where can we get the 1 cube?* [from the train of 7 cubes] Once again, emphasize that students are reorganizing the cubes, not adding to or taking from the total number of cubes they had at the beginning.

- Instruct students to take 1 cube from the train of 7 and add it to the train of 9. Ask how many are in each train now. Connect the process and outcome to the model and diagram on the page in the student book.

Think You can make a 10 to subtract.

Subtract 14 − 6.

Start with 14 counters.

When I have 14, I have 10 and 4 more.

✎ Put an X over the counters in the second 10-frame. How many counters do you subtract to get to 10? __4__

✎ How many more counters need an X to subtract a total of 6? __2__ Put an X over this number of counters in the first 10-frame.

✎ Use the 10-frames to complete each equation.

$$14 - \underline{}^{4} = 10$$

$$10 - \underline{}^{2} = 8$$

Subtracting 6 is the same as subtracting 4 and then subtracting 2 more. So, 14 − 6 = 8.

▶ **Reflect** Work with a partner.

1 Talk About It How can you make a 10 to help you add 8 + 7?

Write About It Possible answer: I know that 8 is 2 away from 10.

Add 2 to 8 to get 10. I need to add 5 more to add a total of 7. 10 + 5 = 15,

so 8 + 7 = 15.

19

▶ Hands-On Activity

Use connecting cubes to understand subtraction.

Materials: connecting cubes (10 of one color and 10 of another color, per student)

- Have students make a cube train of 10 with one color and connect 4 cubes of the other color onto the train of 10.

- Ask students to use the cubes to show the thinking involved in making a 10 to subtract 6 from 14 and explain to a partner what was done.

▶ English Language Learners

During whole-group discussions or when giving oral directions, assist students by either writing the given numbers on the board or repeating the numbers in students' native language.

▶ Mathematical Discourse

4 *How is the make-a-ten strategy for subtraction like counting back?*

You count back from the number you start with until you get to ten and then count back some more until you have subtracted the entire number.

5 *Think about the Reflect question. What are two ways you can make a 10 to find the sum?*

8 + 7 = 8 + 2 + 5; or
7 + 8 = 7 + 3 + 5

6 *Which way do you think is easier? Why?*
Answers will vary. Listen for accurate mathematical reasoning.

Step By Step

- Write the subtraction expression from the **Think** section on the board. Ask students to share strategies they know to calculate the difference.

- Put the subtraction problem into a real-life context with the following: *Sam has a new pack of 10 baseball cards and 4 extra cards. He gives his little brother 6 cards. How could he do this?* Allow students to share ideas and strategies they would use.

- Complete the 10-frame model as a class. Make sure students understand that 6 can be broken apart into 4 + 2, allowing them to subtract 4 from 14 and then the additional 2. Relate the model to the situation posed above. You may want to use the Hands-On Activity to reinforce this concept.

▶ **Hands-On Activity**

▶ **Mathematical Discourse 4**

- Read the **Reflect** question with the class. Ask students to discuss ideas with a partner before writing an answer. Invite students to share responses with the class, using a model to justify their reasoning.

▶ **Mathematical Discourse 5 and 6**

▶ **English Language Learners**

Ready Mathematics
PRACTICE AND PROBLEM SOLVING

Assign *Practice and Problem Solving* **pages 21–22** after students have completed this section.

Guided Instruction

At A Glance

Students model the make-a-ten strategy for addition and subtraction on an open number line. Then students analyze the make-a-ten strategy and represent it using a ladder model.

Step By Step

Let's Explore the Idea

- Work through Problem 2 with the class. Ask students how the numbers in $8 + 8 = 16$ were broken apart to get the two equations in Problem 2. Use the Concept Extension to reinforce the associative property of addition.

▶ **Concept Extension**

> **SMP TIP Use Structure**
> Formal exploration of the associative property validates the structure informally used by students and provides a foundation for future applications of the property. *(SMP 7)*

- Tell students they will have time to work individually on the remainder of the problems on this page and then share their responses in groups.
- As students work individually, circulate among them. This is an opportunity to assess student understanding and address student misconceptions. Use Mathematical Discourse questions 1–3 to stimulate thinking. Relate the third question to the Hands-On activity in the previous lesson.

▶ **Mathematical Discourse 1–3**

- Take note of students who are still having difficulty and wait to see if their understanding progresses as they work with a partner during the next part of the lesson.

Think About **The Strategy of Making a Ten**

🔍 **Let's Explore the Idea** Use open number lines to add and subtract.

Answer Problems 2 through 4 to help you think about $8 + 8 = 16$.

2 Complete the equations.

$8 + \underline{\ \ 2\ \ } = 10$ $\qquad$ $10 + \underline{\ \ 6\ \ } = 16$

3 Use your answers from Problem 2 to fill in the boxes on the open number line.

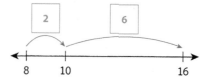

4 Complete the equation. $8 + 8 = 10 + \underline{\ \ 6\ \ }$

Answer Problems 5 through 7 to help you think about $13 - 7 = 6$.

5 Fill in the boxes.

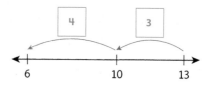

6 Use the open number line to complete the equations.

$13 - \underline{\ \ 3\ \ } = 10$ $\qquad$ $10 - \underline{\ \ 4\ \ } = 6$

7 Complete the equation. $13 - \underline{\ \ 7\ \ } = 6$

20

▶ **Mathematical Discourse**

1 *When subtracting 7 from 13, how do you know where to begin on the number line?*

Start at the 13 because it is the greatest number. When you subtract, you have to move backward.

2 *How did you choose the first number you subtracted from 13? Where did you get it?*

I subtracted 3 first, since $13 - 3 = 10$. I took 3 from the 7 that I need to subtract.

3 *How do you know how many more to subtract?*

Since $3 + 4 = 7$, I have to subtract 4 more after subtracting 3 so that I subtract a total of 7.

▶ **Concept Extension**

Explore an application of the associative property of addition.

Materials: connecting cubes or Activity Sheet 21 (10-Frames)

- Write the expression $7 + 5$ on the board. Instruct students to model adding the numbers with connecting cubes or 10-frames using the make-a-ten strategy.

- Invite a volunteer to explain his or her thinking, and record it on the board. Example: Student says, "I broke apart the 5 into 3 and 2 to add to 7." Write: $7 + 5 = 7 + (3 + 2)$. Student says, "I added the 3 to the 7 to make 10 and then added the other 2." Write: $(7 + 3) + 2$.

- Discuss the function of the parentheses and that the addends don't change, just the way they are grouped.

Let's Talk About It
Work with a partner.

8 Look at the open number line in Problem 3.
Why do you add 2 to 8?

to make a 10

Why do you add 6 next?

You need to add 8 in all, and 2 + 6 = 8.

9 Look at the open number line in Problem 5.
Why do you first subtract 3 from 13?

to make a 10

Why do you subtract 4 next?

You need to subtract 7 in all. You have only

subtracted 3, so you need to subtract 4 more.

▶ **Try It Another Way** **Use a ladder model.**

Fill in the blanks to add or subtract.

10 Find 8 + 6 by adding up.

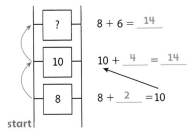

$8 + 6 = \underline{14}$

$10 + \underline{4} = \underline{14}$

$8 + \underline{2} = 10$

start

11 Find 14 − 6 by subtracting down.

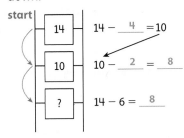

$14 - \underline{4} = 10$

$10 - \underline{2} = 8$

$14 - 6 = \underline{8}$

21

▶ Concept Extension

Help students recognize patterns in addition and subtraction.

- Write the following on the board:

$9 + 9 = 10 + \underline{}$ $17 − 8 = 10 − \underline{}$

$9 + 8 = 10 + \underline{}$ $16 − 8 = 10 − \underline{}$

$9 + 7 = 10 + \underline{}$ $15 − 8 = 10 − \underline{}$

$9 + 6 = 10 + \underline{}$ $14 − 8 = 10 − \underline{}$

- Ask students to fill in the blanks and describe the patterns they notice. Accept all responses, but then lead students to connect a pattern to the make a 10 strategy. Help them notice that the number they write is what is left over after making a 10. Relate the decreasing pattern of the second addend in the addition equations, the decreasing pattern of the minuend in the subtraction equations, and the pattern found among the numbers in the blanks.

▶ Mathematical Discourse

4 *How are the two ladder models the same? How are they different? Explain.*

The numbers you add or subtract are the same but are in a different order (+ 2 is first in the addition, − 4 is first in the subtraction). Students should notice that since the two expressions are related (fact families), one ladder model adds 6 while the other subtracts 6. In both cases, 6 is broken into 2 and 4. In the addition problem, 8 is 2 away from 10; in the subtraction problem, 14 is 4 away from 10. Some students may notice that since 14 is 4 away from 10, after adding 2 in the first problem, you then add the 4. The process is reversed for subtraction.

Step By Step

Let's Talk About It

- Instruct students to work with a partner to complete Problems 8 and 9. Walk around to each pair. Listen to and join in on discussions at different points.

- As students work on Problem 9, allow them to draw a picture or use 10-frames to help them articulate their mental process.

Try It Another Way

- Direct students' attention to **Try it Another Way**. Have them discuss the model with a partner. As students share their interpretations, ask them to write + 2 and + 4 next to the arrows on the left and − 4 and − 2 next to the arrows on the right. Connect this model to the open number line. Use Mathematical Discourse question 4 to expand students' reasoning.

▶ **Mathematical Discourse 4**

- Replicate the ladder model on the board and ask students to complete it for expressions such as 7 + 8 and 9 + 5 and then model each related subtraction expression.

▶ **Concept Extension**

SMP TIP Repeated Reasoning
Encourage students to look for consistencies in patterns by following the structure of the Concept Extension, but beginning with a different set of numbers like 8 + 8 = 10 + ____ . *(SMP 8)*

Ready Mathematics
PRACTICE AND PROBLEM SOLVING

Assign *Practice and Problem Solving* **pages 23–24** after students have completed this section.

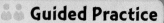
At A Glance

Students demonstrate their understanding of the make-a-ten strategy. They compare and analyze applications of the strategy. Then students select numbers to add and subtract and show how to make a 10 to find the sum and difference.

Step By Step

- Discuss each problem as a class using the discussion points outlined below.

Demonstrate

- Allow students to work with a partner to share strategies. Encourage them to explain their thinking using words, numbers, and/or pictures. Have students work together to make their explanations clear.

- As students share their strategies with the class, ask questions like: *Why did you begin with the 6? Why did you begin with the 9? Why did you break apart the number the way you did? How is adding 6 + 4 + 5 the same as adding 6 + 9? How is it like adding 10 + 5?* Listen for responses that demonstrate students' understanding of the commutative and associative properties of addition. Help students refine their responses to clearly articulate the math concepts used.

Compare

- Ask two volunteers (one male and one female) to come to the front of the class. Ask the female student to explain to the class Greta's strategy in words and/or pictures. Then ask the male student to explain Chuck's strategy in words and/or pictures.

- As students are sharing the strategies, ask questions such as: *Why doesn't it matter that Greta and Chuck broke apart the numbers differently?* [The order and grouping in addition don't matter.] *Why do you think they chose to break apart the numbers the way they did?* [People have their own way of thinking. They use the strategy that makes sense to them. Greta thought of 7 + 3 for making a ten, and Chuck thought of 5 + 5 for making a ten.]

Talk about these questions as a class. Then write your answers.

12 **Demonstrate** Show how to make a 10 to find 6 + 9. Explain your thinking.

Possible answer: 6 is 4 away from 10. Think of 6 + 9

as 6 + 4 + 5. Add 6 + 4 to make a 10. Add 5 more to

add 9 in all. 6 + 9 = 10 + 5, or 15.

13 **Compare** Greta and Chuck each added 5 + 7 by making a 10.

Greta 5 + 7	Chuck 5 + 7
Break apart 5. 2 + 3	Break apart 7. 5 + 2
7 + 3 = 10	5 + 5 = 10
Add 2 more. 10 + 2 = 12	Add 2 more. 10 + 2 = 12
7 + 5 = 12	7 + 5 = 12

Did they both make a 10 correctly? Explain.

Possible answer: Yes. Greta started with the 7 and

made a 10. Chuck started with the 5 and made a 10. Both

ways are correct.

14 **Analyze** Ming added 9 + 8. See her work at the right. What did she do wrong? What is the correct answer?

$$9 + 1 = 10$$
$$10 + 8 = 18$$
$$9 + 8 = 18$$

Possible answer: Ming added 1 to 9 to make a 10.

Then she added 8 more instead of only 7 more. So she

found 9 + 9, not 9 + 8. 9 + 8 = 17.

Analyze

- If students are unable to identify the error, model the situation with 10-frames.

- Ask: *Why do you think Ming made the error she did?* Make sure students realize that when making a 10, the amount added to the first number to make it a 10 must be taken away from the second number. You may want to model with connecting cubes by adding 1 to make a 10 and then adding the additional 8. Ming actually adds 9 to 9.

Scoring Rubrics

Part A	
Points	**Expectations**
2	The student selects two numbers with a sum greater than 10 and uses a model to accurately represent the make-a-ten strategy.
1	Either the number selection or modeling is correct, but not both.
0	Both the number selection and modeling are inaccurate.

Apply ▶ **Ideas About Making a Ten**

Put It Together   Use what you have learned to complete this task.

15 Think about making a 10 to add or subtract.

Part A Choose two numbers you can add by making a 10. Write an addition equation using your numbers.

Draw a model to show how to answer your addition problem by making a 10. Then solve your addition problem.

____ + ____ = ?
Answers will vary.
Sample: 8 + 5 = ?

____ + ____ = ____
Answers will vary.
Sample: Use a ladder model to add up.
8 + 5 = 13
10 + 3 = 13
8 + 2 = 10

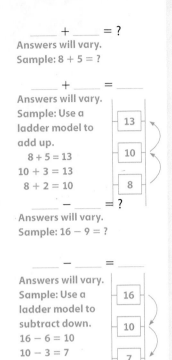

Part B Choose two numbers you can subtract by making a 10. Write a subtraction equation using your numbers.

Draw a model you could use to solve your subtraction equation by making a 10. Then solve your subtraction problem.

____ − ____ = ?
Answers will vary.
Sample: 16 − 9 = ?

____ − ____ = ____
Answers will vary.
Sample: Use a ladder model to subtract down.
16 − 6 = 10
10 − 3 = 7
16 − 9 = 7

Part C How can making a 10 help you add or subtract in your head?

Possible answer: Adding to 10 or taking away from 10 is easy to do in

your head. You can also picture an open number line or 10-frames

in your head.

23

Step By Step

Put It Together

- Direct students to complete the **Put It Together** task on their own.
- Read the directions with students and make sure they understand each part of the task before proceeding. Suggest that students might use a 10-frame or an open number line as models.
- As students work on their own, walk around to assess their progress and understanding, to answer their questions, and to give additional support, if needed. Some students may choose numbers with a sum greater than 20. You may want to allow this if you feel students are capable of completing the task.
- If time permits, ask students to share the numbers they chose and justify their choices.

Ready Mathematics
PRACTICE AND PROBLEM SOLVING

Assign *Practice and Problem Solving* **pages 25–26** after students have completed Guided Practice.

Part B	
Points	**Expectations**
2	The student writes a subtraction equation that can be solved using the make-a-ten strategy and accurately models how to solve it.
1	Either the number selection or modeling is correct, but not both.
0	Both the number selection and modeling are inaccurate.

Part C	
Points	**Expectations**
2	The student's response shows a clear understanding of the make-a-ten strategy.
1	The student's response shows some understanding of the strategy.
0	The student was not able to articulate proper use of the strategy.

Lesson 3
Understand Mental Math Strategies (Make a Ten)

Differentiated Instruction

▶ Intervention Activity

Model making a 10 on a 1–20 chart.

Materials: 1–20 chart (the first two rows of Activity Sheet 2, Hundreds Chart), 2 counters, paper and pencil

• Provide each student with a chart and counters.

• Write the problem $8 + 3 = ?$ on the board. Show students how to use the chart and counters to solve. They place one counter on the first addend, which is 8. They use the second counter to count forward on the chart the number of the second addend. So they count forward 3 spaces and place the second counter on 11, which is the sum.

• Have students write the number sentences that show how to make a 10 to find the sum. For example: $8 + 3 = 8 + 2 + 1$ and $10 + 1 = 11$.

• Repeat with other addition and subtraction problems.

▶ On-Level Activity

Play a make-a-10 game.

Materials: For each pair or group: counters, 3 sets of number cards 1–9 from Digit Cards (Activity Sheet 1)

• Put students in pairs or groups of 3 and give them counters and number cards.

• Place the number cards facedown in a pile. Turn over the top card and place it next to the pile. This number is the first addend. A player picks a card from the pile and mentally adds it to the first addend. If the sum is less than 10, place the card at the bottom of the pile and move to the next player. If the sum is greater than 10, the student describes how to make a 10 to find the sum.

• Students check the sum. They may choose to use counters for this. If students agree that the sum is correct, the player keeps the card and play continues. Use the same first addend until each player has had an opportunity to make a 10 with it. After that, draw a new card for the first addend. Continue until all cards are gone.

• Adapt for subtraction by using 2 stacks of cards, one with numbers greater than 10 and the other less than 10.

▶ Challenge Activity

Model making a 10 on a hundreds chart.

Materials: For each pair or group: Hundreds Chart (Activity Sheet 2), counters, paper and pencil

• Instruct students to work in pairs or small groups. Write the equation $26 + 7 = ?$ on the board or on an individual card for each pair or group. Ask students to use the hundreds chart and counters to solve the problem, showing how the make-a-ten strategy can be applied to numbers greater than 20.

• Tell students to show their thinking and explain what they did using words and/or pictures. Repeat with other problems, such as $27 + 8 = ?$ and $39 + 6 = ?$.

• You may want to have students make up similar problems that they can exchange among themselves and solve.

Teacher Notes

Teacher-Toolbox.com

Overview

Assign the Lesson 3 Quiz and have students work independently to complete it.

Use the results of the quiz to assess students' understanding of the content of the lesson and to identify areas for reteaching. See the Lesson Pacing Guide at the beginning of the lesson and the Differentiated Instruction activities that follow for suggested instructional resources.

Tested Skills

Assesses 2.OA.B.2

Problems on this assessment form require students to use the Make a Ten strategy when adding and subtracting numbers within 20 as well as to interpret models that represent the reasoning behind the Make a Ten strategy. Students will also need to add numbers within 20 and break apart numbers as the sum of two other numbers.

Ready® **Mathematics**

Lesson 3 **Quiz**

Solve the problems.

1 Anna wants to find $13 - 8$. She makes a ten to solve the problem.

$13 - 3 = 10$

$10 - 5 = 5$

$13 - 8 = 5$

Is Anna right? Tell how you know. Circle the correct answer.

A Anna is right. She subtracted 3 from 13 to make a ten and then subtracted 5.

B Anna is right. $13 - 8 = 5$ and $10 - 5 = 5$.

C Anna is wrong. She should have broken apart the 13 instead of breaking apart the 8.

D Anna is wrong. She should have subtracted 3 from 10 in the second step.

2 Luke makes 6 cards for his family. He makes 9 cards for his friends. He wants to find how many cards he has made in all. Fill in the model below to find $6 + 9$.

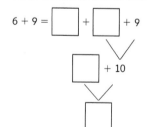

Lesson 3 Quiz continued

3 Bella bakes 14 cookies. Her family eats 6 cookies. How many cookies are left?

Make a ten to find $14 - 6$. Complete each equation using a number from the box.

$14 - \underline{\hspace{1cm}} = 10$

$10 - \underline{\hspace{1cm}} = 8$

| 1 | 2 | 4 | 6 | 8 | 16 | 20 |

$14 - 6 = \underline{\hspace{1cm}}$

4 Jacob is trying to solve some equations.

Tell if each equation shows how to make a ten to find the sum. Circle *Yes* or *No* for each equation.

a. $4 + 8 = 4 + 6 + 2 = \square$ Yes   No

b. $7 + 7 = 4 + 3 + 7 = \square$ Yes   No

c. $9 + 8 = 9 + 2 + 6 = \square$ Yes   No

d. $5 + 9 = 5 + 5 + 4 = \square$ Yes   No

e. $6 + 7 = 6 + 5 + 2 = \square$ Yes   No

5 Complete the open number line to find $14 - 7$.

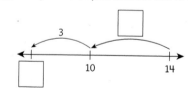

Common Misconceptions and Errors

Errors may result if students:

- break apart a number to subtract, but subtract one of the lesser numbers and the original number.
- think the first step in using the Make a Ten strategy is to add or subtract 10.
- break apart an addend into two lesser numbers that cannot be used to make a ten with the other addend.

Ready® **Mathematics**

Lesson 3 Quiz Answer Key

1. A
DOK 3

2. 5, 1
5
15
DOK 2

3. 4
2
8
DOK 1

4. a. Yes
b. Yes
c. No
d. Yes
e. No
DOK 2

5. Top box: 4, bottom box: 7
DOK 2

CCSS Focus

Domain
Operations and Algebraic Thinking

Cluster
C. Work with equal groups of objects to gain foundations for multiplication.

Standards
2.OA.C.3 Determine whether a group of objects (up to 20) has an odd or even number of members, e.g., by pairing objects or counting them by 2s; write an equation to express an even number as a sum of two equal addends.

Additional Standards
2.NBT.A.2 (see page B3 for full text)

Standards for Mathematical Practice (SMP)

2 Reason abstractly and quantitatively.

3 Construct viable arguments and critique the reasoning of others.

4 Model with mathematics.

7 Look for and make use of structure.

Lesson Objectives

Content Objectives

• Identify odd and even numbers.

• Relate doubles and doubles +1 facts to odd and even numbers.

• Use skip counting by 2s to identify even numbers.

Language Objectives

• Tell whether a number is odd or even.

• Draw a picture to show whether a number is odd or even.

• Skip count by 2s to name even numbers.

Prerequisite Skills

• Know doubles facts to 20.

• Skip count by 2s.

• Understand the meaning of equal groups.

Lesson Vocabulary

• **even number** an even number of objects can be put into pairs or into two equal groups without any leftovers. An even number always has 0, 2, 4, 6, or 8 in the ones place.

• **odd number** an odd number of objects cannot be put into pairs or into two equal groups without a leftover. An odd number always has 1, 3, 5, 7, or 9 in the ones place.

Learning Progression

In Grade 1 students learn to skip count by 2s and learn doubles and doubles +1 facts. They also examine the concept of equality and equal shares.

In Grade 2 students continue to develop skip-counting abilities and deepen understanding of equality.

In this lesson students connect skip counting by 2s to the concept of odd and even numbers. They learn that even numbers can be seen as equal groups of 2 or as 2 equal groups of any number.

Students relate the concept of 2 equal groups to doubles, examine doubles +1 facts, and relate both to the structure of even and odd numbers. They examine odd and even numbers in a 1–20 chart and study patterns.

In Grade 3 students continue the exploration of patterns in number charts. They examine patterns in addition and observe the structure found in multiplication tables.

Lesson Pacing Guide

Whole Class Instruction

Day 1 *45–60 minutes*	Toolbox: Interactive Tutorial* *Odd and Even Numbers* **Introduction** • Opening Activity *20 min* • Think It Through Question *5 min* • Think *10 min* • Think *10 min* • Reflect *5 min*	**Practice and Problem Solving** Assign pages 29–30.
Day 2 *45–60 minutes*	**Guided Instruction** **Think About Identifying Even and Odd Numbers** • Let's Explore the Idea *15 min* • Let's Talk About It *20 min* • Try It Another Way *10 min*	**Practice and Problem Solving** Assign pages 31–32.
Day 3 *45–60 minutes*	**Guided Practice** **Connect Ideas About Even and Odd Numbers** • Evaluate *15 min* • Analyze *15 min* • Explain *15 min*	**Practice and Problem Solving** Assign pages 33–34.
Day 4 *45–60 minutes*	**Independent Practice** **Apply Ideas About Even and Odd Numbers** • Put It Together *30 min* • Pair/Share *15 min*	
Day 5 *45–60 minutes*	• On-Level, Intervention, or Challenge Activity *20 min* **Toolbox: Lesson Quiz** Lesson 4 Quiz	

Small Group Differentiation

Teacher-Toolbox.com

Reteach
Ready Prerequisite Lessons *45–90 min*

Grade 1
• Lesson 6: Doubles and Doubles Plus 1

Student-led Activities
Math Center Activities *30–40 min*

Grade 2 *(Lesson 4)*
• 2.7 Even or Odd?
• 2.8 Facts for Even and Odd Numbers

Personalized Learning

i-Ready.com

Independent
i-Ready Lessons* *10–20 min*

Grade 1 *(Lesson 6)*
• Addition Facts: Doubles

---

*We continually update the Interactive Tutorials. Check the Teacher Toolbox for the most up-to-date offerings for this lesson.

Opening Activity

Equal and Unequal Groups

Objective Examine equal and unequal groups of objects to explore the concept of odd and even numbers.

Time *20–30 minutes*

Materials for each student
- a set of 20 connecting cubes
- pencil and paper or whiteboards

Overview

Students explore the concept of odd and even numbers by breaking cube trains into equal groups. Students will develop the understanding that not all numbers can be divided into two equal groups.

Step By Step

1 Prepare students for the activity.

- Give each student or student group a set of connecting cubes.

- Ask students to follow along as you give instructions and model the activity.

2 Work with an even number of cubes.

- Instruct students to connect 6 cubes to make a train. Model this with your set of cubes.

- Tell students to break the train into 2 equal groups. Ask them how they know the groups are equal. Listen for ideas such as counting the cubes in each group or matching them up to see that they are the same.

- Repeat with a train of 10 cubes.

3 Work with an odd number of cubes.

- Tell students to make a train of 13 cubes. Have them try to break the train into 2 equal groups. Tell students to get the groups as even as possible. Ask what they notice about the groups. [They are not equal.]

- Repeat with a train of 7 cubes.

4 Work independently with different numbers of cubes.

- Give students about 5 minutes to make trains with different numbers of cubes and try to break them into 2 equal groups. Have them record the numbers of cubes that can and cannot divide equally into 2 groups.

5 Discuss the results.

- Have students take turns giving you a number and telling if it did or did not divide equally. Write the numbers on the board in a vertical column in order from least to greatest. Write *yes* or *no* next to each number. For incorrect responses, ask students to justify with the cubes and correct the error.

- Discuss any observations students make about the numbers. Listen for reference to counting by 2s or other patterns.

- Ask: *What did you notice about the leftovers every time there were not 2 equal groups?* [There was 1 extra cube.] *What do you think it means when we say a number is even?* [The numbers can be divided *evenly* into 2 groups.]

Teacher Notes

Introduction

At A Glance

Students explore the concept of odd and even numbers by breaking apart numbers of items into groups of 2. Then students explore ways of thinking about odd and even numbers.

Step By Step

- Introduce the question at the top of the page. Remind students of what they discovered in the opening activity.
- Draw attention to the socks that are circled. Guide students to see that there are 4 groups of 2 socks each with no leftovers.
- Read the **Think** section together. Instruct students to circle groups of 2 shoes and answer the question.
- Use the Mathematical Discourse questions to reinforce the relationship between even and odd numbers.

▶ **Mathematical Discourse 1–3**

▶ **Hands-On Activity**

💭 Think It Through

What are even and odd numbers?

You can break apart some numbers into groups of 2. Look at these 8 socks.

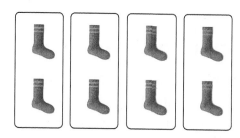

Think **Sometimes when you make groups of 2, there is a leftover.**

Look at these 7 shoes.

✏️ Circle groups of 2.

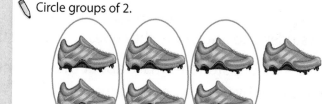

✏️ How many shoes are NOT in a group of 2? ___1___

24

▶ Mathematical Discourse

1 *How are the leftover shoes you found on this page like the leftover blocks in the opening activity?*

Students should notice that in both cases there is 1 leftover.

2 *What would happen if you added 1 more shoe to the group of 7? Why?*

If you added 1 more shoe, you could make another group of 2.

3 *What would happen if you took away 1 shoe from the group of 7? Explain.*

If you took away 1 shoe, you could make 3 groups of 2 and have no leftovers.

▶ Hands-On Activity

Use models to understand odd and even numbers.

Materials: connecting cubes

- Ask each student to take a handful of cubes. Make sure there is variation in how many they end up with. Have students organize the cubes into groups of 2.

- Invite students to tell whether their cubes divided evenly or if there was a leftover. Help them recognize that students started with different numbers of cubes but there are only two possible outcomes: equal groups of 2 or 1 leftover.

- Ask students if they think this would happen if they combined cubes with a partner or if they grouped all the cubes in the classroom. Help them generalize that no matter how many cubes are used, they can either be grouped evenly into groups of 2 or there will be 1 leftover.

Think Make groups of 2 to tell if a number is even or odd.

A number is **even** if you make groups of 2 and have no leftovers.

There are no leftovers, so 6 is even.

A number is **odd** if you make groups of 2 and have 1 leftover.

There is 1 leftover, so 5 is odd.

Think Try making 2 equal groups to tell if a number is even or odd.

A number is **even** if you can make 2 equal groups.

Each group has the same number, so 6 is even.

A number is **odd** if you cannot make 2 equal groups.

Each group has a different number, so 5 is odd.

▶ Reflect Work with a partner.

1 Is 9 an even or odd number? Why?

Possible answer: 9 is an odd number because when I make groups of 2,

there is 1 leftover.

25

Step By Step

- Read the first **Think** section together. Ask students how this relates to what they discovered on the previous page.
- Read the second **Think** section together. Make sure that students understand the difference between groups of 2 and 2 equal groups.
- Have students discuss the **Reflect** question with a partner and write their reply in the space provided.

▶ **Real-World Connection**

> **SMP TIP Model with Mathematics**
> Have students consider the scenarios described in the Real-World Connection and ask whether it is possible for there to be more than one person left over. Have students use a model to explain their thinking. *(SMP 4)*

▶ **Concept Extension**

Ready Mathematics
PRACTICE AND PROBLEM SOLVING

Assign *Practice and Problem Solving* **pages 29–30** after students have completed this section.

▶ Concept Extension
Examine unequal groups of cubes.

Materials For each pair: connecting cubes

- Put students in pairs. Have partners make a train of 12 cubes, then break it into a group of 7 and a group of 5. Ask partners to discuss why this would or would not be a good way to show if 12 is odd or even.
- Call on volunteers to share their ideas with the class. Help students recognize that by moving 1 cube from the group of 7 to the group of 5, you can make 2 groups of 6.
- Repeat the activity using 11 cubes in 4 groups of 2 and 1 group of 3. Ask students to rearrange the cubes to show whether 11 is odd or even.

▶ Real-World Connection

Relate the concept of odd and even numbers to a familiar situation. Ask students what happens when they are picking two teams for an outdoor game or a game in gym class and there is an even number of students. What happens when there is an odd number of students?

Encourage students to think of other real-world situations that involve odd and even numbers. They may think of pairing up for math activities or pairing up with a "buddy" on a field trip. Discuss what happens when there is an even or odd number of students.

Guided Instruction

At A Glance

Students model the concept of even and odd numbers by dividing groups of items into groups of 2 or into 2 equal groups. Then students use doubles and doubles + 1 facts to identify odd and even numbers. They skip count by 2s to identify even numbers.

Step By Step

Let's Explore the Idea

- Tell students that they will have time to work individually on the problems on the page and then share their responses in groups.

▶ **Mathematical Discourse 1**

- Remind students that in Problems 2 and 3, they are circling groups of 2. In Problems 4 and 5, they are circling 2 equal groups, if possible. Since each picture has 2 rows, suggest that students circle each row to try to find 2 equal groups.

▶ **Mathematical Discourse 2**

▶ **Visual Model**

▶ **English Language Learners**

Think About Identifying Even and Odd Numbers

🔍 **Let's Explore the Idea** Tell if a number is *even* or *odd*.

Circle groups of 2. Then tell if the number is *even* or *odd*.

2 15 is ___odd___ .

3 12 is ___even___ .

Show whether you can make 2 equal groups. Then tell if the number is *even* or *odd*.

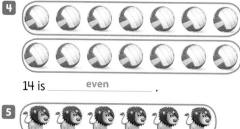

4 14 is ___even___ .

5 11 is ___odd___ .

26

▶ **Mathematical Discourse**

1 *How can you tell if a number is even or odd?*

   If there are no leftovers after making groups of 2, the number is even. If there is a leftover, the number is odd.

2 *In Problem 5, how did you know the number of lions to circle?*

   Students might recognize that 5 lions match up in each row, but the top row has 1 more lion.

▶ **English Language Learners**

Help ELL students connect an everyday meaning of *even* and *odd* to the mathematical use of the word. *Odd* can mean *different*. The leftover means that the groups are not the same (they are different). The word *even* relates to equality, for example, *evenly* dividing some cookies.

▶ **Visual Model 1**

Analyze even/odd structure in dominoes.

- Project a domino block or draw a large domino with 8 dots. Ask students if they can tell without counting whether the number of dots is an even or odd number. They should recognize that the way the dots are lined up, you can see equal groups of 2 or 2 equal groups.

- Repeat the activity, showing dominoes with a variety of even and odd numbers of dots. Ask students to determine whether the number shown is even or odd and justify their responses.

- This activity builds visual/spatial skills and reinforces the concept of the structure of even and odd numbers.

Let's Talk About It
Work with a partner.

6 Write a doubles fact for 8.

$\underline{4} + \underline{4} = 8$

7 Write a doubles + 1 fact for 9.

$\underline{4} + \underline{4} + 1 = 9$

8 Write these doubles or doubles + 1 facts.

$\underline{5} + \underline{5} = 10 \qquad \underline{3} + \underline{3} + 1 = 7$

$\underline{6} + \underline{6} = 12 \qquad \underline{7} + \underline{7} + 1 = 15$

9 Are sums of doubles odd or even numbers? Are sums of doubles + 1 odd or even numbers? Explain.

Possible answer: Doubles show 2 equal groups, so sums of doubles are

even. Doubles + 1 show 2 equal groups and 1 leftover, so sums of

doubles + 1 are odd.

▶ **Try It Another Way** **Skip count by 2s to find even numbers.**

You can skip count by 2s to find even numbers.

10 Skip count by 2s to finish this list. Stop at 20.

2, 4, 6, 8, 10, 12, 14, 16, 18, 20

11 Numbers on your list in Problem 10 are even. Numbers less than 20 that are not on your list are odd.

Circle the even numbers. Underline the odd numbers.

<u>11</u>   (14)   (16)   <u>17</u>

27

Let's Talk About It

- Organize students in pairs to complete this section. You may choose to work through Problem 6 with the class.

- As students work in pairs, walk around to each pair. Listen to and join in on discussions at different points.

▶ **Mathematical Discourse 3 and 4**

Try It Another Way

- Direct students' attention to **Try It Another Way**. Have volunteers come to the board and share their solutions on the number line used in the Visual Model.

▶ **Visual Model**

> **SMP TIP   Look for Structure**
> Emphasize the structure of even and odd numbers on the number line, leading students to recognize the AB pattern that is formed. *(SMP 7)*

Ready Mathematics
PRACTICE AND PROBLEM SOLVING

Assign *Practice and Problem Solving* **pages 31–32** after students have completed this section.

▶ **Visual Model 2**

See even and odd numbers on a number line.

- Draw a 0–20 number line on the board.

- Point to 0 and ask students to tell you where your first "jump" will land if you skip count by 2s. Make an arc from 0 to 2 on the number line.

- Continue to model skip counting on the number line by 2s. Lead students to notice that the numbers you landed on are even and the numbers in between are odd.

- On the same number line, make two arcs below the line, from 0 to 3 and from 3 to 6. Ask if 6 is odd or even. [even] Have students add 1 more, tell where you will land, and identify this number as odd or even. [7; odd] Repeat using other doubles and doubles + 1 facts from the student page.

▶ **Mathematical Discourse**

3 *How is using doubles and doubles + 1 like using the pictures in Let's Explore the Idea?*

Doubles are like finding 2 equal groups. When you add them, the sum is always even. The 1 in a doubles + 1 fact is like the leftover when you circle groups of 2.

4 *What would happen if you subtracted 1 from a doubles fact?*

It would be an odd number. If you take 1 away, one of the groups will have 1 less than the other.

👥 Guided Practice

At A Glance

Students analyze pictures and real-world situations to determine whether numbers are even or odd. Then students demonstrate their understanding of even and odd numbers by identifying and generalizing a pattern on a 1–20 chart.

Step By Step

- Discuss each problem as a class using the discussion points outlined below.

Evaluate

- Ask: *When there are two apples left over, what does that tell you? How can you help Pat organize his apples differently?* Students should realize that Pat can put 1 leftover in each of the 2 groups to make 2 equal groups.

Analyze

- If students struggle to make sense of the scenario presented, lead them to choose an appropriate tool to help visualize the problem. Allow each student to select the representation that he or she finds most meaningful and then share it with the class.
- Some students may solve the problem by displaying 9 groups of 2 and 1 extra, while others may show 2 groups of 9 with 1 extra. Display models for both and discuss why they show the same total number.
- Show a third model by drawing a row of 9 dots below a row of 10 dots on the board. Ask volunteers to show how to find the total using all three models, and then write the corresponding equations. This investigation sets the stage for arrays that are presented in the next lesson.

Explain

- Draw two rows of 4 circles. Ask: *How many are in each row?* [4] *Is this number even or odd?* [even] *What is the total? Is it even or odd?* [8; even]
- Draw one more circle in each row. Ask the same questions as above. Point out that there is an odd number of circles in each row, but the total is still an even number.

Connect ▶ Ideas About Even and Odd Numbers

Talk about these questions as a class. Then write your answers.

12 **Evaluate** Pat looks at this picture of 14 apples. He says that 14 is an odd number. Do you agree? Explain.

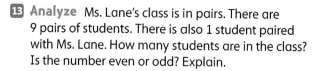

Possible answer: No. There are 2 leftovers, not 1.

Each leftover can be added to a group of 6. Then

there are 2 equal groups of 7. So 14 is even.

13 **Analyze** Ms. Lane's class is in pairs. There are 9 pairs of students. There is also 1 student paired with Ms. Lane. How many students are in the class? Is the number even or odd? Explain.

Possible answer: 9 groups of 2 students plus 1 with

Ms. Lane is 9 + 9 + 1 = 19. 19 is odd. If you make

groups of 2, the class has 1 leftover.

14 **Explain** Mimi says that when she adds doubles, the sum is always even. It doesn't matter if the doubles are odd or even numbers. Do you agree? Explain.

Possible answer: I agree. Doubles form two equal

groups, which tells me a number is even. The

addends of a doubles fact can be even or odd.

28

Scoring Rubrics

Part A	
Points	**Expectations**
2	The student completes the color pattern accurately and describes at least one pattern, clearly articulating the even/odd structure.
1	The student completes most of the color pattern accurately and describes some kind of an even/odd pattern, although not clearly.
0	The student does not complete the color pattern accurately and does not describe an even/odd pattern.

Apply ▶ **Ideas About Even and Odd Numbers**

Put It Together **Use what you have learned to complete this task.**

15 Use this table to answer the questions.

1	2	3	4	5	6	7	8	9	10
11	12	13	14	15	16	17	18	19	20

Odd numbers should be colored red. Even numbers should be colored blue.

Part A Color squares with odd numbers red. Color squares with even numbers blue. What patterns do you see in the numbers?

Possible answer: Every other number is odd. Every other number is even.

Part B Look at 15. Is the ones digit odd or even? Is 15 odd or even?

The ones digit, 5, is odd. 15 is odd.

Part C Look at 16. Is the ones digit odd or even? Is 16 odd or even?

The ones digit, 6, is even. 16 is even.

Part D Amy says that if a two-digit number has an even number in the ones place, the number is also even. Is she correct? Why or why not?

Possible answer: Amy is correct. When you skip count by 2, you get

even numbers, and all of those numbers have an even number in the

ones place.

29

Step By Step

Put It Together

- Direct students to complete the **Put It Together** task on their own. Make sure they have red and blue crayons or pencils.
- Read the directions with students and make sure they understand each part of the task before proceeding.
- As students work on their own, walk around to assess their progress and understanding, to answer their questions, and to give additional support, if needed. Encourage students to list all the patterns they see in the chart. Some may notice that every other column contains even numbers and every other column contains odd numbers. Allow them to also explore other even/odd patterns, such as the pattern found in the diagonals.
- If time permits, ask students to share their observations and ideas about Amy's statement with the class.

Ready· Mathematics
PRACTICE AND PROBLEM SOLVING

Assign *Practice and Problem Solving* **pages 33–34** after students have completed Guided Practice.

Parts B and C	
Points	**Expectations**
2	The student identifies 5 and 15 as odd and 6 and 16 as even.
1	The student identifies either 5 and 15 as odd or 6 and 16 as even, but does not answer both questions correctly.
0	The student is not able to correctly identify the digits or numbers as odd or even.

Part D	
Points	**Expectations**
2	The student justifies the statement by using logical reasoning or a model.
1	The student agrees with the statement, but the justification is not clear or lacks logical reasoning.
0	The student's response indicates a lack of understanding of the statement.

Differentiated Instruction

▶ Intervention Activity

Model odd and even numbers with rectangles.

Materials: 20 counters; 1-inch grid paper cut into various sizes of rectangles, each containing 2 rows (Activity Sheet 3, 1-Inch Grid Paper)

• Instruct students to select a rectangle and place a counter in each box. Ask if the number of counters is an odd or an even number and why. Direct students to write an equation to show how many counters are in each row and the entire rectangle. (Example: 4 + 4 = 8)

• Discuss why one more counter cannot be placed inside the rectangle. Then have students place 1 counter outside the rectangle and write an equation that shows the total number of counters inside and outside of the rectangle. (Example: 4 + 4 + 1 = 9) Talk about how this shows doubles + 1, which is an odd number.

• Have students select a different rectangle and repeat the above activities.

▶ On-Level Activity

Describe doubles and doubles + 1 strips.

Materials: 1-centimeter grid paper cut into strips of different lengths (1 × 6 up to 1 × 20; Activity Sheet 4, 1-Centimeter Grid Paper), crayons or colored pencils

• Ask each student to fold a 1 × 8 strip of grid paper in half. Model how to fold the strip so the grid lines are visible. Have students color each group of 4 squares with a different color. Discuss how this relates to doubles. Then ask students to refold the same strip in 4 groups of 2 squares. Emphasize that the entire strip is divided into groups of 2 with no leftovers. Ask students to describe how the model shows an odd or an even number.

• Tell students to fold a 1 × 11 strip so the fold is on a line, coming as close as possible to dividing the strip in half. Have them color only the squares that are part of the double, leaving one square blank. Then ask students to refold in groups of 2 squares starting at the colored end. Discuss how this relates to doubles + 1. Compare the odd and even strips they made.

• Repeat using different strips.

▶ Challenge Activity

Explore numbers that have more than two digits.

Materials: poster board or large paper

• Remind students of the statement made in Part D of Independent Practice: *If a two-digit number has an even number in the ones place, the number is also even.*

• Challenge students to determine if this generalizes to all numbers no matter how many digits the numbers have. Tell them that to prove the statement doesn't apply to numbers with more than two digits, they must find an example of a number with more than two digits that doesn't follow the statement.

• Allow students to use whatever tools they need to try to prove or disprove the statement. They should create a poster displaying their findings and be prepared to present it to the class.

Teacher Notes

Teacher-Toolbox.com

Overview

Assign the Lesson 4 Quiz and have students work independently to complete it.

Use the results of the quiz to assess students' understanding of the content of the lesson and to identify areas for reteaching. See the Lesson Pacing Guide at the beginning of the lesson and the Differentiated Instruction activities that follow for suggested instructional resources.

Tested Skills

Assesses 2.OA.C.3

Problems on this assessment form require students to identify odd and even numbers and relate even and odd numbers to doubles and doubles + 1 facts. Students will need to know how to skip count by 2s and know their doubles facts to 20.

Ready® Mathematics

Lesson 4 **Quiz**

Solve the problems.

1 Are the number of dots on each card odd or even?
Circle *Odd* or *Even* for each card.

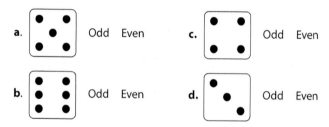

a.   Odd   Even   c.   Odd   Even

b.   Odd   Even   d.   Odd   Even

2 Cheng has 2 pails of fish. Each pail has the same number of fish. Which could be the number of fish that Cheng has in all? Circle all the correct answers.

A   5

B   9

C   10

D   13

E   18

Lesson 4 Quiz continued

3 Write a doubles fact to show that 12 is even.
Write a doubles + 1 fact to show that 15 is odd.

12 = _____ + _____

15 = _____ + _____ + 1

4 Ethan adds 3 and 3. Sarah adds 7 and 7.
Which statement is true? Circle the correct answer.

A   Ethan's sum is odd and Sarah's sum is even.

B   Sarah's sum is odd and Ethan's sum is even.

C   Both sums are odd.

D   Both sums are even.

5 Farah looks at the picture and says that 16 must be an odd number.

Is Farah correct? Explain why or why not.

_____

_____

_____

_____

_____

Common Misconceptions and Errors

Errors may result if students:

- confuse the meaning of *even* and *odd*.

- count the number of rows, instead of the number of items, in a diagram.

- think a number is odd if the doubles fact involves odd numbers.

- do not understand that the sum of two even or two odd numbers is even.

Ready® **Mathematics**

Lesson 4 Quiz Answer Key

1. a. Odd
   b. Even
   c. Even
   d. Odd
   DOK 1

2. C, E
   DOK 2

3. 6, 6
   7, 7
   DOK 2

4. D
   DOK 2

5. Farah is not correct. Possible explanation: If you place the 16 dots into 2 equal groups, there will be none left over. So 16 is even, not odd.
   DOK 3

CCSS Focus

Domain
Operations and Algebraic Thinking
Number and Operations in Base Ten

Cluster
C. Work with equal groups of objects to gain foundations for multiplication.
A. Understand place value.

Standards
2.OA.C.4 Use addition to find the total number of objects arranged in rectangular arrays with up to 5 rows and up to 5 columns; write an equation to express an even number as a sum of equal addends.
2.NBT.A.2 Count within 1000; skip-count by 5s, 10s, and 100s.

Standards for Mathematical Practice (SMP)

1 Make sense of problems and persevere in solving them.

3 Construct viable arguments and critique the reasoning of others.

4 Model with mathematics.

5 Use appropriate tools strategically.

7 Look for and make use of structure.

8 Look for and express regularity in repeated reasoning.

Lesson Objectives

Content Objectives
• Describe an array of up to 5 rows and 5 columns.
• Calculate the number of items in an array using repeated addition and skip counting.
• Write an equation to express the sum of items in an array.

Language Objectives
• Tell the number of rows in an array.
• Tell the number of objects in each row of an array.

Prerequisite Skills

• Add 3 one-digit numbers.
• Visually recognize groups of 2 through 6.
• Skip count by 2s and 5s.
• Write an addition equation.

Lesson Vocabulary

• **array** a set of objects arranged in equal rows and equal columns
• **row** the horizontal groups of objects in an array
• **column** the vertical groups of objects in an array

Learning Progression

In Grade 1 students add up to 3 one-digit numbers. They use equations to express a variety of situations that involve addition. Students also apply counting skills to add, including skip counting.

In Grade 2 students work toward fluency with sums to 20. They continue to use addition equations and skip counting to model addition.

In this lesson students apply their knowledge of addition and skip counting to an array. They analyze arrays,

recognizing them as sets of objects organized in equal rows and columns. They recognize that adding 3 groups of 4 or adding 4 groups of 3 results in the same sum. This structure lays the foundation for the extension of the commutative property to multiplication.

In Grade 3 arrays are used as a tool to help students understand the structure of multiplication and division of whole numbers. The array is used to model the commutative and associative properties and as an introduction to area concepts.

Lesson Pacing Guide

Whole Class Instruction

Day 1
45–60 minutes

Toolbox: Interactive Tutorial*
Add Using Arrays

Introduction

- Opening Activity 15 min
- Use What You Know 10 min
- Find Out More 15 min
- Reflect 5 min

Practice and Problem Solving
Assign pages 37–38.

Day 2
45–60 minutes

Modeled and Guided Instruction

Learn About Adding Using Arrays

- Picture It/Model It/Model It 15 min
- Connect It 20 min
- Try It 10 min

Practice and Problem Solving
Assign pages 39–40.

Day 3
45–60 minutes

Guided Practice

Practice Adding Using Arrays

- Example 5 min
- Problems 7–9 15 min
- Pair/Share 15 min
- Solutions 10 min

Practice and Problem Solving
Assign pages 41–42.

Day 4
45–60 minutes

Independent Practice

Practice Adding Using Arrays

- Problems 1–6 20 min
- Quick Check and Remediation 10 min
- Hands-On or Challenge Activity 15 min

Toolbox: Lesson Quiz
Lesson 5 Quiz

Small Group Differentiation

Teacher-Toolbox.com

Reteach
Ready Prerequisite Lessons 45–90 min

Grade 1
- Lesson 13 *Understand* Sums Greater than 10
- Lesson 14 Make a Ten to Add

Teacher-led Activities
Tools for Instruction 15–20 min

Grade 1 *(Lessons 13 and 14)*
- Doubles Addition Facts
- Make a Ten to Add within 20

Student-led Activities
Math Center Activities 30–40 min

Grade 2 *(Lesson 5)*
- 2.13 Skip Count by 5s
- 2.9 Use Array Vocabulary
- 2.10 Use Arrays to Add

Personalized Learning

i-Ready.com

Independent
i-Ready Lessons* 10–20 min

Grade 1 *(Lessons 13 and 14)*
- Addition Number Sentences
- Addition Facts for 10

*We continually update the Interactive Tutorials. Check the Teacher Toolbox for the most up-to-date offerings for this lesson.

Opening Activity

Build Arrays

Objective Learn the terms *row* and *column*, and arrange a set of objects in equal rows and columns.

Time *20–30 minutes*

Materials for each student
- Square tiles (cut from Activity Sheet 3, 1-Inch Grid Paper)

Overview

Students arrange square tiles in equal rows and equal columns. They discover that there can be more than one way to do this.

Step By Step

1 Model equal rows and columns.

- Model an array with 2 rows and 3 columns of tiles. Ask students how many tiles there are going across and down. Then have students find the total number of tiles. [3 across; 2 down; 6 total]

- Move the tiles to make an array with 3 rows and 2 columns. Encourage students to compare this array with the previous one. Help them recognize that the total number of tiles is the same in both arrays, but the number going across and down is different.

2 Introduce the terms *row* and *column*.

- Explain that the tiles are arranged in *rows* (going across) and *columns* (going down).

- Ask students what they notice about the number of tiles in each row. [The number of tiles in each row is the same.] Ask what they notice about the number of tiles in each column. [The number of tiles in each column is the same.]

3 Make equal rows and columns with 8 tiles.

- Give individual students 8 tiles, and ask them to arrange the tiles in equal rows and equal columns.

- Once students have finished making their arrays, invite volunteers to describe what the arrays look like by telling the number of tiles in each row and column.

- Draw pictures of the arrays on the board. Guide students to understand that there is more than one way to arrange objects to make an array. Encourage them to find all possible ways to arrange the 8 tiles. [1 $\times$ 8, 8 $\times$ 1, 2 $\times$ 4, 4 $\times$ 2]

- You may want to challenge students to think of an easy way of finding the total number of tiles in the array.

Teacher Notes

Introduction

At A Glance

Students analyze an array and write an equation with equal addends to find the total number of objects in the array. Then students examine a different representation of the array, using dots instead of pictures of hats. They learn array vocabulary and analyze an array.

Step By Step

- Work through **Use What You Know** as a class.
- Instruct students to look at the picture of hats on shelves. Ask what they notice about the way the hats are arranged.
- Have students read the problem at the top of the page. Complete Parts a–e together.
- If necessary, instruct students to circle the group of 4 hats on each shelf for visual reinforcement.
- Make sure students write the equation as a sum of the addend 4 repeated 3 times.

Note: Repeated addition is an underlying concept of multiplication and division. Recognizing 12 in terms of 3 groups of 4 leads to the understanding of multiplication as the process of combining equal-sized groups and division as the process of separating into equal-sized groups.

> **SMP TIP   Model with Mathematics**
> Help students recognize that writing an equation is a way to represent the addition found in the visual model by asking them to explain how the equation relates to the picture of the hats. (SMP 4)

▶ **Mathematical Discourse**

▶ **Concept Extension**

⟳ Use What You Know

Review adding 3 one-digit numbers.

Rob's team has shelves for their hats. How many hats are there in all?

a. Does each shelf have the same number of hats? _____ yes

b. How many hats are on each shelf? _____ 4

c. How many shelves are there? _____ 3

d. Look at the lines at the right. Each line shows one shelf. Use numbers to write how many hats are on each shelf.

_____ 4

_____ 4

_____ 4

e. Use your answer to Problem d. Write an equation to show the total number of hats.

$4 + 4 + 4 = 12$

30

▶ **Mathematical Discourse**

Why is it helpful to add 4 three times rather than just counting all the hats on the shelves?

Listen for responses that indicate students recognize that the repeated addition is a faster way to calculate.

▶ **Concept Extension**

Develop the concept of an array as a rectangular shape.

- Ask: *How would the hats be arranged if there were 4 shelves and each shelf had an equal number of hats? Why?* Provide students with small counters to explore this idea. You may want to provide lined paper for them to use as shelves.

- Watch to make sure students arrange the counters on their paper to form 3 columns and then point out the rectangular shape of the hats on the shelf.

- Challenge students to arrange the 12 counters in different numbers of equal rows and columns. Students can make the following arrays: 1×12, 12×1, 2×6, 6×2.

▷▷ Find Out More

The hats on shelves on the previous page show an **array**. An array has **rows** and **columns**. Here is the same array made out of dots instead of hats.

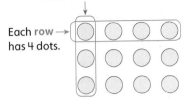

Each **column** has 3 dots.

Each **row** → has 4 dots.

In an array,

- every row has the same number of objects.
- every column has the same number of objects.

▷ Reflect **Work with a partner.**

1 **Talk About It** Kimi makes an array using 10 stamps. Her array has 2 rows. How many stamps are in each column? Explain how you know.

Write About It Each column has 2 stamps. Possible answer:

Put 10 objects into 2 rows. There are 5 stamps in each row. So there

are 5 columns in the array and 2 stamps in each column.

31

▶ English Language Learners

Reinforce the vocabulary by replicating the array of 12 dots on the board. Write the word *array* above it and label the rows and columns. Keep the drawing on display throughout the lesson.

▶ Hands-On Activity

Use classroom objects to make arrays.

Using a variety of classroom objects, ask students to replicate the array of 12 dots. Students might use connecting cubes, counters, tiles, and so on. Discuss how all of these arrays are alike. [They all have 3 rows with 4 objects in each row, and 4 columns with 3 objects in each column.] Tell students that the array of dots can be used as a picture to stand for any of the arrays of real objects they made.

▶ Real-World Connection

Arrays are used in the real world as an organizational structure. Encourage students to generate ideas of places where they have seen arrays. Responses may include: desks in a classroom, seats in a theater, eggs in a carton, stamps on a sheet, boxed items such as glassware, etc. You may want to have some array examples available for students to examine.

Step By Step

- Read and discuss **Find Out More** as a class.
- Draw attention to the vocabulary words *array*, *row*, and *column*. Discuss each term, ensuring students understand their meanings.

▶ **English Language Learners**

- To reinforce the idea that the dots on the page represent any object, use the Hands-On Activity.

▶ **Hands-On Activity**

- Instruct students to complete the **Reflect** question with a partner. Allow students to use tiles or counters, if necessary, to make sense of the problem.

- Encourage students to share their solutions using the vocabulary words they learned. If no one mentions it, point out that the number of rows is the same as the number in each column. Also, the number of columns is the same as the number in each row.

▶ **Real-World Connection**

Ready· Mathematics
PRACTICE AND PROBLEM SOLVING

Assign *Practice and Problem Solving* **pages 37–38** after students have completed this section.

Modeled and Guided Instruction

At A Glance

Students use an array as a representation for solving an addition problem. They write an equation and use skip counting to model the number of objects in the array. Then students use an equation and skip counting to find the total number of items in the array.

Step By Step

- Read the problem at the top of the page together as a class. Make sure students understand the situation posed.

Picture It

- Instruct students to look at the array and tell how many rows and how many columns they see. If necessary, project the array or draw it on the board and ask students to come up and point to and count each row and column.

- Use Mathematical Discourse question 1 to reinforce the concept of an array.

▶ **Mathematical Discourse 1**

Model It

- Direct students to look at the equation. Ask how many 5s are added together. [4] Connect this to the 4 groups of 5, or 4 rows of 5, in the array.

Model It

- Ask students to relate the skip counting to both the array and the equation. It is important that they understand the relationship among all representations.

> **SMP TIP Model with Mathematics**
> The representations on the page reinforce that repeated addition and skip counting by a number are both ways to find the total items in an array. (SMP 4)

Learn About Adding Using Arrays

Read the problem. Then you will look at ways to use an array.

> Mike puts some stickers into an array. Each row has 5 stickers. Each column has 4 stickers. How many stickers are there in all?

▶ **Picture It You can draw an array.**

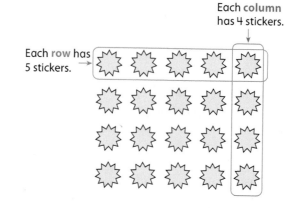

Each **row** has 5 stickers.

Each **column** has 4 stickers.

▶ **Model It You can use the rows in the array to write an equation.**

Add the number of stickers in each row.
Each row has 5 stickers ⟶ $5 + 5 + 5 + 5 = ?$

▶ **Model It You can use the rows in the array to skip count.**

There are 5 stickers in each row. Skip count by 5s ⟶ 5, 10, 15, 20.

32

▶ **Mathematical Discourse**

1 *If Mike had 3 more stickers, could he make another row or column in this array? Why or why not?*

Students should respond that he could not make another row or column because there aren't enough extra stickers to fill up an entire row or an entire column.

▶ **Connect It** Use the array and models to solve the problem.

2 Look at the first *Model It* on the previous page. Why is 5 written four times in the equation?

I have to add the four rows of 5 stickers.

3 Write an equation you could use to find the total number of stickers using the columns.

4 + 4 + 4 + 4 + 4 = ?

4 Look at the second *Model It* on the previous page. Why do you skip count by 5s?

You skip count by 5s to add each row of 5 stickers.

5 **Talk About It** **Work with a partner.**

Do you need to see the array from *Picture It* to solve the problem on the previous page?

Write About It Possible answer: No. You don't have

to see the array if you know how many rows and columns

it has.

▶ **Try It** **Try another problem.**

6 Write two equations you could use to find the total number of shapes in this array.

3 + 3 = 6

2 + 2 + 2 = 6

33

▶ **Mathematical Discourse**

2 *Why do you think adding the stickers in the columns gives you the same answer as adding the stickers in the rows?*

Listen for responses that indicate students recognize that the total number of stickers remains the same no matter how they are added.

3 *How could you skip count to find the total number of stickers by using the columns?*

Students should recognize that they can skip count by 4s, since there are 4 stickers in each column: 4, 8, 12, 16, 20.

Step By Step

Connect It

- Organize students in pairs to complete the questions.
- Remind students that the questions in **Connect It** refer to the problem on the previous page.
- Tell students that Problem 3 asks them to think about the array in a different way. Make sure they understand that they are now adding the number in each column.

> **SMP TIP** **Look for Structure**
> Adding both the number of objects in each row and in each column to get the same total can help students recognize the commutative nature of an array. (SMP 7)

▶ **Mathematical Discourse 2**

- After students complete Problem 4, ask Mathematical Discourse question 3 to help students recognize that they can also skip count using the columns.

▶ **Mathematical Discourse 3**

Try It

6 **Solution**
3 + 3 = 6 and 2 + 2 + 2 = 6; Students write one equation in which the addends are the number of shapes in each row and another equation in which the addends are the number of shapes in each column.
Error Alert Students who write the equation 2 + 3 = 5 added the number of rows and number of columns in the array.

Ready® Mathematics
PRACTICE AND PROBLEM SOLVING

Assign *Practice and Problem Solving* **pages 39–40** after students have completed this section.

👥 Guided Practice

At A Glance

Students practice what they know about repeated addition and skip counting to solve array problems.

Step By Step

- Draw students' attention to the example problem. Lead them to recognize that when there is an even number of rows or columns, grouping doubles can make mental calculation easier.

- Instruct students to solve the problems individually. Direct their attention to the hints given to help them think about and solve the problems. For Problem 9, encourage students to use the open space to draw the array and check the given response for reasonableness. Then they can look back at the original problem to see why Vic may have chosen B.

- **Pair/Share** As students complete the problems, have them Pair/Share with a partner to discuss solutions.

Solutions

7 Solution

15 pieces; Students may add 5 three times or add 3 five times. Students may also skip count.

DOK 2

Practice Adding Using Arrays

Study the model below. Then solve Problems 7–9.

Example

There are 4 rows of crayons in a box. Each row has 4 crayons. How many crayons are in the box?

You can show your work using an array.

4 rows of 4

4 columns of 4

4 + 4 + 4 + 4

8 + 8 = 16

Answer 16 crayons

---

7 In a game, players put pieces in 3 columns. Each column holds 5 pieces. How many pieces fill all 3 columns? Draw an array as part of your answer.

Can you skip count to find the answer?

Show your work.

Possible student work:

5 + 5 + 5 = 15

Answer 15 pieces

Teacher Notes

8 A package has 2 rows of soup cans. Each row has 3 cans. How many cans of soup are in the package? Draw an array as part of your answer.

Show your work.

Possible student work:

$2 + 2 + 2 = 6$

You can add the numbers in each row or the numbers in each column.

Answer ___6 cans of soup___

9 Some students line up in 2 rows to play catch. Each row has 8 students. How many students play catch?

A 8

B 10

(C) 16

D 18

What number can you skip count by to find the answer?

Vic chose **B** as the answer. This answer is wrong. How did Vic get his answer?

Possible answer: Vic added $8 + 2$. He should have added $8 + 8$.

35

Solutions

8 **Solution**

6 cans; Encourage students to describe the strategy they used to solve the problem.

DOK 2

9 **Solution**

C; Add 8 (the number of students in a row) 2 times (the number of rows).

Explain to students why the other two answer choices are not correct:

A is not correct because 8 is the number in only 1 row.

D is not correct because $8 + 8 = 16$, not 18.

DOK 3

Ready® Mathematics
PRACTICE AND PROBLEM SOLVING

Assign *Practice and Problem Solving* **pages 41–42** after students have completed this section.

Teacher Notes

Independent Practice

At A Glance

Students solve problems involving arrays that may appear on a mathematics test.

Solutions

1 Solution

A and **B**; Adding the number in each row or column will result in the correct response.

DOK 1

2 Solution

B; The array is organized in 2 rows of 5.

DOK 1

3 Solution

B and **C**; Adding the number in each row or column will result in the correct response.

DOK 2

Practice Adding Using Arrays

Solve the problems.

1 Which equation shows the total number of hearts in this array? Circle all the correct answers.

(A) 6 + 6 + 6 = 18

(B) 3 + 3 + 3 + 3 + 3 + 3 = 18

C 6 + 3 = 9

D 3 + 3 + 3 = 9

2 Which doubles fact can you use to find the total number of shapes in this array? Circle the correct answer.

A 5 + 2 = 7

(B) 5 + 5 = 10

C 2 + 2 = 4

D 10 + 10 = 20

3 Olga draws an array of dots. The array has 3 columns. The first column has 4 dots. Which equation can you use to find the total number of dots? Circle all the correct answers.

A 3 + 3 + 3 = ?

(B) 3 + 3 + 3 + 3 = ?

(C) 4 + 4 + 4 = ?

D 4 + 4 + 4 + 4 = ?

36

Quick Check and Remediation

- Jeremy makes an array of marbles. He makes 4 rows and 5 columns. How many marbles does he have? [20]

- For students who are still struggling, use the chart to guide remediation.

- After providing remediation, check students' understanding by posing the following problem: There are 8 juice boxes in a package. There are 2 rows of boxes. How many are in each row? [4] Ask students to explain how they found the total number in each row. Help students recognize that the number in each row is the same as the number of columns.

If the error is . . .	Students may . . .	To remediate . . .
9	have added the given numbers.	Ask students to draw the array, ensuring they are making equal-sized rows and columns. Help them understand how to use addition to find the answer.
10	have added two 5s instead of four 5s.	Have students reread the problem. Ask how many rows there are and how many are in each row. Lead them to see that 5 is added 4 times, or 10 is added 2 times.
any other number	have drawn the array incorrectly.	Remind students that an array has the same number of items in each row and the same number in each column. Help students correct their drawings and try to solve the problem again.

4 Dana makes an array using these rules.

- The number in each row is different from the number in each column.
- There is more than one row and more than one column.

Tell if each number could be the number of objects in Dana's array. Circle *Yes* or *No* for each number.

a. 6   (Yes)   No

b. 17   Yes   (No)

c. 9   Yes   (No)

d. 15   (Yes)   No

5 Draw an array with 5 rows. Put 6 objects in each row. Show how to use doubles facts to find the total number of objects.   Possible answer:

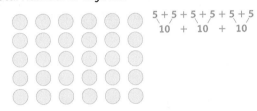

$$5 + 5 + 5 + 5 + 5 + 5$$
$$10 + 10 + 10 = 30$$

6 Show or explain how you can use skip counting to check your answer to Problem 5.

Possible answer: There are 6 columns with 5 in each

column. I can count by 5 six times. 5, 10, 15, 20, 25, 30

✓ **Self Check**   **Now you can solve problems using an array. Fill this in on the progress chart on page 1.**

37

Solutions

4 Solution
a. **Yes**; b. **No**; c. **No**; d. **Yes**; 6 objects can be arranged in an array with three rows of two; 15 objects can be arranged in five rows of three objects.
DOK 3

5 Solution
The arrays should be in a rectangular shape with 5 rows, 6 in each row. Students might add the number in each column since there is an even number of columns.
DOK 3

6 Solution
Students may count by 5s or by 6s.
DOK 2

▶ Hands-On Activity

Create and record arrays.

Materials: counters

- Give each student 18 counters and have them arrange the counters in 2 equal rows. Check to make sure the counters are arranged in 2 rows, with 9 counters in each row. Discuss how many counters are in each row and column, and how many there are in all.
- Challenge students to work with a partner to find as many arrays as possible for the number 18. [Possible arrays: 1 × 18, 18 × 1, 2 × 9, 9 × 2, 3 × 6, 6 × 3]

▶ Challenge Activity

Search for prime numbers.

Materials: counters

- Provide students with 20 counters. Ask them to arrange groups of 2, 3, and 5 counters in separate arrays. Ask what all these arrays have in common. [Each array has only 1 row or 1 column.]
- Challenge students to find other numbers (to 20) that can only be arranged in either 1 row or 1 column when making an array. [7, 11, 13, 17, 19]
- Discuss students' findings.

Teacher-Toolbox.com

Overview

Assign the Lesson 5 Quiz and have students work independently to complete it.

Use the results of the quiz to assess students' understanding of the content of the lesson and to identify areas for reteaching. See the Lesson Pacing Guide at the beginning of the lesson for suggested instructional resources.

Tested Skills

Assesses 2.OA.C.4

Problems on this assessment form require students to be able to interpret an array with up to 8 rows and 8 columns, calculate the number of items in an array using repeated addition and skip-counting, and write an equation to express the sum of items in an array. Students will also need to be familiar with adding 3 one-digit numbers, and skip-counting by numbers up to 10.

Ready® **Mathematics**

Lesson 5 **Quiz**

Solve the problems.

1 Clara makes an array with lemons. She puts 3 lemons in each row. She has 4 rows of lemons.

Which equation can be used to find how many lemons are in Clara's array?

Circle all the correct answers.

A $4 + 4 + 4 = ?$

B $4 + 4 + 4 + 4 = ?$

C $3 + 3 + 3 = ?$

D $3 + 3 + 3 + 3 = ?$

2 Josh makes this array.

He finds the number of dots in all by skip-counting the columns. What numbers does Josh use to skip-count?

Circle the correct answer.

A 3, 6, 9, 12, 15

B 5, 10, 15, 20, 25

C 6, 12, 18, 24

D 36, 42, 48, 54

Lesson 5 **Quiz** continued

3 Mark makes an array using these rules:

- The number in each row is the same as the number in each column.
- There are more than two rows and more than two columns.

Tell if each number can be the total number of objects in Mark's array.

Circle *Yes* or *No* for each number.

a. 25   Yes   No

b. 12   Yes   No

c. 10   Yes   No

d. 4   Yes   No

4 Reba has rows of flowers in her garden. Each row has the same number of flowers.

Reba says there are $8 + 8 + 8 = 24$ flowers.

Draw an array that shows Reba's equation.

Common Misconceptions and Errors

Errors may result if students:

• mistakenly add the number of rows and columns instead of the number of objects in each row.

• began skip-counting from the wrong number or by the wrong number.

• confuse the terms *rows* and *columns*.

• count the number of objects in a row or column incorrectly.

Ready® **Mathematics**

Lesson 5 Quiz Answer Key

1. A, D
  DOK 2

2. B
  DOK 1

3. a. Yes
  b. No
  c. No
  d. No
  DOK 3

4. Students should draw an array with 3 rows of 8 objects or an array with 8 rows of 3 objects.
  DOK 2

Lesson 6
Solve Two-Step Word Problems

CCSS Focus

Domain
Operations and Algebraic Thinking

Cluster
A. Represent and solve problems involving addition and subtraction.

Standards
2.OA.A.1 Use addition and subtraction within 100 to solve one- and two-step word problems involving situations of adding to, taking from, putting together, taking apart, and comparing, with unknowns in all positions, e.g., by using drawings and equations with a symbol for the unknown number to represent the problem.

Additional Standards
2.OA.B.2, 2.NBT.B.5 (see page B3 for full text)

Standards for Mathematical Practice (SMP)

1 Make sense of problems and persevere in solving them.

2 Reason abstractly and quantitatively.

4 Model with mathematics.

7 Look for and make use of structure.

8 Look for and express regularity in repeated reasoning.

Lesson Objectives

Content Objectives

• Analyze two-step problems to determine the series of operations needed to solve them.

• Apply the commutative property of addition as a strategy to solve two-step problems and build number sense.

• Interpret models that represent a two-step problem.

Language Objectives

• Draw two tape diagrams to model a two-step word problem.

• Draw a picture to model a two-step word problem.

• Restate what information a word problem is asking for.

Prerequisite Skills

• Solve one-step problems.

• Interpret a number line.

Lesson Vocabulary

There is no new vocabulary.

Learning Progression

In Grade 1 students represent a simple one-step word problem and identify the unknown in all three positions.

In Grade 2 students expand on what they have learned about solving one-step problems by seeing a two-step problem as a sequence of one-step problems.

In this lesson students solve two-step problems by using pictures, diagrams, and an open number line and then describing the situation as an equation. The concept of a variable is explored in more depth, preparing students for its formal use in future grades.

In Grade 3 students use problem-solving strategies to solve multi-step problems involving all four operations, fractions, and measurement. They represent problems in an equation and use a letter as the variable for the unknown quantity.

Lesson Pacing Guide

Whole Class Instruction

Day 1
45–60 minutes

Toolbox: Interactive Tutorial*
Solve Two-Step Problems

Introduction
- Opening Activity *10 min*
- Use What You Know *10 min*
- Find Out More *10 min*
- Reflect *10 min*

Practice and Problem Solving
Assign pages 45–46.

Day 2
45–60 minutes

Modeled and Guided Instruction
Learn About Ways to Solve Two-Step Problems
- Picture It/Model It *15 min*
- Connect It *20 min*
- Try It *10 min*

Practice and Problem Solving
Assign pages 47–48.

Day 3
45–60 minutes

Modeled and Guided Instruction
Learn About More Ways to Solve Two-Step Problems
- Picture It/Model It *15 min*
- Connect It *20 min*
- Try It *10 min*

Practice and Problem Solving
Assign pages 49–50.

Day 4
45–60 minutes

Guided Practice
Practice Solving Two-Step Word Problems
- Example *5 min*
- Problems 15–17 *15 min*
- Pair/Share *15 min*
- Solutions *10 min*

Practice and Problem Solving
Assign pages 51–52.

Day 5
45–60 minutes

Independent Practice
Practice Solving Two-Step Word Problems
- Problems 1–6 *20 min*
- Quick Check and Remediation *10 min*
- Hands-On or Challenge Activity *15 min*

Toolbox: Lesson Quiz
Lesson 6 Quiz

Small Group Differentiation

Teacher-Toolbox.com

Reteach
Ready Prerequisite Lessons *45–90 min*

Grade 1
- Lesson 3 Add and Subtract in Word Problems
- Lesson 5 Subtract to Compare in Word Problems

Student-led Activities
Math Center Activities *30–40 min*

Grade 2 *(Lesson 6)*
- 2.1 Solve Word Problems

Personalized Learning

i-Ready.com

Independent
i-Ready Lessons* *10–20 min*

Grade 1 *(Lessons 3 and 5)*
- Counting On to Solve Addition Problems
- Subtraction Concepts: Comparisons

*We continually update the Interactive Tutorials. Check the Teacher Toolbox for the most up-to-date offerings for this lesson.

Opening Activity

Model a Two-Step Word Problem

Objective Model a two-step addition problem and write a corresponding equation.

Time *10–15 minutes*

Materials for each student

• counters

• paper

• crayons

Overview

Students use counters to model a two-step addition problem and then draw a picture to represent the same problem. They examine equations for the problem and see that the addends can be ordered in different ways, illustrating the properties of operations.

Step By Step

1 Pose the problem.

• Manny is going to the zoo with his family. There are 2 parents and 4 children in the van. They stop at Robby's house to pick up Robby and his sister. How many people are in the van now?

2 Model the problem.

• Instruct students to use counters to model the problem. You may want to repeat the problem slowly so students have time to count and gather the appropriate number of counters. Then ask students to draw a picture of the problem.

3 Write equations for the problem.

- Ask volunteers to share their pictures with the class and describe the action in the problem. You may want to suggest that students name the people who are in the van in varying order. Write an equation on the board that follows the progression of each description. [2 + 4 + 2 = 8; 2 + 4 + 1 + 1 = 8; 4 + 2 + 2 = 8, etc.]

4 Talk about the equations.

- Have students compare the different equations written on the board. Ask what they notice about the equations. [They are all different, but they all equal 8.] Reinforce the concept that the number 8 can be broken apart in many different ways.

Teacher Notes

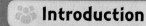 Introduction

At A Glance

Students explore two-step problems by examining a series of one-step problems. Then students analyze the process of solving a two-step problem and apply it to solving problems with both addition and subtraction.

Step By Step

- Work through **Use What You Know** as a class.
- Tell students that this page will help them understand two-step problems by separating them into one-step problems. You may want to remind them of one-step problems by providing an example, such as: Joe has 3 toy cars. He gets 2 more for his birthday. How many does he have now?
- Have students read the problem at the top of the page. Ask a volunteer to tell what they know based on the information given.

▶ **Mathematical Discourse 1 and 2**

- Ask students to work in pairs to think about how they could model this problem using only one tape diagram and one equation. [3 + 3 + 7 = 13] Have student pairs share their ideas with the class, justifying their equations.

Solve Two-Step Word Problems

Use What You Know

You know how to solve one-step word problems.

Eve had 3 striped banners and 3 dotted banners. Then she made 7 white banners. How many banners does Eve have now?

a. How many striped and dotted banners are there? Fill in the model at the right.

b. Now write an equation. How many striped and dotted banners are there in all?

$\underline{\quad 3 \quad} + \underline{\quad 3 \quad} = \underline{\quad 6 \quad}$

6	
3	3
striped banners	dotted banners

c. How many white banners are there? ___7___

d. Add the white banners to the total in Problem b. Fill in the model at the right to show this.

e. Now write an equation. How many banners are there in all?

$\underline{\quad 6 \quad} + \underline{\quad 7 \quad} = \underline{\quad 13 \quad}$

13	
6	7
striped and dotted banners	white banners

38

▶ **Mathematical Discourse**

1 *Why does it make sense to add 3 + 3 first?*

In the problem, Eve has 3 striped and 3 dotted banners before she makes more.

2 *Would the answer be different if you started with 7 and then added the 3s? Why or why not?*

No, it would not. The order of adding doesn't matter. The answer is always the same.

>> Find Out More

The problem on the previous page is a two-step problem.
First, you added the striped and dotted banners.
Then you added the white banners to the sum.

Step 1: $3 + 3 = $ ⑥ **Step 2:** $6 + 7 = 13$

Now look at this two-step problem.

> Juan had 3 pink markers and 7 green markers.
> He lost 2 markers. How many markers does
> he have now?

Step 1: Add to find the total number of markers $3 + 7 = $ ⑩
Juan had.

Step 2: Subtract the number of markers Juan lost $10 - 2 = 8$
to find how many he has now.

Juan has ___8___ markers now.

▶ Reflect **Work with a partner.**

1 **Talk About It** Suki had 17 grapes. She gave 8 grapes to her
sister. Then she gave 3 grapes to her friend. Would you add or
subtract to find how many grapes Suki has now?

Write About It Possible answer: Suki gave away 8 grapes and 3

grapes. So I would subtract twice.

39

▶ Mathematical Discourse

3 *For the problem about Juan's markers,
why does the equation in Step 2 start
with 10?*

The equation starts with 10 because
Juan had a total of 10 markers before
he lost 2 of them.

4 *How do you know Juan had a total of
10 markers?*

I know because in Step 1, Juan's 3 pink
markers and 7 green markers are
added. The total is 10 markers.

▶ Concept Extension

Try subtracting first.

Ask students: *Do you think it matters if we
subtract 2 from 3 first and then add the 7?*
Have students work together in pairs to try
this. Tell one student to solve $3 + 7 - 2$
and the other $3 - 2 + 7$. Remind them to
add or subtract in order from left to right.
Compare the results.

Step By Step

- Read **Find out More** as a class.

- Emphasize that in a two-step problem, there
  are always two parts that must be solved
  before arriving at the final answer.

- Read and discuss the steps involved in solving
  the two-step problem on the previous page.
  You may want to refer to the picture of the
  banners to clarify each step.

- For the problem about Juan's markers,
  remind students that they must read
  carefully to decide what numbers to add
  and what numbers to subtract.

- Read the problem together. Ask students to
  tell what operations they will use and why.

- Ask Mathematical Discourse questions 3
  and 4 to make sure students recognize
  how Steps 1 and 2 are connected.

▶ **Mathematical Discourse 3 and 4**

▶ **Concept Extension**

- Have student pairs read and reply to the
  Reflect question. Encourage students to
  draw a picture, if necessary, to make sense
  of the problem. Expect students to
  recognize that subtraction is used twice in
  this problem.

 **Ready** Mathematics
PRACTICE AND PROBLEM SOLVING

Assign *Practice and Problem Solving*
pages 45–46 after students have
completed this section.

Modeled and Guided Instruction

At A Glance

Students explore different ways of modeling a two-step problem. They write equations to represent what is shown in the models. Then students use addition and subtraction to solve the problem.

Step By Step

- Read the problem at the top of the page as a class. Make sure students recognize that this is an "add to" and "take from" problem.

Picture It

- Draw students' attention to **Picture It**. Ask them to describe what is happening in the picture. Help them understand that in each step, a change occurs. If necessary, allow students to use counters to model the problem.

▶ **English Language Learners**

Model It

- Ask students to work with a partner to interpret the tape diagram in **Model It**. Have them discuss what each number in the diagram represents in the problem.

- Ask students what the 14 shows in the first tape diagram. [total number of pears in the basket after Meg picks 6 more] Ask what the unknown is in Step 2. [9; number of pears left in the basket after Meg gives away 5] Remind students that 8 + 6 and 5 + 9 are two ways of representing the sum 14.

▶ **Mathematical Discourse**

Learn About Ways to Solve Two-Step Problems

Read the problem. Then you will model a two-step problem.

Meg had 8 pears in her basket. Then she picked 6 more pears. After that, she gave away 5 pears to her friends. How many pears are in the basket now?

▶ **Picture It** You can draw a picture.

Step 1: 8 pears + 6 more pears

Step 2: 14 pears − 5 pears given away

▶ **Model It** You can make a tape diagram.

Step 1:

8	6

14

Step 2: 14

5	?

40

▶ **Mathematical Discourse**

How might fact families help you find the unknown in the tape diagram in Step 2?
Since 5 + 9 = 14, 14 − 5 must equal 9.

▶ **English Language Learners**

Some students may struggle to comprehend the language used in a word problem. You may want to pair an English language learner with a proficient reader to complete this task and the ones that follow. Another option is to write each sentence of the problem on a separate line followed by a picture that represents it. Then underline the important words.

Connect It Write equations.

2 What happens in Step 1 of the problem?

Meg picks 6 more pears.

3 Look at *Picture It*. Write an equation for Step 1.

$$\underline{8} + \underline{6} = \underline{14}$$

4 What happens in Step 2 of the problem?

Meg gives away 5 pears.

5 Look at *Model It*. Write an equation for Step 2.

$$\underline{14} - \underline{5} = \underline{9}$$

6 **Talk About It Work with a partner.**

How is a two-step problem different from a one-step problem?

Write About It Possible answer: A two-step problem

has two equations and two models to show both steps of

the problem.

Try It Try another problem.

7 There were 12 boys in the pool. Then 3 went home. Then 6 more boys jumped in the pool. How many boys are in the pool now? Show your work.

There are 15 boys in the pool now. Possible work: $12 - 3 = 9$; $9 + 6 = 15$.

41

▶ Visual Model

Draw a picture.

• Tell students that drawing a picture can help them solve Problem 7.

• Show students how stick figures or tally marks can be used to quickly represent the 12 boys in the pool.

• As you read each part of the problem, ask students to tell you what should be done to the picture. Complete the drawing or ask a student volunteer to do this and explain what is being done and why.

• Guide students to make the connection between the drawing and the equations used to solve the problem.

Connect It

• Read **Connect It** as a class. Make sure students understand that the questions refer to the problem on the previous page.

> **SMP TIP Reason Abstractly and Quantitatively**
> As students describe each step in the solution process, they begin to recognize the relationships among equations and reason about quantities and the varied ways to represent them. *(SMP 2)*

• After students complete Problems 2–6, discuss their answers as a class. Then ask students to work with a partner to write the two steps in this problem as a single equation. [$8 + 6 - 5 = 9$] Ask pairs to justify their equation.

• Instruct students to work in pairs to discuss the question in Problem 6. Invite them to share ideas with the class before completing *Write About It*.

Try It

• For **Try It**, tell students to write equations to represent the steps in the problem. Use the Visual Model activity to assist students in making sense of the problem.

▶ Visual Model

7 **Solution**

15; Students should write equations showing each step of the problem: $12 - 3 = 9$, $9 + 6 = 15$. Some students might write a single equation: $12 - 3 + 6 = 15$.

Error Alert Students who wrote $12 + 6 = 18$ missed the step of subtracting the 3 boys who went home.

Ready Mathematics
PRACTICE AND PROBLEM SOLVING

Assign *Practice and Problem Solving* **pages 47–48** after students have completed this section.

Modeled and Guided Instruction

Learn About More Ways to Solve Two-Step Problems

At A Glance

Students model a two-step word problem using pictures and number lines. Then they model the problem using equations.

Step By Step

- Read the problem at the top of the page as a class.

- Ask students what they need to find out. Use the Mathematical Discourse question 1 to emphasize that in this problem, the result is known but the change is unknown.

▶ **Mathematical Discourse 1**

Picture It

- Guide students to look at the drawing in Step 1 of **Picture It**. Ask how many quarters were left after Russ took 6 out. [10] In Step 2 ask: *What do the counters that are shown tell you?* [how many quarters are in the jar after Dad added some]

> **SMP TIP Make Sense of Problems**
> Ask students to look at the drawing in Step 2 of Picture it. Have students circle the quarters they think Dad put in the jar and then explain their thinking to a partner. Analyzing a model to find a solution and then justifying it builds perseverance in making sense of a mathematical situation. *(SMP 1)*

Model It

- Direct students to look at the open number lines. Discuss that the arrow in Step 1 is moving "backward" to indicate subtraction. In Step 2, ask how the number line is used to find the number of quarters Dad put in the jar.

▶ **Mathematical Discourse 2 and 3**

- Ask students to work in pairs to model the problem on a single number line. Have volunteers share their ideas and discuss their models.

Read the problem. Then you will model a two-step problem.

> There were 16 quarters in a jar. Russ took 6 quarters. Then Dad added more quarters to the jar. Now there are 18 quarters in the jar. How many did Dad put in?

▶ **Picture It You can draw a picture.**

Step 1:   There were 16 quarters in a jar. Russ took 6 quarters.

Step 2:   Then Dad added more quarters to the jar. Now there are 18 quarters in the jar.

▶ **Model It You can use open number lines.**

Step 1:   There were 16 quarters in a jar. Russ took 6 quarters.

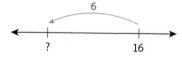

Step 2:   Then Dad added more quarters to the jar. Now there are 18 quarters in the jar.

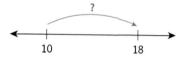

42

▶ **Mathematical Discourse**

1   *How is this two-step problem different from the other two-step problems you solved so far?*

Students should respond that in the previous problems, they were finding how many there are in all after adding and/or subtracting. In this problem, they already know how many quarters in all are in the jar and need to find out how many were put in it.

2   *Do you think it is easier to use pictures or open number lines for this problem? Why?*

Accept responses that relate to solving the problem.

3   *When might it be easier to use open number lines?*

Students might recognize that when greater numbers are involved, using open number lines is more efficient than using pictures. Number lines also help show the computation that is necessary.

▶ **Connect It** Understand what the models mean.

8 What happens in Step 1 of the problem?

Russ takes 6 quarters.

9 Look at the number line in Step 1 of *Model It*.
Complete the equation. $16 - 6 = \underline{10}$

10 What happens in Step 2 of the problem?

Dad adds more quarters to the jar.

11 Write an equation for Step 2.

$\underline{10} + ? = \underline{18}$

12 How many quarters did Dad put in the jar? $\underline{8}$

13 **Talk About It** **Work with a partner.**

Explain how to solve a two-step problem.

Write About It Possible answer: Find the answer to

the first part. Use your answer to the first part in another

equation to find the answer to the problem.

▶ **Try It** **Try another problem.**

14 Gus had 7 shells. Then he found 4 more. Then some shells broke. Now Gus has 9 shells. How many shells broke? Show your work.

2 shells broke; Possible work: $7 + 4 = 11$. Subtract some to get to 9;

$11 - ? = 9$; $11 - 2 = 9$.

43

▶ **Concept Extension**

Explore various symbols that can be used for variables.

- In the problem $10 + ? = 18$, the unknown is shown by using a question mark. A variable or unknown can be shown in many ways.

- Write $10 + ? = 18$ on the board. Ask students if a box or a blank line could be used to show the unknown. Discuss whether a "*q*" could be used to show that you need to find the number of quarters. Challenge students to suggest what else might be used as a variable.

Step By Step

Connect It

- Tell students that **Connect It** will help them learn how to write equations for the problem on the previous page.

- After students complete Problem 9, invite them to explain how both Picture It and Model It on the previous page show that 6 quarters are taken away. Then ask: *How do the words in the problem tell you that 6 quarters are taken away?* [The word "took" refers to take away.]

- After students complete Problem 11, lead a discussion about how both Picture It and Model It on the previous page show Step 2 of the problem.

- Have students solve Problem 12 on their own. Then ask a volunteer to share the answer.

- Have students discuss *Talk About It* in pairs and then write an answer using their own words.

Try It

- Remind students that for the **Try It** problem, they can use a picture or number line to help them make sense of the problem, but they should also try to write equations.

▶ **Concept Extension**

14 **Solution**
2 shells; $7 + 4$ more $= 11$. Break some to get 9, so $11 - ? = 9$. Gus broke 2 shells.

Error Alert Students who answer 20 added all the numbers.

Ready **Mathematics** PRACTICE AND PROBLEM SOLVING

Assign *Practice and Problem Solving* **pages 49–50** after students have completed this section.

Guided Practice

At A Glance

Students model and solve two-step problems involving addition and subtraction.

Step By Step

- Ask students to solve the problems individually and show all their work, including the equations they wrote.

- **Pair/Share** When students have completed each problem, have them Pair/Share to discuss their solutions with a partner.

Solutions

Example Bar models and equations are used to solve this problem. Students may also act it out using counters or playing cards.

15 **Solution**

12 toys in the box; Students may act out the problem by drawing a picture or using a number line model. Students may also write a single equation: $6 - 2 + 8 = 12$.

DOK 2

Practice Solving Two-Step Word Problems

Study the model below. Then solve Problems 15–17.

Example

Emma had 12 cards and Stan had 0. Stan took some of Emma's cards. Now Emma has 9 cards. How many more cards does Emma have than Stan?

Look at how you can show your work.

Emma starts with 12 cards and ends up with 9.

$12 - ? = 9$ $12 - 3 = 9$
So, Stan has 3 cards.

12	
9	?

Emma has 9 cards. Stan has 3 cards.

$9 - 3 = ?$ $9 - 3 = 6$

9	
3	?

Answer Emma has 6 more cards than Stan.

---

15 There were 6 toys in a box. Fritz took 2 toys out of the box. Then he put 8 toys into the box. How many toys are in the box now?

Show your work.

Possible work: $6 - 2 = 4$
$\qquad$ $4 + 8 = 12$

Try acting out the problem.

Answer There are 12 toys in the box.

Teacher Notes

16 Rob had 16 crayons. He gave 8 crayons to Troy. Ella gave Rob some crayons. Now Rob has 17 crayons. How many crayons did Ella give to Rob?

Show your work.

Possible work:

16 − 8 = 8, so Rob had 8 crayons after he gave 8 to Troy.

Now Rob has 17 crayons after getting some from Ella.

8 + ? = 17

8 + 9 = 17

> How many crayons did Rob have after he gave some away? How many does he have now?

Answer ___Ella gave Rob 9 crayons.___

---

17 Bev got 6 dollars from her mom and 4 dollars from her dad. She wants to buy a game that costs 18 dollars. How many more dollars does Bev need?

A 2

(B) 8

C 10

D 14

> How can you find how much money Bev has?

Allie chose **C** as the answer. This answer is wrong. How did Allie get her answer?

Possible answer: She added 6 + 4 = 10. That's only the first step. She

needs to find 18 − 10 to find how many more dollars Bev needs.

45

Solutions

16 **Solution**

Ella gave Rob 9 crayons. See possible work on Student Book page. Students may also try modeling with a number line or by drawing a picture.

DOK 2

17 **Solution**

B; Add the money she got from her parents and subtract that from 18 to find out how much more money she needs.

Explain to students why the other two choices are not correct:

A is not correct because 10 + 2 ≠ 18.

D is not correct because 14 is equal to 18 − 4, not 18 − 10.

DOK 3

Ready Mathematics
PRACTICE AND PROBLEM SOLVING

Assign *Practice and Problem Solving* **pages 51–52** after students have completed this section.

Teacher Notes

Independent Practice

At A Glance

Students will use addition and subtraction to solve two-step word problems that might appear on a mathematics test.

Solutions

1 Solution

C; Cara picked 11 big and 7 small apples. Add $11 + 7 = 18$. Dan picked 5 fewer. $18 - 5 = 13$.

DOK 2

2 Solution

B and **D**; 15 birds and 6 fly away, $15 - 6 = 9$ (**B**); 3 more birds land, $9 + 3 = 12$. (**D**)

DOK 2

3 Solution

C; Ana has 10 beads, Beth has 3 more, so $10 + 3 = 13$. 13 altogether $- 7$ small $= 6$ big.

DOK 2

Practice Solving Two-Step Word Problems

Solve the problems.

1 Cara picked 11 big apples and 7 small apples. Dan picked 5 fewer apples than Cara. How many apples did Dan pick? Circle the correct answer.

A 18   (C) 13

B 6   D 2

2 There were 15 birds on a branch. Then 6 birds flew away. Then 3 birds landed on the branch. How many birds are on the branch now?

Fill in the blanks. Then circle all the answers that show a step in solving the problem.

A $15 + 6 =$ ___21___

(B) $15 - 6 =$ ___9___

C $9 - 3 =$ ___6___

(D) $9 + 3 =$ ___12___

3 Ana has 10 beads. Beth has 3 more beads than Ana. Beth has 7 small beads. The rest of her beads are big. How many big beads does Beth have? Circle the correct answer.

A 20   (C) 6

B 13   D 0

46

Quick Check and Remediation

- There were 9 dogs playing in the dog park. Then 2 dogs went home. Then 4 more dogs came to the park. Ask students to find the number of dogs that are in the park now. [11]

- For students who are still struggling, use the chart to guide remediation.

- After providing remediation, check students' understanding using the following problem: Jenna put 7 toys in a box. Then she put 8 more toys in the box. Her little sister took out 3 toys. How many toys are left in the box? [12]

If the error is ...	Students may ...	To remediate ...
15	have added all the numbers.	Provide students with counters to act out the problem to see that when 2 dogs go home, subtraction is involved.
3	have written the equation $9 - 2 + 4 = ?$ and added $2 + 4$ before subtracting.	Read the problem again with the students, asking them to think about what is happening in the problem to make sense of the equation. Remind them to add and subtract in the order in which they are shown.
3	have subtracted all the numbers.	Reread the problem and help students build an equation that shows each step. Talk about why both addition and subtraction are involved.

4 Lee had 8 square blocks and 9 triangle blocks. Jon took some of Lee's blocks. Then Lee had 10 blocks left. How many blocks did Jon take? Circle the correct answer.

A 2

C 17

(B) 7

D 27

5 A star card is worth 10 points. A moon card is worth 4 fewer points. How many points are a star card and moon card worth together?

Show your work.

Possible work: moon = star − 4
                    10 − 4 = 6

                    star + moon: 10 + 6 = 16

The two cards are worth 16 points.

6 Write a two-step word problem that uses addition and subtraction. Then solve the problem.

Show your work.

Answers will vary. Word problem should include addition in one step and

subtraction in the other step.

✓ **Self Check** Now you can solve two-step problems. Fill this in on the progress chart on page 1.

47

Solutions

4 **Solution**

B; 8 squares + 9 triangles = 17 shapes. 17 − ? = 10 and 17 − 10 = 7. Jon takes 7 shapes.

DOK 2

5 **Solution**

16 points together; star is 10, moon is 10 − 4 = 6; 10 + 6 = 16.

DOK 2

6 **Solution**

Word problems should include addition in one step and subtraction in the other step.

DOK 3

▶ **Hands-On Activity**

Use an act-it-out strategy to understand two-step word problems.

Materials: For each pair: counters, half sheets of paper with problems written on them

• Write two-step problems on a sheet of paper, one problem on each half. Write a total of four different problems. Make enough copies so that each pair has 2 or 3 problems to solve. Cut the paper in half so one problem is on each piece.

• Put students into pairs, and give each pair 2–3 problems and a set of counters.

• Instruct students to read a problem. One partner uses counters to act out the first part of the problem. Then the partner uses counters to act out the second part of the problem. Next, they draw a picture on the paper showing what they did. Finally, students write one or two equations and solve the problem.

▶ **Challenge Activity**

Solve more difficult two-step problems.

The following problem includes an unknown start.

• Stella took her rock collection to school. On the way home, 8 rocks fell out of her box of rocks. The next day, her mom gave her 12 more rocks to add to her collection. She now has 35 rocks. How many rocks did she have to begin with? [31]

The following problem requires organizing information to solve the multi-step problem.

• There are 10 hot dogs in each package and 8 hot dog buns in each package. Marcus has 3 packages of hot dogs and 3 packages of hot dog buns. He needs 40 hot dogs and 40 buns for his birthday picnic. How many packages of hot dogs and how many packages of buns does he need to buy? [1 package of hot dogs and 2 packages of buns]

Teacher-Toolbox.com

Overview

Assign the Lesson 6 Quiz and have students work independently to complete it.

Use the results of the quiz to assess students' understanding of the content of the lesson and to identify areas for reteaching. See the Lesson Pacing Guide at the beginning of the lesson for suggested instructional resources.

Tested Skills

Assesses 2.OA.A.1

Problems on this assessment form require students to be able to analyze two-step problems to determine the series of steps needed to solve the problem and be able to interpret a model that represents a two-step problem. Students will also need to be familiar with solving one-step problems and interpreting number lines and tape diagrams.

Ready® Mathematics

Lesson 6 Quiz

Solve the problems.

1 Write an equation for each step to solve the problem. Then answer the question.

Tina picks 18 flowers.

She throws away 3 flowers. _____

She gives 8 flowers to her mother. _____

How many flowers does Tina have now? _____ flowers

2 Oscar gets 9 books from school. Then he takes 5 books back and gets 2 more books. How many books does Oscar have now?

Fill in the boxes to complete the open number lines. Then solve the problem.

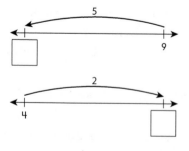

Answer: Oscar has _____ books now.

Lesson 6 Quiz continued

3 Stella has 6 big balloons and 5 small balloons. Bill has 8 balloons. How many more balloons does Stella have than Bill?

Complete each model and the answer using a number from the box below. Numbers may be used more than once.

1	3	5	6	8

Step 1: Find the number of balloons Stella has.

Step 2: Find how many more balloons Stella has than Bill.

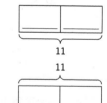

Answer: Stella has _____ more balloons than Bill.

4 Dasha is filling baskets with eggs. A full basket holds 9 eggs. There are 5 eggs in the first basket. She has 8 more eggs to put in the baskets.

If she fills the first basket, how many eggs will go in the second basket?

Circle the correct answer.

A 3   C 6

B 4   D 11

Common Misconceptions and Errors

Errors may result if students:

• stop solving after the first step.

• represent a two-step problem with pictures or models incorrectly.

• think both steps must involve the same operation.

• use the wrong operation in one or both steps.

Ready® **Mathematics**

Lesson 6 Quiz Answer Key

1. $18 - 3 = 15$
$15 - 8 = 7$
7
DOK 2

2. Top number line: 4, bottom number line: 6
6
DOK 2

3. 5, 6 or 6, 5
8, 3 or 3, 8
3
DOK 2

4. B
DOK 3

Use Equal Groups and Add

CCSS Focus

Domain
Operations and Algebraic Thinking
Number and Operations in Base Ten

Cluster
2.OA.A Represent and solve problems involving addition and subtraction.
2.OA.B Add and subtract within 20.
2.OA.C Work with equal groups of objects to gain foundations for multiplication.
2.NBT.A Understand place value.
2.NBT.B Use place value understanding and properties of operations to add and subtract.

Standards
2.OA.A.1, 2.OA.B.2, 2.OA.C.3, 2.OA.C.4, 2.NBT.A.2, 2.NBT.B.5

Standards for Mathematical Practice (SMP)
1 Make sense of problems and persevere in solving them.
2 Reason abstractly and quantitatively.
3 Construct viable arguments and critique the reasoning of others.

Additional SMPs
6, 7, 8

Lesson at a Glance

Students apply skills from the unit to solve real-world problems related to collections of objects. Problems involve skip counting, making equal groups, using arrays to add, writing addition and subtraction equations, and identifying odd or even numbers.

Lesson Pacing Guide

Whole Class Instruction

Day 1
45–60 minutes

Introduction
Problem and Solution *45 min*

Task	Key Skills	Mathematical Practices
Analyze a solution to a problem about putting 20 motors on shelves so that each shelf has an equal number of motors.	• Understand skip counting. • Understand using an array to add. • Understand writing and solving addition equations.	• Organize information. • Express regularity in repeated reasoning. • Critique a given solution.

Day 2
45–60 minutes

Modeled and Guided Instruction
Try Another Approach
Plan It *15 min* • Solve It *20 min* • Reflect *10 min*

Task	Key Skills	Mathematical Practices
Use another approach to identify a way to put 20 motors on shelves so that each shelf has the same number of motors.	• Skip count by 2s, 4s, 5s, and 10s. • Draw an array to show equal groups. • Write an addition equation.	• Reason abstractly and quantitatively. • Make use of structure. • Draw a model to show equal groups.

Day 3
45–60 minutes

Guided Practice
Discuss Models and Strategies
Plan and Solve It *35 min* • Reflect *10 min*

Task	Key Skills	Mathematical Practices
Sort rocks onto 4 trays, 2 with an even number of rocks, 2 with an odd number, with no more than 20 rocks on a tray.	• Identify a number as odd or even. • Break apart a number into doubles or doubles + 1. • Draw an array to show equal groups.	• Make sense of the problem. • Draw a model to show equal groups. • Check that the solution makes sense.

Whole Class Instruction continued

Day 4
45–60 minutes

Independent Practice

Persevere on Your Own

Problem 1

Solve It *35 min* • Reflect *10 min*

Task

Determine a way to place 18 bolts in 3 boxes so that there are at least 3 bolts in each box.

Key Skills

- Add with three addends.
- Use doubles to add.
- Know that addition and subtraction are inverse operations.

Mathematical Practices

- Make sense of the problem.
- Draw a picture to model addition.
- Write an explanation to justify choices.

Day 5
45–60 minutes

Independent Practice

Persevere on Your Own

Problem 2

Solve It *35 min* • Reflect *10 min*

Task

Determine a way to distribute 17 jars so that an even number are used for a project and the rest are put on a shelf.

Key Skills

- Identify odd and even numbers.
- Show an even number as 2 equal groups.
- Show an odd number as 2 equal groups and 1 left over.

Mathematical Practices

- Make sense of the problem.
- Reason abstractly and quantitatively.
- Calculate precisely.

Unit Resources

Practice
Practice and Problem Solving

Grade 2
- Unit 1 Game
- Unit 1 Practice
- Unit 1 Performance Task
- Unit 1 Vocabulary

Assess
Ready Instruction

Grade 2
- Unit 1 Interim Assessment

Introduction

At A Glance

Students examine a problem about deciding how many shelves to build and how many items to put on each shelf. The math involves skip-counting and repeated addition. Students discuss the problem to understand what it is asking and brainstorm different approaches. Then they refer to a problem-solving checklist to analyze a sample solution and identify what makes it a good solution.

Step By Step

- Read the problem aloud with students.

- Direct students' attention to the numbers given in the problem. Invite volunteers to explain what each number means within the context of the problem. [20 is how many motors, more than 1 shelf could be 2, 3, 4, or any greater number.]

- Invite volunteers to rephrase what Beau wants to do. Ask clarifying questions such as: *How many shelves is "more than 1 shelf?"* [any number more than 1] *Could he put 19 motors on one shelf and 1 on another shelf?* [No, 19 and 1 aren't the same number.]

▶ **Mathematical Discourse 1**

- Invite students to share their ideas about how they might begin or approach solving this problem. [for example, draw a picture, use 20 counters, try 2 shelves] Write these on the board. Allow students to describe different approaches without carrying through with an actual solution yet.

- Explain that students will look at the sample solution on the next page to see one way the problem could be solved. Then they will read the solution again and discuss what makes it a good solution by using the **Problem-Solving Checklist.**

Study an Example Problem and Solution

Read this problem about adding to solve real-world problems. Then look at Beau's solution to the problem.

Robot Motors

Beau wants to build a shelf to store his 20 robot motors. Look at his plan.

Shelf Plan
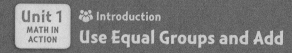
- Use more than 1 shelf.
- Put the same number of motors on each shelf.

How many shelves should Beau make? How many motors should he put on each shelf?

Show how Beau's solution matches the checklist.

✏️ **Problem-Solving Checklist**

- ☐ Tell what is known.
- ☐ Tell what the problem is asking.
- ☐ Show all your work.
- ☐ Show that the solution works.

- a. **Circle** something that is known.
- b. **Underline** something that you need to find.
- c. **Draw a box around** what you do to solve the problem.
- d. **Put a checkmark** next to the part that shows the solution works.

48

▶ **Mathematical Discourse**

1 *Can you think of another situation where someone might put things on shelves, or in boxes, with the same number in each group?*

Students might be able to come up with ideas about displaying items, or packing objects. For example, they might put 4 crackers on each plate at snack time, or they might hang pictures on a wall with 3 pictures in each row.

Beau's Solution

Hi, I'm Beau. Here's how I solved the problem.

▷ **I know** I have 20 robot motors to put on more than 1 shelf. Each shelf has the same number of motors.

▷ **I need to find** how many to put on each shelf.

▷ **I can skip count** to add the same number to try to get to 20.

  By 2s: 2, 4, 6, 8, 10, 12, 14, 16, 18, **20**

  By 3s: 3, 6, 9, 12, 15, 18, 21, 24

  By 5s: 5, 10, 15, **20**

Skip counting by 3s does not work, but 2s and 5s work.

▷ **I will try 5** motors on each shelf.

▷ **I can draw a picture** of 5 motors on 1 shelf. Then I can draw more shelves with 5 motors on each shelf.

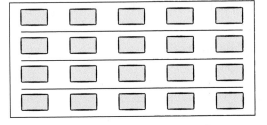

After I drew 4 shelves I had 20 motors.

▷ **I need** 4 shelves.

▷ **Add** all the rows to check. 5 + 5 + 5 + 5 = 20.

▷ **Use 4 shelves.** Put 5 motors on each shelf.

49

▶ Hands-On Activity

Act out placing 5 motors on each of 4 shelves.

Materials: 20 buttons or centimeter cubes, 1 sheet of paper

Have students fold the paper in half horizontally and, without unfolding, fold in half horizontally again. The resulting 4 rows will model the 4 shelves. Guide students to place 5 buttons across the top row, counting aloud. Repeat with remaining rows. Have a volunteer count to verify that there are 20 buttons.

▶ Mathematical Discourse

2 *How are the shelves like the rows of an array? How are the robot parts like the columns?*

Students may see that the shelves go across, like rows. If they struggle to connect the motors to columns, have them draw rings around each column of 4 squares in the illustration.

3 *Why is it helpful to use skip counting?*

If there are the same number of motors on each shelf, the total is found by repeated addition. Skip counting is one way to find the sum in repeated addition.

Step By Step

- Explain that this page shows one way to solve the problem.

- Read through Beau's solution together, one section at a time. Read for understanding, helping students with any language challenges.

- Tell students that the speech bubbles tell what Beau was thinking about as he wrote his solution. Read through the speech bubbles, and help students see how Beau is "talking to us" about what he wrote.

- Make sure students recognize where the '4' and the '5' come from in the solution. [4 shelves, 5 motors on each shelf]

▶ Hands-On Activity

- Be sure everyone agrees that this solution works. Encourage students to recognize that both the drawing and the addition equation help show that it works.

▶ Mathematical Discourse 2 and 3

- Then, as a class, go back to do a close read, using the **Problem-Solving Checklist** to help analyze Beau's solution.

- Explain that a really good answer to a problem like this does all the things on the checklist. Ask: *Where does Beau's answer tell information from the problem?* ["I have 20 robot motors to put on more than 1 shelf."] Have students circle that part.

- Then say: *In a really good answer, you want to write what you are going to figure out. Where did Beau write what he is going to figure out?* ["how many to put on each shelf"] *Underline that.*

- Similarly, lead students to mark where Beau showed his work, and where he checked his work. [Skip counting shows some work, and the drawing shows some work. Both the drawing and the equation show how he checked his work.]

- Tell students that since this is a good answer, they can look at it to get ideas when they write their own answers for this problem.

Modeled and Guided Instruction

Try Another Approach

At A Glance

Students plan and solve the Robot Motors problem from the Introduction using different numbers. Students demonstrate that the problem has more than one solution.

Step By Step

- Review and summarize the steps in Beau's solution. [Skip count to 20 by 2s, 5s, and 10s. Decide how many motors to put on each shelf. The number of shelves is how many times you count that number to get to 20.]

- Have students brainstorm some different steps than these that they might use to solve the problem. They might start by recognizing that 20 is an even number. Or they might begin by trying repeated addition with different numbers.

Plan It

- Read the **Plan It** question aloud. Invite students to share some initial responses. [For example, they might say they can try 5 or 10 shelves since you say 20 when you count by 5s or 10s.]

- Remind students that this problem has many correct answers.

▶ **Mathematical Discourse 1 and 2**

- Have students work independently to write an answer to the **Plan It** question. Tell students they will use their answers along with the **Problem-Solving Tips** on the next page to plan their answer.

- As students work on their plan, circulate to provide support and answer questions. Encourage them to look back at the sample solution for ideas.

> **SMP TIP Reason Abstractly and Quantitatively**
> Encourage students to use numbers and math words in their plans. Ask them to explain what the numbers mean and how these relate to the problem context. *(SMP 2)*

There are many ways to solve problems. Think about how you might solve the Robot Motors problem in a different way.

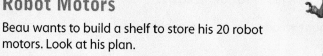

Robot Motors

Beau wants to build a shelf to store his 20 robot motors. Look at his plan.

> **Shelf Plan**
> - Use more than 1 shelf.
> - Put the same number of motors on each shelf.

How many shelves should Beau make? How many motors should he put on each shelf?

▶ **Plan It Answer this question to help you start thinking about a plan.**

What numbers can you use for the number of shelves? Explain how you know.

_____

_____

_____

_____

50

▶ **Mathematical Discourse**

1 *How might skip counting help you answer these questions?*
Students should see the connection between skip counting repeated addition, and equal groups.

2 *What are some numbers that you can't use? Explain why you can't use them.*
Help students extend their thinking to recognize inappropriate or incorrect solutions. They should be able to provide mathematical reasons why these numbers don't work. For example, you can't have 6 shelves because there is no whole number that you can add six times to get 20. Or, you can't put 8 motors on each shelf, because you will have 4 left over after 2 shelves and you don't have enough to fill 3 shelves.

▶ **Solve It** Find a different solution for the Robot Motors problem. Show all your work on a separate sheet of paper.

You may want to use the problem-solving tips to get started.

Problem-Solving Tips

● **Models**

Problem-Solving Checklist

Make sure that you . . .

☐ tell what you know.

☐ tell what you need to do.

☐ show all your work.

☐ show that the solution works.

● **Word Bank**

| skip count | add | total |
| array | row | column |

● **Sentence Starters**

• I can use two _____

• Each shelf holds _____ motors.

▶ **Reflect**

Use Mathematical Practices Talk about this question with a partner.

• **Use a Model** What addition equations can you use to check your answer? What do they show?

51

Scoring Rubric

Points	Expectations
4	The student's response is accurate and complete. All calculations are correct. The solution steps are complete and correct. Students show their work, including adding the number of motors on each shelf.
3	The solution steps and calculations are correct but might not be complete. The addition equation is correct but the number of motors and number of shelves might be reversed.
2	The student's response contains several mistakes. The explanation is inaccurate and might be missing details. The addition equation does not correctly represent the solution.
1	The student's response contains an incorrect solution. The explanation is incomplete and inaccurate. The student does not represent the solution with an addition equation.

Step By Step

Solve It

• Introduce the **Problem-Solving Tips** as ideas students may use to explain their thinking when they write their solution.

• Invite students to share ideas about how they might use the model shown. Ask if there are other words that might be useful. Solicit suggestions for how they might complete each of the sentence starters.

• Model writing out the full solution shown below on the board or on chart paper.

• Discuss the **Reflect** question about using Mathematical Practices.

• Then have students write their own solutions. (They might be different or the same as the one on the board.)

• Encourage students to work out their ideas on scrap paper and try different approaches as necessary. Have them show their complete solution on a copy of Activity Sheet 23 (Solution Sheet 2).

• Provide materials such as buttons, centimeter cubes, small boxes, and paper rectangles for students to use to model their ideas.

• If time permits, students can explain their solutions to the class.

Possible Solution

I have an even number of robot motors (20). So I know I can use 2 shelves. Using doubles addition facts, I know that $10 + 10 = 20$. So I can put 10 motors on each shelf. The picture shows 2 rows with 10 motors in each row for a total of 20.

Guided Practice

At A Glance

With **Problem-Solving Tips** as support, students understand, plan, and solve an open-ended, multi-step problem. They choose appropriate models and strategies to solve the problem, checking their thinking with a partner.

Step By Step

- Read the problem aloud with students. As you read, encourage students to ask clarifying questions about the number of rocks.

▶ **Mathematical Discourse 1**

- Direct students' attention to the illustration. Emphasize that two trays will hold an even number of rocks and two trays will hold an odd number of rocks. Be sure students understand the meaning of "20 or fewer."

- Discuss with students what they need to do [Write an appropriate number, even or odd, in each tray and explain how they know each number is even or odd].

- Write several numbers on the board, some that are odd and some that are even. Discuss with students.

▶ **Mathematical Discourse 2**

> **SMP TIP Model with Mathematics**
> Encourage students to look for patterns and explain their strategies when identifying odd and even numbers. Some examples: doubles and doubles + 1, skip counting by 2s, making equal groups, drawing arrays, etc. **(SMP 4)**

Solve the problem on a separate sheet of paper. There are different ways you can solve it.

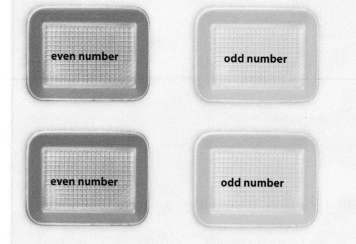

Rock Collection

Beau is sorting some of the rocks in his rock collection. He puts the rocks on the 4 trays below.

Two trays have an even number of rocks. Two trays have an odd number of rocks. Each tray can hold 20 or fewer rocks.

> **even number**
>
> **odd number**
>
> **even number**
>
> **odd number**

What are some ways Beau can put rocks on these trays?

52

▶ **Mathematical Discourse**

1 *How many rocks do you think Beau has in all? Explain why you think this.*

Listen for explanations that address the idea of each tray holding 20 or fewer rocks. Note that Beau can have no more than 78 rocks [max of 20 in the even number trays and max of 19 in the odd number trays].

2 *Look at these numbers: 35, 16, 98, 42, 7, 63. Which numbers could you write on Beau's trays? How do you know?*

Students should recognize that only numbers that are 20 or less can go in the trays.

▶ **Plan It and Solve It** **Find a solution to Beau's Rock Collection problem.**

Use a separate sheet of paper.

• Write two different odd numbers and two different even numbers.

• Show how you know each number is even or odd.

You may want to use the problem-solving tips to get started.

Problem-Solving Tips

• **Questions**

  • What are the numbers I can choose from?

  • Which numbers can make equal groups?

• **Word Bank**

odd number	equal groups	doubles
even number	leftover	doubles + 1

Problem-Solving Checklist

Make sure that you . . .

☐ tell what you know.

☐ tell what you need to do.

☐ show all your work.

☐ show that the solution works.

• **Sentence Starters**

  • I can make equal groups with _____

  • There are _____ in each group.

  • Skip count by _____

▶ **Reflect**

Use Mathematical Practices Talk about this question with a partner.

• **Use a Model** How can you use pictures to show that your answers make sense?

53

Scoring Rubric

Points	Expectations
4	The student's response is accurate and complete. All explanations are correct. It tells what is known and what the problem asks. The solution steps are complete and correctly explain the odd and even numbers in the solution. There is an accurate picture that verifies the solution.
3	The solution is substantially complete and reflects the information given. The solution steps are correct but do not completely explain the solution. The picture shows correct numbers but does not identify them as odd or even.
2	The student's response contains several mistakes. It does not identify the known information or the task. The steps do not explain how to identify the odd and even numbers. The diagram shows rocks but does not identify odd or even numbers.
1	The student's response contains an incorrect solution. The diagram is only partially completed and the numbers and drawings in the boxes do not reflect understanding of odd and even numbers.

Step By Step

Plan It and Solve It

• Discuss the **Problem-Solving Tips** as ideas students may use to explain their thinking when they write their solution.

• Invite students to share ideas about answers to the questions, other words they might use, and how they might complete the sentences. It can also be helpful to look back at Beau's solution.

• Put students in pairs to discuss solution ideas. Ask them to also discuss the **Reflect** questions about Mathematical Practices.

• Discuss a variety of approaches as a class.

• When students are confident that their plans make sense, tell them to write their complete solution on a copy of Activity Sheet 23 (Solution Sheet 2) or a blank sheet of paper.

• If time permits, share and discuss student solutions or the one below.

Possible Solution

20 or fewer rocks go in each tray. Two trays get odd numbers and two get even numbers.

Skip count by 2s starting from 0 to find the even numbers.

2, 4, 6, 8, 10, 12, 14, 16, 18, 20

All the other numbers are odd.

1, 3, 5, 7, 9, 11, 13, 15, 17, 19

For even numbers, use 6 and 8. For odd numbers, use 9 and 5. Draw rocks in two rows to show if the numbers are even or odd. Even numbers have equal rows. For odd numbers, one row has 1 more than the other row.

Independent Practice

At A Glance

Students find and share solutions to multi-step, open-ended problems.

Step By Step

Solve It

- Have students read the problem. Help them with any language issues. Encourage them to come up with some ideas, and ask any questions they may have.

- Then put students in pairs to discuss their preliminary solutions. When they are confident that their plan will work, have students independently write their solutions on a copy of Activity Sheet 23 (Solution Sheet 2) or a blank sheet of paper.

- After students complete their solutions, put them in pairs to discuss the **Reflect** question about Mathematical Practices.

- If time permits, invite various students to explain their solutions for the class to discuss, compare, and critique. Alternatively, share the solution below and invite the class to discuss.

Possible Solution

I have 18 bolts and need to put them into 3 boxes, with at least 3 in each box.

Start by putting 3 bolts into each box. $3 + 3 + 3 = 9. 9 + 9 = 18$ so I have 9 left.

I put all of them into one of the boxes. This box now has $3 + 9 = 12$ bolts.

The other boxes each have 3 bolts.

$12 + 3 + 3 = 18$.

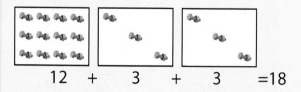

12   +   3   +   3   =18

Persevere On Your Own

Solve the problem on a separate sheet of paper.

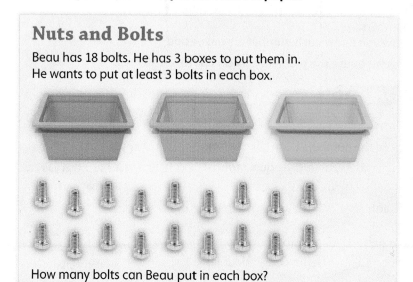

Nuts and Bolts

Beau has 18 bolts. He has 3 boxes to put them in. He wants to put at least 3 bolts in each box.

How many bolts can Beau put in each box?

▶ **Solve It** **Show one way that Beau can put the bolts in the boxes.**

- Draw a picture.
- Tell how many bolts to put in each box.
- Explain why your answer works.

▶ **Reflect**

Use Mathematical Practices Talk about this question with a partner.

- **Make Sense of Problems** How did you decide how many bolts to put in each box?

54

Scoring Rubric	
Points	**Expectations**
4	The student's response is accurate and complete. It tells what is known and what the problem asks. The steps are complete and calculations are accurate. The picture accurately shows how many are in each box. The explanation is clear and includes an appropriate mathematical rationale.
3	The solution is substantially complete and reflects the information given. The picture shows correct quantities but there may be some numbers missing. The explanation might not be thorough.
2	The student's response contains several mistakes. It does not identify the known information or the task. The picture is partially correct but it is incomplete. The explanation is unclear or incomplete.
1	The student's response contains an incorrect solution. The steps are incorrect and do not match the picture. The picture is incomplete and does not accurately reflect a correct solution. The explanation is incomplete and incorrect.

Science Project

Beau has 17 jars. He needs an even number of jars for a science project. He will put the rest of the jars on a shelf.

How many jars could Beau use for the science project?

How many will be left to put on the shelf?

▶ **Solve It** **Tell how many jars Beau could use and how many will be left to put on the shelf.**

- Draw a picture.
- Circle an even number of jars Beau can use.
- Find the number of jars Beau will put on the shelf.
- Show that the total number of jars is 17.

▶ **Reflect**

Use Mathematical Practices Talk about this question with a partner.

- **Check Your Answer** What did you do to check that your answer makes sense?

55

Step By Step

Solve It

- Have students work through this problem entirely on their own.
- Remind students that there are many different ways to solve a problem.
- Invite them to look back at the **Problem-Solving Checklist** to get started and help them stay on track. They might also want to look at the **Problem-Solving Tips** and sample solution on other pages to get some ideas for how to start. Have students write their complete solution on Activity Sheet 22 (Solution Sheet 1) or a blank sheet of paper.
- After students complete their solutions, put them in pairs to discuss the **Reflect** question about Mathematical Practices. Students may also describe other Math Practices they used.
- If time permits, invite various students to explain their solutions for the class to discuss, compare, and critique. Alternatively, share the solution below and invite the class to discuss.

Possible Solution

There are 17 jars. I need to use an even number of the jars that is less than 17. The rest of the jars go on a shelf.

10 is an even number because $5 + 5 = 10$. That's two equal groups.

I started with 17 jars and used 10. $17 - 10 = 7$. So put 7 jars on the shelf. $10 + 7 = 17$.

10 jars

7 jars

Scoring Rubric

Points	Expectations
4	The student's response is accurate and complete. It tells what is known and what the problem asks. The solution steps are complete and calculations are accurate. The picture accurately shows the even number of jars that were used and the odd number on the shelf. The explanation is clear and shows that the sum is 17.
3	The solution reflects the information given. The steps are correct but do not completely explain how the problem was solved. The picture shows correct quantities. The student shows the correct sum but does not explain the numbers used.
2	The student's response contains several mistakes. It does not identify the known information or the task. The steps do not adequately explain what the student did. The picture shows the correct number of jars but the jars are not arranged correctly. The student did not correctly show that the total is 17.
1	The student's response contains an incorrect solution. The steps are incorrect. The picture does not match the steps and does not reflect a correct solution. The student did not show that the total is 17.

Differentiated Instruction

▶ Intervention Activity

Provide support for the Independent Practice.

Nuts and Bolts

Make a tally chart to organize information.

Demonstrate for students how a tally chart like the one below could help them plan a solution. Across the top, label the 3 different boxes. In the next row, write *Start with 3* and show 3 tally marks. Then, in the next row, write *Add more* and show additional tally marks. In the last row, write *Total* and show the equation for the tally marks in that box. Here is one example, showing too few nuts:

	Box #1	Box #2	Box #3
Start with 3	|||	|||	|||
Add more	++++			||
Total	3 + 5 = __	3 + 1 = __	3 + 2 = __

Students can use this example to help them think about correct ways to fill the boxes.

Science Project

Help students think about ways to represent a solution.

This problem is about separating a whole [the jars] into two parts, so it focuses on subtraction. Help students understand this aspect of the problem by discussing visual models and equations. Discuss the following before assigning independent work:

• *How can you model the jars that Beau used?* [Draw a circle around the jars he used, or cross out each jar he used.]

• *How can you write an equation to show how many jars are left after he used those jars?* [17 − used jars = jars left.]

• *What equation could you use to show that the total number of jars is 17?* [used jars + jars on shelf = 17.]

▶ Challenge Activity

Solve extensions to the Independent Practice.

Nuts and Bolts

Extension

Beau finds another box, so now he has 4 boxes. He still wants at least 3 nuts and bolts in each box. Take some nuts and bolts out of the other boxes and put them in the new box. Tell how many nuts you took from each box and how many are now in each box. Show that your answer works.

Possible Solution

Assume that there were 6 nuts and bolts in each box. Take 3 out of the first box and put them in the new box. Take 2 out of the second box and put them in the new box. Keep the 6 in the third box. Now the first box has 6 − 3 = 3. The second box has 6 − 2 = 4. The third box has 6 − 0 = 6. And the new box has 3 + 2 = 5. 3 + 4 + 6 + 5 = 18, so this works.

Science Project

Extension

Beau needs more jars for his science project. He takes 3 jars from the shelf. Now does he have an even number or an odd number of jars left on the shelf?

Possible Solution

Beau starts with an odd number of jars on the shelf. When he removes 1 jar from the shelf, he has an even number of jars. When he removes a second jar, he now has an odd number left. But if he removes one more, for a total of 3, he will have an even number of jars on the shelf.

Teacher Notes

Assessment

Solutions

1 **Solution**
a. **No**
b. **No**
c. **Yes**
d. **Yes**
Correct equations will add the number of equal rows or number of equal columns to find a sum of 20.
DOK 1

2 **Solution**
A, C; Correct equations are part of the fact family that includes $9 - 3 = 6$ and $3 + 6 = 9$.
DOK 2

Solve the problems.

1 Mason put his toy cars in equal rows.

Circle *Yes* or *No* to tell if the equation can be used to find the total number of cars.

a. $4 + 5 + 4 + 5 = ?$ Yes (No)

b. $5 + 5 + 5 + 5 + 5 = ?$ Yes (No)

c. $4 + 4 + 4 + 4 + 4 = ?$ (Yes) No

d. $5 + 5 + 5 + 5 = ?$ (Yes) No

2 Lynda scored 9 goals this season. Becca scored 3 fewer goals than Lynda. Which equation can be used to find the number of goals Becca scored? Circle all the correct answers.

(A) $9 - 3 = 6$

B $12 - 3 = 9$

(C) $3 + 6 = 9$

D $9 + 3 = 12$

56

Teacher Notes

3 Fill in the boxes to show two ways you can find 8 + 6.

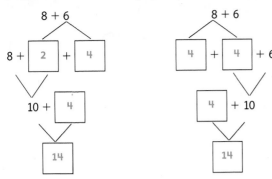

4 Write each number in the correct box below.

12   13   15   18

Odd Numbers	Even Numbers
13	12
15	18

5 Write a word problem that can be solved using this bar model. Then solve your word problem.

7	
?	2

Answers will vary. Possible answer: Ms. Winn has 7 pens. 2 are red.

The rest are blue. How many blue pens does Ms. Winn have? 2 + ? = 7;

7 − 2 = 5; Ms. Winn has 5 blue pens.

57

Solutions

3 **Solution**
8 + 2 + 4; 10 + 4; 14; and 4 + 4 + 6; 4 + 10; 14. In the expression on the left, the addend 6 is broken into 2 + 4 so that a ten can be made with the addend 8. In the expression on the right, the addend 8 is broken into 4 + 4 so that a ten can be made with the addend 6.
DOK 2

4 **Solution**
Odd Numbers: 13, 15
Even Numbers: 12, 18
DOK 1

5 **Solution**
Check students' word problems and solutions. An equation from the fact family that includes 2 + 5 = 7 should be part of the solution.
DOK 3

Teacher Notes

Assessment

Performance Task

Answer the questions. Show all your work on separate paper.

Your school has asked you to read 20 books over the summer.

- You need to read 6 books about animals.
- You need to read 3 books about people.
- The rest of the books have to be about places or hobbies.
- You have to read at least 1 book about places and 1 book about hobbies.

Make a plan about the books that you will read over the summer.

- Tell how many books about places you will read.
- Tell how many books about hobbies you will read.
- Explain why your numbers work.

▶ Reflect

Make an Argument How did you check to see that your numbers work?

Checklist

Did You . . .
- ☐ add or subtract correctly?
- ☐ check your answers?
- ☐ explain your answers?

58

Standards: 2.OA.A.1, 2.OA.B.2, 2.NBT.B.5
DOK: 3
Materials: (optional) tiles or counters
Standards for Mathematical Practice
1, 2, 4, 5

Step By Step

About the Task

Students use equations to represent and solve a multi-step problem. This task calls for students to be able to add and subtract within 20.

Getting Started

Read the problem aloud with students. Review with them the information about the number of books in each category that need to be read over the summer. Throughout the task, encourage struggling students to model numbers with tiles or counters. Students may also draw number bonds or other models. **(SMP 1, 4, 5)**

Completing the Task

Discuss with students the steps they need to take to complete the task. Guide them to recognize that they must first find how many books need to be about places or hobbies. Encourage students to write equations to find this number. Some students may break the problem into steps, writing two equations such as $3 + 6 = ?$ and $20 - 9 = ?$, to find the answer. Other students may write a single equation, such as $3 + 6 + ? = 20$. **(SMP 4)**

Students should find that the total number of books that need to be about places or hobbies is 11. To decide how many books will be about each topic, they must select a pair of addends with the sum of 11. One addend represents the number of books about places, and the other addend represents the number of books about hobbies. Any pair of addends that does not include zero is acceptable. **(SMP 2)**

▶ Extension

4-Point Solution

I will read 6 books about places and 5 books about hobbies.

This is why my numbers work. The total number of books to read over the summer is 20. Of those books, 6 will be about animals and 3 will be about people. $6 + 3 = 9$, and $20 - 9 = 11$. So 11 books will be about places or hobbies. 6 books about places + 5 books about hobbies = 11 books.

	Scoring Rubric	
Points	**Expectations**	
4	The student selects a number of books about places and a number of books about hobbies that add up to 11. All equations, calculations, and explanations are complete and correct.	
3	The student selects a number of books about places and a number of books about hobbies that add up to 11. All equations and calculations are correct, but some explanations are incomplete or unclear.	
2	The student's response contains up to two mistakes in equations or calculations. The student may determine that 11 books need to be about places or hobbies but suggest numbers of books in each category that do not add up to 11. Explanations are incorrect or incomplete.	
1	The student's response is only partially complete. Equations or calculations are incomplete, or they contain more than 2 mistakes. Explanations are missing or incorrect, showing limited understanding of how to use equations to solve problems.	

▶ **Extension**

Take the performance task further.

Jayla wants to read 8 extra books over the summer. She wants some to be about science and some to be about sports. She also wants a greater number to be about science than to be about sports. How many books about each topic can she read? Explain why your numbers work.

Solution

Answers will vary. Possible answer: Jayla can read 6 books about science and 2 books about sports. My numbers work because 6 books about science + 2 books about sports = 8 books. Also, Jayla wants a greater number to be about science than about sports, and 6 is greater than 2.

Reflect

Possible answer: First, I added my 6 books about places and 5 books about hobbies to get 11 books. Then I added the 6 books about animals to the 3 books about people to get 9 books. $11 + 9 = 20$, which is the total number of books to read over the summer. So I know my numbers work.

Unit 2 Number and Operations in Base Ten

Which lessons are students building upon?

Grade 1, Lesson 23
Add Tens to Any Number
1.NBT.C.4

Grade 1, Lesson 24
Add Tens and Add Ones
1.NBT.C.4

Grade 1, Lesson 25
Add and Regroup
1.NBT.C.4

Grade 1, Lesson 19
Understand 10 More and 10 Less
1.NBT.C.5

Grade 1, Lesson 20
Add and Subtract Tens
1.NBT.C.6

Grade 1, Lesson 25
Add and Regroup
1.NBT.C.4

Grade 1, Lesson 3
Add and Subtract in Word Problems
1.OA.A.1

Grade 1, Lesson 14
Make a Ten to Add
1.OA.C.6

Grade 1, Lesson 24
Add Tens and Add Ones
1.NBT.C.4

Grade 1, Lesson 17
Understand Tens
1.NBT.B.2a, 1.NBT.B.2c

Grade 1, Lesson 21
Understand Tens and Ones
1.NBT.B.2a, 1.NBT.B.2c

Grade 1, Lesson 22
Compare Numbers
1.NBT.B.3

Grade 1, Lesson 21
Understand Tens and Ones
1.NBT.B.2a, 1.NBT.B.2c

Grade 1, Lesson 22
Compare Numbers
1.NBT.B.3

Grade 2, Lesson 10
Understand Three-Digit Numbers
2.NBT.A.1a, 2.NBT.A.1b,
2.NBT.A.2

Grade 1, Lesson 22
Compare Numbers
1.NBT.B.3

Grade 2, Lesson 10
Understand Three-Digit Numbers
2.NBT.A.1a, 2.NBT.A.1b,
2.NBT.A.2

Grade 2, Lesson 11
Read and Write Three-Digit Numbers
2.NBT.A.3

Grade 1, Lesson 25
Add and Regroup
1.NBT.C.4

Grade 2, Lesson 10
Understand Three-Digit Numbers
2.NBT.A.1a, 2.NBT.A.1b,
2.NBT.A.2

Grade 2, Lesson 11
Read and Write Three-Digit Numbers
2.NBT.A.3

Unit 2

Lesson 7
Add Two-Digit Numbers
2.NBT.B.5, 2.NBT.B.8

Lesson 8
Subtract Two-Digit Numbers
2.NBT.B.5, 2.NBT.B.8

Lesson 9
Solve One-Step Word Problems with Two-Digit Numbers
2.NBT.B.5, 2.OA.A.1

Lesson 10
Understand Three-Digit Numbers
2.NBT.A.1a, 2.NBT.A.1b, 2.NBT.A.2

Lesson 11
Read and Write Three-Digit Numbers
2.NBT.A.3

Lesson 12
Compare Three-Digit Numbers
2.NBT.A.4

Lesson 13
Add Three-Digit Numbers
2.NBT.B.7, 2.NBT.B.9

Which lessons are students preparing for?

Grade 3, Lesson 9
Use Place Value to Add and Subtract
3.NBT.A.2

Grade 4, Lesson 3
Add and Subtract Whole Numbers
4.NBT.B.4

Grade 3, Lesson 9
Use Place Value to Add and Subtract
3.NBT.A.2

Grade 4, Lesson 3
Add and Subtract Whole Numbers
4.NBT.B.4

Grade 3, Lesson 11
Solve One-Step Word Problems Using Multiplication and Division
3.OA.A.3

Grade 3, Lesson 12
Model Two-Step Word Problems Using the Four Operations
3.OA.D.8

Grade 3, Lesson 8
Use Place Value to Round Numbers
3.NBT.A.1

Grade 3, Lesson 9
Use Place Value to Add and Subtract
3.NBT.A.2

Grade 3, Lesson 8
Use Place Value to Round Numbers
3.NBT.A.1

Grade 3, Lesson 9
Use Place Value to Add and Subtract
3.NBT.A.2

Grade 3, Lesson 8
Use Place Value to Round Numbers
3.NBT.A.1

Grade 3, Lesson 9
Use Place Value to Add and Subtract
3.NBT.A.2

Grade 3, Lesson 9
Use Place Value to Add and Subtract
3.NBT.A.2

Grade 4, Lesson 3
Add and Subtract Whole Numbers
4.NBT.B.4

Which lessons are students building upon?

Grade 1, Lesson 25
Add and Regroup
1.NBT.C.4

Grade 2, Lesson 13
Add Three-Digit Numbers
2.NBT.B.7, 2.NBT.B.9

Grade 1, Lesson 25
Add and Regroup
1.NBT.C.4

Grade 2, Lesson 7
Add Two-Digit Numbers
2.NBT.B.5, 2.NBT.B.8

Unit 2

Lesson 14
Subtract Three-Digit Numbers
2.NBT.B.7, 2.NBT.B.9

Lesson 15
Add Several Two-Digit Numbers
2.NBT.B.6

Which lessons are students preparing for?

Grade 3, Lesson 9
Use Place Value to Add and Subtract
3.NBT.A.2

Grade 4, Lesson 3
Add and Subtract Whole Numbers
4.NBT.B.4

Grade 3, Lesson 9
Use Place Value to Add and Subtract
3.NBT.A.2

Grade 4, Lesson 3
Add and Subtract Whole Numbers
4.NBT.B.4

Unit 2
Number and Operations in Base Ten

Unit 2
Number and Operations in Base Ten

Let's learn about adding and subtracting with two-digit and three-digit numbers.

Real-World Connection Have you ever counted like this: 10, 20, 30, 40, 50, . . . ? Skip counting by 10s is a fast and easy way to count to 100. You can skip count by 100s too: 100, 200, 300, 400, and so on. Skip counting by 10s and 100s will help you add and subtract two-digit and three-digit numbers.

In This Unit You will learn many ways to add and subtract two-digit and three-digit numbers. You will also learn to add more than 2 two-digit numbers at once!

✓ Self Check

Before starting this unit, check off the skills you know below.

I can:	Before this unit	After this unit
add two-digit numbers.	☐	☐
add tens and add ones.	☐	☐
subtract two-digit numbers.	☐	☐
regroup a ten.	☐	☐
solve a one-step word problem by adding or subtracting two-digit numbers.	☐	☐
read and write three-digit numbers.	☐	☐
compare three-digit numbers.	☐	☐
add three-digit numbers.	☐	☐
subtract three-digit numbers.	☐	☐
add more than 2 two-digit numbers.	☐	☐

Ready Mathematics
PRACTICE AND PROBLEM SOLVING

Practice and Problem Solving Resources

Use the following resources from *Practice and Problem Solving* to engage students and their families and to extend student learning.

- **Family Letters** Send Family Letters home separately before each lesson or as part of a family communication package.

- **Unit Games** Use partner Unit Games at classroom centers and/or send them home for play with family members.

- **Unit Practice** Assign Unit Practice as homework, as independent or small group practice, or for whole class discussion.

- **Unit Performance Tasks** Have students solve real-world Unit Performance Tasks independently or in small groups.

- **Unit Vocabulary** Use Unit Vocabulary throughout the unit to personalize student's acquisition of mathematics vocabulary.

- **Fluency Practice** Assign Fluency Skills Practice and Fluency Repeated Reasoning Practice worksheets throughout the unit.

At A Glance

- This page introduces students to the general ideas behind adding and subtracting two-digit and three-digit numbers.

- The checklist allows them to see what skills they will be learning and take ownership of their progress.

Step By Step

- Explain to students that they are going to begin a new unit of lessons. Tell them that in all the lessons in this unit they will be learning about adding and subtracting with two-digit and three-digit numbers.

- Have the class read together the introduction to the unit in their books. Invite and respond to comments and questions, if any.

- Then take a few minutes to have each student independently read through the list of skills.

- Ask students to consider each skill and check the box if it is a skill they think they already have. Remind students that these skills are likely to all be new to them, but it's still possible some students have some of the skills.

- Engage students in a brief discussion about the skills. Invite students to comment on which ones they would most like to learn, or which ones seem similar or related to something they already know. Remind them that the goal is to be able to check off one skill at a time until they have them all checked.

LESSON OVERVIEW

Lesson 7
Add Two-Digit Numbers

CCSS Focus

Domain
Number and Operations in Base Ten

Cluster
B. Use place value understanding and properties of operations to add and subtract.

Standards
2.NBT.B.5 Fluently add and subtract within 100 using strategies based on place value, properties of operations, and/or the relationship between addition and subtraction.
2.NBT.B.8 Mentally add 10 or 100 to a given number 100-900, and mentally subtract 10 or 100 from a given number 100-900.

Additional Standards
2.NBT.B.9 (see page B3 for full text)

Standards for Mathematical Practice (SMP)

2 Reason abstractly and quantitatively.
3 Construct viable arguments and critique the reasoning of others.
4 Model with mathematics.
5 Use appropriate tools strategically.
6 Attend to precision.
7 Look for and make use of structure.

Lesson Objectives

Content Objectives

• Break apart two-digit numbers as a place-value strategy for adding.
• Recognize that in adding, tens are added to tens and ones to ones.
• Determine when regrouping a ten is necessary and carry out the regrouping to find a sum.

Language Objectives

• Record sums found by modeling addition with base ten blocks.
• Draw an open number line to model adding two-digit numbers.
• Make a quick drawing to model adding two-digit numbers.
• Write an addition problem to solve a word problem involving two-digit addition.

Prerequisite Skills

• Identify place value in two-digit numbers.
• Model two-digit numbers.
• Fluently add within 20.

Lesson Vocabulary

There is no new vocabulary. Review the following key terms.

• **regroup** to compose or decompose ones, tens, or hundreds. For example, 10 ones can be regrouped as 1 ten, or 1 hundred can be regrouped as 10 tens.

• **sum** the result of addition

Learning Progression

In Grade 1 students explore the concept of place value by bundling groups of ten ones into one group of ten. They add two-digit numbers with and without composing a ten and mentally find 10 more or 10 less than a given number.

In Grade 2 students are expected to become fluent in two-digit addition and subtraction. They model two-digit numbers and write them in expanded form. Students fluently count by tens, applying that skill to the counting-on strategy for adding numbers.

In this lesson students add two-digit numbers that require regrouping a ten. They break apart numbers into tens and ones and record the addition of partial addends before calculating the sum. Students interpret picture models, number models, and an open number line to understand addition of two-digit numbers.

In Grade 3 students gain fluency with addition and subtraction of numbers within 1,000. They apply concepts of place value to multiplying two-digit numbers and add two-digit numbers when combining partial products.

Lesson Pacing Guide

Whole Class Instruction

Day 1
45–60 minutes

Toolbox: Interactive Tutorial*
Two-Digit Sums with Base-Ten Models

Introduction
- Opening Activity *10 min*
- Use What You Know *10 min*
- Find Out More *10 min*
- Reflect *10 min*

Practice and Problem Solving
Assign pages 73–74.

Day 2
45–60 minutes

Modeled and Guided Instruction
Learn About Different Ways to Show Addition
- Picture It/Model It/Model It *15 min*
- Connect It *20 min*
- Try It *10 min*

Practice and Problem Solving
Assign pages 75–76.

Day 3
45–60 minutes

Modeled and Guided Instruction
Learn About More Ways to Show Addition
- Picture It/Model It *10 min*
- Connect It *25 min*
- Try It *10 min*

Practice and Problem Solving
Assign pages 77–78.

Day 4
45–60 minutes

Guided Practice
Practice Adding Two-Digit Numbers
- Example *5 min*
- Problems 13–15 *15 min*
- Pair/Share *15 min*
- Solutions *10 min*

Practice and Problem Solving
Assign pages 79–80.

Day 5
45–60 minutes

Independent Practice
Practice Adding Two-Digit Numbers
- Problems 1–6 *20 min*
- Quick Check and Remediation *10 min*
- Hands-On or Challenge Activity *15 min*

Toolbox: Lesson Quiz
Lesson 7 Quiz

Small Group Differentiation

Teacher-Toolbox.com

Reteach
Ready Prerequisite Lessons *45–90 min*

Grade 1
- Lesson 24 Add Tens and Add Ones
- Lesson 25 Add and Regroup

Teacher-led Activities
Tools for Instruction *15–20 min*

Grade 1 *(Lessons 24 and 25)*
- Two-Digit Addition without Regrouping

Grade 2 *(Lesson 7)*
- Two-Digit Addition with Regrouping

Personalized Learning

i-Ready.com

Independent
i-Ready Lessons* *10–20 min*

Grade 1 *(Lessons 24 and 25)*
- Regrouping Tens as Ones
- Adding a Two-Digit Number and a One-Digit Number

*We continually update the Interactive Tutorials. Check the Teacher Toolbox for the most up-to-date offerings for this lesson.

Opening Activity

Regrouping a Ten

Objective Model and solve addition equations, with and without regrouping.

Time *10–15 minutes*

Materials for each student
- base-ten blocks

Overview

Students use base-ten blocks to add two numbers, exploring the purpose for regrouping 10 ones into 1 ten.

Step By Step

1 Build and add numbers without regrouping.

- Write "57 + 32 = ?" on the board. Ask students to show 57 in tens and ones using base-ten blocks.

- Instruct students to add 32 blocks in tens and ones to the 57 blocks.

- Ask: *What is the sum?* [89] *How many tens and how many ones are there?* [8 tens and 9 ones]

- On the board, write "8 tens and 9 ones is 89."

2 Build and add numbers with regrouping.

- Have students separate the blocks. Then write "46 + 38 = ?" on the board. Ask students to show 46 in tens and ones using the base-ten blocks.

- Tell them to add 38 blocks.

- Ask: *What is the sum?* [84] *How many tens and how many ones are there?* [7 tens and 14 ones]

- Say: *When we added to get 89 blocks we put the 8 tens and 9 ones together to make 89.*

- On the board, write "7 tens and 14 ones is 714." Ask: *Can I write 7 tens and 14 ones like this? Why or why not?* [Students should respond that there is a total of 84 blocks; 714 is not 84.]

- Say and record on the board: *So you are telling me that 7 tens and 14 ones is 84? I don't see an 8 anywhere. Where did it come from?* [Students should respond that there is another group of ten in 14 ones.]

3 Pull it together.

- Ask students to compare the two addition equations and tell what is the same and what is different about them. Discuss that in both cases they combined tens and ones, but in the second case another ten needed to be made from the ones. You might press them to explain why it is useful to group the tens and ones separately instead of just counting how many blocks there are altogether. [Students may say that counting tens and ones is faster than counting individual unit cubes.]

4 Generalize the concept.

- Ask: *When you look at two numbers to add, what tells you whether you will have to make another ten?* [If the sum of the numbers in the ones place is ten or greater, another ten is formed.]

Teacher Notes

Introduction

At A Glance

Students examine a model of two-digit numbers. They add the numbers by combining tens and ones. Then students connect various models for adding two-digit numbers.

Step By Step

- Work through **Use What You Know** as a class.
- Read the problem at the top of the page. Ask students what operation will help them answer the question.
- Make sure students are circling groups of ten. To ensure they count groups of ten accurately, have them mark each can as it is counted.
- Use the Hands-On Activity to reinforce the concept of building tens and connect it to the problems on this page.

▶ **Hands-On Activity**

- Tell students they may use numbers, pictures, or both to show how they thought about the question in Part e.

▶ **Mathematical Discourse 1**

Ⓖ Use What You Know

You know how to add one-digit numbers.

One day, Jack found 27 cans to recycle. The next day, he found 15 cans to recycle. How many cans did Jack find altogether?

Possible work:

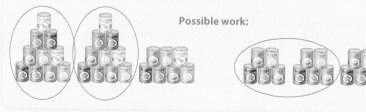

a. Circle groups of ten in the picture of 27 cans.
   There are ___2___ tens and ___7___ ones in 27.

b. Circle groups of ten in the picture of 15 cans.
   There is ___1___ ten and ___5___ ones in 15.

c. How many tens are there in all? ___3___ tens

d. How many ones are there in all? ___12___ ones
   12 ones = ___1___ ten and ___2___ ones

e. How many cans did Jack find? Show your work.

   Jack found 42 cans. Possible work: 3 tens + 1 ten = 4

   tens and 4 tens = 40. Add 2 more ones. 40 + 2 = 42

60

▶ **Mathematical Discourse**

1 *Why does it make sense to break numbers into tens and ones to add?*
Students may respond that counting tens and ones is faster than just counting all the ones.

▶ **Hands-On Activity**
   Model two-digit numbers.

Materials: connecting cubes

- Tell the students to count 27 cubes and lock together groups of 10. Have them compare the tens and ones with what they found in the picture of the cans they circled.

- Have students count 15 cubes, lock together groups of 10, and compare to the picture of cans they circled.

- Guide students in a discussion about how their cubes might be used to show the number of cans that Jack found altogether.

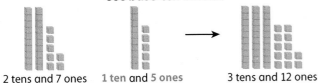

▶▶ Find Out More

You can add two-digit numbers in many ways.
Here are some ways to find 27 + 15.

Use base-ten blocks.

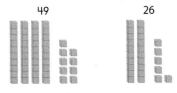

2 tens and 7 ones   1 ten and 5 ones   3 tens and 12 ones

Go to the next ten.
27 + 3 = 30
30 + 10 = 40
40 + 2 = 42

Add tens, then ones.
20 + 7
10 + 5
—————
30 + 12 = 42

▶ Reflect **Work with a partner.**

1 Talk About It Show two ways to add 49 + 26.

49   26

Write About It Possible answer: 4 tens and 9 ones + 2 tens and

6 ones = 6 tens and 15 ones, or 75. 40 + 9 + 20 + 6 = 60 + 15, or 75.

61

▶ Mathematical Discourse

2 *Which of the models helps you add in your head? Why?*
Listen for responses that indicate that students are using mental
calculation. Putting the tens together first and then adding on the
ones is a commonly used mental strategy. Some students might
also be able to go to the next ten and add up mentally.

Step By Step

- Read **Find Out More** as a class. Connect the
picture of base-ten blocks to the work
students did on the previous page.

- Compare the number models shown on this
page. Students should recognize that these
are all ways of representing the same
addition problem. Ask why it might make
sense to write 20 + 7 and 10 + 5 vertically.
Explain that while it might make sense, it
isn't required.

> **SMP TIP Look for Structure**
> Exposing students to a variety of models
> reinforces the concept of the place value
> structure found in our base-ten number
> system. Students use this structure to
> become fluent in mental calculation.
> *(SMP 7)*

- Write the vertical form of the addition
problem 27 + 15 on the board. Ask students
to explain where the 30 and the 12 came
from. Point out that these partial sums are
added to get 42. Invite volunteers to tell
how they know the total of the partial
sums is 42.

- Ask Mathematical Discourse question 2 to
emphasize the importance of being able to
add mentally. Listen to and accept all ideas.
Although there are commonly used
strategies, a mental strategy is an individual
choice. To be effective, it must make sense
to the person using it.

▶ Mathematical Discourse 2

- After students complete the **Reflect**
question, have them share their responses
with the class.

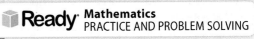
Ready **Mathematics**
PRACTICE AND PROBLEM SOLVING

Assign *Practice and Problem Solving*
pages 73–74 after students have
completed this section.

Modeled and Guided Instruction

At A Glance

Students break apart addends to evaluate an addition problem involving regrouping. Then students revisit this problem, regrouping a ten to add.

Step By Step

- Read the problem at the top of the page together as a class.

Picture It

- Draw attention to the base-ten blocks in **Picture It**.

> **SMP TIP Use Tools**
> Ask why base-ten blocks are a good model to use for adding two-digit numbers. Students should recognize that the tens are already grouped. When using connecting cubes, beans, or other counters, the tens have to be grouped first to be counted. *(SMP 5)*

Model It

- Instruct students to look at the sum in the **Model It** section. Ask how it relates to the way the sum is written in **Picture It**.

▶ **Mathematical Discourse 1**

▶ **Visual Model**

Model It

- Direct attention to **Model It**. Ask students to describe how this way of adding is different from the ways in **Picture It** and the first **Model It**.

▶ **Mathematical Discourse 2**

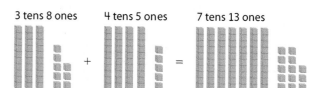

Read the problem. Then you will explore different ways to show addition.

> Before lunch, Maria read for 38 minutes. After lunch, she read for 45 minutes. How many total minutes did Maria read?

▶ **Picture It You can use base-ten blocks.**

3 tens 8 ones   4 tens 5 ones   7 tens 13 ones

▶ **Model It You can add tens and add ones.**

$$38 = 30 + 8$$
$$45 = \underline{40 + 5}$$
$$70 + 13$$

▶ **Model It You can go to the next ten.**

$$38 + 2 = 40$$
$$40 + 40 = 80$$
$$80 + 3 = ?$$

62

▶ **Mathematical Discourse**

1 *Would it make sense to write the sum of 7 tens + 13 ones as* (write on the board) *713? Explain.*

Students should respond that no, it would not make sense. The 7 is not in the tens place so the number cannot be written this way.

2 *Can you find a different way to break up the numbers to add 38 and 45?*

Possible answer: Add 38 + 2, to get 40. Then add 43 to 40 to get 83.

▶ **Visual Model**

Use a place-value chart.

- Draw the following chart on the board:

	Tens	Ones
	3	8
	4	5
Total	7	13

- Write: 3 tens and 8 ones = 30 + 8
         4 tens and 5 ones = 40 + 5
         7 tens and 13 ones = 70 + 13

- Guide students in a discussion of why a place-value chart can be helpful.

▶ Connect It Add tens and ones.

2 Look at *Picture It* on the previous page.
What is the total number of tens and ones?

___7___ tens + ___13___ ones

3 How many tens and ones are in 13?

13 = ___1___ ten and ___3___ ones, or ___10___ + 3

4 Add both tens. Then add the ones.

70 + 10 + 3 = ___80___ + ___3___

= ___83___

5 **Talk About It** Explain how you would add 38 + 45.

Write About It Possible answer: Add the tens. 30 + 40 = 70. Add the

ones. 8 + 5 = 13. Make tens and ones for 13. 10 + 3. Add tens, then ones.

70 + 10 + 3 = 83.

▶ Try It Try another problem.

6 Mr. Dane has 17 pens and 37 pencils. How many pens
and pencils does he have in all? Show your work.

Possible answer: 10 + 7 + 30 + 7 = 40 + 14, or 54 pens and pencils

63

▶ Hands-On Activity

Use base-ten blocks to understand regrouping.

Materials: base-ten blocks

• Have students model the addends 38 and 45 with the blocks.

• Tell them that addition means they combine both groups of blocks.

• Have students use the blocks to model making a ten as they answer
Problem 3.

Connect It

• Read **Connect It** as a class. Make sure
students understand that the questions
refer to the problem on the previous page.

• To reinforce the regrouping process, you
may want to use the Hands-On Activity as
students answer Problem 3.

▶ Hands-On Activity

• Discuss the answer to Problem 5 together
as a class. Allow students who employed
different strategies to show their work on
the board, describing the strategy they used
to find a sum.

• Ask students to describe the mental strategy
they used (or could use) to find the sum of
8 and 5. Discuss how when they use the
make-a-ten strategy, they think in terms of
tens and ones. To make a ten, take 2 from
the 5 to add to 8 and then add the extra 3,
or add 10 + 3. Helping students make this
connection will build confidence in applying
mental calculation strategies.

Try It

6 **Solution**

54 pens and pencils; Break each number
into tens and ones. Add the tens and then
add the ones. Regroup the one ten from
the sum of the ones to the tens place.

Error Alert Watch for students who do not
regroup the ten from the sum of the ones.
Students who either wrote the sum as 414 or
44 did not regroup.

 **Ready** Mathematics
PRACTICE AND PROBLEM SOLVING

Assign *Practice and Problem Solving*
pages 75–76 after students have
completed this section.

Modeled and Guided Instruction

At A Glance

Students examine a quick drawing and an open number line that are used to model a two-digit addition problem involving regrouping. They revisit this problem, using the models to solve it. Then students apply the strategies they have learned to a new problem.

Step By Step

- Read the problem at the top of the page together as a class. Ask students what operation will help them solve the problem.

Picture It

- Draw attention to **Picture It**. Remind students that a quick drawing is an easy way for them to show tens and ones when adding numbers. You may want them to use whiteboards to replicate the addends as a quick drawing.

Model It

- Draw attention to the **Model It** section. Have students evaluate the open number line by explaining what is happening. Tell them that this model shows one way to count up by making a ten first.

▶ **Mathematical Discourse 1**

- Discuss other counting up strategies students may use, such as first adding 40 to 48 and then adding the 3 ones by going to the next ten and adding one more, or first counting on by tens (58, 68, 78, 88) and then adding the 3 ones.

▶ **Mathematical Discourse 2**

▶ **English Language Learners**

Learn About More Ways to Show Addition

Read the problem. Then you will explore different ways to show addition.

> There are 48 students on Bus A and 43 students on Bus B. How many students are on both buses?

▶ **Picture It** **You can use a quick drawing.**

Show each number with a quick drawing.

It is easier to add when one number has no ones. So, make a ten.

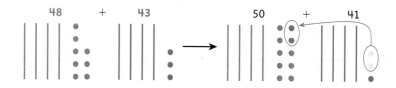

▶ **Model It** **You can use an open number line.**

Start with 48. Add 2 to go to the next ten. To add 40, count on by tens from 50: 60, 70, 80, 90. Then add 1 more.

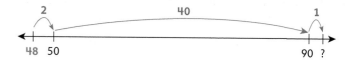

64

▶ **Mathematical Discourse**

1 *How is the strategy used in Model It like the make-a-ten strategy?*

Students should notice that when two is taken from 43 to add to 48, it is like taking 2 from the 3 to add to the 8. 8 + 2 = 10 so 48 + 2 = 50 (the next ten).

2 *Do you think it is easier mentally to add the tens and then the ones, or count up? Why?*

Students will have a variety of responses showing personal preference. If students respond that one way is easier, ask them to tell you what makes it easier. Help struggling students articulate their reasoning.

▶ **English Language Learners**

ELL students may find it difficult to express themselves in sharing strategies, so they may not offer ideas. Yet it is important to get a sense of their thinking. Encourage them to share ideas with a partner whom they trust, or talk to you later when they do not have to speak in front of the class.

▶ **Connect It** Make a ten to add.

Look at *Picture It* on the previous page.

7 Why do you add 2 to 48? _____to make a 10_____

8 What does the drawing show? Fill in the blanks.

$$48 \quad + \quad 43$$
$$+ \boxed{2} \quad - \boxed{2}$$
$$50 \quad + \quad 41 \quad = \quad \boxed{91}$$

Look at *Model It* on the previous page.

9 Why do you first jump 2 spaces?

You want to get to the next ten. Jumping 2 from 48 gets you to 50.

10 What number should you get if you add all the jumps? Why?

You should get 43 if you add all the jumps. That's the number you are

adding to 48. 2 + 40 + 1 = 43

11 Where is the answer on this open number line?

The answer is the number you land on after the last jump, which is 91.

▶ **Try It** Try another problem.

12 Sam drives 39 miles north. Then she drives 28 miles east. How far does she drive altogether? Show your work.

Sam drove 67 miles. Possible work: 39 + 1 = 40. Take away 1 from 28.

Add 40 + 27 = 67.

65

Hands-On Activity

Use base-ten blocks to understand a number line model.

Materials: base-ten blocks

- Direct students' attention to Problem 9.

- Have students model the addends using base-ten blocks. Ask them to demonstrate what is happening when you add 2 to 48 on the number line. [Students should take 2 unit cubes from 43 and move them to 48.] The number 2 is subtracted from the total being added, so the next two jumps on the number line should total 41. Discuss how reorganizing the blocks doesn't change the sum.

Step By Step

Connect It

- Tell students that **Connect It** will help them think about the problem and models on the previous page.

- You may want to complete the Hands-On Activity before students complete Problem 9. It shows that if they first jump 2 (add 2), they have to remember to subtract 2 from the total amount being added (43 − 2 = 41). That's why 40 + 1 is added next.

▶ **Hands-On Activity**

- Make sure students understand in Problem 10 that when making jumps to count up, a number is broken apart to make the addition easier.

Try It

- Have students discuss **Try It** in pairs and then write an answer using their own strategy. Suggest that they think about the strategies they have learned in this lesson.

12 **Solution**

Sam drove 67 miles; Take one from 28 and add to 39: 39 + 1 = 40; Add the remaining 27 to 40: 40 + 27 = 67.

Error Alert Students who answer 57 did not regroup a ten.

Ready Mathematics
PRACTICE AND PROBLEM SOLVING

Assign *Practice and Problem Solving* **pages 77–78** after students have completed this section.

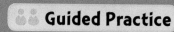
Guided Practice

At A Glance

Students use strategies to solve two-digit addition problems.

Step By Step

- Ask students to solve the problems individually and show all their work, including the equations they wrote. Encourage students to describe their thinking.

- **Pair/Share** When students have completed each problem, have them Pair/Share to discuss their solutions with a partner.

Solutions

Example A picture model is used as an example for employing the counting on strategy. Students may also think of an open number line to count on.

13 Solution
96 flags; 59 + 1 = 60; 60 + 36 = 96.
DOK 2

Practice **Adding Two-Digit Numbers**

Study the model below. Then solve Problems 13–15.

Example

Lucas had 47 rocks in his collection. He got 34 more rocks. How many rocks does Lucas have now?
You can count on by tens and ones to add.

47   57 67 77 78 79 80 81

Answer 81 rocks

13 Bailey sold 59 flags at a parade. She has 37 flags left. How many flags did she have before the parade?

Show your work.

Possible work: 30 + 7 + 50 + 9
80 + 16 = 96

How many tens are in each number? How many ones?

Answer 96 flags

66

---

14 Kory used 47 blocks to build a tower. Then he used 28 more blocks to make it bigger. How many blocks did Kory use altogether?

Show your work.

Possible work:

Answer 75 blocks

15 Jenny got 53 points in her first card game. She got 38 points in her second game. What is the total number of points Jenny got?

A 81

B 93

C 91

D 83

Does it matter which number you start with?

Brady chose **A** as the answer. This answer is wrong. How did Brady get his answer?

Possible answer: He forgot to add the group of 10 from the 11 ones to the

other tens.

67

Solutions

14 **Solution**

75 blocks: $47 + 3 = 50$; $50 + 25 = 75$.

DOK 1

15 **Solution**

C; $53 + 7 = 60$; $60 + 31 = 91$.

Explain to students why the other two choices are not correct:

B is not correct because $8 + 3 = 11$ not 13.

D is not correct because $53 + 30 = 83$. One addend is 38 not 30.

DOK 3

Ready Mathematics
PRACTICE AND PROBLEM SOLVING

Assign *Practice and Problem Solving* **pages 79–80** after students have completed this section.

Teacher Notes

Independent Practice

At A Glance

Students use strategies to add two-digit numbers that might appear on a mathematics test.

Solutions

1 **Solution**
A, B, and **C;** Break each addend into tens and ones to add (**A**). Reorganize the tens and ones from each addend to add (**B**). Add the sum of the combined tens and combined ones (**C**).
DOK 2

2 **Solution**
B; $36 + 4 = 40$; $40 + 23 = 63$.
DOK 1

3 **Solution**
a. **Yes**; Break 24 into tens and ones, and then add the numbers; b. **No**; c. **No**; d. **Yes**; Break 24 into tens and ones, add 1 to 9 to make a ten, and then add the numbers.
DOK 2

Practice ▶ Adding Two-Digit Numbers

Solve the problems.

1 Which addition problem shows a way to add $78 + 16$? Circle all the correct answers.

- Ⓐ $70 + 8 + 10 + 6$
- Ⓑ $70 + 10 + 8 + 6$
- Ⓒ $80 + 14$
- D $70 + 8 + 6$

2 Jo did 36 sit-ups. Then she did 27 more. How many sit-ups did Jo do in all? Circle the correct answer.

- A 73
- Ⓑ 63
- C 53
- D 9

3 Tell if the equation shows how to find $24 + 9$. Circle *Yes* or *No* for each problem.

a. $20 + 4 + 9 = 33$	⟨Yes⟩	No
b. $2 + 4 + 9 = 15$	Yes	⟨No⟩
c. $20 + 40 + 9 = 69$	Yes	⟨No⟩
d. $20 + 10 + 3 = 33$	⟨Yes⟩	No

68

Quick Check and Remediation

- Taylor picked 39 apples and Jordan picked 47 apples. How many apples did they pick altogether? [86]

- For students who are still struggling, use the chart to guide remediation.

- After providing remediation, check students' understanding using the following problem: On Saturday morning 48 children and 35 adults visited the museum. How many people visited the museum on Saturday morning? [83]

If the error is ...	Students may ...	To remediate ...
76	have failed to regroup ten ones.	Provide students with base-ten blocks to model the problem. Make sure they recognize that a ten needs to be regrouped. Have students revisit the strategy they used, adding the ten that was regrouped.
87	have counted on from 39 but failed to subtract 1 from 47.	Help the student use a quick drawing to see that 1 is taken from 47 and added to 39. Remind the student that adding 1 without subtracting from the other addend makes the sum incorrect.
89	have added 3 to 47 to make 50 but failed to subtract 3 from 39.	Use the strategy discussed above to help students recognize the need for subtracting from one addend when adding to the other.

4 Each day Seth runs 1 more minute than the day before. Yesterday he ran for 18 minutes. How many total minutes did he run yesterday and today? Circle the correct answer.

A 17   **C** 35

B 19   **(D)** 37

5 Ms. Ames shows her students the problem at the right. What did she do? Explain. Then show how to solve the problem a different way.

Possible work showing another way:

59 + 1 = 60
25 − 1 = 24
60 + 24 = 84

$$\begin{array}{r} 25 \\ + 59 \\ \hline 14 \\ + 70 \\ \hline 84 \end{array}$$

Possible answer: Ms. Ames added the ones first.

Then she added the tens. Then she added the two sums together.

6 Find 47 + 24 the way Ms. Ames did in Problem 5. Then use a different way. What do you notice?

Possible work:

$$\begin{array}{r} 47 \\ + 24 \\ \hline 11 \\ + 60 \\ \hline 71 \end{array} \qquad \begin{array}{l} 47 = 40 + 7 \\ + 24 = 20 + 4 \\ \hline 60 + 11 = 71 \end{array}$$

Possible answer: If you add the ones first or the tens first you get the

same sum.

✓ Self Check Now you can add two-digit numbers.
Fill this in on the progress chart on page 59.

69

Solutions

4 **Solution**
D; 18 + 19 = 18 + 2 + 17 = 20 + 17 = 37.
DOK 2

5 **Solution**
She added the ones first and recorded the sum. Then she added the tens and recorded the sum. Then she added the partial sums. Student strategies will vary.
DOK 3

6 **Solution**
Ms. Ames' way; 47 + 24 = 11 + 60 = 71. Students' methods will vary. Check for accuracy.
DOK 3

▶ **Hands-On Activity**

Use a hundreds chart to add two-digit numbers.

Materials: Activity Sheet 2 (Hundreds Chart), 1 counter

• Distribute a hundreds chart and counter to each student.

• Write the addition problem 36 + 27 on the board.

• Tell students to find 36 on the chart and place the marker on it. Ask how they might use the chart to count on by tens first.

• Lead students to see that in the hundreds chart, moving vertically adds or subtracts 10. They can add 20 by moving the counter vertically down the chart from 36 to 46 to 56 and then count on the additional 7.

• Write several problems on the board for the students to model with their hundreds chart and counter.

▶ **Challenge Activity**

Devise a new addition strategy.

Challenge students to think of a strategy for adding two-digit numbers that no one in the class has discussed yet. Tell them to:

• Explain the strategy step-by-step so others can use it.

• Test the strategy on three or four addition problems to make sure it works all the time.

• Explain the strategy and give an addition problem to a classmate to see if he or she can use the strategy.

• Change any part of the strategy, if necessary, so that it is clear and will work all the time.

Teacher-Toolbox.com

Overview

Assign the Lesson 7 Quiz and have students work independently to complete it.

Use the results of the quiz to assess students' understanding of the content of the lesson and to identify areas for reteaching. See the Lesson Pacing Guide at the beginning of the lesson for suggested instructional resources.

Tested Skills

Assesses 2.NBT.B.5

Problems on this assessment form require students to be able to decompose two-digit numbers into tens and ones, add two-digit numbers using a variety of strategies, and regroup correctly when necessary. Students will also need to be familiar with the meaning of the word "sum," using base-ten blocks to represent two-digit numbers, and writing an addition problem to solve a word problem involving two-digit addition.

Ready® Mathematics

Lesson 7 Quiz

Solve the problems.

1 Does the addition problem show a way to add $27 + 38$?
Circle *Yes* or *No* for each addition problem.

a. $20 + 7 + 30 + 8$ Yes   No

b. $20 + 70 + 38$ Yes   No

c. $20 + 30 + 7 + 8$ Yes   No

d. $50 + 10 + 5$ Yes   No

2 Li reads 64 pages of her book on day one. On day two she reads 17 pages. Li says the sum of 64 and 17 is 71 pages.

Explain what Li did wrong. How many pages did Li read in all?

Show your work.

_____

_____

_____

Li read _____ pages in all.

Lesson 7 Quiz continued

3 Look at the base-ten blocks.

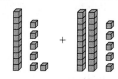

Complete an equation that the blocks can help you solve. Use three of the numbers in the box to fill in the blanks.

| 15 | 16 | 25 | 26 | 31 | 41 |

_____ + _____ = _____

4 Mr. Diaz has 49 red blocks and 33 blue blocks on a table. He asks his class to find the total number of blocks.

Which addition problem shows a way to find $49 + 33$?

Circle all the correct answers.

A $40 + 9 + 3$

B $40 + 30 + 9 + 3$

C $40 + 10 + 9 + 3$

D $70 + 2$

E $70 + 9 + 3$

F $50 + 32$

Common Misconceptions and Errors

Errors may result if students:

- add or subtract single-digit numbers incorrectly.

- regroup ones incorrectly or forget to regroup the ones.

- decompose numbers into tens and ones incorrectly.

- add the correct number to one addend to make the next ten, but then forget to subtract it from the other addend, or subtract an incorrect number.

Ready® **Mathematics**

Lesson 7 Quiz Answer Key

1. a. Yes
   b. No
   c. Yes
   d. Yes
   DOK 2

2. Possible explanation:
   Li forgot to add the group of 10 from the 11 ones to the other tens:
   6 tens + 1 ten = 7 tens
   4 ones + 7 ones = 11 ones or 1 ten + 1 one
   She should have added 7 tens + 1 ten + 1 one = 8 tens + 1 one or 81.
   81
   DOK 3

3. 16 + 25 = 41 or 25 + 16 = 41
   DOK 1

4. B, E, F
   DOK 2

Lesson 8
Subtract Two-Digit Numbers

CCSS Focus

Domain
Number and Operations in Base Ten

Cluster
B. Use place value understanding and properties of operations to add and subtract.

Standards
2.NBT.B.5 Fluently add and subtract within 100 using strategies based on place value, properties of operations, and/or the relationship between addition and subtraction.

2.NBT.B.8 Mentally add 10 or 100 to a given number 100-900, and mentally subtract 10 or 100 from a given number 100-900.

Additional Standards
2.NBT.B.9 (see page B3 for full text)

Standards for Mathematical Practice (SMP)
2 Reason abstractly and quantitatively.

3 Construct viable arguments and critique the reasoning of others.

4 Model with mathematics.

5 Use appropriate tools strategically.

6 Attend to precision.

7 Look for and make use of structure.

Lesson Objectives

Content Objectives
- Decompose a ten as a strategy for subtracting.
- Recognize that addition can be used to solve a subtraction problem.
- Evaluate mental strategies for subtracting a number from a two-digit number.

Language Objectives
- Orally describe how to add up to solve subtraction problems.
- Draw an open number line to model subtracting two-digit numbers.
- Write a subtraction problem to solve a word problem.

Prerequisite Skills

- Identify place value in two-digit numbers.
- Fluently add and subtract within 20.
- Apply the commutative property of addition.

Lesson Vocabulary

There is no new vocabulary. Review the following key terms.

- **regroup** to compose or decompose ones, tens, or hundreds. For example, 10 ones can be regrouped as 1 ten, or 1 hundred can be regrouped as 10 tens.
- **difference** the result of subtraction.

Learning Progression

In Grade 1 students subtract within 20, recognizing when decomposing a number leads to a ten and utilizing addition to solve subtraction problems. Students subtract multiples of ten within 100 and mentally find 10 more or 10 less than a given number.

In Grade 2 students gain fluency adding and subtracting within 20. Students apply concepts of fact families as they explore how inverse operations can be a tool in solving addition and subtraction problems.

In this lesson students subtract a two-digit number from another two-digit number by counting back to a ten and by decomposing a ten. Students interpret picture models, number models, and open number lines to understand subtraction of two-digit numbers.

In Grade 3 students fluently add and subtract numbers within 1,000. They apply concepts of place value to division and recognize the role of subtraction in division with a remainder, and later in division of multi-digit numbers.

Lesson Pacing Guide

Whole Class Instruction

Day 1 *45–60 minutes*	Toolbox: Interactive Tutorial* *Subtracting Two-Digit Numbers* **Introduction** • Opening Activity *15 min* • Use What You Know *10 min* • Find Out More *10 min* • Reflect *5 min*	Practice and Problem Solving Assign pages 83–84.
Day 2 *45–60 minutes*	**Modeled and Guided Instruction** **Learn About Subtracting by Adding Up** • Model It/Model It *15 min* • Connect It *20 min* • Try It *10 min*	Practice and Problem Solving Assign pages 85–86.
Day 3 *45–60 minutes*	**Modeled and Guided Instruction** **Learn About Subtracting by Regrouping** • Model It/Model It *15 min* • Connect It *20 min* • Try It *10 min*	Practice and Problem Solving Assign pages 87–88.
Day 4 *45–60 minutes*	**Guided Practice** **Practice Subtracting Two-Digit Numbers** • Example *5 min* • Problems 14–16 *15 min* • Pair/Share *15 min* • Solutions *10 min*	Practice and Problem Solving Assign pages 89–90.
Day 5 *45–60 minutes*	**Independent Practice** **Practice Subtracting Two-Digit Numbers** • Problems 1–6 *20 min* • Quick Check and Remediation *10 min* • Hands-On or Challenge Activity *15 min* Toolbox: Lesson Quiz Lesson 8 Quiz	

Small Group Differentiation

Teacher-Toolbox.com

Reteach
Ready Prerequisite Lessons *45–90 min*

Grade 1
• Lesson 19 *Understand* 10 More and 10 Less
• Lesson 20 Add and Subtract Tens

Teacher-led Activities
Tools for Instruction *15–20 min*

Grade 1 *(Lessons 19 and 20)*
• Patterns on the Hundred Chart
• Using Models to Subtract

Grade 2 *(Lesson 8)*
• Two-Digit Subtraction with Regrouping
• Two-Digit Subtraction without Regrouping

Student-led Activities
Math Center Activities *30–40 min*

Grade 2 *(Lesson 8)*
• 2.19 Add and Subtract within 100
• 2.20 Solve a Subtraction Sentence

Personalized Learning

i-Ready.com

Independent
i-Ready Lessons* *10–20 min*

Grade 1 *(Lessons 19 and 20)*
• Counting On: 1 to 100
• Addition Facts

*We continually update the Interactive Tutorials. Check the Teacher Toolbox for the most up-to-date offerings for this lesson.

Opening Activity

Explore Subtraction Strategies

Objective Model and solve subtraction problems involving regrouping.

Time *15–20 minutes*

Materials for each student
- connecting cubes (at least 53 per student)

Overview

Students use connecting cubes to subtract a two-digit number from another two-digit number, exploring and evaluating student-directed strategies.

Step By Step

1 Explore the concept of subtraction.

- Tell students to count out 42 connecting cubes.

- Ask: *Is it possible to take 17 cubes away? Why?* [Make sure students understand that since there is a group of 17 within 42, it can be subtracted.]

- Ask: *What will you do to take 17 cubes away?* [Students will most likely respond that they will count out 17 and remove them one by one.] Discuss that trying to use the strategy of counting back 17 is not an efficient way to subtract two-digit numbers.

2 Use strategies to subtract.

- Have students construct 4 trains of 10 cubes each. They should now have 4 ten-cube trains and 2 single cubes.

- Instruct students to take 17 cubes away. Observe their actions. You may want students to record each step on a whiteboard to help them remember the process used.

❸ Share and interpret strategies.

- Ask students to share the strategies used. Some students may have subtracted 2 first, then a 10, and finally the additional 5. Some may have subtracted 2, then 5, and finally 10. Others may have subtracted 10, then the 2, and an additional 5. Allow students to express the strategy in their own way. If a student responds that 17 were taken away all at once, present him or her with 4 cube trains of ten and 2 additional cubes. Have the student demonstrate taking 17 away while you record each movement.

- As students share their strategies, record their processes on the board. Have them compare and contrast each strategy, recognizing that in each case 17 was broken into a 10, a 2, and a 5.

❹ Generalize strategies.

- Write the problem 53 − 25 on the board and tell students to apply the strategy they used with the previous problem to this one.

- Tell students that some strategies, such as doubles + 1, can only be used in certain situations. Other strategies can be used in many situations. This lesson will help them explore several different strategies that they might use for subtracting numbers. Make sure students understand that after learning about various subtraction strategies, they can choose the ones they want to use in different situations.

Teacher Notes

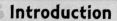
Introduction

At A Glance

Students examine models of a two-digit number and evaluate a subtraction problem based on the models.

Step By Step

- Work through **Use What You Know** as a class.

- Read the problem at the top of the page. Ask students what operation will help them answer the question.

- For Part c, ask: *Are there enough art projects to subtract 9?* Explain. [Yes. Since there are 34 art projects, there is a group of 9 that can be subtracted.]

- Help students understand that within the set of whole numbers, a lesser number can be subtracted from a greater number. However, our place-value system breaks numbers into tens and ones. If the tens are kept together, as in the first set of base-ten blocks, then 9 ones cannot be subtracted because there are only 4 ones.

▶ **Mathematical Discourse 1**

- As students complete Parts d–f, use the Hands-On Activity to connect the concept of decomposing a ten to the problem on this page.

▶ **Hands-On Activity**

Lesson 8 👥 Introduction
Subtract Two-Digit Numbers

2.NBT.B.5
2.NBT.B.8

Use What You Know

You know how to count tens and ones.

There are 34 art projects in a contest.
There are 9 paintings.
The rest are drawings.
How many art projects are drawings?

a. How many tens and ones are in 34?
    ___3___ tens and ___4___ ones

b. Solve 34 − 9 to find the number of drawings.
    How many ones do you need to subtract? ___9___

c. Are there enough ones in 34 to subtract? ___no___
    Explain. _Possible explanation: There are only 4 ones in 34._

    4 is less than 9.

d. Look at the model at the right.
    How many tens blocks are there? ___2___ tens
    How many ones blocks are there? ___14___ ones

e. Now take away 9 ones. How many tens and ones
    are left? ___2___ tens and ___5___ ones

f. How many art projects are drawings? ___25___

70

▶ **Mathematical Discourse**

1 *We know that there is a group of 9 in 34, so why are there not enough ones to subtract 9?*

Students should respond that since the blocks are grouped in tens and ones, there are not enough ones blocks to subtract 9.

▶ **Hands-On Activity**
Model the subtraction problem.

Materials: base-ten blocks

- Distribute base-ten blocks to students.

- Tell students to show 34 in tens and ones.

- Have students model decomposing a ten by trading 1 tens block for 10 ones blocks. Then have them model subtracting 9 by taking away 9 ones blocks.

▷▷ Find Out More

Here are two ways to find $34 - 9$.

✎ **Start at 9 and add up to 34.**

Go to the next 10. $9 + \underline{\quad 1 \quad} = 10$

Add to get to 30. $10 + \underline{\quad 20 \quad} = 30$

Add to get to 34. $30 + \underline{\quad 4 \quad} = 34$

Total the jumps. ——→ $\underline{\quad 25 \quad}$

$9 + \underline{\quad 25 \quad} = 34$, so $34 - 9 = \underline{\quad 25 \quad}$.

✎ **Subtract to make a ten.**

34 has 4 ones, so subtract 4 first. Then subtract 5.

$34 - 4 = 30$

$30 - 5 = 25$

$34 - 9 = \underline{\quad 25 \quad}$

▷ Reflect

1 **Talk About It** How can you subtract $46 - 8$? Explain one way.

Write About It Possible answer: Make a ten. $46 - 6 = 40$

and $40 - 2 = 38$.

71

▷ Concept Extension

Subtract 10 and then add 1.

- After students examine the second strategy shown for subtraction, say: *Dominick says that to subtract 9, he subtracts 10 and then adds 1. Do you think his strategy works? Why or why not?*

- Lead students to recognize that the strategy works. Even though one too many is subtracted at first, it gets added back. You may want to use connecting cubes or a hundreds chart to model the strategy.

▷ Mathematical Discourse

2 *How are the arrows showing jumps on the first number line different from the arrows on the second number line?*

Students should notice that the arrows on the first number line jump to the right, or "go up" the number line. The arrows on the second number line jump to the left, or "go down" the number line. Students may also notice that each number line has a different number of jumps.

3 *What does the direction of the arrows tell you about each number line?*

Because the arrows on the first number line go to the right, the first number line shows addition. Because the arrows on the second number line go to the left, the second number line shows subtraction.

Step By Step

- Read **Find Out More** as a class. Revisit the concept of fact families to justify using addition to solve a subtraction problem. You may want to write the problem on the board: $34 - 9 = ?$. Ask students what an addition equation would look like in this fact family. They should remember that $9 + ? = 34$ is related to $34 - 9 = ?$.

- Discuss with students that when they count up, it is important to keep track of the jumps so they know how much they added to 9 to get to 34.

▶ **Mathematical Discourse 2 and 3**

▶ **Concept Extension**

- Tell students that for the **Reflect** question, they can explain any strategy that makes sense. Choosing one from this page is acceptable but not required. Remind them that their strategy must make sense to their partner before they write it.

> **SMP TIP Construct Arguments**
> As students discuss their strategies in the **Reflect** question, roam the room encouraging students to ask about each other's strategies and to justify their own strategies using reasoning and/or models. *(SMP 3)*

📦 **Ready** Mathematics
PRACTICE AND PROBLEM SOLVING

Assign *Practice and Problem Solving* **pages 83–84** after students have completed this section.

Modeled and Guided Instruction

At A Glance

Students examine two counting-up strategies and apply them to subtracting a two-digit number. Then students revisit this problem, using the counting-up strategies to find the difference. Finally, they select a strategy and apply it to a new problem.

Step By Step

- Read the problem at the top of the page together as a class.

Model It

- Remind students that they are trying to find a part of a whole. Girls + boys = children at camp. To find the number of boys, subtract the number of girls from the total: $54 - 27 = ?$, or add the number of boys to the number of girls: $27 + \text{boys} = 54$.

Model It

- Discuss how 27 is broken into $20 + 3 + 4$ in both situations. Ask Mathematical Discourse questions 1 and 2 to reinforce use of these strategies. Discuss their value in performing mental calculations.

▶ **Mathematical Discourse 1 and 2**

▶ **Concept Extension**

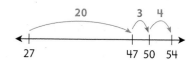

Learn About Subtracting by Adding Up

Read the problem. Then you will add up to subtract two-digit numbers.

> There are 54 children at camp. Of these, 27 are girls. How many boys are at camp?

▶ **Model It** You can add tens first.

$54 - 27 = ?$ is the same as $27 + ? = 54$.

$27 + 20 = 47$
$47 + 3 = 50$
$50 + 4 = 54$

$20 + 3 + 4 = ?$

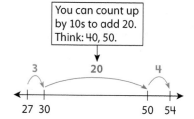

▶ **Model It** You can add up to the next ten.

Find $54 - 27$.

Start with 27 and add 3.
Then add 20 to get to 50.
Finally, add 4 to get to 54.

$27 + 3 = 30$
$30 + 20 = 50$
$50 + 4 = 54$

$3 + 20 + 4 = ?$

> You can count up by 10s to add 20. Think: 40, 50.

72

▶ Mathematical Discourse

1 *Why doesn't it matter if you add up 20 first or 3 first?*

A total of 27 is added. Numbers can be added in any order, and the sum remains the same.

2 *Which way of adding up do you think is easiest to do in your head? Why?*

Listen for responses that show personal preference and justification. Make sure students understand that both ways are mathematically accurate.

▶ Concept Extension

Explore order when subtracting down.

- Say: *It doesn't matter the order you use when adding up. What about when you subtract down? Is $54 - 20 - 7$ the same as $54 - 7 - 20$? Why?*

- Allow students to use connecting cubes and discuss their ideas in pairs before sharing with the class. Students should see that in both cases, they are subtracting a total of 27 cubes and that $20 + 7$ is being subtracted, not $20 - 7$.

- Ask: *Does $20 - 7 = 7 - 20$? Explain.*

Make sure students understand that $20 - 7$ does not equal $7 - 20$, and have them justify their responses.

Teacher Note: This subtraction problem can be modeled as $54 - (20 + 7)$ or $54 - (7 + 20)$, not $54 - (7 - 20)$, in which case the subtraction in the parentheses would occur first.

▶ **Connect It** Understand adding up.

Look at the first *Model It*.

2 What number do you start with? _27_

What number do you stop at? _54_

Look at the second *Model It*.

3 Why do you add 3 first? _You add 3 to get to the_

next ten. It is easy to add tens.

4 What is 54 − 27? How did you get your answer?

27; Find the sum of all the numbers you added to get

_to 54._

5 **Talk About It** How are the two models on the previous page alike? How are they different?

Write About It _Possible answer: Both ways add the_

same numbers, 20 + 3 + 4. But they are added in a

different order in each way.

▶ **Try It** Try another problem.

6 Subtract 71 − 36 by adding up. Show your work.

Possible work: 36 + 4 = 40

_40 + 30 = 70_

_70 + 1 = 71_

_4 + 30 + 1 = 35_

_71 − 36 = 35_

73

Step By Step

Connect It

- Read **Connect It** as a class. Make sure students understand that the questions refer to the problem on the previous page.

- For each **Model It**, discuss why each jump is made on the number line. For the first **Model It**, help students think about why it can be helpful to add tens first.

- For the second **Model It**, help students think about why it can be helpful to add up to the next ten first. Also, make sure students connect the numbers on the number line with the numbers in the equations.

▶ **Visual Model**

Try It

- For **Try It**, remind students that they may use any add up strategy that they prefer, but should show the process they used with an open number line or equations.

6 **Solution**

35; Start at 36. Possible solutions include: 36 + 30 + 4 + 1; 36 + 4 + 30 + 1; 36 + 40 − 5.

Error Alert Watch for students who may lose track of the number of tens added on. They may try using taps or finger counts and, in doing so, add an additional ten.

📦 **Ready** Mathematics
PRACTICE AND PROBLEM SOLVING

Assign *Practice and Problem Solving* **pages 85–86** after students have completed this section.

▶ **Visual Model**

Explore a different strategy.

- Draw an open number line on the board.

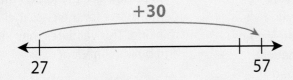

+30

27   57

- Tell students that Kim says her strategy is to add 30 first. Ask: *Does Kim's strategy work?* Allow students to share and justify their ideas.

- Then ask a volunteer to show where the arrow that shows the jump would stop if 30 were added. Ask: *What might be confusing about adding 30?* [It stops at 57 which is greater than 54.] *What could we do after adding 30 to make Kim's strategy work?* Students should see that after adding 30, 3 must be subtracted so that you end at 54, making 27 the total number added.

Modeled and Guided Instruction

At A Glance

Students explore subtracting a two-digit number by decomposing a ten first and by subtracting tens first. Then students revisit this problem, evaluating the models and applying the strategies to a new problem.

Step By Step

- Read the problem at the top of the page together as a class.

Model It

- Draw attention to **Model It**. Have students explain what the model shows. You may want to have base-ten blocks available for students to physically model, if necessary.

- Ask: *Why is one ten decomposed into ten ones?* [It makes it easier to subtract 5 ones.]

Model It

- Have students evaluate the **Model It** picture. Ask: *Why can we take away a ten first?* [There are enough tens to subtract one ten.]

- In the second step, a ten is decomposed to subtract 5 ones. Some students may prefer to subtract 5 from 32 by counting back 2 to 30 and another 3 to 27. There are many ways to think about subtraction, and this model is showing one of those ways.

▶ **Mathematical Discourse**

▶ **English Language Learners**

Note: The strategies on this page develop the thinking associated with the standard algorithm for subtraction. The algorithm itself is not introduced until Grade 4.

> **SMP TIP Use Structure**
> Encourage students to attempt to use varied strategies in solving subtraction problems. Each strategy engages them in working within the structure of our number system somewhat differently, promoting flexibility in thinking as students search for the structure that allows them to solve problems fluently. (*SMP 7*)

Learn About ▶ **Subtracting by Regrouping**

Read the problem. Then you will subtract in different ways.

> Ming had 42 toy animals. She gave 15 toy animals to her friends. How many toy animals does Ming have left?

▶ **Model It** **You can regroup a ten first and then subtract.**

Find $42 - 15$.

Step 1: Make 10 ones with 1 ten in 42.

Step 2: Subtract.

$$\begin{array}{r} 3 \text{ tens and } 12 \text{ ones} \\ - 1 \text{ ten and } 5 \text{ ones} \\ \hline \end{array}$$

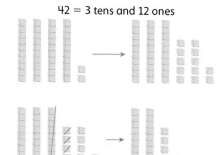

42 = 3 tens and 12 ones

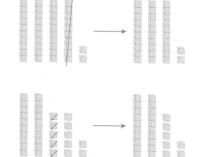

▶ **Model It** **You can subtract tens first.**

Find $42 - 15$.

Step 1: $15 = 1$ ten and 5 ones. Take away 1 ten.

$42 - 10 = 32$

Step 2: Make 10 ones with 1 ten. Then take away 5 ones.

74

▶ **Mathematical Discourse**

Do you think it is easier to regroup a ten first or subtract tens first? Why?

Students will have a variety of responses showing personal preference. Make sure all preferences are justified using mathematical reasoning and equally valued.

▶ **English Language Learners**

ELL students may have learned a strategy differently, or represented it differently than presented. Encourage them to demonstrate for the class their ways of thinking. This validates their strategies and builds confidence.

Connect It Understand ways to subtract.

Look at the first *Model It* on the previous page.

7 Why do you make 10 ones with 1 ten in 42?

You need more ones to subtract 5 ones from 42.

8 How many tens and ones are left after you subtract in Step 2? __2__ tens and __7__ ones

Look at the second *Model It* on the previous page.

9 How many tens and ones are left after you subtract 1 ten? __3__ tens and __2__ ones

10 How many tens and ones are left after you subtract 5 ones? __2__ tens and __7__ ones

11 How many toy animals does Ming have left? __27__

12 **Talk About It** How is Step 1 in the first *Model It* different from Step 1 in the second *Model It*? Does it matter what you do first?

Write About It Possible answer: The first Model It trades a 10 for 10 ones first. The second Model It subtracts the tens first and then the ones. The answer is the same.

Try It Try another problem.

13 Subtract 82 − 63 by taking away tens and ones. Show your work.

Possible work: 8 tens and 2 ones is the same as 7 tens and 12 ones. 7 tens and 12 ones − 6 tens and 3 ones = 1 ten and 9 ones, or 19.

75

Step By Step

Connect It
- Tell students that **Connect It** will help them think about the problem and models on the previous page.
- Remind students that you want them to think about why the strategies on the previous page work, rather than a strategy they may prefer to use.
- Have students discuss *Talk About It* in pairs and then write an answer using their own words.

Try It
- You may want to have base-ten blocks available for students to use as they complete **Try It**. Ask them to include either a quick drawing or an equation to show how they thought about the subtraction problem.

▶ **Concept Extension**

13 **Solution**
19; 82 can be broken into 7 tens and 12 ones. 12 − 3 = 9 and 70 − 60 = 10, 10 + 9 = 19; or 82 − 60 = 22, 22 can be broken into 1 ten and 12 ones, 12 − 3 = 9, 10 + 9 = 19.

Error Alert Students who answer 21 attempted to subtract mentally by subtracting 60 from 80 and 2 from 3.

Ready Mathematics
PRACTICE AND PROBLEM SOLVING

Assign *Practice and Problem Solving* **pages 87–88** after students have completed this section.

▶ Concept Extension

Consider multiple strategies.

- Have students review the subtraction strategies modeled on the previous two pages, which are used to solve the problem about camp, and the subtraction strategies modeled on these two pages, which are used to solve the problem about toy animals.

- Ask: *Why do you think the counting up strategy was used for the first problem and a take away strategy used for the second problem?* Students may respond that the first problem is a part-of-the-whole problem, so it is like a number bond. You can think of the missing part as an addition or subtraction problem. The second problem is a take away situation, so it makes sense to model subtraction as taking something away.

- Discuss with students that either strategy could be used in both situations. Have students talk in pairs about how they could use the "take away" strategy in the first problem and the "counting up" strategy in the second problem and then share their ideas with the class.

Guided Practice

At A Glance

Students use strategies to solve two-digit subtraction problems.

Step By Step

- Ask students to solve the problems individually and show all their work, including the equations they wrote. Encourage students to describe their thinking.

- **Pair/Share** When students have completed each problem, have them Pair/Share to discuss their solutions with a partner.

Solutions

Example An open number line is used to demonstrate the counting back strategy. Remind students that the jumps could be shown as $20 + 2 + 2$.

14 Solution
23 pear trees; $92 - 60 = 32$; $32 - 9 = 23$.
DOK 1

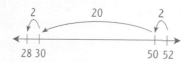

Practice Subtracting Two-Digit Numbers

Study the model below. Then solve Problems 14–16.

Example

Joe has 52 cards. He puts 28 cards in one pile and the rest in a second pile. How many cards are in the second pile? Find $52 - 28$.

You can show your work on an open number line.

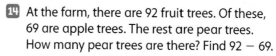

Jump down $2 + 20 + 2$, or 24, to get to 28.
So, $52 - 28 = 24$.

Answer ___24 cards___

14 At the farm, there are 92 fruit trees. Of these, 69 are apple trees. The rest are pear trees. How many pear trees are there? Find $92 - 69$.

Show your work.

Possible work: $92 - 69$ is the same as
$69 + ? = 92$
$69 + 1 = 70$
$70 + 20 = 90$
$90 + 2 = 92$
$1 + 20 + 2 = 23$

If you add up, what number do you start with?

Answer ___23 pear trees___

76

Teacher Notes

15 There are 71 students on two buses. One bus has 38 students. How many are on the other bus? Find 71 − 38.

Show your work.

Possible work: 71 − 30 = 41
41 − 1 = 40
40 − 7 = 33

> What number can you subtract if you subtract tens first?

Answer 33 students

16 Pedro does 27 jumping jacks. Ray does 8 fewer jumping jacks than Pedro. How many jumping jacks does Ray do? Find 27 − 8.

A 9

(B) 19

C 20

D 35

> How many do you take away from 27 to make a ten?

Mia chose **D** as the answer. This answer is wrong. How did Mia get her answer?

Possible answer: Mia added 27 and 8. She should have subtracted

8 from 27.

77

Solutions

15 **Solution**
33 students; 38 + 30 = 68; 68 + 3 = 71; 30 + 3 = 33.
DOK 1

16 **Solution**
B; Break 8 into 7 + 1; 27 − 7 = 20; 20 − 1 = 19.

Explain to students why the other two choices are not correct:

A is not correct because 8 + 9 ≠ 27. One more ten is needed.

C is not correct because 27 − 7 = 20, one more needs to be subtracted.

DOK 3

Ready Mathematics
PRACTICE AND PROBLEM SOLVING

Assign *Practice and Problem Solving* **pages 89–90** after students have completed this section.

Teacher Notes

👤 Independent Practice

At A Glance

Students use strategies to subtract two-digit numbers that might appear on a mathematics test.

Solutions

1 **Solution**
B Count back a total of 17; **D** Add up a total of 18.
DOK 2

2 **Solution**
D; $48 - 8 - 10 - 1$.
DOK 2

3 **Solution**
C; $22 - 2 = 20$; $20 - 3 = 17$.
DOK 1

Practice **Subtracting Two-Digit Numbers**

Solve the problems.

1 How can you find $35 - 17$? Circle all the correct answers.

  A $35 - 5 = 30$ and $30 - 2 = 28$

  (B) $35 - 10 = 25$ and $25 - 7 = 18$

  C $17 + 10 = 27$ and $27 + 7 = 34$

  (D) $17 + 3 = 20$ and $20 + 15 = 35$

2 Jamie drew this model to solve a problem. Which problem did she solve? Circle the correct answer.

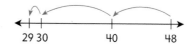

29 30   40   48

  A $40 - 11 = 29$

  B $48 - 18 = 29$

  C $48 - 18 = 30$

  (D) $48 - 19 = 29$

3 Don had 22 shells. He gave 5 to his brother. How many shells does Don have now? Find $22 - 5$. Circle the correct answer.

  A 7

  B 12

  (C) 17

  D 29

Quick Check and Remediation

- Stan has 53 stickers, and his brother has 38 stickers. How many more stickers does Stan have than his brother? [15]

- For students who are still struggling, use the chart to guide remediation.

- After providing remediation, check students' understanding using the following problem: 46 children are on the school playground. At the first bell, 27 children go inside. How many children are left on the playground? [19]

If the error is . . .	Students may . . .	To remediate . . .
91	have added instead of subtracted.	Model the two numbers on an open number line. Point out that when you are looking for "how many more," you are finding the difference between the two numbers. Help students write the subtraction problem and solve it.
13	have counted on from 38 to 48 and then added the extra 3.	Use a hundreds chart to help students see the two numbers that need to be counted to get from 48 to 50 before counting up 3.
25	have subtracted 30 from 50 and 3 from 8.	Model the subtraction problem using base-ten blocks. Students should see that after subtracting 30, 23 blocks are left. Guide students to see their error and encourage them to write down each step to make sense of the subtraction problem.

4 Circle *Yes* or *No* to tell if you can use the method to find 56 − 17.

a. 56 − 6 = 50 and
50 − 1 = 49   Yes   (No)

b. 56 − 10 = 46 and
46 − 7 = 39   (Yes)   No

c. 17 + 3 = 20 and
20 + 36 = 56   (Yes)   No

d.   4 tens and 16 ones
 − 1 ten and 7 ones   (Yes)   No
   3 tens and 9 ones

5 Greg subtracted 73 − 44. He forgot the last step. Write the last step and the answer in the boxes. Explain how Greg subtracted.

$$\begin{array}{r} 73 \\ -\ 40 \\ \hline 33 \\ -\ 3 \\ \hline 30 \\ -\ \boxed{1} \\ \hline \boxed{29} \end{array}$$

Possible answer: First Greg subtracted the 4 tens in 44.

Then he subtracted 3 ones to make a ten. 44 has 4

ones, so he has to subtract 1 more one.

6 Show another way to subtract 73 − 44. Make sure it is different from what you did in Problem 5.

Possible answer: 44 + ? = 73
44 + 20 = 64
64 + 6 = 70
70 + 3 = 73
20 + 6 + 3 = 29

✓ **Self Check** **Now you can subtract two-digit numbers. Fill this in on the progress chart on page 59.**

79

Solutions

4 **Solution**
a. **No**; Only 7 was subtracted. 10 needs to be subtracted, too; b. **Yes**; c. **Yes**; d. **Yes**.
DOK 2

5 **Solution**
The last step is 30 − 1 to have subtracted a total of 44.
DOK 3

6 **Solution**
Students may subtract in the following ways: 73 − 3 = 70; 70 − 1 = 69; 69 − 40 = 29; or 44 + 20 + 9 = 73; or 44 + 6 + 20 + 3 = 73.
DOK 3

▶ **Hands-On Activity**

Use a hundreds chart to subtract two-digit numbers.

Materials: Activity Sheet 2 (Hundreds Chart), 1 counter

- Distribute a hundreds chart and counter to each student and write the subtraction problem 63 − 27 on the board.
- Tell students to find 63 on the chart and place the counter on it. Ask how they might use the chart to subtract 27.
- Students subtract 27 by moving the counter vertically up the chart from 63 to 53 to 43 and then count back the additional 7. Color in the 27 squares that were subtracted. You may want students to use one color for the tens, another for the 3 ones subtracted to get to 40 and another color for the additional 4.
- Repeat the process above using other problems involving subtraction.

▶ **Challenge Activity**

Devise a new subtraction strategy.

Challenge students to think of a strategy for subtracting two-digit numbers that no one in the class has discussed yet. Tell them to:

- Explain the strategy step-by-step so others can use it.
- Test the strategy on three or four subtraction problems to make sure it works all the time.
- Give the explanation and a subtraction problem to a classmate to see if they can use the strategy.
- Revise the strategy as needed so that it will work all the time and is explained clearly.

Teacher-Toolbox.com

Overview

Assign the Lesson 8 Quiz and have students work independently to complete it.

Use the results of the quiz to assess students' understanding of the content of the lesson and to identify areas for reteaching. See the Lesson Pacing Guide at the beginning of the lesson for suggested instructional resources.

Tested Skills

Assesses 2.NBT.B.5

Problems on this assessment form require students to be able to represent two-digit subtraction using equations and number lines, and to recognize and use a variety of strategies when subtracting two-digit numbers. Students will also need to be familiar with the meaning of *difference*, and with regrouping 1 ten into 10 ones.

Ready® Mathematics

Lesson 8 Quiz

Solve the problems.

1 George has 64 baseball cards. He gives 28 of them to his brother. Which method shows a way to find $64 - 28$?

Circle all the correct answers.

A $28 + 2 = 30$
$30 + 30 = 60$

B $64 - 4 = 60$
$60 - 4 = 56$
$56 - 20 = 36$

C $64 - 40 = 24$
$24 + 8 = 32$

D $64 - 4 = 60$
$60 - 8 = 52$
$52 - 20 = 32$

E   5 tens 14 ones
  $-$ 2 tens 8 ones
    $\overline{}$

2 Jessica made this model to subtract two numbers. What problem is she solving?

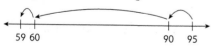

Fill in the blanks to complete the subtraction problem.

_____ $-$ _____ $=$ _____

Lesson 8 Quiz continued

3 Vivian says that the difference of 63 and 27 is 37. Her work is shown below.

$63 - 3 = 60$

$60 - 20 = 40$

$40 - 3 = 37$

Her teacher says her answer is not right. What should Vivian do to fix her work?

_____

_____

_____

_____

_____

4 Alex adds to find $45 - 17$.

Finish Alex's work. Use numbers from the box to fill in the blanks.

2	3	4	5	10	20	22	28	30

$17 +$ _____ $= 37$

$37 +$ _____ $= 40$

$40 +$ _____ $= 45$

$45 - 17 =$ _____

Common Misconceptions and Errors

Errors may result if students:

• leave out any step in a multi-step method of subtraction.

• subtract incorrectly by subtracting a quantity more than once or not at all, or by adding instead of subtracting.

• subtract the smaller digit from the larger digit instead of regrouping 1 ten as 10 ones.

• forget to subtract 1 from the digit in the tens place when regrouping 1 ten as 10 ones.

Ready® **Mathematics**

Lesson 8 Quiz Answer Key

1. B, E
DOK 2

2. 95, 36, 59
DOK 2

3. Possible explanation: Vivian subtracted 3 to make a ten, 60. Then she subtracted 20 to get to 40. So far, she has subtracted 23 and she needs to subtract a total of 27. She now needs to subtract 4 instead of only 3. The last step should be $40 - 4 = 36$.
DOK 3

4. 20
3
5
28
DOK 2

Lesson 9 Solve One-Step Word Problems with Two-Digit Numbers

CCSS Focus

Domain
Number and Operations in Base Ten
Operations and Algebraic Thinking

Cluster
B. Use place value understanding and properties of operations to add and subtract.
A. Represent and solve problems involving addition and subtraction.

Standards
2.NBT.B.5 Fluently add and subtract within 100 using strategies based on place value, properties of operations, and/or the relationship between addition and subtraction.

2.OA.A.1 Use addition and subtraction within 100 to solve one- and two-step word problems involving situations of adding to, taking from, putting together, taking apart, and comparing, with unknowns in all positions, e.g., by using drawings and equations with a symbol for the unknown number to represent ·the problem.

Standards for Mathematical Practice (SMP)

1 Make sense of problems and persevere in solving them.
2 Reason abstractly and quantitatively.
3 Construct viable arguments and critique the reasoning of others.
4 Model with mathematics.
5 Use appropriate tools strategically.
6 Attend to precision.

Lesson Objectives

Content Objectives
- Analyze word problems to determine the operation needed to solve them.
- Apply the use of fact families as a strategy to solve one-step problems and build number sense.
- Interpret models that represent a one-step problem with two-digit numbers.

Language Objectives
- Write an equation to represent a word problem.
- Talk with a partner about strategies used to solve a problem.
- Compare two models for solving a problem and tell how they are the same or different.

Prerequisite Skills

- Add and subtract within 100.
- Use fact families fluently

Lesson Vocabulary

There is no new vocabulary.

Learning Progression

In Grade 1 students solve simple one-step problems involving addition and subtraction within 20. They represent problems with objects, drawings, and equations that use a symbol to represent the unknown.

In Grade 2 students are expected to master solving one- and two-step problems with the unknown in all positions. They model problems using physical objects and diagrams, and write equations using a symbol to represent the unknown.

In this lesson students interpret and solve problems involving two-digit numbers. They utilize concepts of fact families by representing a problem using more than one equation.

In Grade 3 students apply problem-solving strategies to problems involving multiplication and division. At this level and beyond, students recognize mathematics as a tool for solving problems that arise within the context of a lesson and in daily life.

Lesson Pacing Guide

Whole Class Instruction

Day 1
45–60 minutes

Toolbox: Interactive Tutorial*
Money Problems: Addition and Subtraction

Introduction
- Opening Activity 20 min
- Use What You Know 10 min
- Find Out More 10 min
- Reflect 5 min

Practice and Problem Solving
Assign pages 93–94.

Day 2
45–60 minutes

Modeled and Guided Instruction

Learn About Ways to Model Word Problems
- Picture It/Model It/Model It 15 min
- Connect It 20 min
- Try It 10 min

Practice and Problem Solving
Assign pages 95–96.

Day 3
45–60 minutes

Modeled and Guided Instruction

Learn About More Ways to Model Word Problems
- Model It/Model It 15 min
- Connect It 20 min
- Try It 10 min

Practice and Problem Solving
Assign pages 97–98.

Day 4
45–60 minutes

Guided Practice

Practice Modeling and Solving Word Problems
- Example 5 min
- Problems 12–14 15 min
- Pair/Share 15 min
- Solutions 10 min

Practice and Problem Solving
Assign pages 99–100.

Day 5
45–60 minutes

Independent Practice

Practice Modeling and Solving Word Problems
- Problems 1–6 20 min
- Quick Check and Remediation 10 min
- Hands-On or Challenge Activity 15 min

Toolbox: Lesson Quiz
Lesson 9 Quiz

Small Group Differentiation

Teacher-Toolbox.com

Reteach
Ready Prerequisite Lessons 45–90 min

Grade 1
- Lesson 24 Add Tens and Add Ones
- Lesson 25 Add and Regroup

Teacher-led Activities
Tools for Instruction 15–20 min

Grade 1 *(Lessons 24 and 25)*
- Two-Digit Addition without Regrouping

Grade 2 *(Lesson 9)*
- Solve Subtraction Word Problems
- Solve Subtraction Comparison Problems

Student-led Activities
Math Center Activities 15–20 min

Grade 2 *(Lesson 8)*
- Add and Subtract within 100
- Solve a Subtraction Sentence

Personalized Learning

i-Ready.com

Independent
i-Ready Lessons* 10–20 min

Grade 1 *(Lessons 24 and 25)*
- Regrouping Tens as Ones
- Adding a Two-Digit Number and a One-Digit Number

*We continually update the Interactive Tutorials. Check the Teacher Toolbox for the most up-to-date offerings for this lesson.

Explore One-Step Problems with Two-Digit Numbers

Objective Solve a problem involving two-digit numbers using student-selected strategies and models.

Time *20–30 minutes*

Materials for each student

- plain paper, crayons or colored pencils
- access to manipulative materials

Overview

Students are challenged to solve a one-step problem by interpreting the problem, representing it in a way that is meaningful to them, and finding a solution. Solutions and solution strategies are shared and analyzed by the class.

Step By Step

1 Introduce the problem.

- Simon has a piece of ribbon 85 inches long. Simon needs 67 inches for the tail of his kite. How much ribbon should he cut off?

- Tell students they can use any representation: a picture, a model, or manipulative materials. They should show their thinking clearly on paper and find a solution. You may remind them of the problems they solved in Lesson 2, asking if any of those strategies would work here.

- Give students ample time to complete the task, allowing them to work in pairs, if they choose.

2 Support students as they solve the problem.

- Roam the room as students work, making sure they understand the problem and helping them find a meaningful representation and solution strategy. Ask questions like: *What kind of drawing or model would make sense to use to show a piece of ribbon? What part of the ribbon does Simon need? How can you show that?*

3 Share solutions and solution strategies.

- Have students or student pairs take turns sharing their strategy and showing the representation they used.

- Ask: *Why do you think this is a good way to show the problem? What strategy did you use to solve the problem? Did you think of any other strategy that might work? Why did you choose the one you did?*

- As students share solutions, guide them in using mathematical vocabulary and clearly articulating the strategy they employed.

4 Critique the work of others.

- Invite the class to ask questions of each other, seek clarification, and acknowledge the work of their peers. Highlight innovative strategies or representations as an encouragement for all students to attempt diverse ways of thinking.

Teacher Notes

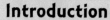

Introduction

At A Glance

Students explore a one-step word problem involving two-digit numbers by examining a bar model. Then students use varied models to represent the problem and analyze the three positions for an unknown.

Step By Step

- Work through **Use What You Know** as a class.

- Review with students the possible positions for an unknown. You may want to refer to the models on the next page.

- Ask: *In this problem, are you trying to find the start, the change, or the total?* [the change] *How do you know?* [They need 75, so that's the total. They have 49, so that's the start. We need to find how many more are needed to get to 75 from 49.]

- Discuss with students how the top bar in the model shows the whole and the bottom boxes are the parts that make up the whole.

▶ **Mathematical Discourse 1**

SMP TIP Use Tools

Asking students to evaluate the use of a model makes them aware of the types of models that are appropriate to use in this kind of problem situation as well as which models are useful for organizing the information found in the problem. Further, asking students to select a model for solving a problem independently promotes good decision-making. *(SMP 5)*

- Ask: *What operation will you use to find the missing part?* [addition] Some students may respond that they could subtract 49 from 75. Discuss that subtraction is an acceptable operation since the three numbers are part of a fact family.

- As students complete Part d, use Mathematical Discourse question 2 to encourage flexible thinking.

▶ **Mathematical Discourse 2**

↻ Use What You Know

Review solving one-step word problems.

Mr. Soto's students can trade 75 box tops for school supplies. They have 49 box tops. How many more do they need to get to 75?

a. What is the total number of box tops the class can trade? Write this number in the model.

b. How many box tops does the class start with? Write this number in the model.

75	
49	?

c. Use the model. Fill in the blanks below to write an equation.

$\underline{49} + ? = \underline{75}$

d. Find the missing number. Show your work.

Possible work: $49 + 1 = 50$
$50 + 25 = 75$
$1 + 25 = 26$

e. How many more box tops does the class need? _26_

▶ **Mathematical Discourse**

1 *Why might this be a good model to use for this problem?*

We are looking for a part of the whole, and this model shows the parts and the whole.

2 *What are some ways you could mentally solve this problem?*

Students may suggest strategies such as counting up from 49 to 75, or subtracting 50 from 75 and adding 1 back.

▶▶ Find Out More

You can use models for *start, change,* and *total* problems.

Here is one way to think of the problem on the previous page.

- **Start** with a number. (49 box tops)
- **Change** happens. (Collect more box tops.)
- Get a **total**. (75 box tops)

You can use any of these models to show the problem.

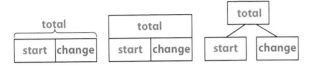

You can use any of these equations to solve the problem.

Addition	**Subtraction**
$49 + ? = 75$	$75 - 49 = ?$
$? + 49 = 75$	$75 - ? = 49$

▶ **Reflect** **Work with a partner.**

1 **Talk About It** Look at the equations above. The ? and numbers are in different places. Why is the answer to all the equations 26?

Write About It Possible answer: The equations are like fact families

with two-digit numbers. Each can be used to find the number you add to

49 to get 75, so the answer will always be 26.

81

▶ **Hands-On Activity**

Use physical models to understand visual models.

Materials: 1 set of 3 rectangles (9×3, $4\frac{1}{2} \times 3$, $4\frac{1}{2} \times 3$) and a set of +, −, and = cards (Activity Sheet 1, Digit Cards)

- Tell students to place the two small rectangles below the large one to resemble the models on this page.

- Instruct students to print a 75 on the long rectangle at the top, a 49 on the rectangle representing the start, and a ? on the third rectangle. You may want students to reposition the rectangles to resemble each model shown.

- Tell students to use the operation and equal signs to show each equation on this page.

▶ **Mathematical Discourse**

3 *How are the models on this page alike? How are they different?*

Listen for responses such as: They are alike because the whole is at the top and the two parts are under it.

They are different because some are put together next to each other and one is spread apart.

4 *How is finding the unknown part like using fact families?*

You can either add the parts to get the whole or subtract the known part from the whole to get the unknown part.

Step By Step

- Ask students to look at the models in **Find Out More**. Ask: *What shows the parts in each model?* [the two boxes at the bottom] *What shows the whole?* [the box or number at the top] Encourage students to describe how each model shows addition and how it shows subtraction.

▶ **Mathematical Discourse 3**

- Ask: *In the problem on the previous page, is the unknown the start, the change, or the total?* [The unknown is the change.] Point out that these models can also be used for problems in which the unknown is the total or the start.

- Discuss the positions of the question marks in the addition and subtraction equations. You may want to use the Hands-On Activity to physically model each of these situations. Reinforce the fact that these models and equations resemble the ones they explored in Lesson 2. Students should recognize that the models used here can be applied to any fact family and used with numbers of any size.

▶ **Mathematical Discourse 4**

▶ **Hands-On Activity**

- Have student pairs read and solve the **Reflect** problem.

📦 **Ready** Mathematics
PRACTICE AND PROBLEM SOLVING

Assign *Practice and Problem Solving* **pages 93–94** after students have completed this section.

Modeled and Guided Instruction

Learn About Ways to Model Word Problems

At A Glance

Students use a bar model and equations to show a one-step word problem. Then students solve the problem using a subtraction equation and an open number line.

Step By Step

- Read the problem at the top of the page as a class. Ask students to tell if this is a "find the total," "find the change," or "find the start" question and how they know. Then ask: *What would the table look like if we needed to find the change? The total?* [The question mark would be on Level 2 for the change and in place of 55 for the total.]

Picture It

- Draw students' attention to **Picture It** and relate it to the models from the previous page.

Model It

- Have students look at the two equations in **Model It**. Ask why the problem can be modeled both ways. Listen for responses showing students understand that the bar model can be represented by either addition or subtraction, and that either addition or subtraction can be used to find the start.

- Say: *I really like to use the counting up strategy. I'm wondering if I could use counting up to find the start?* Encourage students to "assist" you in using the counting up strategy. Reinforce the application of the commutative property of addition that allows them to begin at 16 and count up to 55.

- Provide students time to share their methods of counting up from 16 to 55, listening for accurate calculations. If no student employs the following strategy say: *Janell said she could count up by adding 40 to 16 to get 56 and then subtract 1 from 40. Does this strategy make sense? Why?*

▶ **Visual Model**

Read the problem. Then you will use addition and subtraction equations to model the problem.

Todd plays a game. The table shows his points.

Level 1	?
Level 2	16 points
Total	55 points

How many points did Todd get in Level 1?

▶ **Picture It** You can draw a bar model.

55	
?	16

▶ **Model It** You can use an addition equation.

Level 1 Score	+	Level 2 Score	=	Total Score
?	+	16	=	55

▶ **Model It** You can use a subtraction equation.

Total Score	−	Level 2 Score	=	Level 1 Score
55	−	16	=	?

▶ **Visual Model**

Use a hundreds chart to find the start.

- Project a hundreds chart (Activity Sheet 2) and use a colored pencil or marker to trace the right side of the square containing the number 55. Ask students what 55 represents.

- Trace around the entire block of 55 squares to indicate the total. Lead students to recognize that since the start is unknown, you can count back 16 squares and shade them in to represent the change.

- Students should notice that the first 39 squares are not shaded. This represents the start.

- You may want to use the chart to model some of the strategies students employed to calculate.

Connect It Understand addition and subtraction equations.

2 Look at *Picture It*. What does the ? mean?

The ? means you do not know the Level 1 Score and want to find it.

3 Look at the second *Model It*. Write a different subtraction equation that you could use to solve the problem.

$$55 - ? = 16$$

4 Solve the problem from the previous page. Show your work on the open number line. Then write your answer.

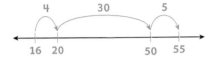

Possible work:

Todd got 39 points in Level 1.

5 **Talk About It** How did you make your number line in Problem 4? What is another way to find the answer?

Write About It Possible answer: I started at 16 and jumped 4 to get to 20. Then I jumped 30 and 5 to get to 55. Another way is to subtract 16 from 55. $55 - 5 = 50$, $50 - 10 = 40$, $40 - 1 = 39$.

Try It Try another problem.

6 Matt had 72 sports cards. Then he got more cards. Now he has 90 cards. How many more cards did Matt get? Show your work.

18 more cards. Possible work: $72 + 8 = 80$; $80 + 10 = 90$; $8 + 10 = 18$.

83

Step By Step

Connect It

- Read **Connect It** as a class. Make sure students understand that the questions refer to the problem on the previous page.

- As students complete Problem 3, remind them to think of what they know about fact families to help them find a different equation. It may also be helpful to have students look at the bar model on the previous page.

> **SMP TIP Attend to Precision**
> Encourage students to share responses to Problem 5, articulating the strategy used to solve and the steps involved in accurately calculating the answer using an open number line. *(SMP 6)*

▶ **Concept Extension**

Try It

6 **Solution**
18; $72 + ? = 90$; $72 + 8 = 80$;
$80 + 10 = 90$; $8 + 10 = 18$.

Error Alert Students who wrote $72 + 90 = 162$ added the numbers shown in the problem to find a whole rather than finding an unknown part.

Ready Mathematics
PRACTICE AND PROBLEM SOLVING

Assign *Practice and Problem Solving* **pages 95–96** after students have completed this section.

▶ **Concept Extension**

Extend calculation strategies.

- After students complete Problem 5, say: *I'm wondering if it would make sense to subtract 20 from 55 to get 35 and then add 4 to get 39?*

- Lead students to recognize that since 20 is greater than 16, subtracting 20 is subtracting 4 too many. So 4 needs to be added back to the 35 so that only 16 has been subtracted.

- You may want to use an open number line or hundreds chart to help students visualize this calculation strategy.

- Encourage students to be creative in their strategies.

Modeled and Guided Instruction

At A Glance

Students solve a word problem using a number bond model. Students revisit this problem, writing equations to model the situation. Then students solve another one-step word problem involving two-digit numbers.

Step By Step

- Read the problem at the top of the page as a class. Discuss what is known and what is unknown. Since the information given refers to the parts, the total is unknown.

Model It

- Direct attention to the models shown. Ask: *Is this an "add to" or "take from" problem? How do you know?* [It is a "take from" problem. Some of the books were taken from the shelf.]

Model It

- Have students tell you equations that would make sense for this problem. Write them on the board and discuss why each equation would or would not make sense.

- Discuss that $? - 24 = 38$ makes sense because 24 books were taken from the total number on the shelf, leaving 38 books. This equation models what occurs in the problem. For some students, this is the easiest way to interpret the problem.

- Students might also suggest the equation $? - 38 = 24$. If a student suggests using addition, ask the Mathematical Discourse question.

▶ **Mathematical Discourse**

▶ **English Language Learners**

Learn About **More Ways to Model Word Problems**

Read the problem. Then you will use words and numbers to model the problem.

Some books were on a shelf. Students took 24 books from the shelf. Then there were 38 books on the shelf. How many books were on the shelf to begin with?

▶ **Model It** You can show the problem with words.

You can model the problem with words.

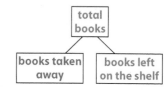

▶ **Model It** You can show the problem with numbers.

You can model the problem with numbers.

84

▶ **Mathematical Discourse**

You told me this is a "take from" problem, so why can you add to find the answer?

Students may respond that the number bond shows the addends. Accept this response, but help students see how addition applies to the problem situation. Some books were taken and some books were left. Their sum represents all the books that were on the shelf.

▶ **English Language Learners**

Some students may struggle to comprehend the language used in a word problem. You may want to pair an English language learner with a proficient reader to complete this task and the ones that follow. You may want to write the information given in the problem on the board:

24 books taken away.
38 books left.
How many books to start with?

▶ **Connect It** **Write an equation to solve the problem.**

7 Look at the second *Model It*. Write an addition equation and a subtraction equation for the problem.
Possible answer:

$\underline{}\ =\ \underline{24}\ +\ \underline{38}$ $\qquad$ $\underline{}\ -\ \underline{38}\ =\ \underline{24}$

8 Write a different addition equation that you could use to solve the problem. Possible answer:

$\underline{38}\ +\ \underline{24}\ =\ \underline{}$

9 What was the total number of books on the shelf to begin with? Show your work.

There were 62 books on the shelf at the start.
Possible work: ? = 24 + 38. 20 + 30 = 50 and
4 + 8 = 12. 50 + 12 = 62.

10 **Talk About It** How did your partner solve the problem?

Write About It Possible answer: My partner added 38 + 24 by

adding up: 38 + 2 = 40 and 40 + 22 = 62.

▶ **Try It** **Try another problem.**

11 Students are helping clean the park. At noon, 33 students went home. There are 48 students left. How many students started? Show your work.

81 started. Possible work: ? = 33 + 48; 30 + 40 = 70, 3 + 8 = 11;

70 + 11 = 81.

85

Step By Step

Connect It

- Read **Connect It** as a class. Remind students that the questions on this page refer to the problem on the previous page.

- Allow students to complete Problems 7–9 independently. For Problem 9, make sure students describe the step-by-step procedure they used to calculate the answer.

- Listen to students as they discuss *Talk About It*. They should have both arrived at the same answer but possibly in different ways. Make sure each student describes the strategy used clearly enough so the partner can write it out.

- If the partners did not arrive at the same answer for Problem 9, have them check each other's work to see if a calculation error or an error in thinking was made. Make sure students know that if they are not able to find an error, they should ask for assistance.

Try It

SMP TIP Make Sense of Problems
Remind students that for Problem 11, they can use a picture or manipulatives to help them make sense of the problem, but they should also try to write an equation and show how they calculated their answer. *(SMP 1)*

11 **Solution**
81 students started. ? − 33 = 48;
48 + 33 = ?; 48 + 30 = 78; 78 + 3 = 81.

Error Alert Students who answer 15 subtracted 33 from 48.

Ready **Mathematics**
PRACTICE AND PROBLEM SOLVING

Assign *Practice and Problem Solving* **pages 97–98** after students have completed this section.

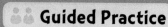

Guided Practice

At A Glance

Students model and solve one-step problems involving addition and subtraction of two-digit numbers.

Step By Step

- Ask students to solve the problems individually and show all their work including the equations they write. Encourage students to describe their thinking.

- **Pair/Share** When students have completed each problem, have them Pair/Share to discuss their solutions with a partner.

Solutions

Example An open number line and an equation are used as examples for solving this problem. Students may also use a number bond or hundreds chart to make sense of the problem.

12 Solution

29 people got on the train; Students may use a number line or number bond model. Students may also write a subtraction equation; $51 - 22 = 29$.

DOK 2

Practice Modeling and Solving Word Problems

Study the model below. Then solve Problems 12–14.

Example

Keesha's math test score is 95. John's score is 13 points less than Keesha's score. What is John's score?

You can show your work on an open number line.

Keesha's score − 13 = John's score   95 − 13 = ?

Answer _John's score is 82._

12 There were 22 people on a train. More people got on at the next stop. Now there are 51 people on the train. How many people got on at the stop?

Show your work.

Possible work:

51	
22	?

$22 + ? = 51$
$22 + 8 = 30$
$30 + 21 = 51$
$8 + 21 = 29$

Can you make a model to help you think about the problem?

Answer 29 people got on the train at the stop.

86

Teacher Notes

13 There are 27 small dogs and 26 big dogs in the pet show. How many dogs are in the pet show?

Show your work.

Possible work:

$27 + 26 = ?$

$20 + 20 = 40$

$7 + 6 = 13$

$40 + 13 = 53$

> Do you add or subtract to solve the problem?

Answer ___There are 53 dogs in the pet show.___

---

14 Liz makes 42 jumps with a jump rope. Tia makes 17 fewer jumps. How many jumps does Tia make?

A 15

B 22

(C) 25

D 59

> Which girl makes more jumps?

Ramin chose **D** as the answer. This answer is wrong. How did Ramin get his answer?

Possible answer: Ramin added $42 + 17$. He should have subtracted

$42 - 17$.

87

Solutions

13 **Solution**

There are 53 dogs in the pet show; See possible work on student book page. Students may also use a number bond to model the problem.

DOK 1

14 **Solution**

C; 42 jumps $-$ 17 jumps $=$ 25 jumps.

Explain to students why the other two choices are not correct:

A is not correct because $17 + 15 \neq 42$.

B is not correct because $42 - 22 = 20$, not 17.

DOK 3

Ready Mathematics
PRACTICE AND PROBLEM SOLVING

Assign *Practice and Problem Solving* **pages 99–100** after students have completed this section.

Teacher Notes

Independent Practice

At A Glance

Students use addition and subtraction to solve one-step word problems involving two-digit numbers that might appear on a mathematics test.

Solutions

1 **Solution**
B Ty's height + additional inches = Meg's height; **C** Meg's height = Ty's height + additional inches; **D** Meg's height − additional inches = Ty's height.
DOK 2

2 **Solution**
C; 26 − 8 = 18.
DOK 2

3 **Solution**
Students find the unknown addend; 26 + 26; 29 + 23; 25 + 27; 34 + 18.
DOK 1

Practice Modeling and Solving Word Problems

Solve the problems.

1 Ty is 47 inches tall. Meg is 56 inches tall. How much taller is Meg?

Which equation can you use to solve this problem? Circle all the correct answers.

A 56 + ? = 47

B 47 + ? = 56

C 56 = 47 + ?

D 56 − ? = 47

2 A beagle weighs 26 pounds. A pug weighs 8 pounds less than the beagle. How many pounds does the pug weigh? Circle the correct answer.

A 34

B 20

C 18

D 13

3 Sara has 52 pens. She puts them into two cups. Complete each equation to show some of the ways Sara could put her pens into the two cups.

26 + __26__ = 52   __25__ + 27 = 52

__29__ + 23 = 52   34 + __18__ = 52

Quick Check and Remediation

- Sue collects 27 cans of food for the food drive. Her goal is to collect 65 cans. How many cans does she still need to collect? [38]

- For students who are still struggling, use the chart to guide remediation.

- After providing remediation, check students' understanding using the following problem: There are 79 people sitting in a movie theater. The theater has enough seats for 93 people. How many seats are empty? [14]

If the error is . . .	Students may . . .	To remediate . . .
42	have subtracted 20 from 60 and 5 from 7.	Have students check their work by adding 42 to 27. Once they realize the answer is incorrect, lead them to use a strategy such as counting up to insure accuracy.
92	have added the numbers instead of subtracting.	Ask students to tell you the total number of cans Sue wants to collect. Ask if it makes sense that she still needs to collect 92. Then help students organize the information using a number bond or hundreds chart.
any other number	have subtracted inaccurately or misrepresented the problem.	As students read each sentence, have them describe what the sentence says and model with base-ten blocks or a drawing. Have students write an equation, solve, and check for computational accuracy.

4. There are 32 students in a school play. There are 17 girls. The rest are boys. How many boys are in the play? Circle the correct answer.

   A 49

   (B) 15

   C 13

   D 12

5. There are 64 balls and 58 bats in the gym. How many more balls are there than bats?

   Circle *Yes* or *No* to tell if each equation can be used to solve the problem.

   a. $58 + ? = 64$ (Yes) No

   b. $64 - 58 = ?$ (Yes) No

   c. $64 + 58 = ?$ Yes (No)

   d. $64 - ? = 58$ (Yes) No

6. Write a one-step word problem that uses addition or subtraction with two-digit numbers. Then solve the problem.

   Answers will vary. Word problems should include either addition or

   subtraction of two-digit numbers.

✔ **Self Check** Now you can solve problems using two-digit numbers. Fill this in on the progress chart on page 59.

89

Solutions

4. **Solution**
   B; $32 - 17 = 15$.
   DOK 2

5. **Solution**
   a. **Yes**; b. **Yes**; c. **No**; $64 + 58 = $ total; d. **Yes**.
   DOK 2

6. **Solution**
   Word problems should include either addition or subtraction of two-digit numbers.
   DOK 3

▶ **Hands-On Activity**

Solve one-step word problems.

Materials: Activity Sheet 5 (Number Bond Mat), blank paper squares to fit number bond mat

- Write 2–3 word problems involving two-digit numbers with the unknown in different positions on a piece of paper. Photocopy so that there are enough for each student. Cut the problems apart and distribute them to students.

- Tell students to write the known numbers from one of the problems on the paper squares and arrange them on the number bond mat.

- Have students glue the problem on a plain sheet of paper, draw the number bond under it, and then write an equation that models the problem.

- Have students solve the problem and show their strategy. Repeat for each problem.

▶ **Challenge Activity**

Write one-step word problems.

Write two-digit numbers such as 53, 67, 46, etc., on separate cards.

Have each student select a card. Provide the following directions:

- Make up 3 word problems in which the number the student selected is the answer in each problem.

- The unknown must be in a different position in each problem.

- Each problem must be about a different topic and the numbers used must be different from those used in the other problems.

- When finished, give each problem to a different classmate to solve. If they do not each have the same solution, students work together to look for possible errors.

Overview

Assign the Lesson 9 Quiz and have students work independently to complete it.

Use the results of the quiz to assess students' understanding of the content of the lesson and to identify areas for reteaching. See the Lesson Pacing Guide at the beginning of the lesson for suggested instructional resources.

Tested Skills

Assesses 2.OA.A.1

Problems on this assessment form require students to be able to determine the operation (addition or subtraction) needed to solve a one-step problem, interpret models and write equations that represent a one-step problem, and solve a one-step problem. Students will also need to be familiar with adding and subtracting within 100 and identifying situations that involve adding and subtracting.

Ready® Mathematics

Lesson 9 Quiz

Solve the problems.

1 Alya has 33 dolls in a box. She has 17 dolls on her bed.

How many dolls does Alya have in all?

Complete the model and find the answer.

33	

Answer: Alya has _____ dolls in all.

2 At the animal park, the price of an adult ticket is $19. The price of a child ticket is $12.

- Eli pays $31 for tickets.
- Grace pays $38 for tickets.

Which types of tickets did each person buy?

_____ buys 1 adult and 1 child ticket.

_____ buys 2 adult tickets.

3 Mateo wants to put 93 pennies into two coin banks. What are two ways Mateo can put the pennies into the banks?

Fill in the blanks to complete the equations.
Use the numbers from the box.

_____ + 50 = 93

_____ + 49 = 93

51	44	43	42
41	39	34	32

Lesson 9 Quiz continued

4 Kimi has 56 cows and 17 horses on her farm. How many more cows than horses are there?

Which equations can you use to solve the problem?

Circle all the correct answers.

A 56 + _____ = 17

B 56 − 17 = _____

C 56 + 17 = _____

D 17 + _____ = 56

5 Miss Rogers asks her students to write and solve a word problem for this equation.

28 + _____ = 52

Which could be a word problem and answer for the equation?

Circle the correct answer.

A Bob sells 28 snack bars. Juan sells 52 snack bars. How many more snack bars does Bob sell than Juan? Answer: 24 bars

B Bob sells 28 snack bars. Juan sells 52 more snack bars than Bob. How many snack bars does Juan sell? Answer: 80 bars

C Bob sells 28 snack bars. Juan sells some snack bars. Together they sell 52 snack bars. How many snack bars does Juan sell? Answer: 24 bars

D Bob sells 28 snack bars. Juan sells 52 snack bars. How many snack bars do Bob and Juan sell in all? Answer: 80 bars

Common Misconceptions and Errors

Errors may result if students:

• interpret a start or change unknown problem as a result unknown problem.

• misidentify the operation needed to solve the problem.

• identify the parts and whole in a problem incorrectly.

• do not understand how to represent a word problem using a number bond or a tape diagram.

Ready® **Mathematics**

Lesson 9 Quiz Answer Key

1. Model: 50 (top), 17 (bottom)
Answer: 50
DOK 2

2. Eli
Grace
DOK 2

3. 43
44
DOK 1

4. B, D
DOK 2

5. C
DOK 3

CCSS Focus

Domain
Number and Operations in Base Ten

Cluster
A. Understand place value.

Standards
2.NBT.A.1 Understand that the three digits of a three-digit number represent amounts of hundreds, tens, and ones; e.g., 706 equals 7 hundreds, 0 tens, and 6 ones. Understand the following as special cases:

a. 100 can be thought of as a bundle of ten tens—called a "hundred."

b. The numbers 100, 200, 300, 400, 500, 600, 700, 800, 900 refer to one, two, three, four, five, six, seven, eight, or nine hundreds (and 0 tens and 0 ones).

2.NBT.A.2 Count within 1000; skip-count by 5s, 10s, and 100s.

Standards for Mathematical Practice (SMP)

2 Reason abstractly and quantitatively.

3 Construct viable arguments and critique the reasoning of others.

7 Look for and make use of structure.

Lesson Objectives

Content Objectives

• Identify ones, tens, and hundreds in a three-digit number.

• Interpret models to determine the combinations of hundreds, tens, and ones in a number.

• Write a three-digit number in terms of varied combinations of hundreds, tens, and ones.

Language Objectives

• Tell how many hundreds, tens, and ones are in a given three-digit number.

• Tell how many tens are in 100 and in 200.

Prerequisite Skills

• Count to 100.

• Count by 10s and by 100s.

• Understand the concept of place value in two-digit numbers.

Lesson Vocabulary

There is no new vocabulary.

Learning Progression

In Grade 1 students are introduced to the concept of place value as it applies to two-digit numbers. This concept is reinforced in Grade 2 as students add and subtract two-digit numbers.

In this lesson students use base-ten blocks to understand that one hundred can be seen as 100 ones or 10 groups of ten. As students count groups of blocks, they record the number in a chart to aid in connecting the concept that a digit is used to indicate the number of groups of objects within a number. This leads to the realization that a digit's value is dependent upon its placement in a number. The 4 in 420 represents 4 groups of one hundred, while the 4 in 42 represents 4 groups of ten. This concept will be further developed in the next lesson as students learn to accurately read and write three-digit numbers.

As early as kindergarten, students are led to recognize the inclusive nature of numbers. Within 7 there is a group of 3 and a group of 4, or 2 groups of three and 1 more, etc. This concept is extended into Grade 1 with two-digit numbers and in Grade 2 with three-digit numbers. This understanding is foundational for upcoming work with subtraction and other operations in the future.

Lesson Pacing Guide

Whole Class Instruction

Day 1 45–60 minutes	Toolbox: Interactive Tutorial* *Place Value to 1,000*	Practice and Problem Solving Assign pages 103–104.
	Introduction • Opening Activity *15 min* • Think It Through Question *5 min* • Think *5 min* • Think *10 min* • Reflect *5 min*	
Day 2 45–60 minutes	**Guided Instruction** **Think About Hundreds, Tens, and Ones** • Let's Explore the Idea *15 min* • Let's Talk About It *20 min* • Try It Another Way *10 min*	Practice and Problem Solving Assign pages 105–106.
Day 3 45–60 minutes	**Guided Practice** **Connect Ideas About Place Value in Three-Digit Numbers** • Evaluate *15 min* • Analyze *15 min* • Identify *15 min*	Practice and Problem Solving Assign pages 107–108.
Day 4 45–60 minutes	**Independent Practice** **Apply Ideas About Place Value in Three-Digit Numbers** • Put It Together *30 min* • Pair/Share *15 min*	
Day 5 45–60 minutes	• On-Level, Intervention, or Challenge Activity *20 min* Toolbox: Lesson Quiz Lesson 10 Quiz	

Small Group Differentiation

Teacher-Toolbox.com

Reteach
Ready Prerequisite Lessons *45–90 min*

Grade 1
• Lesson 17 *Understand* Tens
• Lesson 21 *Understand* Tens and Ones

Teacher-led Activities
Tools for Instruction *15–20 min*

Grade 1 *(Lessons 17 and 21)*
• Patterns on the Hundred Chart
Grade 2 *(Lesson 10)*
• Model Three-Digit Numbers

Student-led Activities
Math Center Activities *30–40 min*

Grade 2 *(Lesson 10)*
• 2.14 Skip Count by 10s and 100s
• 2.11 Three-Digit Number Vocabulary
• 2.12 Understand Three-Digit Numbers

Personalized Learning

i-Ready.com

Independent
i-Ready Lessons* *10–20 min*

Grade 1 *(Lessons 17 and 21)*
• Grouping into Tens and Ones

*We continually update the Interactive Tutorials. Check the Teacher Toolbox for the most up-to-date offerings for this lesson.

Tens and Hundreds

Objective Explore three-digit numbers.

Time *20–30 minutes*

Materials for each student

• connecting cubes

Overview

Students explore hundreds as 10 groups of ten by connecting cubes into groups of ten and bundling into groups of hundreds.

Step By Step

1 Build stacks of cubes.

• Organize students into pairs and provide them with connecting cubes.

• Ask students to build 4 stacks of 10 cubes each.

• Ask: *How many cubes did you stack?* [40] *How do you know?* [I counted them all; I counted by tens.]

• Tell students to combine their stacks with a partner. Ask: *How many cubes do you have now?* [8 stacks or 80 cubes]

2 Build hundreds.

• Ask partners to discuss how many more stacks they will need to have 100 cubes. Then have them make the extra stacks.

• Ask: *How many extra stacks did you make?* [2] *How many total stacks do you have?* [10] *How can you be sure you have 100 cubes stacked?* [count by tens]

• Ask: *How many stacks would you need to show 200 cubes?* [20] Have partners discuss this question and explain how they know.

• Share students' ideas as a class. You may want them to think about and suggest how many stacks would be needed to show 300, 400, 500, . . . cubes.

3 **Apply the concept to multiples of ten.**

- Have student pairs build 3 more stacks of 10 and combine them with the 10 stacks they made earlier. Ask partners to identify the total number of cubes they have both in terms of ones and tens, and in terms of hundreds and tens.

4 **Extend the concept.**

- Engage students in thinking about how they would show other multiples of 10 cubes. You may want to challenge them to think beyond the 100s using numbers such as 240, 350, etc.

Teacher Notes

Introduction

At A Glance

Students explore the meaning of one hundred through different models. They see that 100 can be expressed as 100 ones or 10 tens.

Step By Step

- Introduce the question at the top of the page. Emphasize that there are many ways to count to 100. Have students generate ideas of how they could count to 100. [by 1s, 2s, 5s, 10s, and so on]

- Draw students' attention to the number 100 shown on the chart. Ask students to share what they know about the number 100. [Students may respond that it is a "big" number, that it is "worth more" than 99, and so on.]

▶ **Mathematical Discourse 1**

- Read the **Think** section together. After students circle groups of 10 ones, compare what they did to the model of the 10 tens. Students should notice that they circled ten groups of 10 and the model shows ten groups of 10.

- Refer students back to the hundreds chart on the page. Ask if they can find groups of 10 in the chart. Students may identify groups either horizontally or vertically. Although both are accurate, you may want to point out that the horizontal groups include the counting numbers within each ten.

▶ **Mathematical Discourse 2**

SMP TIP Look for Structure

Analyzing a hundreds chart for skip counting and identifying groups of ten helps students recognize the patterns and structure inherent in our number system, enabling them to become proficient with the base-ten number system. *(SMP 7)*

Think It Through

What is one hundred?

You can count to one hundred. After 99 is **100**.

1	2	3	4	5	6	7	8	9	10
11	12	13	14	15	16	17	18	19	20
21	22	23	24	25	26	27	28	29	30
31	32	33	34	35	36	37	38	39	40
41	42	43	44	45	46	47	48	49	50
51	52	53	54	55	56	57	58	59	60
61	62	63	64	65	66	67	68	69	70
71	72	73	74	75	76	77	78	79	80
81	82	83	84	85	86	87	88	89	90
91	92	93	94	95	96	97	98	99	100

Think One hundred is 100 ones. One hundred is 10 tens.

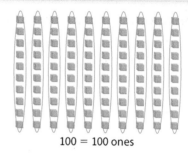 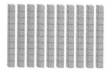

100 = 100 ones   100 = 10 tens

Circle groups of 10 ones in 100.

90

▶ **Mathematical Discourse**

1 *Look at the hundreds chart. How is the number 100 different from the other numbers in its column?*

Answers will vary. Help students recognize that it has two zeros instead of only one.

2 *How does counting by tens help you think about 100?*

Instead of counting all the ones, I can count groups of ten to get to 100 much more quickly. I only have to count by tens 10 times, but it is equal to 100 ones.

Think One hundred can be shown as hundreds, tens, or ones.

Fill in the blanks.

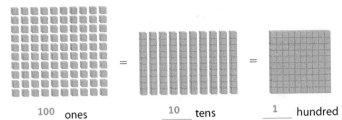

<u>100</u> ones = <u>10</u> tens = <u>1</u> hundred

Ways to Show 100			
Hundreds	**Tens**	**Ones**	
0	0	100	0 hundreds + 0 tens + 100 ones
0	10	0	0 hundreds + 10 tens + 0 ones
1	0	0	1 hundred + 0 tens + 0 ones

100
↑
hundreds place

A three-digit number has a hundreds place. It tells how many hundreds there are in a number.

▶ **Reflect** **Work with a partner.**

1 **Talk About It** Think about 200. How many hundreds does 200 have? How many tens? How many ones?

Write About It The number 200 has 2 hundreds, or 20 tens, or

200 ones.

91

Step By Step

- Read aloud the **Think** statement about one hundred at the top of the page. Then draw students' attention to the three picture models and ask what each one represents. Instruct students to fill in the blank under each model.

▶ **Mathematical Discourse 3 and 4**

- Instruct students to look at the chart and talk to a partner to decide which of the pictures matches each row on the chart. As they share ideas, make sure they understand that the hundreds block is locked together; it has no separate tens and ones. Similarly, each tens block has no separate ones.

- Read the sentence underneath the chart. Direct students' attention to the bottom row of the chart and discuss it. Use Mathematical Discourse question 5 to emphasize what the zeros in 100 represent.

▶ **Mathematical Discourse 5**

▶ **Hands-On Activity**

- Have students reply to the *Talk About It* question. Allow students to draw pictures, if necessary, but encourage them to use number representations also.

Ready Mathematics
PRACTICE AND PROBLEM SOLVING

Assign *Practice and Problem Solving* **pages 103–104** after students have completed this section.

▶ **Hands-On Activity**

Use base-ten blocks to understand one hundred.

Materials: base-ten blocks

- Distribute the blocks so that each student has at least 30 ones blocks, 10 tens blocks, and 1 hundreds block.

- Instruct students to use their blocks to show 3 groups of 10. Ask students to show how many ones are in 3 groups of 10. Ask them to show 6 groups of 10. Ask: *How many ones do you think there are in 6 groups of 10?* [60] Make sure students justify their answers.

- Have students show a hundreds block. Ask how many ones they would have if they could break apart the block. [100] Then have them use tens blocks to show how many tens are in a hundreds block. [10]

▶ **Mathematical Discourse**

3 *How are the three pictures on this page alike?*

They all show 100.

4 *How are the pictures on this page different from each other?*

In the first one, all the pieces are separate. In the second one, the pieces are locked together in groups of ten, but there are spaces between each group. In the third one, all the pieces are locked together.

5 *Why do you think there are two zeros after the 1 in 100?*

Students should recognize that the zeros indicate that there are no tens or ones.

At A Glance

Students use counting strategies to understand three-digit numbers. Then students interpret models and organize three-digit numbers in varied ways.

Step By Step

Let's Explore the Idea

- Tell students that they will have time to work individually on the problems on this page and then share their responses in pairs. Ask students to look at the first set of models and count the groups of 100. Ask: *How many groups of 100 are shown?* [3] Instruct students to write that number on the blank. Encourage students to continue counting by hundreds to 900. Use Mathematical Discourse question 1 to connect counting strategies.

▶ **Mathematical Discourse 1**

- For Problem 3, reinforce the concept that the zeros following the 3 indicate that there are no separate tens or ones. You may want to write the following addition problem on the board: 100 + 100 + 100 = 300. Explain that they are putting groups together just as they do when adding.

- Have students look at the second group of models and ask how these compare to the first group. They should note that in this case, there are groups of ten that are not connected.

- As students complete this page individually, circulate among them. This is an opportunity to assess student understanding and address student misconceptions.

▶ **Mathematical Discourse 2**

- Take note of students who are still having difficulty and wait to see if their understanding progresses as they work in pairs during the next part of the lesson.

> **SMP TIP** Reason Abstractly and Quantitatively
> Using counting strategies to interpret three-digit numbers builds a sense of quantities in students and enables them to use symbolic representations in a meaningful way. *(SMP 2)*

🔍 **Let's Explore the Idea** You can count three-digit numbers by hundreds, tens, and ones.

You can count hundreds.

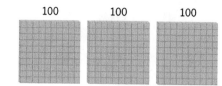

100   100   100

2 Count: 1 hundred, 2 hundreds, __3__ hundreds

3 __3__ hundreds = 300

You can count hundreds and tens.

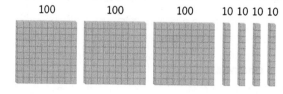

100   100   100   10 10 10 10

4 __3__ hundreds + __4__ tens = 300 + 40 = 340

You can count hundreds, tens, and ones.

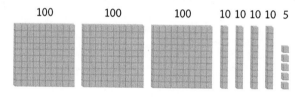

100   100   100   10 10 10 10 5

5 __3__ hundreds + __4__ tens + __5__ ones = 300 + 40 + 5 = 345

92

▶ **Mathematical Discourse**

1 *How is counting by hundreds like counting by tens?*

You count 1 group of one hundred, 2 groups of one hundred, 3 groups of one hundred, and so on, just like you count 1 group of ten, 2 groups of ten, 3 groups of ten, and so on.

2 *Why doesn't it make sense to write 300 instead of 3 on the first blank, or 40 instead of 4 on the second blank?*

There aren't 300 groups of one hundred, but 3 groups of 100; and there aren't 40 groups of ten, but 4 groups of ten.

Let's Talk About It
Work with a partner.

6 This model shows 300 in tens. 300 = __30__ tens

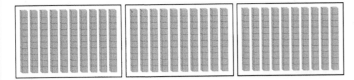

7 This model shows 340 in tens. 340 = __34__ tens

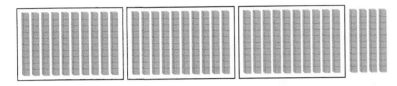

8 This model shows 345 in tens. There are ones left over.

345 = __34__ tens and __5__ ones

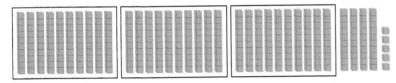

▶ **Try It Another Way** **Write hundreds, tens, and ones in a chart.**

Example
3 hundreds + 5 tens + 8 ones

Hundreds	Tens	Ones
3	5	8

9 5 hundreds + 3 tens

Hundreds	Tens	Ones
5	3	0

10 7 hundreds + 8 ones

Hundreds	Tens	Ones
7	0	8

93

Step By Step

Let's Talk About It

- Organize students in pairs to answer Problems 6–8 on this page. You may choose to work through Problem 6 together.
- Walk around to each pair. Listen to and join in on discussions at different points. Use Mathematical Discourse questions 3 and 4 to help support or extend students' thinking.

▶ **Mathematical Discourse 3 and 4**

Try It Another Way

- Direct students' attention to **Try It Another Way**. Instruct them to continue to work in pairs to fill in the charts.
- Invite volunteers to come to the board to show how they completed the charts for Problems 9 and 10.
- Make sure students include a zero as a placeholder in each of the problems. Discuss that in the chart, it may not seem important to include the zero, but when the number is written out of the chart, it is very important.
- Write 260 on the board and ask students to read the number. Then write the number 26 on the board and ask them to read it. Ask: *Why is it important to add the zero on the end of 260?* [It makes the 26 mean 26 tens, not 26 ones.]

▶ **Visual Model**

Assign *Practice and Problem Solving* **pages 105–106** after students have completed this section.

▶ **Visual Model**

Draw models to show the importance of placeholders.

- Tell students that you will draw some simple models to help them understand placeholders. Draw the following on the board:

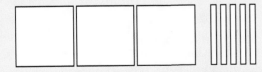

- Write 100 inside each square and 10 under each rectangle. Then write 3 hundreds + 5 tens = 350.
- Draw the following:

- Ask students to write the number shown by the model. [35] Compare the models to show that they are not equal.

▶ **Mathematical Discourse**

3 *Why do you think there is a box around some of the tens? What does it represent?*

Students should recognize that there are 10 tens in each box, which represents 100. The boxes make it easier to count the groups.

4 *How do the models help you think about the number 345?*

It is easy to see the 10 tens in each hundred, and the extra tens and ones. In 345, there are 3 hundreds, 4 tens, and 5 ones, which is equal to 34 tens and 5 ones. Or 345 could be broken apart into 345 ones.

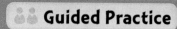
Guided Practice

At A Glance

Students demonstrate their understanding of three-digit numbers by analyzing different ways to represent them. Then students represent quantities in different ways.

Step By Step

- Discuss each problem as a class using the discussion points outlined below.

Evaluate

- Ask students to explain the error Lana made. [She didn't write a zero in the tens place to show there are no separate tens.]
- Then ask: *How would you help Lana understand what she did wrong?* Encourage volunteers to share their ideas with the class.

Analyze

- Write the way each student represented the number 572 on separate sections of the board. Ask students to talk to a partner about what each student did.
- Encourage volunteers to come to the board to draw models showing what Sam and Lev did. You may want to ask students to draw □ for 100, | for 10, and • for one. Make sure that for the 57 tens, groups of 10 tens are boxed to represent a group of 100. This will make the models more visually similar.

Identify

- Draw the completed chart from the student page on the board. Add several blank rows to the bottom of the chart.
- Ask: *Can you think of another way to show 256?* If there are no viable responses, make suggestions such as: *How would you complete the rest of the row if there were 20 tens?* Or: *What if I put 126 in the ones column?*
- Write those numbers in additional rows at the bottom of the chart and allow students to determine how they might complete each row.

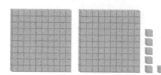
Connect **Ideas About Place Value in Three-Digit Numbers**

Talk about these questions as a class. Then write your answers.

11 Evaluate Lana did this homework problem. What did she do wrong?

2 hundreds + 6 ones = 26

Possible answer: Lana didn't put a 0 in the tens place. So she wrote the

2 hundreds as 2 tens.

12 Analyze Look at how Sam and Lev wrote 572. Explain what each person did.

Sam   572 = 57 tens + 2 ones

Lev   572 = 5 hundreds + 7 tens + 2 ones

Sam used only tens and ones to write the number. 57 tens is 570.

570 + 2 = 572. Lev used hundreds, tens, and ones. 500 + 70 + 2 = 572.

13 Identify Fill in the blanks to show 256 in different ways.

Hundreds	Tens	Ones
0	0	256
0	25	6
2	5	6

94

Scoring Rubrics

Part A		
Points	**Expectations**	
2	The student draws an accurate model to represent the situation.	
1	The student is partially correct. Some elements of the model may be accurate but not all of them.	
0	The student is not able to accurately complete the model.	

Apply ▶ **Ideas About Place Value in Three-Digit Numbers**

Put It Together **Use what you have learned to complete this task.**

14 Nate puts his coins in stacks of ten. He has 12 stacks of coins with 4 coins left over.

Part A Draw a picture to show Nate's coins.

Possible drawing:

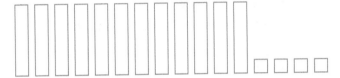

Part B How many coins does Nate have? Write the answer in two different ways.

Possible answer: 12 tens + 4 ones; 120 + 4, or 124 coins

Part C Nate gets 30 more coins from a friend. Nate says that he now has 190 coins. Do you agree or disagree? Explain.

Possible answer: I disagree. Nate had 124 coins and got 30 more.

124 + 30 = 154, not 190. So Nate now has 154 coins.

95

Step By Step

Put It Together

- Direct students to complete the **Put It Together** task on their own.
- Have counters or tiles available for students to stack, if necessary, to make sense of the problem.
- Suggest that students draw rectangles or simple cylinders to represent the stack of coins. It is not necessary to show the ten coins in each stack; however, some students may need to do this. Encourage students to focus on the task rather than on making an artistic drawing.
- For Part C, students may use a drawing or equation to solve. Remind them to explain why they agree or disagree.
- As students work on their own, walk around to assess their progress and understanding, to answer their questions, and to give additional support, if needed.
- If time permits, have students share the strategies they used in completing the task.

📦 **Ready**· Mathematics
PRACTICE AND PROBLEM SOLVING

Assign *Practice and Problem Solving* **pages 107–108** after students have completed Guided Practice.

Part B	
Points	**Expectations**
2	The student answers correctly and writes the number in two different ways.
1	The answer is correct, but only one written representation is accurate.
0	The student is not able to accurately answer or write the number in two ways.

Part C	
Points	**Expectations**
2	The student disagrees with Nate and justifies this response by using an accurate model, correct equation, or logical reasoning.
1	The student disagrees with Nate but does not fully justify this response with an accurate model, correct equation, or logical reasoning.
0	The student agrees that Nate now has 190 coins or disagrees and does not provide a logical reason.

Lesson 10
Understand Three-Digit Numbers

Differentiated Instruction

▶ Intervention Activity

Break apart numbers.

Materials: base-ten blocks, Place-Value Mat (Activity Sheet 6), Three-Digit Cards (Activity Sheet 7), and a blank card

• Provide each student with base-ten blocks, a blank card, and a place-value mat. Place the three-digit number cards facedown. Each student draws a card.

• Have students use the blank card to cover the tens place and ones place on the three-digit number card. Then students place hundreds blocks on the mat to represent the hundreds digit in the number. Slide the blank card to show the number of tens blocks to place on the mat. Finally, slide the blank card again and place the number of ones shown. You may want to repeat this activity several times.

▶ On-Level Activity

Play three-digit number "around the table."

Materials: For each student: base-ten blocks and Place-Value Mat (Activity Sheet 6); For each group: Three-Digit Cards (Activity Sheet 7)

• Place students in groups of 3. Provide each student with a place-value mat and base-ten blocks. Place the cards facedown in a pile. Allow one student to pick a card and use blocks to represent the number on the mat. The student to the right must represent the same number in a different way, and then the last student must represent the number in another way.

• The only rule is that no one can use *all* ones to represent the number. Once students have agreed that all the representations are accurate, they record each representation. The second student in the group picks a card and play resumes as in the first round. Continue until time is up or the cards have all been used.

▶ Challenge Activity

Find all the ways to show a three-digit number.

Materials: paper and pencil

• Refer back to the **Identify** activity students did as a class during Guided Practice. Help students draw a similar chart, or have one drawn for each of them. Ask them to label the columns Hundreds, Tens, and Ones. (You will need to have extra paper or extra charts available.)

• Tell students you want them to try to find *all* the ways to show 127 on the chart. Encourage them to think of possible strategies they may use before beginning. Allow students to discuss those strategies with each other or with you.

• After students have completed the task, evaluate their charts to determine if they have included all the ways to show 127. Then have them present their charts to the class. Ask them to discuss the patterns they used and then display the charts on the wall or bulletin board.

Teacher Notes

Teacher-Toolbox.com

Overview

Assign the Lesson 10 Quiz and have students work independently to complete it.

Use the results of the quiz to assess students' understanding of the content of the lesson and to identify areas for reteaching. See the Lesson Pacing Guide at the beginning of the lesson and the Differentiated Instruction activities that follow for suggested instructional resources.

Tested Skills

Assesses 2.NBT.A.1a, 2.NBT.A.1b, 2.NBT.A.2

Problems on this assessment form require students to be able to skip count by 10 and 100; represent a base-ten model with a standard form number, expanded form number, or number name; and write a three-digit number as varied combinations of hundreds, tens, and ones.

Ready® **Mathematics**

Lesson 10 Quiz

Solve the problems.

1 Hannah is working with blocks to show numbers. What does this set of blocks show?

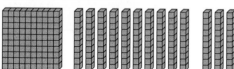

Circle all the correct answers.

A 20 hundreds + 3 tens + 0 ones

B 0 hundreds + 23 tens + 0 ones

C 2 hundreds + 3 tens + 0 ones

D 1 hundred + 13 tens + 0 ones

E 1 hundred + 10 tens + 3 ones

F 0 hundreds + 0 tens + 230 ones

2 Diego makes a model to show the value of a number. What is this same value in tens and in ones?

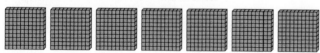

Fill in the blanks to answer.

The model shows _____ hundreds. This is the same value

as _____ tens or _____ ones.

Lesson 10 Quiz continued

3 A sticker book has 100 stickers. A sticker paper has 10 stickers. Ellen and Nick have 5 sticker books and 4 sticker papers. Ellen says they have 450 stickers. Nick says they have 504 stickers. Who is right and why?

Circle the correct answer.

A Ellen is right. When you count by 100 four times and then count by 10 five times, you get 450 stickers.

B Nick is right. When you count by 100 five times and then add 4, you get 504 stickers.

C Neither is right. When you count by 100 five times and then add 4, you get 54 stickers.

D Neither is right. When you count by 100 five times and then count by 10 four times, you get 540 stickers.

4 What value does the model show?

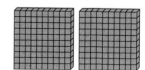

Circle *Yes* or *No* to tell if the model shows the value.

a. 2 ones   Yes   No

b. 200   Yes   No

c. 20   Yes   No

d. 2 hundreds   Yes   No

Common Misconceptions and Errors

Errors may result if students:

• skip count by 10 or 100 incorrectly or by an incorrect value.

• count a number of objects incorrectly.

• confuse the tens and hundreds place-value positions.

• regroup ones as tens or tens as hundreds incorrectly.

Ready® **Mathematics**

Lesson 10 Quiz Answer Key

1. B, C, D, F
DOK 2

2. 7, 70, 700
DOK 1

3. D
DOK 3

4. a. No
   b. Yes
   c. No
   d. Yes
   DOK 2

Lesson 11
Read and Write Three-Digit Numbers

CCSS Focus

Domain
Number and Operations in Base Ten

Cluster
A. Understand place value.

Standards
2.NBT.A.3 Read and write numbers to 1000 using base-ten numerals, number names, and expanded form.

Standards for Mathematical Practice (SMP)
2 Reason abstractly and quantitatively.
4 Model with mathematics.
7 Look for and make use of structure.

Lesson Objectives

Content Objectives

• Identify the place value of each digit in a three-digit number.
• Model three-digit numbers.
• Interpret a model and write the number value.

Language Objectives

• Read aloud three-digit numbers.
• Write three-digit numbers in expanded form.
• Write a three-digit number shown with base ten blocks.

Prerequisite Skills

• Understand two-digit numbers.
• Count by tens and hundreds.
• Add two-digit numbers.

Lesson Vocabulary

• **digit** any one of the ten symbols used to write numbers: 0, 1, 2, 3, 4, 5, 6, 7, 8, 9.

Review the following key term.

• **place value** the value assigned to a digit based on its position in a number. For example, the 2 in 324 is in the tens place and has a value of 2 tens or twenty.

Learning Progression

In Grade 1 students explore the concept of place value by bundling 10 ones to make groups of ten. They learn to read numbers between 9 and 99, and write them using proper digit placement.

In this lesson this concept is extended to include the hundreds place as a group of 10 tens. Through active involvement, students make sense of the place-value system, recognizing a digit as a symbol that tells the number of groups of

hundreds, tens and ones in a number. They then learn to read the numbers accurately.

In Grades 3 and 4 a firm grasp of this concept is essential for students to fully understand addition and subtraction of numbers with more than three digits, as well as to understand multiplication and division of multi-digit numbers. Place-value concepts are then extended to decimal places in Grade 5.

Lesson Pacing Guide

Whole Class Instruction

Day 1 *45–60 minutes*	**Toolbox: Interactive Tutorial*** *Place Value and Writing Numbers in Standard Form*	**Practice and Problem Solving** Assign pages 111–112.
	Introduction • Opening Activity *10 min* • Use What You Know *10 min* • Find Out More *10 min* • Reflect *10 min*	
Day 2 *45–60 minutes*	**Modeled and Guided Instruction** **Learn About Finding the Value of Three-Digit Numbers** • Picture It/Picture It/Model It *10 min* • Connect It *25 min* • Try It *10 min*	**Practice and Problem Solving** Assign pages 113–114.
Day 3 *45–60 minutes*	**Guided Practice** **Practice Reading and Writing Three-Digit Numbers** • Example *5 min* • Problems 7–9 *15 min* • Pair/Share *15 min* • Solutions *10 min*	**Practice and Problem Solving** Assign pages 115–116.
Day 4 *45–60 minutes*	**Independent Practice** **Practice Reading and Writing Three-Digit Numbers** • Problems 1–6 *20 min* • Quick Check and Remediation *10 min* • Hands-On or Challenge Activity *15 min* **Toolbox: Lesson Quiz** Lesson 11 Quiz	

Small Group Differentiation

Teacher-Toolbox.com

Reteach
Ready Prerequisite Lessons 45–90 min

Grade 1
• Lesson 21 *Understand* Tens and Ones
• Lesson 22 Compare Numbers

Teacher-led Activities
Tools for Instruction 15–20 min

Grade 1 *(Lessons 21 and 22)*
• Compare Two-Digit Numbers
Grade 2 *(Lesson 11)*
• Model Three-Digit Numbers

Student-led Activities
Math Center Activities 30–40 min

Grade 2 *(Lesson 11)*
• 2.15 Three-Digit Number Vocabulary Match
• 2.16 Ways to Write a Number

Personalized Learning

i-Ready.com

Independent
i-Ready Lessons* 10–20 min

Grade 1 *(Lessons 21 and 22)*
• Grouping into Tens and Ones
• Comparing Numbers to 100 Using Symbols

*We continually update the Interactive Tutorials. Check the Teacher Toolbox for the most up-to-date offerings for this lesson.

Opening Activity

Put Together Hundreds, Tens, and Ones

Objective Express three-digit numbers in terms of hundreds, tens, and ones.

Time *10–15 minutes*

Materials for each student

- base-ten blocks
- Activity Sheet 6 (Place-Value Mat)
- Activity Sheet 1 (Digit Cards)

Overview

Students build numbers involving hundreds, tens, and ones and express the value of each one.

Step By Step

1 Build a number.

- Provide students with base-ten blocks and a place-value mat.

- Ask students to place 3 hundreds blocks, 2 tens blocks, and 7 ones blocks in their proper locations on the mat.

2 Read a number.

- Hold up a hundreds block. Ask: *What does this show?* [one hundred ones] *How many hundreds are on your mat?* [3] Have students place the digit card "3" under the hundreds place.

- Display a tens block. Ask: *What does this show?* [10 ones] *How many tens blocks are on your mat?* [2] Have students place the digit card "2" under the tens place.

- Ask: *What does a ones block show?* [one] *How many ones blocks are on your mat?* [7] Have students place the digit card "7" under the ones place.

3 **Put it all together.**

- Ask: *What number is used to show 3 hundreds?* [300] *What number is used to show 2 tens?* [20] *What number is used to show 7 ones?* [7]

- Now put together the numbers you just used for hundreds, tens, and ones. How do you say this new number? [three hundred twenty-seven]

4 **Repeat with other numbers.**

- Repeat the steps above using other numbers such as 452, 691, and 758.

- Tell students that in this lesson, they will learn more about reading and writing numbers in the hundreds.

Teacher Notes

Introduction

At A Glance

Students use what they know about hundreds, tens, and ones to solve a problem. Then students determine the value of a digit based on its placement in a number.

Step By Step

- Work through **Use What You Know** as a class.

- Tell students that this page shows them how to think about and write a three-digit number.

- Have students read the problem at the top of the page. Ask: *Is the number of packs Jan buys the same as the number of balloons she buys? Explain.* Students should recognize that since each pack contains more than one balloon, she buys many more balloons than packs.

- You may wish to show hundreds blocks, tens blocks, and ones blocks to represent the balloons in the problem. Discuss that each hundreds block contains 100 ones just as each pack of 100 contains 100 balloons. The *value* of the block or the pack is in terms of ones. Repeat with the value of a tens block and ten pack.

- After students complete Part d, ask them to tell what numbers they wrote in the blanks and explain why.

- Instruct students to circle the 2, the 7, and the 5 that they wrote to fill in the first blank in Part a, Part b, and Part c. Discuss that in the sum of Part d, the 2 is in the hundreds place, the 7 is in the tens place, and the 5 is in the ones place.

> **SMP TIP Reason Abstractly and Quantitatively**
> Seeing three-digit numbers in a variety of contexts enables students to make sense of the values represented by digit placement and the quantity as a whole. *(SMP 2)*

▶ **Real-World Connection**

🄖 Use What You Know

Write three-digit numbers with hundreds, tens, and ones.

Jan buys 2 packs of 100 balloons. She also buys 7 packs of 10 balloons and 5 single balloons. How many balloons does Jan buy?

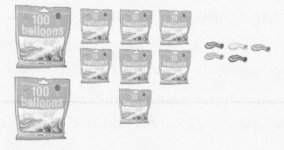

a. 2 packs of 100 = ___2___ hundreds
The number of balloons in 2 packs of 100 is ___200___.

b. 7 packs of 10 = ___7___ tens
The number of balloons in 7 packs of ten is ___70___.

c. 5 single balloons = ___5___ ones
The number of single balloons is ___5___.

d. Complete the equation to find the total number of balloons.

$$\underline{\ 200\ } + \underline{\ 70\ } + \underline{\ 5\ } = \underline{\ 275\ }$$
$$\ \ \ 100s \quad\quad 10s \quad\quad 1s$$

96

▶ **Real-World Connection**

Show students a ten dollar bill (you may use realistic play money). Ask: *How many bills do you see?* [1] *If I traded this in for one dollar bills, how many would I get?* [10] Hold the ten dollar bill in one hand and 10 one dollar bills in the other and ask which is more—the 1 ten or the 10 ones. Students should recognize that they represent the same amount of money. Then show a one hundred dollar bill and ask how many ten dollar bills you would get if you traded it in for tens. How many ones? Reinforce the concept that one bill can have a value of more than one dollar.

▶▶ Find Out More

The **digits** 0, 1, 2, 3, 4, 5, 6, 7, 8, and 9 make up all numbers. The digit's place in a number tells its value.

The same digit can have different values. Look at the value of each 4 in this number.

Hundreds	Tens	Ones
4	4	4

↓	↓	↓
400	40	4

▶ Reflect   Work with a partner.

1 **Talk About It**   When does the digit 8 have a value of 8? 80? 800? What are some three-digit numbers that show these values?

Write About It   Possible answer: 8 has a value of 8 when it is in the ones place, like in 218. 8 has a value of 80 when it is in the tens place, like in 281. 8 has a value of 800 when it is in the hundreds place, like in 812.

97

▶ Concept Extension

Discuss digits as symbols.

- Explain to students that we use many symbols in our world. For example, they might see a ⟲ on a bike trail to tell them to turn right. In math, we use symbols like + and = to tell us what to do or what something means.

- A digit is a symbol that tells how many groups of ones, tens, hundreds, and so on, there are in a number. The digits we use are 0–9.

- In a two-digit number, such as 37, the digits 3 and 7 tell how many groups there are within the number—the "3" means there are 3 groups of 10, and the "7" means there are 7 groups of one.

- Write several two- and three-digit numbers on the board. Ask students to tell you what the number is and identify the digits and their values.

▶ Mathematical Discourse

1 *Why isn't the number 23 called a digit?*

Students should respond that 23 uses two symbols or digits. A digit is only one symbol.

2 *Why might a student write two hundred seventy-five as 200705? Why is it incorrect?*

The student just wrote all the values next to each other. It is not correct because the number is too great. The 7 is in the hundreds place instead of the 2, and the zero is in the tens place instead of the 7.

Step By Step

- Read **Find Out More** as a class.
- Use the Concept Extension and Mathematical Discourse question 1 to reinforce the concept of digits.

▶ **Concept Extension**

▶ **Mathematical Discourse 1**

- Help students interpret the information in the place-value chart. Explain that a 4 in the tens place means 4 tens, or 40. A 4 in the ones place means 4 ones, or 4. You may want to use base-ten blocks to support these ideas.

- Ask students to work with a partner to answer the *Talk About It* questions. After students complete *Write About It*, have them share their numbers, evaluating them for accuracy.

▶ **Mathematical Discourse 2**

Ready Mathematics
PRACTICE AND PROBLEM SOLVING

Assign *Practice and Problem Solving* **pages 111–112** after students have completed this section.

Modeled and Guided Instruction

At A Glance

Students examine a three-digit number represented in pictures and in a chart. Then students revisit this problem by connecting the digits to the values they represent.

Step By Step

- Read the problem at the top of the page as a class. Refer back to the Real-World Connection in Part One, reminding students that 1 ten dollar bill is equal to 10 one dollar bills, so its value is ten dollars. Then remind them of the value of a one hundred dollar bill in a similar manner.

▶ **English Language Learners**

Picture It

- Draw students' attention to **Picture It**. Ask them to describe what the picture shows. Ask how many bills they see. [6] Ask: *Do the number of bills tell how much money Amir has? Explain.* [Students should be able to articulate that since each one hundred dollar bill is equal to 100 ones and the ten dollar bill is equal to 10 ones, Amir must have more money than 6 dollars.]

Picture It

- Connect the quick drawing to the bills by asking students to write 100, 10, or 1 next to each part of the quick drawing.

▶ **Visual Model**

Model It

- Help students connect the place-value chart in **Model It** to the picture and quick drawing.

> **SMP TIP Model with Mathematics**
> To reinforce modeling, use the problem on this page, but change Amir's winnings to 6 hundreds bills, 3 tens bills, and 5 ones bills. Draw on the board the bills of play money that Amir wins. Instruct students to make a quick drawing to represent the winnings and then show the amount in a place-value chart. *(SMP 4)*

Learn About ▶ **Finding the Value of Three-Digit Numbers**

Read the problem. Then you will show hundreds, tens, and ones in different ways.

> Amir plays a board game that uses play money.
> He wins 2 hundreds bills, 1 tens bill, and 3 ones bills.
> What is the total value of the bills Amir wins?

▶ **Picture It You can draw a picture to show the problem.**

▶ **Picture It You can make a quick drawing to show hundreds, tens, and ones.**

▶ **Model It You can show hundreds, tens, and ones in a chart.**

Hundreds	Tens	Ones
2	1	3

98

▶ **English Language Learners**

For students who are not familiar with American dollars, use money from their native country whose denominations are in powers of ten, such as the Mexican 1 peso coin, 10 peso coin, and 100 peso bill.

▶ **Visual Model**

Use quick drawings as a visual model of base-ten blocks.

Materials: base-ten blocks

- Distribute base-ten blocks to students and ask them to show the amount of money Amir wins using the blocks.

- Have students tell the blocks they used and justify their choices.

- Ask how they know each of the hundreds blocks is equal to 100. [Students should see that each hundreds block is divided into 100 units.] Point out the similar shape of the hundreds blocks and the quick drawing squares, and the similar shape of the tens blocks and the vertical line.

- Tell students that the quick drawings are like the blocks but without all the ones shown, to make them "quick" to draw.

▶ **Connect It** **Write the number as hundreds, tens, and ones.**

2 Look at the models on the previous page. How many hundreds, tens, and ones are there?

___2___ hundreds ___1___ ten ___3___ ones

3 What is the value of the hundreds bills? ___200___ dollars

What is the value of the tens bill? ___10___ dollars

What is the value of the ones bills? ___3___ dollars

4 Write an equation to find the total value of all the bills.

___200___ + ___10___ + ___3___ = ___213___ dollars

5 **Talk About It** Amir wins 2 more tens bills. How would you write the new total value of Amir's play money? Explain how you found your answer.

Write About It ___233. Possible answer: Amir has 2 more___

___tens. I added 2 to the tens digit. The value of Amir's bills___

___was 213. When I added 2 to the tens digit, the value___

___became 233.___

▶ **Try It** **Try another problem.**

6 What is another way to show each number? Draw lines to connect each number to another way to write the number.

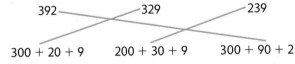

392   329   239

300 + 20 + 9   200 + 30 + 9   300 + 90 + 2

99

▶ **Hands-On Activity**

Connect base-ten blocks and digit placement.

Materials: base-ten blocks, Activity Sheet 6 (Place-Value Mat), and Activity Sheet 1 (Digit Cards)

• Distribute the materials and ask the students to show the number 324 with base-ten blocks. (Do not write the number.)

• Have them place the digit cards in the proper places on their chart to show the number. To connect the digits and their placement with the 3 hundreds blocks, 2 tens blocks, and 4 ones blocks, have students write the expanded form and sum 300 + 20 + 4 = 324.

• Repeat as necessary to solidify the concept. Include numbers such as 420 and 205 to reinforce the concept of 0 as a placeholder.

Step By Step

Connect It

• Read **Connect It** as a class. Make sure students understand that the questions refer to the problem on the previous page.

• For Problem 3, ensure students understand that the value they are finding is the combined value of each kind of bill, not the value of only one bill.

• As students complete Problem 4, ask them why it makes sense to add all the values together.

▶ **Hands-On Activity**

• For Problem 5, make sure students understand that the 2 tens Amir wins are in addition to the money he has already won.

Try It

• Tell students that they may use a picture or other model to help solve the **Try It** problem. Have students explain the thinking they used in solving the problem.

6 **Solution**

392 = 300 + 90 + 2; 329 = 300 + 20 + 9; 239 = 200 + 30 + 9

Error Alert Watch for students who may invert the 9 and 2 in 329 and 392.

SMP TIP **Look for Structure**

Ask students to describe the structure that is inherent in our place-value system. In a three-digit number, the first digit represents the number of hundreds, the second digit represents the number of tens, and the third digit represents the number of ones that together equal the number. *(SMP 7)*

Ready **Mathematics**
PRACTICE AND PROBLEM SOLVING

Assign *Practice and Problem Solving* **pages 113–114** after students have completed this section.

Guided Practice

At A Glance

Students connect various representations to three-digit numbers.

Step By Step

- Ask students to solve the problems individually and show all their work. Tell students to describe their thinking.
- For Problem 7, encourage students to describe how they found each digit. For students who are struggling with Problem 9, suggest that they draw a place-value chart.
- **Pair/Share** When students have completed each problem, have them Pair/Share to discuss their solutions with a partner.

Solutions

Example A place-value chart is used to help students organize the digits in a number that is described in written form. Students could also write the number in expanded form: 500 + 90 + 4 = 594.

7 Solution
The secret number is 942; 9 is one more than 8, 40 equals 4 tens, and 2 ones is 2.
DOK 2

Practice Reading and Writing Three-Digit Numbers

Study the model below. Then solve Problems 7–9.

Example

Mrs. Cole wrote this number on a check.
five hundred ninety-four
What is this number?

You can show your work in a chart.

Hundreds	Tens	Ones
5	9	4

↓ ↓ ↓

five hundred ninety-four

Answer The number is 594.

---

7 Pat wrote these clues about his secret number.
- The hundreds digit is 1 more than 8.
- The tens digit has a value of 40.
- The number has 2 ones.

What is the secret number?

Show your work.

Possible work: 9 is 1 more than 8. 40 is 4 tens. 2 ones is 2.

Hundreds	Tens	Ones
9	4	2

How many digits are in the number?

Answer The secret number is 942.

Teacher Notes

8 Jim is playing a board game. This is Jim's play money. Write the amount in two different ways.

What is the value of each kind of bill in the problem?

___100___ dollars + ___30___ dollars + ___2___ dollars

___132___ dollars

9 Which number is the same as 700 + 6?

A 76

B 607

(**C**) 706

D 760

How many tens does the number have?

Zoey chose **A** as the answer. This answer is wrong. How did Zoey get her answer?

Possible answer: She didn't put a zero in the tens place to show that

there are 0 tens.

101

Solutions

8 **Solution**

100 dollars + 30 dollars + 2 dollars is 132 dollars.

DOK 2

9 **Solution**

C; 700 + 6 = 706.

Explain to students why the other choices are not correct:

B is not correct because 607 = 600 + 7 ≠ 700 + 6.

D is not correct because 760 = 700 + 60 ≠ 700 + 6.

DOK 3

Ready Mathematics
PRACTICE AND PROBLEM SOLVING

Assign *Practice and Problem Solving* **pages 115–116** after students have completed this section.

Teacher Notes

👤 Independent Practice

At A Glance

Students solve problems about three-digit numbers that might appear on a mathematics test.

Solutions

1 Solution
A 2 hundreds = 200, and 5 ones = 5;
D The 2 is in the hundreds place, and the 5 is in the ones place.
DOK 2

2 Solution
3, 4, 6; 300, 40, 6; 346
DOK 2

3 Solution
B 36 tens = 360 ones; **C** 300 + 60 = 360;
D 360 = 300 + 60 or 3 hundred and 6 tens.
DOK 2

> **Practice** **Reading and Writing Three-Digit Numbers**

Solve the problems.

1 What is another way to show 2 hundreds and 5 ones? Circle all the correct answers.

Ⓐ 200 + 5

B 25

C 200 + 50

Ⓓ 205

2 What does the model show? Fill in the table and the blanks.

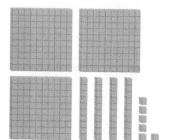

Hundreds	Tens	Ones
3	4	6

Value: ___300___ + ___40___ + ___6___

Total: ___346___

3 A bear at the zoo weighs 360 pounds. What is true about this number? Circle all the correct answers.

A It is 300 + 6.

Ⓑ It equals 36 tens.

Ⓒ It is 300 + 60.

Ⓓ It has 3 hundreds and 6 tens.

102

Quick Check and Remediation

- Jamie is collecting coins. She has 4 jars with one hundred coins in each jar and 7 more coins. How many coins does Jamie have? [407]

- For students who are still struggling, use the chart to guide remediation.

- After providing remediation, check students' understanding using the following problem: Sam is the banker for a board game. Each player gets $240 to start the game. How many hundreds bills and tens bills could he give each player? [Possible answer: 2 hundreds bills and 4 tens bills]

If the error is ...	Students may ...	To remediate ...
47	have placed the digits 4 and 7 together.	Provide students a place-value chart. Help them model the situation by writing in the chart the digit that represents the number of jars and the number of extra coins Jamie has. Assist students in writing the number correctly.
470	have written the 7 in the tens place instead of the ones place.	Help students write the value of the total number of coins in the jars and the extra coins in expanded form: 400 + 7. Help them see that there are no groups of ten, so they should write 400 with a 7 in the ones place.
11	have added the two numbers shown.	Use base-ten blocks to model the situation, ensuring the student recognizes the 100 ones in each hundreds block. Have students count by 100s to find the total in the 4 hundreds blocks (or 4 jars) and then add the additional ones. Write the total in a place-value chart and as a sum.

4 Here are clues about a number.

- The number has 7 hundreds.
- The tens digit has a value of 30.
- The ones digit is less than any other digit in the number.

What could the number be? Explain.

Possible answer: The number could be 732. The number has 7 hundreds,

so the hundreds digit is 7. 30 is 3 tens, so the tens digit is 3. The ones digit

is less than 7 and less than 3. So the ones digit could be 2.

5 Write the value of each digit in the two numbers.

275	527
200 + 70 + 5	500 + 20 + 7

6 Look at Problem 5. Why do the 2, 5, and 7 have a different value in each number? Explain.

Possible answer: The 2, 5, and 7 are in different places in each number.

So, the values are different in each number.

✓ **Self Check** **Now you can write three-digit numbers. Fill this in on the progress chart on page 59.**

103

Solutions

4 **Solution**
7 hundreds = 700, 30 is 3 tens, 0, 1, and 2 are less than both 3 and 7. So students may list 730, 731, or 732. Check students' explanations.
DOK 3

5 **Solution**
200 + 70 + 5; 500 + 20 + 7
DOK 1

6 **Solution**
Possible answer: The 2, 5, and 7 are in different places in each number. The place it is in gives the digit its value.
DOK 2

▶ Hands-On Activity

Race to 500.

Materials: [For each student] Activity Sheet 6 (Place-Value Mat); [For each pair] base-ten blocks, at least 2 sets of 0–9 cards from Activity Sheet 1 (Digit Cards), and 2 number cubes (1 white and 1 colored)

- Organize students into pairs and distribute the materials. Instruct students to take turns rolling the number cube and using base-ten blocks to model what they roll.

- The number on the white cube tells how many ones blocks they take, and the number on the colored cube tells how many tens blocks. They place digit cards on the place-value mat to show the total.

- On the next and subsequent rolls, students add the number of blocks rolled to what they already have, organize their blocks into groups of ones, tens, and hundreds, and display with digit cards on the place-value chart. Continue until one player reaches 500.

▶ Challenge Activity

Explore beyond hundreds.

Materials: place-value chart showing at least 6 place-value positions with only the Ones, Tens, and Hundreds columns labeled

- Challenge students to explore numbers greater than 999 by giving them a place-value chart showing at least 6 place-value positions.

- Ask them to fill in the place values they already know. They should be able to fill in ones, tens, and hundreds.

- Tell them that their task is:

1. to find out what label belongs in the remainder of the place-value positions on the chart (using whatever resources they need).

2. to figure out the value of each of the labels.

3. to write numbers with six or more place values in expanded form and read them using the proper place-value names.

Teacher-Toolbox.com

Overview

Assign the Lesson 11 Quiz and have students work independently to complete it.

Use the results of the quiz to assess students' understanding of the content of the lesson and to identify areas for reteaching. See the Lesson Pacing Guide at the beginning of the lesson for suggested instructional resources.

Tested Skills

Assesses 2.NBT.A.3

Problems on this assessment form require students to be able to write a 3-digit number using given criteria for the numbers of hundreds, tens, and ones, and to show 3-digit numbers in a variety of ways, including base-ten numerals, number names, standard form, and in terms of varied combinations of hundreds, tens, and ones.

Ready® Mathematics

Lesson 11 Quiz

Solve the problems.

1 Kate's family drives 198 miles to the lake. Write 198 in the chart and as a sum of the value of the digits. Then write the sum.

Hundreds	Tens	Ones

Value: _____ + _____ + _____

Total: _____

2 Cheng has 25 ten-dollar bills and 9 one-dollar bills. How much money does Cheng have?

Show your work.

Answer: Cheng has $ _____.

3 Lydia's room number has 3 ones. The hundreds digit has a value of 40 tens. The tens digit is more than 6. What could Lydia's room number be?

Circle all the correct answers.

A 347   D 483

B 446   E 493

C 463   F 494

Lesson 11 Quiz *continued*

4 Look at the model.

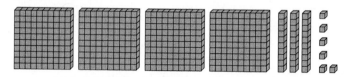

Write the value of the blocks shown as a sum of hundreds, tens, and ones. Then show another way to write the sum.

Fill in the blanks. Use numbers from the box below.

3	4	6	30	40	60	300	400	600

_____ hundreds + 3 tens + _____ ones

_____ + _____ + 6

5 Kyle, Liam, Emma, and Abby each write 315 in a different way.

• Kyle writes: three hundred fifteen

• Liam writes: 31 tens and 5 ones

• Emma writes: 3 + 1 + 5

• Abby writes: 315 ones

Who writes 315 the wrong way?

Circle the correct answer.

A Kyle   C Emma

B Liam   D Abby

Common Misconceptions and Errors

Errors may result if students:

• confuse the hundreds, tens, or ones places.

• identify digits instead of naming their value.

• assume criteria in the problem are listed in place value order.

• misinterpret the value of the ones, tens, or hundreds digit as the number of ones, tens, or hundreds.

Ready® **Mathematics**

Lesson 11 Quiz Answer Key

1.

Hundreds	Tens	Ones
1	9	8

Value: 100, 90, 8
Total: 198
DOK 2

2. $259
DOK 1

3. D, E
DOK 3

4. 4, 6
400, 30
DOK 2

5. C
DOK 2

Lesson 12
Compare Three-Digit Numbers

CCSS Focus

Domain
Number and Operations in Base Ten

Cluster
A. Understand place value.

Standards
2.NBT.A.4 Compare two three-digit numbers based on meanings of the hundreds, tens, and ones digits, using >, =, and < symbols to record the results of comparisons.

Standards for Mathematical Practice (SMP)

2 Reason abstractly and quantitatively.

3 Construct viable arguments and critique the reasoning of others.

4 Model with mathematics.

6 Attend to precision.

7 Look for and make use of structure.

Lesson Objectives

Content Objectives
- Evaluate models of three-digit numbers to determine whether numbers are greater than, less than, or equal to each other.
- Express equalities and inequalities using proper notation.
- Solve problems involving inequalities and justify solutions.

Language Objectives
- Tell which of two three-digit numbers is greater and which is lesser.
- Write inequalities to compare three-digit numbers using > and < symbols.
- Listen to the ideas of others and ask questions to clarify.

Prerequisite Skills

- Identify place value in three-digit numbers.
- Model three-digit numbers.
- Understand the concepts of greater than, less than, and equal to.

Lesson Vocabulary

There is no new vocabulary. Review the following key terms.

- **compare** to decide if one number is greater than, less than, or equal to another number.
- **greater than symbol (>)** a symbol used to compare two numbers when the first is greater than the second.
- **less than symbol (<)** a symbol used to compare two numbers when the first is less than the second.
- **equal sign (=)** a symbol used to compare two numbers that have the same value.

Learning Progression

In Grade 1 students explore the concept of greater than and less than, comparing place values of two-digit numbers. They record comparisons using the symbols for inequalities. Students learn the meaning of the equal sign and apply it to number sentences.

In Grade 2 students expand their understanding of numbers and place value as they explore three-digit numbers. They model three-digit numbers, attending to the additional place-value position of the hundreds place. The concept of inequality is explored further as students measure and compare lengths.

In this lesson students compare three-digit numbers through picture models, charts, and number sentences. Numbers are applied to a variety of settings, extending the concept of number beyond physical quantity. Students model situations involving inequalities using the appropriate symbol.

In Grade 3 and beyond, students apply their understanding of inequalities to fractions and decimals. They model inequalities on a number line and explore the meaning of the greater than or equal to symbol used in algebraic sentences.

Lesson Pacing Guide

Whole Class Instruction

Day 1 *45–60 minutes*	**Toolbox: Interactive Tutorial*** *Comparing and Ordering Three-Digit Numbers* **Introduction** • Opening Activity *15 min* • Use What You Know *10 min* • Find Out More *10 min* • Reflect *5 min*	**Practice and Problem Solving** Assign pages 119–120.
Day 2 *45–60 minutes*	**Modeled and Guided Instruction** **Learn About Ways to Compare Three-Digit Numbers** • Picture It/Model It *10 min* • Connect It *25 min* • Try It *10 min*	**Practice and Problem Solving** Assign pages 121–122.
Day 3 *45–60 minutes*	**Modeled and Guided Instruction** **Learn About More Ways to Compare Three-Digit Numbers** • Picture It/Model It *15 min* • Connect It *20 min* • Try It *10 min*	**Practice and Problem Solving** Assign pages 123–124.
Day 4 *45–60 minutes*	**Guided Practice** **Practice Comparing Three-Digit Numbers** • Example *5 min* • Problems 13–15 *15 min* • Pair/Share *15 min* • Solutions *10 min*	**Practice and Problem Solving** Assign pages 125–126.
Day 5 *45–60 minutes*	**Independent Practice** **Practice Comparing Three-Digit Numbers** • Problems 1–6 *20 min* • Quick Check and Remediation *10 min* • Hands-On or Challenge Activity *15 min* **Toolbox: Lesson Quiz** Lesson 12 Quiz	

Small Group Differentiation

Teacher-Toolbox.com

Reteach
Ready Prerequisite Lessons *45–90 min*

Grade 1
• Lesson 22 Compare Numbers

Teacher-led Activities
Tools for Instruction *15–20 min*

Grade 1 *(Lesson 22)*
• Compare Two-Digit Numbers
Grade 2 *(Lesson 12)*
• Compare and Order Three-Digit Numbers

Student-led Activities
Math Center Activities *30–40 min*

Grade 2 *(Lesson 12)*
• 2.17 Compare Three-Digit Number Vocabulary
• 2.18 Compare Three-Digit Numbers

Personalized Learning

i-Ready.com

Independent
i-Ready Lessons* *10–20 min*

Grade 1 *(Lesson 22)*
• Comparing Numbers to 100 Using Symbols

*We continually update the Interactive Tutorials. Check the Teacher Toolbox for the most up-to-date offerings for this lesson.

Opening Activity

Compare Two-Digit Numbers

Objective Compare two-digit numbers using *greater than* and *less than*.

Time *15–20 minutes*

Materials for each pair

- a set of all the number cards from both pages of Activity Sheet 8 (Two-Digit Cards)

Overview

Students practice the concepts of *greater than* and *less than* by playing a card game comparing two-digit numbers.

Step By Step

1 Prepare the game.

- Make a set of all the two-digit number cards from both pages of Activity Sheet 8 for each student pair.

- Put students in pairs and give them a set of cards.

2 Play the game.

- Instruct students to divide their cards into two equal piles, placing them facedown. Tell them how many cards to put in each pile. Each partner takes a pile. Tell them they are going to play a game of Greater Than.

- Have students turn the card from the top of their pile face-up. They compare the cards and decide whose number is greater. The player with the greater number keeps both cards.

- Students continue to play until all cards have been played. To avoid excessive competition, you can have students mix the cards back together without counting the number each student "won."

- Have students play the game again as a game of Less Than.

- As students play, make sure they understand the concepts of *greater than* and *less than*. Have a hundreds chart available for reference, if necessary.

- You may want students to replay the game when finished. Allow them to trade cards with another group for variety.

3 Discuss the game.

- Use this question to assess students' understanding of comparing two-digit numbers: *How did you know if your number was greater than or less than your partner's number?* Make sure students can analyze by comparing the tens place. If the tens digits are the same, then compare the ones digits. You can use a hundreds chart to reinforce this concept.

Teacher Notes

Introduction

At A Glance

Students use what they know about place value to interpret and compare two numbers. Then students compare numbers by starting with the greatest place value. They examine the equality and inequality symbols used to write number sentences.

Step By Step

- Work through **Use What You Know** as a class.

- Have students read the problem at the top of the page. Tell them that the number in each box represents a digit. When the digits are written one next to the other, they form a number. Use Mathematical Discourse question 1 to reinforce this concept. Write the numbers the students generate on the board.

▶ **Mathematical Discourse 1**

- You may want to suggest that students use quick drawings of hundreds, tens, and ones, if they find this helpful. Use Mathematical Discourse question 2 and the Hands-On Activity to help students review using place value to read and write numbers.

▶ **Mathematical Discourse 2**

▶ **Hands-On Activity**

Compare Three-Digit Numbers

🅖 Use What You Know

Compare hundreds and tens.

Kim and Jon tossed beanbags at a target. What is the greatest number each person can make using the digits they landed on? Whose number has more hundreds?

a. What is the greatest number Kim can make? Why?

421; Possible answer: Kim has 3 numbers, so put the greatest number in

the hundreds place. Then put the next greatest number in the tens place.

b. One of Jon's beanbags did not land on the board, so he can only use two numbers. What is the greatest number Jon can make? Why?

97; Possible answer: Jon has 2 numbers, so put the greatest number

in the tens place.

c. How many hundreds, tens, and ones are in each number?

Kim's number: __4__ hundreds + __2__ tens + __1__ one

Jon's number: __0__ hundreds + __9__ tens + __7__ ones

d. Compare the numbers. Which has more hundreds?

421 has 4 hundreds. 97 has 0 hundreds. So Kim's number has more hundreds.

104

▶ Mathematical Discourse

1 *What other numbers could Kim have made with her tosses? What other number could Jon have made? Why is there only one other number Jon could make?*

Kim could have made 124, 142, 214, 241, 412; Jon could have made 79. Jon could only make one other number because there are only 2 digits and only 2 ways to arrange them.

2 *How would you show the hundreds, tens, and ones for the other numbers Kim could have made? For the other number Jon could have made?*

Student responses should indicate that they understand place value by expressing the correct number of ones, tens, and hundreds for each number.

▶ Hands-On Activity

Use base-ten blocks to model two- and three-digit numbers.

Materials: base-ten blocks, number cards 0–9 from Activity Sheet 1 (Digit Cards), and Activity Sheet 6 (Place-Value Mat)

- Record the numbers generated from Mathematical Discourse question 1 on the board. Ask students to put base-ten blocks on the place-value mat to show the number of ones, tens, and hundreds contained in each number.

- Have students place a corresponding 0–9 card under each group of blocks.

- Compare each number Kim might have made to the number Jon might have made and ask: *Which number has more hundreds? Why?* [Kim's numbers always have more hundreds since Jon can only make a two-digit number.]

▶ Connect It Understand how to compare numbers.

2 Look at the models on the previous page. Can you use the numbers in the hundreds place to decide which number is greater? Why or why not?

No, the hundreds are the same.

3 Now compare the tens. Which number has more tens?

352 has 5 tens and 328 has 2 tens. 352 has more tens.

4 Complete the number sentence to compare 352 and 328.

328 $<$ 352

5 **Talk About It** Bart says 2 $<$ 8, so 352 $<$ 328. Is this correct? Explain.

Write About It No; Possible explanation: The 2 and 8 are in the ones

place. You have to compare hundreds first. They are the same, so

compare tens. 2 $<$ 5, so 328 $<$ 352.

▶ Try It Try another problem.

6 Write a number sentence to compare 761 and 716. Explain why the number sentence is true.

Possible answer: 761 $>$ 716 or 716 $<$ 761. Both numbers have

7 hundreds, but the tens are different. Six tens is more than 1 ten.

So, 761 $>$ 716.

107

▶ Visual Model

Compare numbers on a diagram.

- Write the names of two towns/cities on the board whose distances from your school are greater than 100 miles, but have the same number of hundreds of miles.

- Draw a diagram similar to the one shown, using the names of the towns selected.

```
Our town                Town A
  o────────────────────o
          (distance)

Our town                   Town B
  o─────────────────────────o
          (distance)
```

- Ask: *Which town is a greater distance from our town?* [Town B] *How do you know?* [The line is longer.]

- Have students write the inequality that represents this situation on whiteboards or paper. Ask a volunteer to share the number sentence that was written. Discuss how two sentences, one using $>$ and another using $<$, can both represent the same situation.

Step By Step

Connect It

- Read **Connect It** as a class. Make sure students understand that the questions refer to the problem on the previous page.

- After students complete Problem 4, ask them to write a different number sentence using $>$ to compare the two numbers.

> **SMP TIP Construct Arguments**
> Ask students to describe Bart's faulty reasoning in Problem 5, using what they have learned about comparing numbers. *(SMP 3)*

▶ Visual Model

Try It

6 **Solution**
761 $>$ 716 or 716 $<$ 761; both numbers have 7 hundreds, but the tens are different. Six tens is more than 1 ten so 761 is greater than 716.

Error Alert Watch for students who may invert the 1 and 6 in one of the numbers, seeing the numbers as equal.

Ready Mathematics
PRACTICE AND PROBLEM SOLVING

Assign *Practice and Problem Solving* **pages 121–122** after students have completed this section.

Modeled and Guided Instruction

At A Glance

Students examine models of three-digit numbers in which the hundreds and tens are equal. Then students evaluate the number of hundreds, tens, and ones and write number sentences comparing two numbers.

Step By Step

- Tell students that they will find out how to decide which number is greater than or less than the other when both the hundreds and the tens are the same.

- Read the problem at the top of the page together as a class. Ask students what number they are supposed to find, the greater or the lesser.

Picture It

- Draw attention to the quick drawing models. Use Mathematical Discourse question 1 to help students recognize that there are an equal number of hundreds and tens.

▶ **Mathematical Discourse 1**

Model It

- Have students compare the quick drawings to the place-value chart.

- Use Mathematical Discourse question 2 to help students recognize that the only difference between these two numbers is found in the ones place.

▶ **Mathematical Discourse 2**

- Replicate the chart on the board. Use a piece of paper to cover the digits in the hundreds place since the number of hundreds are the same. Cover the digits in the tens place since the number of tens are the same. Students can now compare the ones place to determine which number is greater.

> **SMP TIP Model with Mathematics**
> Have students compare the models they have seen in this lesson. Ask them to tell which model or models make it easier to write a number sentence comparing two numbers and why. *(SMP 4)*

Learn About > **More Ways to Compare Three-Digit Numbers**

Read the problem. Then you will compare in different ways.

These two paintings are in the school art contest. Which painting has more votes?

Painting A: 467 Votes   Painting B: 463 Votes

▶ **Picture It** You can show the numbers in a quick drawing.

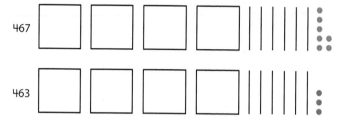

467

463

▶ **Model It** You can model the numbers in a chart.

Hundreds	Tens	Ones
4	6	7
4	6	3

108

▶ **Mathematical Discourse**

1 *How are these models different from the other models in this lesson?*
Listen for or encourage responses that identify the models on this page as having both an equal number of hundreds and tens.

2 *How can thinking about the number of tens and ones help you decide which of these numbers is greater?*
Since they both have 46 tens, the ones place will tell you which number is greater.

▶ Connect It Compare hundreds, tens, and ones.

7 Look at the models on the previous page. Compare the hundreds and tens. What do you notice?

Both numbers have 4 hundreds and 6 tens.

8 Which place do you need to look at to compare the numbers? Why?

You need to look at the ones. The hundreds and tens are the same in

both numbers.

9 Use the numbers 467 and 463 to complete each number sentence.

467 > 463   463 < 467

10 Why can you write two different number sentences to compare 467 and 463?

Possible answer: If 467 is greater than 463, then 463 is less than 467.

11 Which painting has more votes? How do you know?

Painting A has more votes because 467 is greater than 463.

▶ Try It Try another problem.

12 Write > or < in each blank.

a. 264 __<__ 462   c. 954 __>__ 950   e. 718 __<__ 788

b. 372 __<__ 379   d. 876 __>__ 867   f. 653 __>__ 553

109

▶ English Language Learners

- Students may struggle with the terms *greater than* and *less than*. Try using terms more familiar to them like *bigger* and *smaller*. When a term is found that makes sense, provide each student with a card that has the words *greater than* printed on it. Write the synonym that is most familiar to the student under it. Do the same for *less than*.

- Also check for understanding of the terms *least* and *greatest*. Have students compare 3 one-digit numbers, such as 2, 9, and 5. Write the numbers on the board. First, ask students to compare 2 and 9, guiding them as necessary to say "2 is less than 9." Then ask them to compare 2 and 5, guiding them as necessary to say "2 is less than 5." Explain that because 2 is less than both 9 and 5, 2 is the *least* number.

- On the board, write "2 < 9" and the sentence "2 is less than 9." Then point to the 2, 9, and 5 that you originally wrote, and circle the 2. Write the sentence "2 is the least number." Underline *less than* and *least* in the two sentences you wrote. Explain that *less than* is used when comparing two numbers, and *least* is used when comparing more than two numbers. Then focus on the word *greatest*, using the same numbers and process.

Step By Step

Connect It

- Read **Connect It** as a class. Make sure students understand that the questions refer to the problem on the previous page.

- For Problem 9, write the two number sentences on the board. Ask a volunteer to read the number sentence from left to right, attending to the direction of the inequality sign.

Try It

- After students complete the **Try It** section, ask them to tell how they knew which direction to write the inequality sign. Use this opportunity to correct student misunderstandings. Help struggling students find a method that is personally meaningful for remembering how to properly position the symbol.

▶ **English Language Learners**

12 Solution

a. 264 < 462   b. 372 < 379

c. 954 > 950   d. 876 > 867

e. 718 < 788   f. 653 > 553

SMP TIP Attend to Precision
Have students describe the strategy they used in Problem 12 to determine which number was greater and which one was lesser, and explain how they know they are correct. *(SMP 6)*

Ready Mathematics
PRACTICE AND PROBLEM SOLVING

Assign *Practice and Problem Solving* **pages 123–124** after students have completed this section.

👥 Guided Practice

At A Glance

Students solve problems involving the comparison of three-digit numbers.

Step By Step

- Ask students to solve the problems individually and show all their work. Review the sample problem together telling students that using a visual or number model can help them compare numbers. They should choose a model that makes the most sense to them.

- **Pair/Share** When students have completed each problem, have them Pair/Share to discuss their solutions with a partner.

Solutions

Example A number model is used to describe each situation, demonstrating that 25 tens is equal to 250. Therefore, the answer to the question is that neither person packs more. They pack the same number of oranges.

13 **Solution**
Sarita and Chen; 92 has no hundreds, so it's the least. The other numbers all have 2 hundreds, so compare tens. 233 and 236 have 3 tens, and 213 has only 1 ten.
DOK 2

Practice ▶ Comparing Three-Digit Numbers

Study the model below. Then solve Problems 13–15.

Example

Yen packs 250 oranges in a box. Gia packs 25 bags of oranges. She puts 10 oranges in each bag. Who packs more oranges?

Look at how you can show your work.

25 bags with 10 in each bag = 25 tens

25 tens = 250

250 oranges in bags
250 oranges in a box
250 = 250

Answer They each pack 250 oranges. Neither person packs more than the other.

13 Which two players have the greatest scores? Write the number of hundreds and tens in the table.

Player	Score	Hundreds	Tens
Eden	92	0	9
Sarita	233	2	3
Paul	213	2	1
Chen	236	2	3

Remember to look at the hundreds place first.

Show your work.

92 has no hundreds. 233 and 236 have the greatest number of hundreds and tens. 213 has the same number of hundreds as 233 and 236 but fewer tens than those numbers. So, 233 and 236 are the greatest scores.

Answer Sarita and Chen have the greatest scores.

110

Teacher Notes

14 Bella biked 122 miles. Ariel biked 126 miles. Who biked fewer miles?

Show your work.

Possible work:

122 = 1 hundred 2 tens 2 ones

126 = 1 hundred 2 tens 6 ones

The hundreds and tens are the same. Compare ones. Since 2 < 6, 122 < 126.

Are you looking for the lesser or greater number?

Answer Bella biked fewer miles.

15 Jill and Iman each write a three-digit number.

    Jill's number: 305

    Iman's number: 3 hundreds 5 tens

Which number sentence compares their numbers correctly?

A 305 < 305

B 305 = 305

C 350 > 305

D 350 < 305

What number is the same as 3 hundreds 5 tens?

Dan chose **B** as the answer. This answer is wrong. How did Dan get his answer?

Possible answer: Dan wrote 3 hundreds 5 tens as

305, but it should be 350.

111

Solutions

14 Solution

Bella biked fewer miles; The hundreds and tens are the same. Compare the ones. Since 2 < 6, 122 < 126.

DOK 1

15 Solution

C; 3 hundreds 5 tens = 350, 350 > 305. Explain to students why the other two choices are not correct.

A is not correct because 305 = 305.

D is not correct because the inequality symbol should be pointing at the lesser number. This sentence is read *350 is less than 305*.

DOK 3

Ready· **Mathematics**
PRACTICE AND PROBLEM SOLVING

Assign *Practice and Problem Solving* **pages 125–126** after students have completed this section.

Teacher Notes

Independent Practice

At A Glance

Students compare numbers to answer questions that might appear on a mathematics test.

Solutions

1 Solution

A 431 has one more ten;
C 772 has more tens.
DOK 2

2 Solution

C 252 has 5 tens, which is more than 4 tens;
D 260 has 6 tens, which is more than 4 tens.
DOK 2

3 Solution

a. **True**; 551 has more tens than 539;
b. **False**; 924 has more hundreds than 889;
c. **False**; There are more tens in 770 than in 707; d. **True**; There are fewer ones in 422.
DOK 1

Practice Comparing Three-Digit Numbers

Solve the problems.

1 Which comparison is true? Circle all the correct answers.

(A) 431 > 427

B 540 < 5 hundreds 4 ones

(C) 727 < 772

D 9 hundreds 6 tens < 906

2 Phil has 248 trading cards. Sean has more trading cards than Phil. How many cards could Sean have? Circle all the correct answers.

A 239

B 245

(C) 252

(D) 260

3 Choose *True* or *False* for each comparison.

a. 551 > 539   (True)   False

b. 924 < 889   True   (False)

c. 770 = 707   True   (False)

d. 422 < 425   (True)   False

Quick Check and Remediation

- Tory and Sam are playing a video game. They get points for moves they make. At the end of the game, Tory has 228 points and Sam has 241 points. Write a comparison to show who has more points.
  [Sam: 241 > 228]

- For students who are still struggling, use the chart to guide remediation.

- After providing remediation, check students' understanding using the following problem: Juan and his family travel 498 miles on a trip. Jay and his family travel 568 miles on a trip. Write a comparison to show who travels the lesser distance. [Juan: 498 < 568]

If the error is . . .	Students may . . .	To remediate . . .
241 < 228	not understand which inequality symbol should be used.	Review how the inequality symbol is always "gobbling up" the greater number or "points to" the lesser number.
241 < 228	have compared the ones place rather than the tens place.	Have the student write each number in a place-value chart. Compare the digits in each place value, reinforcing the importance of starting with the hundreds place. Remind the student that the digits in the tens place are only compared if the digits in the hundreds place are the same, and that the digits in the ones place are only compared if the digits in the tens place are the same.
other answers	not understand the concept of greater than and less than.	Use physical models or models such as a hundreds chart or a number line with one- and two-digit numbers to review and reinforce what it means to be greater than or less than. Put the number comparisons into situations familiar to the student to provide a meaningful context.

4 Write one of the numbers below in each box to make a true comparison.

308   380   390

$\boxed{390}$ > 386   38 tens = $\boxed{380}$ $\boxed{308}$ < 384

5 Use the digits below to make the greatest three-digit number you can. Explain how you got your answer.

$\boxed{4}$ $\boxed{1}$ $\boxed{8}$

841; Possible explanation: I put the greatest digit in the

hundreds place and the least digit in the ones place.

6 Josh wants to use the digits from Problem 5 to make the least number he can. He writes 184. Is this the least number he can make? Explain.

No; Possible explanation: The least number he can make is

148. Since 148 has 4 tens and 184 has 8 tens, 148 < 184.

✓ Self Check   Now you can compare three-digit numbers. Fill this in on the progress chart on page 59.

113

Solutions

4 Solution
390, 380, 308
DOK 1

5 Solution
841; When the digits are ordered from greatest to least, the higher place value always has the greater number in it.
DOK 3

6 Solution
No, 148 is the least number; Order the digits from least to greatest to write the least number possible.
DOK 3

▶ **Hands-On Activity**

Is it greater or lesser?

Materials: For each pair: 3 sets of 0–9 number cards and 1 set of >, <, and = cards from Activity Sheet 1 (Digit Cards), 10 three-digit number cards from Activity Sheet 7 (Three-Digit Cards)

• Organize students into pairs. Have them place all 3 sets of the 0–9 cards facedown in one pile, and the set of three-digit cards facedown in another pile. Either label the piles or color code them.

• One student turns 1 three-digit card face-up and places it on the table. The other student turns 3 one-digit cards face-up, places them together to form a 3-digit number, and puts those cards next to the 3-digit card—leaving a space. The first student then places one of the inequality symbols (or possibly an equal sign) between the numbers and explains the reasoning for the selection. Then students mix the one-digit cards back into their pile and repeat the activity, changing roles until all of the three-digit cards have been used.

▶ **Challenge Activity**

How far is it?

Materials: a list of 5–10 cities throughout the United States

• Challenge students to explore greater than and less than as they relate to distances.

• Give each student a list of cities in the United States and tell them to find the distance to that city from the town or city in which they live.

• Once they find the distances, they compare to determine which city is the greatest and least distance.

• Ask students to record their findings and share them with each other, justifying their answers.

• Challenge them further by asking them to find a destination whose distance is greater than the greatest distance among the cities they researched.

Teacher-Toolbox.com

Overview

Assign the Lesson 12 Quiz and have students work independently to complete it.

Use the results of the quiz to assess students' understanding of the content of the lesson and to identify areas for reteaching. See the Lesson Pacing Guide at the beginning of the lesson for suggested instructional resources.

Tested Skills

Assesses 2.NBT.A.4

Problems on this assessment form require students to be able to compare three-digit numbers, including pairs of numbers that have the same hundreds, tens, or ones digit, and to determine whether or not a written comparison is true. Students will also need to be familiar with the symbols <, =, and >; the words *more than*, *less than*, *greater than*, and *equal*; the value of numbers written as varied combinations of hundreds, tens, and ones; and using base-ten blocks to model three-digit numbers.

Ready® Mathematics

Lesson 12 Quiz

Solve the problems.

1 Mrs. Jackson asks her students to compare the numbers in the box to 650. Is the number greater than 650 or less than 650?

| 660 | 640 | 506 | 604 | 565 | 656 |

Write each number in the correct column.

Less than 650	Greater than 650

2 Charlie makes this model to show the number of cars in a parking lot on Saturday.

There are more cars in the parking lot on Sunday than on Saturday. How many cars could be in the parking lot on Sunday?

Circle all the correct answers.

A 233   **D** 246

B 137   **E** 263

C 300   **F** 204

Lesson 12 Quiz continued

3 There are 528 students in Bella's school. There are 546 students at Jake's school. Bella says there are more students at her school than at Jake's school.

Is Bella right? Explain why or why not.

_____

_____

_____

4 Mr. Avery asks his students to write and compare three-digit numbers using only the digits 2, 4, 7, and 9.

- Saul writes: $247 < 724$
- Mark writes: $479 < 497$
- Janelle writes: $274 > 247$
- Sam writes: $947 > 974$

Which student writes a number sentence that is **not** true?

Answer: _____

5 Which number sentence is true?

Circle *Yes* or *No* for each number sentence.

a. 3 hundreds 4 tens > 3 hundreds 41 ones   Yes   No

b. $675 < 679$ Yes   No

c. 130 = 1 hundred 3 tens   Yes   No

d. $754 > 745$ Yes   No

Common Misconceptions and Errors

Errors may result if students:

- confuse the meaning of < and >, *greater than* and *less than*, or *more* and *fewer*.

- compare only the digits in a lower place value, when the digits in a higher place value also differ.

- ignore the order or place value of the digits, and think that two numbers with the same digits are equal.

Ready® **Mathematics**

Lesson 12 Quiz Answer Key

1.

Less than 650	Greater than 650
640, 506, 604, 565	660, 656

DOK 1

2. C, D, E
DOK 2

3. No, Bella is not right. Possible explanation: The number of hundreds is the same in both numbers, but 546 has more tens than 528, so 528 < 546.
DOK 3

4. Sam
DOK 1

5. a. No
   b. Yes
   c. Yes
   d. Yes
   DOK 2

Lesson 13
Add Three-Digit Numbers

CCSS Focus

Domain
Number and Operations in Base Ten

Cluster
B. Use place value understanding and properties of operations to add and subtract.

Standards
2.NBT.B.7 Add and subtract within 1000, using concrete models or drawings and strategies based on place value, properties of operations, and/or the relationship between addition and subtraction; relate the strategy to a written method. Understand that in adding or subtracting three-digit numbers, one adds or subtracts hundreds and hundreds, tens and tens, ones and ones; and sometimes it is necessary to compose or decompose tens or hundreds.
2.NBT.B.9 Explain why addition and subtraction strategies work, using place value and the properties of operations.

Additional Standards
2.NBT.B.8 (see page B3 for full text)

Standards for Mathematical Practice (SMP)
2 Reason abstractly and quantitatively.
3 Construct viable arguments and critique the reasoning of others.
4 Model with mathematics.
6 Attend to precision.
7 Look for and make use of structure.

Lesson Objectives

Content Objectives
- Break apart three-digit numbers as a place-value strategy for adding.
- Recognize that in adding, hundreds are added to hundreds, tens to tens, and ones to ones.
- Determine when regrouping a hundred or a ten is necessary, and carry out the regrouping to find the sum.

Language Objectives
- Write two numbers in a place value chart to find their sum.
- Write two numbers in expanded notation to find their sum.
- Record partial sums as a step toward finding the sum of two numbers.

Prerequisite Skills

- Identify place value in three-digit numbers.
- Model three-digit numbers.
- Perform two-digit addition with and without regrouping.

Lesson Vocabulary

There is no new vocabulary. Review the following key terms.

- **regroup** to compose or decompose ones, tens, or hundreds. For example, 10 ones can be regrouped as 1 ten, or 1 hundred can be regrouped as 10 tens.

- **sum** the result of addition.

Learning Progression

In Grade 1 students explore the concept of place value by bundling groups of ten ones into one group of ten. They add two-digit numbers with and without composing a ten and mentally find 10 more or 10 less than a given number.

In Grade 2 students extend their understanding of numbers and place value as they explore three-digit addition and subtraction. They model three-digit numbers and write them in the expanded form. Students fluently skip count by hundreds and tens using that skill to count on.

In this lesson students add three-digit numbers with and without regrouping a hundred and/or a ten. They break apart numbers to add, and record the addition of partial addends before calculating the sum. Students interpret picture models, number models, and an open number line to understand addition of multi-digit numbers. They apply models to addition and select models they find most meaningful.

In Grade 3 students gain fluency with addition and subtraction of numbers within 1,000. In later years, students will draw on the understanding of place value as they multiply and divide multi-digit numbers and apply place-value concepts to decimal numbers.

Lesson Pacing Guide

Whole Class Instruction

Day 1 *45–60 minutes*	Toolbox: Interactive Tutorial* *Adding Three-Digit Numbers* **Introduction** • Opening Activity *15 min* • Use What You Know *10 min* • Find Out More *10 min* • Reflect *5 min*	**Practice and Problem Solving** Assign pages 129–130.
Day 2 *45–60 minutes*	**Modeled and Guided Instruction** **Learn About Adding Hundreds, Tens, and Ones** Picture It/Model It *10 min* Connect It *15 min* Try It *20 min*	**Practice and Problem Solving** Assign pages 131–132.
Day 3 *45–60 minutes*	**Modeled and Guided Instruction** **Learn About Adding Three-Digit Numbers** Model It/Model It/Model It *10 min* Connect It *20 min* Try It *15 min*	**Practice and Problem Solving** Assign pages 133–134.
Day 4 *45–60 minutes*	**Guided Practice** **Practice Adding Three-Digit Numbers** Example *5 min* Problems 12–14 *15 min* Pair/Share *15 min* Solutions *10 min*	**Practice and Problem Solving** Assign pages 135–136.
Day 5 *45–60 minutes*	**Independent Practice** **Practice Adding Three-Digit Numbers** • Problems 1–6 *20 min* • Quick Check and Remediation *10 min* • Hands-On or Challenge Activity *15 min* Toolbox: Lesson Quiz Lesson 13 Quiz	

Small Group Differentiation

Teacher-Toolbox.com

Reteach
Ready Prerequisite Lessons 45–90 min

Grade 1
• Lesson 25 Add and Regroup

Teacher-led Activities
Tools for Instruction 15–20 min

Grade 1 *(Lesson 25)*
• Two-Digit Addition without Regrouping

Grade 2 *(Lesson 13)*
• Three-Digit Addition

Student-led Activities
Math Center Activities 30–40 min

Grade 2 *(Lesson 13)*
• 2.25 Add 10 or 100 to a Three-Digit Number
• 2.23 Add Three-Digit Numbers
• 2.27 Use Addition Strategies to Solve

Personalized Learning

i-Ready.com

Independent
i-Ready Lessons* 10–20 min

Grade 1 *(Lesson 25)*
• Adding a Two-Digit Number and a One-Digit Number

*We continually update the Interactive Tutorials. Check the Teacher Toolbox for the most up-to-date offerings for this lesson.

Explore Addition with Three-Digit Numbers

Objective Students explore adding three-digit numbers through an open-ended problem.

Time *15–20 minutes*

Materials for each student
- paper and crayons or colored pencils
- manipulative materials

Overview

Students practice adding three-digit numbers by solving a problem with two unknown addends. They find different combinations of addends that result in a given sum.

Step By Step

1 Introduce the problem.

- Students set up chairs for the winter program. They set up a total of 465 chairs. They set up some chairs on one day and the rest the next day. How many chairs did they set up each day?

- Write the given information on the board: 465 chairs. Ask students to tell you what they are supposed to find out.

- Organize students into pairs and give them paper and writing/coloring tools. Set out the manipulatives so all students have access.

2 Support students as they solve the problem.

- Tell students they can work in pairs and use any models they want to solve the problem. They then record their solution on paper and tell how they know it is correct.

- You may need to discuss that this is a problem with many correct answers. Make sure students understand that they are finding two numbers whose sum is 465.

- Watch out for students who struggle to find an entry point into the problem. To break 465 in two groups, suggest a number that they might begin with, such as 200.

- As students work, circulate and make sure they understand the task and are recording their solutions.

- Once students find and record one answer, encourage them to try to find others.

3 Share solutions and solution strategies.

- When students are finished, ask them to share their solutions. Ask how they know their solution is correct. Encourage students to share the solution strategy they used. Listen for accurate mathematical language and sound reasoning. Write each solution on the board as an equation.

4 Extend the problem.

- Ask students if it is possible to set up the chairs in equal rows and columns, like an array. Let them explore the idea using models. They should notice that they can make rows of 10 using the base-ten blocks, but there will be 5 left over. Lead them to see that they could break each of the rows of 10 into rows of 5 to form an array.

Teacher Notes

👥 Introduction

At A Glance

Students complete a place-value chart for two three-digit numbers. They add the numbers by combining each place value. Then students break apart addends and use an open number line to find the sum of two three-digit numbers.

Step By Step

- Work through **Use What You Know** as a class.

- Tell students that this page will help them add three-digit numbers.

- Have students read the problem at the top of the page. Ask students what operation will help them answer the question.

- Remind students of what they learned about digits and their values in Lesson 11. The digit tells how many groups of hundreds, tens, or ones are in a number. The value of the digit depends on its place in the number.

- Guide students to understand that writing the digits of the numbers in the place-value chart helps them to focus on the value of each digit. As they answer the questions on the page, make sure they refer to the column headings of the place-value chart.

▶ **Mathematical Discourse 1**

▶ **Concept Extension**

🔄 Use What You Know

Add hundreds, tens, and ones.

There are 214 fish in the giant tank at an aquarium. There are 131 other sea animals in the tank. How many animals live in the giant tank?

a. How many hundreds, tens, and ones are in each number? Fill in the table.

	Hundreds	Tens	Ones
214	2	1	4
131	1	3	1

b. What is the total number of hundreds, tens, and ones in the chart?

_____3_____ hundreds _____4_____ tens _____5_____ ones

c. What is the value of the total number of hundreds, tens, and ones?

_____300_____ + _____40_____ + _____5_____

d. How many animals live in the giant tank?

$214 + 131 = $ _____345_____

114

▶ **Mathematical Discourse**

1 *Why does it make sense to break numbers into hundreds, tens, and ones to add?*

Students may respond that it makes it easier to see the value of each digit in order to add hundreds to hundreds, tens to tens, and ones to ones.

▶ **Concept Extension**

Evaluate a different strategy.

- Tell the students: *Stuart remembers that there are 21 tens in 214 and 13 tens in 131. He wonders if he can write, 21 tens + 13 tens + 5 ones = 34 tens and 5 ones. What should I tell him?*

- Ask students to discuss this situation in pairs and decide if Stuart's strategy will work, and explain why or why not.

- Invite students to share their ideas with the class. They should notice that within 21 tens, there are 2 groups of 100, and within 13 tens, there is one group of 100. So adding the tens is like adding the hundreds and tens. In the sum of 34 tens, there are 3 groups of 100 and 4 groups of ten.

▷▷ Find Out More

There are other ways to find the sum of 214 and 131.

Here are two ways to break apart addends.

$$
\begin{array}{rcl}
214 & \to & 200 + 10 + 4 \\
+ 131 & \to & 100 + 30 + 1 \\
\hline
345 & \leftarrow & 300 + 40 + 5
\end{array}
\qquad
\begin{array}{rcl}
214 & \to & 2 \text{ hundreds} + 1 \text{ ten} + 4 \text{ ones} \\
+ 131 & \to & 1 \text{ hundred} + 3 \text{ tens} + 1 \text{ one} \\
\hline
345 & \leftarrow & 3 \text{ hundreds} + 4 \text{ tens} + 5 \text{ ones}
\end{array}
$$

You can also show jumps on an open number line.

(open number line: 214 — jump of 100 → 314 — jump of 30 → 344 — jump of 1 → 345)

▶ Reflect **Work with a partner.**

1 Talk About It Do you always have to add hundreds, then tens, then ones? Why or why not?

Write About It _No; Possible explanation: You can add in any order._

Add ones, then tens, and then hundreds. 214 + 1 = 215; 215 + 30 = 245;

_245 + 100 = 345_

115

▶ Hands-On Activity

Use base-ten blocks to understand a number line model.

Materials: base-ten blocks

- Replicate the open number line from this page on the board.

- Distribute base-ten blocks to students.

- Tell students to place 214 blocks in front of them, showing 2 hundreds blocks, 1 tens block, and 4 ones blocks.

- Have students use the blocks to model the thinking involved in the open number line. Adding 1 hundreds block changes the hundreds, but not the tens or ones.

- Repeat, adding the tens blocks either as a group or individually. Adding tens blocks changes the number of tens, but not the number of hundreds or ones. Then add on the ones block.

▶ Mathematical Discourse

2 _How is using the open number line like counting on by hundreds, tens, and ones?_

Students should notice that when starting at 214, two hundreds have already been counted, so count on another hundred to get **3**14. There is already one ten in 314, so adding the thirty is like counting on by tens—324, 334, 3**4**4. Then count on the extra one to get 34**5**.

3 _Do you think it is easier to add in your head starting with the hundreds or starting with the ones? Why?_

Listen for students to demonstrate the flexible use of mental strategies, honoring each idea presented. As students hear the strategies of others, they will refine their own mental approach to calculations.

Step By Step

- Read **Find Out More** as a class. Refer to the place-value chart on the previous page, making the connection to the expanded form shown on this page.

- Write the vertical form of the addition problem on the board, leaving a small amount of space between each digit. Draw vertical lines to separate each place value.

- Ask students why adding the columns makes sense. They should notice that adding the digits in each column preserves place value.

- Ask students to examine the open number line. Help them to interpret it by using the Hands-On Activity.

▶ **Hands-On Activity**

▶ **Mathematical Discourse 2**

- After students discuss and answer the **Reflect** question, ask Mathematical Discourse question 3.

▶ **Mathematical Discourse 3**

Ready Mathematics
PRACTICE AND PROBLEM SOLVING

Assign _Practice and Problem Solving_ **pages 129–130** after students have completed this section.

Modeled and Guided Instruction

At A Glance

Students use a quick drawing and break apart addends to evaluate an addition problem involving regrouping in the ones place. Then students revisit this problem, regrouping a ten to add.

Step By Step

- Read the problem at the top of the page together as a class.

Picture It

- Draw attention to the quick drawing in **Picture It**, asking students to describe what they see.

Model It

- Instruct students to look at the sum in the **Model It** section. Ask the Mathematical Discourse question to help students recognize that this addition problem requires more steps than the previous addition problem.

▶ **Mathematical Discourse**

- Ask students what they might do with the 12 ones to make the sum make sense. Listen for responses that show they understand that 12 is 1 ten and 2 ones. The 1 ten needs to be grouped with the other tens.

- Ask: *How would you know, just by looking at the sum of the ones, that you need to regroup?* Help them recognize that when there is a two-digit sum, regrouping is necessary since there can only be one digit in each place-value position.

- Encourage students to show the addition problem on their whiteboards or paper using an open number line. Have volunteers show their models on the board. Discuss how when adding on the ones, another ten was composed, leaving 2 extra ones.

> **SMP TIP** Look for Structure
> Exposing students to a wide variety of models reinforces the concept of the place-value structure found in our base-ten number system. *(SMP 7)*

Learn About **Adding Hundreds, Tens, and Ones**

Read the problem. Then you will show the addends in different ways.

> There are 254 adults and 328 children helping to clean up their city. How many people are helping to clean up the city?

▶ **Picture It** You can show the numbers in a quick drawing.

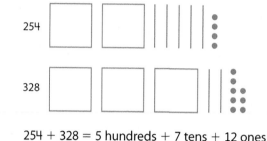

254

328

$$254 + 328 = 5 \text{ hundreds} + 7 \text{ tens} + 12 \text{ ones}$$

▶ **Model It** You can break apart addends.

$$
\begin{array}{r}
254 \\
+\ 328
\end{array}
\longrightarrow
\begin{array}{r}
200 + 50 + 4 \\
\underline{300 + 20 + 8} \\
500 + 70 + 12
\end{array}
$$

▶ **Mathematical Discourse**

Would it make sense to write the sum of 5 hundreds + 7 tens + 12 ones as (write on the board) *5712? Explain.*

Students should respond that the 5 is not in the hundreds place and the 7 is not in the tens place, so the number cannot be written this way.

▶ **Connect It** Make a ten to add.

2 Look at *Picture It*. How do you write 12 ones as tens and ones?

12 ones = ___1___ ten + ___2___ ones

3 Look at *Model It*. What is the total number of tens in 70 + 12? Explain.

8; Possible explanation: There are 7 tens in 70 and

another ten in 12. So, there are 8 tens in all.

4 How many people are helping to clean the city? Show how to find the sum.

582 people; Possible work: 500 + 70 + 12 = 500 + 82,

or 582.

▶ **Try It** Try more problems.

Find each sum. Show your work.

5
```
  526
+ 235
```
Possible answer:

500 + 20 + 6
200 + 30 + 5
700 + 50 + 11 = 761

6 167 + 426

Possible answer:

100 + 60 + 7
400 + 20 + 6
500 + 80 + 13 = 593

117

Step By Step

Connect It

- Read **Connect It** as a class. Make sure students understand that the questions refer to the problem on the previous page.

- To reinforce the regrouping process, use the Hands-On Activity before moving on to the **Try It** problems.

▶ **Hands-On Activity**

Try It

- Discuss the solutions to Problems 5 and 6 together as a class. Allow students who used different strategies to show their work on the board, describing the strategy they used to find the sum.

5 **Solution**
761; Add the hundreds, tens, and ones, then regroup the ten from the sum of the ones and add to the tens place.

Error Alert Watch for students who do not regroup the ten from the sum of the ones. Students who either wrote the sum as 7511 or 751 did not regroup.

6 **Solution**
593; Add the hundreds, tens, and ones, then regroup the ten from the sum of the ones and add to the tens place.

Ready Mathematics
PRACTICE AND PROBLEM SOLVING

Assign *Practice and Problem Solving* **pages 131–132** after students have completed this section.

▶ **Hands-On Activity**

Use base-ten blocks to understand regrouping.

Material: base-ten blocks

- Have students model the two addends with their blocks. Ask them to organize all the blocks together into groups of hundreds, tens, and ones and count each group.

- When they count the ones blocks, help them recognize that they can regroup 10 of the ones blocks into 1 tens block, making a total of 8 tens blocks.

Modeled and Guided Instruction

Learn About **Adding Three-Digit Numbers**

Read the problem. Then you will model addition in different ways.

> There are 476 rocks and 148 minerals in a museum display. What is the total number of rocks and minerals in the display?

At A Glance

Students evaluate models of a three-digit addition problem involving regrouping in the ones and tens places. Then students revisit this problem to find the sum.

Step By Step

- Read the problem at the top of the page together as a class. Ask students what operation will help them solve the problem.

▶ **Model It** **You can show each number as hundreds, tens, and ones.**

$$476 \longrightarrow 4 \text{ hundreds } + 7 \text{ tens } + 6 \text{ ones}$$
$$+ 148 \longrightarrow 1 \text{ hundred } + 4 \text{ tens } + 8 \text{ ones}$$
$$\overline{\quad\quad\quad 5 \text{ hundreds } + 11 \text{ tens } + 14 \text{ ones}}$$

Model It

- Have students evaluate **Model it** by asking what they notice about the sums of the tens and ones. They should see that there are two-digit sums in both places; therefore, the tens and ones need to be regrouped.

- Ask students to write 5 hundreds + 11 tens + 14 ones as numbers on whiteboards or paper. Help students check their work to make sure they included the correct number of zeros.

▶ **Model It** **You can add hundreds, then tens, then ones.**

$$\begin{array}{r} 476 \\ + 148 \\ \hline 500 \longrightarrow 400 + 100 \\ 110 \longrightarrow 70 + 40 \\ 14 \longrightarrow 6 + 8 \end{array}$$

$$500 + 110 + 14$$

> **SMP TIP** **Attend to Precision**
> Asking students to check their work facilitates the attention to precision and accuracy in calculation that plays a vital role in computational fluency. *(SMP 6)*

▶ **Model It** **You can add ones, then tens, then hundreds.**

$$\begin{array}{r} 476 \\ + 148 \\ \hline 14 \longrightarrow 6 + 8 \\ 110 \longrightarrow 70 + 40 \\ 500 \longrightarrow 400 + 100 \end{array}$$

$$14 + 110 + 500$$

Model It

- Draw attention to **Model It**. Have students evaluate the model by explaining each row. Help them see that 500 + 110 + 14 is the same as what they wrote on their whiteboards or paper.

▶ **Mathematical Discourse**

Look at the second Model It. Why do you think it is helpful to line up the sums in three separate rows?

The extra ten from the addition of the ones and the extra hundred from the addition of the tens can be added to the other tens and hundreds to get the sum, instead of writing 500 + 110 + 14 and then regrouping to find the sum.

Model It

- Direct attention to **Model It**. Ask students if the sum is the same or different if they add and record the ones place first. Guide students to see that the partial sums are the same, and the order in which they are added doesn't matter.

▶ **Connect It** **Make a ten and a hundred to add.**

7 Look at the first *Model It*. Write the value of the total hundreds, tens, and ones.

5 hundreds = __500__   11 tens = __110__   14 ones = __14__

8 Look at the last *Model It*. How many ones, tens, and hundreds are there? Fill in the blanks.

14 = __14__ ones   110 = __11__ tens   500 = __5__ hundreds

9 What is the same about the numbers in Problems 7 and 8? What is different?

Possible answer: They have the same number of hundreds, tens, and

ones. The hundreds, tens, and ones are shown in a different order.

10 What is the total number of rocks and minerals in the display? Show your work.

Possible work: 500 + 110 + 14
500 + 100 = 600
10 + 10 = 20
0 + 4 = 4
600 + 20 + 4 = 624

There are 624 rocks and minerals.

▶ **Try It** **Try another problem.**

11 What is 649 + 184? Show your work.

Possible work: 600 + 40 + 9
                100 + 80 + 4
                700 + 120 + 13 = 833

833

119

Step By Step

Connect It

- Read **Connect It** as a class. Make sure students understand that the questions refer to the problem on the previous page.

- For Problem 9, make sure students recognize that there are multiple ways to think about or write numbers. Have students think of other ways to write the sums and record them on the board.

- If no ideas are generated, write: 500 + 100 + 10 + 10 + 4 and ask how this could represent the sums. Help students see that you broke apart the 110 and the 14 to clearly see the hundred and ten that need to be regrouped.

Try It

- After students complete the **Try It** section, ask them to share their calculations on the board. Try to have as many different strategies displayed as possible. This validates students' strategies and allows all students to see that there are many ways to calculate, all resulting in the same sum.

SMP TIP Construct Arguments
Have students compare the strategies used to calculate the sum. Discuss the similar elements and differences of each one and ask students to justify their computational approaches. *(SMP 3)*

11 **Solution**
833; Add the hundreds, tens, and ones, then regroup a hundred and a ten.

Ready **Mathematics**
PRACTICE AND PROBLEM SOLVING

Assign *Practice and Problem Solving* **pages 133–134** after students have completed this section.

Guided Practice

At A Glance

Students solve word problems involving the addition of two three-digit numbers.

Step By Step

- Ask students to solve the problems individually and show all their work. Review the example problem together, telling students that using a visual or number model can help them think about breaking apart numbers to add. Make sure they know they can use whatever strategy is most meaningful to them.

- **Pair/Share** When students have completed each problem, have them Pair/Share to discuss their solutions with a partner.

Solutions

Example An open number line is used to interpret the problem by adding on 146 to 158 to arrive at 304.

12 Solution
515 tickets; $400 + 100 + 15 = 515$.
DOK 1

Practice ▶ Adding Three-Digit Numbers

Study the model below. Then solve Problems 12–14.

Example

There are 146 firefighters and 158 police officers marching in a parade. What is the total number of firefighters and police officers marching in the parade?

You can show your work on an open number line.

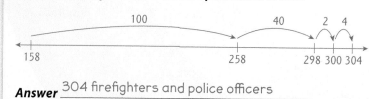

Answer 304 firefighters and police officers

---

12 A basketball team sells 379 tickets before game day. Another 136 people buy tickets at the door. How many tickets does the team sell in all?

Show your work.

Possible work:
```
  379
+ 136
  400
  100
   15
  515
```

How many hundreds, tens, and ones does each number have?

Answer The team sells 515 tickets.

120

Teacher Notes

13 Ms. Stone's students work in the school garden. They plant 267 beet plants and 278 onion plants. What is the total number of plants?

Remember, you can add in any order.

Show your work.

Possible work:

$$267 = 200 + 60 + 7$$
$$278 = 200 + 70 + 8$$
$$400 + 130 + 15 = 545$$

Answer There are 545 plants.

14 There is a box of foam shapes in the art room. It has 356 squares and 304 circles. Which addition problem shows how many foam shapes there are in all?

What does the 0 mean in 304?

A $600 + 5 + 10$

(B) $600 + 50 + 10$

C $600 + 90 + 6$

D $300 + 50 + 6$

Dean chose **A** as the answer. This answer is wrong. How did Dean get his answer?

Possible answer: He thought the 5 in 356 means 5 ones. It means 5 tens.

121

Solutions

13 **Solution**
545 plants; $400 + 130 + 15 = 545$.
DOK 1

14 **Solution**
B; $300 + 300 = 600$, $50 + 0 = 50$, $6 + 4 = 10$.
DOK 3

Explain to students why the other two choices are not correct.

C is not correct because the numbers in the tens and ones places were miscalculated.

D is not correct because the numbers in the hundreds and ones places were miscalculated.

Ready **Mathematics** PRACTICE AND PROBLEM SOLVING

Assign *Practice and Problem Solving* **pages 135–136** after students have completed this section.

Teacher Notes

Independent Practice

At A Glance

Students solve three-digit addition problems that might appear on a mathematics test.

Solutions

1 **Solution**
A 300 + 60 + 3 = 363; **C** 200 + 100 + 60 + 3 = 363; **D** 3 + 60 + 300 = 363.
DOK 1

2 **Solution**
C; 500 + 200 = 700, 70 + 20 = 90, 1 + 8 = 9.
DOK 2

3 **Solution**
690; Break apart 563 and 127 into hundreds, tens, and ones, then add to find the sum.
DOK 2

Practice Adding Three-Digit Numbers

Solve the problems.

1 How can you show 203 + 160?
Circle all the correct answers.

(A) 300 + 60 + 3

B 300 + 90

(C) 200 + 100 + 60 + 3

(D) 3 + 60 + 300

2 Jane writes 700 + 90 + 9 to add two three-digit numbers. What two numbers could she be adding? Circle the correct answer.

A 354 + 455

B 396 + 313

(C) 521 + 278

D 590 + 290

3 Find 563 + 127. Fill in the chart. Then complete the equation.

Hundreds	Tens	Ones
5	6	3
1	2	7

___6___ hundreds + ___8___ tens + ___10___ ones = ___690___

Quick Check and Remediation

- There were 278 people at the art fair on the first day and 364 people the second day. How many people went to the two-day art fair? [278 + 364 = 500 + 130 + 12 = 642 people]

- For students who are still struggling, use the chart to guide remediation.

- After providing remediation, check students' understanding using the following problem: In Park City, the nature club planted 158 trees for Arbor Day. The garden club planted 65 trees. How many trees did they plant in all? [158 + 65 = 100 + 110 + 13 = 223 trees]

If the error is . . .	Students may . . .	To remediate . . .
532	not have regrouped the hundred and the ten.	Provide the student with base-ten blocks to model the problem. The student records the number of hundreds, tens, and ones in the sum. Lead the student to notice that 10 tens blocks can be regrouped into 1 hundreds block, and 10 ones blocks can be regrouped into 1 tens block.
632	have regrouped the hundred but not the ten.	Check the student's partial sums to make sure the addition was completed accurately. If so, ask the student what was done with the extra ten found in the ones place. Lead the student to recognize the error by writing the partial sums vertically.
other answers	have miscalculated.	Have the student check for accuracy by solving the problem using an addition strategy other than the one originally employed.

4　Write the missing numbers on the open number line. Then write the addition equation that the number line shows.

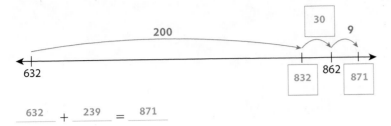

632　+　239　=　871

Use the information in the box for Problems 5 and 6.

5　Carmen has 172 photos of her family. She also has 153 photos of friends. Which photo album will hold all of her pictures?

Show your work.

> **Choose an album!**
>
> Album A holds 225 photos.
>
> Album B holds 275 photos.
>
> Album C holds 375 photos.

Possible work: 172 + 153 = 200 + 120 + 5, or 325

Carmen could put all of her photos in album C.

6　Write your own problem about the photo albums in Problem 5. Have a partner solve your problem.

Possible problem and solution: Hal has Albums A and C. How many photos

can the albums hold in all? 225 + 375 = ?; 200 + 300 = 500; 20 + 70 = 90;

5 + 5 = 10; 500 + 90 + 10 = 600. Albums A and C can hold 600 photos.

✓ Self Check　**Now you can add three-digit numbers. Fill this in on the progress chart on page 59.**

123

Solutions

4　**Solution**
632 + 239 = 871; Jump +200 to 832, then +30 to 862, and finally +9 to 871.
DOK 2

5　**Solution**
Album C; 172 + 153 = 200 + 120 + 5 = 325. Carmen needs an album that holds at least 325 pictures.
DOK 2

6　**Solution**
Answers will vary.
DOK 3

▶ Hands-On Activity

Play a target number game.

Materials: For each pair: 3 number cubes, 5–10 number cards from Activity Sheet 7 (Three-Digit Cards), and a whiteboard

- Organize students into pairs and distribute the materials.
- Students turn up one of the number cards. This is the target number. The first player rolls the number cubes, arranges the digits to form a three-digit number, and records it on the whiteboard.
- The second player rolls the number cubes and tries to make a three-digit number that, when added to the first number, has a sum that is close to but does not go over the target number.
- If the student is successful, 1 point is awarded.
- The first player rolls 3 number cubes and tries to make a number, that when added to the number on the whiteboard, has a total even closer to the target. If successful, this player gets 2 points.
- Students switch turns and the game continues until the number cards have all been used.

▶ Challenge Activity

Can you switch the tens?

- Show students the following sum:
360 + 230 = 330 + 260. Make sure they notice that the groups of tens have been switched around, being paired with a different hundred.
- Challenge students to determine if switching the tens in this way will always work, even when there are digits other than zero in the ones places.
- Require students to justify whether switching the tens does or does not always work, using at least 10 examples.
- If they find that it does always work, have them explain, using visual models and/or blocks to justify their solutions.
- If students find that it does not always work, they should provide examples and tell when it will and when it will not work.

Teacher-Toolbox.com

Overview

Assign the Lesson 13 Quiz and have students work independently to complete it.

Use the results of the quiz to assess students' understanding of the content of the lesson and to identify areas for reteaching. See the Lesson Pacing Guide at the beginning of the lesson for suggested instructional resources.

Tested Skills

Assesses 2.NBT.B.7, 2.NBT.B.8, 2.NBT.B.9

Problems on this assessment form require students to be able to decompose three-digit numbers into hundreds, tens, and ones, determine when regrouping is necessary and carry out the regrouping to find the sum, and mentally add 10 or 100 to a given three-digit number. Students will also need to be familiar with place-value charts, the word *sum*, and writing an addition expression to solve a word problem.

Ready® **Mathematics**

Lesson 13 **Quiz**

Solve the problems.

1 Which addition problems in the box have a sum of 593? Which have a sum of 503?

493 + 100	100 + 403	493 + 10	583 + 10	10 + 393

Write the addition problem in the correct column. Not all problems will be used.

Sum of 593	Sum of 503

2 Ethan works at the library. He has 184 picture books and 152 soft-cover books to put away. How many books does Ethan have to put away in all?

Complete the chart. Then write the sum.

	Hundreds	Tens	Ones
Picture books	1		
Soft-cover books			2

Answer: Ethan has to put away _____ books.

Lesson 13 **Quiz** continued

3 Maria has 584 students at her school. Noah has 364 students at his school. Noah wants to find out how many students are at both schools together.

Part A

Noah breaks apart each addend to add. Fill in the blanks to show how he breaks apart the numbers.

584 = _____ hundreds + _____ tens + _____ ones

364 = _____ hundreds + _____ tens + _____ ones

Part B

How many students are at both schools together? Circle the correct answer.

A 828   **C** 948

B 848   **D** 968

4 Cora has 150 buttons. Her friend Emily has 265 buttons. They want to know how many buttons they have together.

Cora adds 300 + 110 + 5 to get 415 buttons.

Emily adds 300 + 11 + 5 to get 316 buttons.

Which friend is correct? Explain your answer.

_____

_____

_____

_____

Common Misconceptions and Errors

Errors may result if students:

• forget to regroup 10 tens as a hundred or 10 ones as a ten.

• regroup but also include an additional, unnecessary ten or hundred.

• misidentify which digit of an addend represents hundreds, tens, or ones.

Ready® Mathematics

Lesson 13 Quiz Answer Key

1.

Sum of 593	Sum of 503
493 + 100	100 + 403
583 + 10	493 + 10

DOK 1

2. Picture books: 8, 4
   Soft-cover books: 1, 5
   336
   DOK 2

3. *Part A:*
   5, 8, 4
   3, 6, 4
   DOK 1

   Part B:
   C
   DOK 2

4. Cora is correct. Possible explanation: To add the tens, add 6 tens + 5 tens to get 11 tens or
   110 as Cora did, and not 11 as Emily did. They have 415 buttons together.
   DOK 3

Lesson 14
Subtract Three-Digit Numbers

CCSS Focus

Domain
Number and Operations in Base Ten

Cluster
B. Use place value understanding and properties of operations to add and subtract.

Standards
2.NBT.B.7 Add and subtract within 1000, using concrete models or drawings and strategies based on place value, properties of operations, and/or the relationship between addition and subtraction; relate the strategy to a written method. Understand that in adding or subtracting three-digit numbers, one adds or subtracts hundreds and hundreds, tens and tens, ones and ones; and sometimes it is necessary to compose or decompose tens or hundreds.
2.NBT.B.9 Explain why addition and subtraction strategies work, using place value and the properties of operations.

Additional Standards
2.NBT.A.1 (see page B3 for full text)

Standards for Mathematical Practice (SMP)
1 Make sense of problems and persevere in solving them.
2 Reason abstractly and quantitatively.
3 Construct viable arguments and critique the reasoning of others.
4 Model with mathematics.
6 Attend to precision.
7 Look for and make use of structure.

Lesson Objectives

Content Objectives
• Determine when regrouping a ten and/or a hundred is necessary to subtract, and carry out the regrouping to find the difference.
• Recognize that in subtracting, hundreds are subtracted from hundreds, tens from tens, and ones from ones.
• Explore subtraction as a process of taking away or adding up.

Language Objectives
• Write two numbers in a place-value chart to find their difference.
• Write two numbers in expanded notation to find their difference.
• Record the steps for adding up to subtract on an open number line.
• Compare two approaches to subtraction to describe how they are alike and different.

Prerequisite Skills

• Identify place value in three-digit numbers.
• Model three-digit numbers.
• Perform two-digit subtraction with and without regrouping.

Lesson Vocabulary

There is no new vocabulary. Review the following key terms.

• **regroup** to compose or decompose ones, tens, or hundreds. For example, 10 ones can be regrouped as 1 ten, or 1 hundred can be regrouped as 10 tens.

• **difference** the result of subtraction.

Learning Progression

In Grade 1 students explore the concept of two-digit subtraction using physical models and drawings. They subtract multiples of 10, applying strategies based on place value and the relationship between addition and subtraction.

In Grade 2 students subtract two- and three-digit numbers with and without regrouping. They use varied models to represent subtraction and connect models and strategies to a written expression.

In this lesson students subtract three-digit numbers with and without regrouping a hundred and/or a ten. They analyze subtraction problems to determine when a ten or hundred needs to be decomposed before subtracting. Students interpret picture models, number models, and an open number line to understand subtraction of multi-digit numbers.

In Grade 3 students gain fluency with subtraction of numbers within 1,000. They rely less on concrete models and pictures, focusing on the numerical representation in preparation for learning standard algorithms in the following year.

Lesson Pacing Guide

Whole Class Instruction

Day 1 *45–60 minutes*	**Toolbox: Interactive Tutorial*** *Subtracting Three-Digit Numbers* **Introduction** • Opening Activity *20 min* • Use What You Know *10 min* • Find Out More *10 min* • Reflect *5 min*	**Practice and Problem Solving** Assign pages 139–140.
Day 2 *45–60 minutes*	**Modeled and Guided Instruction** **Learn About Subtracting Hundreds, Tens, and Ones** • Picture It/Model It *15 min* • Connect It *15 min* • Try It *15 min*	**Practice and Problem Solving** Assign pages 141–142.
Day 3 *45–60 minutes*	**Modeled and Guided Instruction** **Learn About Regrouping to Subtract** • Picture It/Model It *15 min* • Connect It *15 min* • Try It *15 min*	**Practice and Problem Solving** Assign pages 143–144.
Day 4 *45–60 minutes*	**Guided Practice** **Practice Subtracting Three-Digit Numbers** • Example *5 min* • Problems 12–14 *15 min* • Pair/Share *15 min* • Solutions *10 min*	**Practice and Problem Solving** Assign pages 145–146.
Day 5 *45–60 minutes*	**Independent Practice** **Practice Subtracting Three-Digit Numbers** • Problems 1–6 *20 min* • Quick Check and Remediation *10 min* • Hands-On or Challenge Activity *15 min* **Toolbox: Lesson Quiz** Lesson 14 Quiz	

Small Group Differentiation

Teacher-Toolbox.com

Reteach
Ready Prerequisite Lessons *45–90 min*

Grade 1
• Lesson 25 Add and Regroup

Teacher-led Activities
Tools for Instruction *15–20 min*

Grade 1 *(Lesson 25)*
• Two-Digit Addition without Regrouping
Grade 2 *(Lesson 14)*
• Three-Digit Subtraction

Student-led Activities
Math Center Activities *30–40 min*

Grade 2 *(Lesson 14)*
• 2.26 Subtract 10 or 100 from a Number
• 2.24 Subtract Three-Digit Numbers
• 2.28 Use Subtraction Strategies to Solve

Personalized Learning

i-Ready.com

Independent
i-Ready Lessons* *10–20 min*

Grade 1 *(Lesson 25)*
• Adding a Two-Digit Number and a One-Digit Number

*We continually update the Interactive Tutorials. Check the Teacher Toolbox for the most up-to-date offerings for this lesson.

Explore Three-Digit Subtraction

Objective Solve a subtraction problem using any form of representation.

Time *20–30 minutes*

Materials for each student
- paper and crayons or colored pencils
- manipulative materials

Overview

Students are challenged to solve a subtraction problem by interpreting the problem, representing it in a way that is meaningful to them, and finding a solution. Solutions and solution strategies are shared and analyzed by the class.

Step By Step

1 Introduce the problem.

- Pablo's family takes a trip to his grandma's house. Pablo's grandmother lives 213 miles away. They drive 127 miles and stop for lunch. How much farther do they have to drive to get to his grandma's house?

- Tell students they can use any representation: a picture, a drawing (such as a map or diagram), or manipulatives. They should show their thinking clearly on paper and find a solution.

- Give students ample time to complete the task and allow them to work in pairs, if they choose.

2 Support students as they solve the problem.

- Circulate the room as students work, making sure they understand the problem. Help them find a meaningful representation and reasonable solution strategy, if necessary. Ask questions like: *What kind of drawing or model would make sense to use to show how far they drove? What part of the drive do you need to find out about? What might you do to find out?*

3 **Share solutions and solution strategies.**

- Have students or student pairs take turns sharing their strategy and showing the representation they used.

- Ask: *Why did you choose this way to show the problem? What strategy did you use to solve the problem?*

- As students share solutions, guide them in using mathematical vocabulary and clearly articulating the strategy they employed.

4 **Critique the work of others.**

- Invite the class to ask questions of each other, seek clarification, and acknowledge the work of their peers. Highlight innovative strategies or representations as an encouragement for all students to attempt diverse ways of thinking.

Teacher Notes

👥 Introduction

At A Glance

Students model a take-away strategy for finding the difference between two three-digit numbers. Then students explore regrouping tens as a strategy.

Step By Step

- Work through **Use What You Know** as a class.
- Tell students that this page will help them understand subtracting three-digit numbers.
- Have students read the problem at the top of the page.
- Make sure students understand that they are crossing out the number of cards Dora has. Discuss how hundreds are subtracted from hundreds, tens from tens, and ones from ones.

▶ **Mathematical Discourse 1**

- Complete the remainder of the problems. Use the Visual Model activity to reinforce the concept of subtraction as finding the difference between two numbers.

▶ **Visual Model**

⟳ Use What You Know

Use base-ten blocks to subtract.

Holly has 368 pet pal cards. Dora has 243 cards. How many more cards does Holly have than Dora?

a. How many cards does Dora have? Write the number as hundreds, tens, and ones.

____2____ hundreds ____4____ tens ____3____ ones

b. The model shows Holly's cards. Cross out hundreds, tens, and ones to subtract Dora's cards.

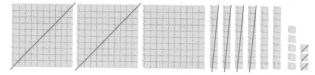

c. What blocks are left?

____1____ hundred ____2____ tens ____5____ ones

d. What do the blocks that are left show?

They show how many more cards Holly has.

e. How many more cards does Holly have? ___125___

124

▶ **Mathematical Discourse**

1 *Why do you subtract to find how many more?*

Students may respond that when you take away the number of cards Dora has, what is left is the number of cards that Holly has that Dora does not.

▶ **Visual Model**

Use a bar graph to model the concept of the difference between two numbers.

- On the board, draw this graph without the horizontal line at 243.

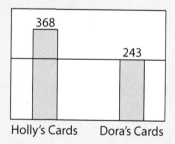

Holly's Cards   Dora's Cards

- Discuss how to use the graph to show how many more cards Holly has. Draw a line as shown. Point out that the portion above the line shows how many more cards Holly has than Dora. Cover the portion that is equal and tell students that when you subtract the amount that is equal, what's left is the difference.

▷▷ Find Out More

Sometimes you have to regroup three-digit numbers to subtract.

There are enough hundreds, tens, and ones to subtract 368 − 243 without regrouping.

100s	10s	1s
3	6	8
2	4	3

$3 > 2$ $6 > 4$ $8 > 3$

There are not enough ones in 368 to subtract 249 without regrouping.

100s	10s	1s
3	6	8
2	4	9

$3 > 2$ $6 > 4$ $\boxed{8 < 9}$

> You need more ones to subtract 9.

Regroup a ten in 368 to get 10 more ones.

100s	10s	1s
3	~~6~~5	18
− 2	4	9
1	1	9

> Think:
> $300 + 60 + 8 = 300 + 50 + 18$

The difference is 1 hundred, 1 ten, 9 ones, or 119.

▶ Reflect   Work with a partner.

1 **Talk About It** Are there enough ones in 465 to subtract 328? What do you need to do?

Write About It There are not enough ones. Possible answer: Regroup

a ten in 465 to make 10 more ones. Then subtract 15 ones − 8 ones to get

7 ones. 465 − 328 = 137.

125

▶ English Language Learners

The term *regroup* may not be familiar to ELL students. In some cultures the terms *compose* and *decompose* are used. Explain that regrouping can mean putting blocks together to make a larger block or breaking a block into smaller parts.

▶ Mathematical Discourse

2 *Would it make sense to subtract the 8 from the 9? Why? or why not?*

Students should respond no. The problem instructs them to take 9 from 8. Subtraction is not commutative.

3 *What would happen if you forgot to cross out the 6 and write 5 to show a ten was decomposed?*

You would have too many tens in the answer. It would be like adding a ten to Holly's cards.

Step By Step

- Read **Find Out More** as a class. Refer to the models on the previous page, reminding students that there were enough blocks in each group to cross out ones, tens, and hundreds.

- Read the inequalities shown with the class. Make sure students understand they are comparing digits that are in the same place-value position. Discuss that the purpose of comparing is to determine whether there are enough hundreds, tens, or ones to subtract.

- Ask: *If Dora had 249 cards, could you cross out 9 ones on the model shown on the previous page?* [No. There would not be enough.] *How could you get enough ones to cross out?* [Trade 1 tens block for 10 ones blocks.]

▶ **Mathematical Discourse 2**

- Direct students' attention to the number model showing the regrouping. Ask why a 5 and 18 are shown in the tens and ones places. Discuss how when adding, 10 ones can be regrouped, or composed, into 1 tens block. To regroup when subtracting, we can break apart, or decompose, 1 ten into 10 ones.

▶ **Mathematical Discourse 3**

▶ **English Language Learners**

- After students discuss and answer the **Reflect** question, have them share their answers with the class.

> **SMP TIP Attend to Precision**
> Ask students to help you calculate 368 − 239. Write the calculation on the board. Ask them what the calculation would be if you forgot to record the regrouped ten. Ask if the answer makes sense and have students explain their thinking. *(SMP 6)*

Ready Mathematics
PRACTICE AND PROBLEM SOLVING

Assign *Practice and Problem Solving* **pages 139–140** after students have completed this section.

Modeled and Guided Instruction

At A Glance

Students examine a picture of base-ten blocks that shows subtraction with regrouping, as well as a model that shows the subtraction of hundreds, tens, and ones. Then students revisit this problem, regrouping a ten to subtract.

Step By Step

- Read the problem at the top of the page together as a class.

Picture It

- Draw attention to the model shown in **Picture It**. Have students describe what they see and help them interpret the model. Make sure they interpret the ones blocks as the decomposed (regrouped) ten. Ask: *Does this show taking a ten away from 5 tens?* [No. It shows taking a ten away from 4 tens. One ten was broken apart into ones to take away 8 ones.]

▶ **Hands-On Activity**

Model It

- Instruct students to look at and interpret the subtraction in the **Model It** section. Ask the Mathematical Discourse questions to reinforce mental strategies.

▶ **Mathematical Discourse 1 and 2**

Learn About ▶ **Subtracting Hundreds, Tens, and Ones**

Read the problem. Then you will show subtraction in different ways.

There are 450 campers at Camp Cody. One day, 218 campers did art projects. The rest did sports. How many campers did sports that day?

▶ **Picture It** You can subtract using base-ten blocks.

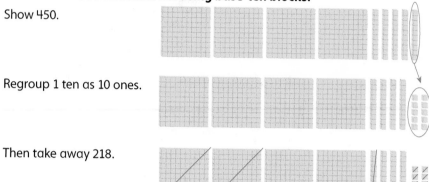

Show 450.

Regroup 1 ten as 10 ones.

Then take away 218.

▶ **Model It** You can subtract hundreds, tens, and ones.

Think: 218 = **200 + 10 + 8**

$$
\begin{array}{r}
450 \\
-\ 200 \\
\hline
250 \\
-\ 10 \\
\hline
240 \\
-\ 8 \\
\hline
? \\
\end{array}
$$

126

▶ **Mathematical Discourse**

1 *How might the Model It strategy help you subtract in your head?*

It is easy to count back hundreds and count back tens. Then just subtract the extra ones.

2 *How can you subtract 8 from 240 in your head?*

Some students may say they need to regroup a ten because there aren't enough ones. Others may recognize that 8 fewer than 40 is 32, so 8 fewer than 240 is 232.

▶ **Hands-On Activity**

Use base-ten blocks to model subtraction.

Materials: base-ten blocks and Activity Sheet 6 (Place-Value Mat)

- Have students use base-ten blocks to show 450 on the place-value mat.

- Ask: *What do you need to think about when subtracting 218?* [You need to figure out if there needs to be regrouping.] *Why does the picture in the book show a ten being regrouped?* [There aren't enough ones to take 8 from.] *Where can you find some ones?* [from the tens place]

- Have students use their blocks to demonstrate the regrouping. Ask: *Can you subtract now? Why?* [Yes, there are enough ones now to subtract.]

- Allow students to model the subtraction shown in the book with their base-ten blocks.

▶ **Connect It** **Find the difference.**

2 Look at *Picture It.* Why do you need to trade 1 ten for 10 ones?

0 ones < 8 ones, so you need to regroup to be able to

subtract.

3 Fill in the boxes to find 450 − 218.

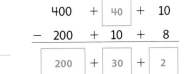

$$
\begin{array}{r}
400 + \boxed{40} + 10 \\
-\ \ 200 + 10 + 8 \\
\hline
\boxed{200} + \boxed{30} + \boxed{2}
\end{array}
$$

4 How many campers did sports? ___232___

5 **Talk About It** Look at *Model It.* How is the way the problem is solved like the way shown in *Picture It*? How is it different?

Write About It Possible answer: In both, you start

with 450. Then you subtract the hundreds, then the tens,

and then ones. In the way shown in Model It, you do not

need to regroup.

▶ **Try It** **Try another problem.**

6 Jim has 572 stamps. Leo has 347 stamps. How many more stamps does Jim have than Leo? Show your work.

Jim has 225 more stamps. Possible work:

572 − 300 = 272; 272 − 40 = 232; 232 − 7 = 225

127

Step By Step

Connect It

• Read **Connect It** as a class. Make sure students understand that the questions refer to the problem on the previous page.

• Discuss how the partial sums shown in Problem 3 are a recording of what was done when the regrouping was shown with base-ten blocks on the previous page.

Try It

• As students complete **Try It**, remind them that they can use either of the strategies they learned on the previous page or one of their own. Tell them to be sure and include an equation or recording of their work to show how they subtracted.

• Discuss students' answers to Problem 6. Encourage students to share their strategies. Some may choose to regroup while others may use subtraction of hundreds, tens, and then ones. If one of these is not employed, ask a volunteer to come to the board and show how it could be used to solve the subtraction problem.

SMP TIP Attend to Precision
As students explain their thinking, guide them to use accurate vocabulary and clear explanations. Help them evaluate their solutions to ensure that they make sense in the context of the problem. *(SMP 6)*

6 **Solution**
225; Either regroup a ten or subtract hundreds, tens, and then ones.

Error Alert Students who wrote 235 subtracted the 2 from the 7 rather than regrouping.

Ready· Mathematics
PRACTICE AND PROBLEM SOLVING

Assign *Practice and Problem Solving* **pages 141–142** after students have completed this section.

Modeled and Guided Instruction

At A Glance

Students evaluate two different models of a three-digit subtraction problem. Then students revisit this problem, regrouping a ten and a hundred to subtract.

Step By Step

- Read the problem at the top of the page together as a class.

> **SMP TIP Reason Quantitatively**
> Have students restate the problem, making sure they understand the context of the problem, what they need to find, and what number to subtract. (SMP 2)

Picture It

- Have students evaluate the model in **Picture It**. Ask how this model is different from the previous model showing base-ten blocks. They should notice that in this model, both a ten and a hundred have been regrouped.

▶ **Mathematical Discourse**

- Reinforce the concept of regrouping by having students add the value of each addend in the regrouped "Think" numbers to see that they still represent 305.

Model It

- Draw attention to the **Model It** section. Put the addition back into the context of the problem to help students make sense of the correlation.

- Ask: *If you add how many more girls there are than boys to the number of boys, what number should you get? Why?* [You should get 305, the number of girls since there are more girls than boys.]

- Have students describe what is happening in the open number line. Make sure they understand the counting up strategy that is used.

Learn About ▶ Regrouping to Subtract

Read the problem. Then you will model subtraction.

> At Brown School, there are 305 girls and 276 boys. How many more girls are there than boys?

▶ **Picture It You can use base-ten blocks to regroup.**

$305 = 300 + 5$

$305 = 200 + 100 + 5$

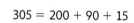

$305 = 200 + 90 + 15$

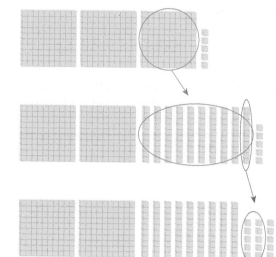

▶ **Model It You can use an open number line.**

Think of subtraction as addition: $276 + ? = 305$.

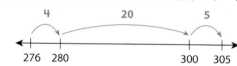

276 280   300 305

128

▶ **Mathematical Discourse**

How is subtracting three-digit numbers like subtracting two-digit numbers? How is it different?

Students should recognize that in both cases, they subtract tens from tens and ones from ones and they need to decide if a ten needs to be regrouped.

When subtracting three-digit numbers, they need to subtract hundreds from hundreds and may need to regroup a hundred.

▶ Connect It Subtract two different ways.

7 Compare the digits in each place in 305 and 276.
Write < or > in each box.

3 hundreds + 0 tens + 5 ones
2 hundreds + 7 tens + 6 ones

3 [>] 2   0 [<] 7   5 [<] 6

8 How can you tell from your answer to Problem 7
that you need to regroup two times?

You need more tens and more ones because 0 < 7

and 5 < 6.

9 How many hundreds, tens, and ones are
there after you regroup? Fill in the chart.
Then subtract.

100s	10s	1s
2	9	15
− 2	7	6
0	2	9

10 How many more girls are there
than boys? _____ 29

▶ Try It Try another problem.

11 At Taylor School, students go to school for 180 days.
They have already been in school for 136 days. How
many school days are left? Show your work.

44 days. Possible work: 136 + 4 = 140; 140 + 40 = 180;

40 + 4 = 44

129

Step By Step

Connect It

- Read **Connect It** as a class. Make sure students understand that the questions refer to the problem on the previous page.

- Connect Problem 9 to the model of base-ten blocks on the previous page. The number students record in each place-value position represents the regrouped number.

Try It

- For the **Try It** problem, encourage students to attempt a solution strategy that they have not yet tried independently.

- After students complete the **Try It** section, ask them to share their calculations on the board.

> **SMP TIP Construct Arguments**
> Have students compare the strategies used to calculate. Discuss the similar elements and differences of each one and ask students to justify their computational approaches. (SMP 3)

11 **Solution**
44 days; Students may subtract by regrouping a ten or use the counting up strategy demonstrated in the number line model.

Ready· Mathematics
PRACTICE AND PROBLEM SOLVING

Assign *Practice and Problem Solving*
pages 143–144 after students have
completed this section.

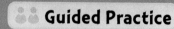 Guided Practice

At A Glance

Students solve word problems involving the subtraction of three-digit numbers.

Step By Step

- Ask students to solve the problems individually and show all their work. Review the example problem together, discussing how the number line shows the subtraction problem as an addition problem.

- Draw attention to the Study Buddies on each page. Tell students that the buddies help them think of a strategy to use. Encourage students to attempt a variety of strategies in solving the problems.

- **Pair/Share** When students have completed each problem, have them Pair/Share to discuss their solutions with a partner.

Solutions

Example An open number line is used to interpret the problem by adding $142 + ? = 725$.

12 Solution

147 pennies; $872 - 700 = 172$; $172 - 20 = 152$; $152 - 5 = 147$.

DOK 1

Practice **Subtracting Three-Digit Numbers**

Study the model below. Then solve Problems 12–14.

Example

Carla had 725 roses. She used some to make a float for a parade. Now she has 142 roses. How many roses did she use for the float?

You can show your work on a number line.

$725 - 142$ is the same as $142 + ? = 725$

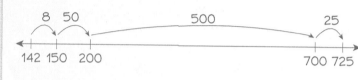

$8 + 50 + 500 + 25 = 583$

Answer Carla used 583 roses.

---

12 Gus had 872 pennies. He gave 725 pennies to the pet shelter. How many pennies does Gus have left?

Show your work.

Possible work:

$$
\begin{array}{r}
872 \\
-700 \\
\hline
172 \\
-20 \\
\hline
152 \\
-5 \\
\hline
147
\end{array}
$$

Do you need to regroup? If so, how?

Answer Gus has 147 pennies left.

Teacher Notes

13 Students need to paint 500 pumpkins for the fair. They have painted 193 so far. How many pumpkins are left to paint?

Show your work.

Possible work:

How could you add up to find the answer?

$300 + 7 = 307$

Answer There are 307 pumpkins left to paint.

14 Ms. Diaz had 185 stickers. She gave some away. Now she has 139 stickers. How many stickers did Ms. Diaz give away?

(A) 46

B 54

C 56

D 146

You can add or subtract to find the answer.

Ria chose **D** as the answer. This answer is wrong. How did Ria get her answer?

Possible answer: She did not subtract the hundreds.

131

Solutions

13 **Solution**

307 pumpkins; $193 + 300 = 493$; $493 + 7 = 500$; $300 + 7 = 307$.

DOK 2

14 **Solution**

A; $185 - 139 = 46$.

Explain to students why the other choices are not correct.

B is not correct because $139 + 54 = 193$; $193 \neq 185$. $5 - 9 \neq 9 - 5$.

C is not correct because the number of tens should be 4, not 5.

DOK 3

Ready Mathematics
PRACTICE AND PROBLEM SOLVING

Assign *Practice and Problem Solving* **pages 145–146** after students have completed this section.

Teacher Notes

Independent Practice

At A Glance

Students solve three-digit subtraction problems that might appear on a mathematics test.

Solutions

1 **Solution**
a. **Yes, Yes**; b. **No, Yes**; c. **No, No**;
d. **Yes, No**
DOK 2

2 **Solution**
191; hundreds place should read 7 − 6.
DOK 1

3 **Solution**
A; 215 − 132 = 83.
DOK 2

Practice ▶ Subtracting Three-Digit Numbers

Solve the problems.

1 For each subtraction problem, tell if you need to regroup tens to get more ones. Then tell if you need to regroup hundreds. Circle *Yes* or *No* for Tens and for Hundreds for each problem.

		Tens	Hundreds
a.	932 − 845	(Yes) No	(Yes) No
b.	673 − 581	Yes (No)	(Yes) No
c.	392 − 270	Yes (No)	Yes (No)
d.	557 − 148	(Yes) No	Yes (No)

2 Fill in the blanks to find 826 − 635.

100s	10s	1s
7	12	6
− 6	3	5
1	9	1

3 Kali had some shells. She found 132 more. Now she has 215 shells. How many shells did she have to begin with? Circle the correct answer.

(A) 83   **C** 223

B 123   **D** 347

Quick Check and Remediation

- Cody wants to buy a bike that costs 250 dollars. He has saved 169 dollars. How many more dollars does he need to save to be able to buy the bike? [81 dollars]

- For students who are still struggling, use the chart to guide remediation.

- After providing remediation, check students' understanding using the following problem: Students at the Park City School are collecting cans for a food drive. They would like to collect 575 cans. So far, they have collected 237 cans. How many more cans do they need to collect to reach their goal? [575 − 237 = 338]

If the error is . . .	Students may . . .	To remediate . . .
119	have subtracted 0 from 9 and 50 from 60 rather than regrouping.	Provide students with base-ten blocks to model the problem. When trying to remove 9 blocks, the students should notice there are no ones to take away. Demonstrate how regrouping in an equation is a recording of what was done with the blocks.
91	have regrouped a ten but failed to record one less ten in the tens place.	Ask students to review their work to see if it makes sense. Point out the tens place and ask what the error is with that calculation. Guide students to self-correct.
other answers	have miscalculated.	Have students check their answers using addition. After they recognize an error was made, have them check their work to find the error. You may need to point out where the error was made, but allow each student to identify it.

4 Add up to find the difference. Fill in the blanks.

524 − 395 = ?

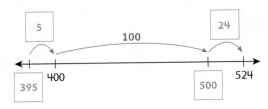

524 − 395 = __129__

5 Any class that earns 750 reading points gets a pizza party. Which class has more points? How many more points?

Class	Reading Points
A	585
B	612

Show your work.

Possible work:

585 + 5 = 590; 590 + 10 = 600;
600 + 12 = 612; 5 + 10 + 12 = 27

Class B has 27 more points than Class A.

6 Look at Problem 5. Ben says Class B needs 148 more points to get a pizza party. Is Ben correct? Explain.

Ben is not correct. Possible answer: A class needs 750 points in all to get a

pizza party. Class B has 612 points. Add up: 612 + 8 = 620, 620 + 80 = 700,

and 700 + 50 = 750. Class B needs 8 + 80 + 50, or 138 more points.

✓ **Self Check** Now you can subtract three-digit numbers. Fill this in on the progress chart on page 59.

133

Solutions

4 **Solution**
129; 395 + 5 = 400; 400 + 100 = 500; 500 + 24 = 524.
DOK 1

5 **Solution**
Class B has 27 more points than class A. 612 − 585 = 27.
DOK 2

6 **Solution**
No, Ben is not correct; Class B needs 138 more points; 750 − 612 = 138.
DOK 3

▶ Hands-On Activity

Model subtraction using base-ten blocks.

Materials: base-ten blocks and Activity Sheet 6 (Place-Value Mat)

- Distribute base-ten blocks to each student.
- Write several subtraction problems on the board involving regrouping a ten, a hundred, or both.
- Have students copy one problem at a time, using base-ten blocks to solve. Students may use the blocks to think about regrouping or to subtract hundreds, then tens, then ones.
- Make sure students record on their paper what they did in number form.

▶ Challenge Activity

Write subtraction problems for a given difference.

Materials: one card from Activity Sheet 7 (Three-Digit Cards); Each student should be given a different number.

- Give each student a card containing a three-digit number. Make sure each student has a different number.
- Challenge students to write as many subtraction problems as they can think of in which their number is the difference.
- Have them record the equations and see if they notice any patterns or consistencies. Have them, describe what they notice.

Teacher-Toolbox.com

Overview

Assign the Lesson 14 Quiz and have students work independently to complete it.

Use the results of the quiz to assess students' understanding of the content of the lesson and to identify areas for reteaching. See the Lesson Pacing Guide at the beginning of the lesson for suggested instructional resources.

Tested Skills

Assesses 2.NBT.B.7, 2.NBT.B.8, 2.NBT.B.9

Problems on this assessment form require students to be able to use a variety of strategies to subtract three-digit numbers, mentally subtract 10 or 100 from a given number, and determine when it is necessary to regroup tens or hundreds to subtract and carry out the regrouping correctly. Students will also need to be familiar with open number lines and writing subtraction equations to solve word problems.

Ready® Mathematics

Lesson 14 Quiz

Solve the problems.

1 Lucy had 372 flowers. She put 287 into baskets to give away. How many flowers does Lucy have left?

Add up to find 372 − 287. Write the correct numbers in the boxes. Then write the difference.

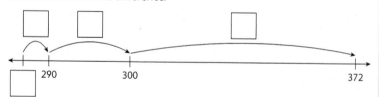

290   300   372

372 − 287 = _____

2 Leo is subtracting 475 − 358. Which tells how Leo should regroup and why?

Circle the correct answer.

A Leo needs to regroup 4 hundreds as 3 hundreds and 1 ten in order to subtract 5 in the tens place.

B Leo needs to regroup 4 hundreds as 3 hundreds and 10 tens in order to subtract 5 in the tens place.

C Leo needs to regroup 7 tens as 6 tens and 10 ones in order to subtract 8 in the ones place.

D Leo needs to regroup 7 tens as 6 tens and 1 one in order to subtract 8 in the ones place.

Lesson 14 Quiz continued

3 Raj has 128 cards. Ed has 274 cards. How many more cards does Ed have than Raj?

Show your work.

Answer: Ed has _____ more cards.

4 Dan wants to know if he should regroup the hundreds to subtract the tens in each problem. For which problems does Dan need to regroup the hundreds?

Circle all the correct answers.

A 496 − 375

B 852 − 571

C 538 − 219

D 326 − 184

5 Bea has 250 jelly beans. She and her friends eat 105 of them. How many jelly beans are left?

Use the numbers in the box to correctly fill in the blanks.

| 1 | 10 | 45 | 55 | 105 | 140 | 145 | 150 | 155 |

To subtract 250 − 105, Bea needs to regroup _____ ten as _____ ones. There are _____ jelly beans left.

Common Misconceptions and Errors

Errors may result if students:

• add the numbers in the problem instead of subtracting them.

• forget to regroup 1 hundred as 10 tens or 1 ten as 10 ones, and instead subtract the lesser digit from the greater digit.

• regroup 1 ten as 1 one instead 10 ones, or regroup 1 hundred as 1 ten instead of 10 tens.

Ready® **Mathematics**

Lesson 14 Quiz Answer Key

1. Above the arrows: 3, 10, 72
Below the line: 287
85
DOK 2

2. C
DOK 3

3. 146
DOK 2

4. B, D
DOK 2

5. 1, 10, 145
DOK 1

CCSS Focus

Domain
Number and Operations in Base Ten

Cluster
B. Use place value understanding and properties of operations to add and subtract.

Standards
2.NBT.B.6 Add up to four two-digit numbers using strategies based on place value and properties of operations.

Additional Standards
2.NBT.B.5, 2.NBT.B.9 (see page B3 for full text)

Standards for Mathematical Practice (SMP)

2 Reason abstractly and quantitatively.

3 Construct viable arguments and critique the reasoning of others.

4 Model with mathematics.

5 Use appropriate tools strategically.

6 Attend to precision.

7 Look for and make use of structure.

8 Look for and express regularity in repeated reasoning.

Lesson Objectives

Content Objectives

• Break apart three or more two-digit numbers as a place-value strategy for adding.

• Develop strategies for adding more than two numbers.

• Apply the commutative and associative properties of addition.

Language Objectives

• Rewrite two-digit numbers in expanded notation to add three or more numbers.

• Draw lines to group addends that are easy to add.

• Describe a mental math strategy used to add three or more numbers.

• Justify conclusions and communicate the conclusions to others.

Prerequisite Skills

• Identify place value in two-digit numbers.

• Model two-digit numbers in expanded form.

• Perform two-digit addition with and without regrouping.

• Use addition facts fluently.

Lesson Vocabulary

There is no new vocabulary.

Learning Progression

In Grade 1 students add one- and two-digit numbers within 100 using concrete models and pictures. They apply strategies based on place value and properties of operations. Students at this level develop strategies for computing mentally and learn tens facts.

In Grade 2 students build on their knowledge of number and place value through a wide variety of models. Number models are used more extensively, transitioning students into abstract thinking and mental computation. They notice consistencies in addition and subtraction that enable them to become proficient in computation.

In this lesson students add three or more two-digit numbers with and without regrouping a hundred and/or a ten. Students interpret number models and explore strategies including breaking apart numbers and making tens and hundreds.

In Grade 3 students gain fluency with addition of numbers within 1,000. They apply the strategy of breaking apart numbers to multiplication of whole numbers and use place value to round numbers.

Lesson Pacing Guide

Whole Class Instruction

Day 1 *45–60 minutes*	**Toolbox: Interactive Tutorial*** *Add up to Four Two-Digit Numbers* **Introduction** • Opening Activity *20 min* • Use What You Know *10 min* • Find Out More *10 min* • Reflect *5 min*	**Practice and Problem Solving** Assign pages 149–150.
Day 2 *45–60 minutes*	**Modeled and Guided Instruction** **Learn About Adding Four Two-Digit Numbers** • Model It/Model It *10min* • Connect It *20 min* • Try It *15 min*	**Practice and Problem Solving** Assign pages 151–152.
Day 3 *45–60 minutes*	**Guided Practice** **Practice Adding Several Two-Digit Numbers** • Example *5 min* • Problems 7–9 *15 min* • Pair/Share *15 min* • Solutions *10 min*	**Practice and Problem Solving** Assign pages 153–154.
Day 4 *45–60 minutes*	**Independent Practice** **Practice Adding Several Two-Digit Numbers** • Problems 1–6 *20 min* • Quick Check and Remediation *10 min* • Hands-On or Challenge Activity *15 min* **Toolbox: Lesson Quiz** Lesson 15 Quiz	

Small Group Differentiation

Teacher-Toolbox.com

Reteach
Ready Prerequisite Lessons *45–90 min*

Grade 1
• Lesson 25 Add and Regroup

Teacher-led Activities
Tools for Instruction *15–20 min*

Grade 1 *(Lesson 25)*
• Two-Digit Addition without Regrouping

Student-led Activities
Math Center Activities *30–40 min*

Grade 2 *(Lesson 15)*
• 2.21 Use Place Value to Add Two-Digit Numbers
• 2.22 Use Properties to Add Two-Digit Numbers

Personalized Learning

i-Ready.com

Independent
i-Ready Lessons* *10–20 min*

Grade 1 *(Lesson 25)*
• Adding a Two-Digit Number and a One-Digit Number

*We continually update the Interactive Tutorials. Check the Teacher Toolbox for the most up-to-date offerings for this lesson.

Opening Activity

Making Hundreds

Objective Recognize patterns involved in combinations of two numbers with a sum of 100.

Time *20–30 minutes*

Materials for each student
- sheet with 2 to 4 10 × 10 grids printed on it
- colored pencils or crayons

Overview

Students apply their knowledge of tens facts to hundreds facts. They then create facts on a 10 × 10 grid and search for the structure and patterns that enable them to easily recognize any two numbers with a sum of 100.

Step By Step

1 Relate tens facts to hundreds facts.

- Ask students to recite tens facts together. Help them start by saying: *0 + 10, 10 + 0, 1 + 9, 9 + 1...*

- Ask students how many tens facts there are. [11] Ask: *How many hundred facts do you think there are?* Allow students to respond and justify their responses. Tell them that in this activity, they will find out what the hundreds facts are.

- Ask students if they can think of a way to use their tens facts to find some hundreds facts. Listen for them to tell you that 50 + 50 = 100, 60 + 40 = 100, etc. Make sure students tell how each hundred fact relates to a tens fact.

2 Explore hundreds facts on a 10 × 10 grid.

- Distribute the 10 × 10 grids and colored pencils or crayons.

- Have students use a hand or another piece of paper to cover 5 rows of ten on the grid and tell how many rows are showing; cover 3 rows of ten and tell how many are showing. Have them relate this to facts such as 50 + 50 and 30 + 70, and find all combinations. This will reinforce the connection between these hundreds facts and tens facts.

- Ask students if they can think of other ways to combine two numbers to make 100. Listen to ideas and then show students how to model on the grid combinations such as 53 + 47 and 28 + 72.

- Ask students to use their own grids to find two more combinations of 100. Suggest that they shade two sections of each grid with a different color and count the squares of each color to identify the hundreds fact.

3 Search for consistencies among the facts.

- Under each grid, have students write an expression for the fact the shading shows.

- Tell students to work with a partner. Ask them to look at all the expressions they wrote to find an easy way to decide if two numbers equal 100. You may want to provide a hint that leads them to add the tens and add the ones in the numbers in each expression.

4 Conjecture about hundreds facts.

- Encourage students to conjecture about what they found and justify it using their grids. Students should recognize that the sum of the tens place is almost always 90 (or is 100) and the sum of the ones place is almost always 10 (or is 0). Find a grid that has just one row shaded in two different colors. On that grid, show students how one of the rows of ten is divided into two numbers that make a 10, and the rest of the rows of ten are solid. Since 10 less than 100 is 90, the sum of those rows will always be 90.

5 Test the conjecture.

- Write the following expressions on the board: 32 + 68, 78 + 12, 47 + 53. Ask students which, if any of them, equal 100 and why.

- Challenge students to determine the number of hundreds facts there are and justify their responses. [101]

Introduction

At A Glance

Students examine a break-apart model of three two-digit numbers. They add the tens and then the ones. Then students examine the strategy of adding two numbers first to make a ten or a hundred, before adding the third number.

Step By Step

- Work through **Use What You Know** as a class.

- Have students read the problem at the top of the page. Ask students to restate the problem and describe what they are to find.

- Ask students to share their mental strategies for adding the tens and adding the ones. Discuss how finding numbers that are easy to add makes mental calculation more accurate.

▶ **Mathematical Discourse 1**

▶ **Concept Extension**

- Tell students that breaking apart numbers is one way to add numbers. Discuss strategies that students may have for adding a series of numbers. Encourage students to devise their own methods of calculating and compare them to the methods explored in the lesson.

Use What You Know

Add three numbers.

Gia follows directions to find a secret code for a treasure hunt.

- Start at the oak tree. Take 36 steps toward the fence.

- Turn right. Take 28 steps.

- Turn left. Take 42 steps.

- The total number of steps is the secret code.

What is the secret code?

a. Break each number into tens and ones. Write your answers in the box.

b. Add the tens. What do you get? __90__

c. Add the ones. What do you get? __16__

$$36 = 30 + 6$$
$$28 = 20 + 8$$
$$42 = 40 + 2$$

d. What is the secret code? Explain how you got your answer.

The secret code is 106. Possible explanation: I added

the total tens and total ones: 90 + 16 = 106.

134

▶ **Mathematical Discourse**

1 *How is adding three numbers like adding two numbers?*

Students may respond that they still add the numbers based on place value and add hundreds to hundreds, tens to tens, and ones to ones.

▶ **Concept Extension**

Apply the commutative property.

- Write the numbers 30, 6, 20, 8, 40, and 2 on separate squares of paper.

- Project the numbers arranged with addition signs: 30 + 6 + 20 + 8 + 40 + 2. You may want to model each of the numbers with base-ten blocks. Make sure students are aware that these are the numbers shown in the problem at the top of the page, but arranged horizontally instead of vertically.

- Ask: *Susan says that if we added 22, 38, and 46 we would get the same sum as that of the numbers on this page. What do you think about Susan's idea?*

- Allow students to share ideas and ask them to use an equation and/or models to justify their thinking. This is an extension of the commutative property of addition. Since addition is the process of combining groups, the order in which they are combined does not affect the sum.

⟫ Find Out More

There are many ways to add three numbers.

You have learned how to break apart all three numbers and then add the tens and ones.

You can also add two numbers at a time.

$$36 \quad + \quad 28 \quad + \quad 42$$

$$64 \quad + \quad 42 \quad = 106$$

You can look for two numbers that make a ten. Add those first. Then add the third number.

$$36 \quad + \quad 28 \quad + \quad 42 \quad \longleftarrow \quad \boxed{\begin{array}{l} 8 + 2 = 10, \\ \text{so add} \\ 28 + 42 \text{ first.} \end{array}}$$

$$36 \quad + \quad 70 \quad = 106$$

Sometimes there are two numbers that make 100. Add these first. Then add the third number.

$$25 \quad + \quad 59 \quad + \quad 75$$

$$100 \quad + \quad 59 \quad = 159$$

▶ **Reflect** **Work with a partner.**

1 **Talk About It** Why would you change the order that you add three numbers? Explain using 37 + 21 + 63.

Write About It Possible answer: Change the order to make it easier to

add. Add 37 + 63 first to make 100. Then add 100 and 21 to get 121.

135

▶ Mathematical Discourse

2 *Why is it easy to add when you make a hundred first?*

After you have a hundred, the other addend goes after the one in the hundreds place so you have one hundred "something."

3 *Do you think it is easier to break apart numbers or to add two numbers first and then the third one? Why?*

Allow students to share personal preferences, listening for mathematical reasoning.

Step By Step

- Read **Find Out More** as a class. Ask students if this is a strategy any of them thought about on the previous page. When students are encouraged to devise their own strategies first, they take ownership of the strategy and then the text validates the strategy.

- Ask: *What must you remember to do when you add numbers by finding a ten in the ones place?* [You need to add an extra ten to the tens place.]

- Ask students to remember the opening activity as they examine the strategy of making a hundred. Have them tell you how they know when two numbers equal 100.

▶ **Mathematical Discourse 2**

> **SMP TIP** **Look for Structure**
> Exploring the strategies of breaking apart numbers and finding numbers whose sum is 100 reinforces the structure of the base-ten number system. *(SMP 7)*

- Have students work in pairs to complete the **Reflect** question. Then ask Mathematical Discourse question 3.

- Have students think of numbers that may not be easy to add by making a ten or a hundred. Discuss strategies they could use in those situations. Listen for strategies such as counting on by tens and then adding the ones.

▶ **Mathematical Discourse 3**

📦 **Ready** **Mathematics**
PRACTICE AND PROBLEM SOLVING

Assign *Practice and Problem Solving* **pages 149–150** after students have completed this section.

Modeled and Guided Instruction

At A Glance

Students examine breaking apart numbers and applying the commutative property as strategies for the addition of four two-digit numbers. Then students revisit this problem, applying the strategies of breaking apart numbers and grouping compatible numbers to add.

Step By Step

- Read the problem at the top of the page together as a class.

Model It

- Draw attention to **Model It**. Ask students how this model differs from the one on the first page of the lesson.

- Discuss the value of each digit in the tens column. Remind them that when they see a digit in the tens place, they should always think of its value; 4 tens is 40. This will prepare them for attending to place value when they multiply two- and three-digit numbers in the future.

Model It

- Tell students to look at **Model It** and ask: *Why does it make sense to group the numbers this way?* [9 + 1 makes ten, so add 41 and 39. It makes a ten number that is easy to add to other numbers.]

▶ **Mathematical Discourse**

> **SMP TIP Repeated Reasoning**
> As students analyze strategies for adding numbers, they recognize the structure and regularity of those strategies. By generalizing and applying strategies to new situations, they gain fluency in mental computation. *(SMP 8)*

▶ **English Language Learners**

Learn About ▶ Adding Four Two-Digit Numbers

Read the problem. Then you will explore different ways to add four numbers.

> Ray and Cho fill water balloons for a game. Ray fills 16 red balloons and 41 white balloons. Cho fills 22 red balloons and 39 white balloons. How many balloons do they fill in all?

▶ **Model It** **You can break the numbers into tens and ones.**

Break each number into tens and ones. Then add pairs of numbers.

Tens	Ones
1 ⟩ 5 4	6 ⟩ 7 1
2 ⟩ 5 3	2 ⟩ 11 9

5 + 5 tens   7 + 11 ones

▶ **Model It** **You can add two numbers at a time.**

Look for ones that make a 10. Add those numbers first.

16   +   41   +   22   +   39

38   +   80

136

▶ **Mathematical Discourse**

When would you want to use the make a ten or make a hundred strategy and when would it be easier to break apart numbers to add?

Students may respond that if they can see two digits whose sum is 10 or two numbers whose sum is 100, use that strategy. If there aren't any of those combinations, it is easier to break apart the numbers.

▶ **English Language Learners**

Engage ELL students in sharing their strategies with the class. Students from other cultures may have learned strategies other than the ones presented in your class. ELL students may fear calling attention to themselves. Provide a nonthreatening environment for them to do so and give them recognition for their ideas.

Connect It Add four two-digit numbers.

2 Look at the first *Model It*. Fill in the blanks to find the total number of balloons.

___10___ tens + ___18___ ones = ___118___

3 The box shows how Ella added the numbers. How is this like adding in the first *Model It*?

Possible answer: In both ways you add the tens, and

then add the ones. With Ella's way, you write the value of

each digit.

$$\begin{array}{r} 10 + 6 \\ 40 + 1 \\ 20 + 2 \\ 30 + 9 \\ \hline 100 + 18 \end{array}$$

4 Look at the second *Model It*. Why are 41 and 39 grouped together?

Possible answer: You can make a ten with the ones digits.

It's easier to add tens with no ones.

5 Complete the work in the second *Model It* to find the number of balloons Ray and Cho fill in all.

38 + 80 = 118. Ray and Cho fill 118 ballons in all.

Try It Try another problem.

6 Yuri's bowling scores are 45, 62, 68, and 55. What is the total of Yuri's four scores? Show your work.

Possible work:

$$\begin{array}{lll} 40 + 5 & 60 + 2 & 100 \\ 50 + 5 & 60 + 8 & + 130 \\ \hline 90 + 10 = 100 & 120 + 10 = 130 & 230 \end{array}$$

The total of Yuri's four scores is 230.

137

▶ Hands-On Activity

Model with base-ten blocks.

Materials: base-ten blocks and Activity Sheet 6 (Place-Value Mat)

• Organize the class in pairs. Have each student model the four numbers in the **Try It** problem with base-ten blocks on his or her own place-value mat.

• One student in the pair combines some of his or her blocks to make two numbers, trading 10 tens blocks for 1 hundreds block, and 10 ones blocks for 1 tens block, as needed. The student records the two new numbers.

• Then the other student in the pair combines his or her blocks in a different way to make two numbers, trading 10 tens blocks for 1 hundreds block, and 10 ones blocks for 1 tens block, as needed. The student records the two new numbers.

• Finally, ask each student to combine all the blocks on his or her place-value mat, recording the total. Have the students in each pair compare the numbers they recorded and their sum.

• Discuss how, when adding numbers, the order in which they are added or the way they are grouped to add will not affect the sum no matter what number of addends are used. Make sure they understand that place-value position does matter. They can move the tens and ones around, but tens will still always be added to tens and ones will always be added to ones.

Step By Step

Connect It

• Read **Connect It** as a class. Make sure students understand that the questions refer to the problem on the previous page.

• For Problem 2, have students share mental strategies they could use to add the tens and the ones.

• The model already shows that in the tens place, 10 + 40 = 50 and 20 + 30 = 50. Students should see that 50 + 50 = 100 or that 30 + 40 = 70 and 20 + 10 = 30. 70 + 30 = 100.

• Ask students to tell you how the ones could be added a different way than is already shown. [The 9 and 1 in the ones place make a ten.]

• After students complete Problem 5, have them compare their total to Ella's. Discuss that it doesn't matter how you group or order numbers when you add.

Try It

• After students complete the **Try It** question, ask them to share their calculations with the class. Reiterate that there is more than one way to order and group the numbers, all resulting in the same sum.

▶ Hands-On Activity

6 Solution

230; Possible solution: 45 + 55 = 100; 62 + 68 = 130; 100 + 130 = 230.

Error Alert Students who wrote 220 may have failed to include the composed ten when adding 62 + 28 = 130.

Ready Mathematics PRACTICE AND PROBLEM SOLVING

Assign *Practice and Problem Solving* **pages 151–152** after students have completed this section.

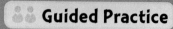

Guided Practice

At A Glance

Students solve word problems using strategies to add three or four two-digit numbers.

Step By Step

- Ask students to solve the problems individually and show all their work. Review the sample problem together, asking students to identify the strategy that was used. Remind them to try to practice the strategies they learned in this lesson when solving the remainder of the problems.

- **Pair/Share** When students have completed each problem, have them Pair/Share to discuss their solutions with a partner.

Solutions

Example The strategy of finding and adding two numbers whose sum is 100, and then adding the remaining two numbers, and finally finding the sum is applied.

7 Solution
98 birds; Students may add $28 + 22 = 50$, $23 + 25 = 48$, $50 + 48 = 98$.
DOK 1

Practice **Adding Several Two-Digit Numbers**

Study the model below. Then solve Problems 7–9.

Example

Mr. Carey's class took a nature walk. The chart shows what they collected. How many objects did they collect in all?

Rocks	Pinecones	Feathers	Acorns
52	37	12	63

You can add two numbers at a time.

$$37 + 63 = 100$$
$$52 + 12 = \underline{64}$$
$$164$$

Answer The class collected 164 objects.

7 There are 28 parrots and 23 macaws in the zoo's jungle birdhouse. There are also 22 toucans and 25 hornbills. What is the total number of birds?

Show your work.

Possible work: $28 + 22 = 50$ and $23 + 25 = 48$

$50 + 48 = 98$

Do any ones digits make a ten?

Answer There are 98 birds in all.

138

Teacher Notes

8 It is race day at the city park. The chart shows how many people sign up for each race. What is the total number of people who sign up?

You can break the numbers into tens and ones.

1-Mile Race	Bike Race	Swim Race
66	49	37

Show your work.

Possible work: $60 + 40 + 30 = 130$
$6 + 9 + 7 = 22$
152

Answer   There are 152 people who sign up.

9 Gita adds the number of cans in the school recycling bins. What is the total?

$28 + 16 + 32 + 2 = ?$

How many tens are in each number?

A 68

B 76

C 78

D 96

Jeff chose **D** as the answer. This answer is wrong. How did Jeff get his answer?

Possible answer: Jeff added 2 tens for 2. He should have added 2 ones.

139

Solutions

8 Solution

152; students may add $60 + 40 + 30 = 130$, $6 + 9 + 7 = 22$, $130 + 22 = 152$.

DOK 1

9 Solution

C; $28 + 2 = 30$, $32 + 16 = 48$, $48 + 30 = 78$.

DOK 3

Explain to students why the other two choices are not correct.

A is not correct because 1 ten was not added.

B is not correct because the 2 was not added.

Ready· **Mathematics**
PRACTICE AND PROBLEM SOLVING

Assign *Practice and Problem Solving* **pages 153–154** after students have completed this section.

Teacher Notes

Independent Practice

At A Glance

Students solve two-digit addition problems involving three or four addends that might appear on a mathematics test.

Solutions

1 **Solution**

55, 77, and 39; In each case, the sum of the ones place is 10 and the sum of the tens place is 90.

DOK 1

2 **Solution**

A 25 + 15 = 40; **C** 25 + 18 + 24 + 15 = 82, 82 < 100; **D** The sum is 82.

DOK 2

3 **Solution**

C; 25 + 25 + 25 + 32 = 107.

DOK 1

Practice **Adding Several Two-Digit Numbers**

Solve the problems.

1 Complete each equation using a number from the box at the right.

a. 45 + 55 = 100

b. 77 + 23 = 100

c. 61 + 39 = 100

> 39
> 55
> 77

2 A train has four cars. The number of people in each car is 25, 18, 24, and 15. Which of the sentences below are true? Circle all the correct answers.

(A) The number of people in two of the cars add up to 40.

B More than 100 people are on the train.

(C) Fewer than 100 people are on the train.

(D) There are 82 people on the train.

3 A park has 25 oak trees, 25 maple trees, 25 elm trees, and 32 pine trees. What is the total number of trees? Circle the correct answer.

A 57

B 97

(C) 107

D 117

140

Quick Check and Remediation

- Ben read 37 minutes on Monday, 29 minutes on Tuesday, 35 minutes on Wednesday, and 13 minutes on Thursday. How many minutes did he record on his reading log that he turned in on Friday? [114; 30 + 20 + 30 + 10 = 90; 7 + 9 + 5 + 3 = 24; 90 + 24 = 114]

- For students who are still struggling, use the chart to guide remediation.

- After providing remediation, check students' understanding using the following problem: Joni made a necklace using red, yellow, and orange beads. She used 46 red beads, 25 yellow beads, and 54 orange beads. How many beads did she use in all? [125; 46 + 54 = 100; 100 + 25 = 125]

If the error is . . .	Students may . . .	To remediate . . .
104	have added 37 + 13 and failed to add the regrouped ten.	Provide students with base-ten blocks to model the addition, pointing out that the ten ones composed into a ten is added to the sum of the tens.
132	have inverted the 1 and 3, recording 13 as 31.	Have students break apart each number into tens and ones and then compare them to the numbers that were added.
other answers	have miscalculated either the ones or the tens.	Have students rework the problem utilizing a different strategy to check for accuracy.

Use these number cards for Problems 4–6.

| 27 | 48 | 43 | 29 | 34 | 35 |

4 Pablo picks two cards with ones digits that make a ten. Which two cards does he pick? Explain.

Possible answer: Pablo picks 27 and 43. The ones digits

make a ten. The sum is 70.

5 Pablo loses the 29 card. Taj picks three of the cards that are left. His cards have a sum less than 100. What are the three cards? Show how to find the sum by adding tens and ones.

Possible answer: Taj picks 27, 34, and 35.

$20 + 30 + 30 + 7 + 4 + 5 = 80 + 16$, or $96. 96 < 100$

6 Explain how you decided which cards to use for Problem 5. Check your answer by adding two numbers at a time.

Possible answer: I crossed out 29 because that card

was lost. Then I added the remaining numbers with

the least value. $27 + 34 = 61; 61 + 35 = 96. 96 < 100$

✓ **Self Check** Now you can add many two-digit numbers. Fill this in on the progress chart on page 59.

141

Solutions

4 **Solution**
27 and 43; $7 + 3 = 10$.
DOK 2

5 **Solution**
Possible answer: 27, 34, and 35; $20 + 30 + 30 = 80, 7 + 4 + 5 = 16, 80 + 16 = 96$. $96 < 100$.
DOK 2

6 **Solution**
Answers will vary. Possible answer shown on Student Book page.
DOK 3

▶ **Hands-On Activity**

Practice strategies using base-ten blocks.

Materials: For each pair: base-ten blocks, Activity Sheet 8 (Two-Digit Cards), paper, and pencils

• Organize students in pairs. Distribute the materials.

• Have each partner pick two cards and model his or her numbers with base-ten blocks. Students work together to decide which two of their four numbers to add first.

• Have students combine blocks to show the addition of the two numbers they decided to add first, replacing 10 ones blocks with 1 tens block, and 10 tens blocks with 1 hundreds block, whenever possible. Ask students to record what they did as an equation.

• Then have students work together to show with base-ten blocks the addition of the other two numbers they picked.

• Finally, ask students to combine all their base-ten blocks and work together to record what they did.

• Repeat as time allows or until all the number cards are used.

▶ **Challenge Activity**

Generalize strategies to add three-digit numbers.

Challenge students to generalize the strategies they learned in this lesson to adding a series of three-digit numbers and/or find a new strategy for adding three-digit numbers. Tell them to think of ways to add more than two three-digit numbers and record their ideas.

Give students the following instructions:

• Write the numbers you added.

• Tell the strategy you used to add them.

• Explain how the strategy works so that your classmates could use it.

• Show that it works every time by using it to add other numbers.

Tell students to follow this list for each strategy they find.

Teacher-Toolbox.com

Overview

Assign the Lesson 15 Quiz and have students work independently to complete it.

Use the results of the quiz to assess students' understanding of the content of the lesson and to identify areas for reteaching. See the Lesson Pacing Guide at the beginning of the lesson for suggested instructional resources.

Tested Skills

Assesses 2.NBT.B.6

Problems on this assessment form require students to be able to recognize and use a variety of strategies to add several two-digit numbers. Students will also need to be familiar with the commutative and associative properties of addition, reading information presented in a table, and decomposing two-digit numbers into tens and ones.

Ready® Mathematics

Lesson 15 Quiz

Solve the problems.

1 Olivia is playing a game. She gets 33 points on her first turn. She gets 29 points on her second turn. She gets 27 points on her third turn. How many points does Olivia have in all?

Show your work.

Answer: _____ points

2 The table shows how many pets Caden counts at the pet store. How many pets are there in all?

Pet	Number
Dog	26
Cat	44
Rabbit	38

Show how to find the sum by adding tens and ones.
Write a number in each blank.

_____ tens + _____ ones = _____

Lesson 15 Quiz continued

3 Avery wants to add these numbers.

22 + 35 + 38

Explain how she can find the sum by making a ten. What is the sum?

_____

_____

The sum is _____ .

4 Mia wants to add 42 + 31 + 59 + 18. Which problems show a way Mia can find the sum?
Circle all the correct answers.

A 60 + 90

B 4 + 3 + 5 + 1 + 20 + 10 + 90 + 80

C 40 + 30 + 50 + 10 + 2 + 1 + 9 + 8

D 132 + 18

5 Lucas is adding these numbers. Can Lucas make a ten to help him find the sum?
Circle *Yes* or *No* for each problem.

a. 46 + 12 + 34 + 63   Yes   No

b. 29 + 54 + 55 + 61   Yes   No

c. 45 + 27 + 62 + 74   Yes   No

d. 44 + 91 + 37 + 10   Yes   No

Common Misconceptions and Errors

Errors may result if students:

• forget to regroup, or forget to add the extra tens that came from regrouping the ones.

• add only some of the addends, or add an addend more than once.

• do not notice that two numbers can make a 10 if the numbers are not next to each other.

• attempt to use the making ten strategy, but look in the tens place, rather than the ones place, for numbers that add up to ten.

Ready® **Mathematics**

Lesson 15 Quiz Answer Key

1. 89
DOK 1

2. 9, 18, 108 (or 10, 8, 108)
DOK 2

3. Possible explanation: Avery can add 22 and 38 first because the numbers 8 and 2 in the ones place add to 10. She can add $22 + 38 = 20 + 30 + 10 = 60$. She can then add $60 + 35 = 95$. The sum is 95.
DOK 3

4. A, C, D
DOK 2

5. a. Yes
b. Yes
c. No
d. No
DOK 2

Add, Subtract, and Compare Numbers

CCSS Focus

Domain
Number and Operations in Base Ten

Clusters
2.NBT.A Understand place value.
2.NBT.B Use place value understanding and properties of operations to add and subtract.

Standards
2.NBT.A.1, 2.NBT.A.3, 2.NBT.A.4, 2.NBT.B.5, 2.NBT.B.6, 2.NBT.B.7, 2.NBT.B.8, 2.NBT.B.9, 2.OA.A.1

Standards for Mathematical Practice (SMP)
1 Make sense of problems and persevere in solving them.
2 Reason abstractly and quantitatively.
3 Construct viable arguments and critique the reasoning of others.

Additional SMPs
4, 6, 7

Lesson at a Glance

Students apply skills from the unit to solve real-world problems related to a food shop. Problems involve comparing and ordering 3-digit numbers, and adding and subtracting 1-, 2-, and 3-digit numbers with and without regrouping.

Lesson Pacing Guide

Whole Class Instruction

Day 1 45–60 minutes	**Introduction** Problem and Solution 45 min		
	Task Analyze a solution to a problem about ways to make equal groups of 3 kinds of cookies with a total between 400 and 500.	**Key Skills** • Understand comparing 3-digit numbers. • Understand equal groups. • Recognize how a quick drawing shows place value.	**Mathematical Practices** • Organize information. • Draw a model to show place value. • Critique a given solution.
Day 2 45–60 minutes	**Modeled and Guided Instruction** Try Another Approach Plan It 15 min • Solve It 20 min • Reflect 10 min		
	Task Use another approach to make equal groups of 3 kinds of cookies with a total between 400 and 500.	**Key Skills** • Compare 3-digit numbers. • Add three 3-digit numbers. • Regroup to add.	**Mathematical Practices** • Make use place-value structure. • Reason quantitatively. • Check that a solution makes sense.
Day 3 45–60 minutes	**Guided Practice** Discuss Models and Strategies Plan It and Solve It 35 min • Reflect 10 min		
	Task Find a way to pack 145 cookies in boxes that hold different quantities.	**Key Skills** • Compare 3-digit numbers. • Add 1- and 2-digit numbers. • Subtract 2- and 3-digit numbers.	**Mathematical Practices** • Make sense of assorted problem information. • Calculate precisely. • Justify and explain choices.

Whole Class Instruction continued

Day 4
45–60 minutes

Independent Practice

Persevere on Your Own

Problem 1

Solve It *35 min*   •   Reflect *10 min*

Task	**Key Skills**	**Mathematical Practices**
Determine amounts of 2 types of food given criteria about the total and about the quantities of each type used.	• Compare 3-digit numbers. • Add 3-digit numbers with and without regrouping. • Subtract 3-digit numbers with and without regrouping.	• Make sense of the problem. • Reason quantitatively. • Justify choices.

Day 5
45–60 minutes

Independent Practice

Persevere on Your Own

Problem 2

Solve It *35 min*   •   Reflect *10 min*

Task	**Key Skills**	**Mathematical Practices**
Find the number of extra fruit salads and allocate them between donations and given out free to customers.	• Subtract 3-digit numbers. • Add 3-digit numbers. • Write subtraction and addition equations.	• Make sense of the problem. • Calculate precisely. • Construct an argument to defend decisions.

Unit Resources

Practice
Practice and Problem Solving

Grade 2
• Unit 2 Game
• Unit 2 Practice
• Unit 2 Performance Task
• Unit 2 Vocabulary

Assess
Ready Instruction

Grade 2
• Unit 2 Interim Assessment

Introduction

At A Glance

Students examine a problem about a cookie order at a bakery in which the math involves comparing and adding 3-digit numbers. Students discuss the problem to understand what it is asking and brainstorm different approaches. Then they refer to a **Problem-Solving Checklist** to analyze a sample solution and identify what makes it a good solution.

Step By Step

- Read the problem out loud with students. Explain that "Sweet T" is a boy's name. The Bake Stars is a group of his friends who work in a bakery.

- Invite volunteers to describe in their own words what they need to figure out [how many of each kind of cookie to make] and what information is given that will be useful [between 400 and 500 altogether, 3 kinds, the same number of each].

- Direct students' attention to Sweet T's notes about the cookie order.

▶ **Mathematical Discourse 1**

- Invite students to share their ideas about how they might solve this problem. Allow them to describe different approaches, without carrying through with an actual solution yet.

▶ **Mathematical Discourse 2**

- Invite students to discuss how a drawing might help them solve the problem.

▶ **Visual Model**

- Explain that students will look at the sample solution on the next page to see one way the problem could be solved. Then they will read the solution again and discuss what makes it a good solution by using the **Problem-Solving Checklist.**

Study an Example Problem and Solution

Read this problem about adding numbers. Then look at Sweet T's solution to the problem.

Cookie Order

Sweet T is in the Bake Stars' kitchen. He takes notes about a cookie order.

> **Cookie Order**
> - Make between 400 and 500 cookies.
> - Make chocolate chip, peanut butter, and oatmeal cookies.
> - Make the same number of each kind of cookie.

How many of each kind of cookie should the Bake Stars make? Show why your numbers work.

Show how Sweet T's solution matches the checklist.

> **Problem-Solving Checklist**
> - ☐ Tell what is known.
> - ☐ Tell what the problem is asking.
> - ☐ Show all your work.
> - ☐ Show that the solution works.
>
> **a. Circle** something that is known.
> **b. Underline** something that you need to find.
> **c. Draw a box around** what you do to solve the problem.
> **d. Put a checkmark** next to the part that shows the solution works.

142

▶ **Mathematical Discourse**

1 *How many different kinds of cookies do the Bake Stars need to make? How do you know?*

Students should note that the illustration shows 3 kinds of cookies and that the notes list 3 kinds of cookies.

2 *What could you do to start solving this problem? How would doing this help you think about the solution?*

Some might first choose a total between 400 and 500. Others might begin with the idea of 3 numbers that are the same; these students might use numbers or visual models to depict the quantities.

▶ **Visual Model**

Use a drawing to show three equal quantities.

- Draw three large circles to represent the three different kinds of cookies. Label the circles *chocolate chip*, *peanut butter*, and *oatmeal*. Relate this model to the task requirement to make about the same number of each kind of cookie.

- Write "10" in one of the circles and ask students what numbers to put in the other two circles [10]; then fill in these circles. Point out that the sum is only 30, not even near 400.

- Erase those numbers and elicit some additional examples. Don't solve the problem, but just model learning from mistakes, using a trial and error approach.

Sweet T's Solution

Hi, I'm Sweet T. Here's how I solved this problem.

▷ **I know** there are 3 kinds of cookies. The total is between 400 and 500 cookies.

▷ **I need to find** 3 numbers that have a sum between 400 and 500.

 Try 100: 100 + 100 + 100 = 300.
 Try 200: 200 + 200 + 200 = 600.

Using 100 makes too few cookies. Using 200 makes too many cookies.

▷ 150 is between 100 and 200.

▷ **I can make a quick drawing** to help me add.

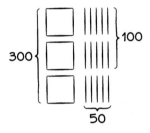

I drew 100 + 100 + 100 and 50 + 50 + 50.

▷ 300 + 100 + 50 = 450 and 450 is between 400 and 500.

The numbers total 450. So 150 works.

▷ **Here is what the Bake Stars can make:**

 150 chocolate chip cookies
 150 peanut butter cookies
 150 oatmeal cookies

143

▶ Hands-On Activity

Build a model to match the visual.

Materials: 3 hundreds blocks, 15 tens blocks

• Have students build 150 using 1 hundreds block and 5 tens blocks. Elicit that this represents the number of chocolate chips cookies used in the solution.

• Have students build 150 twice more to represent the other kinds of cookies.

• Discuss how their model is like the drawing in the book. Have students put their hands over 300 [3 hundreds blocks], then over 100 [10 tens blocks], and finally over 50 [5 tens blocks].

▶ Mathematical Discourse

3 *What does the quick drawing show? What do the numbers in the quick drawing mean?*

Students may need help recognizing that it shows 150 three times, representing 150 of each type of cookie. The numbers show how Sweet T grouped the hundreds to get 300, grouped 10 tens to get 100, and grouped the last 5 tens to get 50.

4 *How does trying different numbers help solve this problem?*

Trying 100 and 200 of each kind of cookie first provides a range within which to look for a solution.

Step By Step

• Explain that this page shows one way to solve the problem.

• Read through Sweet T's solution together, one section at a time. Read for understanding, helping students with any language challenges.

• Tell students that the speech bubbles tell what Sweet T was thinking about as he wrote his solution. Read through the speech bubbles, and help students see how Sweet T is "talking to us" about what he wrote.

• Discuss the sample solution with students. Make sure students can see how the diagram represents 150 of each cookie, and how the diagram shows the sum.

▶ **Mathematical Discourse 3 and 4**

• Be sure everyone agrees that this solution works.

▶ **Hands-On Activity**

• Then, as a class, go back to do a close read, using the **Problem-Solving Checklist** to help analyze Sweet T's solution.

• Remind students that a really good answer to a problem like this does all the things on the checklist. Ask: *Where does Sweet T's answer tell information from the problem?* [the first two sentences] Have students circle that part.

• Then say: *In a really good answer, you want to write what you are going to figure out. Where did Sweet T write what he is going to figure out?* [the second bullet] *Underline that.*

• Similarly, lead students to mark where Sweet T showed his work, and where he checked his work. [He showed his work with the quick drawing, and checked his answer when he found the sum and compared it to 400 and 500.]

• Tell students that since this is a good answer, they can look at it to get ideas when they write their own answers for this problem.

• When students are finished with the page, have them find a partner and read or describe the parts of the solution that they marked for each item on the checklist. Encourage them to justify the choices that they made.

Modeled and Guided Instruction

At A Glance

Students plan and solve the Cookie Order problem from the Introduction using different numbers. Students demonstrate that the problem has more than one solution.

Step By Step

- Review and summarize the steps in Sweet T's solution shown. [Look for a number you can add three times to get a sum between 400 and 500. Try a number. Make a model with 3 groups of that number. See if the total is between 400 and 500.]

- Have students brainstorm some different steps than these that they might use to solve the problem. For example, they might use a place-value table instead of a diagram to model numbers.

▶ **Mathematical Discourse 1**

> **SMP TIP** **Model with Mathematics**
> Invite students to use a variety of representations (quick drawings, place-value charts, base-ten blocks) as they try different numbers of cookies. Prompt them to compare how each representation shows how many there are of each kind and the total. **(SMP 4)**

Plan It

- Read the question in **Plan It** aloud. Invite students to share some initial responses. [For example, they might say more is possible because the total can be more than 450, and less is possible because the total can be less than 450.]

▶ **Mathematical Discourse 2**

- Have students work independently to write an answer to the **Plan It** question. Tell students they will use their answers along with the **Problem-Solving Tips** on the next page to plan their answer.

▶ **English Language Learners**

Try **Another Approach**

There are many ways to solve problems. Think about how you might solve the Cookie Order problem in a different way.

Cookie Order

Sweet T is in the Bake Stars' kitchen. He takes notes about a cookie order.

> **Cookie Order**
> - Make between 400 and 500 cookies.
> - Make chocolate chip, peanut butter, and oatmeal cookies.
> - Make the same number of each kind of cookie.

How many of each kind of cookie should the Bake Stars make? Show why your numbers work.

▶ **Plan It** **Answer this question to help you start thinking about a plan.**

Look at the numbers for each kind of cookie in the sample answer. Could you use numbers greater than these? Less than these? Explain.

_____

_____

_____

_____

144

▶ **Mathematical Discourse**

1 *What are some other ways you could represent the number of each kind of cookie?*

Listen for how each representation shows that the three numbers will add to between 400 and 500.

2 *How can you tell if a different number of cookies fits the problem?*

Students should be able to point out that the total number of cookies must be between 400 and 500. They can determine if a given number fits by using models and addition to add three of a chosen number.

▶ **English Language Learners**

Review the meaning of *between*. Draw a number line and label 100 and 200. Have students plot examples of numbers that are between 100 and 200. Provide some examples of numbers that are not between 100 and 200.

▶ **Solve It** Find a different solution for the Cookie Order problem. Show all your work on a separate sheet of paper.

You may want to use the problem-solving tips to get started.

Problem-Solving Tips

- **Models**

Hundreds	Tens	Ones
1	?	?

Problem-Solving Checklist

Make sure that you . . .
- ☐ tell what you know.
- ☐ tell what you need to do.
- ☐ show all your work.
- ☐ show that the solution works.

- **Word Bank**

  add   subtract   total   greater than
  sum   difference   compare   less than

- **Sentence Starters**
  - I can look for numbers _____
  - I can try numbers _____

▶ **Reflect**

Use Mathematical Practices Talk about this question with a partner.

- **Reason with Numbers** How can the numbers in the sample answer help you solve this problem?

145

Step By Step

Solve It

- Introduce the **Problem-Solving Tips** as ideas students may use to explain their thinking when they write their solution.

- Invite students to share ideas about how they might use the model shown. Ask if there are other words that might be useful. Solicit suggestions for how they might complete each of the sentence starters.

- Encourage students to share their ideas with a partner. Suggest that partners also discuss the **Reflect** on Mathematical Thinking questions before writing their complete solution on a copy of Activity Sheet 23 (Solution Sheet 2) or a blank sheet of paper.

- If time permits, selected students can explain their solutions to the class. Alternatively, you can share the solution below and invite the class to discuss it.

Possible Solution

Try a number that is between 100 and 150. Use 140 and show the work in a table.

	Hundreds	Tens	Ones
Choc. Chip	1	4	0
Peanut B.	1	4	0
Oatmeal	1	4	0
Total	3	12	0

3 hundreds, 12 tens, and 0 ones is the same as 4 hundreds, 2 tens, and 0 ones, which is 420. This is between 400 and 500, so the solution works.

Scoring Rubric

Points	Expectations
4	The student's response is accurate and complete. The solution steps and calculations are complete and correct. Students show their work, tell how many of each kind to make, and verify the solution.
3	Student's solution is substantially complete and reflects the information given. The steps are correct but might be incomplete. The solution is correct but may not be verified correctly.
2	The student's response contains several mistakes. The model may have errors. The total is between 400 and 500 but does not depict equal groups.
1	The student's response contains an incorrect solution. The model is incomplete and inaccurate. The total is not between 400 and 500 and does not reflect equal groups. There is no verification.

👥 **Guided Practice**

At A Glance

With **Problem-Solving Tips** as support, students understand, plan, and solve an open-ended, multi-step problem. They choose appropriate models and strategies to solve the problem, checking their thinking with a partner.

Step By Step

- Read the problem out loud with students. As you read, encourage students to ask clarifying questions. Help them understand that boxes can be full or partially full, they can use as many or as few of each size as they like, etc.

- Direct students' attention to the various sizes of the boxes. Discuss advantages and disadvantages of using different boxes.

▶ **Mathematical Discourse 1**

> **SMP TIP Reason Quantitatively**
> Engage students in a discussion about why they might want to use more or fewer boxes. Encourage them to use mathematical concepts to bolster their arguments. **(SMP 2)**

- Point out that students can make their own choices about which boxes to use, for any reason.

- Discuss that the bakery needs to keep track of how many cookies they pack and how many boxes they use.

▶ **Mathematical Discourse 2 and 3**

Discuss **Models and Strategies**

Solve the problem on a separate sheet of paper. There are different ways you can solve it.

Cookie Boxes

Sweet T is packing an order of 145 chocolate chip cookies. The pictures below show the different-size boxes there are at the shop. Each box holds a different number of cookies.

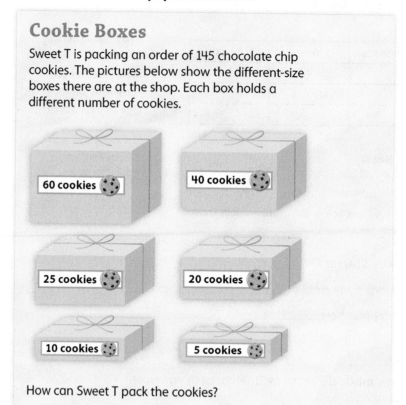

60 cookies 40 cookies

25 cookies 20 cookies

10 cookies 5 cookies

How can Sweet T pack the cookies?

146

▶ Mathematical Discourse

1 *Why would you, or wouldn't you, use the 60-cookie box? The 5-cookie box? Other boxes?*

   Students may cite advantages and disadvantages of different boxes, such as breakage, freshness, convenience, size, shape, weight, stackability, etc.

2 *How will you know when you have packed enough cookies?*

   Possible answer: Keep a running total of the cookies in each box as you pack.

3 *How will you keep track of the number and types of boxes you use?*

   Students should be able to explain how their plan tracks data accurately, for example, by writing the box sizes in a table and making tally marks to show how many of each size they use.

▶ **Plan It and Solve It** **Find a solution to Sweet T's Cookie Boxes problem.**

Decide which boxes Sweet T should use to pack the cookies.
• Tell why you chose these boxes.
• Show that your answer works.

You may want to use the problem-solving tips to get started.

Problem-Solving Tips

● **Questions**
  • Would I rather use fewer boxes or more boxes?
  • Do I want to make sure that every box I use is full?

● **Word Bank**

add	sum	total
hundred	tens	ones

● **Sentence Starters**
  • I can use _____ boxes.
  • The box holds _____
  • I used these boxes because _____

Problem-Solving Checklist

Make sure that you . . .
□ tell what you know.
□ tell what you need to do.
□ show all your work.
□ show that the solution works.

▶ **Reflect**
Use Mathematical Practices Talk about this question with a partner.
  • **Make an Argument** How can you explain the reason for the boxes that you chose?

147

Scoring Rubric

Points	Expectations
4	The student's response is accurate and complete. The solution tells what is known and what the problem asks. The steps are complete. Calculations are accurate. The explanation is clear. The student explains the decisions about the boxes and verifies that the solution works.
3	The solution is substantially complete and reflects the information given. Solution steps are correct. The explanation does not clearly explain the decisions about the boxes. The solution is correct but may not be verified correctly.
2	The solution is incomplete and contains several mistakes. Some calculations are inaccurate. The student does not fully explain the decisions about the boxes or does not show that their answer works.
1	The solution is incorrect. Solution steps are incomplete and do not correctly reflect the task; calculations are mostly incorrect. The decisions about the boxes are not explained. The solution is not verified.

Step By Step

Plan It and Solve It

• Discuss the **Problem-Solving Tips** as ideas students may use to explain their thinking when they write their solution.

• Invite students to share ideas about answers to the questions, other words they might use, and how they might complete the sentences.

• Put students in pairs to discuss solution ideas. Ask them to also discuss the **Reflect** questions about Mathematical Practices. Remind students that there are always different ways to answer these questions.

• Discuss a variety of approaches as a class. Let students revise their plans and discuss again with a partner. Provide support for any issues students have discussed but can't resolve.

• When students are confident that their plans make sense, tell them to write a complete solution on a copy of Activity Sheet 22 (Solution Sheet 1) or a blank sheet of paper.

• If time permits, share and discuss student solutions or the one below.

Possible Solution

I need to pack 145 cookies. I want to use fewer boxes to save on the cost of boxes. I will fill each box so I don't waste space. This will also keep the cookies from rattling around inside.

I know that $6 + 4 = 10$, so I can see that 6 tens + 4 tens = 10 tens. This means $60 + 40 = 100$. I can use one 60-cookie box and one 40-cookie box.

I still have 45 cookies left because $145 - 100 = 45$.

$25 + 20 = 45$ so I will use one 25-cookie box and one 20-cookie box.

$60 + 40 + 25 + 20 = 145$

60 cookies

40 cookies

25 cookies

20 cookies

Independent Practice

At A Glance

Students find and share solutions to a multi-step, open-ended problem.

Step By Step

▶ Solve It

- Have students use their plan to begin solving the problem. Encourage them to work out their ideas and note any questions or difficulties they encounter.

- Then put students in pairs to discuss their preliminary solutions. When they are confident that their plan will work, have students independently write their solutions on a copy of Activity Sheet 22 (Solution Sheet 1) or a blank sheet of paper.

- After students complete their solutions, put them in pairs to discuss the **Reflect** question about Mathematical Practices.

- If time permits, invite various students to explain their solutions for the class to discuss, compare, and critique. Alternatively, share the solution below and invite the class to discuss.

Possible Solution

The total weight of fruit and vegetables must be between 500 and 550 pounds. They used less than 300 pounds of fruit. So let's say they used 250 pounds of fruit. $250 < 300$.

They used more than 200 pounds of vegetables. Since $250 > 200$, I can try using 250 pounds of vegetables.

250 pounds of fruit + 250 pounds of vegetables = 500 pounds of fruit and vegetables

The total amount of fruits and vegetables is greater than 500 pounds. So I'll say they used 280 pounds of vegetables. 280 pounds is greater than 200 pounds.

Check: $280 + 250 = 530$, $530 > 500$ and $530 < 550$, so 530 is between 500 and 550.

Persevere ⟩ On Your Own

Solve the problem on a separate sheet of paper.

Fruits and Vegetables

Sweet T likes to talk about numbers with the Bake Stars.

Here are some of the things he said at the end of last month.

- We used more than 200 pounds of vegetables this month.
- We used less than 300 pounds of fruit this month.
- The total amount of fruit and vegetables we used was between 500 and 550 pounds.

How many pounds of fruit could the Bake Stars have used? How many pounds of vegetables?

▶ Solve It **Find the amount of fruit and vegetables that the Bake Stars could have used.**

- Tell how many pounds of fruit they might have used.
- Tell how many pounds of vegetables they might have used.
- Show that the total weight is between 500 and 550 pounds.

▶ Reflect

Use Mathematical Practices Talk about this question with a partner.

- **Be Precise** How did you use words or symbols to show that your answer works?

148

Scoring Rubric

Points	Expectations
4	The student's response is accurate and complete. The solution steps and calculations are complete and correct. Students show their work, tell how many pounds of fruit and vegetables were used, and verify the solution.
3	The solution is substantially complete and reflects the information given. Solution steps are correct but do not detail all the comparisons. The solution is correct but may not be verified completely.
2	The student's response contains several mistakes. Some calculations are incorrect. The solution may be between 500 and 550 but the pounds of fruit or vegetables is not in the correct range. The verification is incomplete.
1	The solution is incorrect. Most or all calculations and comparisons are incorrect. The solution is not between 500 and 550 and the pounds of fruit and/or vegetables are not in the correct range. The solution is not verified.

Fruit Salads

Sweet T found a mistake that the Bake Stars made. They made 448 fruit salads for a customer. The customer only ordered 248 fruit salads. Here is what they plan to do with the extra food.

- Donate some fruit salads to the youth center.
- Keep some fruit salads at the shop. Give them out for free to customers.

How many fruit salads should the Bake Stars donate? How many should they give out for free?

▶ **Solve It** **Decide what to do with the extra fruit salads.**
- Tell how many to give to the youth center.
- Tell how many to keep at the shop.
- Explain why your numbers work.

▶ **Reflect**

Use Mathematical Practices Talk about this question with a partner.
- **Make Sense of Problems** What was the first thing that you did to solve this problem? Why?

149

Scoring Rubric

Points	Expectations
4	The solution is accurate and complete. Students show their work and tell how many fruit salads go to the youth center and stay in the shop. They use an equation to verify their solution.
3	The solution is substantially complete and reflects the information given. Solution steps are correct but all work may not be shown. The solution is correct but may not be verified correctly.
2	The solution contains several mistakes. The student may not tell how many fruit salads go to the youth center or stay at the shop. Solution steps may not be appropriate for the problem. Some calculations are set up incorrectly and may be calculated incorrectly.
1	The solution is incomplete and incorrect. The steps are incomplete and inaccurate. Calculations are incorrect. There is no verification.

Step By Step

▶ **Solve It**

- Have students work through this problem entirely on their own.

- Remind students that there are many different ways to solve a problem.

- Invite them to look back at the **Problem-Solving Checklist** to get started and help them stay on track. They might also want to look at the **Problem-Solving Tips** on other pages to get some ideas for how to start.

- Suggest that students try different numbers or different approaches. Have them write their complete solution on a copy of Activity Sheet 22 (Solution Sheet 1) or a blank sheet of paper.

- After students complete their solutions, put them in pairs to discuss the **Reflect** question about Mathematical Practices. Students may also describe other Math Practices they used.

- If time permits, invite various students to explain their solutions for the class to discuss, compare, and critique. Alternatively, share the solution below and invite the class to discuss.

Possible Solution

There are 448 fruit salads and 248 are for a customer. I need to figure out how many of the extra fruit salads to donate to the youth center and how many to keep at the shop.

$448 - 248 = 200$, so there are 200 to donate to the youth center or keep. They can give 100 fruit salads to the youth center and keep 100 at the shop.

$100 + 100 = 200$ and $100 + 100 + 248 = 448$

Differentiated Instruction

▶ Intervention Activity

Provide support for the Independent Practice.

Fruits and Vegetables

Use base-ten blocks to model the problem.

Help students understand the problem by modeling it with base-ten blocks. Have them draw three rectangles on a piece of paper and label them "< 300," "> 200," and "between 500 and 550." Then have students fill the < 300 and > 200 boxes with base-ten blocks that fit the requirements. See if they can make numbers that will be between 500 and 550. To see if they succeeded, have them combine the base-ten blocks in the "between 500" box and identify the sum.

Fruit Salads

Help students make sense of the problem with word equations and diagrams.

Begin by having students discuss what they know [how many fruit salads were made, how many the customer gets] and what they need to find out [how many of the leftovers to give to the youth center and how many to keep at the store]. Use word equations and/or diagrams to show that students first need to find how many fruit salads are leftover.

number made − number customer gets = number left over

448 fruit salads

| number customer gets | number left over |

number for youth center + number kept at store = number left over

448 fruit salads

| number customer gets | youth center |
| | store |

▶ Challenge Activity

Solve extensions to the Independent Practice.

Fruits and Vegetables

Extension

Not only did Bake Stars use < 300 pounds of fruit and > 200 pounds of vegetables, but they also used more than 100 pounds of flour. In total, they used between 700 and 800 pounds of fruit, vegetables, and flour. Tell how many pounds of fruit, vegetables, and flour they used and show that the solution works.

Possible Solution

Start with the fruit. Let's say they used 200 pounds of fruit. That's < 300. Now use vegetables to get to 600 pounds. 600 − 200 = 400. So they used 400 pounds of vegetables. 400 > 200. 100 pounds of flour gives a total of 700, but the total needs to be between 700 and 800. Try 150 pounds of flour. 150 > 100, and 200 + 400 + 150 = 750, which is > 700 and < 800.

Fruit Salads

Extension

The problem is the same, except the customer wants between 218 and 238 fruit salads and the youth center has to have an odd number of fruit salads. Come up with a solution that works for the customer, the youth center, and the store.

Possible Solution

I can start by using numbers that are easy to work with. Then I can add or subtract 1 to change an even number to an odd number. Give the customer 220 fruit salads.

448 − 220 = 228. Give the youth center 128 and keep 100 at the store. 220 + 128 + 100 = 448. But the youth center needs an odd number. So take 1 from the youth center and leave it at the store. Now the customer gets 220, the youth center gets 127, and the store gets 101: 220 + 127 + 101 = 448.

Teacher Notes

Solutions

1 Solution

Less than 436: 398, 430
Greater than 436: 442, 535
DOK 1

2 Solution

B; Break apart both addends by place value.
C; Break apart 386 by place value.
D; Add the hundreds, tens, and ones.
DOK 2

3 Solution

A; To subtract 236 − 118, regroup 3 tens as 2 tens 10 ones.
D; To subtract 862 − 523, regroup 6 tens as 5 tens 10 ones.
DOK 2

Solve the problems.

1 Compare each number below to 436.

442   430   398   535

Write each number in the correct box below.

Less Than 436	Greater Than 436
398	442
430	535

2 Shelby has 517 baseball cards and 386 football cards. She wants to find how many cards she has in all. How could she add 517 + 386? Circle all the correct answers.

A 386 + 51 + 7

B 500 + 300 + 10 + 80 + 7 + 6

C 517 + 300 + 80 + 6

D 800 + 90 + 13

3 Paige solved a subtraction problem. She had to regroup tens to subtract ones. She did not regroup hundreds. Which of these could be the problem Paige solved? Circle all the correct answers.

A   236
    − 118

B   520
    − 427

C   634
    − 251

D   862
    − 523

150

Teacher Notes

4 Ken's book has 343 pages. He has read 228 pages. How many pages does Ken have left to read?

Draw a model and write an equation to solve the problem.

Possible answer:

$343 - 228 = ?$

```
        ┌─────┐
        │ 343 │
        └─────┘
         ╱    ╲
    ┌─────┐  ┌─────┐
    │ 228 │  │  ?  │
    └─────┘  └─────┘
```

Answer ___115___ pages

5 Complete the table to show 863 in different ways. In the last row, show a way that is different from the others.

Hundreds	Tens	Ones
8	6	3
0	86	3
6	6	203

Possible answer:

Hundreds	Tens	Ones
0	0	863

151

Solutions

4 **Solution**
115; Models and equations will vary. The problem situation involves a known whole, one known part, and one unknown part. The model should show a total of 343. It should also show two parts, which are the number 228 and a variable, in either order.
DOK 2

5 **Solution**
6; 86; 203
Possible last row: 0; 0; 863; The last row should show hundreds, tens, and ones with a combined value of 863.
DOK 2

Teacher Notes

Assessment

Standards: 2.NBT.A.1a, 2.NBT.A.1b, 2.NBT.A.3, 2.NBT.B.7

DOK: 3

Materials: (optional) base-ten blocks

Standards for Mathematical Practice
2, 4, 5, 6, 7

Step By Step

About the Task

In this task, students read and write numbers using their understanding of place value. Students break apart 3-digit numbers based on the number of hundreds, tens, and ones that make up those numbers.

Getting Started

Read the problem aloud with your students. Be sure they understand that the tickets must be ordered in groups of 100, 10, and 1. Guide students to recognize the parallels between the number of tickets and the place-value system. If students are having trouble visualizing how the tickets are grouped, you might have them model a pack of 100, sheet of 10, and single ticket with base-ten blocks. *(SMP 4)*

Completing the Task

Students first need to copy the table onto a separate sheet of paper. You might suggest that they use the edge of a ruler to help them draw straight lines. Remind students to fill in the labels at the top of the table, as well as the names in the first column and the total tickets in the last column. *(SMP 5, 6)*

Students should use place-value concepts to complete the rest of the table. To determine how many packs of 100, sheets of 10, and single tickets each student can order, they need to think of the total number of tickets each student wants in terms of hundreds, tens, and ones. Have struggling students model the totals with base-ten blocks. *(SMP 4, 7)*

▶ **Extension**

Performance Task

Answer the questions. Show all your work on separate paper.

Four students want to order tickets to play their favorite games at the school fair. They have to order some packs of 100, some sheets of 10, and some single tickets.

- The table below shows the total number of tickets each student wants.

- Copy the table onto a separate sheet of paper.

How many packs of 100, sheets of 10, and single tickets can the students order to get the total number of tickets they want? Fill in your table.

Name	Packs of 100	Sheets of 10	Single Tickets	Total
Lori				555
Penn				662
Maria				656
Antoine				593

Checklist

Did You . . .

☐ use place value correctly?

☐ check your answers?

☐ explain your answers with words and numbers?

▶ **Reflect**

Look for Structure How did you use what you know about place value to solve this problem?

152

4-Point Solution

Name	Packs of 100	Sheets of 10	Single Stickers	Total
Lori	5	5	5	555
Penn	6	6	2	662
Maria	6	5	6	656
Antoine	5	9	3	593

Scoring Rubric

Points	Expectations
4	The student accurately completes the entire table, correctly determining how many packs of 100, sheets of 10, and single tickets can be ordered for each total.
3	The student completes the entire table, but makes one or two errors in determining how many packs of 100, sheets of 10, and single tickets can be ordered for each total.
2	The student only partially completes the table, and makes at least three errors in determining how many packs of 100, sheets of 10, and single tickets can be ordered for each total.
1	The student partially completes the table, but makes only limited connections to place value in determining how many packs of 100, sheets of 10, and single tickets can be ordered for each total.

▶ **Extension**

Take the performance task further.

Pedro orders 4 packs of 100 tickets, 18 sheets of 10 tickets, and 65 single tickets. What is the total number of tickets Pedro orders? Show your work.

Solution

Pedro orders 645 tickets; Possible work: 4 packs of 100 tickets = 400 tickets; 18 sheets of 10 tickets = 180 tickets; 65 single tickets = 65 tickets; 400 + 180 + 65 = 645.

Reflect

Possible Answer: The tickets come in groups of 100, 10, and 1, which is just like the place value in numbers. So I broke the total number of tickets each student wants into hundreds, tens, and ones. I wrote the number of hundreds in the column for packs of 100. I wrote the number of tens in the column for sheets of 10. And I wrote the number of ones in the column for single tickets.

Unit 3 Measurement and Data

Which lessons are students building upon?

Grade 1, Lesson 31
Order Objects by Length
1.MD.A.1

Grade 1, Lesson 32
Compare Lengths
1.MD.A.1

Grade 1, Lesson 31
Order Objects by Length
1.MD.A.1

Grade 1, Lesson 32
Compare Lengths
1.MD.A.1

Grade 1, Lesson 33
Understand Length Measurement
1.MD.A.2

Grade 1, Lesson 33
Understand Length Measurement
1.MD.A.2

Grade 2, Lesson 16
Understand Length and
Measurement Tools
2.MD.A.1

Grade 2, Lesson 17
Measure Length
2.MD.A.1

Grade 1, Lesson 31
Order Objects by Length
1.MD.A.1

Grade 2, Lesson 16
Understand Length and
Measurement Tools
2.MD.A.1

Grade 2, Lesson 17
Measure Length
2.MD.A.1

Grade 1, Lesson 31
Order Objects by Length
1.MD.A.1

Grade 1, Lesson 32
Compare Lengths
1.MD.A.1

Grade 2, Lesson 19
Understand Estimating Length
2.MD.A.3

Grade 1, Lesson 33
Understand Length Measurement
1.MD.A.2

Grade 2, Lesson 17
Measure Length
2.MD.A.1

Grade 2, Lesson 20
Compare Lengths
2.MD.A.4

Grade 1, Lesson 29
Sort and Count
1.MD.C.4

Grade 1, Lesson 30
Compare Data
1.MD.C.4

Unit 3

Lesson 16
Understand Length and Measurement Tools
2.MD.A.1

Lesson 17
Measure Length
2.MD.A.1

Lesson 18
Understand Measurement with Different Units
2.MD.A.2

Lesson 19
Understand Estimating Length
2.MD.A.3

Lesson 20
Compare Lengths
2.MD.A.4

Lesson 21
Add and Subtract Lengths
2.MD.B.5, 2.MD.B.6, 2.OA.A.1

Lesson 22
Understand Reading and Making Line Plots
2.MD.B.6, 2.MD.D.9

Which lessons are students preparing for?

Grade 3, Lesson 22
Liquid Volume
3.MD.A.2

Grade 3, Lesson 23
Mass
3.MD.A.2

Grade 3, Lesson 22
Liquid Volume
3.MD.A.2

Grade 3, Lesson 23
Mass
3.MD.A.2

Grade 3, Lesson 14
Understand What a Fraction Is
3.NF.A.1

Grade 3, Lesson 26
Measure Length and Plot Data on Line Plots
3.MD.B.4

Grade 3, Lesson 26
Measure Length and Plot Data on Line Plots
3.MD.B.4

Grade 3, Lesson 26
Measure Length and Plot Data on Line Plots
3.MD.B.4

Grade 3, Lesson 26
Measure Length and Plot Data on Line Plots
3.MD.B.4

Grade 3, Lesson 29
Add Areas
3.MD.C.7c, 3.MD.C.7d

Grade 3, Lesson 26
Measure Length and Plot Data on Line Plots
3.MD.B.4

Which lessons are students building upon?

Grade 1, Lesson 29
Sort and Count
1.MD.C.4

Grade 1, Lesson 30
Compare Data
1.MD.C.4

Grade 1, Lesson 34
Tell Time
1.MD.B.3

Unit 3

Lesson 23
Draw and Use Bar Graphs and Picture Graphs
2.MD.D.10

Lesson 24
Tell and Write Time
2.MD.C.7, 2.NBT.A.2

Lesson 25
Solve Problems Involving Money
2.MD.C.8, 2.NBT.A.2

Which lessons are students preparing for?

Grade 3, Lesson 24
Solve Problems Using Scaled Graphs
3.MD.B.3

Grade 3, Lesson 25
Draw Scaled Graphs
3.MD.B.3

Grade 3, Lesson 20
Tell and Write Time
3.MD.A.1

Grade 3, Lesson 21
Solve Problems About Time
3.MD.A.1

Grade 4, Lesson 24
Time and Money
4.MD.A.2

Unit 3
Measurement and Data

Unit 3
Measurement and Data

Let's learn about different measurement tools and units.

Real-World Connection You use measurements in many parts of your life. You and a friend might measure your heights. You subtract to find how much taller you are. Maybe you have 30 minutes for lunch each day. You might have 8 coins that are worth 48 cents.

In This Unit You will learn how to use measurement tools. You will measure lengths using different units. You will also compare measurements like length, time, and money.

✓ Self Check

Before starting this unit, check off the skills you know below.

I can:	Before this unit	After this unit
use a ruler to measure an object.	☐	☐
choose the correct tool for measuring an object.	☐	☐
measure the same object using different units.	☐	☐
estimate the length of an object.	☐	☐
compare lengths to tell which object is longer and how much longer it is.	☐	☐
add and subtract lengths to solve problems.	☐	☐
measure lengths and show data on a line plot.	☐	☐
draw and solve problems with picture graphs and bar graphs.	☐	☐
tell and write time to the nearest 5 minutes.	☐	☐
solve problems about money.	☐	☐

▣ Ready Mathematics
PRACTICE AND PROBLEM SOLVING

Practice and Problem Solving Resources

Use the following resources from *Practice and Problem Solving* to engage students and their families and to extend student learning.

- **Family Letters** Send Family Letters home separately before each lesson or as part of a family communication package.

- **Unit Games** Use partner Unit Games at classroom centers and/or send them home for play with family members.

- **Unit Practice** Assign Unit Practice as homework, as independent or small group practice, or for whole class discussion.

- **Unit Performance Tasks** Have students solve real-world Unit Performance Tasks independently or in small groups.

- **Unit Vocabulary** Use Unit Vocabulary throughout the unit to personalize student's acquisition of mathematics vocabulary.

- **Fluency Practice** Assign Fluency Skills Practice and Fluency Repeated Reasoning Practice worksheets throughout the unit.

At A Glance

- This page introduces students to the general ideas behind measurement tools and units.

- The checklist allows them to see what skills they will be learning and take ownership of their progress.

Step By Step

- Explain to students that they are going to begin a new unit of lessons. Tell them that in all the lessons in this unit they will be learning about different measurement tools and units.

- Have the class read together the introduction to the unit in their books. Invite and respond to comments and questions, if any.

- Then take a few minutes to have each student independently read through the list of skills.

- Ask students to consider each skill and check the box if it is a skill they think they already have. Remind students that these skills are likely to all be new to them, but it's still possible some students have some of the skills.

- Engage students in a brief discussion about the skills. Invite students to comment on which ones they would most like to learn, or which ones seem similar or related to something they already know. Remind them that the goal is to be able to check off one skill at a time until they have them all checked.

Lesson 16
Understand Length and Measurement Tools

CCSS Focus

Domain
Measurement and Data

Cluster
A. Measure and estimate lengths in standard units.

Standards
2.MD.A.1 Measure the length of an object by selecting and using appropriate tools such as rulers, yardsticks, meter sticks, and measuring tapes.

Standards for Mathematical Practice (SMP)
5 Use appropriate tools strategically.
6 Attend to precision.

Lesson Objectives

Content Objectives
- Understand that objects can be measured using different units.
- Understand that measuring with standard units makes comparing lengths easier.
- Represent and measure the length of an object using tiles and a ruler.

Language Objectives
- Describe how to use a ruler to measure an object by lining up one end of the object with the zero mark on the ruler.
- Tell the reason for using standard units of measure.
- Create an inch ruler using a strip of paper and 1-inch tiles.

Prerequisite Skills

- Count fluently from 0 to 20.
- Understand that a model can represent a length.

Lesson Vocabulary

- **standard unit** a unit of measure, such as a centimeter or a foot that has a defined length, as compared to a non-standard unit such as a shoe-length.
- **inch** the smallest unit of length in the U.S. customary system. A quarter is about 1 inch across. 12 inches is equivalent to 1 foot.
- **centimeter** a unit of length in the metric system. Your little finger is about 1 centimeter across. 100 centimeters is equivalent to 1 meter.

Review the following key terms.

- **length** a measurement that tells the distance from one point to another.
- **measure** to determine the length of an object by comparing it to a standard.

Learning Progression

In Grade 1 students compare the lengths of two objects directly, by placing the objects next to each other. They use words such as taller, shorter, and longer to compare and describe lengths.

In Grade 2 students measure the lengths of objects using a variety of tools. They learn about different units of length, and compare and estimate lengths. Students also solve problems involving adding and subtracting lengths, and they organize length data in a line plot.

In this lesson students investigate why we use standardized units for measuring lengths and why we use numbers to describe lengths. They use rulers and tiles to measure the lengths of objects to the nearest inch or centimeter.

In Grade 3 students measure objects more precisely, using half-inches and quarter-inches, when appropriate. They use what they know about length to solve problems involving perimeter and area. They also extend their use of standard units to measures of liquid volume and mass.

Lesson Pacing Guide

Whole Class Instruction

Day 1 *45–60 minutes*	**Introduction** • Opening Activity *20 min* • Think It Through Question *5 min* • Think *10 min* • Think *10 min* • Reflect *5 min*	**Practice and Problem Solving** Assign pages 171–172.
Day 2 *45–60 minutes*	**Guided Instruction** **Think About Measuring with Tiles and Rulers** • Let's Explore the Idea *25 min* • Let's Talk About It *10 min* • Try It Another Way *10 min*	**Practice and Problem Solving** Assign pages 173–174.
Day 3 *45–60 minutes*	**Guided Practice** **Connect Ideas About Measuring with Tiles and Rulers** • Create *15 min* • Compare *15 min* • Analyze *15 min*	**Practice and Problem Solving** Assign pages 175–176.
Day 4 *45–60 minutes*	**Independent Practice** **Apply Ideas About Measuring with Tiles and Rulers** • Put It Together *30 min* • Pair/Share *15 min*	
Day 5 *45–60 minutes*	• On-Level, Intervention, or Challenge Activity *20 min* **Toolbox: Lesson Quiz** Lesson 16 Quiz	

Small Group Differentiation

Teacher-Toolbox.com

Reteach
Ready Prerequisite Lessons *45–90 min*

Grade 1
• Lesson 31 Order Objects by Length
• Lesson 32 Compare Lengths

Student-led Activities
Math Center Activities *30–40 min*

Grade 2 *(Lesson 16)*
• 2.29 Measurement Vocabulary Match

Opening Activity

Measuring on Grid Paper

Objective Experiment with measuring lengths.

Time *20–30 minutes*

Materials for each student
- Activity Sheet 3 (1-Inch Grid Paper)

Overview

Students are asked to find objects in the classroom that fit inside a rectangle.

Step By Step

1 Describe the situation.

- Tell students that a company is designing a new pencil box that is 2 inches by 7 inches. Model how to draw a 2-inch by 7-inch rectangle on the 1-inch grid paper. Have students do the same on their own grids.

- Tell students they need to find out which classroom objects will fit in the box.

2 Measure objects.

- Have students work in pairs.

- Ask each pair to find at least five different objects that fit in the box and one that does not fit.

3 Collect the data.

- As students find and measure the objects, have them keep a list of what fits in the box and what does not.

4 Discuss the results as a class.

- Invite students to show the objects they found that will fit in the box.

- Ask: *How could you tell that an object will fit in the box?* Students might place the object on the grid paper, or place the grid paper on the object.

- Explain that you want to find the longest of all their objects that will fit in the box. Ask: *How can we tell which is the longest object? What is the longest object?* Students might suggest putting two objects next to each other to see which is the longest.

- Ask: *Do you think that the company should make a pencil box this size? Do you have any suggestions about changing the shape or size of the box?* Answers will vary. Have students explain their responses.

Teacher Notes

👥 Introduction

At A Glance

Students explore how to measure an object using paper clips. Then students learn how to use standard units to measure length.

Step By Step

- Work through **Think It Through** as a class.

- Discuss the question at the top of the page. Ask students to describe different ways they have measured length in real life.

- Read the **Think** section together.

- Invite students to suggest why each of the four guidelines in the **Think** section must be followed when measuring an object.

- Ask Mathematical Discourse questions 1 and 2 to be certain that students understand the importance of using the same unit and not a combination of units to measure an object.

▶ **Mathematical Discourse 1 and 2**

▶ **Real-World Connection**

💭 Think It Through

What does it mean to measure length?

You can find the length of objects, like a marker.

length

Think You can use objects to measure length.

You can use paper clips to measure the length of a marker.

Line up the edge of the first paper clip with the edge of the marker.

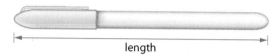

- Do not put the marker in the middle of the paper clips. ✕

- Do not use paper clips that are different sizes. ✕

- Do not have any spaces between the paper clips. ✕

- Do not have any paper clip on top of another paper clip. ✕

✏️ How many paper clips fit under the marker? ___5___

154

▶ Mathematical Discourse

1 *Suppose we had 3 big paper clips and 3 small paper clips, and they all fit under the marker exactly. Would it be correct to say that the marker is 6 paper clips long? Why or why not?*

Students' responses should indicate that to make an accurate measurement, all the paper clips need to be the same size.

2 *Do you think that paper clips are good tools for measuring? Why or why not?*

Students may point out that keeping the paper clips in a straight line could be difficult, or that we can't be sure that everyone uses paper clips of the same length.

▶ Real-World Connection

Ask students to think of some examples of lengths that they know and use in their daily life.

Examples: how many blocks students travel to school, who is the tallest in the class, the length of a sports field, how deep a swimming pool is, how many miles to a grandparent's home, etc.

Students may describe lengths using comparisons: *I'm tall enough to stand up in the shallow end of the pool.* They might also use units: *It's four blocks from my house to my friend's house.* Listen for and talk about different types of units, both standard and non-standard.

Think **You can use units of the same size to measure objects.**

Inches and centimeters are two units used to measure length.

The length of a quarter is about 1 **inch** (in.).

Your little finger is about 1 **centimeter** (cm) across.

1 inch is a little longer than 2 centimeters.

A ruler is a tool used to measure length.

This ruler is not life-sized.

▶ **Reflect** **Work with a partner.**

1 **Talk About It** Why would you measure the length of your shoe with a ruler instead of paper clips?

Write About It Possible answer: Using a ruler is easier than lining up paper clips next to my shoe. Also, I know the units on a ruler are the same for everyone.

155

Step By Step

- Give each student a ruler, and allow time for free exploration with the rulers. Read the **Think** section together. Have each student find both the inches and the centimeters on the rulers.

- If students are using separate rulers for inches and centimeters, explain that some rulers show both units, such as the ruler shown on the student page.

- Discuss with students how a ruler is similar to a number line. The left edge is 0. Each tick mark represents the distance from that mark to 0. The 0 should always line up with one side of whatever object is being measured.

- Read the **Reflect** question together. Ask students to discuss the question with a partner and then write their answer.

- Invite students to share their answers to the **Reflect** question with the class.

▶ **Mathematical Discourse 3–5**

▶ **English Language Learners**

- **Note:** Students may be familiar with the U.S. customary system of measurement (inches, feet, yards), the metric system (centimeters, meters, kilometers), or both.

- U.S. customary units are used in the United States. The metric system is used in most countries outside the United States. In the United States, the metric system is used in the areas of science, medicine, and other industries.

Ready **Mathematics**
PRACTICE AND PROBLEM SOLVING

Assign *Practice and Problem Solving* **pages 171–172** after students have completed this section.

▶ **English Language Learners**

ELL students may be more familiar with the metric system than with the U.S. customary system. Assure students that they will have many opportunities to practice measuring in both systems.

▶ **Mathematical Discourse**

3 *What if "one inch" meant "the length of an eraser"?*

Students should understand that since erasers come in many different sizes, a measurement such as "3 inches" could mean different lengths, depending on the size of your eraser.

4 *What if you use inches to measure your shoe, and your friend uses paper clips to measure her shoe? Can you compare the lengths of the two shoes?*

Listen to be sure that students understand that if two people use different units, it is more difficult to compare lengths correctly. They may suggest that if you know the length of a paper clip in inches, you could compare the lengths.

5 *Why do we need standard units such as inches and centimeters?*

We need standard units so that we all agree on what a length such as "10 inches" means.

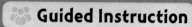

Guided Instruction

At A Glance

Students measure length with inch tiles and line up the tiles with an inch ruler. Then students analyze these measurements and measure the length of a piece of yarn in centimeters.

Step By Step

Let's Explore the Idea

- Give each student some inch tiles cut from Activity Sheet 3 (1-Inch Grid Paper).

- Work through Problems 2 and 3 as a class. You may want to put the measurement activity in a context, such as, "Audrey needs 4 inches of yarn for a craft project. Does she have enough yarn?"

▶ **Mathematical Discourse 1–3**

- Have students complete Problems 4–6 individually.

- As students work, circulate among them. As they place the tiles above the ruler, check that they don't leave spaces between the tiles and don't overlap the tiles. Make sure students understand that the number of tiles needed to measure the yarn is the same as the length of the yarn in inches.

▶ **Hands-On Activity**

> **SMP TIP Use Tools**
> Students use appropriate tools as they measure. Encourage students to think about how using tiles and using a ruler are similar, and about how they could measure if neither one were available. *(SMP 5)*

Think About ▶ **Measuring with Tiles and Rulers**

🔍 **Let's Explore the Idea** You can use 1-inch tiles to help you understand a ruler.

2 Use the tiles your teacher gives you to find the length of the yarn.

How many tiles did you use? __6__

3 Each tile is 1 inch long.
How long is the yarn? __6 inches__

4 Number the tiles you used in order from 1 to 6.

5 Place Tile 1 above the ruler below. Place it so the left side of the tile lines up with 0.
Then put the other tiles in order next to Tile 1.

| 0 | | 1 | | 2 | | 3 | | 4 | | 5 | 6 |
| inches | | | | | | | | | | | |

6 What do you notice about the numbers on your tiles and on the ruler?

Tile 1 ended at 1 on the ruler, tile 2 ended at 2 on the ruler, and so on.

156

▶ **Mathematical Discourse**

1 *How do you know where to put the first tile when you measure the yarn?*
It is important to line up one edge of the tile with one end of the yarn.

2 *What would happen if you left spaces between the tiles or overlapped the tiles when measuring the yarn?*
The measurement would be incorrect.

3 *If you put your inch tiles in a different order, would you still need the same number of tiles?*
Yes, the order of the tiles does not matter.

▶ **Hands-On Activity**

Practice measuring with inch tiles.

Materials: For each pair: inch tiles cut from Activity Sheet 3 (1-Inch Grid Paper), assorted classroom objects

- Have students work in pairs. Ask them to measure items in the classroom with the inch tiles. Both students in the pair should measure the same object, and then agree on the length.

- Students record lengths in a table.

Object	Length (in inches)
Short side of notebook	8

- Discuss the results. What is the longest length they found? What is the shortest? What are some problems with measuring using inch tiles?

Let's Talk About It
Work with a partner.

7 Where do you put the first tile when you measure the yarn?

at the edge of the yarn

8 How do you find the length of the yarn using tiles?

Count how many tiles there are. Each tile is 1 inch. There are 6 tiles,

so it is 6 inches long.

9 Use your ruler to measure the yarn. What number on the ruler should you line up with the left end of the yarn? _____ the 0

10 Now how do you find the length of the yarn?

Look at the number that lines up with the other end of the yarn. The

number is 6, so the yarn is 6 inches long.

▶ **Try It Another Way** **Now use 1-centimeter tiles.**

11 Use 1-centimeter tiles to measure the length of this yarn. How many tiles do you use? _____ 11

12 Each tile is 1 centimeter long.
How long is the yarn? _____ 11 centimeters

13 Now use the centimeter side of your ruler to measure.
Based on the ruler, how long is the yarn? 11 centimeters

157

Step By Step

Let's Talk About It

- Have students work with a partner to complete Problems 7–10.

- For Problem 9, some students may think that they should line up the end of the yarn with the tick mark at 1 on the ruler, instead of at 0. Remind the class that the number 1 at the first tick mark represents a distance of 1 inch from the 0 edge of the ruler. The number 1 is not a starting point.

▶ **Mathematical Discourse 4 and 5**

Try It Another Way

- Direct students' attention to **Try It Another Way**. Make sure that all students have centimeter tiles cut from Activity Sheet 4 (1-Centimeter Grid Paper). Have students complete the problems individually, then compare their results with a partner.

> **SMP TIP Attend to Precision**
> When lining up tiles and counting them, students attend to precision. They should apply the same precision to measuring with rulers. *(SMP 6)*

▶ **Mathematical Discourse 6**

▶ **Real-World Connection**

Ready Mathematics
PRACTICE AND PROBLEM SOLVING

Assign *Practice and Problem Solving* **pages 173–174** after students have completed this section.

▶ **Real-World Connection**

Share with students some ways in which measurements are used in different careers. For example, a surveyor measures land. A biologist might use a stage micrometer (a microscope slide with a scale on it) to take very small measurements. A carpenter uses a tape measure to measure and cut pieces of wood.

▶ **Mathematical Discourse**

4 *Will you get the same result if you measure the yarn with inch tiles and then with a ruler?*

Yes, the result should be the same.

5 *Which tool do you think is easier to use for measuring, the inch tiles or the ruler?*

Students may suggest that the ruler is easier to handle, more accurate, and better for measuring an object that is vertical.

6 *Do you think it is easier to measure in inches or in centimeters?*

Answers will vary. Students may prefer inches because the tiles are larger and easier to handle, or centimeters because they seem more accurate.

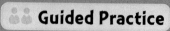

Guided Practice

At A Glance

Students demonstrate their understanding of measuring tools. Then students create rulers in both inches and centimeters.

Step By Step

- Discuss each problem as a class using the discussion points outlined below.

Create

- This problem focuses on the concept that measuring a length with a ruler corresponds to counting the number of tiles that align with the length.

- As students share their completed rulers, ask questions like: *What does the number 4 represent on the ruler?* Listen for responses that demonstrate the recognition that each number on a ruler represents the distance from the 0 point of the ruler to the corresponding mark on the ruler.

Compare

- This problem asks students to notice that the units on a ruler must be equal in size. Make sure students understand that after they circle the ruler that was made correctly, they should write below how they know it was made correctly.

- Ask: *Could you use a ruler that is made with a mixture of inch tiles and centimeter tiles?* Students should recognize that the units on one side of a ruler are either all inches or all centimeters.

Analyze

- As students analyze the error, ask them to look at where the crayon and the tiles line up with the ruler.

- Ask: *Why do you think Tony made the error he did?* Students may suggest that it seems natural to start a sequence at 1 rather than 0. Remind students that the mark at number 1 represents a distance of 1 unit from the 0 mark. Students should notice that the crayon and the tiles need to line up with 0 on the ruler.

Connect Ideas About Measuring with Tiles and Rulers

Talk about these problems as a class. Then write your answers.

14 Create Macie lined up 1-centimeter tiles along a strip of paper. She marked the end of each tile. Write numbers on the blanks to finish making the ruler.

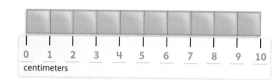

15 Compare Ty and Lynn each made a ruler.

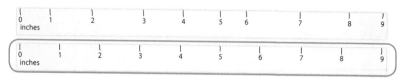

Circle the ruler that was made correctly. How do you know?

These rulers are not life-sized.

It has units (or spaces) that are all the same size.

16 Analyze Tony says the crayon is 8 centimeters long.

What did Tony do wrong?

Tony lined up the crayon with the 1 instead of the 0.

158

Scoring Rubrics

	Part A	
Points	**Expectations**	
2	The student lines up the inch tiles starting at the 0 mark. The ends of the tiles are marked and numbered correctly, and the correct length of the ruler is given.	
1	The student is partially correct. The completed ruler may have some extra spaces between the tick marks or be numbered incorrectly.	
0	The student was not able to create the ruler.	

Apply **Ideas About Measuring with Tiles and Rulers**

Put It Together **Use what you have learned to complete this task.**

17 For this task, you will need 1-inch tiles and 1-centimeter tiles.

    Part A Use 1-inch tiles to make a ruler. Check students' rulers.

    How long is your ruler?   6 inches

    Part B Use 1-centimeter tiles to make a ruler. Check students' rulers.

    How long is your ruler?   15 centimeters

    Part C Explain the steps you took to make the rulers.

    Possible answer: First I lined up a tile with the 0. Then I placed more

    tiles to the right of it with no spaces. I stopped when another tile would

    not fit inside the rectangle. Then I marked the end of each tile. Then I

    numbered the marks.

159

Step By Step

Put It Together

- Direct students to complete the **Put It Together** task on their own.

- Read the directions with students and make sure they understand each part of the task before proceeding.

- As students work on their own, walk around to assess their progress and understanding, to answer their questions, and to give additional support, if needed.

- If time permits, ask students to share the rulers they created and explain why they are good measurement tools.

 **Mathematics**
PRACTICE AND PROBLEM SOLVING

Assign *Practice and Problem Solving* **pages 175–176** after students have completed Guided Practice.

Part B	
Points	**Expectations**
2	The student lines up the centimeter tiles starting at the 0 mark. The ends of the tiles are marked and numbered correctly, and the correct length of the ruler is given.
1	The student is partially correct. The completed ruler may have some extra spaces between the tick marks or be numbered incorrectly.
0	The student was not able to create the ruler.

Part C	
Points	**Expectations**
2	The student's response accurately describes all steps the student took to make the ruler.
1	The student's response omits one or more steps used to create the ruler.
0	The student was not able to describe how the ruler was made.

Differentiated Instruction

► Intervention Activity

Model rulers with grid paper.

Materials: 1-Inch Grid Paper (Activity Sheet 3), 1-Centimeter Grid Paper (Activity Sheet 4), crayons (including red), scissors, and objects to measure

• Tell students to position the 1-inch grid paper horizontally and color the first square in one row red. They then use a different color to shade the remaining 7 squares.

• Have students cut out and use this homemade ruler to measure several different objects. If possible, choose objects with dimensions that are whole inches. Tell students to make sure that the red square always lines up with the left edge of the object they are measuring. Then they should count all of the squares to find the length of the object.

• Repeat the activity using 20 squares on 1-centimeter grid paper and a different set of objects, if necessary.

► On-Level Activity

Measure your foot.

Materials: ruler, paper and pencil

• Have students work in groups of 3 or 4.

• Tell students they will measure the length of each person's foot in their group, to the nearest inch.

• Have each student trace around his or her own foot on a piece of paper. Then students use a ruler to measure the longest length on their own tracing, to the nearest inch. Have another student in the group check the measurement.

• Record each student's name and foot length. When all the groups are finished, compare all the lengths. Who has the longest foot?

► Challenge Activity

Model proportional reasoning.

Materials: For each group: at least 12 of the same measureable object, such as unused crayons, index or playing cards, or pieces of paper; yardstick or meter stick

• Have students work in small groups to complete the following steps.

• Measure the length of one crayon, to the nearest inch or centimeter, and record the length in a table like the one below. Put two crayons end to end and measure the total length. Add a third crayon to the chain and measure the total length again.

Number of Crayons	Total Length (inches)
1	
2	

• Continue adding crayons, measuring, and recording until the chain of crayons is longer than the yardstick or meter stick.

• Ask students to look for patterns in the lengths they recorded. Can they predict the length of a line of 100 crayons? Ask them to explain their reasoning using diagrams or words.

Teacher Notes

Overview

Assign the Lesson 16 Quiz and have students work independently to complete it.

Use the results of the quiz to assess students' understanding of the content of the lesson and to identify areas for reteaching. See the Lesson Pacing Guide at the beginning of the lesson and the Differentiated Instruction activities that follow for suggested instructional resources.

Tested Skills

Assesses 2.MD.A.1

Problems on this assessment form require students to be able to measure lengths using different tools (tiles, ruler) and different units (inches, centimeters), determine if a certain tool is appropriate for measuring a given object, and create a paper ruler. Students will also need to be familiar with counting from 0 to 20 and measuring length by iterating the same-sized unit with no gaps or overlaps, and understand that objects can be measured with different units.

Ready® Mathematics

Lesson 16 Quiz

Solve the problems.

1 Which objects have a length that would be easy to measure with one ruler marked only in inches?

Circle *Yes* or *No* for each object.

a. a book   Yes   No

b. a kitten   Yes   No

c. a road   Yes   No

d. a telephone pole   Yes   No

e. a carrot   Yes   No

2 Mateo makes a ruler using 1-inch tiles. How should Mateo label the ruler?

Fill in the blanks to label Mateo's ruler.

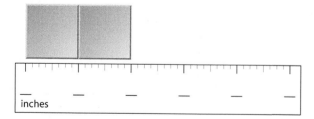

inches

Lesson 16 Quiz continued

3 Steven uses 1-centimeter tiles to measure the length of a pretzel. How long is the pretzel in centimeters?

Fill in the blank.

Answer: The pretzel is _____ centimeter(s) long.

4 Leila and Becky each make a ruler. Whose ruler was made the correct way?

Leila's Ruler

| 0 | 1 | 2 | 3 | 4 | 5 | 6 | 7 |

Becky's Ruler

| 0 | 1 | 2 | 3 | 4 | 5 | 6 | 7 |

Circle the correct explanation.

A Leila's ruler is made the correct way. It starts at the zero mark and the marks are numbered in order.

B Neither ruler is made the correct way. The numbers should start at 1, not 0.

C Becky's ruler was made the correct way. The marks have equal space between them.

D Both rulers are made the correct way. They both have the same starting and ending numbers and each mark is counted correctly.

Common Misconceptions and Errors

Errors may result if students:

• measure an object from 1 instead of 0 when using a ruler, misalign the ruler with the object, or read the ruler incorrectly.

• confuse units (inches and centimeters).

• count all marks, not just the whole-unit marks, when labeling a ruler.

• incorrectly estimate the length of a common object.

Ready® **Mathematics**

Lesson 16 Quiz Answer Key

1. a. Yes
   b. Yes
   c. No
   d. No
   e. Yes
   DOK 2

2. 0, 1, 2, 3, 4, 5
   DOK 2

3. 6
   DOK 1

4. C
   DOK 3

CCSS Focus

Domain
Measurement and Data

Cluster
A. Measure and estimate lengths in standard units.

Standards
2.MD.A.1 Measure the length of an object by selecting and using appropriate tools such as rulers, yardsticks, meter sticks, and measuring tapes.

Additional Standards
2.NBT.B.5 (see page B3 for full text)

Standards for Mathematical Practice (SMP)

3 Construct viable arguments and critique the reasoning of others.

4 Model with mathematics.

5 Use appropriate tools strategically.

6 Attend to precision.

7 Look for and make use of structure.

Lesson Objectives

Content Objectives

• Learn about rulers, yardsticks, meter sticks, and tape measures.

• Measure lengths using different tools.

• Learn how to use a ruler repeatedly to measure a length.

• Choose a tool for measuring the length of a given object.

Language Objectives

• Record the lengths of objects measured with a ruler, tape measure, or meter stick.

• Tell which measuring tool would be best for measuring a particular object.

• Justify answers and communicate the results to others.

Prerequisite Skills

• Understand that objects can be measured with different units.

• Add multiples of 10.

Lesson Vocabulary

• **foot** a unit of length in the U.S. customary system. 1 foot is equal to 12 inches.

• **yard** a unit of length in the U.S. customary system. 1 yard is equal to 3 feet or 36 inches.

• **meter** a unit of length in the metric system. 1 meter is equal to 100 centimeters.

Review the following key terms.

• **inch** the smallest unit of length in the U.S. customary system. A quarter is about 1 inch across. 12 inches is equivalent to 1 foot.

• **centimeter** a unit of length in the metric system. Your little finger is about 1 centimeter across. 100 centimeters is equivalent to 1 meter.

Learning Progression

In Grade 1 students learn about length as a measurable attribute. They use non-standard units, such as tiles and paper clips, to measure length by iterating the same-sized unit with no gaps or overlaps. They compare and order lengths of objects.

In the previous lesson students began using standardized units to measure lengths. They discovered that standard units are useful for comparing and recording measurements.

In this lesson students learn about measuring with different tools, such as rulers, yardsticks, and measuring tapes. They learn how to choose which tool to use, and how to measure an object longer than a ruler by using the ruler repeatedly.

In the next lesson students will compare measurements in different types of units. They will find that the smaller the unit, the greater the number needed to measure an object.

Lesson Pacing Guide

Whole Class Instruction

Day 1 45–60 minutes	**Toolbox: Interactive Tutorial*** *Using a Ruler: Inches* **Introduction** • Opening Activity *15 min* • Use What You Know *10 min* • Find Out More *10 min* • Reflect *5 min*	**Practice and Problem Solving** Assign pages 179–180.
Day 2 45–60 minutes	**Modeled and Guided Instruction** **Learn About Measuring Length** • Measure It/Measure It *10 min* • Connect It *25 min* • Try It *10 min*	**Practice and Problem Solving** Assign pages 181–182.
Day 3 45–60 minutes	**Modeled and Guided Instruction** **Learn About More Ways to Measure Length** • Measure It/Measure It *20 min* • Connect It *20 min* • Try It *5 min*	**Practice and Problem Solving** Assign pages 183–184.
Day 4 45–60 minutes	**Guided Practice** **Practice Measuring Length** • Example *5 min* • Problems 14–16 *15 min* • Pair/Share *15 min* • Solutions *10 min*	**Practice and Problem Solving** Assign pages 185–186.
Day 5 45–60 minutes	**Independent Practice** **Practice Measuring Length** • Problems 1–6 *20 min* • Quick Check and Remediation *10 min* • Hands-On or Challenge Activity *15 min* **Toolbox: Lesson Quiz** Lesson 17 Quiz	

Small Group Differentiation

Teacher-Toolbox.com

Reteach
Ready Prerequisite Lessons 45–90 min

Grade 1
• Lesson 32 Compare Lengths
• Lesson 33 *Understand* Length Measurement

Student-led Activities
Math Center Activities 30–40 min

Grade 2 *(Lesson 17)*
• 2.30 Measure Lengths of Objects

*We continually update the Interactive Tutorials. Check the Teacher Toolbox for the most up-to-date offerings for this lesson.

Opening Activity

Measuring Paths on a Grid

Objective Practice measuring in inches.

Time *15–20 minutes*

Materials for each student
- Activity Sheet 3 (1-Inch Grid Paper)
- colored pencils
- ruler

Overview

Students will explore finding and measuring different paths between two locations on grid paper.

Step By Step

1 Present the situation.

- Have students draw a rectangle that is 3 inches by 4 inches on their grid paper. Then have them draw two points labeled "Home" and "School" at two opposite vertices of the rectangle.

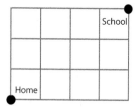

- Tell students that they are going to find the lengths of different paths from a teacher's home to her school. The paths have to stay on the grid lines and cannot go outside the 3 × 4 rectangle.

2 Sketch some possible paths.

- On the board, draw some examples of paths that the teacher might take.

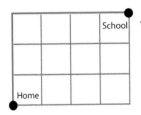 This is one path the teacher could take from home to school. Its length is 7 inches on the grid paper.

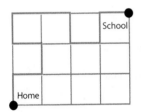 This is a longer path that the teacher could take from home to school. Its length is 11 inches on the grid paper.

- Give students time to find at least 6 different paths that the teacher could take. They may prefer to use different colors to draw the paths, or draw more rectangles. As they finish each path, have them find its length in inches. They can use rulers to confirm the lengths.

3 Share results.

- After students have finished, compile their path lengths. What is the shortest path length they could find? What is the longest? Did anyone find a path that is 8 inches long? Did any path cross itself, or hit the same intersection twice?

4 Extend the problem.

- Have students measure directly from the point labeled "Home" to the point labeled "School," along the diagonal of the rectangle. [5 inches]

- Ask students to suppose that each grid square represents 10 blocks. How could you find how many blocks long any of the paths are? [Find how long the path is in inches. Count by 10 that many times.]

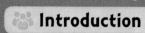

Introduction

At A Glance

Students review measuring with a centimeter ruler. Then students learn about different types of measuring tools.

Step By Step

- Work through **Use What You Know** as a class.

- Tell students that this page shows how to measure in centimeters with a ruler.

- Read the problem at the top of the page as a class. Then have students answer Questions a–d on their own.

- As students work, circulate among them to assess understanding and address any misconceptions about aligning a ruler correctly.

▶ **Mathematical Discourse 1**

- Once students have completed the questions, go through the results with the class.

▶ **Mathematical Discourse 2**

- Draw lines of different lengths on the board, and ask pairs of students to measure them in centimeters. One student can hold the ruler, and the other can read the measurement.

- If students are using rulers that have centimeters on one edge and inches on the other, make sure they use the side with centimeters.

> **SMP TIP** Use Tools
> Throughout this lesson, students use tiles, rulers, yardsticks, and meter sticks to measure. This gives them the opportunity to find out how the different tools look and feel and to practice using appropriate tools strategically. *(SMP 5)*

☺ Use What You Know

Review how a ruler measures length.

Alex uses his scissors to cut out some shapes.

What is the length of the scissors in centimeters?

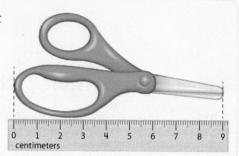

a. What units are shown on the ruler? _____centimeters_____

b. What number is lined up with the handle of the scissors? ___0___

c. How do you use a ruler to measure the scissors?

Possible answer: Make sure one end of the scissors lines

up with the 0 on the ruler. Read the number on the ruler

below the other end.

d. What is the length of the scissors?

The length of the scissors is 9 centimeters.

160

▶ Mathematical Discourse

1 *What do you notice about how the ruler is lined up with the scissors?*

Students should know that the 0 mark on the ruler is correctly placed to align with one end of the scissors. Also, students should recognize that the ruler is lined up to measure the longest possible length of the scissors.

2 *How did you decide that the scissors are 9 centimeters long instead of 8 centimeters or 10 centimeters?*

Answers may vary, but students should know that the tip of the scissors is closest to the 9 centimeter mark on the ruler.

▶▶ Find Out More

Rulers often show both inches and centimeters.

Many rulers show 12 inches. This is equal to 1 **foot**.

This ruler is not life-sized.

How many inches are on the ruler? _____ 12 inches

How many centimeters are on the ruler? _____ 30 centimeters

Some measuring tools are longer than a ruler.

- A yardstick shows 36 inches.
  There are 36 inches in a **yard**.

- A meter stick shows 100 centimeters.
  There are 100 centimeters in a **meter**.

- A tape measure can show inches and centimeters.

▶ Reflect **Work with a partner.**

1 **Talk About It** How is a yardstick like an inch ruler? How is it different?

Write About It Possible answer: They both show

inches. A yardstick is longer than an inch ruler.

161

Step By Step

- Read **Find Out More** as a class. If possible, have rulers, yardsticks, meter sticks, and tape measures available for students to use.

▶ **English Language Learners**

- Have students examine each type of tool that you have available. Ask them to find the 0 mark on each tool and to determine which type of units each tool measures. Then ask: *How many inches are on a yardstick?* [36 inches] *How many centimeters are on a meter stick?* [100 centimeters]

- Explain that a tape measure is useful for measuring very long lengths, such as the length of a room.

- If your classroom rulers have both centimeters and inches, have students find both units on the rulers. Discuss with students how they can check to make sure they are using the correct units each time they measure.

- Ask students to tell you which of the measuring tools is the shortest and which is the longest.

- Have students work in pairs to read and answer the **Reflect** question.

▶ **Real-World Connection**

▶ **Visual Model**

Ready Mathematics
PRACTICE AND PROBLEM SOLVING

Assign *Practice and Problem Solving* **pages 179–180** after students have completed this section.

▶ Visual Model

Create a representation of your measuring tools.

- On the board or on a large sheet of paper, have different pairs of students trace and label each of the measuring tools that you have in the classroom. One student can hold the tool while the other traces.

Inch ruler

Centimeter ruler

Yardstick

- If possible, leave this diagram on the board throughout the measurement lessons.

▶ English Language Learners

Discuss with students that the word *foot* has two different meanings. It can refer to either the unit of measure or to the part of your body that is below the ankle. Students may find it helpful to know that the unit of measure was originally based on the length of an adult's foot.

▶ Real-World Connection

Discuss jobs in which workers might use the measuring tools shown in this lesson. Students may have noticed the measuring tape being used by plumbers or architects, or by employees in fabric stores. Point out that measuring length is a very common use of mathematics in everyday life.

Modeled and Guided Instruction

At A Glance

Students compare measuring with inch tiles and measuring with a ruler. Then students complete this problem and use centimeters to measure a key.

Step By Step

- Read the problem at the top of the page as a class. Make sure that students have inch tiles cut from Activity Sheet 3 (1-Inch Grid Paper), rulers, and paper. You may also wish to provide students with centimeter tiles cut from Activity Sheet 4 (1-Centimeter Grid Paper).

Measure It

- Draw students' attention to **Measure It**. Have students align their inch tiles with the paper as shown in the diagram. Use Mathematical Discourse questions 1 and 2 to emphasize the importance of lining up the tiles right next to each other, without any extra spaces between them and without overlapping.

▶ **Mathematical Discourse 1 and 2**

Measure It

- Draw students' attention to **Measure It**. Have them line up their rulers with the paper.

> **SMP TIP Attend to Precision**
> Lining up the 0 mark of a measuring tool correctly is a good opportunity for students to attend to precision. You may want to have students move objects to the left and right of the 0 mark to see how this affects the measurement. *(SMP 6)*

▶ **Mathematical Discourse 3 and 4**

- Point out that students can use centimeters to measure the paper instead of inches. If you have them measure using centimeter tiles, note that the last tile does not align with the right edge of the paper. Tell students that we say the paper is "almost 28 centimeters long" in this case.

Learn About ▶ Measuring Length

Read the problem. Then you will look at ways to measure.

> Erin wants to measure the length of a sheet of notebook paper. What is the length in inches?

▶ **Measure It** You can use 1-inch tiles to find the length.
Line up the edge of the paper with the first tile.

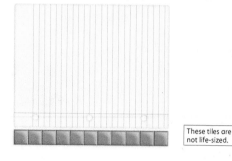

These tiles are not life-sized.

▶ **Measure It** You can use a ruler to find the length.
Line up the edge of the paper with the 0 on the inch ruler.

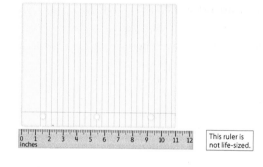

This ruler is not life-sized.

162

▶ Mathematical Discourse

1 *Why is it important to make sure that the tiles are lined up right next to each other?*
If there are spaces or gaps between the tiles, the measurement will be incorrect.

2 *What would happen if parts of some tiles were on top of other tiles?*
The measurement would be incorrect.

3 *How do you know that the inch tiles and ruler are lined up with the paper correctly?*
When measuring with inch tiles, one edge of a tile should line up with one edge of the paper. When measuring with a ruler, the 0 mark on the ruler should line up with the edge of the paper.

4 *What do the two methods of measuring shown on this page have in common? How are they different?*
They both use inches. The ruler is in one piece, the tiles are many pieces.

Connect It Use the models to solve the problem.

2 Look at the first *Measure It*. How many inch tiles are used? ___11___

3 Look at the second *Measure It*. What is the length of the paper? ___11 inches___

4 Do you think it is easier to measure with tiles or a ruler? Explain.

> Answers will vary. Students might choose the ruler

> because there is only one thing to line up.

5 **Talk About It** Would the length of the paper be the same if you measured it using a yardstick? Why or why not?

Write About It Possible answer: The length would be

the same number of inches. A yardstick shows inches, too.

Try It Measure the key using centimeters.

6 Look at the centimeter tiles. The key has a length of ___5___ centimeters.

7 Look at the centimeter ruler. The key has a length of ___5___ centimeters.

163

▶ Hands-On Activity

Measure classroom objects.

Materials: rulers or meter sticks, classroom objects such as books, folders, and pencils

- Have students measure and record the lengths of a variety of objects in the classroom with the rulers or meter sticks.

- Then give them target lengths, such as 10 centimeters, 20 centimeters, or 100 centimeters, that are different from the lengths of the objects they already measured. Ask students to find objects that are those target lengths.

- Encourage students to share their results. Do students who measured the same objects during the first part of the activity agree on their lengths? For the second part of the activity, were they able to find objects with the given lengths?

▶ Mathematical Discourse

5 *What would happen if you used a mix of inch tiles and centimeter tiles to measure the key or the sheet of paper?*

Students should recognize that combining customary and metric units to measure any object is not correct.

Step By Step

Connect It

- Read the first two **Connect It** problems as a class. Make sure students understand that the problems refer to the previous page.

- Ask students to answer Problems 2–4 on their own. Invite individual students to share their answers to Problem 4.

- For Problem 5, have students work in pairs. Ask them to think about the type of units they see on a yardstick. Have yardsticks available for students to look at if they are unsure about the units.

Try It

- For the **Try It** questions, have students work in pairs. When they are finished, discuss the answers as a class. Then ask: *What would the length of the key be if you measured it with a meter stick?* [5 centimeters]

▶ Mathematical Discourse 5

▶ Hands-On Activity

6 **Solution**
5

7 **Solution**
5

Error Alert Students who wrote 6 centimeters may have counted all the tick marks on the ruler for 0–6.

Ready Mathematics
PRACTICE AND PROBLEM SOLVING

Assign *Practice and Problem Solving* **pages 181–182** after students have completed this section.

Modeled and Guided Instruction

At A Glance

Students explore measuring with a centimeter ruler and a meter stick. Then students learn how to add ruler lengths to find measures, and compare using a centimeter ruler to using a meter stick.

Step By Step

- Read the problem at the top of the page as a class. Tell students that they will learn about measuring an object that is longer than a ruler.

Measure It

- Draw students' attention to **Measure It**. Use Mathematical Discourse question 1 to ensure students understand that it is important to lay the ribbon flat before measuring it.

▶ **Mathematical Discourse 1**

- Give students lengths of string that are 90 centimeters long, and draw a line segment on the board that is also 90 centimeters long. Tell students they will practice using a ruler to measure a length longer than the ruler.

- Align a centimeter ruler at the left end of the segment on the board, and draw a tick mark at the 30 centimeter mark. Have students do the same thing with the string, holding an index finger in place instead of drawing a tick mark. Move the ruler so the 0 mark aligns with the tick mark or index finger. Repeat the marking and moving to measure the segment.

Measure It

- Read and discuss **Measure It**. Ask Mathematical Discourse question 2 to encourage students to think about other measuring tools.

▶ **Mathematical Discourse 2**

▶ **Concept Extension**

Learn About ▷ More Ways to Measure Length

Read the problem. Then you will look at ways to measure.

Jonah wants to measure the length of the ribbon he used to wrap this present.

What is the length of the ribbon in centimeters?

▷ **Measure It** **You can use a ruler to find the length.**

The rulers and meter stick on this page are not life-sized.

Line up the left edge of the ribbon with the 0 on the ruler.

Mark where the ruler ends. Then move the ruler so that 0 is at your mark. Repeat this until you find the length.

▷ **Measure It** **You can use a meter stick to find the length.**

Line up the left edge of the ribbon with the 0 on the meter stick.

164

▶ Mathematical Discourse

1 *Why is it important to lay the ribbon flat before measuring it with a ruler?*

Students may say that since the rulers are flat, the ribbon must be also. If we are using a paper or fabric tape measure, we could leave the ribbon on the package and wrap the tape measure around it.

2 *Can you think of another way to measure the ribbon when it is flat?*

We could use a tape measure.

▶ Concept Extension

Use string to measure around boxes.

Materials: For each group: a small box (or a book), a meter stick, and a long piece of string

- Have students work in small groups. Give each group one box, a meter stick, and a long length of string.

- Show students how to measure around a box. Wrap the string around the box, mark or hold the point on the string where it meets the end of the string, and unwrap the string. Then use the meter stick to measure from the end of the string to the point you have marked or are holding.

- Have students measure their boxes, then trade boxes with other groups to measure again.

Connect It Use the models to solve the problem.

8 Look at the first *Measure It*. The length of the ribbon is equal to how many rulers? ___3___

9 How many centimeters are on each ruler? ___30 cm___

10 Write an equation to find the length of the ribbon.

___30___ cm + ___30___ cm + ___30___ cm = ___90___ cm

11 Look at the meter stick. How long is the ribbon?

___90___ centimeters

12 **Talk About It** Why is it easier to measure the ribbon with a meter stick than with a ruler?

Write About It Possible answer: The meter stick is long

enough to measure the ribbon without having to move it.

You can just line it up and read the length.

Try It Try another problem.

13 Circle the objects that are easier to measure with a centimeter ruler. Underline the objects that are easier to measure with a meter stick.

(a hot dog)   a jump rope   (a pencil)

your height   (this book)

165

Step By Step

- Tell students that this page will help them find lengths of objects that are longer than one ruler's length.

Connect It

- Work through the **Connect It** section as a class.

> **SMP TIP Model with Mathematics**
> In Problem 10, when students add 30 cm + 30 cm + 30 cm, they are modeling a situation with an equation. *(SMP 4)*

- For Problem 12, have students work with a partner. You may want to have students mimic what is shown on the student page and measure an actual 90-centimeter piece of string with a ruler and meter stick.

▶ **English Language Learners**

Try It

- After students complete the **Try it** problem, ask volunteers to share their answers with the class. Have students discuss why they circled or underlined each object.

▶ **Hands-On Activity**

13 **Solution**
Circled terms: *a hot dog*, *this book*, and *a pencil*. Underlined terms: *your height* and *a jump rope*.

Error Alert Students who underlined "book" may have incorrectly estimated the length of an average book.

> **Ready** · **Mathematics**
> PRACTICE AND PROBLEM SOLVING
>
> Assign *Practice and Problem Solving* **pages 183–184** after students have completed this section.

▶ **English Language Learners**

Pair English language learners with proficient readers for Problem 12. Before students begin the **Try It** question, demonstrate circling and underlining words on the board.

▶ **Hands-On Activity**

Write equations to find the lengths of line segments.

Materials: For each group: centimeter ruler

- Draw several line segments on the board, or put several lengths of painter's tape or strips of paper on the floor. Use lengths that are multiples of the length of your centimeter rulers, such as 30 centimeters, 60 centimeters, and 150 centimeters.

- Have students work in small groups to measure the lengths of the segments. Make sure that they write the equation they are using to find the total length of each segment.

- When they are done, have them share the results. Write the complete equation for each length on the board or on each piece of tape or paper.

Guided Practice

At A Glance

Students practice measuring objects and answer questions about length and measuring tools.

Step By Step

- Ask students to solve the problems individually and show all their work. Before they begin, point to the unit abbreviations after the answer blanks in the Example and Problem 14. Remind them that *cm* is the abbreviation for "centimeters" and that *in.* is the abbreviation for "inches."

- **Pair/Share** When students have completed each problem, have them Pair/Share to discuss their solutions with a partner.

Solutions

Example A centimeter ruler is used to find the length of the shell in centimeters by aligning one side with 0 on the ruler.

14 **Solution**
2 inches
DOK 1

Practice **Measuring Length**

Study the model below. Then solve Problems 14–16.

Example

Dawson found a shell. How long is the shell in centimeters?
You can use a centimeter ruler. Make sure to line up the shell at 0.

Answer _____5_____ centimeters

14 Measure the length of the eraser in inches using a ruler.

What side of the ruler should you use?

Answer ___2___ inches

166

Teacher Notes

15 Think about the length of the actual objects. Draw lines to match each object with the best tool for measuring it.

a watch

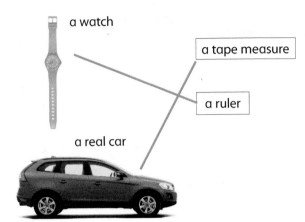

a tape measure

a ruler

a real car

Which tool is used to measure very long objects?

16 What is the length of the craft stick in inches?

Did Jake measure with a unit that is smaller or bigger than inches?

(A) 4 inches

B 5 inches

C 10 inches

D 11 inches

Jake chose **C** as the answer. This answer is wrong. How did Jake get his answer?

Possible answer: He used the wrong side of the ruler. He used

centimeters instead of inches.

167

Solutions

15 Solution
watch: ruler
car: tape measure
DOK 2

16 Solution
A; Students use an inch ruler to measure.
DOK 3
Explain to students why the other two choices are not correct:
If a student chose **B**, make sure the student is measuring from 0 on the ruler, not 1.
If a student chose **D**, make sure that the student uses inches and aligns the ruler correctly.

Ready Mathematics
PRACTICE AND PROBLEM SOLVING

Assign *Practice and Problem Solving* **pages 185–186** after students have completed this section.

Teacher Notes

Independent Practice

At A Glance

Students solve measurement problems that might appear on a mathematics test.

Solutions

1 **Solution**

A, C, and D; all of these measuring tools except the yardstick can be used to measure the calculator in centimeters.

DOK 2

2 **Solution**

A; 2 inches

DOK 1

3 **Solution**

a. **No**; b. **Yes**; c. **Yes**; d. **Yes**

DOK 1

Quick Check and Remediation

- Draw a line segment that is 10 inches long and ask students to measure it in inches. [10 inches]

- For students who are still struggling, use the chart to guide remediation.

- After providing remediation, check students' understanding by drawing a line segment of a different length and having them measure its length.

Solve the problems.

1 Leah wants to measure the length of her calculator in centimeters. Which tool could she use? Circle all the correct answers.

(A) ruler

B yardstick

(C) meter stick

(D) tape measure

2 What is the length of the worm in inches? Circle the correct answer.

(A) 2 inches   C 4 inches

B 3 inches   D 5 inches

3 Ruby measured each line in centimeters. She wrote the length of each line next to it. Did she measure correctly? Choose *Yes* or *No* for each length.

a. ——————————— 5 cm   Yes (No)

b. ———— 3 cm   (Yes) No

c. ——— 2 cm   (Yes) No

d. ——————— 4 cm   (Yes) No

168

If the error is ...	Students may ...	To remediate ...
11 inches	have started measuring from 1 on the ruler instead of from 0.	Have students find 1 inch on the ruler, then measure a line segment 1 inch long. Repeat with 2 inches, then 3 inches.
25 inches	have used centimeters instead of inches.	Have students find the side of the ruler with inches on it, and the side with centimeters.
any other number	have read the ruler incorrectly.	Have students align the ruler with the line segment correctly, then place one finger at each end of the segment. One finger should be at 0 and the other should be at 10.

4 Marcus says the length of the stick is 6 centimeters.
What did Marcus do wrong?
Circle the correct answer.

A He measured in inches.

B He used the wrong side of the ruler.

C He didn't line up one end of the stick at 0.

D He should have used a yardstick.

5 Kayla started to draw a rectangle that is 4 inches
long. Complete Kayla's rectangle to make it the
correct length.

6 Brian wants to measure the length of his bed in
centimeters. He says the best tool to use is a ruler.
Do you agree? Why or why not?

Possible answer: I do not agree. A bed is a very long

object. So a tape measure that shows meters is the best

tool to use.

✓ **Self Check** **Now you can solve problems using a ruler.**
Fill this in on the progress chart on page 153.

169

Solutions

4 **Solution**
C; He didn't line up one end of the stick at 0.
DOK 2

5 **Solution**
Check students' drawings.
DOK 2

6 **Solution**
Check students' answers, which should
explain why a ruler is not the best tool.
DOK 3

▶ **Hands-On Activity**

Estimate the length of a beanbag toss.

Materials: For each pair or group: beanbags; yardstick, meter stick,
or tape measure

• Students should work in pairs or small groups.

• One student will guess how far he or she can (gently) toss a
beanbag, and then toss it.

• Students work together to measure the length of the toss.
They should record the student's guess and the actual length
of the toss.

• Repeat until each student in the group has had a chance to guess,
toss, and measure at least two times.

• Ask the following questions: *Who had the longest toss? Who had the
toss that was closest to his or her guess? Did you change your guess
before you tossed the beanbag the second time?*

▶ **Challenge Activity**

Find a length indirectly.

Materials: strips of paper as described in activity

• Cut four strips of paper whose lengths are multiples of 8, such as 32,
40, 56, and 72 centimeters, or 16, 24, 32, and 48 inches.

• Fold two of the strips in half three times, so they are one-eighth of
their original length.

• Give students the other two strips. Have students measure the
strip, fold it in half, measure the folded length, and then record the
folded length. Repeat the folding and measuring until it has been
folded in eighths. Ask what they notice about the lengths they
recorded, and if they see a pattern.

• Give students the strips you folded, and have them measure the
folded length. Can they predict the length of the strips when they
are completely unfolded?

Teacher-Toolbox.com

Overview

Assign the Lesson 17 Quiz and have students work independently to complete it.

Use the results of the quiz to assess students' understanding of the content of the lesson and to identify areas for reteaching. See the Lesson Pacing Guide at the beginning of the lesson for suggested instructional resources.

Tested Skills

Assesses 2.MD.A.1

Problems on this assessment form require students to be able to use a ruler to measure lengths in different units (inches, centimeters). Students will also need to be familiar with counting fluently from 0 to 20, and understand that objects can be measured with different units.

Ready® Mathematics

Lesson 17 Quiz

Solve the problems.

1 Zain measures the lengths of some toy bugs. Use a ruler to decide if his measurements are correct.

Circle *Yes* or *No* for each bug's measurement.

a. 4 centimeters   Yes   No

b. 2 centimeters   Yes   No

c. 8 centimeters   Yes   No

Lesson 17 Quiz continued

2 How long is Miguel's toy car?

Fill in the blanks.

Answer: The toy car is _____ _____ long.

3 Kelsey lines up her hair clip this way to find its length.

Is Kelsey correct? Explain.

_____

_____

_____

Common Misconceptions and Errors

Errors may result if students:

- measure an object from 1 instead of 0 when using a ruler.

- misalign the ruler with the object.

- read the ruler incorrectly.

- confuse units (inches and centimeters).

Ready® **Mathematics**

Lesson 17 Quiz Answer Key

1. **a.** No
   b. No
   c. Yes
   DOK 1

2. 3, inches
   DOK 1

3. Kelsey is not correct. Possible explanation: Kelsey needs to line up the left end of the hair clip with the 0 mark on the ruler.
   DOK 3

CCSS Focus

Domain
Measurement and Data

Cluster
A. Measure and estimate lengths in standard units.

Standards
2.MD.A.2 Measure the length of an object twice, using length units of different lengths for the two measurements; describe how the two measurements relate to the size of the unit chosen.

Standards for Mathematical Practice (SMP)

2 Reason abstractly and quantitatively.

5 Use appropriate tools strategically.

6 Attend to precision.

Lesson Objectives

Content Objectives

- Compare lengths measured in different units.
- Understand the relationship between feet and inches.
- Understand the relationship between centimeters and meters.
- Explore how the number of units in a measurement is related to the size of the units used.

Language Objectives

- Compare given lengths measured in different units.
- Predict whether a given object would be more inches in length or more feet in length.
- Describe the relationship between centimeters and meters.

Prerequisite Skills

- Measure lengths in inches and centimeters

Lesson Vocabulary

There is no new vocabulary. Review the following key terms.

- **inch** the smallest unit of length in the U.S. customary system. A quarter is about 1 inch across. 12 inches is equivalent to 1 foot.
- **foot** a unit of length in the U.S. customary system. 1 foot is equal to 12 inches.
- **yard** a unit of length in the U.S. customary system. 1 yard is equal to 3 feet or 36 inches.
- **centimeter** a unit of length in the metric system. Your little finger is about 1 centimeter across. 100 centimeters is equivalent to 1 meter.
- **meter** a unit of length in the metric system. 1 meter is equal to 100 centimeters.

Learning Progression

In Grade 1 students developed their understanding of measuring in different units, using nonstandard units. They compared lengths directly and put lengths in order without using units such as inches or centimeters.

In Grade 2 students extend their knowledge of measuring lengths to the use of standard units, focusing on inches and centimeters.

In this lesson students compare measurements made in inches and feet, inches and centimeters, and other units. For example, students measure an object in both feet and inches, and learn that more inches are needed to measure the object than feet.

In Grade 3 choosing an appropriate unit will continue to be important as students begin to measure volumes and weights in addition to lengths. Students will apply what they know about measuring lengths to problems involving perimeter and area.

Lesson Pacing Guide

Whole Class Instruction

Day 1
45–60 minutes

Toolbox: Interactive Tutorial*
Understand Measurement with Different Units

Introduction
• Opening Activity *20 min*
• Think It Through Question *5 min*
• Think *15 min*
• Think *5 min*
• Reflect *5 min*

Practice and Problem Solving
Assign pages 189–190.

Day 2
45–60 minutes

Guided Instruction
Think About Comparing Units of Measure
• Let's Explore the Idea *10 min*
• Let's Talk About It *25 min*
• Try It Another Way *10 min*

Practice and Problem Solving
Assign pages 191–192.

Day 3
45–60 minutes

Guided Practice
Connect Ideas About Comparing Units of Measure
• Analyze *15 min*
• Compare *15 min*
• Explain *15 min*

Practice and Problem Solving
Assign pages 193–194.

Day 4
45–60 minutes

Independent Practice
Apply Ideas About Comparing Units of Measure
• Put It Together *30 min*
• Pair/Share *15 min*

Day 5
45–60 minutes

• On-Level, Intervention or Challenge Activity *20 min*

Toolbox: Lesson Quiz
Lesson 18 Quiz

Small Group Differentiation

Teacher-Toolbox.com

Reteach
Ready Prerequisite Lessons *45–90 min*

Grade 1
• Lesson 33 *Understand* Length Measurement

Grade 2
• Lesson 17 Measure Length

Student-led Activities
Math Center Activities *30–40 min*

Grade 2 *(Lessons 17 and 18)*
• 2.30 Measure Lengths of Objects
• 2.31 Measure with Different Units
• 2.32 Compare Units

Personalized Learning

i-Ready.com

Independent
i-Ready Lessons* *10–20 min*

Grade 2 *(Lesson 17)*
• Using a Ruler: Inches

*We continually update the Interactive Tutorials. Check the Teacher Toolbox for the most up-to-date offerings for this lesson.

Opening Activity

Comparing Measurements

Objective Measure using centimeters and inches, and compare measurements of the same objects using different units.

Time *20–30 minutes*

Materials for each student

• ruler

• Activity Sheet 9 (Measuring Worksheet)

Overview

Students measure lengths using inches and centimeters. They then compare the measurements and look for a pattern.

Step By Step

1 Activate students' knowledge about measuring lengths.

• Draw a line segment on the board. Ask students to describe all the different ways they could use to find out how long it is. [Use a ruler, a tape measure, a yardstick, or a meter stick.]

• Ask students what units are on each of the measuring tools they just described.

2 Take some measurements.

• Give each student a copy of Activity Sheet 9.

• *Option 1:* Each student can measure each object twice, once in inches and once in centimeters.

• *Option 2:* Half the students can use inches to measure the objects and half can use centimeters.

- Remind students to find each length to the nearest inch or nearest centimeter. Record the lengths the students find on the board in a table like this one:

Object	Length in inches	Length in centimeters
Seedling		
Slanted side of triangle		
Marker		
Paper clip		

3 Talk about the results.

Ask questions about the lengths that the students measured.

- *What do you notice about the lengths we found?* [For each object, the number in the inch column is different from the number in the centimeter column. Students may also notice that the numbers in the centimeter column are greater than the numbers in the inch column.]

- *Does changing the units change how big or how small the object is?* [No, the objects stay the same lengths, but the number of units changes.]

Teacher Notes

Introduction

At A Glance

Students compare measuring in inches with measuring in feet. They find out more about the relationship between feet and inches, then examine the relationship between centimeters and meters.

Step By Step

- Tell students they will learn about measuring an object in two different ways.
- Read the text at the top of the page together as a class.
- Have students find 24 inches and 2 feet on a yardstick or tape measure, and compare the two lengths.
- Read and complete the **Think** section as a class.

▶ **Mathematical Discourse 1–3**

▶ **Hands-On Activity**

💭 Think It Through

What happens when you measure the same object in both inches and feet?

Kim measures a piece of fabric. She says that the length is 24 inches.

Nadia measures the same piece of fabric. She says that the length is 2 feet.

Think   It takes different numbers of each unit to measure an object.

Kim's number and Nadia's number are different.

 Did the length of the fabric change? ___no___

The girls measured using different units.
Kim measured in inches.
The fabric has a length of 24 inches.
Nadia measured in feet.
The fabric has a length of 2 feet.

> The yardsticks on this page are not life-sized.

170

▶ Mathematical Discourse

1 *Can you think of other ways to measure the fabric?*

Students may suggest using centimeters to measure the fabric, or using inch tiles or centimeter tiles instead of a yardstick.

2 *How does using a different unit change the measurement?*

Switching from inches to feet means that the number changes, although the size of the fabric does not.

3 *Why is it important to say what units you are using when you measure something?*

If you just say, "The fabric is 2," it's unclear whether it is 2 inches long or 2 feet long.

▶ Hands-On Activity

Measure objects in feet and inches.

Materials: For each group: yardstick or ruler, large classroom objects such as tables and chairs

- Have students work in small groups. Give each group a yardstick or a ruler.
- Make a list of large objects in the classroom on the board, such as a student's table, the teacher's desk, or the base of a window. If possible, choose things that are taller or longer than 2 feet.
- Have students work together to measure each of the objects in inches and in feet.
- Record the lengths they measured on the board, with inches in one column and feet in the other.
- Have students put each column of lengths in order from shortest to longest. Ask: *Is the order the same for the measurements in inches and in feet?*

Think It takes more of a smaller unit to measure an object.

Think about the fabric on the previous page.
It took 24 inches to measure the fabric.
But it only took 2 feet to measure the fabric.

✏️ Look at the ruler. Which unit is greater,
1 inch or 1 foot?

___1 foot___

> When you measure in feet, you say "1 foot" instead of "1 feet." Say "feet" if the length is not 1.

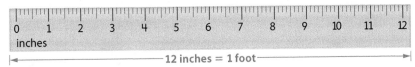

12 inches = 1 foot

This ruler is not life-sized.

An inch is shorter than a foot.

So you need more inches than feet
to measure the fabric.

▶ **Reflect** Work with a partner.

1 **Talk About It** Josie measured the length
of her bed using both centimeters and meters.
Did it take more meters or more centimeters
to measure its length?

Write About It Possible answer: Centimeters are smaller than meters,

so it took more centimeters to measure the bed.

171

- Tell students that they will learn more about how inches are related to feet.

- Read the **Think** section together as a class. Then have students find 2 feet and 24 inches on the yardsticks shown on the previous page. Also have them find 1 foot and 12 inches. You may also wish to have students find 1 foot and 12 inches on actual yardsticks.

- Write "1 foot = 12 inches" and "2 feet = 24 inches" on the board, and have students line up 12 one-inch tiles next to a customary ruler.

▶ **Mathematical Discourse 4–5**

▶ **Visual Model**

- To prepare for the **Reflect** question, have students find 100 centimeters and 1 meter on a meter stick. Invite a student to read the **Reflect** question to the class, then have students work with a partner to answer the question.

- When students have finished answering the **Reflect** question, discuss their responses as a class. Some students may assume that using a larger unit leads to using a larger *number* of units. In this lesson, they learn that the opposite is actually true: Measuring with a larger unit means the number of units needed is smaller.

📦 **Ready** Mathematics
PRACTICE AND PROBLEM SOLVING

Assign *Practice and Problem Solving* **pages 189–190** after students have completed this section.

▶ **Visual Model**

Draw a ruler.

- Draw a ruler on the board showing 12 inches. Under the ruler write "1 foot."

- Ask students: *Which is longer, 1 foot or 12 inches?* [They are the same length.] Then ask: *Which measurement uses more units, 1 foot or 12 inches?* [12 inches has a greater number of units than 1 foot does.]

▶ **English Language Learners**

- ELL students may be more familiar with centimeters than with inches. Provide support for students to learn about both types of units by having meter sticks and yardsticks available when needed.

- Pair ELL students with strong readers for the Reflect question.

▶ **Mathematical Discourse**

4 *Why would you measure something in feet instead of inches?*

You might use feet to measure something very large, like a building. It would be easier than measuring it in inches.

5 *Why would you measure something in inches instead of feet?*

You might choose inches to measure more accurately, or to measure a smaller object, like a coin.

👥 Guided Instruction

At A Glance

Students use rulers to compare measuring in inches with measuring in centimeters. Then students describe the relationship between the size of a unit and the number of units needed to measure an object.

Step By Step

Let's Explore the Idea

• Tell students that now they will look at what happens when you measure an object in both inches and centimeters.

• Make sure students have centimeter and inch rulers available for use. Have students identify which ruler is for inches and which is for centimeters, or which side is for each unit if the classroom rulers have both units on them.

• Work through Problems 2 and 3 as a class. Model good measuring skills: Point out that the 0 is aligned correctly, check the units, and measure to the nearest unit.

▶ **Mathematical Discourse 1**

• Have students work together in small groups to complete Problems 4 and 5.

▶ **Mathematical Discourse 2**

SMP TIP Use Tools/Attend to Precision
When students measure objects on this page with inches and centimeters, they are attending to precision. Point out that Problem 4 states that the leaf is 8 centimeters long and Problem 5 states that the leaf is about 3 inches long. Ask students to explain which is a more precise measurement and explain why. *(SMP 6)*

Think About ▶ **Comparing Units of Measure**

🔍 **Let's Explore the Idea** You can measure an object in inches and in centimeters.

Use the paper clip for Problems 2 and 3.

2 Measure the length of the paper clip in inches.
The paper clip is ___2___ inches long.

3 Measure the length of the paper clip in centimeters.
The paper clip is about ___5___ centimeters long.

Use the leaf for Problems 4 and 5.

4 Measure the length of the leaf in centimeters.
The leaf is ___8___ centimeters long.

5 Measure the length of the leaf in inches.
The leaf is about ___3___ inches long.

172

▶ **Mathematical Discourse**

1 *Can the measurement in inches and the measurement in centimeters both be accurate, even though they are not the same number?*
Yes, the number of inches should be different from the number of centimeters because the units are not the same size.

2 *Can you explain why you should say whether the measurement is in inches or centimeters?*
Saying that the leaf is "8" doesn't tell the unit that was used for measuring the leaf, so it doesn't tell enough about the leaf's size. An 8-inch leaf would be much larger than the leaf on this page, which is 8 centimeters.

Let's Talk About It
Work with a partner.

6 Does it take fewer inches or fewer centimeters to measure the length of the paper clip?

_____fewer inches_____

7 Does it take fewer inches or fewer centimeters to measure the length of the leaf?

_____fewer inches_____

8 If you measure the length of your math book, will it take fewer inches or fewer centimeters? Why?

___It will take fewer inches. Possible answer: Inches are___

___bigger, so you don't need as many of them as centimeters.___

▶ **Try It Another Way** **Compare other units.**

9 Would it take fewer erasers or fewer buttons to measure the length of your pencil? Circle the correct answer.

10 Would it take more hair clips or more crayons to measure the length of your desk? Circle the correct answer.

173

▶ **Hands-On Activity**

Compare measurements with nonstandard units.

Materials: connecting cubes and sticky notes

- Have students measure one connecting cube, telling if it is longer or shorter than one inch. Ask students to predict whether it will take fewer or more connecting cubes than inches to measure the eraser and the crayon. Measure to check the predictions.

- Repeat using a different nonstandard measuring tool, such as a sticky note.

▶ **English Language Learners**

Discuss with students that *fewer* means there are not as many. Write a short sentence such as "There are fewer ○s than □s" on the board and draw a picture of 4 circles and 8 squares.

▶ **Mathematical Discourse**

3 *In Problem 8, how did you decide that it takes fewer inches than centimeters to measure the book?*

Students may reply that they followed the pattern they noticed in measuring the paper clip and the leaf.

4 *How could you check whether your answer to Problem 8 is correct?*

We could measure the book in inches and in centimeters, and then see whether fewer inches or centimeters were needed.

5 *Justin says that the length of his book is about 24 centimeters. Why does he say about?*

His book does not measure exactly 24 centimeters.

Let's Talk About It
- Work through Problem 6 as a class.

▶ **English Language Learners**

- Have students work with a partner for the rest of the questions.

- Check students' understanding with questions such as: *If you have some very small units, do you need many of them or just a few of them to measure an object? If you have larger units, do you need many or just a few to measure the same object?*

▶ **Mathematical Discourse 3–5**

Try It Another Way

- Read the **Try It Another Way** questions as a class. Make sure students notice that for Problem 10, they need to circle the object it would take more of to measure their desk. Then have students answer the questions individually.

▶ **Hands-On Activity**

Ready **Mathematics**
PRACTICE AND PROBLEM SOLVING

Assign *Practice and Problem Solving* **pages 191–192** after students have completed this section.

👥👥 Guided Practice

At A Glance

Students demonstrate what they have learned about how the size of a unit affects the number of units needed to measure an object. Then students apply their understanding of measuring in different units.

Step By Step

- Read and discuss the problems as a class, using the discussion points below.

Analyze

- Have students work with a partner to discuss which item goes with which number of units. You may wish to have students draw a line below the quarter to help them visualize its length and compare it to the length of the comb.

- Ask students to share their responses with the class. Listen for responses that show that a greater number of smaller-sized units are needed to measure the picture, or that students visualized measuring the picture with the given items.

Compare

- Ask students to describe how they decided that more feet are needed to measure the bedroom than yards.

- Ask: *How could you find out if your answer is correct?* Students may respond that they could measure the bedroom in feet, or make a model showing three feet for each yard.

Explain

- Have students discuss the problem and their responses with a partner.

- Ask one pair of students to draw a diagram on the board, using rulers if they like, to support their answers. Have the class discuss the diagram, which should show that 12 inches are longer than 12 centimeters.

Connect ▶ Ideas About Comparing Units of Measure

Talk about these questions as a class. Then write your answers.

11 **Analyze** Ed measures a picture using combs and quarters as his units. The length of the picture is 3 units of one item and 18 units of the other. Which item does he use to get a length of 3 units? Explain.

He uses 3 combs. Possible answer: Combs are longer

than quarters, so he needs fewer of them.

12 **Compare** Joe's bedroom is 4 yards long. He also measures it in feet. Is the length of Joe's bedroom more yards or more feet? Explain.

It is more feet. Possible answer: Feet are smaller than

yards, so it takes more of them.

13 **Explain** Kit's red ribbon is 12 inches long. Her blue ribbon is 12 centimeters long. Kit says they are the same length. Do you agree? Explain.

Possible answer: I don't agree. The numbers are the same, but the units

are different. Inches are longer than centimeters, so the red ribbon is

longer.

174

Apply > **Ideas About Comparing Units of Measure**

Put It Together **Use what you have learned to complete this task.**

14 Eric measures the length of his model car.

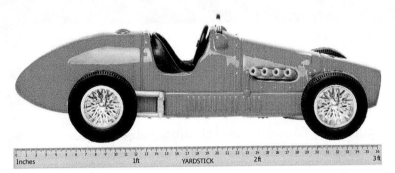

This yardstick is not life-sized.

Part A What is the length of Eric's car? ___3___ feet

Part B What is the length of Eric's car? ___1___ yard(s)

Part C Which units would you need the most of to measure the length of Eric's car? Circle the correct answer.

    inches   (centimeters)   yards   feet

Part D Which units would you need the least of to measure the length of Eric's car? Circle the correct answer.

    inches   centimeters   (yards)   feet

175

Step By Step

Put It Together

- Tell students they will complete the **Put It Together** task on their own.
- Read the directions and the four parts to the question before students begin.
- Have rulers and yardsticks available for students to use if they want them.
- As students work on their own, walk around to assess their progress and understanding, to answer their questions, and to give additional support, if needed.
- If time permits, ask students to share their answers and justify their choices.

📦 **Ready** Mathematics
PRACTICE AND PROBLEM SOLVING

Assign *Practice and Problem Solving* **pages 193–194** after students have completed Guided Practice.

Scoring Rubrics

Parts A to D

Points	Expectations
2	The student completes the measurements and the unit choices correctly.
1	Some measurement and unit choices are correct and some are incorrect.
0	Neither the measurements nor the unit choices are correct.

Differentiated Instruction

▶ Intervention Activity

Measure lengths and compare units.

Materials: rulers

- Provide each student with a ruler that shows both inches and centimeters, or two rulers.

- Have students use the rulers to draw line segments that are the following lengths:

  2 inches
  6 inches
  10 inches
  12 inches

- Help students measure each of the segments to the nearest centimeter, and have them record the lengths. [about 5 cm, 15 cm, 25 cm, and 30 cm]

- Ask students which is longer, 2 inches or 5 centimeters? [They are about the same.] Which uses more units, 2 inches or 5 centimeters? [5 centimeters] Which uses a larger unit, 2 inches or 5 centimeters? [2 inches]

- Repeat the questions using the other lengths.

▶ On-Level Activity

Measure objects and choose units.

Materials: For each group: classroom objects, ruler, yardstick, and meter stick

- Have students work in small groups.

- Before beginning the activity, make a list of about 6 objects in the classroom that students can measure. Include some larger objects, such as the length of one side of the room, and some smaller objects, such as a paper clip.

- Students decide which unit to use to measure each object on the list. For example, they might choose feet to measure the length of one side of the room, and centimeters to measure the paper clip. They work together to measure the objects and record the lengths.

- For each length they record, students explain how they decided which unit to use.

▶ Challenge Activity

Invent a measurement system.

Materials: large plain paper

- Students have now had practice measuring length using the U.S. customary system, which is based on 1 foot equaling 12 inches, and the metric system, which is based on 1 meter equaling 100 centimeters.

- Ask students to make up a measurement system of their own, based on a number different from 12 or 10. The invented measurement system should include at least two different units, and students can decide how big the units are, how they are related, and what their names are.

- Have students make a chart showing the units they have invented, their approximate size, and how they are related to each other. Have them include benchmark measurements, giving the lengths of three common objects in their invented units. Invite students to present their new measurement systems to the class.

Teacher Notes

Teacher-Toolbox.com

Overview

Assign the Lesson 18 Quiz and have students work independently to complete it.

Use the results of the quiz to assess students' understanding of the content of the lesson and to identify areas for reteaching. See the Lesson Pacing Guide at the beginning of the lesson and the Differentiated Instruction activities that follow for suggested instructional resources.

Tested Skills

Assesses 2.MD.A.2

Problems on this assessment form require students to be able to compare lengths measured in different units, understand how feet, inches, and yards are related, and how the size of a unit relates to the number of units needed to measure a length (e.g., will more inches or more feet will be needed to measure a length). Students will also need to be familiar with measuring length in inches and centimeters.

Ready® Mathematics

Lesson 18 Quiz

Solve the problems.

1 Laura, Alex, and their father take a walk. Laura's steps are shorter than her father's. Alex's steps are shorter than Laura's.

Which statements about their steps are true?

Circle *True* or *False* for each statement.

a. Laura takes fewer steps than her father.	True	False
b. Alex takes the most number of steps.	True	False
c. Laura takes fewer steps than Alex.	True	False
d. Alex and his father take the same number of steps.	True	False

2 Dr. Roland plans to measure the length of a shark in feet and also in yards.

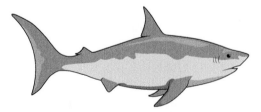

Use words from the box to complete the sentence.

Dr. Roland will use more _____ than _____ to measure the shark.

feet   yards

Lesson 18 Quiz continued

3 Ken wants to measure the length of the door in his classroom. Which object should Ken use if he wants the length to be the fewest number of units?

Circle the correct answer.

A  MARKER

B (pencil)

C ERASER

D  POINTER

4 Claire, Nona, and Talia use different objects to measure the length of a table.

Claire uses 6 math books to measure the length.

Nona uses 18 erasers to measure the length.

Talia uses 9 new pencils to measure the length.

Explain how you know that the pencil is shorter than the math book.

_____

_____

_____

_____

_____

Common Misconceptions and Errors

Errors may result if students:

- assume the larger/longer a unit is, the more that are needed to measure a length.

- confuse units (e.g., inches with centimeters or feet with yards).

Ready® **Mathematics**

Lesson 18 Quiz Answer Key

1. **a.** False
   b. True
   c. True
   d. False
   DOK 2

2. feet, yards
   DOK 2

3. D
   DOK 1

4. Possible explanation: The pencil is shorter than the math book because it takes more pencils than math books to measure the length of the table. It takes more of a smaller unit than a larger unit to measure an object.
   DOK 3

Lesson 19
Understand Estimating Length

CCSS Focus

Domain
Measurement and Data

Cluster
A. Measure and estimate lengths in standard units.

Standards
2.MD.A.3 Estimate lengths using units of inches, feet, centimeters, and meters.

Standards for Mathematical Practice (SMP)

1 Make sense of problems and persevere in solving them.

3 Construct viable arguments and critique the reasoning of others.

4 Model with mathematics.

5 Use appropriate tools strategically.

Lesson Objectives

Content Objectives

• Estimate lengths in inches, centimeters, feet, and meters.

• Use benchmark objects when estimating.

Language Objectives

• Define the key vocabulary term *estimate* when discussing measurement with a partner.

• Justify conclusions and communicate conclusions to others.

Prerequisite Skills

• Measure lengths in inches and centimeters.

• Add numbers less than 10.

Lesson Vocabulary

• **to estimate** to give an approximate number or answer based on mathematical thinking.

• **an estimate** a close guess made using mathematical thinking.

Learning Progression

In Grade 1 students develop their understanding of measuring in different units, using nonstandard units. This prepares them to make reasonable estimates of lengths in different units.

In Grade 2 students learn more about measuring in standard units. Being able to estimate lengths, as they learn in this lesson, is good practice for estimating answers to many types of math problems.

In Grade 3 estimating in appropriate units continues to be important as students begin to measure volumes and weights in addition to lengths. Students apply what they know about measuring lengths to problems involving perimeter and area. Students extend their estimation skills by estimating volumes, masses, and intervals of time.

Lesson Pacing Guide

Whole Class Instruction

Day 1 *45–60 minutes*	**Toolbox: Interactive Tutorial*** *Inches, Feet, and Yards* **Introduction** • Opening Activity *15 min* • Think It Through Question *5 min* • Think *10 min* • Think *10 min* • Reflect *5 min*	**Practice and Problem Solving** Assign pages 197–198.
Day 2 *45–60 minutes*	**Guided Instruction** **Think About Using Different Units to Estimate Length** • Let's Explore the Idea *20 min* • Let's Talk About It *15 min* • Try It Another Way *10 min*	**Practice and Problem Solving** Assign pages 199–200.
Day 3 *45–60 minutes*	**Guided Practice** **Connect Ideas About Estimating Length** • Explain *15 min* • Analyze *15 min* • Identify *15 min*	**Practice and Problem Solving** Assign pages 201–202.
Day 4 *45–60 minutes*	**Independent Practice** **Apply Ideas About Estimating Length** • Put It Together *30 min* • Pair/Share *15 min*	
Day 5 *45–60 minutes*	• On-Level, Intervention or Challenge Activity *20 min* **Toolbox: Lesson Quiz** Lesson 19 Quiz	

Small Group Differentiation

Teacher-Toolbox.com

Reteach
Ready Prerequisite Lessons *45–90 min*

Grade 1
• Lesson 31 Order Objects by Length

Grade 2
• Lesson 17 Measure Length

Teacher-led Activities
Tools for Instruction *15–20 min*

Grade 2 *(Lessons 17 and 19)*
• Estimate and Measure Lengths

Student-led Activities
Math Center Activities *30–40 min*

Grade 2 *(Lessons 17 and 19)*
• 2.30 Measure Lengths of Objects
• 2.33 Estimate Lengths
• 2.34 Estimated and Actual Lengths

Personalized Learning

i-Ready.com

Independent
i-Ready Lessons* *10–20 min*

Grade 1 *(Lesson 17)*
• Using a Ruler: Inches

*We continually update the Interactive Tutorials. Check the Teacher Toolbox for the most up-to-date offerings for this lesson.

Opening Activity

One-Unit Scavenger Hunt

Objective Find benchmark objects that can be used as estimates for some common unit measures.

Time *15–20 minutes*

Materials for each student
- ruler
- classroom objects

Overview

Students estimate the length of a variety of objects in order to find objects that measure about one inch, one centimeter, one foot, and one meter.

Step By Step

1 Activate students' knowledge about standard units.

- Have students use rulers to draw lengths of one inch, one centimeter, and one foot. (A length of one foot can be drawn diagonally on a regular sheet of notebook paper.) Draw a length of one meter on the board.

- Have students suggest some objects or distances that they think are about the length of each of the units they drew.

2 Hunt for objects.

- Tell students that they are going to search for things that are close to the length of each of the units. They can use objects or groups of objects, such as a book or two connecting cubes, or distances, such as the height from the floor to a doorknob. They should not use objects whose locations can change, such as the distance from a pencil to a book.

- Give students time to make suggestions, measure, and suggest again until they find objects in the classroom to match all four units.

- Record the objects students find on the board in a table like the one below.

Unit	Object
One centimeter	
One inch	
One foot	
One meter	

3 Check the results.

- Have students check the lengths of each other's suggested benchmark objects. Discuss which ones are closest to the unit measures.

Teacher Notes

Introduction

At A Glance

Students explore what it means to estimate a length. Then students find out how to estimate lengths using benchmarks that are not equal to one unit.

Step By Step

- Tell students they will learn about estimating length.

- Read the introductory text as a class. Use the word *estimate* in a couple of sentences, one in which the word is used as a noun and one in which it is used as a verb. Help students understand the differences between the two uses of the word.

▶ **Mathematical Discourse 1**

- Read the **Think** section as a class. Talk with students about how estimates are not exact. On this page, for example, a quarter is not exactly one inch at its widest part, and the toy car is not exactly the same length as two quarters.

- Use Mathematical Discourse question 2 to begin a discussion of items that might be used to estimate length.

▶ **Mathematical Discourse 2**

- Have students measure the toy car with a ruler. Tell them that following up each estimate with a measurement will help them become better at estimating.

▶ **English Language Learners**

💭 **Think It Through**

What does it mean to estimate?

Sometimes you don't need an exact measurement. You can use the math you know to make an **estimate**.

Here are some items you can use to make estimates.

1 centimeter	1 inch	1 foot	1 meter or 1 yard
about the width of your little finger	about the width of a quarter	about the length of a loaf of bread	about the width of a door

Think Use what you know about units to estimate length.

Ty wants to estimate the length of his toy car. He thinks about 2 quarters would fit under his car.

🖊 Is the length of the toy car longer or shorter than 2 quarters?   ___shorter___

🖊 What do you think is a good estimate for the length of Ty's car in inches?   Possible answer: a little less than 2 inches

176

▶ **Mathematical Discourse**

1 *Can you think of why we might estimate a length instead of measuring it directly?*

Students may point out that we don't always have a ruler available, that we can't always handle an object to measure it, or that we might not need to know the exact length.

2 *What other items could Ty use to estimate the length of the toy car?*

Students may suggest using the benchmark for one inch that they found in the Opening Activity, or they may have another way of estimating one inch.

▶ **English Language Learners**

Discuss the difference between an *exact* measurement and an *estimated* measurement. Tell students that for an exact measurement, they will use a measuring tool such as a ruler, yardstick, or meter stick. For an estimated measurement, they will not use a measuring tool. Point out that in this lesson, students will follow up each estimate with an exact measurement.

Think Use measurements you already know to estimate length.

Julia wants to estimate the length of her pencil box. She knows a marker is about 14 centimeters long.

Julia thinks about how a marker would look next to her pencil box.

✏️ Which best describes the length of the pencil box? Mark all the correct answers.

☐ less than 14 cm   ☒ more than 14 cm

☒ less than 28 cm   ☐ more than 28 cm

▶ **Reflect** Work with a partner.

1 Talk About It Hannah estimates that Julia's pencil box is 30 centimeters long. Is this a good estimate? Explain why or why not.

Write About It Possible answer: It is not a good estimate.

30 centimeters would be more than 2 markers long, and the pencil box is

less than 2 markers long.

177

Step By Step

- Read the **Think** section together.
- Have students look at the drawing of the pencil box in the **Think** section. Discuss how Julia could use the marker to estimate the pencil box's length.

▶ **Mathematical Discourse 3–5**

- Have students work in pairs to complete the **Reflect** question. Invite a volunteer to read the question aloud before students begin.
- After students answer the **Reflect** question, discuss their responses. Then have them measure the pencil box with a centimeter ruler and compare their estimate to the actual measurement to check for reasonableness.

SMP TIP Use Tools
When students measure the lengths of the pencil box on this page and the toy car on the previous page, they are using appropriate tools strategically. *(SMP 5)*

▶ **Visual Model**

▶ **Real-World Connection**

Ready· Mathematics
PRACTICE AND PROBLEM SOLVING

Assign *Practice and Problem Solving* **pages 197–198** after students have completed this section.

▶ **Visual Model**

Draw diagrams.

Throughout this lesson, encourage students to make and label simple diagrams that compare the estimated length to a known length. For example, if they estimate that a book is about two pencil lengths, sketch two pencils in a row and write each pencil's length to help students visualize the length and an addition problem.

▶ **Real-World Connection**

Ask students if they can think of any jobs in which estimates of lengths might be made. [A truck driver might estimate how far he or she can drive in one day, and a mover might estimate how big a truck is needed to deliver a large piece of furniture.] List suggested jobs, and discuss the units each worker might use.

▶ **Mathematical Discourse**

3 *What are some reasonable estimates for the length of the pencil box?*

Students' answers should be greater than 14 centimeters but less than 28 centimeters.

4 *How is using the marker to estimate different from using two quarters?*

The marker is 14 units long, and the quarter is only 1 unit long. Instead of thinking about lining up the marker two or three times, as Ty did with the quarter, Julia is deciding if the box is longer or shorter than the marker.

5 *What are some other items we could use to help us make good estimates?*

Students may suggest common objects that are reliably all the same length, such as unused crayons or playing cards.

At A Glance

Students practice estimating lengths in centimeters and inches. Then students examine how a reasonable estimate is developed.

Step By Step

Let's Explore the Idea

- Tell students that they can become good at estimating lengths by practicing using both centimeters and inches.

- Work through the page together as a class. Students can measure the width of their own little fingers to see how they compare to one centimeter.

- Reinforce that an estimate of a length does not have to equal the exact length. However, an estimate should not be a random guess. It should be based on reasoning and known object or unit lengths.

▶ **Mathematical Discourse 1–2**

▶ **Hands-On Activity**

Think About Using Different Units to Estimate Length

🔍 **Let's Explore the Idea** Use different units to help you estimate length.

Use the stamp to answer Problems 2 and 3.

2 Use the width of your little finger to help you estimate the length of the stamp.

The stamp is about <u>3 or 4</u> cm long.

3 Use a centimeter ruler to measure the length of the stamp.

What is the actual length?

<u>3</u> cm long

length

Use the hair clip and ribbon to answer Problems 4 and 5.

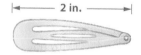

|← 2 in. →|

4 Estimate the length of the ribbon.

The ribbon is about <u>4 or 5</u> inches long.

5 Use an inch ruler to measure the length of the ribbon.

What is the actual length? <u>5</u> inches long

178

▶ **Mathematical Discourse**

1 *What do you notice about the estimate in Problem 4 and the measured length in Problem 5?*

Students might find that they are not the same. An estimate and an exact length do not have to be equal, but they should be reasonably close to each other.

2 *Can you explain why you should tell what units you are using when you estimate?*

If I just say that the stamp is 3, without saying whether it is 3 inches or 3 centimeters, other people won't know if it is a reasonable estimate.

▶ **Hands-On Activity**

Estimate lengths of classroom objects.

Materials: For each pair: ruler and classroom objects

- Have students work in pairs. Give each pair a list of about 4 classroom objects such as a table, 10 connecting cubes, an eraser and a stapler.

- Students estimate the length of each object, using benchmark objects if they like. They then measure each object and compare their estimate with the actual length.

- They can record the name of the object, the estimate, and the actual length in a chart.

- After they are finished, compare the results as a class. Ask: *Can you describe how you made your estimates? Did your estimates improve during this activity?*

Let's Talk About It
Solve the problems below as a group.

6 How did you estimate the length of the stamp?

Possible answer: I lined up my little finger on the stamp 4 times.

7 How did you estimate the length of the ribbon?

Possible answer: The ribbon looks as long as 2 hair clips, so I added

2 + 2 to get 4 inches.

8 How does your estimate compare with the actual length of the ribbon?

Possible answer: The actual length was 5 inches. My estimate was a little

less than the actual length.

9 Talk About It **Work with a partner.**
When would you estimate a length instead of measuring the exact length?

Write About It Possible answer: I might estimate a length when I

don't have a ruler or when I don't need to know the exact length.

▶ **Try It Another Way** **Estimate length using different units.**

10 The length of your teacher's desk   Answers will vary.

Estimate: _____ feet   Actual: _____ feet

11 The length of a classroom wall

Estimate: _____ meters   Actual: _____ meters

179

▶ **Mathematical Discourse**

3 *Can you think of other ways to estimate the length of the ribbon?*
Students may suggest using the technique described on the first page of the lesson, imagining how many quarters could line up below the ribbon.

4 *Some teachers say, "An estimate is a guess with a method behind it." What do you think that means, and do you agree?*
Answers will vary, but listen for evidence that students recognize that an estimate of an object's length should include some thought, such as comparing it to a known length, or imagining how many unit lengths would be needed to cover the object.

Step By Step

Let's Talk About It

- Have students work in small groups for Problems 6 through 8.
- After students have completed Problem 8, discuss as a class why an estimate and the actual measure might be different numbers.

▶ **Mathematical Discourse 3 and 4**

- Ask a volunteer to read Problem 9 aloud. Then have students work in pairs to answer the question.

> **SMP TIP Construct Arguments**
> In Problem 9, students are asked to explain when they might choose to estimate rather than measure. This gives students the opportunity to practice clarifying and communicating their thinking, which are important steps in developing strong mathematical arguments. *(SMP 3)*

Try It Another Way

- For the **Try It Another Way** questions, have tape measures or yardsticks and meter sticks available. Have all students make both estimates, then have one student measure the desk, and another measure the wall. Record the actual lengths as a class.

- Check with students to see how close their estimates are to the exact measurements. Discuss with students that if an estimate is very far from the actual measure, it may mean that they made a mistake in either measuring or estimating.

> 📖 **Ready** **Mathematics**
> PRACTICE AND PROBLEM SOLVING

Assign *Practice and Problem Solving* **pages 199–200** after students have completed this section.

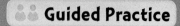 Guided Practice

At A Glance

Students demonstrate their understanding of estimating lengths. They explain their estimation methods, and analyze a method of checking an estimate.

Step By Step

- Discuss each problem as a class, using the discussion points below.

Explain

- Have students complete the problem individually.

- Ask students to share their responses with the class. Students may have valid reasons to choose inches or centimeters instead of feet, so listen for responses that show they compared their arm length to a known length to make their estimate.

Analyze

- Encourage students to talk with a partner about the error Erik may have made. Have rulers with both inches and centimeters available for students to use.

- Point out to students that Erik's estimate and his measurement are very different. Ask: *Do you think that 10 inches is a reasonable length for a crayon?*

- Students should recognize that crayons are shorter than 10 inches, and that the measurement must be incorrect.

- Ask: *How could Erik have measured 10 inches instead of 4?* Students can look at the rulers to see that 4 inches is about the same length as 10 centimeters.

> **SMP TIP Critique Reasoning/Persevere in Problem-Solving**
> In Problem 13, students are asked to critique another's reasoning. Emphasize the importance of supporting their argument by describing known lengths. *(SMP 3)*

Connect ▶ Ideas About Estimating Length

Talk about these questions as a class. Then write your answers.

12 Explain Estimate the length of your arm. Use one of the units in the box to make your estimate.

Write your estimate. Explain how you made your estimate.

> centimeters
> inches
> feet
> meters

Possible answer: I estimate 2 feet. The length from my hand

to my elbow is about the same as the length from my elbow to my

shoulder. Both are about the height of my math book, or 1 foot.

13 Analyze Erik estimates that the length of a crayon is about 4 inches. He measures the crayon and says it has a length of 10 inches. Do you think his estimate or his measurement is wrong? Why?

Possible answer: Crayons are about 4 inches long, so his

estimate is good. His measurement is wrong, probably

because he measured in centimeters.

14 Identify Which is the best estimate for the length of a see-saw? Mark your answer.

☐ 30 inches ☐ 100 yards ☒ 4 meters

Explain how you made your estimate.

Possible answer: 30 inches is shorter than a yardstick.

100 yards is the length of a football field. Neither of these

is a good estimate for the length of a see-saw.

180

Identify

- Have students discuss the problem and their responses with a partner.

- Ask: *What would be a good way to estimate the length of a seesaw?* Encourage students to think about how a seesaw compares to their own height, or to the height of an adult.

Teacher Notes

Teacher-Toolbox.com

Overview

Assign the Lesson 19 Quiz and have students work independently to complete it.

Use the results of the quiz to assess students' understanding of the content of the lesson and to identify areas for reteaching. See the Lesson Pacing Guide at the beginning of the lesson and the Differentiated Instruction activities that follow for suggested instructional resources.

Tested Skills

Assesses 2.MD.A.3

Problems on this assessment form require students to be able to estimate lengths in inches, centimeters, feet, and meters, determine if a certain unit is appropriate for measuring or estimating the length of a given object, and use a common object (benchmark) to estimate a length.

Ready® Mathematics

Lesson 19 **Quiz**

Solve the problems.

1 The width of a door is about 1 meter. Which of the objects below is about 1 meter long in real life?

Circle the correct answer.

A

B

C

D

Lesson 19 Quiz continued

2 Manuel estimates the length of his skateboard, his desk, and his shoe. Use the measurement units in the box to complete the sentences.

Answer choices may be used only once.

inches   feet   meters   centimeters

The length of his skateboard is about 30 _____.

The length of his desk is about 3 _____.

The length of his shoe is about 22 _____.

3 Lucy estimates that a large dog is about 3 feet long.

Is her estimate reasonable?

Explain how Lucy might use a coloring book to make a reasonable estimate.

_____

_____

_____

_____

_____

Common Misconceptions and Errors

Errors may result if students:

- do not have a clear concept of the approximate length of an inch, a foot, a centimeter, or a meter.

- count the number of objects used, instead of using the length of the object, to estimate the length of another object.

- confuse units (e.g., inches with centimeters or feet with meters).

Ready® **Mathematics**

Lesson 19 Quiz Answer Key

1. A
   DOK 2

2. inches
   feet
   centimeters
   DOK 2

3. Yes. Possible explanation: The length of a coloring book is about 1 foot. A large dog is about 3 coloring books long.
   DOK 3

LESSON OVERVIEW

Lesson 20
Compare Lengths

CCSS Focus

Domain
Measurement and Data

Cluster
A. Measure and estimate lengths in standard units.

Standards
2.MD.A.4 Measure to determine how much longer one object is than another, expressing the length difference in terms of a standard length unit.

Standards for Mathematical Practice (SMP)

1 Make sense of problems and persevere in solving them.
2 Reason abstractly and quantitatively.
3 Construct viable arguments and critique the reasoning of others.
4 Model with mathematics.
5 Use appropriate tools strategically.
6 Attend to precision.

Lesson Objectives

Content Objectives

• Compare the lengths of objects by determining which measure is greater than or less than the other.

• Use addition and subtraction to compare lengths, finding how much greater or less the measure of one object is than the other.

Language Objectives

• Tell how to compare the lengths of two objects that are not lined up next to each other.

• Record the lengths of two objects and subtract to tell how much longer or shorter one is than the other.

Prerequisite Skills

• Add and subtract within 20.
• Measure in standard units of measure.
• Use measuring tools to measure to the nearest unit.

Lesson Vocabulary

There is no new vocabulary.

Learning Progression

In Grade 1 students explore measurement as the process of comparing lengths to one another and to a length of iterated (repeated) units.

In Grade 2 students expand on the concept of unit of measure as they measure the length of an object using two different units of measure in whole number units. At this level, they use tools to measure standard units, estimate lengths and determine the appropriate tool to use in measuring.

In this lesson students compare lengths of objects within a specific unit, and use addition and subtraction to find differences in length.

In Grade 3 students increase accuracy by measuring lengths in fractions of an inch. They recognize that the lengths of the sides of a figure can be measured in units and combined to find the perimeter of the figure.

Lesson Pacing Guide

Whole Class Instruction

Day 1
45–60 minutes

Toolbox: Interactive Tutorial*
Compare Lengths

Introduction
• Opening Activity *15 min*
• Use What You Know *10 min*
• Find Out More *10 min*
• Reflect *5 min*

Practice and Problem Solving
Assign pages 205–206.

Day 2
45–60 minutes

Modeled and Guided Instruction
Learn About Finding Differences Between Lengths
• Measure It/Model It *20 min*
• Connect It *15 min*
• Try It *10 min*

Practice and Problem Solving
Assign pages 207–208.

Day 3
45–60 minutes

Modeled and Guided Instruction
Learn About Ways to Compare Lengths
• Measure It/Measure It *15 min*
• Connect It *20 min*
• Try It *10 min*

Practice and Problem Solving
Assign pages 209–210.

Day 4
45–60 minutes

Guided Practice
Practice Comparing Lengths
• Example *5 min*
• Problems 13–15 *15 min*
• Pair/Share *15 min*
• Solutions *10 min*

Practice and Problem Solving
Assign pages 211–212.

Day 5
45–60 minutes

Independent Practice
Practice Comparing Lengths
• Problems 1–5 *20 min*
• Quick Check and Remediation *10 min*
• Hands-On or Challenge Activity *15 min*

Toolbox: Lesson Quiz
Lesson 20 Quiz

Small Group Differentiation

Teacher-Toolbox.com

Reteach
Ready Prerequisite Lessons *45–90 min*

Grade 1
• Lesson 31 Order Objects by Length
• Lesson 32 Compare Lengths

Student-led Activities
Math Center Activities *30–40 min*

Grade 2 *(Lesson 20)*
• 2.35 Compare Centimeter Lengths
• 2.36 Compare Lengths

*We continually update the Interactive Tutorials. Check the Teacher Toolbox for the most up-to-date offerings for this lesson.

Opening Activity

Use a Benchmark to Compare Lengths

Objective Explore comparing lengths by comparing objects to a benchmark.

Time *15–20 minutes*

Materials for each student
• paper and pencil

Overview

Students find objects that are longer than and shorter than a benchmark. They then compare a length in a different orientation to a benchmark and devise a strategy for comparison.

Step By Step

1 Establish a benchmark.

• Ask students to look for something in the room that is longer than their desktop, and something that is shorter than their desktop. Listen to several responses, making sure that students understand what it means to be longer or shorter and that they are all using the same side of the desk as the benchmark length.

• Tell students that they will work with a partner to find things in the room they think are longer than their desktop, and other things they think are shorter than their desktop.

2 Record comparisons.

• Demonstrate how to make a table to record their observations.

• Have students look around the room and find at least 10 different objects that fit each category and record them in the table.

Longer than a desk	Shorter than a desk

3 Share comparisons.

- Invite students to share their ideas with the class. Ask them what they did— or could do—if they weren't certain how an object's length compared to their desk's length. Listen for suggestions that refer to direct comparison such as: "We could lay the object on the desk to see which one is longer."

- Show students an object, such as a lamp or potted plant, that has a height close to the length of a desk. Ask: *Do you think this is taller or shorter than the length of a desk?* Point out the height to make sure students understand the measurement you are referring to.

- Allow students to discuss the situation and offer suggestions of how they could figure out if it is longer or shorter. They may suggest tipping it over to compare or measuring both objects.

4 Devise a strategy.

- Ask students to think of a strategy that would allow them to compare these objects quickly without using a direct comparison or measurement.

- Suggest using something like a string or piece of yarn if no one else does. Invite a volunteer to measure a desk using a piece of string or yarn and another student to measure the height of the other object. Tape the two lengths of string on the board to compare. Discuss how these objects were more difficult to compare because of their orientation.

- Ask: *How much longer (or shorter) is (the object) than your desk? How could you know for sure?* Tell students that this lesson will help them use measuring to compare and find out how much longer or shorter one object is than another.

Introduction

At A Glance

Students measure pictures of objects in centimeters to compare their lengths. Then students compare lengths by looking at a ruler, and explore the use of addition and subtraction for comparing lengths.

Step By Step

- Work through **Use What You Know** as a class.

- Tell students that this page will help them review measuring with a ruler.

- Have students read the problem at the top of the page. Remind students where the centimeters are on their ruler.

- Make sure students are lining up their ruler correctly as they measure.

> **SMP TIP** **Attend to Precision**
> Throughout this lesson, emphasize the importance of precision in measurements. If one measure is inaccurate, the comparison is also inaccurate. *(SMP 6)*

- Following Part c, ask Mathematical Discourse question 1.

▶ **Mathematical Discourse 1**

- For Part d, make sure students are attending to the measurements recorded in Parts a and b, and not relying on visual comparisons.

▶ **Hands-On Activity**

▶ **English Language Learners**

🔄 Use What You Know

You know how to measure length.

Layla found this spoon and fork with her tea set.

Measure each object in centimeters. Which object is longer?

a. What is the length of the spoon? ___8___ centimeters

b. What is the length of the fork? ___10___ centimeters

c. Which object is longer? _the fork_

d. Explain how you know which object is longer.

Possible answer: The length of the fork is 10 cm, and the length of the spoon is 8 cm. 10 is more than 8, so the fork is longer.

182

▶ **Mathematical Discourse**

1 *Why is it a good idea to compare lengths using centimeters rather than just by looking at the objects?*
When objects aren't lined up exactly, it might be difficult to tell which one is longer. Measuring gives numbers to compare.

▶ **Hands-On Activity**

Measure with centimeter cubes.

Materials: centimeter cubes or centimeter tiles cut from Activity Sheet 4 (1-Centimeter Grid Paper)

- Have students line up the cubes beneath the picture of the spoon and the picture of the fork.

- Ask: *How does the number of cubes you used compare to the number of centimeters you measured? Why?* [The numbers are the same because each interval on the ruler and each cube is 1 centimeter long.]

▶ **English Language Learners**

ELL students may be more familiar with the metric system than the U.S. customary system of measure. Encourage them to share what they know about the metric system and be the "experts" in the class. Help them to see that strategies used for comparing in the U.S. customary system are the same as strategies used for comparing in the metric system.

▷▷ Find Out More

What is the difference between the length of the spoon and the length of the fork?

It takes 2 jumps to get from 8 to 10.

The fork is ___2___ centimeters longer than the spoon.

The spoon is ___2___ centimeters shorter than the fork.

▶ **Reflect** **Work with a partner.**

1 **Talk About It** Zuri and Marco want to find the difference in their heights. Explain how they could do this.

Write About It Possible answer: They could measure their

heights and then subtract the lesser number from the greater number.

183

▶ Concept Extension

Understand ruler units.

Materials: centimeter cubes or centimeter tiles cut from Activity Sheet 4 (1-Centimeter Grid Paper)

- Give students an object that is easy to measure, such as a toothpick or straw.
- Instruct students to arrange centimeter cubes one next to the other along the object. Then use a centimeter ruler to check the measurement.
- Model and ask students to move the ruler so that the left side of the object is lined up with the number 2 on the ruler.
- Ask: *How can you measure length starting at 2 on the ruler? Explain.* Students should recognize that they could measure starting at any number by counting the total number of units along the length of the object.

▶ Mathematical Discourse

2 *How is comparing lengths like working with fact families?*

Students should respond that the longer length is like the whole. If you subtract the shorter length, you get the difference. Those are like the parts. If you add the difference and the shorter length, you get the longer length. If you subtract the difference from the longer length, you get the shorter length.

Step By Step

- Ask students to look at the objects in **Find Out More**. Remind students that on the previous page, they compared the spoon and fork to find which one is longer. Explain that when comparing two objects, they can also find how much longer or shorter one object is than the other.
- Ask: *How can you tell that the fork is 2 centimeters longer than the spoon?* Help students recognize that they can count jumps on the ruler as shown on the page, or they can use subtraction or addition to find out the difference.
- Ask Mathematical Discourse question 2 to connect the process used when comparing lengths to fact families.

▶ **Mathematical Discourse 2**

- Have students complete the **Reflect** section. Discuss students' responses.

▶ **Concept Extension**

Ready **Mathematics**
PRACTICE AND PROBLEM SOLVING

Assign *Practice and Problem Solving* **pages 205–206** after students have completed this section.

Modeled and Guided Instruction

At A Glance

Students measure and compare lengths using a bar model. Then students find the difference between the two lengths by writing and solving an equation.

Step By Step

- Read the problem at the top of the page as a class. Ask: *Can you tell just by looking at the pieces of tape which one is longer?* [Yes] *Can you tell how much longer? Why or why not?* [No. You need to measure to find how long they each are and then find the difference.]

▶ **Real-World Connection**

Measure It

- Discuss the **Measure It** section. Ask: *How can you find out how much longer Nate's piece of tape is?* [Either subtract 3 from 8 or find how many more 8 is than 3.]

Model It

- Read **Model It**. Ask how the bar model helps compare the lengths. Students should recognize that the bar model is one way to represent numbers in a fact family.

- Use the Hands-On Activity to help further connect the bar model to comparing lengths.

▶ **Hands-On Activity**

Learn About Finding Differences Between Lengths

Read the problem. Then you will explore ways to find the difference between lengths.

Nate and Jen each have a piece of tape.

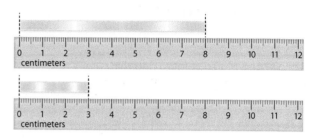

Nate   Jen

Who has the longer piece of tape? How much longer is it?

▶ **Measure It** You can measure each piece of tape.

Measure each piece of tape using centimeters.

▶ **Model It** You can make a bar model.

You can make a bar model to compare the lengths.

Length of Nate's tape	
Length of Jen's tape	?

184

▶ **Real-World Connection**

Discuss that in daily life, sometimes just looking at objects to compare them is good enough, such as knowing that one person is taller than the other. At other times, it is important to be able to tell how much longer one object is than another.

Give this example: Suppose you have an 18-inch piece of ribbon for a craft you are making, but the craft requires only 13 inches of ribbon. You need to know how much longer your piece of ribbon is to know how much to cut off.

▶ **Hands-On Activity**

Use centimeter grid paper to compare lengths.

Materials: 2-row section cut from Activity Sheet 4 (1-Centimeter Grid Paper), crayons or colored pencils, and scissors

- Have students shade one row of 8 squares to represent Nate's a piece of tape.

- Beneath that row, they should shade 3 squares to represent Jen's piece of tape. Show them how to cut off the extra grid squares to make a rectangular grid like the one below.

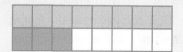

- Discuss that the part of the grid that is unshaded is the difference between the two lengths.

▶ **Connect It** **Write an equation to find the difference.**

2 What is the length of each person's piece of tape?
Write the numbers in the bar model.

Length of Nate's tape	
8 centimeters	
Length of Jen's tape	?
3 centimeters	

3 Who has the longer piece of tape? Explain how
you know.

Nate. Possible answer: 8 cm is more than 3 cm.

4 Write an equation you can use to find the difference
in the lengths. Then find the difference.

3 + ? = 8 or 8 − 3 = ?; The difference is 5.

5 Complete the sentence to compare Nate's and Jen's tape.

<u>Nate's</u> tape is <u>5</u> centimeters

longer than <u>Jen's</u> tape.

▶ **Try It** **Try another problem.**
Use these stickers for Problems 6 and 7.

6 Circle the sticker that is longer.

7 Measure and write the length
of each sticker in centimeters.
How much longer is the long
sticker than the short sticker?

Super Job! Way to go!

The sticker with the star is 5 cm and the sticker of the sun is 3 cm. So the

star sticker is 2 cm longer.

185

Step By Step

Connect It

- Read **Connect It** as a class. Remind students
that the questions refer to the tape shown
on the previous page.

- For Problem 3, invite students to share ideas
of ways they could figure out which piece of
tape is longer. [Just by looking at them;
seeing that one is longer on a bar model;
knowing that 8 is greater than 3, etc.] For
this problem, it is not necessary to include
the numerical difference.

- Have students complete Problem 4 and
discuss the equations they wrote. Reinforce
the idea that the difference can be found
using either an addition or subtraction
equation.

**SMP TIP Reason Abstractly and
Quantitatively**
Encourage students to make connections
to mental strategies they have learned to
help them solve the comparison
problems. This reinforces the relationship
between the concepts of number and
measurement. A length measurement is
the comparison of an object's length to a
set of same-sized units that are counted.
So measurements can be compared in the
same way as other quantities. *(SMP 2)*

Try It

6 **Solution**
The sticker on the left is longer, so it
should be circled.

7 **Solution**
The long sticker is 2 cm longer than the
short sticker. 5 − 3 = 2.

Ready Mathematics
PRACTICE AND PROBLEM SOLVING

Assign *Practice and Problem Solving*
pages 207–208 after students have
completed this section.

Modeled and Guided Instruction

At A Glance

Students compare lengths by measuring each object and by measuring the difference. Then students revisit the problem to find the difference in length.

Step By Step

- Ask students how the question on this page is different from the questions on the previous pages. They should notice that they are asked to find how much shorter rather than how much longer one object is than another.

Measure It

- Help students recognize that whether they are finding how much longer one object is than another or how much shorter one object is than another, they are finding the difference in length.

- However, the comparison statement they make is different for each type of problem. Ask students how they can reword the problem on this page to find which is the longer object.

- Ask students to describe what the model shows. Make sure they recognize that they can use addition or subtraction to find how much longer one object is than another.

Measure It

- Read how to measure the difference. Ask students to describe how this method is different from the one shown in the first Measure It.

▶ Mathematical Discourse 1–2

▶ Hands-On Activity

Learn About ▶ **Ways to Compare Lengths**

Read the problem. Then you will explore ways to compare lengths.

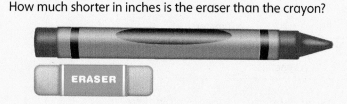

How much shorter in inches is the eraser than the crayon?

▶ **Measure It** You can measure each object and find the difference.

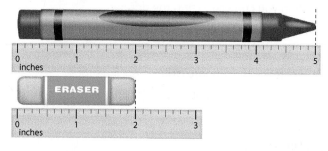

▶ **Measure It** You can measure the difference.

Line up one end of the eraser and the crayon. Then use a ruler to measure the difference.

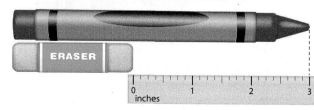

186

▶ Mathematical Discourse

1 *Do you think it is easier to find the difference by subtracting or by measuring it? Why?*

Answers will depend on student preferences, but some may respond that when measuring the difference, only one measurement is made.

2 *Sarah asks, "Why do I need to know if I am finding which object is longer or which object is shorter, since the difference is the same for both questions?" What should I tell her?*

The difference between the lengths of the objects is the same, but if the question asks how much shorter one is than the other, you have to write down the name of the shorter object, not the name of the longer object.

▶ Hands-On Activity

Use inch tiles to measure the difference between lengths.

Materials: inch tiles cut from Activity Sheet 3 (1-Inch Grid Paper)

- Ask students to find two books that are different heights.

- Have them compare the books by placing them next to each other.

- Ask: *If your books were a bar model, what would tell you the difference in their heights?* [The distance from the edge of shortest to the edge of longest book.]

- Instruct students to lay their tiles one next to another to extend from the shortest book to the longest. Have them tell the difference between the books in inches.

- Have students measure the difference with their ruler to see that the measures of the difference are the same.

▶ **Connect It Find the difference.**

8 Look at the first *Measure It*. Explain how to find how much shorter the eraser is than the crayon.

Possible answer: Subtract the length of the eraser from the length

of the crayon.

9 How much shorter is the eraser than the crayon?

The eraser is 3 inches shorter than the crayon.

10 What is measured in the second *Measure It*?

the difference between the length of the crayon and the length

of the eraser

11 **Talk About It** Kelly says that you cannot always use the method shown in the second *Measure It*. Do you agree? Why or why not?

Write About It Possible answer: I agree. This method only works

when the two objects can be lined up next to each other.

▶ **Try It Try another problem.**

12 Henry has two paper clips.

Circle the paper clip that is shorter. How many inches shorter is it?

It is 1 inch shorter.

187

Step By Step

Connect It

- Tell students that **Connect It** will help them explore ways to find the difference between the eraser and the crayon shown on the previous page.

- Discuss *Talk About It* as a group. Use the Hands-On Activity to explore a situation in which lining up lengths may be difficult. Have students share ideas of when lining up to compare works and when it may be difficult to use.

▶ **Hands-On Activity**

Try It

- Make sure students have an inch ruler for solving the **Try It** problem.

12 **Solution**
    Students should circle the shorter paper clip and respond that it is 1 inch shorter.

 **Ready** Mathematics
PRACTICE AND PROBLEM SOLVING

Assign *Practice and Problem Solving* **pages 209–210** after students have completed this section.

▶ **Hands-On Activity**

Use two methods of finding the difference in side lengths.

Materials: 6-inch by 9-inch piece of construction paper, ruler, inch tiles cut from Activity Sheet 3 (1-Inch Grid Paper)

- Give each student a piece of construction paper and ask them to compare the side lengths.

- Ask: *How might you find out how much longer one side is than the other?* Students may suggest that they can measure. *Would it make sense to measure the difference in the lengths?* Explain. [It would not make sense since the sides are not lined up next to each other.]

- Ask students if they could think of a way to use the strategy of measuring the difference in this situation. They may suggest comparing their piece of paper to a classmate's and measuring the difference, or using tiles to extend along each length and then repositioning them next to each other to find the difference.

- Ask students to use the inch side of a ruler to measure each side of the paper, using subtraction to find the difference. Then have them use one of the other strategies. Share results.

- Discuss which strategy makes more sense to use in this situation and why.

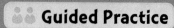
Guided Practice

At A Glance

Students solve problems about the difference between two measures.

Step By Step

- Provide each student with a ruler for measuring centimeters and inches.

- Ask students to solve the problems individually and show all their work, including any equations they write. Remind students to pay attention to whether they are to find which object is longer or shorter.

- For Problem 15, make sure students understand that they are finding a length of yarn that is shorter than the one Tim has.

- **Pair/Share** When students have completed each problem, have them Pair/Share to discuss their solutions with a partner.

Solutions

Example A bar model and an equation are used to model the difference between two given measures.

13 Solution
6 centimeters; $9 - 3 = 6$.
DOK 2

Study the model below. Then solve Problems 13–15.

Example

Jonah is 52 inches tall. His sister Sophia is 43 inches tall. How much taller is Jonah than Sophia?

You can show your work with a bar model and equation.

$52 - 43 = 9$

Answer _Jonah is 9 inches taller than Sophia._

13 Anna measures the paper strips below in centimeters. What is the difference in the lengths of the paper strips?

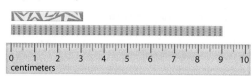

The difference in the lengths of the paper strips is how much longer or shorter one is than the other.

Show your work.
Possible work: $9 - 3 = 6$

188

Answer 6 centimeters

Teacher Notes

14 Circle the nail that is shorter. Then tell how much shorter it is. Measure using centimeters.

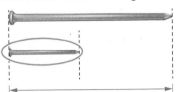

What equation can you write to help you find the answer?

Show your work.
Possible work: 7 − 3 = 4

Answer 4 centimeters

15 Tim has a piece of yarn that is 3 inches long. Which piece of yarn is 1 inch shorter than Tim's yarn?

A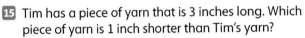

B

C

D

Will the length of the correct piece of yarn be more or less than 3 inches?

Ben chose **A** as the answer. This answer is wrong. How did Ben get his answer?

Possible answer: He found the piece of yarn that is 1 inch longer instead

of shorter.

189

Solutions

14 Solution
4 cm; 7 − 3 = 4. Check that the shorter nail is circled.
DOK 2

15 Solution
D; 2 inches is 1 inch less than 3 inches. Explain to students why the other two choices are not correct:

B is not correct because 1 inch is the difference, not the length of the yarn.

C is not correct because 3 inches is equal to Tim's yarn, not shorter.
DOK 3

Ready Mathematics
PRACTICE AND PROBLEM SOLVING

Assign *Practice and Problem Solving* **pages 211–212** after students have completed this section.

Teacher Notes

Independent Practice

At A Glance

Students solve problems involving the comparison of two lengths that might appear on a mathematics test.

Solutions

1 **Solution**
   A; $4 - 2 = 2$.
   DOK 2

2 **Solution**
   B Longer kite − shorter kite = difference;
   D Shorter kite + difference = longer kite.
   DOK 2

Practice Comparing Lengths

Solve the problems.

1 How much longer in inches is the bottom bandage than the top bandage? Circle the correct answer.

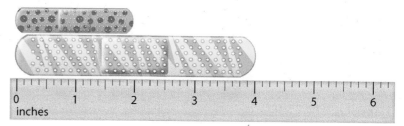

(A) 2 inches

B 3 inches

C 4 inches

D 5 inches

2 The tail on Evan's kite is 85 centimeters long. The tail on Maya's kite is 68 centimeters long. What equation could you use to find the difference in the lengths? Circle all the correct answers.

A $85 + 68 = ?$

(B) $85 - 68 = ?$

C $85 + ? = 68$

(D) $68 + ? = 85$

190

Quick Check and Remediation

- Give students two strips of paper; one 12 cm and one 7 cm long. Have students measure in centimeters to compare the lengths and tell how much longer one is than the other. [5 cm]

- For students who are still struggling, use the chart to guide remediation.

- After providing remediation, check students' understanding by giving them an unused pencil and a new crayon to measure and compare.

If the error is . . .	Students may . . .	To remediate . . .
19 cm	have added the lengths rather than subtracted.	Provide students with centimeter tiles cut from Activity Sheet 4 or centimeter cubes. Ask them to identify where the difference between the paper strips is shown. Have them place the tiles or cubes along the side of the longer strip to find the difference.
4 cm	have measured or subtracted incorrectly.	Have students measure the paper strips again to ensure they measured accurately. If they used subtraction previously to find the difference, have them use addition this time. If they used addition previously, have them use subtraction this time.

3 What is the difference in the lengths of the two straws? Measure using centimeters. Circle the correct answer.

A 3 cm   **C** 7 cm

B 4 cm   **D** 11 cm

4 A table is 10 feet long. A desk is 3 feet long. Circle *True* or *False* for each statement.

a. The table is 7 feet shorter than the desk.   True (False)

b. The table is 7 feet longer than the desk.   (True) False

c. The desk is 7 feet shorter than the table.   (True) False

d. The desk is 7 feet longer than the table.   True (False)

5 Draw a line that is 6 centimeters longer than the line below.

How long is your line in centimeters? How did you know the length your line should be?

My line is 11 centimeters. I measured to find that the line already on the page

is 5 centimeters. Since 5 + 6 = 11, I knew my line should be 11 centimeters.

✓ **Self Check**   Now you can compare lengths. Fill this in on the progress chart on page 153.   **191**

Solutions

3 **Solution**
B; $11 - 7 = 4$.
DOK 2

4 **Solution**
a. **False**; b. **True**; c. **True**; d. **False**
DOK 2

5 **Solution**
Students should draw an 11-cm line; $5 + 6 = 11$. Check students' explanations.
DOK 3

▶ Hands-On Activity

Compare foot length and hand length.

Materials: inch ruler, paper, and pencil

• Tell students that they will each measure the length of their own foot in inches and the length of their own hand in inches. Then they will find the difference in those lengths.

• Have students start by measuring the length of their foot. For measuring the length of their hand, have students place a hand flat on a desk and measure from the middle of their wrist to the tip of their longest finger. Ask students to record their findings in a chart labeled as shown.

Foot	Hand	Difference

• When students have completed their chart, ask them to compare the difference they found with that of other students. Students should find that the difference is fairly consistent.

▶ Challenge Activity

Compare units of measure.

Materials: ruler for measuring inches and centimeters; or yardstick and meter stick

• Have students measure at least ten different objects in both inches and centimeters.

• Tell them to record their measurements in a table.

Object	Inches	Centimeters

• Instruct them to compare each measurement in inches and centimeters. Have them look for a pattern that they can use to estimate the centimeter length of an object if they only know its length in inches. (They should find that the number of centimeters is a little less than 3 times the number of inches.)

• Have them test their strategy and share it with their peers.

Teacher-Toolbox.com

Overview

Assign the Lesson 20 Quiz and have students work independently to complete it.

Use the results of the quiz to assess students' understanding of the content of the lesson and to identify areas for reteaching. See the Lesson Pacing Guide at the beginning of the lesson for suggested instructional resources.

Tested Skills

Assesses 2.MD.A.4

Problems on this assessment form require students to be able to compare the lengths of objects, within one unit type, to determine which one is longer than another, and add and subtract to find how much longer or shorter one object is than another. Students will also need to be familiar with adding and subtracting within 20, measuring length using standard units, and using a measuring tool to measure to the nearest unit.

Ready® Mathematics
Lesson 20 **Quiz**

Solve the problems.

1 How much longer is the bookmark than the paper clip?

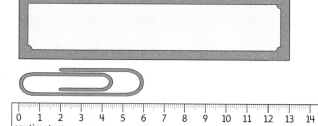

Circle the correct answer.

A 19 centimeters

B 13 centimeters

C 7 centimeters

D 6 centimeters

2 Abby draws a line that is 11 centimeters long. Jim draws a line that is 4 centimeters shorter. What is the length of Jim's line?
Use numbers from the box below to complete the sentence.

15	11	12	8	7	6	4

Jim's line is _____ centimeters long.

Lesson 20 **Quiz** continued

3 Sally has a yellow crayon and a blue crayon.

Yellow

Blue

Use a ruler to measure each crayon in inches. Then write an equation to find the difference of the lengths.

Answer: Yellow crayon: _____ inches

Blue crayon: _____ inches

Equation: _____ inches

4 Megan has a toy green boat that is 5 inches long. She also has a toy red boat that is 1 inch longer than the green boat. Bob says the red boat is 4 inches long.

Bob is not correct. What mistake did he make?

Circle the correct answer.

A Bob measured the red boat in centimeters.

B Bob measured the red boat in feet.

C Bob used addition to find the length.

D Bob used subtraction to find the length.

Common Misconceptions and Errors

Errors may result if students:

• measure an object from 1 instead of 0 or otherwise measure incorrectly when using a ruler.

• incorrectly set up a subtraction equation.

• add instead of subtract, subtract instead of add, or subtract incorrectly.

• confuse the terms *longer* and *shorter*.

Ready® **Mathematics**

Lesson 20 Quiz Answer Key

1. C
DOK 2

2. 7
DOK 2

3. 3
5
$5 - 3 = 2$
DOK 2

4. D
DOK 3

CCSS Focus

Domain
Measurement and Data

Cluster
B. Relate addition and subtraction to length.

Standards
2.MD.B.5 Use addition and subtraction within 100 to solve word problems involving lengths that are given in the same units, e.g., by using drawings (such as drawings of rulers) and equations with a symbol for the unknown number to represent the problem.

2.MD.B.6 Represent whole numbers as lengths from 0 on a number line diagram with equally spaced points corresponding to the numbers 0, 1, 2, . . ., and represent whole-number sums and differences within 100 on a number line diagram.

Domain
Operations and Algebraic Thinking

Cluster
A. Represent and solve problems involving addition and subtraction.

Standards
2.OA.A.1 Use addition and subtraction within 100 to solve one- and two-step word problems involving situations of adding to, taking from, putting together, taking apart, and comparing, with unknowns in all positions, e.g., by using drawings and equations with a symbol for the unknown number to represent the problem.

Standards for Mathematical Practice (SMP)

1 Make sense of problems and persevere in solving them.
2 Reason abstractly and quantitatively.
3 Construct viable arguments and critique the reasoning of others.
4 Model with mathematics.
5 Use appropriate tools strategically.
6 Attend to precision.

Lesson Objectives

Content Objectives

• Use addition and subtraction to solve problems involving lengths.

• Recognize the importance of working within a single unit when adding or subtracting lengths.

• Interpret and apply models that represent measurement problems involving addition and subtraction.

Language Objectives

• Restate the essential information in a measurement word problem.

• Draw a bar model to represent a measurement word problem.

• Discuss with a partner strategies used to solve a problem.

Prerequisite Skills

• Add and subtract within 100.

• Apply concepts of fact families.

• Understand addition and subtraction situations involving adding to, taking from, putting together, taking apart, and comparing.

• Measure in centimeters and inches.

Lesson Vocabulary

There is no new vocabulary.

Learning Progression

In Grade 1 students compare lengths of objects by iterating (repeating) units. They develop the understanding that the length of an object is determined by the number of iterated units that are used to compare.

In Grade 2 students measure and compare objects using more than one unit of measure. They recognize the need for comparing within a single unit and estimate lengths based on an understanding of units of measure.

In this lesson students apply what they have learned about measuring to solve problems involving measurements. They use models to represent problems and devise strategies to organize the information that leads to a solution.

In Grade 3 and beyond, students will apply these skills to problems involving additional units of measure such as miles and kilometers, to fractions of units, and to problems involving area and perimeter.

Lesson Pacing Guide

Whole Class Instruction

Day 1
45–60 minutes

Toolbox: Interactive Tutorial*
Solve Problems Involving Length

Introduction
- Opening Activity *20 min*
- Use What You Know *10 min*
- Find Out More *10 min*
- Reflect *5 min*

Practice and Problem Solving
Assign pages 215–216.

Day 2
45–60 minutes

Modeled and Guided Instruction
Learn About Solving Problems About Lengths
- Picture It/Model It/Model It *15 min*
- Connect It *20 min*
- Try It *10 min*

Practice and Problem Solving
Assign pages 217–218.

Day 3
45–60 minutes

Modeled and Guided Instruction
Learn About Solving Two-Step Problems About Length
- Picture It/Model It/Model It *15 min*
- Connect It *20 min*
- Try It *10 min*

Practice and Problem Solving
Assign pages 219–220.

Day 4
45–60 minutes

Guided Practice
Practice Adding and Subtracting Lengths
- Example *5 min*
- Problems 13–15 *15 min*
- Pair/Share *15 min*
- Solutions *10 min*

Practice and Problem Solving
Assign pages 221–222.

Day 5
45–60 minutes

Independent Practice
Practice Adding and Subtracting Lengths
- Problems 1–6 *20 min*
- Quick Check and Remediation *10 min*
- Hands-On or Challenge Activity *15 min*

Toolbox: Lesson Quiz
Lesson 21 Quiz

Small Group Differentiation

Teacher-Toolbox.com

Reteach
Ready Prerequisite Lessons *45–90 min*

Grade 1
- Lesson 33 *Understand* Length Measurement

Teacher-led Activities
Tools for Instruction *15–20 min*

Grade 2 *(Lesson 21)*
- Solve Word Problems about Measurement Data

Student-led Activities
Math Center Activities *30–40 min*

Grade 2 *(Lesson 21)*
- 2.37 Solve Measurement Word Problems
- 2.38 Measurement Word Problems Equation Match
- 2.39 Whole Numbers as Lengths
- 2.4 Diagram Problem Match

*We continually update the Interactive Tutorials. Check the Teacher Toolbox for the most up-to-date offerings for this lesson.

Opening Activity

Add and Subtract Lengths

Objective Explore addition and subtraction of lengths.

Time *20–30 minutes*

Materials for each pair

- Activity Sheet 10 (Half-Inch Grid Paper) cut into lengths of 6, 8, 9, 10, 12, 14, 15, and 16 squares (preferably each length a different color)
- 12-inch length of string
- tape (optional)

Overview

Students find lengths of units that can be combined to equal a length of string. They devise and compare strategies to find the appropriate lengths.

Step By Step

1 Pose the problem.

- Provide student pairs with grid-paper strips (described in the Materials list) and a 12-inch length of string. You may want them to tape each end of the string to their desk to keep it from moving.

- Tell students they need to find lengths of grid paper that, when combined, are exactly the same length as the string. Have them record each combination on a piece of paper in equation form.

2 Explore the concept.

- As students work through the problem, circulate the room asking questions such as: *How did you know that you needed a length of 8 units to add to a length of 16 units? Can you find 3 lengths that equal the length of the string? What do you need to do to decide?*

3 Share strategies.

- Invite students to share the strategies they used to find lengths, such as subtracting a length from 24, thinking of what length is needed to get to 24, and trying different lengths until finding ones that work (guess and check).

- Ask: *If you put an 8 and a 6 together, what other length would you need to use to equal the length of the string?* [10 squares] Listen for strategies such as add 8 + 6 then subtract the sum from 24. Ask students to explain each strategy and tell how they know they are correct.

4 Connect the concept.

- Ask students to think about other problems they have solved using similar strategies. Discuss with them that doing this activity is like solving the one- and two-step problems they did earlier in the year.

Teacher Notes

Introduction

At A Glance

Students solve a problem involving measurement by using subtraction. Then students add lengths of parts and compare the result to the whole length.

Step By Step

- Work through **Use What You Know** as a class.

- Have students read the problem at the top of the page. Ask a volunteer to tell what they know based on the information given and what they need to find out.

- Ask Mathematical Discourse questions 1–3 to engage student thinking about how to use addition and subtraction.

▶ **Mathematical Discourse 1–3**

- Discuss how this problem resembles the problems from the previous lesson, in which students compared lengths to find the difference. Point out that in this problem, they are given the difference to use to find an unknown length, rather than finding the difference.

▶ **Visual Model**

🔁 Use What You Know

You know how to compare lengths.

The length of a toy alligator's body is 32 inches.
The tail of the alligator is 6 inches shorter than the body.
How long is the tail?

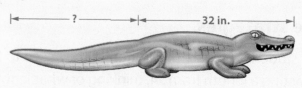

a. What is the length of the alligator's body?

  32 inches

b. Will you add or subtract to find the length of the alligator's tail? Why?

  I will subtract, because the tail is shorter than the body.

c. Write an equation to find the length of the tail.

  _32 − 6 = ?_

d. How long is the alligator's tail? _26 inches_

▶ **Mathematical Discourse**

1 *Why doesn't it make sense to add 32 and 6 for this problem?*

The problem says that the tail is shorter than the body. If we added, the tail would be longer than the body.

2 *How might you use addition to think about this problem?*

Since the tail is 6 inches shorter than the body, you can think of what you need to add to 6 to get 32.

3 *Do you think it is easier to add or subtract? Why?*

Students may respond that subtraction is easier since the difference is so great.

▶ **Visual Model**

Use a bar model to represent the problem.

- Tell students that in this problem, the length of the alligator's tail is being compared to the length of the alligator's body. Make sure students understand that the body does not include the tail.

- Helps students recognize that because the body is the longer of the two parts, it can be considered the whole in this bar model.

alligator body	
tail	?

- Ask students to tell what they know about the tail. [It is 6 inches shorter than the body.] Replace the question mark with 6 and write 32 in the top box. Discuss how to use the model to find the length of the tail.

▶▶ Find Out More

You can add lengths to find a total length.

You can measure the tail and measure the body. Then add to find the total length of the alligator.

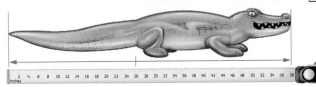

When you add lengths, the units need to be the same.

26 inches   +   32 inches

You can also measure the whole alligator.

The tape measures on this page are not life-sized.

You get the same answer either way.

26 inches + 32 inches = ___58___ inches

▶ **Reflect** **Work with a partner.**

1 **Talk About It** Why does adding the lengths of the parts of the alligator give you the same answer as measuring the whole alligator?

Write About It   Possible answer: When you put the two parts

together, you get the length of the whole alligator.

193

▶ Hands-On Activity

Explore why lengths must be the same unit when they are added.

Materials: inch tiles cut from Activity Sheet 3 (1-Inch Grid Paper), centimeter cubes or centimeter tiles cut from Activity Sheet 4 (1-Centimeter Grid Paper), marker, and crayon

• Ask students to measure a marker with inch tiles and record the length in inches.

• Have students measure the crayon with centimeter cubes or tiles, and record the length in centimeters.

• Show students how to lay the marker and crayon next to each other end to end. Ask: *What is the length of the marker and crayon together?* Discuss why you can't just add two lengths when each is measured in a different unit.

▶ Mathematical Discourse

4 *Suppose you are finding the length of the whole alligator by adding the lengths of the parts, but one of the parts is measured incorrectly. What will happen?*

Students should recognize that using an incorrect length when adding parts will cause the total length to also be incorrect.

Step By Step

• Read **Find Out More** together as a class. Ask: *What are the parts in the first picture?* [the alligator body and tail] *What is the whole?* [the whole alligator]

• Ask Mathematical Discourse question 4 to emphasize the importance of measuring accurately when adding lengths of parts to find the length of a whole.

▶ **Mathematical Discourse 4**

• Then use the Hands-On Activity to help students understand the importance of using a single unit when adding lengths.

▶ **Hands-On Activity**

• Have student pairs read and discuss the **Reflect** question.

• Ask: *How is what you did on this page different from what you did on the first page?* Discuss how, on the first page, they found the length of one of the parts by comparing one part to the other. On this page, they found the length of the whole alligator by adding the two parts of the alligator.

Ready **Mathematics**
PRACTICE AND PROBLEM SOLVING

Assign *Practice and Problem Solving* **pages 215–216** after students have completed this section.

Modeled and Guided Instruction

At A Glance

Students explore how a picture, bar model, and number line can be used to solve a one-step problem involving measurement. Then students revisit this problem by writing equations to represent what is shown in the models.

Step By Step

- Read the problem at the top of the page as a class.

Picture It

- Draw students' attention to **Picture It**. Ask how drawing a picture can help solve the problem. Guide students to see that a picture helps make sense of the problem and leads to a strategy to use.

- Ask: *Does it matter which end the 8 centimeters is cut from? Explain.* [No, it doesn't matter. It is still 8 centimeters shorter than at first.] You may want to demonstrate this by using two equal lengths of yarn and cutting 8 cm off a different end of each.

Model It

- Draw attention to **Model It**. Discuss what each part of the bar model represents. Ask: *What is the total length?* [56 cm] *What is the part Michaela cuts off?* [8 cm]

Model It

- Have students relate the number line to the bar model.

▶ **Mathematical Discourse 1 and 2**

> **SMP TIP Model with Mathematics**
> Discuss with students how the models on this page help them make sense of the problem and lead to an equation. Make sure to emphasize these connections as students work through the problems on the next page. *(SMP 4)*

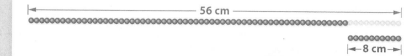

Learn About Solving Problems About Lengths

Read the problem. Then you will explore ways to model it.

> Michaela has a string of beads that is 56 centimeters long. She cuts off 8 centimeters to make it the right length for a necklace. How long is the string of beads now?

▶ **Picture It You can draw a picture.**

The string of beads is **56** centimeters long.

Michaela cuts off **8** centimeters.

▶ **Model It You can make a bar model.**

The total length is **56** centimeters.

The part cut off is **8** centimeters.

56	
?	8

▶ **Model It You can use a number line.**

Start at **56**. Subtract to get a ten.
Then subtract the rest.

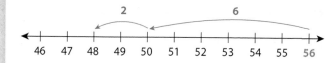

▶ **Mathematical Discourse**

1 *On the number line, why does it make sense to jump backward 6 units and then 2 more units?*

When you jump backward 6 units, you get to a ten, which is 50. Then it is easy to take away 2 more.

2 *Could you use addition instead of subtraction for this problem? Explain.*

Yes. You could think, "What number can I add 8 to for a sum of 56?"

▶ **Connect It** **Add and subtract lengths.**

2 Look at the models on the previous page. Write a subtraction equation you can use to solve the problem.

$56 - 8 = ?$

3 Write an addition equation you can use to solve the problem.

Possible answer: $? + 8 = 56$

4 Explain how the jumps on the number line show that Michaela cuts off 8 centimeters.

Jumps to the left show subtraction. A jump of 6 gets to a

ten. Jump 2 more to take away a total of 8.

5 How long is the string of beads now? 48 cm

6 How much shorter is a string of beads that is 34 centimeters long than a string that is 56 centimeters long? Explain how you found your answer.

22 centimeters; Possible answer: I subtracted 34 from 56.

▶ **Try It** **Try another problem.**

7 Jesse threw a ball 59 feet. Owen threw a ball 15 feet less than Jesse. How far did Owen throw the ball?

44 feet

195

▶ **Mathematical Discourse**

3 *Do you think it is easier to use a subtraction equation or an addition equation to solve the problem? Explain.*

Students' answers will vary. Some students may say that they prefer using a subtraction equation because part of the string of beads is taken away. Other students may say that they prefer using an addition equation so that they can count up to solve. Whatever their preference, make sure students explain their reasoning.

Step By Step

Connect It

- Read and work through the **Connect It** questions as a class. Make sure students understand that the questions refer to the problem on the previous page.

- For Problems 2 and 3, tell students to think of what they know about fact families. Explain that this will help them be able to write both a subtraction equation and an addition equation to solve the problem about Michaela's beads.

- After students answer Problem 3, tell them: *Bill says he can add $56 + 8$ to solve the problem. Do you agree? Why or why not?* Students should recognize that adding $56 + 8$ will result in an incorrect answer because the length of the string of beads is 56 cm at the start, and Michaela cuts off 8 cm.

▶ **Mathematical Discourse 3**

Try It

- Tell students that they may use a picture or other model to help in thinking about the **Try It** problem. Have students explain the thinking they used in solving the problem, sharing strategies and/or equations.

> **SMP TIP Make Sense of Problems**
> As students complete Problem 7, emphasize the importance of taking the time to understand what the problem is asking. Also, encourage students to look back at the problem after they have solved it to make sure the model they used and the answer they found make sense. *(SMP 1)*

7 **Solution**
  44 feet; $59 - 15 = 44$.

📦 **Ready** **Mathematics**
PRACTICE AND PROBLEM SOLVING

Assign *Practice and Problem Solving* **pages 217–218** after students have completed this section.

Modeled and Guided Instruction

At A Glance

Students model a two-step word problem involving measurement using a picture, number line, and diagram. Then students revisit this problem, writing an equation to model the situation. Finally, students solve another two-step word problem involving measurement.

Step By Step

- Read the problem at the top of the page as a class. Have students describe what they know and what they need to find out to solve the problem.

- Relate this problem to the two-step problems they solved in Unit 1. Ask what makes it a two-step problem. They should remember that a two-step problem has two parts that need to be solved in order to get the final answer to the problem.

Picture It

- Ask students to explain **Picture It**. Ask: *When you find the sum of both pieces of border, have you finished the problem? Why or why not?* Make sure students recognize that once the sum is found, it still needs to be compared to 50 in order to determine whether there is enough border to cover the top of the poster.

Model It

- Have students work with a partner to compare the picture and the number line. Then discuss as a class how the number line can be used to think about the problem.

▶ **Visual Model**

Model It

- Help students recognize that the first section of the diagram shows Sam's border and that the other two sections show Sadie's border.

▶ **Mathematical Discourse 1 and 2**

Learn About **Solving Two-Step Problems About Length**

Read the problem. Then you will explore ways to model it.

> Sam and Sadie are making a poster with a border. Sam has a piece of border 23 inches long. Sadie has a border that is 7 inches longer than Sam's. The top of their poster is 50 inches long. Do they have enough border to cover the top of the poster? Explain your reasoning.

▶ **Picture It** You can draw a picture.

Sam's border   Sadie's border

23 inches   23 inches + 7 inches

▶ **Model It** You can use an open number line.

Start at **23**. Add **7** first to get to the next ten.
To add 23 more, jump **20** and then **3**.

23   30   50   ?

▶ **Model It** You can use a diagram.

Add **23 + 7** first to make a ten.

| 23 | 23 | 7 |

23 + 23 + 7

23 +   30

196

▶ Mathematical Discourse

1 *How do the picture and diagram on this page help you make sense of the problem?*

   Students should recognize that they help organize the information so students can easily see what information students have and what they need to find.

2 *Do you think the picture or diagram is easier to use? Why?*

   Students will express personal preferences. Encourage them to justify using reasons that express how their choice helps them organize and make sense of the problem.

▶ Visual Model

Use an open number line.

- Replicate the number line in Model It on the board.

- Tell students that the number line starts at 23 because that is the length of Sam's border. Ask: *Based on the problem, what numbers do you add to find the length of Sadie's border?* [23 + 7] *Why is 7 added first on the number line?* [to get to the next 10] *Why are 20 and 3 the next jumps?* [to add 23 more]

- Help students see that the number line shows the total length of Sadie's border being added to the length of Sam's border.

▶ **Connect It** **Add and subtract lengths.**

8 Explain how you know the length of Sadie's border is 23 + 7.

Possible answer: Sam's border is 23 inches. Since Sadie's

border is 7 inches longer than Sam's, it is 23 + 7.

9 Write an equation you can use to find the length of the two pieces together.

23 + 7 + 23 = 53

10 Do Sam and Sadie have enough border to cover the top of the poster? Explain why or why not.

Yes. They have 53 inches, and the length of the top of the

poster is only 50 inches. 53 inches is more than 50 inches.

11 Ethan has two pieces of border. One is 24 inches long, and the other is 5 feet long. He says that the total length is 29 inches. What did he do wrong?

Possible answer: He added the lengths, but you can only

do that if the units are the same.

▶ **Try It** **Try another problem.**

12 Sarah bought 18 yards of rope. She used 6 yards to hang a swing and 4 yards to hang a birdfeeder. How much rope is left? Show your work.

8 yards; Possible work: 18 − 6 = 12; 12 − 4 = 8

197

Step By Step

Connect It

- Tell students that **Connect It** will help them learn how to write an equation to solve the problem on the previous page.

- Work through **Connect It** together as a class, referring back to the models on the previous page as you do so.

- In Problem 9, ask students to describe the relationship between the equation and the models on the previous page.

Try It

- For **Try It**, remind students that they can use a picture, diagram, or other model to help them make sense of the problem. Ask them to show the equations they use to solve the problem.

12 **Solution**
   8 yards; 18 − 6 = 12; 12 − 4 = 8.

   Error Alert Students who answer 10 yards added the rope used but failed to subtract from 18.

▶ **English Language Learners**

Ready Mathematics
PRACTICE AND PROBLEM SOLVING

Assign *Practice and Problem Solving* **pages 219–220** after students have completed this section.

▶ **English Language Learners**

Read Problem 12 with students. Then draw a simple diagram that shows a 4-yard piece and a 6-yard piece have been cut from an 18-yard piece of rope.

You might also make a drawing of a birdhouse hanging from a 4-yard piece of rope and a swing hanging from a 6-yard piece of rope.

Ask students to use the diagrams and pictures to tell what the problem is asking and what they need to find out.

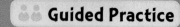

Guided Practice

At A Glance

Students model and solve measurement problems involving addition and subtraction.

Step By Step

- Ask students to solve the problems individually and show all their work, including the equations they write.

- Draw a picture and/or a number line on the board to show students other ways to represent the example problem.

- **Pair/Share** When students have completed each problem, have them Pair/Share to discuss their solutions with a partner.

Solutions

Example A bar model and equations are used as examples for solving this problem.

13 Solution
18 inches tall; 26 − 6 = 20; 20 − 2 = 18; so 26 − 8 = 18.
DOK 2

Practice ▶ Adding and Subtracting Lengths

Study the model below. Then solve Problems 13–15.

Example

Mr. Yee walks 12 feet from his house to the sidewalk. Then he walks 28 feet to the mailbox. Mr. Yee turns around and walks 17 feet back toward his house along the sidewalk. How far does Mr. Yee have to walk to get back to his house now?

Look at how you can show your work with a bar model.

12	28
17	?

$$\begin{array}{r} 12 \\ +28 \\ \hline 30 \\ +10 \\ \hline 40 \end{array} \qquad \begin{array}{r} 40 \\ -17 \\ \hline 30 \\ -7 \\ \hline 23 \end{array}$$

Answer Mr. Yee has to walk 23 feet to get to his house.

---

13 Jude's sunflower grew 8 inches this week. It is 26 inches tall now. How tall was Jude's sunflower at the beginning of the week?

Show your work.

Possible work: Find 26 − 8.
                  26 − 6 = 20
                  20 − 2 = 18
                  So, 26 − 8 = 18

Was the sunflower taller or shorter at the beginning of the week?

Answer The sunflower was 18 inches tall.

Teacher Notes

14 A path in the park was 22 meters long. Then another section was added. Now the path is 50 meters long. How long is the new section?

Show your work.

Possible work:
22 + ? = 50
22 + 20 = 42
42 + 8 = 50

20 + 8 = 28
22 + 28 = 50

> Does the path get longer or shorter?

Answer The new section is 28 meters long.

---

15 Lisa used 37 centimeters of string to hang a picture and 46 centimeters of string to hang another picture. She has 12 centimeters of string left. How much string did she start with?

A 21 cm

B 71 cm

C 83 cm

(D) 95 cm

> The amount of string at the start is the amount of string Lisa used plus what other amount?

Chase chose **C** as the answer. This answer is wrong. How did Chase get his answer?

Possible answer: He only added 37 and 46. He didn't add

the 12 centimeters of string left.

199

Solutions

14 Solution

The new section is 28 meters; 22 + 8 = 30; 30 + 20 = 50; 8 + 20 = 28.

DOK 2

15 Solution

D; 37 + 46 + 12 = 95.

Explain to students why the other two choices are not correct:

A is not correct because you need to find 37 + 46 + 12, not 46 − 37 + 12.

B is not correct because you need to find 37 + 46 + 12, not 37 + 46 − 12.

DOK 3

Ready Mathematics
PRACTICE AND PROBLEM SOLVING

Assign *Practice and Problem Solving* **pages 221–222** after students have completed this section.

Teacher Notes

Independent Practice

At A Glance

Students use addition and subtraction to solve measurement problems that might appear on a mathematics test.

Solutions

1 Solution

D; Add 44 inches to the length of the dresser to find the length of the wall; $44 + 36 = 80$.

DOK 2

2 Solution

B and **C**; These number pairs have a difference of 25.

DOK 2

3 Solution

A; The red line is $55 - 14$, or 41 centimeters, and the green line is $41 - 23$, or 18 centimeters.

DOK 2

Practice Adding and Subtracting Lengths

Solve the problems.

1 Maddie's dresser is 44 inches shorter than her bedroom wall. The length of the dresser is 36 inches. What is the length of the wall? Circle the correct answer.

A 8 inches   **C** 70 inches

B 12 inches   **(D)** 80 inches

2 Jordan has two tracks for his toy cars. One track is 25 inches longer than the other. What could be the lengths of the tracks? Circle all the correct answers.

A 12 inches and 13 inches

(B) 75 inches and 50 inches

(C) 20 inches and 45 inches

D 5 inches and 20 inches

3 Willa draws three lines.

- a blue line that is 55 cm long

- a red line 14 cm shorter than the blue line

- a green line 23 cm shorter than the red line

What is the length of the green line? Circle the correct answer.

(A) 18 cm   **C** 32 cm

B 22 cm   **D** 41 cm

200

Quick Check and Remediation

- Kylie has a red ribbon that is 53 centimeters long. Her blue ribbon is 27 centimeters shorter than the red ribbon. How long is the blue ribbon? [26 cm]

- For students who are still struggling, use the chart to guide remediation.

- After providing remediation, check students' understanding using the following problem: Dom has a piece of yarn that is 34 inches long. It is 16 inches longer than Sadie's yarn. How long is Sadie's yarn? [18 inches]

If the error is ...	Students may ...	To remediate ...
80 inches	have added the given numbers.	Ask students what *shorter than* means. Help students draw a bar model for the problem. Explain why the shorter measurement goes in one of the bottom boxes and the longer measurement goes in the top box. Have students solve using the bar model.
34 inches	have subtracted 20 from 50 and 3 from 7.	Have students check their work by adding 34 and 27. Once they realize the answer is incorrect, help them solve using a different strategy, such as regrouping the tens and then subtracting, or counting up.

4 Bella hangs a string of lights in her room. Then she adds two more strings of lights that are 12 feet and 9 feet long. Altogether, the length of all the lights is 32 feet. How long is the first string of lights?

Fill in the blanks. Then circle all the answers that show a step in solving the problem.

(A) 12 + 9 = _21_   **C** 21 + 32 = _53_

B 12 − 9 = _3_   **(D)** 32 − 21 = _11_

5 Josh was on a path 100 meters long. He ran 35 meters and then started walking. He ran again for the last 15 meters. How far did Josh walk?

Show your work.

Possible work:
100 − 35 = 65
65 − 15 = 50

Answer _He walked 50 meters._

6 Write a word problem that uses lengths. Then solve your problem.

Answers will vary. Word problems should include

lengths.

✓ Self Check Now you can add and subtract lengths. Fill this in on the progress chart on page 153.

201

Solutions

4 **Solution**
A Add 12 and 9 to find the length of the two strings; **D** Then subtract the sum (21) from the total length.
DOK 2

5 **Solution**
Josh walked 50 meters; Subtract the distance he ran (35 + 15) from the total length of the path (100 − 50 = 50).
DOK 2

6 **Solution**
Answers will vary. Possible answer: Rita's ribbon is 48 centimeters long. Josh's ribbon is 61 centimeters long. How much longer is Josh's ribbon? 61 − 48 = 13; Josh's ribbon is 13 centimeters longer than Rita's ribbon.
DOK 3

▶ Hands-On Activity

Model adding lengths.

Materials: strips of squares cut from Activity Sheet 10 (Half-Inch Grid Paper)

• Pose the following problem: Mr. Jones needs to set up tables for a big dinner. He has tables that are 4 feet, 6 feet, and 8 feet long. He sets up an 8-foot and a 6-foot table to make one long table. He needs to make the long table 30 feet long. What other tables can he set up to finish making the long table?

• Write the table sizes on the board. Tell students to cut the grid paper to show the 8-foot table and the 6-foot table that Mr. Jones has set up.

• Instruct students to cut the other paper strips into 4, 6, and 8 squares to show the other tables Mr. Jones has. Tell them to use those strips to show what other table or tables he needs to make a 30-foot long table.

• Have students record their solution and the strategy they used. When they are finished writing, have them share their solutions and strategies.

▶ Challenge Activity

Find all the possible combinations.

Materials: strips of squares cut from Activity Sheet 10 (Half-Inch Grid Paper)

• Challenge students to complete the Hands-On Activity, finding all the possible combinations of tables, Mr. Jones could use.

• Encourage students to organize their information and tell how they know they have found all the possibilities.

• Extend the challenge by having students find the number of **yards** that equals the 30-foot table. Make sure they show their strategy and explain how they solved the problem.

Teacher-Toolbox.com

Overview

Assign the Lesson 21 Quiz and have students work independently to complete it.

Use the results of the quiz to assess students' understanding of the content of the lesson and to identify areas for reteaching. See the Lesson Pacing Guide at the beginning of the lesson for suggested instructional resources.

Tested Skills

Assesses 2.MD.B.5, 2.MD.B.6

Problems on this assessment form require students to be able to use addition and subtraction to solve problems involving lengths, use visual models to represent measurement problems involving addition and subtraction, and identify strategies and essential information in word problems. Students will also need to be familiar with adding and subtracting whole numbers within 100, measuring in centimeters and inches, and using number lines.

Ready **Mathematics**

Lesson 21 **Quiz**

Solve the problems.

1 Carmen has two kites. One kite is 17 centimeters longer than the other kite.

Could the pair of lengths be the lengths of Carmen's kites?

Circle *Yes* or *No* for each pair of lengths.

a.	21 centimeters and 38 centimeters	Yes	No
b.	17 centimeters and 20 centimeters	Yes	No
c.	69 centimeters and 52 centimeters	Yes	No
d.	37 centimeters and 56 centimeters	Yes	No

2 Mrs. Li has a wood board that is 72 inches long. She cuts off 17 inches. How long is the board now?

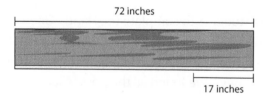

Write + or − in the circle and write numbers from the box on the blanks to write an equation. Then complete the statement. You can use a number more than once.

____ ◯ ____ = ____ | 17 65 89 55 72 |

The board is _____ inches long.

Lesson 21 Quiz continued

3 The body of Charlie's dog, Otto, is 27 inches long. Otto's tail is 13 inches long. What is Otto's length in all?

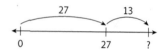

A 14 inches

B 17 inches

C 27 inches

D 40 inches

4 Martin has a blue rug that is 28 inches long. He has a red rug that is 15 inches longer than the blue rug. How can Martin find the length of both rugs in inches?

Circle the correct answer.

A Find the length of the red rug by adding 28 + 15. Add that sum to the length of the blue rug, 28.

B Find the length of the red rug by subtracting 28 − 15. Add that difference to the length of the blue rug, 28.

C Add the length of the blue rug, 28, to the length of the red rug, 15.

D Find the length of the red rug by subtracting 28 − 15. Subtract that difference from the length of the blue rug, 28.

Common Misconceptions and Errors

Errors may result if students:

- regroup numbers incorrectly or unnecessarily when subtracting.

- confuse when to add and when to subtract.

- incorrectly set up or interpret a visual model.

- misread the problem or answer choices, especially regarding use of the word difference in the given context.

Ready® **Mathematics**

Lesson 21 Quiz Answer Key

1. a. Yes
   b. No
   c. Yes
   d. No
   DOK 2

2. $72 - 17 = 55$
   55
   DOK 2

3. D
   DOK 1

4. A
   DOK 3

Lesson 22
Understand Reading and Making Line Plots

CCSS Focus

Domain
Measurement and Data

Cluster
B. Relate addition and subtraction to length.
D. Represent and interpret data.

Standards
2.MD.B.6 Represent whole numbers as lengths from 0 on a number line diagram with equally spaced points corresponding to the numbers 0, 1, 2, . . ., and represent whole-number sums and differences within 100 on a number line diagram.

2.MD.D.9 Generate measurement data by measuring lengths of several objects to the nearest whole unit, or by making repeated measurements of the same object. Show the measurements by making a line plot, where the horizontal scale is marked off in whole-number units.

Standards for Mathematical Practice (SMP)

1 Make sense of problems and persevere in solving them.

2 Reason abstractly and quantitatively.

3 Construct viable arguments and critique the reasoning of others.

6 Attend to precision.

Lesson Objectives

Content Objectives

- Interpret marks on a line plot as data.
- Understand that the numbers on a ruler or number line can be used to represent a given length.
- Represent data on a line plot.

Language Objectives

- Describe how the number line on a line plot is like a ruler.
- Label the number line on a line plot with numbers to represent given data.
- Tell what each *X* on a line plot represents.

Prerequisite Skills

- Know how to measure in inches, feet, centimeters, and meters.
- Differentiate among and compare lengths in inches, feet, centimeters, and meters.
- Understand that a number line is a series of intervals organized on a line.

Lesson Vocabulary

- **data** a set of collected information; often numerical information such as a list of measurements.
- **line plot** a data display that shows the frequencies of the data as marks above a number line.

Learning Progression

In Grade 1 students organize and interpret data within categories. They compare lengths to analyze data, determining whether a length is greater than or less than the others.

In Grade 2 students represent lengths and whole-number sums on a number line. They measure to the whole-number unit, and represent and interpret data.

In this lesson students organize lengths on a line plot. They read charts, interpret the data, and represent the data. They recognize that a number line can be used as tool for organizing information.

In Grade 3 students measure in fractions of an inch and create line plots using fractional values. Line plots are seen as one of many ways to display data.

Beyond Grade 3 students explore applications of line plots other than to record measurements and extend the concept of creating a scale.

Lesson Pacing Guide

Whole Class Instruction

Day 1
45–60 minutes

Toolbox: Interactive Tutorial*
Line Plot and Measuring Length

Introduction
- Opening Activity *20 min*
- Think It Through Question *5 min*
- Think *5 min*
- Think *15 min*
- Reflect *5 min*

Practice and Problem Solving
Assign pages 225–226.

Day 2
45–60 minutes

Guided Instruction
Think About Reading and Making Line Plots
- Let's Explore the Idea *20 min*
- Let's Talk About It *15 min*
- Try It Another Way *10 min*

Practice and Problem Solving
Assign pages 227–228.

Day 3
45–60 minutes

Guided Practice
Connect Ideas About Line Plots
- Identify *15 min*
- Explain *15 min*
- Analyze *15 min*

Practice and Problem Solving
Assign pages 229–230.

Day 4
45–60 minutes

Independent Practice
Apply Ideas About Line Plots
- Put It Together *30 min*
- Pair/Share *15 min*

Day 5
45–60 minutes

- On-Level, Intervention or Challenge Activity *20 min*

Toolbox: Lesson Quiz
Lesson 22 Quiz

Small Group Differentiation

Teacher-Toolbox.com

Reteach
Ready Prerequisite Lessons *45–90 min*

Grade 1
- Lesson 29 Sort and Count
- Lesson 30 Compare Data

Teacher-led Activities
Tools for Instruction *15–20 min*

Grade 1 *(Lessons 29 and 30)*
- Representing Data: Tally Charts

Grade 2 *(Lesson 22)*
- Data Collection: Line Plots

Student-led Activities
Math Center Activities *30–40 min*

Grade 2 *(Lesson 22)*
- 2.47 Complete a Line Plot
- 2.48 Measure Objects and Make a Line Plot

Personalized Learning

i-Ready.com

Independent
i-Ready Lessons* *10–20 min*

Grade 1 *(Lessons 29 and 30)*
- Picture Graphs

*We continually update the Interactive Tutorials. Check the Teacher Toolbox for the most up-to-date offerings for this lesson.

Opening Activity

Explore a Number Line

Objective Develop the concept of a number line.

Time *20–30 minutes*

Materials for each student
- blank piece of unlined paper
- pencil
- ruler
- half-inch strip of heavy paper or tag board

Overview

Students create a number line with equally-spaced intervals.

Step By Step

1 Interpret an open number line.

- Draw a horizontal line on the board and ask students how they would make an open number line to solve the addition problem 8 + 7.

- Invite a volunteer to the board to model the addition on the number line.

- Ask: *Why did you start at 8?* Point to the left of the 8 and ask: *What is on this side of the 8?* Students may reply that nothing is there. If so, ask what numbers come before 8 when counting. Ask: *Why didn't you show those numbers?* [It isn't necessary since 8 is the first number used in the addition problem.] Make sure students understand that even though they aren't recorded on the number line, those numbers still exist.

- Discuss what the jump from 8 to 15 on the number line represents. Ask: *How do you know there are 7 spaces between 8 and 15?* [The 7 above the curved arrow tells you.]

2 Create a number line.

- Demonstrate positioning the paper horizontally and have students follow on their own paper as you use a ruler to draw a line across the entire length of the paper. Place an arrowhead at each end of the line. Tell students that the arrows mean the line keeps going in both directions, but we only have room on the paper for some of the line.

- Use the half-inch paper strip to make a hash mark on the far left side of the line, slightly to the right of the arrow. Have students do the same. Show students how to make a hash mark at every half inch by marking the right side of the strip and then continuing to move and mark the right side of the strip along the length of the line.

- Tell students to write a 0 under the first mark and then write numbers in sequence under each of the remainder of the marks.

3 Add on the number line.

- Tell students to show the addition problem 8 + 7 on this number line using a curved arrow like on the open number line.

- Ask: *How is adding on this number line like adding on an open number line? How is it different?* [Students should notice that they can show the jump using a curved arrow like on the open number line, but this number line shows all the numbers before, after, and in between the curved arrow that the open number line does not.]

Teacher Notes

Introduction

At A Glance

Students explore the concept of a number line used in creating line plots by comparing it to a tape measure. Then students explore the structure of a line plot.

Step By Step

- Read the Study Buddy question and answer at the top of the page.

- Ask students to recall ways they have organized data and the kinds of data they have looked at. They may recall bar graphs displaying kinds of pets, ways to come to school, colors of balloons, types of leaves, etc.

- Tell students that this lesson will help them explore a way to organize lengths. Observe the lengths listed. Ask questions such as: *What is the length of the longest sea lion? The shortest sea lion? What are the lengths of the sea lions that are the same length?*

- Draw attention to the tape measure and number line in **Think**. Ask students what the numbers on the tape measure represent. [lengths] Have students compare the visual representations of the tape measure and the number line.

- Ask Mathematical Discourse questions 1 and 2. Following the second question, extend a tape measure if you have one, and discuss that a tape measure includes numbers greater than and less than those shown on this page.

▶ **Mathematical Discourse 1 and 2**

Think It Through

What is a line plot?

A **line plot** is a way to organize a set of measurements, like the lengths of young sea lions at an aquarium.

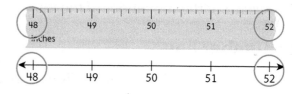

52 inches   49 inches   50 inches   52 inches   52 inches   48 inches   49 inches

Think **You can use a number line to make a line plot.**

A number line is like a ruler or tape measure.

- The numbers have equal spaces between them.
- The numbers are in order.
- No numbers are skipped.

48 inches   49   50   51   52

48   49   50   51   52

Circle the lengths of the shortest and longest sea lions on the ruler and the number line.

202

▶ **Mathematical Discourse**

1 *How is the number line shown here like an open number line? How is it different?*

Students may note that on an open number line and on this number line, the numbers are organized from least to greatest. However, this number line shows each number in sequence, while on an open number line, there are large intervals between one number to the next.

2 *Look at the tape measure and number line on this page. Why do you think only some of the numbers on the tape measure and number line are shown?*

Students should respond that the other numbers are not needed, since there are no lengths greater than 52 inches or less than 48 inches. Make it clear that more numbers *could be* shown, but the book uses only the numbers that are needed in order to fit them all on the page.

Think A line plot can help you show measurements.

This line plot shows the lengths of sea lions.

The number line starts at 48 because the shortest length is 48 inches.

Why does the number line end at 52? The greatest

length is 52 inches.

There are 7 lengths, so there should be 7 *X*s on the line plot.

The title tells what the graph is about. → **Sea Lions' Measurements**

```
                        x
            x           x
    x   x   x           x
    48  49  50  51  52
```

There is an *X* for each sea lion length.

The numbers along the bottom show all the lengths. → **Length (inches)** ← The label tells what the numbers mean.

The line plot shows that 2 sea lions are 49 inches long.

▶ **Reflect** Work with a partner.

1 **Talk About It** How is the number line on a line plot like a ruler? How is it different?

Write About It Possible answer: Like: Both show numbers. Both have

numbers in order without any missing. Different: A line plot shows many

measurements at one time. You don't use it to measure length.

203

Step By Step

- Draw students' attention to the **Think** section. Discuss the function of each part of the plot as described. After pointing out that there is an *X* on the line plot for each length, ask: *How many sea lions are 52 inches long?* [3 sea lions] *How many sea lions are 51 inches long?* [No sea lions are 51 inches long.]

▶ **Mathematical Discourse 3 and 4**

- Complete the Hands-On Activity to reinforce the concept of a line plot.

▶ **Hands-On Activity**

- Have students complete *Talk About It* and share their responses with the class.

 **Ready** Mathematics PRACTICE AND PROBLEM SOLVING

Assign *Practice and Problem Solving* **pages 225–226** after students have completed this section.

▶ **Hands-On Activity**

Build a line plot.

Materials: inch ruler, ten straws in varying lengths (at least 3 the same length), ten small counters (such as beans), paper, and pencil

- Instruct students to measure each straw to the nearest inch and record the lengths on their paper. Then ask students to organize the straws from shortest to longest.

- Have them lay the ruler in front of them horizontally and show the length of each straw by placing a counter above the number on the ruler that shows the length.

- Discuss how the plot they made compares to the way they ordered the straws. Ask: *What does the line plot tell you that you cannot see by looking at the straws?* [the lengths of the straws and the exact difference in inches between them]

▶ **Mathematical Discourse**

3 *Why is it important to include a title and label for a line plot?*

Students should explain that the title lets anyone who sees the line plot know what the data represent. The label tells what unit, such as inches or centimeters, was used to measure.

4 *Paige asks, "Why do you have to put the 51 on the plot when no sea lion is 51 inches, but you don't have to put 53 on the plot since no sea lion is 53 inches?" What could you tell her?*

Listen for responses that indicate students understand that numbers greater or less than those in the data set don't need to be included. However, all the numbers between the greatest and least number in the data set must be included.

👥 Guided Instruction

At A Glance

Students construct a line plot by recording lengths they measure. Then students analyze the line plot.

Step By Step

Let's Explore the Idea

- Discuss this section as a class. Tell students to make sure they use the centimeter side of their ruler when measuring.

- Discuss possible strategies for measuring and recording data on the line plot. Ask Mathematical Discourse question 1. Make sure students know that both strategies are acceptable. They need to use the way that works best for them.

▶ **Mathematical Discourse 1**

- Ask the Mathematical Discourse question 2 as students are measuring for Problem 2.

▶ **Mathematical Discourse 2**

- Provide students time to work individually on the rest of the problems on this page and then share their responses in groups.

SMP TIP   Attend to Precision
Encourage students to be precise when measuring the pieces of spaghetti on this page. Remind them of the importance of lining up one end of the ruler to one end of the spaghetti to measure. *(SMP 6)*

- Watch for students who are having difficulty. See if their understanding progresses as they work in their groups during the next part of the lesson.

▶ **Hands-On Activity**

Think About ▶ Reading and Making Line Plots

🔍 **Let's Explore the Idea** Measure lengths and make a line plot.

Julia spilled a box of spaghetti. She picked up the broken pieces shown below. She measured each piece using centimeters.

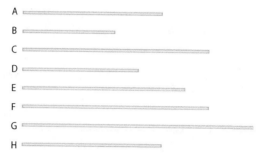

2 What is the length of piece A? ____6____ centimeters

3 Draw an *X* above that number on the line plot below.

4 Measure the rest of the spaghetti pieces. After you measure each piece, draw an *X* above the correct number on the line plot below.

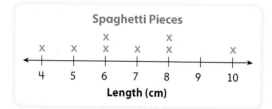

Spaghetti Pieces

Length (cm)

204

▶ **Mathematical Discourse**

1 *Why might it be easier to record each piece of spaghetti on the line plot as you measure?*

Students may respond that if they record each one as they measure, it doesn't take as much time as writing measures first and then plotting.

2 *How does the care you take in measuring affect your line plot?*

Students should respond that if they don't measure correctly, they might put a mark on the plot in the wrong place.

▶ **Hands-On Activity**

Model with strips of paper.

Materials: For each pair: $\frac{1}{4}$-inch paper strips cut into lengths of 4 cm, 5 cm, 6 cm, 6 cm, 7 cm, 8 cm, 8 cm, and 10 cm; ruler

- Have students work in pairs. Ask them to compare the lengths of the strips of paper to the lengths of the spaghetti shown on this page to see that they correspond to each other.

- Demonstrate and have students follow as you line up the paper strips along the cm side of the ruler from shortest to longest, one above the other.

- Compare the strips lined up above the ruler to the line plot. Discuss how there is one *X* above each number that corresponds to the length of a single strip, and two *X*s above each number that corresponds to the length of two strips.

Let's Talk About It
Work with a partner.

5 What does each number on the line plot show?

the length of pieces of spaghetti in centimeters

6 What does each *X* on the line plot show?

the length of a piece of spaghetti

7 How many *X*s should be on the line plot? Why?

8, because there are 8 pieces of spaghetti.

8 Why does the line plot start at 4 instead of 0?

There aren't any pieces shorter than 4, so we don't need to show any

shorter lengths.

9 Why aren't there any *X*s above the 9?

There aren't any pieces of spaghetti 9 cm long.

▶ **Try It Another Way** **Answer these questions about the spaghetti line plot.**

10 What is the length of the shortest spaghetti piece? __4__ cm

11 What is the length of the longest spaghetti piece? __10__ cm

12 How many spaghetti pieces are 6 cm long? __2__

13 How many spaghetti pieces are longer than 7 cm? __3__

205

Step By Step

Let's Talk About It

- Have students work in small groups to complete Problems 5–9. Walk around to each group. Listen to and join in on discussions at different points.

- As students work on Problem 8, remind them that 0, 1, 2, 3 could be shown on the plot, but these numbers are not necessary since there are no lengths shorter than 4 cm.

▶ **Mathematical Discourse 3**

Try It Another Way

- For Problems 10–13, make sure students use the data on the line plot to answer the questions.

▶ **Concept Extension**

> **SMP TIP Reason Abstractly and Quantitatively**
> The Concept Extension activity focuses on the unit as an interval, which reinforces the concept of the accumulation of distance. A measure is the quantity of a collection of iterated units. Therefore, a measure can be taken from any starting point on a ruler. *(SMP 2)*

Ready Mathematics
PRACTICE AND PROBLEM SOLVING

Assign *Practice and Problem Solving*
pages 227–228 after students have completed this section.

▶ **Concept Extension**

Compare lengths in a line plot.

- Draw and display a completed line plot from the previous page.

- Ask: *How much longer is the longest piece of spaghetti than the shortest piece?* [6 cm] *How can you tell?* Students may suggest subtracting 4 from 10.

- Erase or cover the scale on the line plot and ask students if they can still find the difference between lengths of the spaghetti.

- Discuss that since the units used in measuring are represented by the intervals between the numbers, the number of intervals between each length tells how much longer one piece is than another.

- Have students find the difference between two pieces of spaghetti that you indicate on the plot.

▶ **Mathematical Discourse**

3 *How would the line plot change if there were a piece of spaghetti 14 cm long in this group?*

Students should respond that the line would be longer and would have to include at least 11, 12, 13, and 14.

At A Glance

Students solve problems involving line plots. Then students demonstrate their understanding of line plots by creating a line plot and analyzing it.

Step By Step

- Discuss each problem as a class using the discussion points outlined below.

Identify

- Allow students to work with a partner to share ideas. Encourage them to explain and justify their thinking.

- As students share their ideas, make sure they have ordered the lengths from least to greatest and included all values between and including 6 and 11. Explain that these are the values that MUST be included, but it would be acceptable to include all the numbers from 0 to 11 or greater.

Explain

- Ask: *What do the Xs on the line plot represent?* [the number of people who jumped each distance]

- Tell students that it is easy to misunderstand what a graph is showing. Discuss the importance of creating a graph that others can read and easily understand.

- Have students generate ideas of ways to make sure the line plot they create is clear so someone like Nate doesn't misinterpret it.

- You may want students to draw this line plot on whiteboards with *X*s all the same size.

Analyze

- *What do the numbers along the bottom of the line plot tell you?* [the shortest and longest distances Bo ran, and all the numbers in between]

- Discuss why Tia might make the mistake of reading the three *X*s as the farthest Bo ran.

- Ask: *How might the line plot be read if Bo forgot to include a label for the numbers?* [No one would know if the distances are in meters, feet, yards, or miles.]

Connect | **Ideas About Line Plots**

Talk about these problems as a class. Then write your answers.

14 **Identify** Rachel wants to make a line plot to show the lengths of six rooms. Write the numbers Rachel needs to put in the line plot.

Length (meters)

Room	Length (meters)
A	8
B	6
C	10
D	9
E	11
F	10

15 **Explain** Look at the line plot at the right. Nate says that more people jumped 4 feet than any other length. Explain why Nate is wrong.

Possible answer: The *X*s are different sizes. They are

tallest above the 4. But there are more *X*s above the

3, so more people jumped 3 feet.

Long Jump Results

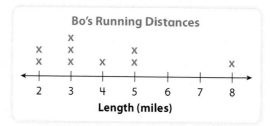

Length (feet)

16 **Analyze** Bo made a line plot to show how far he ran each day. Tia says the farthest Bo ran in one day is 3 miles. Is she correct? Why or why not?

Bo's Running Distances

```
         X
   X     X           X
   X     X     X     X                    X
   ←—————————————————————————————————————→
   2     3     4     5     6     7     8
```

Length (miles)

No. Bo ran 3 miles the most times. The farthest he ran was 8 miles.

Scoring Rubrics

Parts A and B	
Points	**Expectations**
2	The student accurately measures each shell and records the measure in the table. The student creates a line plot that includes all the elements and contains data that is accurately displayed.
1	The student may measure with some accuracy, but is inconsistent. The table may or may not be completed. Some of the line plot may be inaccurate and some may be missing.
0	The student does not accurately measure nor complete the table and line plot.

Apply ▶ **Ideas About Line Plots**

Put It Together **Use what you have learned to complete this task.**

17 Use the page of shells your teacher gives you.

Part A Measure the length of each shell in inches. Write the lengths in the table.

Part B Use your measurements to make a line plot.

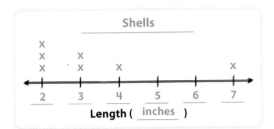

Shells

Shell	Length (inches)
A	3
B	2
C	4
D	2
E	7
F	2
G	3

Part C The length of the longest shell is ___7___ inches.
The length of the shortest shell is ___2___ inches.

The length with the most shells is ___2___ inches.

Part D Two more shells are each 4 inches long. Explain how the line plot would change if the lengths of these shells were added to the line plot.

Possible answer: There would be three Xs above the 4 instead of one X.

207

Step By Step

Put It Together

- Direct students to complete the **Put It Together** task on their own.

- Read the directions with students and make sure they understand each part of the task before proceeding.

- Copy and distribute Activity Sheet 11 (Shells).

- As students work on their own, walk around to assess their progress and understanding, to answer their questions, and to give additional support, if needed.

- If time permits, ask students to share the line plots they made. You may want students to make and share observations based on their line plots, such as: None of the shells are 5 or 6 inches; There are two more 2-inch shells than 4-inch shells.

Ready **Mathematics**
PRACTICE AND PROBLEM SOLVING

Assign *Practice and Problem Solving* **pages 229–230** after students have completed Guided Practice.

Part C	
Points	**Expectations**
2	All responses are accurate.
1	Some responses are accurate.
0	No responses are accurate.

Part D	
Points	**Expectations**
2	The student responds that three *X*s would be above the 4.
1	The student may respond that there would be more *X*s above the 4, but does not articulate the correct number of *X*s.
0	The student does not respond that more *X*s would need to be placed above the 4.

Differentiated Instruction

▶ Intervention Activity

Make a line plot for pencil lengths.

Materials: set of used colored pencils of different lengths (7 inches or shorter), Number Line and Ruler Page (Activity Sheet 12), and squares of paper cut from Half-Inch Grid Paper (Activity Sheet 10)

- Tell students they are to measure each pencil to the nearest inch using the ruler printed on the paper. Have them glue a paper square above the closest inch (you may wish to cut squares from colored paper matching the colors of pencils). If more than one pencil is the same length, glue another paper square above the one(s) recorded.

- Once students have completed measuring the pencils and gluing the squares, have them use the number line to create a line plot. They should replicate the placement of the paper squares above the ruler by drawing *X*s above the number line.

- When finished, have students compare the graphs, explaining similarities between them. Students should notice that the line plot represents the lengths of pencils that were recorded above the ruler.

▶ On-Level Activity

Make a line plot for crayon lengths.

Materials: a blank number line from Blank Number Lines (Activity Sheet 13), 10–12 used crayons, and a centimeter ruler

- Have students measure each crayon to the nearest centimeter and record the length on a separate piece of paper or whiteboard.

- Tell students to examine all the measurements and then decide what number to start with on the number line. Number each interval in sequence.

- Instruct students to mark an *X* above each number on the number line that corresponds to the length of a crayon.

- Tell students to include a label for the numbers and a title for the line plot.

- Have them write three observations they make from analyzing the completed line plot.

- Tell students to measure an unused crayon and compare its length to those on the line plot. Ask: *What does the line plot tell you about the way you have used your crayons this year?* [It may indicate that they have been used a lot or that they have not been used much.]

▶ Challenge Activity

Make a line plot for book heights.

Materials: 10–12 books, ruler, yardstick, blank paper, and pencil

- Select books for students to measure. Make sure some of them are the same height.

- Have students measure the height of each book and create a line plot to display their results. Tell them to make sure they have all the parts labeled and have included a title.

- Have students write observations they make from analyzing the completed line plot. Then present a scenario, such as buying or making a bookshelf, and ask students how the data might help them make a decision.

Teacher Notes

Teacher-Toolbox.com

Overview

Assign the Lesson 22 Quiz and have students work independently to complete it.

Use the results of the quiz to assess students' understanding of the content of the lesson and to identify areas for reteaching. See the Lesson Pacing Guide at the beginning of the lesson and the Differentiated Instruction activities that follow for suggested instructional resources.

Tested Skills

Assesses 2.MD.D.9

Problems on this assessment form require students to be able to plot measurement data in a line plot, interpret marks on a line plot as data, recognize that each X on a line plot represents one data item, and recognize the difference between measurement data and the number of data items. Students must understand the need for equal size intervals on a number line, ruler, or line plot.

Ready® Mathematics

Lesson 22 Quiz

Solve the problems.

1 Ari measures the lengths of some cars on his street.

- One car is 19 feet long.
- Three cars are each 17 feet long.
- Two cars are each 16 feet long.

Ari makes a line plot. Is the sentence about his line plot true?
Circle *Yes* or *No* for each sentence.

a. The 16 has the most Xs.   Yes   No

b. There is 1 X above the 19.   Yes   No

c. There are 3 Xs above the 17.   Yes   No

d. The number 18 is not on the number line.   Yes   No

2 Brianna wants to make a line plot to show the heights of seven plants. Look at her measurements in the table.

Plant	a.	b.	c.	d.	e.	f.	g.
Height (cm)	13	10	13	11	14	14	13

Which heights would have more than one X above it in the line plot?
Circle all the correct answers.

A 10   **D** 13

B 11   **E** 14

C 12   **F** 15

Lesson 22 Quiz continued

3 Jake makes this line plot to show the lengths of some boxes.

Box Lengths

```
X
X                   X
X         X         X
|---------|---------|---------|
5         6         7         8
```
Length (inches)

Marcus says that the longest box is 5 inches long because that is the number with the most Xs above it. Explain the mistake Marcus made and write the correct answer.

_____

_____

_____

4 Jessica measures the lengths of some ribbons. The measurements are shown in the table below. Use the measurements to complete the line plot.

Ribbon	Length (feet)
Red	5
Blue	8
Green	5
Yellow	9
Orange	10
Purple	8
Pink	8
White	6

Ribbon Lengths

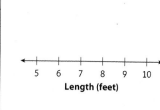

Length (feet)

Common Misconceptions and Errors

Errors may result if students:

• place one X over each number on the line plot, regardless of the data.

• leave out a number that is within the range shown on the line plot but does not have any items associated with it.

• interpret the number of Xs as the measurement of an item.

***Ready*® Mathematics**

Lesson 22   Quiz Answer Key

1. a. No
   b. Yes
   c. Yes
   d. No
   DOK 2

2. D, E
   DOK 2

3. Possible explanation: The number of Xs above the 5 tells the number of boxes that are 5 inches long, not the length of the box. The length with the most boxes is 5 inches. The longest box is 8 inches long because 8 is the largest number with an X above it.
   DOK 3

4.

Ribbon Lengths

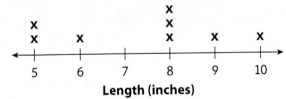

Length (inches)

DOK 1

Lesson 23
Draw and Use Bar Graphs and Picture Graphs

CCSS Focus

Domain
Measurement and Data

Cluster
D. Represent and interpret data.

Standards
2.MD.D.10 Draw a picture graph and a bar graph (with single-unit scale) to represent a data set with up to four categories. Solve simple put-together, take-apart, and compare problems using information presented in a bar graph.

Standards for Mathematical Practice (SMP)

1 Make sense of problems and persevere in solving them.

2 Reason abstractly and quantitatively.

3 Construct viable arguments and critique the reasoning of others.

4 Model with mathematics.

6 Attend to precision.

Lesson Objectives

Content Objectives

• Collect data to display in a bar graph or picture graph.

• Compare data in a tally chart, table, picture graph, and bar graph.

• Interpret graphs by reading and comparing the data shown in the graph.

• Complete a picture graph and bar graph.

• Create a bar graph from a given set of data.

Language Objectives

• Compare a bar graph and a picture graph for the same data.

• Use key mathematical vocabulary terms *picture graph*, *bar graph*, and *data* in discussions.

Prerequisite Skills

• Represent and interpret simple graphs.

• Understand tally marks.

• Identify how many more and how many less.

Lesson Vocabulary

• **data** a set of collected information; often numerical information such as a list of measurements.

• **picture graph** a data display in which pictures are used to represent the number of items in each category.

• **bar graph** a data display in which bars are used to represent the number of items in each category.

Learning Progression

In Grade 1 students organize data into three categories. They represent the data in a bar graph and interpret it by comparing the data from one category to another.

In Grade 2 students organize and represent data in more than one way, recognizing the kinds of data that are best represented in a line plot and those organized into categories and best represented in a bar graph.

In this lesson students organize data into a tally chart and table in order to use it for making a graph. They represent the

data in both a picture graph and bar graph, using a scale in a one-to-one correspondence with the data. Students recognize the relationship of the two forms of graphs and how the shape of the data is consistent when in either form.

In Grade 3 students expand their understanding of scale as they represent data in a graph where the scale is in intervals of twos, fives, etc. They organize data and represent it in a graph, determine an appropriate scale, and use the data to solve one- and two-step problems.

Lesson Pacing Guide

Whole Class Instruction

Day 1
45–60 minutes

Toolbox: Interactive Tutorial*
Picture Graphs and Bar Graphs

Introduction
- Opening Activity *15 min*
- Use What You Know *10 min*
- Find Out More *10 min*
- Reflect *5 min*

Practice and Problem Solving
Assign pages 233–234.

Day 2
45–60 minutes

Modeled and Guided Instruction
Learn About Using a Picture Graph and Bar Graph
- Picture It/Model It *10 min*
- Connect It *25 min*
- Try It *10 min*

Practice and Problem Solving
Assign pages 235–236.

Day 3
45–60 minutes

Modeled and Guided Instruction
Learn About Making Bar Graphs and Picture Graphs
- Model It/Model It *15 min*
- Connect It *20 min*
- Try It *10 min*

Practice and Problem Solving
Assign pages 237–238.

Day 4
45–60 minutes

Guided Practice
Practice Making Bar Graphs and Picture Graphs
- Example *5 min*
- Problems 13–15 *15 min*
- Pair/Share *15 min*
- Solutions *10 min*

Practice and Problem Solving
Assign pages 239–240.

Day 5
45–60 minutes

Independent Practice
Practice Making Bar Graphs and Picture Graphs
- Problems 1–5 *20 min*
- Quick Check and Remediation *10 min*
- Hands-On or Challenge Activity *15 min*

Toolbox: Lesson Quiz
Lesson 23 Quiz

Small Group Differentiation

Teacher-Toolbox.com

Reteach
Ready Prerequisite Lessons *45–90 min*

Grade 1
- Lesson 29 Sort and Count
- Lesson 30 Compare Data

Teacher-led Activities
Tools for Instruction *15–20 min*

Grade 1 *(Lessons 29 and 30)*
- Representing Data: Tally Charts

Grade 2 *(Lesson 23)*
- Solve Word Problems about Measurement Data

Student-led Activities
Math Center Activities *30–40 min*

Grade 2 *(Lesson 23)*
- 2.45 Use Data Vocabulary
- 2.46 Draw and Use a Bar Graph

Personalized Learning

i-Ready.com

Independent
i-Ready Lessons* *10–20 min*

Grade 1 *(Lessons 29 and 30)*
- Picture Graphs

*We continually update the Interactive Tutorials. Check the Teacher Toolbox for the most up-to-date offerings for this lesson.

Opening Activity

Explore a Number Line

Objective Collect and organize data.

Time *15–20 minutes*

Materials for each student
- a 3-inch square of paper or sticky note
- tape

Overview

Students explore the purpose for organizing, displaying, and interpreting data by representing the results of a quick classroom survey in a chart and a bar graph.

Step By Step

1 Collect the data.

- Draw vertical lines to divide the board into four large sections and label each one with the types of books students like to read, such as Animal Stories, Adventure Stories, Mysteries, Biographies, etc. Make sure you limit it to four categories and that students understand what each category means.

- Distribute a square piece of paper to each student. Have them write their name on the paper.

- Ask students to decide which type of story listed is their favorite kind of book to read. Have them come to the board and tape their square piece of paper randomly in the appropriate section.

2 Organize the data.

- If students organized the squares in the form of a bar graph, ask them to explain why they organized them in that way. If not, discuss how they might compare the number of students' names that appear in each group. They should notice that they need to count the number of squares in each group. Ask: *How might we organize the squares so that it is easy to compare the number in each group?* Show how to arrange the squares in a vertical bar so it is easy to compare the data.

- Students should have some experience with bar graphs. If so, ask where the labels you wrote should be placed. Write the labels under the bars they represent. Ask: *What do each of the squares of paper stand for?* [a person in the class who likes that kind of book] Ask: *How do you know the number of students who like each kind of book?* [Count the number of squares.] *What could we do to show others how many are in each group so they don't have to count?* Lead students to see that they can write a number on the board to the left of the "bars" that corresponds with each paper square.

3 Purpose for displaying data.

- Tell students that data or information is collected, organized, and displayed for a reason. The information is used to make decisions.

- Ask: *Who might be interested in this information?* [A teacher or librarian might be interested.] *How might they use this information to make a decision?* [It can help a teacher know what kinds of books to use in the classroom. It might help a librarian decide the kind of books to buy the most and least of for the library.] *Do you think this graph would be the same if we asked another second-grade class to tell their favorite kinds of books? Why or why not?* Discuss that the data may be completely different for students in another class, but second graders generally like many of the same kinds of books. So, on the other hand, it would not be unlikely that another class would have similar results.

Teacher Notes

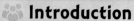

Introduction

At A Glance

Students read a picture graph and then answer questions and write equations about the information in the graph. Then students examine a bar graph that displays the same data.

Step By Step

- Work through **Use What You Know** as a class.

- Draw students' attention to the picture graph. Ask students what they think a picture graph is. Discuss that a picture graph is a display of information using a picture of each piece of data to show the totals in each category or group.

- Ask: *What vegetables do you see listed in this graph?* [carrots, beans, broccoli, corn] Compare the numbers for each category on the graph and ask Mathematical Discourse question 1.

▶ **Mathematical Discourse 1**

- Discuss with students that although we can't be sure the next person surveyed will choose carrots, graphs are often used to make predictions. The predictions then help us make decisions.

- Ask: *If you sold vegetables at a farmer's market, how might this information help you make decisions?* [You might plant more carrots and not as much corn or beans.]

- Work through the questions as a class. Discuss the difference between Problems c and d.

▶ **Mathematical Discourse 2**

▶ **Real-World Connection**

◷ Use What You Know

You know how to add and subtract to solve problems.

Parker asked his friends to tell him their favorite vegetable. He organized their answers in a **picture graph**.

Favorite Vegetables

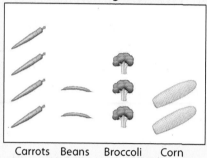

Carrots   Beans   Broccoli   Corn

a. How many carrots are on the graph? ___4___

> This tells how many friends chose carrots.

b. How many beans are on the graph? ___2___

> This tells how many friends chose beans.

c. Write an equation to find how many friends chose carrots and beans in all.

___4___ + ___2___ = ___6___

d. Write an equation to find how many more friends chose carrots than beans.

___4___ − ___2___ = ___2___

208

▶ Mathematical Discourse

1 *If Parker asked one more of his friends to tell their favorite vegetable, what do you think it would be? Why?*

Answers may vary, but students should recognize that since carrots were chosen most often there is a good possibility the next student surveyed will choose carrots.

2 *How might you use an addition equation to solve Problem d? Explain.*

Students should respond that $2 + ? = 4$ could be used to find how many more friends chose carrots than beans. Starting at the number of beans and counting up to the number of carrots results in the difference.

▶ Real-World Connection

- Find samples of graphs in the newspaper or magazines. Discuss how those who make graphs use them to help make decisions.

- Provide real-life scenarios such as: An ice cream shop makes a graph of the flavors of ice cream they sell each day for a month. What kinds of decisions might they make? The city graphs the numbers of cars that drive on 4 different streets in a week. How might that help them make a decision about road repairs?

- If possible, have community members or school personnel such as a principal, secretary, janitor, cook, librarian, etc., come to the classroom and show/tell how they use graphs to help them make decisions.

▶▶ Find Out More

A **bar graph** uses bars to show information.

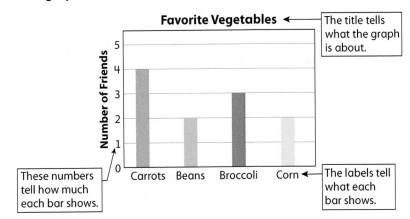

Favorite Vegetables ← The title tells what the graph is about.

These numbers tell how much each bar shows.

The labels tell what each bar shows.

The information shown in graphs is called **data**.

Reflect Work with a partner.

1 **Talk About It** How are the Favorite Vegetables picture graph and bar graph alike? How are they different?

Write About It Possible answer: Both show the same information.

The bar graph uses bars to show the information instead of pictures.

209

Step By Step

- Ask students to read **Find Out More**. Discuss that in the bar graph, bars (rectangles) are used to represent the information from the picture graph. The information is called *data*.

- Discuss each part of the graph shown. Ask students to describe what the numbers on the graph tell them. Compare the parts of the bar graph to the parts of a line plot.

- Remind students of the way they used labels when making line plots.

▶ **Mathematical Discourse 3**

- Have students complete the **Reflect** questions in pairs. Discuss their observations as a class.

▶ **Concept Extension**

Ready Mathematics PRACTICE AND PROBLEM SOLVING

Assign *Practice and Problem Solving* **pages 233–234** after students have completed this section.

▶ Concept Extension

Compare different types of data displays.

- Draw students' attention to the two data displays shown on these pages and ask: *Would it make sense to put the same data on a line plot? Explain.* Listen to student responses, reserving judgment.

- Have students draw a number line with at least 6 intervals and the numbers 0 to 5. Then have students attempt to mark the data on the line plot.

- Ask: *Does the line plot give you information about the vegetables students chose? Explain.* [No. You don't know what the Xs above the numbers mean.]

- Discuss how some kinds of data are best displayed on certain kinds of graphs.

▶ Mathematical Discourse

3 *What might happen if there were no labels on this graph?*

No one would know what the numbers mean. You wouldn't know which vegetable each of the bars represents.

Modeled and Guided Instruction

At A Glance

Students analyze how data presented in a tally chart is used to make a picture graph and a bar graph. Then students interpret the graphs and answer questions about them.

Step By Step

- Read the problem at the top of the page as a class. Ask students what the tally marks in the chart represent. Make sure students know how to read tally marks. Have them write the corresponding number under each set of marks.

Picture It

- Draw students' attention to **Picture It**. Ask them to describe what the picture graph shows. They should recognize that it is displaying the data from the chart using a picture rather than a tally mark to show each response. Ask Mathematical Discourse question 1.

▶ **Mathematical Discourse 1**

Model It

- Discuss with students how to read the bar graph shown in **Model It**. Make sure they either visually line up the bars with a numerical value or use a piece of paper or ruler to line them up.

- Have students compare the bar graph to the picture graph. Discuss how both graphs display the same data. In the picture graph, pictures of sports objects represent the number of students who selected each sport. The bar graph is more abstract—the bars represent numbers of students who selected a sport, but the bars don't look like a student or a sport.

▶ **Mathematical Discourse 2**

Learn About Using a Picture Graph and Bar Graph

Read the problem. Then you will use the graphs to answer questions.

Martin asked the students in his class, "What is your favorite sport?" His results are in the tally chart.

Soccer	Baseball	Tennis	Football
ⲎⲎⳘ ||	||||	|||	ⲎⲎⳘ|

How many students did Martin ask?

Picture It **You can make a picture graph.**

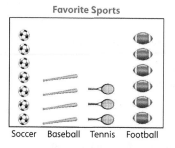

Favorite Sports

Model It **You can make a bar graph.**

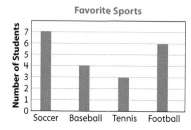

Favorite Sports

210

▶ **Mathematical Discourse**

1 *Why does it make sense for Martin to collect his data in a tally chart rather than in a picture graph?*

To make a picture graph while collecting data, he would either have to have pictures of sports objects and glue with him or take the time to draw the pictures on the graph. Doing this would take longer than just making tally marks as he gathers his information.

2 *Why does the bar graph include numbers but the picture graph does not?*

In the picture graph, the number of pictures tells you how many of each sport were chosen. In the bar graph, you need the numbers in order to know how many each bar shows.

Connect It Use the graphs.

2 How do you use the picture graph to find the number of students who chose soccer?

Possible answer: Count the number of soccer balls.

3 How do you use the bar graph to find the number of students who chose soccer?

Possible answer: Look at the bar above Soccer. Find the top

of the bar and read the number on the left.

4 How many students chose soccer as their favorite? ___7___

5 Explain how to use the bar graph to find the total number of students Martin asked.

Possible answer: Find the number of students who chose each sport and

add them all together.

6 How many students did Martin ask? Show your work.

Martin asked 20 students. Possible work: $7 + 4 + 3 + 6 = 20$

Try It Try more problems.

7 How many fewer students chose tennis than football? ___3___

8 Two students changed their answers from soccer to baseball.

Now how many students chose soccer? ___5___

Now how many students chose baseball? ___6___

211

▶ Hands-On Activity

Make a class graph.

Materials: [For the whole class] a large piece of chart paper or construction paper; [For each student] a 3-inch square of white paper and a 3-inch square of colored paper (all the colored squares should be the same color; you may wish to use sticky notes instead), tape

• Draw a tally chart on the board like the one on the previous page. Ask students to choose their favorite sport from those listed in the chart. Collect data by either a show of hands or having each student come to the board and draw a tally mark under their favorite sport in the chart.

• Write the sports labels along the bottom of the shorter side of a large piece of chart paper or construction paper. Have students draw a stick figure on their 3-inch square of white paper. Have them take turns taping their square on the chart paper above the sport that they chose.

• Discuss how the class picture graph resembles the bar graph on the previous page. Since the pictures are drawn on squares of paper, they look like a bar.

• Have students cover the picture they glued on the picture graph with a colored square. Add numbers, labels, and a title to the bar graph.

• Compare the data from your class to that of Martin's class.

Connect It

• Read **Connect It** as a class. Make sure students understand that the questions refer to the graphs on the previous page.

• For Problem 3, make sure students describe how they can find this information in the bar graph, not from the other displays shown.

> **SMP TIP Reason Abstractly and Quantitatively**
> Discuss how each bar in a bar graph represents a quantity. Point out that the interval between each number on the bar graph on the previous page represents one student. By determining which number lines up with the top of a bar, you can find the number of intervals. This is the number of students who say that a particular sport is their favorite. (SMP 2)

Try It

7 **Solution**
   3; 6 football − 3 tennis = difference of 3.

8 **Solution**
   5; 7 soccer − 2 = 5 soccer; 6;
   4 baseball + 2 = 6 baseball.
   Error Alert Students who wrote 7 for soccer failed to subtract 2 from those who selected soccer.

▶ **Hands-On Activity**

Ready Mathematics
PRACTICE AND PROBLEM SOLVING

Assign *Practice and Problem Solving* **pages 235–236** after students have completed this section.

Modeled and Guided Instruction

At A Glance

Students examine a set of data organized in a tally chart and in a table. Then students use the data to create a picture graph and bar graph.

Step By Step

- Read the problem at the top of the page as a class. Discuss that each color Lynn wrote down represents the color of apple grown by a tree she saw in a row of apple trees.

Model It

- Ask: *How could you make sure all the colors Lynn wrote down are recorded in the tally chart?* Listen for responses that indicate students have developed a strategy such as crossing off each color as it is recorded.

> **SMP TIP Attend to Precision**
> Emphasize the need for precision in recording data when graphing by having students count the total number of trees Lynn saw in the opening problem and compare that to the total number of tallies in the chart and the total number of trees shown in the table. *(SMP 6)*

▶ **Mathematical Discourse 1**

Model It

- Make sure students are aware that both the chart and table are used to organize the data. Ask: *Why do you think it is important to organize the data before making a picture graph or bar graph?* Help students recognize that organizing the data will help them create accurate graphs.

- Ask students which of the organizational tools they think would be easier to use. Discuss with them when it might be easier to make a tally chart than a table. They should recognize that when they are taking a survey or when they first organize the data, a tally chart is quick and simple.

Learn About Making Bar Graphs and Picture Graphs

Read the problem. Then you will show the data in a graph.

> Lynn visited an apple orchard. She looked at one row of trees. She wrote down the color of the apples on each tree.
>
> red, red, yellow, green, red, green, red, red, yellow, red, green, green
>
> First, organize the data. Then make a picture graph and a bar graph to show the data.

▶ **Model It You can organize the data in a tally chart.**

Red	Yellow	Green
卌I	II	IIII

▶ **Model It You can organize the data in a table.**

Color of Apple	Number of Trees
Red	6
Yellow	2
Green	4

212

▶ **Mathematical Discourse**

1 *How are the tally chart and the table alike? How are they different?*

They show the same information. The tally chart uses tally marks to record the data that Lynn collected. The table records the data with numerals rather than with tallies.

▶ **Connect It** Make a picture graph and a bar graph.

For Problems 9–11, use these graphs and the data from the previous page.

Apple Orchard Trees

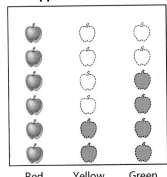

Red   Yellow   Green

Apple Orchard Trees

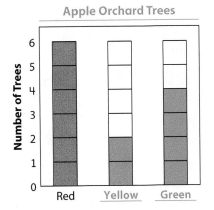

Number of Trees

Red   Yellow   Green

9 Color the picture graph to show how many yellow apple trees and green apple trees Lynn saw.

10 On the bar graph, fill in the title and labels.

11 Color the bar graph to show how many yellow apple trees and green apple trees Lynn saw.

▶ **Try It** Draw a bar graph.

12 Make a bar graph for this data. Show your work on a separate sheet of paper.

Favorite Colors			
Blue	Purple	Green	Red
5	6	2	3

Check students' graphs. Make sure they have the correct labels and bar heights.

213

▶ **Mathematical Discourse**

2 *On your graphs, why did you color the same number of apples and squares yellow?*

Students should recognize that both graphs represent the same data. So since Lynn counted 2 yellow apple trees, the same number of apples and squares on the graphs are colored yellow.

3 *How are the two graphs you made different from each other?*

Answers will vary, but students should recognize that in the picture graph, the numbers of red, yellow, and green apple pictures tell the numbers of red, yellow, and green apple trees Lynn saw. On the bar graph, the heights of the red, yellow, and green bars (or the numbers of squares in each bar) tell how many red, yellow, and green apple trees Lynn saw.

Step By Step

Connect It

• Tell students that **Connect It** will help them learn how to make a picture graph and bar graph for the data from the previous page.

• Read through the **Connect It** problems as a class. Make sure students understand what they need to do on the page. Then instruct students to work in pairs as they follow the directions in the problems to complete the graphs.

• When students are finished, ask questions about how they made their graphs, such as: *On the bar graph, what did you write to fill in the second and third labels?* [yellow and green] *On the picture graph, how many apples did you color yellow?* [2] *On the bar graph, how many squares did you color yellow?* [2]

▶ **Mathematical Discourse 2 and 3**

• Have students analyze the data in their graphs by asking questions such as: *How many more red apple trees than yellow apple trees did Lynn see?* [4] *How many trees that Lynn saw grew red apples or green apples?* [10]

• Discuss why you need to add the total in both categories when the word "or" is used in a question. Ask students more of the same type of question involving the word "or" so that they have a chance to practice this concept.

Try It

• Have students work in pairs to complete **Try It**.

12 **Solution**

Students' bar graphs should include a title, numbers along the vertical axis, and labels for both axes. The graphs should correctly show the data from the table.

Error Alert Watch for students who do not include a title with their bar graph. Ask these students how they know what the bar graph shows.

Ready Mathematics
PRACTICE AND PROBLEM SOLVING

Assign *Practice and Problem Solving* **pages 237–238** after students have completed this section.

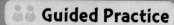

Guided Practice

At A Glance

Students analyze data displays, using them to answer questions.

Step By Step

- Ask students to solve the problems individually and show all their work, including the equations they wrote.

- For Problem 14, make sure students understand that the word "more" used here is not making a comparison, but tells that an additional 2 books were read on Sunday.

- **Pair/Share** When students have completed each problem, have them Pair/Share to discuss their solutions with a partner.

Solutions

Example Equations are used to solve a problem about data shown in a picture graph.

13 Solution

Gavin has 2 more yellow stickers than red stickers; yellow stickers = 1 (moon) + 8 (stars) = 9; red stickers = 5 (hearts) + 2 (dots) = 7; yellow stickers (9) − red stickers (7) = 2.

DOK 2

Study the model below. Then solve Problems 13–15.

Example

Gavin made a picture graph to show the stickers he has. How many more stars does Gavin have than moons and dots combined?

Stickers	
Moon	☾
Heart	♥ ♥ ♥ ♥ ♥
Star	☆ ☆ ☆ ☆ ☆ ☆ ☆ ☆
Dot	● ●

Look at how you can show your work.

$1 + 2 = 3 \qquad 8 - 3 = 5$

Answer He has 5 more stars than moons and dots combined.

---

13 How many more yellow stickers does Gavin have than red stickers?

Show your work.

Yellow stickers $= 1 + 8 = 9$

Red stickers $= 5 + 2 = 7$

$9 - 7 = 2$

How many yellow stickers are there? How many red stickers? Find the total of each and then compare.

Answer Gavin has 2 more yellow stickers than red ones.

214

Teacher Notes

14 Ally made this graph on Sunday morning. Then she read 2 more books that day. Fill in the graph to show that she read 2 more books on Sunday.

What is the total number of books for Sunday?

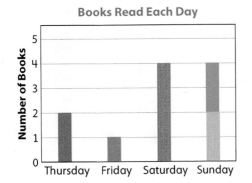

Books Read Each Day

15 How many fewer books did Ally read on Thursday and Friday combined than on Saturday?

(A) 1

B 2

C 3

D 4

This problem has two steps. What do you need to do first?

John chose **C** as the answer. This answer is wrong. How did John get his answer?

Possible answer: He combined Thursday's and Friday's books but didn't

subtract them from Saturday's books.

215

Solutions

14 Solution
The graph should show two additional segments filled in above the label Sunday for a total of 4.
DOK 2

15 Solution
A; $4 - 3 = 1$

Explain to students why the other two choices are not correct:

B is not correct because 2 is the total read on Thursday.

D is not correct because 4 is the total read on Saturday.
DOK 3

Ready Mathematics
PRACTICE AND PROBLEM SOLVING

Assign *Practice and Problem Solving* **pages 239–240** after students have completed this section.

Teacher Notes

Independent Practice

At A Glance

Students use graphs to answer questions that might appear on a mathematics test.

Solutions

1 **Solution**
D; 4 black hair, 3 blonde hair, 5 brown hair, 1 red hair
DOK 1

2 **Solution**
a. **False**; black = 4, brown = 5; b. **False**; brown = 5, black + blonde + red = 8; c. **True**; 3 − 1 = 2; d. **True**; 5 + 3 = 8.
DOK 2

Practice ▶ **Making Bar Graphs and Picture Graphs**

Solve the problems.

Use the graph to solve Problems 1 and 2.

Maggie recorded the hair color of the girls on her softball team. She put her data in a bar graph.

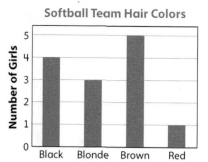

Softball Team Hair Colors

1 Which two colors have the least number of girls with that hair color? Circle the correct answer.

A black and blonde

B brown and black

C black and red

(D) red and blonde

2 Circle *True* or *False* for each sentence.

a. There are more girls with black hair than brown hair. True (False)

b. There are more girls with brown hair than the other three colors combined. True (False)

c. There are 2 fewer girls with red hair than blonde hair. (True) False

d. There are 8 girls with brown hair or blonde hair. (True) False

---

Quick Check and Remediation

- Show students a tally chart containing information about glasses of lemonade flavors sold at a lemonade stand: 6 strawberry, 5 pink, 9 regular, 5 kiwi. Have them make a bar graph, including labels and a title, to display the data.

- For students who are still struggling, use the chart to guide remediation.

- After providing remediation, check students' understanding by changing the numbers and/or flavors used on the lemonade stand chart and asking students to create a graph using the new data.

If the error is ...	Students may ...	To remediate ...
The bars do not correspond to the number of glasses sold.	not understand how to create a scale.	Provide students with paper squares. Have them use one-to-one correspondence to display the data. Remind them that each square represents one glass, so all the numbered intervals need to be the same distance apart.
Labels are missing or inaccurate.	not recognize the importance of appropriate labels or know how to write them.	Ask the students to tell you what the numbers and the bars represent. Then have them write their descriptions in the appropriate positions on the graph. Discuss how someone who hasn't seen the data will not know what the numbers or bars mean if they are not labeled.

3 Wes recorded the weather for one week in the table at the right.

Complete the picture graph below using the data in the table. Draw a ☼ for sunny days and a ☁ for cloudy days.

Day	Weather
Sun.	cloudy
Mon.	cloudy
Tues.	sunny
Wed.	sunny
Thur.	rainy
Fri.	sunny
Sat.	cloudy

Sunny, Cloudy, and Rainy Days	
Sunny	☼ ☼ ☼
Cloudy	☁ ☁ ☁
Rainy	💧

4 Use your completed picture graph from Problem 3 to fill in the blanks below.

There were the same number of ___sunny___ and ___cloudy___ days.

There were ___2___ more sunny days than ___rainy___ days.

5 If Saturday had been sunny, how would the picture graph be different than it is now?

Possible answer: Instead of 3 suns and 3 clouds, there

would be 4 suns and 2 clouds.

✓ **Self Check** Now you can make bar and picture graphs. Fill this in on the progress chart on page 153.

217

Solutions

3 **Solution**
Missing label: Cloudy; 3 sunny and 3 cloudy pictures drawn
DOK 2

4 **Solution**
sunny; cloudy; 2; rainy
DOK 2

5 **Solution**
1 more sunny day and 1 fewer cloudy day; so 4 sunny days and 2 cloudy days; so 4 suns and 2 clouds on the graph
DOK 3

▶ **Hands-On Activity**

Organize and display data.

Materials: concrete objects to sort and graph such as 4 different shapes of dry pasta, 4 different colors of buttons or beads, etc.; 1-inch squares cut from Activity Sheet 3 (1-Inch Grid Paper); plain white paper

• Provide each student with a small cupful of objects and ask them to sort the objects.

• Demonstrate how to do so, and then have students count and record the number of each group in a table.

• Show students how to fold the paper vertically into 4 sections. Have them unfold the paper and write a label at the bottom of each section.

• Tell students to use a ruler to mark and number 1-inch intervals along the left side of the paper.

• Have students use the 1-inch squares to create a bar graph on the paper. Remind students to include labels and a title.

▶ **Challenge Activity**

Collect and display data.

Challenge students to collect data that can be organized in a picture or bar graph. You may want to help them with survey ideas such as favorite game or favorite type of playground equipment.

They must:

• collect the data.

• organize the data in a tally chart and/or table.

• display the data in a graph.

• tell how they (or someone else) might use the data to make a decision.

Overview

Assign the Lesson 23 Quiz and have students work independently to complete it.

Use the results of the quiz to assess students' understanding of the content of the lesson and to identify areas for reteaching. See the Lesson Pacing Guide at the beginning of the lesson for suggested instructional resources.

Tested Skills

Assesses 2.MD.D.10

Problems on this assessment form require students to be able to read and interpret bar graphs and picture graphs to analyze and compare data. They must understand and use conventions for labeling graphs and be able to correctly label a graph. Students will also need to be familiar with collecting data, using tally charts and tables, comparing quantities, and adding within 10.

Ready® **Mathematics**

Lesson 23 **Quiz**

Solve the problems.

1 Rosa makes a picture graph showing the number of some things in her room.

Which statement is true? Circle the correct answer.

A Rosa has 3 more lamps than books.

B Rosa has 2 more books than lamps.

C Rosa has fewer dolls than lamps and chairs combined.

D Rosa has more books than lamps and dolls combined.

Things in Rosa's Room

Book   Chair   Doll   Lamp

2 Sean asks his friends what pets they own. The table shows the data.

Finish the bar graph for Sean's data. Write the labels in the boxes.

Pet	Number of Friends
Dog	4
Rabbit	2
Cat	3

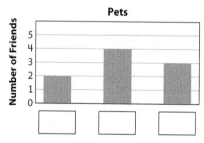

Pets

Number of Friends

---

3 Rob counts 3 different colored trucks at a truck stop. He makes a bar graph to show the data.

Truck Colors		
White	Yellow	Black
3	2	5

Truck Colors

Number of Trucks

White   Yellow   Black

Explain what is wrong with Rob's bar graph.

_____

_____

_____

_____

Common Misconceptions and Errors

Errors may result if students:

• make a computational error when adding or subtracting.

• miscount the number of pictures in a picture graph or misread the height of a bar in a bar graph.

• incorrectly compare two categories or use the wrong operation to compare.

• confuse the meanings of the words *more* and *less*.

Ready® **Mathematics**

Lesson 23 Quiz Answer Key

1. C
DOK 2

2. Rabbit, Dog, Cat
DOK 1

3. The bar graph shows the wrong number of white and yellow trucks. The graph should show 3 white trucks and 2 yellow trucks.
DOK 3

CCSS Focus

Domain
Measurement and Data

Cluster
C. Work with time and money.

Standards
2.MD.C.7 Tell and write time from analog and digital clocks to the nearest five minutes, using AM and PM.

Domain
Number and Operations in Base Ten

Cluster
A. Understand place value.

Standards
2.NBT.A.2 Count within 1000; skip-count by 5s, 10s, and 100s.

Standards for Mathematical Practice (SMP)

2 Reason abstractly and quantitatively.

3 Construct viable arguments and critique the reasoning of others.

7 Look for and make use of structure.

8 Look for and express regularity in repeated reasoning.

Lesson Objectives

Content Objectives

- Read time to the nearest 5-minute interval.
- Write time using proper notation.
- Show time on an analog clock using proper hour-hand and minute-hand placement.
- Determine when a digital clock should read AM or PM.

Language Objectives

- Skip count by 5s to read time on an analog clock.
- Use the terms AM and PM correctly in discussions.

Prerequisite Skills

- Tell and write time in hours and half hours.
- Skip count by 5s and 10s.
- Understand the concept of half.

Lesson Vocabulary

- **AM** the time from midnight until before noon
- **PM** the time from noon until before midnight

Review the following key terms

- **hour** a unit of time equal to 60 minutes
- **minute** a unit of time equal to 60 seconds
- **hour hand** the shorter indicator (or hand) on an analog clock, which shows the hours
- **minute hand** the longer indicator (or hand) on an analog clock, which shows the minutes
- **analog clock** a clock that uses hour and minute hand positions to show time
- **digital clock** a clock that uses digits to display the time

Learning Progression

In Grade 1 students explore time by reading an analog and digital clock, telling time in hours and half hours. They write time using a colon to separate the hours and minutes.

In Grade 2 students expand on their understanding of time and reading a clock as they explore duration and passage of time.

In this lesson students read an analog and digital clock to the nearest 5 minutes. They recognize the structure of an analog clock that enables them to use skip counting to read or place the

minute hand. Students differentiate between and draw clock hands to indicate what the time is between two hours and to show the number of minutes that have passed. Students explore the concept of AM and PM, and determine whether an event occurs in an AM or PM time.

In Grade 3 students tell time to the nearest minute. They read and solve problems involving intervals between two times. Students read minutes shown on a clock as the minutes that follow an hour or as the number of minutes before the next hour.

Lesson Pacing Guide

Whole Class Instruction

Day 1 *45–60 minutes*	**Toolbox: Interactive Tutorial*** *Telling Time to 5 Minutes* **Introduction** • Opening Activity *15 min* • Use What You Know *15 min* • Find Out More *10 min* • Reflect *5 min*	**Practice and Problem Solving** Assign pages 243–244.
Day 2 *45–60 minutes*	**Modeled and Guided Instruction** **Learn About Telling and Writing Time** • Picture It/Picture It *15 min* • Connect It *20 min* • Try It *10 min*	**Practice and Problem Solving** Assign pages 245–246.
Day 3 *45–60 minutes*	**Guided Practice** **Practice Telling and Writing Time** • Example *5 min* • Problems 7–9 *15 min* • Pair/Share *15 min* • Solutions *10 min*	**Practice and Problem Solving** Assign pages 247–248.
Day 4 *45–60 minutes*	**Independent Practice** **Practice Telling and Writing Time** • Problems 1–6 *20 min* • Quick Check and Remediation *10 min* • Hands-On or Challenge Activity *15 min* **Toolbox: Lesson Quiz** Lesson 24 Quiz	

Small Group Differentiation

Teacher-Toolbox.com

Reteach
Ready Prerequisite Lessons *45–90 min*

Grade 1
• Lesson 34 Tell Time

Teacher-led Activities
Tools for Instruction *15–20 min*

Grade 1 *(Lesson 34)*
• Telling Time to the Hour and Half Hour
Grade 2 *(Lesson 24)*
• Telling Time to the Nearest Five Minutes

Student-led Activities
Math Center Activities *30–40 min*

Grade 2 *(Lesson 24)*
• 2.41 Tell Time Vocabulary
• 2.42 Tell Time from Analog and Digital Clocks

*We continually update the Interactive Tutorials. Check the Teacher Toolbox for the most up-to-date offerings for this lesson.

Opening Activity

Time Relationships

Objective Understand time concepts.

Time *15–20 minutes*

Materials for each student

• none

Overview

Students explore the concept of a minute and relate it to an hour. They relate time to activities in their lives.

Step By Step

1 Explore one minute.

• Have students put their heads on their desks and close their eyes. Tell them to stay in that position for one minute and when they think one minute has expired, put up a thumb for you to see.

• After one minute, have students put up their heads and discuss if they thought one minute was a long time or a short time and why. Ask when one minute might *seem* like a long time [waiting for something like your turn or a friend to come over] and when a minute seems like a short time [playing a fun game].

2 Explore one hour.

• Ask: *How long is one hour?* [Some may respond: a long time; longer than a minute; 60 minutes; etc.]

• Write the headings *Longer than one hour* and *Shorter than one hour* on the board.

• Have students generate ideas of activities in their lives that last longer than one hour and shorter than one hour. Activities that take less than one hour might include recess, lunch, reading a book, playing a game, and riding the bus home after school. Activities that take more than one hour might include watching a movie or a sporting event, driving to grandma's house or to a vacation spot, or playing a game of baseball. As students suggest activities and whether they take more or less than one hour, write their ideas on the board under the corresponding heading.

3 Use a clock to tell time.

- Ask the class how they can know whether an activity takes more than an hour or less than an hour. They should respond that they can use a clock.

- Show students an analog and a digital clock or watch and tell them that this lesson will help them tell time using a clock.

Teacher Notes

At A Glance

Students read the time shown on an analog clock by analyzing the placement of the two hands. Then students explore skip counting by 5s to find the number of minutes.

Step By Step

- Work through **Use What You Know** as a class.
- Read the problem at the top of the page.
- Use the Hands-On Activity to help students make sense of reading an analog clock.

▶ **Hands-On Activity**

- Complete the page together as a class.
- Point out the time notation used in Parts c and d.

▶ **Real-World Connection**

⏱ Use What You Know

You know how to tell time to the hour and half hour.

Lucy started her piano lesson at the time shown on the clock.

What time does the clock show?

a. The short hand shows the hour. What number did the short hand just go past?

_____4_____

b. The long hand shows the minutes. It is halfway around the clock. How many minutes are in a half hour?

_____30_____

c. The time is halfway between which two hours?

___4___ : ___00___ and ___5___ : ___00___

d. What time did Lucy start her piano lesson?

___4___ : ___30___
hours   minutes

218

▶ **Hands-On Activity**

Make an analog clock.

Materials: paper plate, $\frac{1}{4}$-inch × 4-inch tag board, $\frac{1}{4}$-inch by 2-inch tagboard, and brass fastener

- Before passing out the materials, poke a hole in the center of each plate and near one end of each piece of tagboard.
- Distribute the materials to students. Have them fold the paper plate in half and in half again. Then have them unfold the plate and write 12, 3, 6, and 9 in the appropriate places. Show them how to fill in the remainder of the numbers.
- Show students how to make clock hands by cutting a tip on the ends without holes. Then show them how to fasten the hands to the center of the plate with the brass fastener so that the long hand is on top of the short hand.
- Demonstrate and have students follow showing 4 o'clock on their clocks.

- Ask: *What does the long hand have to do to get to 5 o'clock?* [move all the way around the clock back to the 12] Remind students that while the minute hand is moving, the hour hand is also moving very slowly toward the 5.
- Have students move the minute hand to the 6. Ask: *How far around the clock has the minute hand moved? How far do you think the hour hand should move?* [halfway; halfway to the 5] Have them move the hands to show 4:30.

▶ **Real-World Connection**

Ask: *When might it be important to know what time it is on a clock?*

Discuss how it is important to know when it is time for recess, when you are supposed to be ready to go to your ballgame, etc. Encourage students to generate ideas of their own.

▷▷ Find Out More

Look at the clock. The short hand is called the **hour hand**.
It tells you the **hour**.

It takes 1 hour for the hour hand to move from one number to the next.

Since the hour hand has gone past the 4 (but isn't to the 5 yet), the hour is 4.

The long hand is called the **minute hand**.
It tells you the number of **minutes**.

It takes 5 minutes for the minute hand to move from one number to the next.

The minute hand is pointing to the **6**. Skip count by five **6** times to find the number of minutes.
5, 10, 15, 20, 25, 30

When writing the time, write the hour, then a colon (:),
then the minutes. The clock shows 4:30.

▶ Reflect   Work with a partner.

1 Talk About It Why can you skip count by five to show there are 60 minutes in an hour?

Write About It   Possible answer: There are 12 numbers on a clock.

Each number shows 5 minutes. If I skip count by five 12 times, I get 60:

5, 10, 15, 20, 25, 30, 35, 40, 45, 50, 55, 60.

219

▶ Mathematical Discourse

Is it possible for a clock to read 5:75? Explain.

Students should respond that it is not possible. A clock is divided into 60 minutes. After the minute hand goes all the way around the clock, the minutes start over.

Step By Step

- Read **Find Out More** as a class.

- Ask students how many little tick marks they see between each number on the clock. Have them add tick marks to the clocks they made in the Hands-On Activity.

- Ask students what they think each of the marks shows. Then ask how many minutes it takes for the minute hand to move from one number on the clock to the next number. [5] Make sure students understand that the interval indicates the minute, not the mark itself.

> **SMP TIP Use Structure**
> Sketch a clock on the board and draw curved lines (jumps) to each number, emphasizing that the spaces or intervals on the clock that are between each number are what are being counted, not the number itself. Discuss how the structure of a clock enables us to read it easily using counting strategies. *(SMP 7)*

▶ Mathematical Discourse

- Ask: *Why is the hour hand going toward the 5 and not the 4 when it is 4:30?* Students should remember that the hour hand moves slowly as the minute hand moves. Show this movement with a demonstration clock or one of the student-made clocks.

- Write 7:30 on the board. Have students model the time on their clocks. Ask students to justify why they modeled it the way they did. Then ask them to read the time out loud.

- Have students discuss the **Reflect** question and then write about it in their own words. Encourage students to use their clocks to skip count around the clock.

> ▣ **Ready** **Mathematics**
> PRACTICE AND PROBLEM SOLVING
>
> Assign *Practice and Problem Solving* **pages 243–244** after students have completed this section.

Modeled and Guided Instruction

At A Glance

Students relate time shown on an analog clock to a digital clock. Then students solve more problems about time.

Step By Step

- Read the problem at the top of the page together as a class.

Picture It

- In **Picture It**, make sure students focus on the 4 intervals past 7 o'clock indicating the time is 20 minutes past 7.

Picture It

- Direct students' attention to **Picture It**. Ask Mathematical Discourse question 1 to help students compare a digital clock to an analog clock.

▶ **Mathematical Discourse 1**

- Direct attention to the AM notation on the digital clock and ask students if they know what it means. Ask them if they know what PM means. Discuss how they know when it is morning or afternoon.

- Explain that the AM and PM come from a foreign language and mean it is morning or afternoon. Tell them they can think of PM as "**P**ast **M**orning," so AM is in the morning.

▶ **Mathematical Discourse 2**

▶ **Concept Extension**

Learn About ▶ **Telling and Writing Time**

Read the problem. Then you will look at ways to tell and write time.

Evan started eating breakfast at the time shown on the clock.

What time does the clock show?

▶ **Picture It** **You can use the clock to find the hour and minutes.**

The hour hand is between the 7 and the 8.

The minute hand is pointed at the 4.
Skip count by five 4 times to find the minutes.

▶ **Picture It** **You can use a digital clock to show the time.**

The same time can be shown on a **digital clock**. It shows the hour first, then the minutes.

A digital clock shows **AM** to mean "during the morning" or **PM** to mean "noon until midnight."

220

▶ **Mathematical Discourse**

1 *How is a digital clock like an analog clock? How are they different?*

Students may respond that both kinds of clocks show the time, but a digital clock shows the time the way we write it, instead of with hands.

2 *When might a digital clock be more helpful than an analog clock?*

Students may share situations when it is important to know whether it is morning or afternoon. They should note that the digital clock tells you when it is morning or afternoon, but the analog clock does not.

▶ **Concept Extension**

What time is one minute after 4:59?

- Show students a demonstration clock with the hands positioned at 4:59. Write 4:59 on the board.

- Ask: *What time will it be when the hand moves one more minute?* [5:00] Write 5:00 on the board.

- Write 29 on the board. Ask students to describe what happens when one more is added. They should remember that the ones are grouped into another ten, making the number 30.

- Then ask students what happens when one more is added to 39, to 49, and then to 59. [Students should recognize that one more than 39 is 40, one more than 49 is 50, and one more than 59 is 60.]

- Discuss how working with minutes is similar, until one more minute is added to 59. On a clock, the minutes go back to zero after 59. One minute after :59 is the next hour, :00.

▶ **Connect It** Understand and use the models to solve a new problem.

2 What time did Evan start eating breakfast?

    7 : 20

3 This clock shows the time Evan finishes breakfast. Tell how you know what the hour is.

Possible answer: The hour hand is past the 7 but not

to the 8, so the hour is still 7.

4 How can you skip count to find the number of minutes on the clock when Evan finishes breakfast?

Possible answer: The minute hand is pointing to the

10, so I can skip count by five 10 times:

5, 10, 15, 20, 25, 30, 35, 40, 45, 50.

5 What time did Evan finish breakfast?

    7 : 50

▶ **Try It** Try another problem.

6 The first clock shows when Mark went to bed. Write the same time on the digital clock. Circle AM or PM.

221

Step By Step

Connect It

- Read **Connect It** as a class.

- Have students model with their clocks the times that Evan started and ended breakfast. Ask students what tells them that they are still in the 7 o'clock hour. [Since the hour hand is still between 7 and 8, it is past 7 but before 8 o'clock.]

- After students complete Problem 5, you may want to use the Concept Extension to engage them in thinking about how they can determine the amount of time that has elapsed between two events.

▶ **Concept Extension**

Try It

- Tell students to complete the **Try It** problem on their own. Remind them that they need to circle AM or PM. When students are done, discuss their representations to ensure they all understand how to show time on both an analog and digital clock.

6 **Solution**
The digital clock should show 8:35 PM.

Error Alert Watch for students who may display 9:35, not recognizing the 9 as the hour the short hand is moving toward.

Ready® Mathematics
PRACTICE AND PROBLEM SOLVING

Assign *Practice and Problem Solving* **pages 245–246** after students have completed this section.

▶ **Concept Extension**

Explore the concept of elapsed time.

- Challenge students to determine the amount of time it took Evan to eat breakfast.

- Allow students to work in groups to find out how much time it took for Evan to eat. [30 minutes] Encourage them to use the clocks they made, or pictures of analog clocks, to help them.

- Ask: *Is it easier to figure this problem out using an analog or digital clock? Why?* Students may respond that the analog is easier since intervals can be counted. There are no intervals to count on the digital clock. Some students may say the digital because they can count by tens from 20 to 50.

Guided Practice

At A Glance

Students show time on analog and digital clocks.

Step By Step

- Ask students to solve the problems independently. Tell them they will use what they learned about telling time during this lesson to complete the problems.

- For Problem 8, make sure students understand that they need to draw hands on the clock. Remind them that the long hand shows the minutes and the short hand tells the hour. Watch to make sure they all represent the time with hands in the proper positions.

- **Pair/Share** When students have completed each problem, have them Pair/Share to discuss their solutions with a partner.

Solutions

Example Analysis of the placement of the hour hand is used to determine the hour. Skip counting is used to determine the minutes.

7 Solution

9:15 AM. The hour is between 9 and 10, and the minute hand is on the 3. Since it is morning, it is AM.

DOK 2

Practice **Telling and Writing Time**

Study the model below. Then solve Problems 7–9.

Example

Dina went on a bike ride at the time shown on the clock. What time does the clock show?

You can skip count.

The hour hand is past the 2, but not to the 3 yet. So, the hour is 2.

The minute hand is on the 9, so skip count by five 9 times to find the number of minutes.

5, 10, 15, 20, 25, 30, 35, 40, 45

Answer ___2:45___

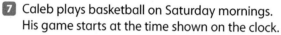

7 Caleb plays basketball on Saturday mornings. His game starts at the time shown on the clock.

Show the same time on the digital clock. Remember to circle AM or PM.

How can you tell if it is AM or PM?

222

Teacher Notes

8 Sophia had a meeting at the time shown on the digital clock below.
Show the same time on the other clock.

What two numbers will the hour hand be between? What number will the minute hand point to?

PM 1:40

9 Jane got home from school at the time shown on the clock. What time did Jane get home?

A 5:15

B 3:05

(C) 3:25

D 4:25

Which hand tells the hour?

Emily chose **B** as the answer. This answer is wrong. How did Emily get her answer?

Possible answer: She thought the minute hand pointed to the number of

minutes. She didn't count by fives to get the minutes.

223

Solutions

8 **Solution**

The hour hand should be a little more than halfway between the 1 and 2, and the minute hand is on the 8.

DOK 1

9 **Solution**

C; 3:25

Explain to students why the other two choices are not correct:

A is not correct because the hour hand (short hand) is between 3 and 4. It is the minute hand that is on 5.

D is not correct because the hour hand is between 3 and 4, so the hour is still 3.

DOK 3

Ready Mathematics
PRACTICE AND PROBLEM SOLVING

Assign *Practice and Problem Solving* **pages 247–248** after students have completed this section.

Teacher Notes

Independent Practice

At A Glance

Students use concepts of telling time to solve problems that might appear on a mathematics test.

Solutions

1 **Solution**
B The hour hand is between the 5 and 6, and the minute hand is at the 9;
D It is in the afternoon, so it is PM.
DOK 2

2 **Solution**
D; 10:30 is halfway between 10 and 11.
DOK 1

3 **Solution**
B and **D**; The minute hand would denote 50 minutes past an hour.
DOK 2

Practice **Telling and Writing Time**

Solve the problems.

1 Elsa went to swim practice after school. She finished at 5:45. Which clock shows the time Elsa finished? Circle all the correct answers.

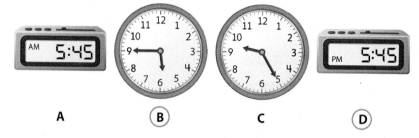

A   B   C   D

2 Where does the hour hand point when a clock shows 10:30? Circle the correct answer.

A at the 6

B at the 10

C between the 9 and the 10

(D) between the 10 and the 11

3 The minute hand on a clock points at the 10. What time could it be? Circle all the correct answers.

A 10:10

(B) 4:50

C 10:30

(D) 8:50

Quick Check and Remediation

- On a demonstration analog clock or on a drawing of an analog clock, show the time 3:50. Ask: *What time is it?* [3:50] Ask students to write the time as it would be shown on a digital clock. [3:50]

- For students who are still struggling, use the chart to guide remediation.

- After providing remediation, check students' understanding using the following problem:

  Display the time 4:15 on a digital clock. Have students say the time and show it on an analog clock face. [hour hand just after the 4, minute hand on the 3]

If the error is . . .	Students may . . .	To remediate . . .
10:20	have read the minute hand as the hour and the hour hand as the minutes.	Show students an analog clock. Ask which hand moves faster than the other. Ask if hours or minutes go by faster. Lead them to see that the short hand displays the hour, and the long hand displays the minutes.
3:10	have read the number on the clock face as the minutes.	Show students an analog clock. Ask how many minutes are in an hour. Model how 60 minutes are counted as the minute hand moves around the clock.
any other answer	have misinterpreted the hour or misread the minutes.	Tell students to show the time on a demonstration analog clock. Point out the placement of the hour hand and count the minutes together.

Dylan finished his afternoon soccer practice at the time shown on the clock at the right.

Which clock below shows the time Dylan finished soccer practice? Circle the correct answer.

A   **B**   **C**   **D**

Solutions

4 **Solution**
B; The clock shows 5 minutes past 4, and it was in the afternoon.
DOK 2

 Robin read until 7:35 in the evening. Draw hands on the clock to show that time. Then write the same time on the digital clock. Be sure to circle AM or PM.

5 **Solution**
The analog clock should show the hour between 7 and 8, and the minute hand on the 7. The digital clock should show 7:35 PM.
DOK 2

 The clock at the right is missing the minute hand. It is either 6:05 or 6:55. Which is correct? Explain how the hour hand can help you know the answer.

6:55 is correct. Possible answer: The hour hand is

almost to the 7, so it is almost 7:00. It is 6:55.

6 **Solution**
The hour hand tells if the time is closer to 6 o'clock or to 7 o'clock. Since it is closer to 7 o'clock, the minutes must be 55. 6:05 would be closer to 6 o'clock.
DOK 3

✓ **Self Check** **Now you can read and write time.**
Fill this in on the progress chart on page 153.

225

▶ Hands-On Activity

Show time on an analog clock and a digital clock.

Materials: For each pair: a student-made clock, paper divided to replicate a digital clock screen, and cards cut from both pages of Activity Sheet 14 (Digital Clock Cards)

- Have students work in pairs.
- One of the students shows a time on the analog clock (make sure the student knows what time is shown) and tells what might be happening at that time (to make evident whether it is morning or afternoon/evening).
- The partner selects and places Digital Clock Cards on the paper to show the time, including AM or PM.
- Students analyze whether the digital clock is correct, say the time, and switch roles.

▶ Challenge Activity

How did people tell time long ago?

Materials: list of time-keeping devices

- Challenge students to search on the computer or in the library to find out about how people told time long ago.
- Give them a list of time-keeping devices including: hourglass, sundial, obelisk, candle clock, time stick.
- Have students:
  - learn everything they can about one timepiece.
  - print a picture of the timepiece to display.
  - report to the class, explaining how the device was used to tell time.

Teacher-Toolbox.com

Overview

Assign the Lesson 24 Quiz and have students work independently to complete it.

Use the results of the quiz to assess students' understanding of the content of the lesson and to identify areas for reteaching. See the Lesson Pacing Guide at the beginning of the lesson for suggested instructional resources.

Tested Skills

Assesses 2.MD.C.7

Problems on this assessment form require students to be able to read and write time from an analog clock to the nearest five minutes, write time from a description of the location of the hands on an analog clock, and determine when a digital clock should read am or pm. Students will also need to be familiar with the concept of half, telling and writing time in hours and half hours (using colon notation), and skip counting by 5s and 10s.

Ready® Mathematics

Lesson 24 Quiz

Solve the problems.

1 Pete goes to a ball game at 2:40. Draw the missing minute hand on the clock to show 2:40.

2 A circus starts at the time shown on the clock. Bea says the circus starts at 2:25.

What is Bea's mistake? What is the right time?
Circle the correct answer.

  A Bea mixed up the hour and the minute hand. The right time is 7:14.

  B Bea read the minute hand wrong. The right time is 2:07.

  C Bea read the hour hand wrong. The right time is 3:35.

  D Bea read the minute hand wrong. The right time is 2:35.

Lesson 24 Quiz continued

3 Cheng will get up in the morning at the time shown on the clock. What time will Cheng get up?

Fill in the blanks. Circle AM or PM.

  Answer: Cheng will get up at ____ : _____ AM PM.

4 Diana saw that the long hand on her watch was pointing at the 9. Which clocks show what time it could be on Diana's watch?

Circle all the correct answers.

  A

  C

  B

  D

Common Misconceptions and Errors

Errors may result if students:

• confuse the minute and hour hands.

• think that when the hour hand is pointing between two numbers, the hour corresponds to the larger number.

• think the number the minute hand is pointing to is the number of minutes past the hour.

• incorrectly skip count by 5s.

Ready® **Mathematics**

Lesson 24 Quiz Answer Key

1.

DOK 1

2. D
DOK 3

3. 6:05 AM
DOK 2

4. A, B
DOK 2

CCSS Focus

Domain
Measurement and Data

Cluster
C. Work with time and money.

Standards
2.MD.C.8 Solve word problems involving dollar bills, quarters, dimes, nickels, and pennies, using $ and ¢ symbols appropriately. Example: If you have 2 dimes and 3 pennies, how many cents do you have?

Domain
Number and Operations in Base Ten

Cluster
A. Understand place value.

Standards
2.NBT.A.2 Count within 1000; skip-count by 5s, 10s, and 100s.

Standards for Mathematical Practice (SMP)

1 Make sense of problems and persevere in solving them.

2 Reason abstractly and quantitatively.

3 Construct viable arguments and critique the reasoning of others.

4 Model with mathematics.

6 Attend to precision.

7 Look for and make use of structure.

8 Look for and express regularity in repeated reasoning.

Lesson Objectives

Content Objectives

• Recognize and name the coins penny, nickel, dime, and quarter.

• Know the value of coins and paper denominations.

• Count the amount of money represented by a set of coins or bills.

Language Objectives

• Write the value of a set of coins.

• Write the value of a set of bills.

• List coins that have a given total value.

Prerequisite Skills

• Count by 5s, 10s, 20s, and 25s.
• Fluently add within 100.

Lesson Vocabulary

• **cent** the smallest unit of money in the U.S.

• **penny** a coin that has a value of 1 cent

• **nickel** a coin that has a value of 5 cents

• **dime** a coin that has a value of 10 cents

• **quarter** a coin that has a value of 25 cents

• **dollar** a unit of money in the U.S. equal to 100 cents

Learning Progression

In Grade 1 students do not formally explore money concepts, but they may informally have experiences with coins and their values.

In Grade 2 students explore concepts of money including coins and denominations of bills.

In this lesson students recognize, name, and count the values of pennies, nickels, dimes, and quarters. They combine coins to equal the value of other coins, determine the coins needed to equal one dollar, and use notation to label dollars and cents. Students use counting strategies to find the value of a set of bills in denominations of $5, $10, $20, $50, and $100.

In Grade 3 and beyond, students will solve problems involving money. They recognize that coins represent a fraction of a dollar and use the decimal point to separate dollars from cents.

Lesson Pacing Guide

Whole Class Instruction

Day 1
45–60 minutes

Toolbox: Interactive Tutorial*
Coin Values

Introduction
- Opening Activity *15 min*
- Use What You Know *10 min*
- Find Out More *10 min*
- Reflect *5 min*

Practice and Problem Solving
Assign pages 251–252.

Day 2
45–60 minutes

Modeled and Guided Instruction
Learn About Finding the Value of Coins
- Picture It/Model It/Model It *20 min*
- Connect It *15 min*
- Try It *10 min*

Practice and Problem Solving
Assign pages 253–254.

Day 3
45–60 minutes

Modeled and Guided Instruction
Learn About Solving Word Problems About Money
- Model It/Model It *20 min*
- Connect It *15 min*
- Try It *10 min*

Practice and Problem Solving
Assign pages 255–256.

Day 4
45–60 minutes

Guided Practice
Practice Solving Word Problems About Money
- Example *5 min*
- Problems 13–15 *15 min*
- Pair/Share *15 min*
- Solutions *10 min*

Practice and Problem Solving
Assign pages 257–258.

Day 5
45–60 minutes

Independent Practice
Practice Solving Word Problems About Money
- Problems 1–6 *20 min*
- Quick Check and Remediation *10 min*
- Hands-On or Challenge Activity *15 min*

Toolbox: Lesson Quiz
Lesson 25 Quiz

Small Group Differentiation

Teacher-Toolbox.com

Reteach
Ready Prerequisite Lessons *15–20 min*

Grade 1
- Lesson 18 The 120 Chart

Teacher-led Activities
Tools for Instruction *15–20 min*

Grade 2 *(Lesson 25)*
- Problem Solving: Money Amounts
- Coin Combinations

Student-led Activities
Math Center Activities *30–40 min*

Grade 2 *(Lesson 25)*
- 2.43 Find the Value of Coins and Bills
- 2.44 Make Change

---

*We continually update the Interactive Tutorials. Check the Teacher Toolbox for the most up-to-date offerings for this lesson.

Add on a Hundreds Chart

Objective Explore strategies for adding on a hundreds chart.

Time *15–20 minutes*

Materials for each student

- Activity Sheet 2 (Hundreds Chart)
- one counter

Overview

Students add groups of 1, 5, 10, and 25. They devise, share, and analyze strategies that will prepare them to add coin values.

Step By Step

1 Add tens on the hundreds chart.

- Provide students with a hundreds chart and a counter.

- Write 10 + 10 on the board. Have students show and describe how they would perform the addition on the hundreds chart. They should place the counter on 10 and then move down one row to the 20.

- Write 25 + 10 on the board and ask students to model and describe how they would perform the addition on the hundreds chart. The counter starts on 25 and jumps down one row to 35.

- Discuss why you can add ten on a hundreds chart by moving down one row. If necessary, have children model several more additions of ten to solidify the concept. Then have students start at 15, add 3 tens, and describe their actions.

2 Add a series of numbers.

- Write 5 + 10 + 10 + 1 + 1 + 5 on the board and have students model the addition on the hundreds chart, moving the counter to the proper position for every number they add.

- Discuss the ways in which students performed the addition on the chart. Some students may have grouped the tens, the fives, and the ones to add. Some may have combined the 2 fives to make a ten to add.

- Write $5 + 10 + 1 + 1 + 25 + 1 + 5 + 25$ on the board and allow students to model the addition on the hundreds chart. (For those who prefer to use mental math, tell them that modeling may help them with the lesson and ask that they show on the chart what they thought about in their head.)

3 Share strategies.

- Discuss the strategies they used to add. Make sure a variety of strategies are shared with the class. Ask questions such as: *Why did you do that? How did that help you find the sum? Is there another way of thinking about the addition problem? How might you combine numbers differently?*

4 Relate the problem situation to money.

- Discuss how the numbers they added on the chart are like the values of coins. Tell them that this lesson will help them count money.

   Note: You may want to refer to or allow students to use the hundreds chart to aid in counting coins during this lesson.

Teacher Notes

Introduction

At A Glance

Students explore and count the value of pennies, nickels, and dimes. Then students examine the values of coins and bill denominations and learn the notation used to represent dollars and cents.

Step By Step

- Work through **Use What You Know** as a class.

- Read the problem at the top of the page together.

- Ask students what they notice about each group of coins. Discuss that each coin has a front and a back. You may want to display real coins and flip them back and forth to show both sides.

- Make sure students understand that they are counting the value of each coin. You may want to practice counting by 5s and 10s.

- Ask Mathematical Discourse question 1 to connect coin values to base-ten blocks and emphasize what it means to find the value of coins.

▶ **Mathematical Discourse 1**

SMP TIP Look for Structure

Show students a ones block, tens block, and hundreds block. Place a penny below the ones block, a dime below the tens block, and a dollar below the hundreds block. Discuss the similarities in the structure of money and our base-ten system of numeration. *(SMP 7)*

- Say: *Susan says the coins are confusing. A nickel is bigger than a dime, but a nickel is only 5 cents and a dime is 10 cents. Shouldn't the bigger coin be worth more?* Explain that dimes used to be made of silver, which was worth more than the material that was used to make nickels. Even though today dimes are no longer made of silver, they are still smaller than nickels and worth more than nickels.

▶ **English Language Learners**

Use What You Know

You know how to count by ones, fives, and tens.

Lee, Seth, and Jack each have five coins.

| **Lee** | **Seth** | **Jack** |

Which child has the most cents?

a. Lee has five pennies. Each penny is worth 1 cent. Count by ones to find how many cents she has.

<u>1</u> , <u>2</u> , 3 , 4 , 5

b. Seth has five nickels. Each nickel is worth 5 cents. Count by fives to find how many cents he has.

<u>5</u> , <u>10</u> , 15 , 20 , 25

c. Jack has five dimes. Each dime is worth 10 cents. Count by tens to find how many cents he has.

<u>10</u> , <u>20</u> , 30 , 40 , 50

d. Who has the most cents? Explain how you know.

Jack. Possible answer: Jack has the most because 50 is the greatest number.

226

▶ **Mathematical Discourse**

1 *How is finding the value of coins like using base-ten blocks?*

When you use base-ten blocks, you don't just count how many hundreds blocks, tens blocks, and ones blocks you have. You count by 100s, 10s, and 1s to find the total value.

▶ **English Language Learners**

Discuss how the money used in the child's native culture compares to that of the U.S. If possible, correlate their money to ours, such as peso = 1; penny = 1.

▶▶ Find Out More

You can learn about the value of money.

Each type of coin and bill has a different value.

Name	Value	Front	Back
penny	1¢		
nickel	5¢		
dime	10¢		
quarter	25¢		many different kinds

We use ¢ to show cents and $ to show dollars. 5¢ is five cents. $5 is five dollars.

A $1 bill is worth the same amount as 100¢.

There are also other types of bills, such as $5, $10, $20, $50, and $100.

Reflect Work with a partner.

1 **Talk About It** Each child in the problem on the previous page has five coins. Why don't they all have the same amount of money?

Write About It Possible answer: because each type of coin is worth a

different amount.

227

Step By Step

- Draw attention to the chart in **Find Out More**. Point out that each coin has a distinct front and back. You may want to show the class special coins such as buffalo head nickels and state quarters, reminding them that even though the images on them are different, the values are the same as those of standard coins.

▶ **Visual Model**

SMP TIP Reason Quantitatively
Use the Visual Model activity to help students make sense of the relationships among the values of coins and find ways of combining them. *(SMP 2)*

- Point out the notation used to show dollars and cents. You may want to model the signs on the board and have students practice drawing them on whiteboards.

- Draw attention to the value of one dollar in cents. Ask: *How many nickels do you think it takes to make a dollar? How many dimes? How many quarters?* Allow students to discuss and/or model each situation.

▶ **Mathematical Discourse 2 and 3**

▶ **Visual Model**

Make a table.

Materials: For each pair: paper, pencils, and play coins

- Have student pairs fold a piece of paper into 4 vertical sections. They should unfold the paper, trace the creases, and label the sections: 25¢, 10¢, 5¢, and 1¢. Give each pair a set of play coins for modeling.

- Tell students to find as many ways as possible to make 25¢. They record in the columns the number of each coin used, separating each row with a horizontal line.

- Have students compare lists. Point out any student pairs who organized their lists and discuss how that can aid in finding all the combinations.

▶ **Mathematical Discourse**

2 *Why does it take more dimes to make a dollar than it does quarters?*

Listen for responses that indicate that students recognize that since a dime is worth less than a quarter, it takes more of them to equal a dollar.

3 *How does knowing that 1 dollar is 100 cents help you to know how many cents are in 2 dollars or 5 dollars or any number of dollars?*

Students may make the connection to base-ten blocks. There are 100 ones in 1 hundreds block, there are 200 ones in 2 hundreds blocks, and there are 500 ones in 5 hundreds blocks. Money is similar. Since there are 100 cents in 1 dollar, there are 200 cents in 2 dollars, 500 cents in 5 dollars, etc.

Ready Mathematics
PRACTICE AND PROBLEM SOLVING

Assign *Practice and Problem Solving* **pages 251–252** after students have completed this section.

Modeled and Guided Instruction

At A Glance

Students explore the strategies of sorting coins, making a model, and writing an equation for determining the value of a set of coins. Then students revisit this problem, using counting and addition strategies to determine the value of the coins.

Step By Step

- Read the problem at the top of the page as a class. Ask students to identify each coin shown and tell its value.

Picture It

- Draw students' attention to **Picture It**. Ask: *What does the picture show?* [The picture shows Erik's coins ordered from greatest value to least value.]

Model It

- Examine the model in **Model It**. Ask students how the size of each section relates to the value of the coin it represents. They should notice that the sections representing a value of 10 (dimes) are twice as long as the sections representing a value of 5 (nickels) and ten times as long as the sections representing a value of 1 (pennies).

▶ **Mathematical Discourse**

Model It

- Direct attention to the addition equation. Ask students to tell how it relates to the model directly above it.

▶ **Hands-On Activity**

Learn About ▶ **Finding the Value of Coins**

Read the problem. Then you will explore ways to find the value of the coins.

Erik found some coins on the floor. How many cents did he find?

▶ **Picture It** You can sort the coins and think about the value of each coin.

| 10¢ | 10¢ | 10¢ | 5¢ | 5¢ | 5¢ | 1¢ | 1¢ |

▶ **Model It** You can make a model.

| 10 | 10 | 10 | 5 | 5 | 5 | 1 | 1 |

▶ **Model It** You can write an addition equation.

$$10 + 10 + 10 + 5 + 5 + 5 + 1 + 1 = ?$$

228

▶ **Mathematical Discourse**

How is the model shown in the first Model It like the coins in Picture It?

The model shows tens, fives, and ones that are ordered like the 10¢, 5¢, and 1¢ coins.

▶ **Hands-On Activity**

Use play coins to show money amounts.

Materials: For each pair: a bag of play money, cards cut from Activity Sheet 15 (Money Amount Cards)

- Have students work in pairs. Give each pair the play money and money amount cards. Tell them to place the cards facedown.

- Students turn a card face up and work together to use the play money to represent the amount in at least 2 different ways.

- Have students record on paper the amount shown on the card and the coins they used.

- You may want students to share solutions with the class, discussing the varied ways of organizing the coins.

Connect It Use skip counting and addition to find the value of the coins.

2 Use skip counting to find the value. Each time the coins change, be sure to change what you are counting by.

10¢   20¢   30¢   35¢   40¢   45¢   46¢   47¢

3 Erik added the values like this. Fill in the sum.

$$10 + 10 + 10 + 5 + 5 + 5 + 1 + 1$$

$$30 \quad + \quad 15 \quad + \quad 2 \quad = \quad 47¢$$

4 Draw another set of coins that has the same value as Erik's set of coins.

Possible answers: one quarter, two dimes, and two pennies; four dimes and seven pennies; nine nickels and two pennies

Try It Try another problem.

5 Blaire has these coins.

How many cents does she have? _85_ ¢

Draw another set of coins that is worth the same amount.

Possible answers: three quarters and one dime; eight dimes and one nickel

229

Step By Step

Connect It

- Read **Connect It** as a class. Make sure students understand that the questions refer to the problem on the previous page.

- For Problem 2, make sure students understand that they are to write the cumulative total under each coin to demonstrate a counting-on strategy.

- Ask: *How does organizing coins help you to count them?* [It is easier to count on and keep track when you start with the greatest value.]

- Draw attention to the way the coins are grouped in Problem 2. Ask: *If you organize the coins a different way, will the total amount change? Explain.* Students should recognize that neither the order nor the way coins are grouped affects the total value.

- Have students complete Problem 4 using open circles with values written inside for coins. Share and count solutions together to check for accuracy. Encourage students to give reasons for coin selection.

- Say: *I notice that all the ways to make 47¢ have at least 2 pennies. Is it possible to make 47¢ with fewer than 2 pennies? Explain.* Students should notice there are many ways to make 45¢, including with pennies, but you will always need 2 pennies to get from 45¢ to 47¢.

Try It

- Read **Try It** together and have students complete the problem independently. Discuss and verify solutions.

5 **Solution**
85 cents; Possible solution: 3 quarters and 1 dime

Note: You may wish to have play coins available for students to handle and count. Hundreds charts can help them develop counting strategies for adding coin values.

Ready Mathematics
PRACTICE AND PROBLEM SOLVING

Assign *Practice and Problem Solving* **pages 253–254** after students have completed this section.

Modeled and Guided Instruction

At A Glance

Students use a tape diagram, bar model, and open number lines to solve a word problem involving denominations of bills. Then students revisit this problem, writing equations and determining the bills needed to represent the solution.

Step By Step

- Read the problem at the top of the page as a class. Ask students to describe the problem and explain what they need to find out.

Model It

- Ask students to explain how the tape diagram in **Model It** relates to Step 1 of the problem. Then ask how the bar model relates to Step 2.

▶ **Mathematical Discourse 1**

- Discuss how the bar model indicates that a part is missing. Ask: *What equations could we write to find the missing part?* [45 + ? = 100; 100 − 45 = ?]

Model It

- Have students examine the open number lines in **Model It** and describe what they are showing. Then ask the Mathematical Discourse question 2 to help students compare both **Model Its**.

▶ **Mathematical Discourse 2**

- Use the Hands-On Activity to provide students another alternative for counting bills.

▶ **Hands-On Activity**

Learn About Solving Word Problems About Money

Read the problem. Then you will explore ways to solve it.

> Liam had a $100 bill. Kane had two $20 bills and one $5 bill. Kane got more bills for his birthday. Then he had the same amount of money as Liam. How much money did Kane get for his birthday?

▶ **Model It** **You can make a tape diagram and a bar model.**

Step 1: Kane had two $20 bills and one $5 bill.

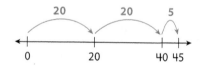

Step 2: Kane got some more bills. Then he had $100.

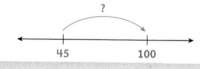

▶ **Model It** **You can use open number lines.**

Step 1: Kane had two $20 bills and one $5 bill.

Step 2: Kane got some more bills. Then he had $100.

230

▶ **Mathematical Discourse**

1 *In the bar model, why is the whole 100?*

The whole shows the total amount that Kane has after he gets some money for his birthday. Kane's total amount is supposed to be the same as the amount that Liam has, which is $100.

2 *How are both Model Its on this page alike?*

They both show that you first add what Kane has. He has $45. Since he is supposed to get to $100, the missing part in each model shows how much more he needs to get from 45 to 100.

▶ **Hands-On Activity**

Show bill amounts on a grid.

Materials: 10 × 10 grid cut from Activity Sheet 10 (Half-Inch Grid Paper) and colored pencils or crayons

- Ask: *If one of the squares on the grid is one dollar, what might represent a ten dollar bill?* [a row or column of 10 squares] *A five dollar bill?* [half of a row of ten or a group of 5 squares] *A twenty dollar bill?* [two rows of ten]

- Show students how to trace around two rows of ten and lightly shade them to represent a $20 bill. Have them write 20 in that block. Then repeat for a group of 5.

- Ask students how they could use the grid to find how many $5, $10, and $20 bills they could use to get to $100. Discuss the various strategies students may use to calculate.

▶ **Connect It** Use the models to solve the problem.

6 What do you find in Step 1?

how much money Kane had to start

7 Write an addition equation for Step 1.

__20__ + __20__ + __5__ = __45__

8 How much money did Kane have after his birthday? How do you know?

He had $100. I know because after his birthday, he had the same

amount of money as Liam.

9 What do you find in Step 2?

how much money Kane got for his birthday

10 Write a subtraction equation for Step 2.

__100__ − __45__ = __55__

11 How much money did Kane get for his birthday? __$55__

Draw a set of bills that he could have received.

Possible answer: one $50 bill and one $5 bill;
five $10 bills and one $5 bill

▶ **Try It** Try another problem.

12 Izzy has two $10 bills and three $5 bills. Matt has two $5 bills and a $20 bill. Who has more money? How much more? Show your work.

Izzy has $5 more than Matt. Izzy: 10 + 10 + 5 + 5 + 5 = 35;

Matt: 5 + 5 + 20 = 30; 35 − 30 = 5

231

▶ **Mathematical Discourse**

3 *Jordan says, "I have 9 bills and Trina only has 3 bills, so I have more money." Is Jordan right?*

Students should realize that Jordan just compared the two numbers shown without paying attention to the value of the bills. Because we don't know the denomination of the bills, we don't have enough information to determine who has more money.

Step By Step

Connect It

- Tell students that **Connect It** will help them learn how to write equations for the problem on the previous page.

- Work through the problems together. Note that in Problem 7, the addends may be ordered in any way.

- For Problem 10, remind students that subtraction is one way to solve. Ask if they prefer to use addition or subtraction and why. For some students, counting up may make more sense or be easier to think about.

- Have students draw open rectangles with the denomination written in each one to represent the bills in Problem 11.

▶ **Mathematical Discourse 3**

SMP TIP Attend to Precision
Discuss with students the importance of accurate calculations in counting money and how failure to count correctly can negatively affect them. Have students discuss situations where not counting accurately can pose a problem, such as planning to purchase something and finding at the checkout stand that you don't have enough money. *(SMP 6)*

Try It

12 **Solution**
Izzy has $5 more; 10 + 10 + 5 + 5 + 5 = 35; 20 + 5 + 5 = 30; 35 − 30 = 5.

▣ **Ready** **Mathematics**
PRACTICE AND PROBLEM SOLVING

Assign *Practice and Problem Solving* **pages 255–256** after students have completed this section.

Guided Practice

At A Glance

Students solve problems involving coins and bills.

Step By Step

- Ask students to solve the problems individually and show all their work, including any equations they write.

- Problem 14 refers to "getting change." Discuss with students what this means. Explain that you may not always have the exact amount of money to pay for an item. When you give the store clerk too much, he or she gives you back the difference between the cost and what you gave.

- **Pair/Share** When students have completed each problem, have them Pair/Share to discuss their solutions with a partner.

Solutions

Example Models are shown to represent the problem, and a subtraction equation is used to solve.

13 Solution
Possible answers: 20 + 5; 10 + 10 + 5; 20 + 1 + 1 + 1 + 1 + 1; 10 + 5 + 5 + 5
DOK 2

Practice Solving Word Problems About Money

Study the model below. Then solve Problems 13–15.

Example

Paige has two quarters, one dime, and one nickel. Andre has six dimes. Which set of coins is worth more? How much more?

You can show your work with models.

Paige	25		25		10	5
Andre	10	10	10	10	10	10

$$65 - 60 = 5$$

Answer Paige's set of coins is worth 5¢ more than Andre's.

13 Anthony has $25 in bills. Name two ways he could have $25.

Show your work.

Possible work: 20 + 5 = 25

10 + 10 + 1 + 1 + 1 + 1 + 1 = 25

Think about ways you could use $1, $5, $10, and $20 bills to add up to $25.

Answer Possible answer: one $20 bill and one $5

bill; two $10 bills and five $1 bills

232

Teacher Notes

---

14 A pen costs 35¢. Logan paid with two quarters. What coins could Logan get back as change?

Show your work.

Possible work: $25 + 25 = 50$

$50 - 35 = 15$

$10 + 5 = 15$

10¢ is a dime; 5¢ is a nickel

What are two quarters worth? How do you figure out the change Logan should get?

Answer Possible answer: a dime and a nickel

---

15 Johanna has these coins in her pocket.

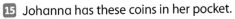

How much are the coins worth?

Try skip counting to find the total.

A 8¢

B 40¢

C 80¢

D \$2

Mary chose **C** as the answer. This answer is wrong. How did Mary get her answer?

Possible answer: She counted the coins as dimes instead of nickels.

233

Solutions

14 **Solution**

Possible answer: a dime and a nickel; $25 + 25 = 50$, $50 - 35 = 15$, $10 + 5 = 15$.

DOK 2

15 **Solution**

B; Eight groups of 5 is 40.

Explain to students why the other two choices are not correct:

A is not correct because 8 represents the number of coins, not their value.

D is not correct because a nickel is 5 cents, not 25 cents.

DOK 3

Ready Mathematics
PRACTICE AND PROBLEM SOLVING

Assign *Practice and Problem Solving* **pages 257–258** after students have completed this section.

Teacher Notes

👤 Independent Practice

At A Glance

Students solve problems involving coins and bills that might appear on a mathematics test.

Solutions

1 **Solution**
C; 25 + 10 + 10 + 10 + 5 + 5 + 1 + 1 = 67.
DOK 1

2 **Solution**
B; 75 − 68 = 7, 5 + 2 = 7.
DOK 2

3 **Solution**
a. **True;** b. **False;** a nickel is worth 5 pennies; c. **True;** d. **True**
DOK 2

Practice **Solving Word Problems About Money**

Solve the problems.

1 What is the total value of these coins?
Circle the correct answer.

A 52¢   (C) 67¢

B 62¢   D 77¢

2 A bookmark costs 68¢. Haley uses 3 quarters to pay for it. Which coins should she get back in change?
Circle the correct answer.

A

(B)

C

D

3 Circle *True* or *False* for each statement.

a. A dime is worth the same as ten pennies.	(True)	False
b. A nickel is worth the same as two dimes.	True	(False)
c. A quarter is worth the same as five nickels.	(True)	False
d. A quarter is worth the same as two dimes and one nickel.	(True)	False

234

Quick Check and Remediation

- Isadora has 2 quarters, 2 dimes, 3 nickels, and 4 pennies. How much money does she have? [89¢]

- For students who are still struggling, use the chart to guide remediation.

- After providing remediation, check students' understanding using the following problem: Tony has 77¢. What coins could he have? [Possible answers include: 3 quarters, 2 pennies; 2 quarters, 2 dimes, 7 pennies; 2 quarters, 2 dimes, 1 nickel, 2 pennies]

If the error is ...	Students may ...	To remediate ...
79¢	have calculated the quarters as 20¢ rather than 25¢.	Remind students that a quarter is 25¢ and have them calculate again.
11¢	have added the number of coins rather than their values.	Show students 3 hundreds blocks, 4 tens blocks, and 2 ones blocks. Ask students if the blocks show a total of 9 ones. Students should recognize that the blocks show more than 9 ones. Relate this to the values of coins and how many cents they are worth. Review the value of each coin in the problem and help students add the values.
any other number	have calculated the value of the coins incorrectly.	To assess the error, have the student show you how the coins were counted. If the error is simple calculation, have the student recount to find the error. If the error involves coin values, review the value of each coin in the problem and have the student solve again.

4 Which set of coins is worth 31¢?
Circle all the correct answers.

A

B

C

D

5 Tess has more than three bills. They have a total value of $30. What bills could Tess have?

Show your work.

Possible work: 10 + 10 + 5 + 5 = 30

Possible answer: She could have two $10 bills and two $5 bills.

6 Jim answers Problem 5. He says Tess could have four $10 bills. Do you agree? Explain why or why not.

I don't agree. Possible answer: 10 + 10 + 10 + 10 = 40, but Tess only

has $30. So Tess could not have four $10 bills.

✓ **Self Check** **Now you can solve problems using money. Fill this in on the progress chart on page 153.**

235

Solutions

4 **Solution**
B 25 + 5 + 1 = 31; **C** 25 + 6 = 31;
D 10 + 10 + 5 + 5 + 1 = 31.
DOK 1

5 **Solution**
Possible answers: 10 + 10 + 5 + 5; 10 + 5 + 5 + 5 + 5; 10 + 10 + 5 + 1 + 1 + 1 + 1 + 1
DOK 2

6 **Solution**
Tess could not have four $10 bills; 10 + 10 + 10 + 10 = 40, but Tess has only $30.
DOK 3

▶ Hands-On Activity

Race for a dollar.

Materials: For each pair or group: a number cube and play coins

- Organize students into pairs or groups of three.

- Have students take turns rolling the number cube and taking the amount of money matching the number rolled.

- On a player's turn, sets of coins may be exchanged for a single coin of equal value.

- Have players check each other's exchanges to make sure they are accurate.

- Play continues until the value of a player's coins reaches one dollar. Have players count the coins together to make sure one dollar has been reached.

▶ Challenge Activity

Make change.

Materials: For each pair: play coins, play one dollar bills, and cards cut from Activity Sheet 15 (Money Amount Cards)

- Have students work in pairs.

- One student is the "cashier" and the other is the "customer."

- The customer gives the cashier a card with the cost of an item written on it and an amount of money that is more than the cost. The cashier counts back the change.

- Challenge students to find easy ways to count back the change. You may want them to record the strategies they use.

Lesson 25
Solve Word Problems Involving Money

Teacher-Toolbox.com

Overview

Assign the Lesson 25 Quiz and have students work independently to complete it.

Use the results of the quiz to assess students' understanding of the content of the lesson and to identify areas for reteaching. See the Lesson Pacing Guide at the beginning of the lesson for suggested instructional resources.

Tested Skills

Assesses 2.MD.C.8

Problems on this assessment form require students to be able to recognize the value of the coins penny, nickel, dime, and quarter, and paper bills of different denominations (using the correct $ and ¢ notation), write the value of a set of coins or bills, and write the coins or bills needed to equal a given or calculated value (e.g., determine the coins/bills needed to equal a calculated amount of change). Students will also need to be familiar with skip counting by 5s, 10s, 20s, and 25s, and fluently adding within 100.

Ready® Mathematics
Lesson 25 **Quiz**

Solve the problems.

1 Use the numbers in the box to help Anna skip count her money. Not all of the numbers will be used.

55	35	15	67	20	40	70

10 ___ 30 ___ 50 ___ 60 65 66 ___

2 Nick says that the value of these bills is $5.

Explain what Nick did wrong.

_____

_____

_____

Lesson 25 Quiz continued

3 Sue buys a basketball for $14. She pays for it with a $20 bill. Which sets of bills could Sue get back as change?

Circle all the correct answers.

A two $5 bills and four $1 bills   **C** one $5 bill and one $1 bill

B six $1 bills   **D** one $10 bill and six $1 bills

4 Chuck wants to buy a pen that costs 99¢. He has these coins.

How much more money does Chuck need to buy the pen?

Answer: Chuck needs _____ ¢.

5 Jonah buys a balloon for 33¢. He pays with two quarters. Jonah receives exactly 5 coins as change.

How many of each coin will Jonah get back in change?

Write a number from the box in each blank. Not all of the numbers will be used.

0	2	3	1	5	4

_____   _____   _____

Common Misconceptions and Errors

Errors may result if students:

• add the number of coins/bills instead of the value of the coins/bills.

• confuse the different coins/bills or the values of the different coins/bills.

• incorrectly skip count by 5s, 10s, 20s, or 25s.

• make an addition or subtraction error or use the incorrect operation.

Ready® **Mathematics**

Lesson 25 Quiz Answer Key

1. 20, 40, 55, 67
DOK 1

2. Possible explanation: Nick has 5 bills. He counted the bills by 1s, but each has a value of $10, not $1. He should count by 10s: $10 + 10 + 10 + 10 + 10 = 50$. Nick has $50.
DOK 3

3. B, C
DOK 2

4. 41
DOK 2

5. 0 dimes, 3 nickels, 2 pennies
DOK 2

CCSS Focus

Domain
Measurement and Data

Clusters
2.MD.A Measure and estimate lengths in standard units.
2.MD.B Relate addition and subtraction to length.
2.MD.C Work with time and money.

Standards
2.MD.A.1, 2.MD.A.4, 2.MD.B.5, 2.MD.C.8

Standards for Mathematical Practice (SMP)

1 Make sense of problems and persevere in solving them.

3 Construct viable arguments and critique the reasoning of others.

4 Model with mathematics.

Additional SMPs
2, 5, 6, 7

Lesson at a Glance

Students apply skills from the unit to solve real-world problems related to making crafts from recycled items. Problems involve measuring length, adding and subtracting length measurements, making and interpreting a line plot or bar graph, adding money amounts, and determining coin values.

Lesson Pacing Guide

Whole Class Instruction

Day 1
45–60 minutes

Introduction
Problem and Solution *45 min*

Task	**Key Skills**	**Mathematical Practices**
Analyze a solution to a problem about ways to decorate a box with buttons given measurements of the box and buttons.	• Understand how to measure with a ruler. • Understand addition equations. • Understand how a diagram represents a situation.	• Model with mathematics. • Use a ruler to measure length. • Critique a given solution.

Day 2
45–60 minutes

Modeled and Guided Instruction
Try Another Approach
Plan It *15 min* • Solve It *20 min* • Reflect *10 min*

Task	**Key Skills**	**Mathematical Practices**
Use another approach to find ways to decorate a box with buttons given measurements of the box and buttons.	• Use a ruler to measure length. • Draw a diagram to represent a situation. • Write and solve addition equations.	• Use a tool. • Persevere in solving a problem. • Check that the solution works.

Day 3
45–60 minutes

Guided Practice
Discuss Models and Strategies
Plan It and Solve It *35 min* • Reflect *10 min*

Task	**Key Skills**	**Mathematical Practices**
Measure lengths, organize them in a line plot or bar graph, and find the difference between the shortest and longest lengths.	• Compare length measurements. • Make and interpret a line plot or bar graph.	• Organize information. • Use an appropriate tool. • Precisely specify units of measure.

Whole Class Instruction continued

Day 4
45–60 minutes

Independent Practice

Persevere on Your Own

Problem 1

Solve It *35 min* • Reflect *10 min*

Task	**Key Skills**	**Mathematical Practices**
Decide how many wooden items to buy using given criteria about the amount of available money and the item prices.	• Add money amounts. • Add two-digit numbers. • Determine a group of coins with a given value.	• Make sense of the problem. • Look for structure to determine the value of money. • Reason quantitatively.

Day 5
45–60 minutes

Independent Practice

Persevere on Your Own

Problem 2

Solve It *35 min* • Reflect *10 min*

Task	**Key Skills**	**Mathematical Practices**
Determine the lengths of two parts of a border using given criteria about the total length and the lengths of each part.	• Add length measurements. • Subtract length measurements. • Write an addition or subtraction equation to represent a situation.	• Make sense of the problem. • Construct an argument to justify choices. • Write an equation to model a situation.

Unit Resources

Practice
Practice and Problem Solving

Grade 2
• Unit 3 Game
• Unit 3 Practice
• Unit 3 Performance Task
• Unit 3 Vocabulary

Assess
Ready Instruction

Grade 2
• Unit 3 Interim Assessment

👥 Introduction

Unit 3
MATH IN
ACTION

👥 Introduction

Use Measurement

SMP1 **Make sense
of problems and
persevere in
solving them.**

At A Glance

Students examine a problem that uses measurement and design to determine how many buttons to put on each edge of a pencil box. The math involves measuring and understanding units of measurement. Students discuss the problem to understand what it is asking and brainstorm different approaches. Then they refer to a **Problem-Solving Checklist** to analyze a sample solution and identify what makes it a good solution.

Step By Step

- Read the problem out loud with students. Invite a volunteer to describe the illustrations.

▶ **Mathematical Discourse 1**

▶ **Hands-On Activity**

- Discuss the measurements in the problem. Elicit that the button's width is unknown. Discuss what to do about that.

▶ **Mathematical Discourse 2**

- Invite volunteers to rephrase what Bella wants to do. Ask clarifying questions such as: *Why do you think Bella wrote how long each side is?* [to know how many buttons would fit] *Do you think she will need more than 4 buttons? Why?* [Yes; There are 4 sides so there would only be one button on each side.] *Do you think she will put the same number of buttons on each side?* [She can, but she might use fewer on the shorter sides.]

- Invite students to share their ideas about how they might plan their design. [For example, put one button in each corner, make a solid line of buttons, use different colors, and so forth. Although color is irrelevant, a student who mentions color is engaged in imagining the end result. Validate all contributions.] Allow them to describe different approaches without carrying through with an actual solution yet.

▶ **Mathematical Discourse 3**

Study an Example Problem and Solution

Read this problem about measuring in centimeters. Then look at Bella's solution to the problem.

Buttons

Bella saves buttons to decorate things she makes. Bella wants to glue some buttons on the front of a pencil box. Each button is the same width.

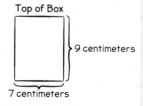

- Put buttons in a line around all 4 edges.
- The buttons do not have to touch.
- Measure the button to help you plan.

Top of Box

9 centimeters

7 centimeters

How can Bella decorate the pencil box? Draw a picture. Tell how many buttons she needs.

Show how Bella's solution matches the checklist.

🖉 Problem-Solving Checklist

- ☐ Tell what is known.
- ☐ Tell what the problem is asking.
- ☐ Show all your work.
- ☐ Show that the solution works.

- **a. Circle** something that is known.
- **b. Underline** something that you need to find.
- **c. Draw a box around** what you do to solve the problem.
- **d. Put a checkmark** next to the part that shows the solution works.

▶ Mathematical Discourse

1 *Where in this problem can you find what the problem is asking? How do you know?*

Students should connect "asking" to the idea of a question and the use of a question mark. Then they can use context to identify the sentences that specify what they need to find out.

2 *Describe how you would find the width of the button.*

Students should suggest measuring the button. They should recognize that the button should be measured using the same units that Bella used to measure the front of the box and explain why this is important.

3 *What are some different ways you could plan the design?*

Students may come up with a variety of approaches. For example: have the buttons touch, put equal space between the buttons, put unequal space between the buttons, have the same number of buttons on each side, etc.

▶ Hands-On Activity

Sort objects according to size.

Materials: a variety of buttons, centimeter ruler

Give pairs of students about 12 buttons of different sizes. Have students measure the buttons using a centimeter ruler, sort them into 3 groups: less than 1 centimeter, exactly one centimeter, and more than 1 centimeter. Ask, *How are your buttons different from Bella's?* [Bella's are all the same size.] This activity can help students understand that the uniformity of Bella's buttons is a key part of the problem.

Bella's Solution

Hi, I'm Bella. Here's how I solved this problem.

▷ **First, I can measure the button.**
It is 1 centimeter wide.

▷ **I need 4 lines of buttons.**
I'll put 1 centimeter of space between the buttons.

▷ **I can make a drawing to show my thinking.**
- Start with the long sides.
- Draw and count 9 centimeters.
- Then make the top and bottom numbers.
- Draw and count 7 centimeters.

I made a drawing to help me solve the problem.

I checked my work by adding.

Both sides have 5 buttons and 4 spaces. 5 + 4 = 9

The bottom and top each have 4 buttons and 3 spaces.
4 + 3 = 7

9 centimeters and 7 centimeters match the drawing.

▷ **I can count all the buttons to see how many I need.**
There are 14 buttons.

237

At A Glance

- Read through Bella's solution together, one section at a time. Read for understanding, helping students with any language challenges.

- Point out that the speech bubbles tell what Bella was thinking about as she wrote her solution. Read through the speech bubbles, and help students see how Bella is "talking to us" about what she wrote.

- Discuss the sample solution with students. Have them describe the design that the solution uses. [1 centimeter between the buttons.] Elicit ideas for other designs.

▶ **Mathematical Discourse 4**

- Discuss the diagram and the equations that accompany it. Have students explain how these help to understand the buttons and spaces.

▶ **Mathematical Discourse 5**

- Then, as a class, go back to do a close read, using the **Problem-Solving Checklist** to help analyze Bella's solution.

▶ **Mathematical Discourse 6**

- Remind students that a very good answer will include all the things on the checklist. Work through each part of the checklist with them. Help students recognize that the lengths of the sides are part of what is known. The size of the button is one of the things Bella needed to find out. She showed her work with the drawing and the addition equations. She checked her work by comparing the equations to the drawing.

- Tell students that since this is a good answer, they can look at it to get ideas when they write their own answers for this problem.

▶ **Visual Model**

SMP TIP Model with Mathematics
Prompt students to look for connections between the addition equations and the diagram. Have them describe what part of the diagram each number represents. *(SMP 4)*

▶ **Mathematical Discourse**

4 *What would happen to the design if you decided to use more space between the buttons? Less space? Explain.*

Listen for responses that show recognition that more space leads to fewer buttons and less space leaves room for more buttons on each side. Ensure that students realize that there could be no space left between buttons, or different amounts of space between them.

5 *How do the equations represent the buttons and the spaces?*

Students should recognize that 7 and 9 represent the width and height, respectively, of the pencil box. The addends represent the buttons and the 1-centimeter spaces between them. The sum of the widths of the buttons and the spaces represents an edge of the box.

6 *How do you know this solution works?*

Responses should indicate that the buttons and spaces on each side use up the entire length of that side.

▶ **Visual Model**

Use grid paper to model a design.

Materials: grid paper, pencils

- Have students outline a rectangle 9 squares tall and 7 squares wide to represent the pencil box. Have students count the squares across the top [7] and down one side [9].

- Students can shade a square to represent a button. Have students model the sample solution and compare their model with the sample.

Modeled and Guided Instruction

At A Glance

Students plan and solve the Buttons problem from the Introduction using a different design. Students demonstrate that the problem has more than one solution.

Step By Step

- Review and summarize the steps in Bella's solution. [Measure the button. Decide to use 1 centimeter between the buttons. Draw the design and write equations to make sure it works. Count the buttons.]

▶ **Mathematical Discourse 1**

- Have students brainstorm some different steps than these that they might use to solve the problem. For example, they might decide not to use any spaces, or they might start by reasoning that they can use 7 or fewer buttons on each side.

Plan It

- Read the **Plan It** question aloud. Invite students to share some initial responses. Record on the board information they find useful, using words or pictures.

▶ **English Language Learners**

- Have students work independently to write an answer to the **Plan It** question. Tell students they will use their answers along with the **Problem-Solving Tips** on the next page to plan their answer.

- As students work on their plan, circulate to provide support and answer questions.

- Remind students that this problem has many correct answers. Using no spaces between buttons is just one choice they could make.

▶ **Mathematical Discourse 2**

Try Another Approach

There are many ways to solve problems. Think about how you might solve the Buttons problem in a different way.

Buttons

Bella saves buttons to decorate things she makes. Bella wants to glue some buttons on the front of a pencil box. Each button is the same width.

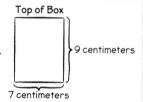

- Put buttons in a line around all 4 edges.
- The buttons do not have to touch.
- Measure the button to help you plan.

Top of Box

9 centimeters

7 centimeters

How can Bella decorate the pencil box? Draw a picture. Tell how many buttons she needs.

▶ **Plan It Answer this question to help you start thinking about a plan.**

The example answer has spaces between each button. How could you make a design with no space between the buttons?

_____

_____

_____

238

▶ **Mathematical Discourse**

1 *Bella's solution has 5 buttons on each side and 4 buttons on top and bottom. Why isn't that a total of 18 buttons?*

You can't count the corner buttons twice. For example, the same button that is at the top of the left column of 5 buttons is also the first button in the row of 4 buttons along the top.

2 *How could you write an equation to show that your design works?*

Encourage students to express their ideas mathematically. Depending on their design plan, their equations will vary.

▶ **English Language Learners**

Discuss the difference between "space" and "no space." Invite students to position two books on a desk with space between them and then with no space between them.

▶ **Solve It** Find a different solution for the Buttons problem. Show all your work on a separate sheet of paper.

You may want to use the problem-solving tips to get started.

Problem-Solving Tips

- **Tools**

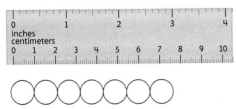

Problem-Solving Checklist

Make sure that you . . .
- ☐ tell what you know.
- ☐ tell what you need to do.
- ☐ show all your work.
- ☐ show that the solution works.

- **Word Bank**

length	ruler	centimeter
measure	count	add

- **Sentence Starters**
  - I can draw _____
  - I can use a ruler _____

▶ **Reflect**

Use Mathematical Practices Talk about this question with a partner.

- **Persevere** What can you do if you get to a difficult part of the problem?

239

Scoring Rubric

Points	Expectations
4	The student's response is accurate and complete. The design, measurements, solution steps, and any calculations are complete, well explained, and correct. The illustration and its explanation are complete and show understanding of the problem and solution.
3	The student has made limited minor errors. The solution is adequate but not detailed. Solution steps, calculations, and measurements are correct. The design and illustration may not be clearly explained. The illustration may not fully reflect the design. The number of buttons is correct for the design shown.
2	The student's response contains several errors. The description and design may not reflect the task. Some measurements may be inaccurate. The number of buttons appears to be correct for the design shown.
1	The solution is incorrect. The plan and design do not match the task requirements. Measurements are inaccurate. The number of buttons is incorrect for the design shown.

Unit 3 Math in Action

Step By Step

Solve It

- Introduce the **Problem-Solving Tips** as ideas students may use to explain their thinking when they write their solution.

- Invite students to share ideas about how they might use one of the models shown. Ask if there are other words that might be useful. Solicit suggestions for how they might complete each of the sentence starters.

- Discuss the **Reflect** question about using Mathematical Practices. [For example, you can try a different model, or try a different plan, or you can discuss it with a partner.]

- Then have students write their own solutions. Encourage them to work out their ideas on scrap paper and try different approaches as necessary. Have students write their complete solution on a copy of Activity Sheet 23 (Solution Sheet 2) or a blank sheet of paper.

- If time permits, selected students can explain their solutions to the class. Alternatively, you can share the solutions below and invite the class to discuss make comments.

Possible Solution

The button is 1 centimeter wide. I need to put buttons around the edge of the box front and tell how many I need. I will make the buttons touch, with no space between.

I can use a ruler to draw the box. There is room for 7 buttons along the top and bottom and 9 along each side.

Count the buttons but only count the corners once. There are 28 buttons.

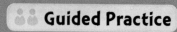

Guided Practice

At A Glance

With **Problem-Solving Tips** as support, students understand, plan, and solve an open-ended, multi-step problem. They choose appropriate models and strategies to solve the problem, checking their thinking with a partner.

Step By Step

- Read the problem aloud with students. As you read, encourage students to ask clarifying questions about the information given and what they need to find.

- Direct students' attention to the lengths of wood. Have students discuss their observations.

▶ **Mathematical Discourse 1**

- Discuss the list of tasks. Invite students to explain how they can find the information Bella wants.

▶ **Mathematical Discourse 2**

- Ask students to discuss with a partner some possible approaches to solving the problem.

- Have both inch rulers and 1-inch squares available for students to use. Also discuss whether students plan to use exact measurement or estimation.

> **SMP TIP Use Tools**
> Allow students to choose their own measuring tool. Understanding the appropriate tool for a task involves important mathematical thinking. *(SMP 5)*

▶ **Mathematical Discourse 3 and 4**

Discuss ▶ Models and Strategies

Solve the problem on a separate sheet of paper. There are different ways you can solve it.

Wood Scraps

Bella saves scraps of wood to reuse. She wants you to find:

- the length of each piece in inches.
- how many pieces there are of each length.
- the length of the shortest and longest pieces.
- the difference between the shortest and longest pieces.

a
b
c
d
e
f
g
h

How can Bella organize the data?

240

▶ Mathematical Discourse

1 *What are some ways you can describe these scraps of wood?*
   Students may notice that there are 8 pieces in 4 different lengths. They may identify shortest and longest pieces.

2 *How will you know which pieces of wood are longest or shortest?*
   First measure each piece and then compare the lengths.

3 *Explain why you would use a line plot or a bar graph to organize the data.*
   Listen for descriptions of similarities and differences between these two representations.

4 *What else might help you organize the data?*
   Students may wish to make a list of the different lengths before making their line plot or bar graph.

▶ **Plan It and Solve It** Find a solution to Bella's **Wood Scraps problem.**

Make sure to do all parts of the task.

• Measure each piece of wood.
• Organize the data in a line plot or bar graph.
• Use words to describe the lengths of the scraps of wood.

You may want to use the problem-solving tips to get started.

Problem-Solving Tips

● **Questions**

• What tool should I use to measure?
• How will I show the data?

Problem-Solving Checklist

Make sure that you . . .

☐ tell what you know.
☐ tell what you need to do.
☐ show all your work.
☐ show that the solution works.

● **Word Bank**

length	longer	shorter
difference	inches	longest
shortest	compare	

● **Sentence Starters**

• The length of _____

• The longest piece _____

▶ **Reflect**

Use Mathematical Practices Talk about this question with a partner.

• **Use Tools** How can you decide what measuring tool to use?

241

Scoring Rubric

Points	Expectations
4	The student's response is accurate and complete. The difference between the longest and shortest lengths is correct. The line plot or bar graph is complete and correctly reflects the data.
3	The student has attempted all measurements and data displays but has made limited minor errors. The solution is substantially complete and reflects the information given. Measurements are correct. Solution steps are correct but some work may be missing. The line plot or bar graph may be missing a title or label.
2	The student's response contains several errors. Most measurements are correct. Solution steps are incomplete and may not reflect the tasks. The line plot or bar graph has some inaccurate information and is missing titles and/or labels.
1	The solution is incorrect. Many measurements are incorrect. Solution steps are incomplete and the data has errors. The difference between the longest and shortest lengths is incorrect. The line plot or bar graph is incorrect or missing.

Step By Step

Plan It and Solve It

• Discuss the **Problem-Solving Tips** as ideas students may use to explain their thinking when they write their solution.

• Invite students to share ideas about answers to the questions, other words they might use, and how they might complete the sentences.

• Put students in pairs to discuss solution ideas. Ask them to also discuss the **Reflect** question about Mathematical Practices. Remind students that there are always different ways to answer these questions.

• Discuss a variety of approaches as a class.

• When students are confident that their plans make sense, tell them to write a complete solution on a copy of Activity Sheet 23 (Solution Sheet 2) or a blank sheet of paper.

• If time permits, share and discuss student solutions or the one below.

Possible Solution

I need to measure each wood scrap and find how many pieces there are of each length. I need to find the shortest and longest lengths and find the difference. I also need to describe the lengths in words and organize the information in some way. I will use a line plot. First, make a table of the lengths to help.

Piece	A	B	C	D	E	F	G	H
Length (inches)	6	5	4	6	5	3	6	4

Three pieces are 6 inches long. Two are 5 inches long. Two are 4 inches long. One is 3 inches long. The shortest piece is 3 inches and the longest is 6 inches. The difference between them is 3 inches.

Lengths of Wood Scraps

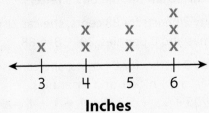

Inches

Independent Practice

At A Glance

Students find and share solutions to multi-step, open-ended problems.

Step By Step

▶ Solve It

- Have students use their plan to begin solving the problem. Encourage them to work out their ideas and note any questions or difficulties they encounter.

- Then put students in pairs to discuss their preliminary solutions. When they are confident that their plan will work, have students independently write their solutions on a copy of Activity Sheet 22 (Solution Sheet 1) or a blank sheet of paper.

- After students complete their solutions, put them in pairs to discuss the **Reflect** question about Mathematical Practices.

- If time permits, invite various students to explain their solutions for the class to discuss, compare, and critique. Alternatively, share the solution below and invite the class to discuss.

Possible Solution

I know that hearts cost 44¢ each and letters cost 28¢ each. I have to decide how many Bella will buy. She has 1 dollar for hearts and 1 dollar for letters.

I think she should buy as many as possible. 2 hearts cost 44 + 44 = 88 cents. 3 hearts cost 88 + 44 = 132 cents, which is more than 1 dollar. So she should buy 2 hearts.

2 letters cost 28 + 28 = 56 cents. 3 letters cost 56 + 28 = 84 cents. 4 letters cost 56 + 56 = 112 cents, which is more than 1 dollar. So she should buy 3 letters.

To buy 2 hearts for 88 cents, she can use 8 dimes and 8 pennies. 80 + 8 = 88.

To buy 3 letters for 84 cents, she can use 3 quarters, 1 nickel, and 4 pennies. 25 + 25 + 25 + 5 + 1 + 1 + 1 + 1 = 84.

Persevere ▶ **On Your Own**

Solve the problem on a separate sheet of paper.

Craft Supplies

Bella likes to recycle items for her projects. But she still has to buy some things. Bella wants to buy some wooden hearts and some wooden letters. She can spend up to $1 on hearts and up to $1 on letters.

Wooden hearts: 44¢ each   **Wooden letters: 28¢ each**

How many hearts and letters can Bella buy?

▶ Solve It   Help Bella decide what to buy.

- Tell how many hearts and letters to buy.
- Give the cost for the hearts and for the letters.
- Name a group of coins she could use to buy hearts.
- Name a group of coins she could use to buy letters.

▶ Reflect

Use Mathematical Practices Talk about this question with a partner.

- **Use Structure** How did you use the values of coins to solve the problem?

242

Scoring Rubric

Points	Expectations
4	The solution is accurate and complete. Student uses equations to verify the solution. The coins are correct for the quantities used.
3	The student has attempted all parts of the problem but has made limited minor errors. The solution is substantially complete and reflects the information given. Some work may not be shown or one of the cost may be more than $1. Calculations are correct and the coins are correct for the quantities given.
2	The solution contains several errors. The number of hearts and/or letters used has a cost of more than $1. Some calculations are either set up or added incorrectly. The coins for hearts and/or letters are incorrect for the quantities given.
1	The solution is incomplete and inaccurate. Calculations are incorrect. The coins are incorrect for the quantities given.

Bella's Bottles

Bella wants to make a garden border.

She will use red and blue recycled bottles to make it.

Read Bella's notes.

My Notes
- The whole border is between 60 and 72 inches.
- Part A is between 45 and 55 inches.
- Part B is between 15 and 25 inches.

Garden

Part A	Part B
Red Bottles	Blue Bottles

How can Bella design her border?

▶ **Solve It** **Help Bella make a plan for her border.**
- Write the length for each part.
- Show all your work.
- Tell why your measurements work.

▶ **Reflect**

Use Mathematical Practices Talk about this question with a partner.

- **Make an Argument** How did you show that your measurements work?

243

▶ **Solve It**

- Have students work through this problem entirely on their own.

- Remind students that there are many different ways to solve a problem.

- Invite them to look back at the **Problem-Solving Checklist** to get started and help them stay on track. They might also want to look at the **Problem-Solving Tips** on other pages to get some ideas for how to start.

- Suggest that students try different numbers or different approaches. Have them write their complete solution on a copy of Activity Sheet 22 (Solution Sheet 1) or a blank sheet of paper.

- After students complete their solutions, put them in pairs to discuss the **Reflect** question about Mathematical Practices. Students may also describe other Math Practices they used.

- If time permits, invite various students to explain their solutions for the class to discuss, compare, and critique. Alternatively, share the solution below and invite the class to discuss.

Possible Solution

The border has 2 parts. Part A is between 45 and 55 inches, Part B is between 15 and 25 inches, and the total has to be between 60 and 72 inches.

Make Part A 50 inches. Try a number between 15 and 25 for Part B.

Try 24. $50 + 24 = 74$, which is greater than 72. Try a smaller number.

Now try 20. $50 + 20 = 70$, which is between 60 and 72. So that solution works.

Part A is 50 inches and Part B is 20 inches.

Scoring Rubric

Points	Expectations
4	The solution is accurate and complete and reflects understanding of the relationship of the parts of the border. Student shows all work and verifies the solution.
3	The student has attempted all parts of the problem but has made limited minor errors. The solution is substantially complete and reflects the information given. Calculations are correct but it is not clear where the numbers come from. The solution is correct.
2	The solution contains several errors. The measurements used do not reflect the problem parameters. Solution steps may not be appropriate for the problem. Some calculations are set up incorrectly and may be calculated incorrectly.
1	The solution is incorrect. The steps are poorly explained and are not appropriate for the problem. Measurements used are also inappropriate. Calculations are incorrect.

Differentiated Instruction

▶ Intervention Activity

Provide support for the Independent Practice.

Craft Supplies

Use hundreds grids to model the 100 cents in each dollar.

Materials: hundreds grids, crayons or pencils in various colors

Have students use a hundreds grid to work out possible solutions. Remind students that $1 is equal to 100 cents. Have students shade 44 grid squares to represent the cost of 1 heart. Ask, *Are there enough squares left to shade 44 more?* [Yes.] Have students shade 44 squares in a different color and ask if they can shade 44 more. [No.]

Repeat the exercise with a fresh hundreds grid but this time shade 28 squares at a time, to represent the wooden letters. Ask students to predict if they will be able to buy fewer, more, or the same number of letters as hearts. [More.]

You may also wish to have students use hundreds grids to figure out what coins to use. They can shade 25 squares to represent one quarter, 10 to represent one dime, 5 for one nickel, and 1 for one penny.

Bella's Bottles

Demonstrate a guess-and-check strategy.

Materials: prepared index cards – 9 cards for Part A, with numbers 46, 47, 48, 49, 50, 51, 52, 53, 54; 9 cards for Part B, with numbers 16, 17, 18, 19 20, 21, 22, 23, 24. Draw a diagram of the two parts of the garden border on a piece of paper.

Use a guess-and-check method to support students for this problem. Have students turn over one card for the length of Part A and one card for the length of Part B. Have students lay each card on the appropriate part of the diagram. Prompt students to combine the lengths (add) to see if the total is between 60 and 72. If it is not, ask how they could change one or both lengths to find numbers that work. Repeat as desired, selecting different cards.

▶ Challenge Activity

Solve extensions to the Independent Practice.

Craft Supplies

Extension

Bella decides to combine her remaining money. How much does she have? Can she buy any more hearts or numbers? If so, what could she buy? What coins could she use?

Possible Solution

Bella had bought 2 hearts for 88 cents, so she has $100 - 88 = 12$ cents left. She got 3 letters for 84 cents, so she has $100 - 84 = 16$ cents left. $12 + 16 = 28$ cents, which is exactly enough to buy one more letter. She could use 2 dimes, 1 nickel, and 3 pennies. $10 + 10 + 5 + 3 = 28$.

Bella's Bottles

Extension

Bella wants to change the border to have 3 parts. Now Part A is between 8 and 12 inches, Part B is between 35 and 45 inches, and Part C is between 15 and 25 inches. The whole garden border is still between 60 and 72 inches.

Write the length for each part. Show all your work. Tell why your measurements work.

Possible Solution

Part A could be 10 inches. Part B could be 40 inches. $10 + 40 = 50$ inches for Parts A and B together. $50 + \underline{\quad}$ has to be greater than 60 inches and less than 72 inches. And Part C has to be between 15 and 25 inches. So try 20 inches. $50 + 20 = 70$, which is greater than 60 and less than 72. So the total works. Part A is 10 inches, Part B is 40 inches, and Part C is 20 inches.

Teacher Notes

Assessment

Solutions

1 **Solution**

Possible answer: 3; 3; 2; 8; 1; 8; 0; 18; 1; 1; 3;
Three quarters have a total value of 75¢;
75 − 57 = 18; Rows should show coins
with a total value of 18¢.
DOK 2

2 **Solution**

4 stars; 7 − 3 = 4
5 dots; 7 + 4 + ? = 16, 11 + ? = 16,
16 − 11 = 5
DOK 2

Solve the problems.

1 Stephanie buys a pen that costs 57¢. She pays
with 3 quarters. Complete the table to show different
ways she could get her change.

Possible answer:

Dimes	Nickels	Pennies
0	3	3
0	2	8
1	0	8
0	0	18
1	1	3

2 Juan counts the paper shapes he has.

- He counts 7 hearts.
- He counts 3 fewer stars than hearts.
- He counts 16 paper shapes in all.

Complete the picture graph to show the paper shapes
Juan has.

Juan's Paper Shapes	
Hearts	♡ ♡ ♡ ♡ ♡ ♡ ♡
Stars	☆ ☆ ☆ ☆
Dots	○ ○ ○ ○ ○

244

Teacher Notes

3 Catelyn has a rope that is 66 inches long. She cuts
it into two pieces. Circle *Yes* or *No* to tell whether each pair
of lengths below could be the lengths of the pieces.

    a. 44 inches and 24 inches   Yes   (No)

    b. 40 inches and 26 inches   (Yes)   No

    c. 35 inches and 32 inches   Yes   (No)

    d. 33 inches and 33 inches   (Yes)   No

4 Which object is about 8 feet long?
Circle the correct answer.

    A math book

    B roller skate

    C football field

    (**D**) cafeteria table

5 The hour hand fell off this clock. Circle *Yes* or *No*
to tell if each time shown below could be the time
shown on the clock.

    a. 3:25   (Yes)   No

    b. 4:05   Yes   (No)

    c. 5:25   (Yes)   No

    d. 6:20   Yes   (No)

245

Solutions

3 **Solution**
a. **No**; 44 + 24 = 68
b. **Yes**; 40 + 26 = 66
c. **No**; 35 + 32 = 67
d. **Yes**; 33 + 33 = 66
DOK 2

4 **Solution**
D; A cafeteria table is the only object
listed that is about 8 feet long.
DOK 2

5 **Solution**
a. **Yes**
b. **No**
c. **Yes**
d. **No**
The minute hand is pointing to the 5,
so the number of minutes after the hour
is 25. The times 3:25 and 5:25 show
25 minutes after the hour.
DOK 2

Teacher Notes

Assessment

Standards: 2.OA.A.1, 2.MD.A.1, 2.MD.A.2, 2.MD.D.9

DOK: 3

Materials: inch and centimeter rulers

Standards for Mathematical Practice
2, 3, 4, 5, 6, 7

Step By Step

About the Task

Students measure the lengths of objects in both inches and centimeters and then display the data on a line plot. Students will use addition to solve problems about the lengths and will explain measuring in different units.

Getting Started

Read the task aloud with students. Review the table and point out the information that needs to be gathered to complete it. You may want to point out some sample objects for measurement and place some parameters on the objects students should measure. You could, for example, limit the lengths of objects to less than the length of one ruler. **(SMP 5)**

Completing the Task

Students first will need to measure the lengths of five objects using both inches and centimeters. Review with students how to use a ruler to measure the length of an object. Point out that the zero mark of the ruler should be placed at one end of the object and then students should find the whole-unit mark nearest the other end of the object. Demonstrate the correct use of the ruler for students who are having trouble with it. Remind students that they will need to measure each object in both inches and centimeters. **(SMP 5)**

Once students have completed the table, they will need to add the measures in both inches and centimeters to find the total lengths of the objects, and then compare the numbers. Encourage students to first compare the numbers in the table for each object. Students should recognize that each

Performance Task

Answer the questions. Show all your work on separate paper.

Measure 5 objects in inches and in centimeters. Make a table like the one below. Write the names of the objects and the lengths in the table.

Object	Length in Inches	Length in Centimeters

- What is the total length of all the objects in inches? What is the total length in centimeters?

- Compare the total lengths. Is there a greater number of centimeters or inches? Explain why.

- Use your measurements to make a line plot like the one below. The line plot can show inches or centimeters.

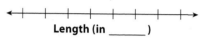

Length (in _____)

▶ **Reflect**

Look for Structure What was different about measuring the objects using inches and measuring them using centimeters? What was the same?

246

number of centimeters is greater than the corresponding number of inches. Guide students to think about the sizes of the units and how that might affect the numbers of inches and centimeters. **(SMP 2, 3, 6, 7)**

Students next need to make a line plot to display their data. Have them copy the line plot onto a separate sheet of paper, and tell them to leave enough space to write a number beneath each hash mark. They should label the scale and write whether the numbers represent inches or centimeters. Remind students that their numbers may differ based on the lengths of the objects they measured. **(SMP 4)**

▶ **Extension**

4-Point Solution

Object	Length in inches	Length in Centimeters
Shoe	7	18
Pencil	6	15
Marker	5	13
Book	11	28
Pencil box	8	20

Total length in inches: 37 inches

Total length in centimeters: 94 centimeters

There is a greater number of centimeters. Centimeters are smaller than inches, so the same length has a greater number of centimeters than inches.

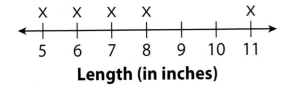

Length (in inches)

Scoring Rubric

Points	Expectations
4	The student's response is accurate and complete, and all calculations are correct. The table of measures is complete, and all measures are correct. The line plot is complete and correct. All explanations are complete and correct, exhibiting an understanding of measuring with different units.
3	The student has completed the table, and all measures are correct. The line plot is correct and complete. The student has attempted all calculations involving the lengths but has made limited minor errors. Explanations are correct, though some might not be complete.
2	The table is not complete, or there are some incorrect measures. The line plot accurately reflects most of the data from the table. The student makes some errors in calculations. Responses show limited understanding of measuring with different units.
1	The table is only partially correctly completed, and the student does not correctly complete the line plot or make calculations involving the lengths. Explanations are missing or incorrect.

▶ **Extension**

Take the performance task further.

Suppose you measured the lengths of the objects instead to the nearest foot and the nearest meter. How would that change the numbers in your table? How would it change your line plot? What does that tell you about which units are better to use when measuring those objects?

Solution

Possible answer: All of the numbers in the middle column of the table would be either 0 or 1, and all of the numbers in the last column of the table would be 0. The line plot would have entries only for 0 and 1. It is better to use the smaller units of inches and centimeters because it tells more about the real lengths of the objects.

Reflect

Possible answer: The number of centimeters was greater than the number of inches. It was easier to find the nearest inch because inches are larger than centimeters. I measured the same way for both units. I lined up one end of the object with the zero mark and then found the nearest whole mark to the other end of the object.

Unit 4 Geometry

Which lessons are students building upon?

Grade 1, Lesson 26
Understand Shapes
1.G.A.1

Grade 1, Lesson 27
Understand Putting Shapes Together
1.G.A.2

Grade 1, Lesson 26
Understand Shapes
1.G.A.1

Grade 1, Lesson 27
Understand Putting Shapes Together
1.G.A.2

Grade 1, Lesson 26
Understand Shapes
1.G.A.1

Grade 1, Lesson 27
Understand Putting Shapes Together
1.G.A.2

Grade 1, Lesson 28
Understand Breaking Shapes
into Parts
1.G.A.3

Unit 4

Lesson 26
Recognize and Draw Shapes
2.G.A.1

Lesson 27
Understand Tiling in Rectangles
2.G.A.2

Lesson 28
Understand Halves, Thirds, and Fourths in Shapes
2.G.A.3

Which lessons are students preparing for?

Grade 3, Lesson 31
Understand Properties of Shapes
3.G.A.1

Grade 3, Lesson 32
Classify Quadrilaterals
3.G.A.1

Grade 3, Lesson 27
Understand Area
3.MD.C.5a, 3.MD.C.5b, 3.MD.C.6

Grade 3, Lesson 31
Understand Properties of Shapes
3.G.A.1

Grade 3, Lesson 33
Divide Shapes Into Parts with Equal Areas
3.G.A.2

Unit 4
Geometry

Unit 4
Geometry

Real-World Connection Look around your classroom. How many shapes can you name? Do you see shapes that you don't know the names of? Can you describe the parts of shapes? Some shapes have straight sides, and some shapes have curves. Some shapes have sides that are all the same length. Others have sides that are different lengths.

In This Unit You will learn the names of shapes and how to describe their parts. You will put shapes together to make new shapes. You will also divide shapes into equal parts.

Let's learn about naming shapes, breaking them apart, and putting them together.

✓ Self Check

Before starting this unit, check off the skills you know below.

I can:	Before this unit	After this unit
recognize and draw different shapes.	☐	☐
break up a rectangle into squares.	☐	☐
divide shapes into equal parts.	☐	☐

Ready Mathematics
PRACTICE AND PROBLEM SOLVING

Practice and Problem Solving Resources

Use the following resources from **Practice and Problem Solving** to engage students and their families and to extend student learning.

- **Family Letters** Send Family Letters home separately before each lesson or as part of a family communication package.

- **Unit Games** Use partner Unit Games at classroom centers and/or send them home for play with family members.

- **Unit Practice** Assign Unit Practice as homework, as independent or small group practice, or for whole class discussion.

- **Unit Performance Tasks** Have students solve real-world Unit Performance Tasks independently or in small groups.

- **Unit Vocabulary** Use Unit Vocabulary throughout the unit to personalize student's acquisition of mathematics vocabulary.

- **Fluency Practice** Assign Fluency Skills Practice and Fluency Repeated Reasoning Practice worksheets throughout the unit.

At A Glance

- This page introduces students to the general ideas behind naming and describing shapes.

- The checklist allows them to see what skills they will be learning and take ownership of their progress.

Step By Step

- Explain to students that they are going to begin a new unit of lessons. Tell them that in all the lessons in this unit they will be learning about naming shapes, breaking them apart, and putting them together.

- Have the class read together the introduction to the unit in their books. Invite and respond to comments and questions, if any.

- Then take a few minutes to have each student independently read through the list of skills.

- Ask students to consider each skill and check the box if it is a skill they think they already have. Remind students that these skills are likely to all be new to them, but it's still possible some students have some of the skills.

- Engage students in a brief discussion about the skills. Invite students to comment on which ones they would most like to learn, or which ones seem similar or related to something they already know. Remind them that the goal is to be able to check off one skill at a time until they have them all checked.

CCSS Focus

Domain
Geometry

Cluster
A. Reason with shapes and their attributes.

Standards
2.G.A.1 Recognize and draw shapes having specified attributes, such as a given number of angles or a given number of equal faces. Identify triangles, quadrilaterals, pentagons, hexagons, and cubes.

Standards for Mathematical Practice (SMP)

3 Construct viable arguments and critique the reasoning of others.

5 Use appropriate tools strategically.

Lesson Objectives

Content Objectives

• Identify triangles, quadrilaterals, pentagons, and hexagons based on the number of sides and angles they have.

• Recognize that one shape can be formed from a composite of other shapes.

• Distinguish among triangles, quadrilaterals, pentagons, and hexagons based on their attributes.

• Draw a shape based on specific attributes.

Language Objectives

• Write the names of shapes based on the number of sides and angles.

• Draw shapes that have a given number of sides or angles.

• Draw lines in a shape to show different ways it can be made from other shapes.

Prerequisite Skills

• Identify the sides and angles of a polygon.

• Sort objects based on attributes.

• Identify and name triangles, circles, squares, and rectangles.

Lesson Vocabulary

• **side** a line segment that forms part of a two-dimensional shape

• **angle** one of the corners of a shape where two sides meet

• **quadrilateral** a two-dimensional closed shape with exactly four sides and four angles

• **square** a quadrilateral with four square corners and all sides the same length

• **rectangle** a quadrilateral with four square corners. Opposite sides of a rectangle are the same length.

• **rhombus** a quadrilateral with all sides the same length

• **pentagon** a two-dimensional closed shape with exactly five sides and five angles

Review the following key terms.

• **triangle** a two-dimensional closed shape with exactly three sides and three angles

• **hexagon** a two-dimensional closed shape with exactly six sides and six angles

Learning Progression

In Grade 1 students examine attributes that distinguish one shape from another and compose polygons from another set of polygons.

In Grade 2 students become more sophisticated in distinguishing among shapes and in their use of attributes.

In this lesson students use the number of sides and angles to identify, name, and classify polygons. They compose and decompose one polygon from a set of

other polygons. Students reason logically when they generalize attributes to sets of shapes, and in determining when an attribute can be applied to all of one kind of polygon, some of them, or none of them.

In Grade 3 students expand their understanding of polygons by categorizing sets within sets. They recognize that quadrilaterals all have four sides, yet possess other distinguishing features that set them apart from other four-sided figures.

Lesson Pacing Guide

Whole Class Instruction

Day 1
45–60 minutes

Toolbox: Interactive Tutorial*
Recognize and Draw Shapes

Introduction
- Opening Activity *20 min*
- Use What You Know *10 min*
- Find Out More *10 min*
- Reflect *5 min*

Practice and Problem Solving
Assign pages 273–274.

Day 2
45–60 minutes

Modeled and Guided Instruction
Learn About Naming and Drawing Shapes
- Picture It/Draw It *15 min*
- Connect It *20 min*
- Try It *10 min*

Practice and Problem Solving
Assign pages 275–276.

Day 3
45–60 minutes

Modeled and Guided Instruction
Learn About Making Shapes
- Model It/Model It *15 min*
- Connect It *20 min*
- Try It *10 min*

Practice and Problem Solving
Assign pages 277–278.

Day 4
45–60 minutes

Guided Practice
Practice Recognizing and Drawing Shapes
- Example *5 min*
- Problems 10–12 *15 min*
- Pair/Share *15 min*
- Solutions *10 min*

Practice and Problem Solving
Assign pages 279–280.

Day 5
45–60 minutes

Independent Practice
Practice Recognizing and Drawing Shapes
- Problems 1–6 *20 min*
- Quick Check and Remediation *10 min*
- Hands-On or Challenge Activity *15 min*

Toolbox: Lesson Quiz
Lesson 26 Quiz

Small Group Differentiation

Teacher-Toolbox.com

Reteach
Ready Prerequisite Lessons *45–90 min*

Grade 1
- Lesson 26 *Understand* Shapes
- Lesson 27 *Understand* Putting Shapes Together

Teacher-led Activities
Tools for Instruction *15–20 min*

Grade 1 *(Lessons 26 and 27)*
- Plane Shapes: Defining Attributes
- Plane Shapes: Making New Shapes

Grade 2 *(Lesson 26)*
- Categories of Plane Figures
- Draw and Describe Shapes

Student-led Activities
Math Center Activities *30–40 min*

Grade 2 *(Lesson 26)*
- 2.49 Geometry Vocabulary Match
- 2.50 Attributes of Shapes

Personalized Learning

i-Ready.com

Independent
i-Ready Lessons* *10–20 min*

Grade 1 *(Lessons 26 and 27)*
- Classifying Plane Shapes by Attributes
- Decomposing Two-Dimensional Shapes

*We continually update the Interactive Tutorials. Check the Teacher Toolbox for the most up-to-date offerings for this lesson.

Opening Activity

Sort Polygons

Objective Recognize similarities and differences among polygons.

Time *20–30 minutes*

Materials for each pair and for the teacher

- For the teacher: a set of all the shapes enlarged and cut from Activity Sheet 16 (Shapes and Angles), a shape of more than six sides, and a circle

- For each pair of students: a set of all the shapes cut from Activity Sheet 16 (Shapes and Angles)

Overview

Students sort polygons by attributes and describe the distinguishing attribute for each group of shapes.

Step By Step

1 Examine and sort shapes.

- Before photocopying the shapes from Activity Sheet 16, label each shape with a number (1, 2, 3, etc.) or a letter (a, b, c, etc.). Enlarge one set of all the shapes. The rest of the photocopies can be made without enlarging.

- Tape the enlarged set of shapes from Activity Sheet 16 to the board. Distribute the other sets of shapes to student pairs.

- Ask student pairs to find shapes that belong together in some way and place them in a group. Have them record the label of the shapes that have a common attribute and write how they belong together. Encourage students to make and record multiple groups.

2 Describe sets created.

- Invite pairs of students to tell you what shapes they put together and why. Move the shapes they identify to one side of the board as a group and write the defining attribute above or below the group.

- Invite students to comment on the grouping, discussing their observations.

- Ask for pairs who have a different group and attribute. Display their suggestions and allow others to discuss. Continue until you have a few different groups and attributes displayed.

3 Analyze sets.

- Ask the class to analyze the groupings and the attributes. Ask: *Do all the shapes in this group have (the attribute listed)? Are there other shapes that could fit into this group? Explain.*

- If the description of a set is not clear, have students think of ways to make it more specific so there is no doubt what might fit into the set. If there are multiple ways of describing a set, analyze which description is most clear. Tell students that often there is more than one way to describe a set. Discuss attributes that may be distinguishing (all have 4 sides) to those that are not (all small).

4 Apply set descriptions to new shapes.

- Display a shape that has more than six sides, and ask if it belongs to one of the sets that students made. Discuss why it does or does not belong. Repeat with the circle.

Teacher Notes

Introduction

At A Glance

Students identify circles, triangles, squares, and rectangles from a set of shapes. They identify polygons based on number of sides and angles.

Step By Step

- Read the problem at the top of the page. Tell students that a collage is a piece of art made by gluing various pictures, objects, or shapes to a sheet of paper or other surface.

- Work through **Use What You Know** together as a class. For Part d, a student may ask if the squares should also be colored green. This child may have learned that squares are special kinds of rectangles.

- Discuss how the squares are like rectangles. [4 sides, 4 angles, square corners (90° angles)] Ask how they are different. [Squares have sides all the same length; rectangles don't.]

- Tell them that squares are a special kind of rectangle, but for this activity, the shapes they should color green are the rectangles that are not squares.

- Do the Hands-On Activity to introduce students to cubes and how they can be identified. After completing the Hands-On Activity, ask Mathematical Discourse question 1 to help students recognize where they see cubes in their daily lives.

▶ **Hands-On Activity**

▶ **Mathematical Discourse 1**

- Complete the Real-World Connection activity to provide students with a sense of geometry in the world around them. Discuss with them that many of the shapes they found were a face of a solid figure.

▶ **Real-World Connection**

🔄 Use What You Know

Find circles, triangles, squares, and rectangles.

Macy makes this collage with cutout shapes. How many circles, triangles, squares, and rectangles does she use?

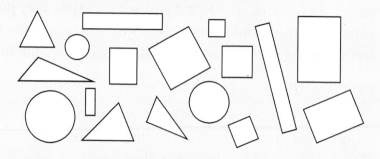

Color the shapes as described below.
Then write how many there are of each shape.

a. Color the circles red. ___3___ circles

b. Color the triangles blue. ___4___ triangles

c. Color the squares yellow. ___4___ squares

d. Color the rectangles green. ___6___ rectangles

Check students' coloring above. Students should color all circles red, all triangles blue, all squares yellow, and all rectangles green.

248

▶ Mathematical Discourse

1 *What are some real-life objects you can think of that are cubes?*

Students may suggest number cubes, blocks, sugar cubes, and connecting cubes. If possible, have some cube-shaped objects available to show students after they answer this question.

▶ Real-World Connection

- Make a chart on the board with the headings *circle, square, triangle,* and *rectangle*. Tell students that they will be going on a shape hunt around the room.

- Students are to find objects in the room that fit each of the labels on the chart. Have them draw a sketch of the object on the chart under the appropriate label. They should find one of each shape.

▶ Hands-On Activity

Learn about cubes.

Materials: For each pair: a cube-shaped block or number cube, paper, and pencil

- Point to one face of a cube-shaped block and tell students that the flat part of a solid figure is called a *face.*

- Have one student in each pair hold a cube-shaped block firmly on a sheet of paper while the partner carefully traces around the block with a pencil.

- Ask: *What shape did you draw?* [a square] *How do you know it is a square?* [It has 4 sides that are all the same length and 4 square corners.]

- Ask students to examine their blocks. Discuss that all the faces on the block are squares. Write the word "cube" on the board, and explain that a solid figure with six square faces is called a *cube.*

▷▷ Find Out More

Most shapes have sides and angles.

Triangles have 3 sides and 3 angles.

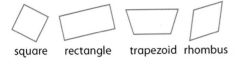

Quadrilaterals have 4 sides and 4 angles.

square   rectangle   trapezoid rhombus

Pentagons have 5 sides and 5 angles.

Hexagons have 6 sides and 6 angles.

Reflect   Work with a partner.

1 **Talk About It** Look at the hexagons above. Can the shape at the right be called a hexagon? Explain.

Write About It Possible answer: The shape is not a

hexagon. It has 8 sides, not 6 sides.

249

Step By Step

- Read **Find Out More** as a class. Review the terms *side* and *angle*. You may want to use the first part of the Hands-On Activity to reinforce these terms. Then have students point to and count the number of sides and angles of each kind of shape on the page.

▶ **Hands-On Activity**

- Display labeled pictures of each shape on a bulletin board or chart to help students with visual recognition of the words.

- Have students discuss the **Reflect** question and then write about it in their own words.

▶ **Mathematical Discourse 2**

Ready· Mathematics
PRACTICE AND PROBLEM SOLVING

Assign *Practice and Problem Solving* **pages 273–274** after students have completed this section.

▶ **Hands-On Activity**

Make string-and-straw shapes.

Materials: 2-foot lengths of string, straws cut in various sizes

- Give each student a string and 8–10 straws of varying lengths. Have students string 3 straws together and tie the ends of the string.

- Identify the *sides* as the straight pieces of straw and the *angles* as the place where the sides meet.

- Ask: *What shape did you all make?* [triangle] Have students compare their triangles. Discuss that the shapes may look different and have sides of different lengths, but they are all triangles.

- Repeat for a quadrilateral, pentagon, and hexagon.

▶ **Mathematical Discourse**

2 *Would a circle belong to any of the groups listed on this page? Explain.*

No. All the shapes on this page have sides and angles. A circle has neither sides nor angles.

Modeled and Guided Instruction

At A Glance

Students examine pictures of real objects and name the shapes based on attributes. Then students draw shapes based on attributes.

Step By Step

- Read the problem at the top of the page together as a class.
- Connect this problem to the Real-World Connection activity from the Introduction.

Picture It

- Have students name each of the shapes on the page. Point out that the triangle has 3 sides and 3 angles. Then say: *The rectangle has 4 sides. How many angles does it have?* [4 angles] *The pentagon has 5 angles. How many sides does it have?* [5 sides]
- Guide students to recognize that a triangle has 3 sides and 3 angles, a rectangle has 4 sides and 4 angles, and a pentagon has 5 sides and 5 angles.

> **SMP TIP Critique Reasoning**
>
> Ask: *Do you think it is possible for a shape to have 4 angles but not 4 sides? Why or why not?* Engage students in a discussion about this question. Encourage them to justify their reasoning and question the reasoning of classmates. If there is unresolved disagreement, give students strings and straws and challenge them to make a figure that has 4 angles but not 4 sides. They will find that if the shape is closed, it is impossible. *(SMP 3)*

Draw It

- Have students look at the **Draw It** section of the page. Discuss how drawing shapes of more than 4 sides can be challenging. Tell them that a drawing doesn't have to be perfect.

▶ **English Language Learners**

Learn About ▶ **Naming and Drawing Shapes**

Read the problem. Then you will explore sides and angles of shapes.

> Some friends hunt for shapes around school. Then they draw pictures of the objects they see. What are the names of the shapes that they draw?

▶ **Picture It You can look for shapes.**

▶ **Draw It You can draw the shapes.**

Shape A   Shape B   Shape C

250

▶ **English Language Learners**

The extensive vocabulary used in this lesson may be overwhelming to ELL students. Provide students with Activity Sheet 16 (Shapes and Angles), which lists the terms *triangle, quadrilateral, rectangle, square, pentagon, hexagon, side,* and *angle*. Allow students to keep the sheet at their desks for visual reference.

Connect It Use the number of sides and angles to name shapes.

2 Look at *Draw It* to complete the chart below.

Shape	Shape Name	Number of Sides	Number of Angles
A	triangle	3	3
B	rectangle	4	4
C	pentagon	5	5

3 What do you notice about the number of sides and the number of angles in each shape?

Possible answer: Each shape has the same number of

sides and angles.

4 What is another name for Shape B? Explain.

Possible answer: The rectangle is also a quadrilateral

because it has 4 sides.

▶ **Try It** Try another problem.

5 Draw 3 shapes. One has 3 angles. One has 4 angles. One has 5 sides. Make the shapes different from those in *Draw It*.

Possible shapes:

251

Step By Step

Connect It

- Read **Connect It** as a class. Make sure students understand that the questions refer to the problem on the previous page

- Some students may identify shape B as a quadrilateral. Tell them that the shape is a quadrilateral, but that it has another name. The Concept Extension can be completed at this time or following Problem 4.

▶ **Concept Extension**

Try It

- Tell students that in the **Try It** problem, their drawings do not need to be exact, but they should try to make the sides as straight as possible.

5 **Solution**

See possible shapes on the student page. Accept any shape that fulfills the requirements even though it may be uncommon.

Error Alert Watch for students who may draw a shape that is not closed, such as the shape below.

The shape has 3 angles, but since it is not closed, it is neither a polygon nor a triangle.

Ready Mathematics
PRACTICE AND PROBLEM SOLVING

Assign *Practice and Problem Solving* **pages 275–276** after students have completed this section.

▶ **Concept Extension**

Explore subsets of quadrilaterals.

- Display a square, trapezoid, rhombus, and rectangle.

- Tell students that all quadrilaterals have 4 sides and 4 angles, but some of them belong to a group of quadrilaterals that have their own name.

- To develop the concept of a subset, you may discuss that they are all second graders. "Second grade boys" is a certain group of second graders. Ask: *Is everyone in the room a second grader? a second grade boy?* Tell them that (Jackson) is a second grader, but because he is also a boy, he also belongs to the group of second grade boys. Repeat for the girls.

- Name each of the shapes and have students compare them based on observations such as: "The rhombus has 4 sides that are all the same length." Listen for attributes that set one shape apart from another.

- Students will learn more about quadrilaterals in third and fourth grade.

Modeled and Guided Instruction

At A Glance

Students explore ways to compose a hexagon from trapezoids, triangles, and rhombuses. They evaluate the composite hexagons, find new ways to make the same shape, and then show how to make a different shape.

Step By Step

- Read the problem at the top of the page together as a class and have students describe the shapes shown.

Model It

- Ask the Mathematical Discourse question and then have students use triangles cut from Activity Sheet 16 (Shapes and Angles) to cover the trapezoid from the same Activity Sheet. They should use three copies of the first triangle on the Activity Sheet.

▶ **Mathematical Discourse**

Model It

- Ask students how many triangles they think will cover the blue rhombus (diamond shape). Ask: *Can you use what you know about the number of triangles that cover a blue rhombus to figure out how many blue rhombuses it will take to cover the hexagon?*

- Instruct students to discuss the question without using the blocks. Help them recognize that since it takes 2 triangles to cover the rhombus and 6 triangles to cover the hexagon, they will need 3 groups of 2 triangles, or 3 rhombuses, to cover the hexagon.

- Allow students to test their reasoning by covering the hexagon with rhombuses.

> **SMP TIP** Use Tools
> Have students construct the composite hexagons shown using shapes cut from Activity Sheet 16 (Shapes and Angles). By physically organizing the shapes into a hexagon, students develop spatial reasoning skills and explore part/whole relationships as well as area concepts. *(SMP 5)*

Learn About ▶ **Making Shapes**

Read the problem. Then explore different ways to make a hexagon.

Meg has these shapes. How can she put them together to make a hexagon?

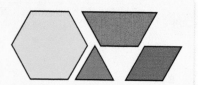

▶ **Model It** **You can make the hexagon with the same shapes.**

Both parts of the hexagon are the same shape.

▶ **Model It** **You can make the hexagon with different shapes.**

Some parts are the same shape but some are different.

252

▶ **Mathematical Discourse**

How is it possible for the same-sized hexagon to be made with either 2 or 6 pieces?

The shapes used are different sizes. Three triangles make up one of the trapezoids.

▶ **Connect It** **Name shapes that make a hexagon.**

6 Look at the first *Model It*. What shapes make up the hexagon? How many of each shape?

The hexagon is made from 2 trapezoids.

7 Look at the second *Model It*. What shapes make up the hexagon? How many of each shape?

The hexagon is made from 4 triangles and 1 rhombus.

8 Find two new ways to make a hexagon. Use the shapes at the top of the previous page. Make a drawing to show each way. Then write how many of each shape make up each hexagon.

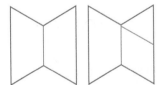

Possible answer: 2 triangles and 2 rhombuses; 6 triangles

▶ **Try It** **Try another problem.**

9 Show how to make this shape two different ways. Use the shapes shown at the top of the previous page.

Possible answer:

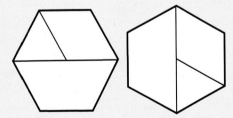

253

Connect It

• Read **Connect It** as a class.

• For Problem 8, allow students to use shapes cut from Activity Sheet 16 (Shapes and Angles) to find ways to cover the hexagons. Remind them that they can use the triangle and rhombus that match the ones shown at the top of the previous page.

• Explain that after drawing to show two new ways to make a hexagon, students need to write how many of each shape they used for the first hexagon and how many of each shape for the second hexagon.

▶ **Concept Extension**

Try It

9 **Solution**
Sample answers are shown on the student page. Accept any configurations that meet the given requirements.

🔲 **Ready**· Mathematics
PRACTICE AND PROBLEM SOLVING

Assign *Practice and Problem Solving* **pages 277–278** after students have completed this section.

▶ **Concept Extension**
Compare figures.

• Display the two configurations shown here and ask if they are the same arrangement of shapes.

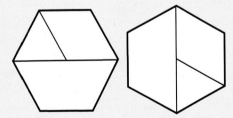

• Although the orientations are different, the shapes used are the same.

• Challenge students' spatial abilities by asking them if it is possible for the two figures to exactly match up. You may want to copy the figures onto lightweight paper and cut them out for each student or student pair to manipulate. Allow students time to flip and turn the figures either mentally or physically.

• Use a transparency or interactive whiteboard to demonstrate how one figure can be flipped and turned to fit exactly over the other figure. This builds the concept of congruence.

👥 Guided Practice

At A Glance

Students use attributes and logical reasoning to answer questions about polygons.

Step By Step

- Ask students to solve the problems independently. Tell them they will use what they learned about shapes during this lesson to complete the problems.

- **Pair/Share** When students have completed each problem, have them Pair/Share to discuss their solutions with a partner.

Solutions

Example Six dots are connected to draw a non-regular hexagon.

10 Solution
A pentagon should be drawn.
DOK 2

Practice ▸ **Recognizing and Drawing Shapes**

Study the model below. Then solve Problems 10–12.

Example

Lin drew a hexagon that is different from the ones on the previous page. What could her shape look like? Make a drawing.

You can use dot paper to show your work.

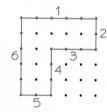

Answer This shape has 6 sides. It is a hexagon.

10 Draw a shape that has 5 sides. Write the name of the shape.

Show your work.

Possible answer:

You can use the dots as the corners of your shape.

Answer The shape is a pentagon.

254

Teacher Notes

11 Solve the riddle.

I have fewer sides than a pentagon.

I am not a quadrilateral.

What am I?

What shapes have fewer sides than a pentagon?

Show your work.

Possible work: A pentagon has 5 sides. The shape has either 3 or 4 sides. It's not a quadrilateral, so it has to have 3 sides.

Answer The shape is a triangle.

12 Which statement is true?

A Rectangles are not quadrilaterals.

B Quadrilaterals can have 5 angles.

C All quadrilaterals have 4 sides.

D All quadrilaterals have 4 equal sides.

Make a picture of all the different quadrilaterals you know.

Alma chose **D** as the answer. This answer is wrong. How did Alma get her answer?

Possible answer: Squares and rhombuses have 4 equal sides. Alma

thought that squares and rhombuses are the only kinds of quadrilaterals.

Rectangles are quadrilaterals that don't have all equal sides.

255

Solutions

11 Solution

A triangle has fewer sides than a pentagon, and it is not a quadrilateral.

DOK 2

12 Solution

C; A quadrilateral is a 4-sided polygon. Explain to students why the other two choices are not correct:

A is not correct because a rectangle has 4 sides, so it is a quadrilateral.

B is not correct because quadrilaterals have exactly 4 sides and 4 angles.

DOK 3

Ready **Mathematics** PRACTICE AND PROBLEM SOLVING

Assign *Practice and Problem Solving* **pages 279–280** after students have completed this section.

Teacher Notes

Independent Practice

At A Glance

Students apply their understanding of attributes of polygons to answer questions that might appear on a mathematics test.

Solutions

1 **Solution**

a. **All**; b. **Some**; c. **No**.

DOK 2

2 **Solution**

B and **D**; A hexagon has 6 sides and 6 angles.

DOK 2

3 **Solution**

A The shape has 5 sides; **C**

DOK 2

Quick Check and Remediation

- Show students a rectangle, square, trapezoid, and rhombus. Ask what name can be used for all of the shapes and have students tell why. [They are all quadrilaterals. They have 4 sides and 4 angles.]

- For students who are still struggling, use the chart to guide remediation.

- After providing remediation, check students' understanding using the following problem: Show students a variety of triangles, quadrilaterals, pentagons, and hexagons and ask them to name them and organize them into groups. [Check for accurate labels.]

Practice **Recognizing and Drawing Shapes**

Solve the problems.

1 Fill in the blanks. Use the words in the box.

   a. <u>All</u> triangles have 3 sides.

   b. <u>Some</u> triangles have sides the same length.

   c. <u>No</u> triangles have 4 angles.

> Some
>
> No
>
> All

2 Ross draws a shape with 6 angles. What is true about his shape? Circle all the correct answers.

   A It is a pentagon.

   (B) It has 6 sides.

   C It has 5 sides.

   (D) It is a hexagon.

3 What is true about the shape below? Circle all the correct answers.

   (A) It is a pentagon.

   B It is a quadrilateral.

   (C) It can be made up of 2 trapezoids.

   D It has 3 angles.

256

If the error is . . .	Students may . . .	To remediate . . .
pentagons or hexagons	not have learned the vocabulary word *quadrilateral* yet.	Ask students to tell you what all the shapes have in common. Guide them to recognize that all the shapes have 4 sides and 4 angles, and remind them that the name for that group of shapes is *quadrilateral*.
rectangles	have misinterpreted the term *rectangle* to mean any 4-sided figures.	Show students several quadrilaterals. Have them identify similarities and differences. Help them to recognize that only some of the shapes share the attributes of a rectangle.

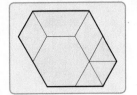

Use the shape in the box for Problems 4 and 5.

4 What is the name of the big shape that is made by putting all the small shapes together? How do you know?

The big shape is a hexagon. It has 6 sides.

5 There are 7 smaller shapes that make up the big shape. How many are there of each smaller shape?

___3___ triangles

___3___ quadrilaterals

___1___ hexagon

6 Draw a shape that has between 3 and 6 sides. Use the dots below. What is the name of your shape? Explain how you know.

Answers will vary. Possible answer: The shape I drew

has 4 sides. So it is a quadrilateral.

✓ Self Check **Now you can count sides and angles. Fill this in on the progress chart on page 247.**

257

Solutions

4 **Solution**
It is a hexagon. It has 6 sides and 6 angles.
DOK 1

5 **Solution**
3 triangles, 3 quadrilaterals, 1 hexagon
DOK 1

6 **Solution**
Answers will vary. Check students' drawings and explanations.
DOK 3

► **Hands-On Activity**

Make shapes using tangram pieces.

Materials: For each pair: tangram pieces copied on heavy paper and cut apart from Activity Sheet 17 (Tangram)

• Draw a chart on the board with the headings *Triangle, Square, Rectangle,* and *Trapezoid.* Have students copy the chart on plain paper.

• Give each student pair a set of tangram pieces. Tell them that they are to put some or all of their shapes together to make each of the shapes listed in the chart. Tell them that there is more than one way to make most of the shapes.

• After students build a shape, they should draw it on their chart showing the pieces they used. Emphasize that exactness is not necessary.

• When everyone is finished, share solutions.

► **Challenge Activity**

Find more ways to make shapes using tangram pieces.

Materials: tangram pieces copied on heavy paper and cut apart from Activity Sheet 17 (Tangram)

• Challenge students to extend the activity done by the class.

• Students should attempt to construct each of the shapes on the chart using 2, 3, 4, 5, 6, and 7 tangram pieces.

• Have them record each set of solutions on a separate sheet of paper showing the tangram pieces they used.

• When everyone is finished, share solutions.

Teacher-Toolbox.com

Overview

Assign the Lesson 26 Quiz and have students work independently to complete it.

Use the results of the quiz to assess students' understanding of the content of the lesson and to identify areas for reteaching. See the Lesson Pacing Guide at the beginning of the lesson for suggested instructional resources.

Tested Skills

Assesses 2.G.A.1

Problems on this assessment form require students to be able to identify and distinguish shapes based on attributes such as the number of sides and angles, identify a shape that is a composite of other shapes, and identify the shapes used to compose a new shape. Students will also need to be familiar with the attributes of triangles, quadrilaterals, squares, rectangles, pentagons, and hexagons.

Ready® Mathematics

Lesson 26 Quiz

Solve the problems.

1 Look at the shapes below.

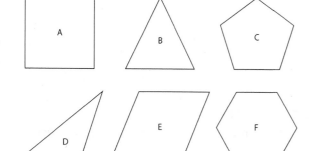

Are the sentences about the shapes true?
Circle *Yes* or *No* for each sentence.

a. Shape E is a square.   Yes   No

b. Shape D is a triangle.   Yes   No

c. Shape A is a hexagon.   Yes   No

d. Shape F is a pentagon.   Yes   No

e. Shape A is a quadrilateral.   Yes   No

Lesson 26 Quiz continued

2 Adam has these shapes.

Which shows how Adam can put the shapes together to make a hexagon?
Circle the correct answer.

A   C

B   D

3 Use a word from the box to make each sentence about quadrilaterals correct.

Words may be used more than once.

| Some   No   All |

_____ quadrilaterals have 5 angles.

_____ quadrilaterals have 4 sides.

_____ quadrilaterals have sides that are not the same length.

_____ quadrilaterals are rectangles.

Common Misconceptions and Errors

Errors may result if students:

• consider only some of the given attributes or assume attributes not given when identifying a shape.

• determine that a shape has a given attribute incorrectly or do not recognize that a shape has a given attribute.

• confuse or incorrectly identify the attributes or names of different shapes.

Ready® **Mathematics**

Lesson 26 Quiz Answer Key

1. a. No
   b. Yes
   c. No
   d. No
   e. Yes
   DOK 1

2. B
   DOK 2

3. No
   All
   Some
   Some
   DOK 3

CCSS Focus

Domain
Geometry

Cluster
A. Reason with shapes and their attributes.

Standards
2.G.A.2 Partition a rectangle into rows and columns of same-size squares and count to find the total number of them.

Standards for Mathematical Practice (SMP)

1 Make sense of problems and persevere in solving them.

2 Reason abstractly and quantitatively.

3 Construct viable arguments and critique the reasoning of others.

4 Model with mathematics.

5 Use appropriate tools strategically.

7 Look for and make use of structure.

Lesson Objectives

Content Objectives

- Analyze a tiling as an array of squares with no gaps or overlaps.
- Determine the number of squares used to tile a rectangle.
- Create a tiling of squares to fit a rectangular shape.

Language Objectives

- Draw lines in a rectangle to make rows of same-sized squares.
- Tell how many same-sized squares of a certain size will tile a rectangle.

Prerequisite Skills

- Know that an array is organized in equal-sized rows and columns.
- Compose a shape from a different shape.
- Know the attributes of a square and a rectangle.

Lesson Vocabulary

There is no new vocabulary.

Learning Progression

In Grade 1 students identify and explore attributes of triangles and squares. They compose two-dimensional shapes to create a composite shape.

In Grade 2 students extend their understanding of shapes and attributes by grouping them into broad categories of triangle, quadrilateral, pentagon, and hexagon. They compose a polygon with other polygons and explore the concept of an array as a rectangular shape.

In this lesson students build on the concept of an array and composing shapes as they tile a rectangular shape using congruent squares.

In Grade 3 students utilize the concept of an array as rows and columns of equal-sized squares as a tool for understanding multiplication and division, and in exploring concepts of area.

Lesson Pacing Guide

Whole Class Instruction

Day 1
45–60 minutes

Toolbox: Interactive Tutorial*
Concepts of Area in Two-Dimensional Shapes

Introduction
• Opening Activity *15 min*
• Think It Through Question *5 min*
• Think *10 min*
• Think *10 min*
• Reflect *5 min*

Practice and Problem Solving
Assign pages 283–284.

Day 2
45–60 minutes

Guided Instruction
Think About Using Squares to Fill a Rectangle
• Let's Explore the Idea *15 min*
• Let's Talk About It *20 min*
• Try It Another Way *10 min*

Practice and Problem Solving
Assign pages 285–286.

Day 3
45–60 minutes

Guided Practice
Connect Ideas About Tiling in Rectangles
• Explain *15 min*
• Evaluate *15 min*
• Analyze *15 min*

Practice and Problem Solving
Assign pages 287–288.

Day 4
45–60 minutes

Independent Practice
Apply Ideas About Tiling in Rectangles
• Put It Together *30 min*
• Pair/Share *15 min*

Day 5
45–60 minutes

• On-Level, Intervention or Challenge Activity *20 min*

Toolbox: Lesson Quiz
Lesson 27 Quiz

Small Group Differentiation

Teacher-Toolbox.com

Reteach
Ready Prerequisite Lessons *45–90 min*

Grade 1
• Lesson 26 *Understand* Shapes
• Lesson 27 *Understand* Putting Shapes Together

Teacher-led Activities
Tools for Instruction *15–20 min*

Grade 1 *(Lessons 26 and 27)*
• Plane Shapes: Defining Attributes
• Plane Shapes: Making New Shapes

Student-led Activities
Math Center Activities *30–40 min*

Grade 2 *(Lesson 27)*
• 2.51 Tile Rectangles
• 2.52 Fill Rectangles with Squares

Personalized Learning

i-Ready.com

Independent
i-Ready Lessons* *10–20 min*

Grade 1 *(Lessons 26 and 27)*
• Classifying Plane Shapes by Attributes
• Decomposing Two-Dimensional Shapes

*We continually update the Interactive Tutorials. Check the Teacher Toolbox for the most up-to-date offerings for this lesson.

Opening Activity

Tile a Rectangle

Objective Explore tiling a rectangle with congruent squares.

Time *15–20 minutes*

Materials for each student

- 1 six-inch × three-inch rectangle cut from Activity Sheet 18 (Shapes for Tiling)

- 6 two-inch squares cut from Activity Sheet 18 (Shapes for Tiling); if possible, the 2-inch squares should be a different color from the rectangle

- 18 one-inch squares cut from Activity Sheet 3 (1-Inch Grid Paper); if possible, the 1-inch squares should be a different color from the rectangle and the 2-inch squares

Overview

Students cover a rectangular shape with 1-inch squares and then with 2-inch squares, leaving no gaps or overlaps. They analyze the tiling to determine the reason one size of square will tile and the other will not.

Step By Step

1 Tile a rectangle.

- Distribute the rectangle and 1-inch squares to students.

- Ask students to cover the rectangle with the 1-inch squares, making sure there are no gaps or overlaps. Point out how the squares cover the paper, lining up perfectly with each side of the rectangle.

2 Try another tiling.

- Distribute the 2-inch squares to students. Have students try to cover the rectangle with the 2-inch squares in the same way they covered it with the 1-inch squares. They should notice that the squares don't fit perfectly in both directions.

3 Talk about the tilings.

- Compare the two tilings. Ask: *What is the same about the two tilings?* [They are both made of squares that are all the same size.] *What is different about the two tilings?* [The 1-inch squares all fit perfectly, but the 2-inch squares hang over on one side.]

- Help students make sense of the concept of a tiling and self-correct faulty reasoning through yes/no questions. Ask: *What would you need to do to make the 2-inch squares fit?* [Students may respond that they would need to cut off part of some of the squares.] Ask: *Would all the tiles still be squares?* [No.] *Would it still be a tiling of squares?* [No.] Some students may respond that they would have to make the rectangle bigger. Remind them that the rectangle cannot change. Some students may respond that they could make one row of 1-inch tiles. Tell them that the idea is a good one, but this kind of tiling must be made of squares that are all the same size. Ask: *If we used some of the 1-inch tiles, would all the tiles be the same size?* [No.]

- Project a tiling where a row of 2-inch tiles overlaps another row of 2-inch tiles. Ask: *What do you think about this strategy?* Guide students to see that it won't work because when you covered some of the squares, it made them into rectangles.

- Summarize the activity by discussing that students have learned how to tile a rectangle using squares that are all the same size, arranging the squares so that there are no gaps and no overlaps.

Teacher Notes

Introduction

At A Glance

Students explore tiling as a series of equal rows of congruent squares. They examine correct and incorrect ways to tile a rectangle with squares.

Step By Step

- Introduce the question at the top of the page. Remind students of how, in the previous lesson, they composed a hexagon with equal-sized trapezoids and with equal-sized triangles.

- Use the Hands-On Activity to engage students in the process of building rectangles.

▶ **Hands-On Activity**

- Reinforce the concept that making a rectangle this way is like covering a rectangle completely, with no gaps or overlaps.

- Use Mathematical Discourse questions 1 and 2 to help students connect the concept of tiling to an array.

▶ **Mathematical Discourse 1 and 2**

> **SMP TIP Look for Structure**
> Here and throughout the lesson, reinforce the structure of an array and how it applies to tiling. This prepares students for concepts involving multiplication and the area of rectangles. *(SMP 7)*

Think It Through

> **How can you break up a rectangle into squares of the same size?**

You know how to put shapes together to make bigger shapes. You can make a rectangle by using just squares.

> **Think** **You can use squares that are the same size to make a rectangle.**

You can put 12 squares in 1 row to make a rectangle.

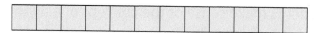

You can also put them in 2 rows to make a rectangle. Each row has 6 squares.

← The top row has 6 squares.
← The bottom row also has 6 squares.

Make a drawing of 12 squares. Put the squares in 3 rows.

There are ___3___ rows of squares.

There are ___4___ squares in each row.

258

▶ Mathematical Discourse

1 *Are the tiles that make up the second rectangle arranged in an array? Explain.*

   Yes, they are arranged in an array because they are lined up in rows and columns, with the same number of squares in each row and the same number in each column.

2 *What would happen to the second rectangle if you removed one of the tiles?*

   It would no longer be a rectangle, and the shape would no longer be made up of squares arranged in an array. There would not be the same number of squares in each row or each column. Students may also respond that the shape would be a hexagon.

▶ Hands-On Activity

Use tiles to build rectangles.

Materials: 12 1-inch tiles cut from Activity Sheet 3 (1-Inch Grid Paper)

- Distribute 12 tiles to each student.

- As students examine the pictures of rectangles on the page, have them use the tiles to build their own rectangles, replicating the ones shown.

- After completing the page, have students use their 12 tiles to create rectangles that are not shown on this page. They should make rectangles with rows of 1, 2, and 3 tiles.

Think Fill a rectangle with squares that are the same size.

Use graph paper to make this rectangle.

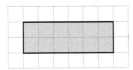

> You can fill a rectangle with squares. All the squares must be the same size. All the shapes have to be squares.

Here are two ways to draw the rectangle using squares that are the same size.

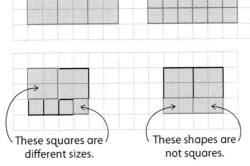

These rectangles are not drawn using squares that are the same size.

These squares are different sizes.

These shapes are not squares.

▶ **Reflect** **Work with a partner.**

1 **Talk About It** You have 9 squares that are the same size. Can you make a rectangle with the squares in 1 row? 2 rows? 3 rows?

Write About It 1 row of 9 squares or 3 rows of 3 squares make

rectangles. You can't make a rectangle with 2 rows. Each row has a

different number of squares.

259

▶ Hands-On Activity

Explore tiling with squares of two different sizes.

Materials: For each pair: 12 1-inch tiles cut from Activity Sheet 3 (1-Inch Grid Paper) and 12 2-inch tiles cut from Activity Sheet 19 (2-Inch Grid Paper)

• Distribute the paper tiles to each student pair. Ask them to try to build a rectangle using some of each of the two different-sized tiles.

• Ask students if they were able to build a rectangle. Invite a volunteer to display a rectangle that was made.

• Ask: *Is this rectangle an array? Explain.* Allow the volunteer to respond or allow the student to call on a classmate to respond. Students should recognize that an array has not been formed since the rectangle is not made up of same-sized squares arranged in rows and columns.

▶ Mathematical Discourse

3 *Could you trace larger squares in this rectangle? Explain why or why not.*

Students should respond that they cannot trace larger squares in the rectangle. There would need to be an equal number of rows and columns of smaller squares within each larger square.

Step By Step

• Read the **Think** section together as a class.

• Direct students' attention to the two ways of drawing a rectangle using same-sized squares. Ask Mathematical Discourse question 3 to engage students in thinking about how squares are composed from other squares.

▶ **Mathematical Discourse 3**

• Examine the rectangle that is divided into squares of different sizes. Discuss that since the squares are not the same size, an array was not made. Use the Hands-On Activity to explore this concept and reinforce the impossibility of creating an array with different sizes of squares.

▶ **Hands-On Activity**

• Read the **Reflect** question with the class. Tell students that they may draw squares or use tiles to help them. When their answers are complete, invite students to share responses with the class, demonstrating their reasoning with tiles.

> **SMP TIP** **Persevere in Problem Solving**
> Encourage students to attempt varied configurations in exploring answers to questions about tiling. This promotes perseverance in problem solving and stimulates spatial reasoning skills. *(SMP 1)*

Ready Mathematics
PRACTICE AND PROBLEM SOLVING

Assign *Practice and Problem Solving* **pages 283–284** after students have completed this section.

Guided Instruction

At A Glance

Students determine the number of tiles used to fill in rectangles. Then they answer questions based on these tiling activities.

Step By Step

Let's Explore the Idea

- Work through Problem 2 with the class. Drawing individual squares may be challenging for students. Encourage them to take care in drawing the missing squares to make sure they all fit inside the rectangle.

- For students with fine motor challenges, it may be easier for them to use a straight edge to extend each line, creating a grid inside of the rectangle.

- Have students work individually on the rest of the problems on this page.

- As students work individually, circulate among them. This is an opportunity to assess student understanding and address student misconceptions.

▶ **Mathematical Discourse 1 and 2**

- Watch for students who are having difficulty. See if their understanding progresses as they work in pairs during the next part of the lesson.

Think About **Using Squares to Fill a Rectangle**

🔍 **Let's Explore the Idea** Fill rectangles with squares. Then find the total number of squares.

2 Dan started drawing squares to fill this rectangle. Draw the rest of the squares.

3 How many rows of squares are there? How many squares are in each row?

> There are 6 rows with 4 squares in each row.

4 How many squares are there in all?

> There are 24 squares in all. $6 + 6 + 6 + 6 = 24$

5 This rectangle is the same size as the one above. Dan started drawing larger squares to fill this rectangle. Draw the rest of the squares.

6 How many rows of squares are there? How many squares are in each row?

> There are 3 rows with 2 squares in each row.

7 How many squares are there in all?

> There are 6 squares in all. $3 + 3 = 6$

260

▶ **Mathematical Discourse**

1 *How do you know where to draw the rest of the squares?*
  I can follow the way the squares were started and make it like an array.

2 *After you drew the squares in the first rectangle, what strategy did you use to find the number of squares in all?*
  Possible responses: I added 6 together 4 times; I added 4 together 6 times; I counted them all.

Let's Talk About It
Work with a partner.

8 How did you know how many squares were missing in the first rectangle?

Possible answer: I saw 4 squares in a row and 6 squares in a column.

So I filled in the rows.

9 How did you know how many squares were missing in the second rectangle?

Possible answer: I drew 1 square to fill the left column. Then I copied the

same number of squares in the right column.

10 The two rectangles are the same size. Why is there a different number of squares in each one?

Possible answer: The squares are different sizes.

▶ **Try It Another Way** **Use dot paper to draw squares in rectangles.**

11 Show two different ways to fill the rectangle with same-sized squares.

Possible answer:

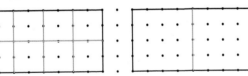

261

Step By Step

Let's Talk About It

- Instruct students to work in pairs to complete Problems 8–10. Walk around to each pair, listening to and joining in on discussions at different points.

▶ **Mathematical Discourse 3**

> **SMP TIP** **Reason Abstractly and Quantitatively**
> Ask groups to share their responses to Problem 10. Engage students in a discussion of how a larger square covers more of the rectangle than a smaller square, so you don't need as many larger squares. This prepares students for concepts of equivalencies of fractions and measuring area using different sized units. *(SMP 2)*

Try It Another Way

- Before students complete the **Try It Another Way** problem, have them discuss with a partner ways in which they could draw the squares.

▶ **Concept Extension**

Ready **Mathematics**
PRACTICE AND PROBLEM SOLVING

Assign *Practice and Problem Solving* **pages 285–286** after students have completed this section.

▶ **Concept Extension**

Find how many smaller squares are in a large square and rectangle.

Materials: Activity Sheet 20 (Dot Paper), colored pencils, and scissors

- Have students use the dots to draw a 6-unit by 6-unit square and cut it out.

- Have students use different colors to divide their large square into same-sized smaller squares in as many ways as they can. They should use 1×1, 2×2, and 3×3 smaller squares.

- Ask students to compare their squares with a partner.

- Show partners how to put their two 6-unit by 6-unit squares together to form a rectangle. Discuss how to find the number of smaller squares in the rectangle they formed. Students should recognize that they can double the

number of smaller squares in a 6×6 square to find the total number of squares in the rectangle.

▶ **Mathematical Discourse**

3 *How could thinking about the rectangles as arrays help you find a strategy for knowing how many squares are missing?*

An array is organized in rows and columns. There are the same number of squares in each row and each column, so you can count the squares in one full column or row and then draw the same number of squares in the rest of the columns or rows.

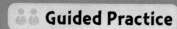
Guided Practice

At A Glance

Students demonstrate their understanding of how to tile a rectangle with squares. Then they apply their understanding of tiling by determining the size of squares that will cover a specific rectangular shape.

Step By Step

- Discuss each problem as a class using the discussion points outlined below.

Explain

- Discuss with students how a tiling is organized like an array. Ask: *Is there more than one way to find the total number of squares used? Explain.* Students should recognize that they might add 6 three times or 3 six times. You can either add the rows or the columns since there are an equal number in each row and in each column.

Evaluate

- Ask students why Tim might have divided the rectangle as he did. Engage them in a discussion of the similarities and differences between squares and rectangles. They both have 4 sides and 4 angles. They both have 4 "square" angles. A rectangle has two sides that are longer than the other two sides, while all the sides of a square are the same size.

- Ask: *How should Tim have divided his rectangle?* [He should have divided it into all squares.] *How many squares would he count?* [12] *How do you know?* [Each of the rectangles could be divided into two squares for a total of 6 squares. Add 6 to the 6 squares already there to get 12 squares.]

Analyze

- Point out how this situation is like **Try It Another Way** on the previous page.

- Ask: *What do Molly and Nina need to remember when filling their poster board with squares?* [They need to remember to use same-sized squares for the whole tiling and make sure there are no empty spaces or pieces that overlap each other.]

Connect **Ideas About Tiling in Rectangles**

Talk about these questions as a class. Then write your answers.

12 Explain What number can you add to find the total number of squares in the rectangle at the right? How many times do you add this number? Why?

> Possible answer: You can add 6 three times, because
>
> there are 3 columns with 6 squares in each column.
>
> 6 + 6 + 6 = 18

13 Evaluate Tim says there are a total of 9 squares in this rectangle. Do you agree? Explain.

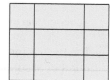

> Possible answer: I don't agree with Tim. Three of the
>
> shapes he drew are rectangles. There are not 9 squares.

14 Analyze Molly and Nina paste squares on posters that are the same size. The sizes of their squares are shown. Who will use more squares to fill her poster? Why?

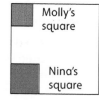

Molly's square

Nina's square

> Possible answer: Molly's squares are smaller, so she
>
> will need more squares to fill the poster.

262

---

262 **Lesson 27** *Understand* Tiling in Rectangles

Apply ▸ **Ideas About Tiling in Rectangles**

Put It Together **Use what you have learned to complete this task.**

15 Sue is making a mosaic design. She has squares that are the sizes below. But she can only use squares that are all the same size.

3 cm   4 cm   5 cm

Sue will use the squares to fill a piece of paper that is 24 centimeters long and 12 centimeters wide.

24 cm

12 cm

Squares and rectangle are not life-sized.

Part A Can Sue use the 3-centimeter squares to make her design? If so, how many squares will she need? Draw a picture at the right to help you explain.

Yes, Sue can use the 3 cm squares to make 4 rows

of squares with 8 squares in each row or 32 total squares.

Part B Repeat Part A for the 4-centimeter squares.

The 4-centimeter squares will fit in 3 rows of 6 squares.

Part C Repeat Part A for the 5-centimeter squares.

The 5-centimeter tiles won't fit exactly in the rectangle.

263

Step By Step

Put It Together

- Direct students to complete the **Put It Together** task on their own.

- Read the directions with students and make sure they understand each part of the task before proceeding.

- Tell students that the pictures of Sue's squares and piece of paper are not life-sized, and that students' drawings don't need to be the exact size either.

- Instruct students to make their drawings in the blank space at the right of Parts A, B, and C. Show how to draw a rectangle, labeling the sides 24 cm and 12 cm.

- In one corner of the rectangle, draw a square with the number 3 in it. Point out that students can see how many squares they need to draw for each row or column by figuring out how many 3s add up to 24 or 12. They can use a similar strategy for the 4 cm and 5 cm squares.

- If time permits, ask students to share the square sizes they chose and justify their choices.

Ready Mathematics
PRACTICE AND PROBLEM SOLVING

Assign *Practice and Problem Solving* **pages 287–288** after students have completed Guided Practice.

Scoring Rubrics

Parts A and B

Points	Expectations
2	The student states that 3 cm squares can be used and 4 cm squares can be used. The student draws rectangles showing 32 and 18 squares respectively.
1	The student states that 3 cm and 4 cm squares can be used, but the drawings are inaccurate. Words may or may not be present to explain reasoning.
0	The student states that 3 cm and 4 cm squares cannot be used.

Part C

Points	Expectations
2	The student states that 5 cm squares cannot be used and clearly articulates his or her reasoning.
1	The student states that 5 cm squares cannot be used but does not provide any reasoning for this answer.
0	The student states that 5 cm squares can be used.

Differentiated Instruction

▶ Intervention Activity

Create a mosaic tiling.

Materials: 1-Inch Grid Paper (Activity Sheet 3), at least 12 2-inch squares in varied colors cut from 2-Inch Grid Paper (Activity Sheet 19), and glue

Note: Tiling with no gaps or overlaps is challenging for students at this level. Providing grid paper as a guide enables students to successfully complete a tiling.

• Before distributing the 1-inch grid paper, cut off one column of squares so that the grid has rows of 6 squares and columns of 8 squares.

• Distribute the 6 × 8 1-inch grid paper and 2-inch squares.

• Tell students they are to make a tiling of squares to cover the grid paper.

• Help them notice that each of the cut-out squares covers 4 squares on the grid paper.

• Suggest that they arrange the squares on the grid paper before gluing to ensure they like the design.

• Have students glue the squares on the paper, reminding them to stay within the grid lines.

• Provide a place for students to display their tilings when completed.

▶ On-Level Activity

Create a mosaic tiling.

Materials: 1-Inch Grid Paper (Activity Sheet 3), at least 56 1-inch squares in varied colors cut from another copy of 1-Inch Grid Paper (Activity Sheet 3), and glue

• Provide students with the grid paper and 1-inch squares.

• Tell students they are to make a tiling of squares to cover the grid paper.

• Students may arrange the squares in any way they choose, staying within the grid lines. Suggest that they place the squares on the grid in the way they would like before gluing.

• Have students glue the squares on the grid paper to create a tiling that has no gaps or overlaps.

• Provide a place for students to display their tilings when completed.

▶ Challenge Activity

Find all the ways to tile a rectangle.

Materials: 12 in. × 18 in. sheet of construction paper and inch ruler

• Distribute the sheets of construction paper, but do not tell students the size of the paper.

• Tell students that their challenge is to find out what size squares they could use to tile this rectangle. They may only consider squares that are whole-inch sizes, such as squares that are 1 inch, 2 inches, 3 inches, etc. They need to find *all* the possible sizes of squares that would work and justify why those are the *only* sizes that would work.

• Provide students with further challenges by telling them to find all the whole-inch sizes of squares that could tile a 16 in. × 24 in. rectangle, a 21 in. × 35 in. rectangle, and a 24 cm × 48 cm rectangle. Have them justify their answers.

Teacher Notes

Teacher-Toolbox.com

Overview

Assign the Lesson 27 Quiz and have students work independently to complete it.

Use the results of the quiz to assess students' understanding of the content of the lesson and to identify areas for reteaching. See the Lesson Pacing Guide at the beginning of the lesson and the Differentiated Instruction activities that follow for suggested instructional resources.

Tested Skills

Assesses 2.G.A.2

Problems on this assessment form require students to be able to recognize when a rectangle has been partitioned into or tiled/filled with same-sized squares with no gaps or overlaps, determine how many same-sized squares of a certain size will tile/fill a rectangle, and determine whether a tiling is possible with a given number of rows/squares. Students will also need to be familiar with attributes of squares and rectangles, and composing shapes from other shapes.

Ready® **Mathematics**

Lesson 27 Quiz

Solve the problems.

1 Rosie is making rectangles. She will use 16 same-sized square tiles to make each rectangle.

Which rectangles can Rosie make?

Circle all the correct answers.

A

D

B

E

C

F

Lesson 27 Quiz continued

2 Sam begins filling a rectangle using same-sized square tiles.

How many square tiles will there be in all after Sam finishes filling the rectangle?

A 10

B 15

C 18

D 24

3 Diana is using square tiles to fill a rectangle. She wants to use the fewest number of tiles possible.

Should Diana use the black tiles or the gray tiles?
Explain your answer.

_____

_____

_____

Common Misconceptions and Errors

Errors may result if students:

- incorrectly count, skip count, or use repeated addition when determining the total number of squares filling a rectangle.

- consider only squares shown or squares missing when determining the total number of squares needed to fill a partially-tiled rectangle.

- do not recognize that each row of a tiling contains the same number of equal-sized squares.

Ready® **Mathematics**

Lesson 27 Quiz Answer Key

1. B, C, D
DOK 1

2. D
DOK 2

3. Diana should use the gray tiles. Possible explanation: The gray tiles are larger than the black tiles, so it will take fewer of them to fill the rectangle.
DOK 3

Lesson 28 *Understand* Halves, Thirds, and Fourths in Shapes

CCSS Focus

Domain
Geometry

Cluster
A. Reason with shapes and their attributes.

Standards
2.G.A.3 Partition circles and rectangles into two, three, or four equal shares, describe the shares using the words halves, thirds, half of, a third of, etc., and describe the whole as two halves, three thirds, four fourths. Recognize that equal shares of identical wholes need not have the same shape.

Standards for Mathematical Practice (SMP)

1 Make sense of problems and persevere in solving them.

3 Construct viable arguments and critique the reasoning of others.

5 Use appropriate tools strategically.

6 Attend to precision.

7 Look for and make use of structure.

Lesson Objectives

Content Objectives
- Identify and name halves, thirds, and fourths as parts into which a shape is divided.
- Recognize that fractional parts are equal in size.
- Understand that the more parts a whole is divided into, the smaller the size of each part.

Language Objectives
- Divide a shape into halves, thirds, and fourths.
- Draw lines in a shape to show 4 equal parts in different ways.
- Label parts of shapes that are cut into same-size pieces with the words *half, third,* or *fourth.*

Prerequisite Skills

- Recognize halves of a whole.
- Know the meaning of ordinals third and fourth.

Lesson Vocabulary

- **one third** one of three equal parts of a whole
- **thirds** the parts formed when a whole is divided into three equal parts

Review the following key terms.

- **one half** one of two equal parts of a whole
- **halves** the parts formed when a whole is divided into two equal parts
- **one fourth** one of four equal parts of a whole
- **fourths** the parts formed when a whole is divided into four equal parts

Learning Progression

In Grade 1 students explore halves and fourths by partitioning circles and rectangles into two and four equal shares. They recognize that the more parts a shape is divided into, the smaller the size of each part.

In Grade 2 students extend their understanding of fractions to thirds.

In this lesson students partition squares, circles, and rectangles into halves, thirds, and fourths, recognizing that equal parts of congruent shapes need not be identical. They name and compare fractional parts based on their shape and the amount of the whole they consume.

In Grade 3 students focus on fractions as equal areas of a shape in preparation for calculating areas in Grade 4. They read and write fractions numerically and explore fractions on a number line. Students expand their understanding of fractions to sixths and eighths. They compare fractions in varied ways and find equivalencies, preparing them for future study of addition of fractions.

Lesson Pacing Guide

Whole Class Instruction

Day 1 45–60 minutes	**Toolbox: Interactive Tutorial*** *Fraction of a Whole: Halves and Fourths* **Introduction** • Opening Activity *20 min* • Think It Through Question *5 min* • Think *10 min* • Think *10 min* • Reflect *5 min*	**Practice and Problem Solving** Assign pages 291–292.
Day 2 45–60 minutes	**Guided Instruction** **Think About Dividing Rectangles into Equal Parts** • Let's Explore the Idea *20 min* • Let's Talk About It *15 min* • Try It Another Way *10 min*	**Practice and Problem Solving** Assign pages 293–294.
Day 3 45–60 minutes	**Guided Practice** **Connect Ideas About Dividing into Parts** • Explain *15 min* • Compare *15 min* • Draw *15 min*	**Practice and Problem Solving** Assign pages 295–296.
Day 4 45–60 minutes	**Independent Practice** **Apply Ideas About Dividing into Parts** • Put It Together *30 min* • Pair/Share *15 min*	
Day 5 45–60 minutes	• On-Level, Intervention or Challenge Activity *20 min* **Toolbox: Lesson Quiz** Lesson 28 Quiz	

Small Group Differentiation

Teacher-Toolbox.com

Reteach
Ready Prerequisite Lessons *45–90 min*

Grade 1
• Lesson 26 *Understand* Shapes
• Lesson 28 *Understand* Breaking Shapes Into Parts

Teacher-led Activities
Tools for Instruction *15–20 min*

Grade 1 *(Lessons 26 and 28)*
• Plane Shapes: Defining Attributes
• Plane Figures: Making Equal Shares

Grade 2 *(Lesson 28)*
• Make Equal Shares

Student-led Activities
Math Center Activities *30–40 min*

Grade 2 *(Lesson 28)*
• 2.53 Equal Shares Vocabulary
• 2.54 Draw Equal Shares

Personalized Learning

i-Ready.com

Independent
i-Ready Lessons* *10–20 min*

Grade 1 *(Lessons 26 and 28)*
• Classifying Plane Shapes by Attributes

*We continually update the Interactive Tutorials. Check the Teacher Toolbox for the most up-to-date offerings for this lesson.

Half of a Square

Objective Find multiple ways of dividing a square into two equal parts.

Time *20–30 minutes*

Materials for each student
- Activity Sheet 4 (1-Centimeter Grid Paper) and a pencil

Overview

Students divide a 4 × 4 square into different arrangements of halves. They compare ways of dividing the square, justifying that the division represents one half of the whole square.

Step By Step

1 Show half of a square.

- Ask students to trace around a 4 × 4 square on grid paper.

- Tell students to draw a line that will divide the square in half. If necessary, remind them that *half* means "two equal parts." Expect horizontal, vertical, and diagonal divisions, and accept any division that can be justified.

- Have students display the way they divided the square and tell how they know they have divided it in half. Listen for reasons such as: The two parts look the same; If I folded the paper they would be the same or one would fit on top of the other. Some students may use area to justify rather than relying on visual comparisons. They will notice that each half contains the same number of little squares.

2 Extend the concept of half.

- Ask students to trace another 4 × 4 square.

- Challenge students to be creative in finding another way that no one has shown yet to divide the square in half. Allow students to collaborate with a partner if they would like to.

- Provide students time to struggle with ideas. Once a student finds a way to divide, have them project their solution for all to see. Ask questions such as: *How do you know the two parts are the same size? Does everyone agree they look the same? Is there something you could do to be sure?* Listen for justification that is becoming more sophisticated. Students may begin focusing on ways to count the little squares, think of folding, recognize a reflection, or identify that a shape has been turned.

3 Analyze half.

- If no student has divided the square in one of the following ways, project one and ask students if they think the square has been divided in half. These squares are divided into visually congruent parts. So if students are not yet thinking in terms of area, they can still reason accurately.

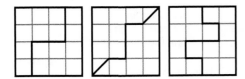

- Ask: *Is this square divided in half? How can you tell?* Listen for some of the reasons listed above. If necessary, have students replicate the square and then cut it out to compare the two halves.

Teacher Notes

Introduction

Understand Halves, Thirds, and Fourths in Shapes

At A Glance

Students explore the concept of equal parts. Then students examine thirds and fourths of squares in which the fractional parts are not the same shape.

Step By Step

- Introduce the question at the top of the page. Remind students that in the opening activity, they explored different ways of dividing a square into halves. Ask: *What is important when dividing a square into halves?* [Both parts must cover the same amount of the square.]

- Draw attention to the circles on the student page. Ask Mathematical Discourse questions 1 and 2 to engage students in thinking about equal parts.

▶ **Mathematical Discourse 1 and 2**

- On the board, draw examples of circles that are not divided into equal parts and discuss how these are different from the ones on the student page.

- Draw attention to the three squares and ask: *Are these squares cut in half?* [The first two are, the third one is not.] *How can you tell?* [In the first two, the parts are the same, but in the third one, the parts are not the same.]

- Make sure students understand that when the terms *half*, *third*, and *fourth* are used, equal-sized parts are implied.

▶ **Real-World Connection**

▶ **English Language Learners**

💭 **Think It Through**

How do you divide shapes into 2, 3, and 4 equal parts?

The circles are divided into equal parts. You use the number of equal parts to name the parts.

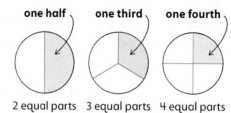

one half   one third   one fourth

2 equal parts   3 equal parts   4 equal parts

Think Equal parts cover an equal amount of the shape.

Think about sharing a sandwich with a friend. You want each piece to be the same size.

These squares show equal parts. So each person gets the same amount.

In this square, one part is bigger than the other.

✏️ Draw another way you could share a sandwich equally with a friend. Use the square at the right.

Possible answer:

264

▶ **Mathematical Discourse**

1 *How is dividing a shape into thirds and fourths like dividing it into halves?*

The parts all have to be the same size so they take up the same amount of the shape.

2 *How could you check that each third takes up the same amount of the shape? How could you check the fourths?*

For the thirds, I could cut out the pieces to see if they matched up. For the fourths, I could cut out the pieces or fold the shape.

▶ **Real-World Connection**

Materials: paper cut into circles, squares, and rectangles

- Ask students to think of things they have seen or used that are in the shape of a circle, square, or rectangle that are divided into equal parts.

- Expect them to name pizza, pie, cake, brownies, and other food items. Steer them to items such as windows divided into panes, a square folded game board, etc.

- Have students draw examples of items they mentioned on the paper cutouts.

▶ **English Language Learners**

Students may struggle with the vocabulary *thirds* and *fourths*. Provide situations in which ordinal numbers are used such as: *You are the third person to come to the board. How many people have come to the board?* [3]

Think Equal parts can have different shapes.

These squares are all the same size. Each smaller shape covers one fourth of the square. So each smaller shape is an equal part of the square.

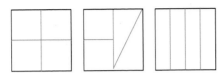

Think: Divide the square in half. Then divide each half in half.

These squares are the same size as the ones above. Each is divided into 3 equal parts, or thirds. So each smaller shape is an equal part of the square.

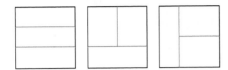

▶ **Reflect** Work with a partner.

1 **Talk About It** Draw two squares that are the same size as the ones above. Divide one into fourths and one into thirds in different ways than above. Which parts are bigger, the fourths or thirds? Explain.

Write About It Check students' drawings. Possible explanation:

Thirds are bigger. Since there are fewer parts, they take up more space

than fourths.

265

▶ Mathematical Discourse

3 *Why does it make sense that dividing each half in half makes fourths?*
When you divide a shape in half, you know those parts are the same size. If you divide a half in half again, it makes two equal-sized parts that take up the same amount of space. If you do this with both halves, there are 4 parts that each take up the same amount of space.

4 *Brayden says, "I don't get it! Four is greater than three, so why aren't fourths bigger than thirds?" What will you tell him?*
Listen for suggestions that reflect student understanding of the concept of fractions. Fourths and thirds tell the number of parts into which a whole is divided. The more parts there are, the smaller each one is.

Step By Step

- Draw student attention to **Think**. Compare the different ways in which the first three squares are divided. Ask students how they could be sure each of the parts is one fourth of the shape. Listen for suggestions such as cutting one of the fourths into smaller pieces to see if they fit on each of the other fourths.

SMP TIP Attend to Precision
Ask Mathematical Discourse question 3 to engage student thinking and encourage precise articulation of a concept. Encourage students to be clear and accurate in describing halves of a half by asking questions such as: *What does it mean that they are the same?* (SMP 6)

▶ **Mathematical Discourse 3**

- Draw the following on a 5 × 5 dot paper square (Activity Sheet 20, Dot Paper). Display it and ask: *Is this square divided into fourths? How do you know?*

Students should notice that the parts don't have an equal area. The two middle sections contain 3 small squares while the triangles at the ends contain only 1 small square.

- Analyze the way in which the squares shown on the student page are divided into thirds by focusing on the amount of space that is consumed by each part.

- For the **Reflect** section, have students draw their squares in the space to the left of each set of squares at the top of the page. Discuss responses.

▶ **Mathematical Discourse 4**

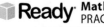 **Ready**· Mathematics
PRACTICE AND PROBLEM SOLVING

Assign *Practice and Problem Solving* **pages 291–292** after students have completed this section.

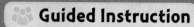

👥 **Guided Instruction**

At A Glance

Students divide a rectangle into halves, thirds, and fourths and identify the parts by name. Then students describe a whole in terms of the number of fractional parts it contains.

Step By Step

Let's Explore the Idea

- Work through Problems 2 and 3 together as a class. Then direct students to work on the rest of the page independently. Tell students to divide each rectangle as carefully as possible.

- Thirds are more challenging to visualize and draw than halves or fourths. Suggest that students check their thirds using a nonstandard measure such as a length on their pencil or finger to ensure the divisions are close to being equal.

- As students work individually, circulate among them. This is an opportunity to assess student understanding and address student misconceptions.

> **SMP TIP Use Structure**
> Focus on the structure of fractions and how that structure relates to the name of the fraction part. *(SMP 7)*

▶ **Mathematical Discourse 1 and 2**

- Watch for students who are still having difficulty. See if their understanding progresses as they work in pairs during the next part of the lesson.

▶ **Concept Extension**

Think About ▶ Dividing Rectangles into Equal Parts

🔍 **Let's Explore the Idea** Follow the directions for each rectangle.

2 Divide this rectangle into two equal parts.

Possible answer:

3 Complete this sentence about the rectangle in Problem 2. Use a word from the box at the right.

Each part is a ___half___ of the whole rectangle.

> half
> third
> fourth

4 Divide this rectangle into three equal parts.

Possible answer:

5 Complete this sentence about the rectangle in Problem 4. Use a word from the box at the right.

Each part is a ___third___ of the whole rectangle.

> half
> third
> fourth

6 Divide this rectangle into four equal parts.

Possible answer:

7 Complete this sentence about the rectangle in Problem 6. Use a word from the box at the right.

Each part is a ___fourth___ of the whole rectangle.

> half
> third
> fourth

266

▶ **Mathematical Discourse**

1 *What tells you the name of the part?*

Third is like three. So when I divide into 3 equal parts, they are thirds. Fourth is like four. So when I divide into four equal parts, they are fourths.

2 *How do you know the parts you drew are equal?*

Listen for responses such as: I measured to make sure they are all the same size; They all look the same.

▶ **Concept Extension**

Explore fraction/size relationships.

- Say: *Josie is confused. She said she knows a half is bigger than a third, but a half of a mini pizza is smaller than a third of a family-sized pizza. Why?*

- You may want to draw a picture on the board of the two pizzas described.

- Discuss that a fraction describes a part of a whole. Even though the amount of pizza is smaller in the pizza divided in half, it is a bigger part of *that* pizza than the third is of the larger pizza.

- Emphasize that when comparing fractions using more than one whole, each whole should be the same size to avoid confusion.

Let's Talk About It
Work with a partner.

8 How many halves are in the big rectangle in Problem 2?

There are 2 halves in the whole rectangle.

9 How many thirds are in the big rectangle in Problem 4?

There are 3 thirds in the whole rectangle.

10 How many fourths are in the big rectangle in Problem 6?

There are 4 fourths in the whole rectangle.

▶ **Try It Another Way** **Show a different way to make halves, thirds, and fourths.**

11 Show another way to divide a rectangle into halves.

Possible answer:

12 Show another way to divide a rectangle into thirds.

Possible answer:

13 Show another way to divide a rectangle into fourths.

Possible answer:

267

▶ **Hands-On Activity**

Divide rectangles on dot paper.

Materials: Activity Sheet 20 (Dot Paper) and pencil

- Demonstrate how to draw a 5 × 4 rectangle on dot paper. Have students draw three of their own 5 × 4 rectangles.

- Then ask them to connect some of the dots to divide one of their rectangles into halves, another into thirds, and another into fourths.

- Discuss that halves cannot be made horizontally on the 5 × 4 rectangle because of the location of the dots. Have students describe any other limitations they notice.

- Ask students to draw a rectangle of a different size on the dot paper. Have them discover which of the fractions they can make.

▶ **Mathematical Discourse**

3 *Would it be possible to have 5 fourths in a rectangle? Explain.*

No. Fourths means the rectangle is divided into 4 equal parts. If there were 5 parts, they would not be fourths.

4 *What if I divided one of the fourths into two equal parts? How many parts would there be? Would the parts be fourths?*

If you divided one of the fourths into two parts, there would be 5 parts in the rectangle, so the parts would not be fourths. You only have fourths if the rectangle is divided into 4 equal-sized parts.

Let's Talk About It

- Instruct students to work in pairs to complete Problems 8–10. Walk around to each pair. Listen to and join in on discussions at different points.

- After students complete Problem 10, ask Mathematical Discourse questions 3 and 4 to reinforce the relationship of fractional parts to the name of the fraction.

▶ **Mathematical Discourse 3 and 4**

Try It Another Way

- Have students discuss **Try It Another Way** with a partner. Tell them to divide each rectangle differently from the way they did on the previous page.

- Invite volunteers to justify that the fractional parts they made within each rectangle are equal in size.

- Discuss whether the rectangles on this page could be used to demonstrate that a half is greater than a third, and that both a half and a third are greater than a fourth.

- Students should respond that since the rectangles are all the same size, it is clear to see which parts are larger in size than the others.

▶ **Hands-On Activity**

Ready **Mathematics**
PRACTICE AND PROBLEM SOLVING

Assign *Practice and Problem Solving* **pages 293–294** after students have completed this section.

Lesson 28 *Understand* Halves, Thirds, and Fourths in Shapes   **267**

👥 Guided Practice

At A Glance

Students demonstrate their understanding of the fractions half, third, and fourth. Then students divide wholes into halves, thirds, or fourths.

Step By Step

- Discuss each problem as a class using the discussion points outlined below.

Explain

- Allow students to work with a partner to share ideas. Encourage them to explain their thinking, using pictures to help justify.

- As students share their ideas with the class, listen to each explanation and help students clarify their thoughts and descriptions.

Compare

- Ask students how they could check to see if the divisions are equal. They should focus on the concept of congruence (matching the parts up) or area (making sure the parts take up the same amount of space).

- Have students justify that the parts in circle B are not equal. You may want to cut out a circle to show that the parts don't match up.

- Make sure students understand that even though two of the parts in circle B are the same size, they can't be thirds since all three parts are not equal in size.

Draw

- Some students may be creative and divide a circle in a way similar to what is shown here.

- Ask how they could be sure the two parts are the same size. Suggest that one way would be to use a straight line to divide the circle in half (see dashed line). Compare the triangles on each side of the line. If the triangles are the same size, the halves are equal.

- Discuss how using a straight dividing line results in equal parts.

Connect ▶ Ideas About Dividing into Parts

Talk about these questions as a class. Then write your answers.

14 **Explain** Carlo and Abe buy the same sandwich. Carlo's sandwich is cut in thirds. Abe's sandwich is cut in fourths. Which sandwich has smaller pieces? Explain.

Possible answer: Abe's sandwich has smaller pieces.

Abe's sandwich is cut into 4 pieces. Carlo's sandwich

is cut into 3 pieces. When you divide a shape into

more pieces, the pieces are smaller.

15 **Compare** Which circle is divided into thirds? Explain.

Possible answer: Circle A is divided into thirds. Both

circles have 3 parts, but the parts in circle B are not

equal. The parts of circle A are equal.

A   B

16 **Draw** Divide the squares in half two different ways. Make the halves of one square different shapes than the halves of the other square. Try doing the same with the circles. What do you notice?

Possible drawing:

Possible answer: I can make the parts of the square

different shapes. The parts of the circle are the

same shape.

Scoring Rubrics

Part A	
Points	**Expectations**
2	The student accurately divides the shapes into halves, thirds, or fourths to make exactly 10 pieces.
1	The student may draw 10 pieces, but the fractional parts within each shape are not equal. Or the fractional parts are equal, but there are not a total of 10 pieces.
0	The student was not able to accurately divide the shapes into fractional parts, and either more or fewer than 10 pieces were made.

Apply **Ideas About Dividing into Parts**

Put It Together **Use what you have learned to complete this task.**

17 Shara and her mom make these 3 pizzas for a party.

Part A Shara will have 10 people at the party. Draw how she could cut each pizza so every person gets 1 piece of pizza. **Possible answer:**

Part B Shara asks more people to the party. Now there will be 12 people. Draw how she could cut each pizza so every person gets 1 piece of pizza.
Possible answer:

Part C Do you think each person gets an equal amount of pizza? Explain.

Possible answer: No, each person does not get an equal

amount of pizza. The pizzas are different shapes and sizes,

so the wholes are not the same size.

269

Step By Step

Put It Together

- Direct students to complete the **Put It Together** task on their own.

- Read the directions with students and make sure they understand each part of the task before proceeding. Explain that students should divide the pizzas into halves, thirds, or fourths. Let them know that they do not have to divide all the pizzas the same way.

- If time permits, ask students to share the divisions they chose and justify their choices.

 Ready· Mathematics
PRACTICE AND PROBLEM SOLVING

Assign *Practice and Problem Solving* **pages 295–296** after students have completed Guided Practice.

Part B	
Points	**Expectations**
2	The student accurately divides each shape into 4 equal parts.
1	The student may draw 12 pieces, but the fractional parts within each shape are not equal. Or the parts are equal, but 12 parts were not made.
0	The student was not able to accurately divide the shapes into fractional parts or into a total of 12 pieces.

Part C	
Points	**Expectations**
2	The student's response demonstrates a clear understanding of fractions. The student recognizes that a fourth of one shape may not be equal in size to a fourth of another shape.
1	The student's response shows some understanding of fractions. The student may respond that each person gets a fourth of a pizza, but may fail to recognize that a fourth of one shape may not be equal to a fourth of a different shape.
0	The student was not able to articulate an understanding of fractional parts or their relationship to each other within a single shape or among different shapes.

Differentiated Instruction

▶ Intervention Activity

Explore with fraction puzzles.

Materials: For each pair: 3 rectangles, 3 circles, and 3 squares cut from heavy paper; each set should be cut apart into halves, thirds, and fourths (cut the parts of rectangles and squares differently from each other); each whole shape should be similarly sized

• Provide student pairs with the cut-out fraction pieces.

• Tell students to find and put together the pieces that make 3 same-sized rectangles. Repeat for the circles and squares. Study each set of shapes, comparing the sizes of halves, thirds, and fourths. Ask students to place a half, third, and fourth of one shape next to each other and order them from largest to smallest. Reinforce the concept that the more pieces a shape is divided into, the smaller each piece will be.

• Ask students to write the word *Halves* at the top of a sheet of paper and then glue all the puzzle pieces that are halves onto the paper. Guide students to place each half with another half to form a whole shape. Ask students to do the same for thirds and fourths.

▶ On-Level Activity

Make paper-folded fractions.

Materials: 3 rectangles and 3 circles drawn on paper or cut out

• Provide students with the rectangles and circles. Ask them to cut out the shapes if necessary.

• Tell students to fold one rectangle into halves. Encourage a variety of ways to fold. Compare the ways students folded.

• Repeat for thirds and fourths, discussing strategies students used, such as folding in half and in half again for fourths. Have students shade one of the fractional pieces on each shape.

• Repeat the above activity with the circles. For thirds, have students fold a circle in half and then fold that piece into three equal parts from the center of the fold. It will make 3 wedges (sectors). Open it all up and notice that two of the folded parts is a third of the whole.

• Display the folded shapes under the headings *Halves, Thirds,* and *Fourths.*

▶ Challenge Activity

Fold rectangles into sixths, eighths, and twelfths.

Materials: at least 4 rectangles drawn on paper or cut out

• Provide students with the rectangles. Ask students to cut them out if necessary.

• Challenge students to find ways of folding the rectangles into sixths, eighths, and twelfths.

• Have them share each rectangle they folded and justify that the parts are the same size.

• Ask students to tell how knowing halves, thirds, and fourths can help them find sixths, eighths, and twelfths.

Teacher Notes

Teacher-Toolbox.com

Overview

Assign the Lesson 28 Quiz and have students work independently to complete it.

Use the results of the quiz to assess students' understanding of the content of the lesson and to identify areas for reteaching. See the Lesson Pacing Guide at the beginning of the lesson and the Differentiated Instruction activities that follow for suggested instructional resources.

Tested Skills

Assesses 2.G.A.3

Problems on this assessment form require students to be able to identify and name half, third, and fourth parts of a divided shape, recognize that halves, thirds, and fourths indicate equal-sized parts, divide a shape into halves, thirds, or fourths, recognize that equal parts of identical wholes can have different shapes, and understand that the more equal parts there are, the smaller each part is. Students will also need to be familiar with how to partition shapes into equal parts and what halves, thirds, and fourths mean.

Ready® **Mathematics**

Lesson 28 Quiz

Solve the problems.

1 The two large rectangles below are the same size. Each rectangle is divided into equal parts in a different way.

Are the shaded parts equal in size?

Circle the correct answer and explanation.

A No. The shaded part in the first rectangle is larger than the shaded part in the second rectangle.

B No. The shaded part in the first rectangle is smaller than the shaded part in the second rectangle.

C Yes. The two shaded parts are different shapes, but each covers one third of the large rectangle so they are equal in size.

D Yes. The two shaded parts are different shapes, but each covers one fourth of the large rectangle so they are equal in size.

2 Mr. Diaz wants to cut a sandwich into fourths to share with his family.

Draw lines on the shape to show one way Mr. Diaz can cut the sandwich into fourths.

Lesson 28 Quiz continued

3 Liza sees a circle in her book. The circle is divided into halves. Which circle could Liza see?

Circle the correct answer.

A   **C**

B   **D**

4 The circle below is divided into equal parts.

Circle *True* or *False* for each statement about the circle.

a. The whole circle is one fourth.   True   False

b. The whole circle is four fourths.   True   False

c. The circle has 4 parts that are one fourth each.   True   False

d. The circle is divided into fourths.   True   False

Common Misconceptions and Errors

Errors may result if students:

- confuse the number of equal parts in halves (two), thirds (three), and fourths (four).

- do not recognize that two halves, three thirds, and four fourths all equal a whole.

Ready® **Mathematics**

Lesson 28 Quiz Answer Key

1. C
DOK 3

2. Possible student answers.

DOK 2

3. A
DOK 1

4. a. False
b. True
c. True
d. True
DOK 2

Recognize and Use Shapes

CCSS Focus

Domain
Geometry

Cluster
2.G.A Reason with shapes and their attributes.

Standards
2.G.A.1, 2.G.A.2, 2.G.A.3

Standards for Mathematical Practice (SMP)

1 Make sense of problems and persevere in solving them.

3 Construct viable arguments and critique the reasoning of others.

4 Model with mathematics.

Additional SMPs
2, 5, 6, 7

Lesson at a Glance

Students apply skills from the unit to solve real-world problems related to cakes. Problems involve naming shapes, dividing shapes into equal parts, naming fractional parts, and composing and decomposing shapes.

Lesson Pacing Guide

Whole Class Instruction

Day 1
45–60 minutes

Introduction

Problem and Solution *45 min*

Task	**Key Skills**	**Mathematical Practices**
Analyze a solution to a problem about ways to cut 3 different-shaped cakes into halves, thirds, or fourths.	• Understand halves as 2 equal parts. • Understand thirds as 3 equal parts. • Understand fourths as 4 equal parts.	• Draw a model to represent fractions. • Make use of structure. • Critique a given solution.

Day 2
45–60 minutes

Modeled and Guided Instruction

Try Another Approach

Plan It *15 min* • Solve It *20 min* • Reflect *10 min*

Task	**Key Skills**	**Mathematical Practices**
Use another approach about ways to cut 3 different-shaped cakes into halves, thirds, or fourths.	• Know that fractions name equal parts of a whole. • Identify the number of equal parts in halves, thirds, and fourths.	• Draw a fractional model to represent a situation. • Critique the geometric reasoning of others. • Persevere in solving a problem.

Day 3
45–60 minutes

Guided Practice

Discuss Models and Strategies

Plan and Solve It *35 min* • Reflect *10 min*

Task	**Key Skills**	**Mathematical Practices**
Determine a way to cut a square cake into equal parts and tell the size of the parts using given measurements.	• Draw a model to represent same-size fractional parts. • Know a square has four equal sides. • Measure length with a ruler.	• Reason abstractly about geometric figures. • Use an appropriate tool. • Precisely describe length measurements.

Whole Class Instruction continued

Day 4
45–60 minutes

Independent Practice

Persevere on Your Own

Problem 1

Solve It *35 min* • Reflect *10 min*

Task	**Key Skills**	**Mathematical Practices**
Determine a way to use specified shapes to make a fish-shaped cake and tell how many of each shape are used.	• Draw a triangle, a square, and a rhombus. • Organize data. • Know that shapes can be composed from other shapes.	• Make sense of the problem. • Construct an argument to justify choices. • Accurately draw shapes.

Day 5
45–60 minutes

Independent Practice

Persevere on Your Own

Problem 2

Solve It *35 min* • Reflect *10 min*

Task	**Key Skills**	**Mathematical Practices**
Find two ways to arrange specified shapes to make a given cake shape.	• Identify triangles, trapezoids, squares, rhombuses, and hexagons. • Organize data. • Know that shapes can be composed to form other shapes.	• Make sense of a problem. • Justify decisions. • Reason about shapes and their attributes.

Unit Resources

Practice
Practice and Problem Solving

Grade 2
• Unit 4 Game
• Unit 4 Practice
• Unit 4 Performance Task
• Unit 4 Vocabulary

Assess
Ready Instruction

Grade 2
• Unit 4 Interim Assessment

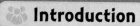
At A Glance

Students examine a problem about baking cakes that involves cutting geometric shapes into equal-size pieces. Students discuss the problem to understand what it is asking and brainstorm different approaches. Then they refer to a problem-solving checklist to analyze a sample solution and identify what makes it a good solution.

Step By Step

• Read the problem out loud with students. Invite volunteers to describe what information is given and what they need to figure out.

▶ **Mathematical Discourse 1**

• Direct students' attention to the illustration of the cakes.

• Invite students to share their ideas about how they might solve this problem. Allow them to describe different approaches, without carrying through with an actual solution yet.

▶ **Mathematical Discourse 2 and 3**

• Explain that students will look at the sample solution on the next page to see one way the problem could be solved. Then they will read the solution again and discuss what makes it a good solution by using the **Problem-Solving Checklist.**

▶ **English Language Learners**

Study an Example Problem and Solution

Read this problem about breaking shapes into equal parts. Then look at Luna's solution to the problem.

Cake Shapes

Luna makes 3 cakes. She wants to cut each cake into equal-size pieces. Read Luna's notes.

My Notes

My cakes are in the shape of a circle, a rectangle, and a square.
• Cut one cake into halves.
• Cut one into thirds.
• Cut one into fourths.

Show one way Luna can cut the cakes.

Show how Luna's solution matches the checklist.

Problem-Solving Checklist

☐ Tell what is known.
☐ Tell what the problem is asking.
☐ Show all your work.
☐ Show that the solution works.

a. Circle something that is known.
b. Underline something that you need to find.
c. Draw a box around what you do to solve the problem.
d. Put a checkmark next to the part that shows the solution works.

270

▶ **Mathematical Discourse**

1 *How many pieces will Luna have after she cuts the cakes? How do you know?*

Students should recognize that she will have 2 halves, 3 thirds, and 4 fourths.

2 *Which cake would you cut into halves? Thirds? Fourths? Why did you choose that cake?*

Any cake can be cut into any fraction, but some cuts are easier to see than others! Listen for students' reasons and explanations for cutting a cake into a certain fraction.

3 *How many ways could you cut the rectangular cake into halves?*

Encourage students to think flexibly. The cake can be cut horizontally, vertically, or diagonally (from upper left or lower left). Be sure that the students show understanding of equal parts.

▶ **English Language Learners**

Discuss with students the words *halves*, *thirds*, and *fourths*. Point out that *fourths* has the word *four* in it and means that a whole is cut into 4 equal parts. The word *thirds* is related to *three* and means that a whole is cut into 3 equal parts. What about the word *halves*? Discuss ways to remember that it means a whole is cut into 2 equal parts.

Luna's Solution

Hi, I'm Luna. Here's how I solved this problem.

▷ **I know what** halves, thirds, and fourths are.
Halves are 2 equal parts.
Thirds are 3 equal parts.
Fourths are 4 equal parts.

I thought about what I already know.

▷ **I need to cut each shape into a different number of equal parts.**

2 half-circles
(2 halves)

3 same-size rectangles
(3 thirds)

4 same-size triangles
(4 fourths)

I labeled the pictures to check my thinking.

▷ **I can tell how I cut the cakes.**
I cut the circle cake in halves.
I cut the rectangle cake in thirds.
I cut the square cake in fourths.

271

▶ Mathematical Discourse

4 *What are some other ways Luna could have cut the circle into halves?*
Take some time to allow students to "play" with this question. Let them struggle a little to describe how many ways they could cut a circle into 2 equal pieces. Some may only consider horizontal or vertical cuts, but others will likely see there are any number of diagonal cuts possible.

5 *Could she have cut the circle into thirds? Fourths?*
Allow students time for productive struggle with how to show thirds on a circle. Redirect if they draw parallel lines creating unequal pieces for either thirds or fourths.

Step By Step

- Explain that this page shows one way to solve the problem.
- Read through Luna's solution together, one section at a time. Read for understanding, helping students with any language challenges.
- Discuss the sample solution with students.

SMP TIP Model with Mathematics
Engage students in a discussion about the illustrations. Have them talk with a partner about how the sample solution uses the illustrations to help solve the problem. **(SMP 4)**

- Have students describe Luna's solution. Invite students to suggest other ways Luna might have decided to cut the cakes.

▶ **Mathematical Discourse 4 and 5**

- Direct students' attention to the last three sentences. Make sure students recognize the importance of showing that the answer works. Be sure everyone agrees that this solution works.
- Then, as a class, go back to do a close read, using the **Problem-Solving Checklist** to help analyze Luna's solution.
- By now students understand that the checklist lists ways to make sure you write a good answer. Ask students to look at the solution again and decide where Luna wrote something that was given in the problem. [The shapes of the cakes were given.] Have them circle that part.
- Then have them look for a place that Luna wrote what she was trying to do. [Break the shapes into halves, thirds, and fourths.] When the class is in agreement, have them underline that part.
- Likewise support students as they mark where Luna showed her work and where she checked her work. [She showed her work inside the shapes and checked her work by numbering the pieces.]

Modeled and Guided Instruction

Try Another Approach

At A Glance

Students plan and solve the Cake Shapes problem from the Introduction by cutting the shapes in different ways. Students demonstrate that the problem has more than one solution.

Step By Step

- Review and summarize the steps in Luna's solution. [Explain what halves, thirds, and fourths are. Cut the circle into halves, the rectangle into thirds, and the square into fourths. Show that the cakes have 2 equal parts, 3 equal parts, and 4 equal parts.]

- Have students brainstorm some different steps than these that they might use to solve the problem. For example, they might cut different cakes into halves, thirds, or fourths.

Plan It

- Read the question in **Plan It** aloud. Invite students to share some initial responses. [For example, cut the rectangle into fourths and cut the square into thirds.]

▶ **Hands-On Activity**

▶ **Mathematical Discourse 1 and 2**

- Have students work independently to answer the **Plan It** question. Tell students they will use their answers along with the **Problem-Solving Tips** on the next page to plan their answer.

- Remind students that this problem has many correct answers.

- As students work on their plan, circulate to provide support and answer questions. Encourage them to use a cutting plan that is different from Luna's answer.

There are many ways to solve problems. Think about how to solve the Cake Shapes problem in a different way.

Cake Shapes

Luna makes 3 cakes. She wants to cut each cake into equal-size pieces. Read Luna's notes.

> **My Notes**
> My cakes are in the shape of a circle, a rectangle, and a square.
> - Cut one cake into halves.
> - Cut one into thirds.
> - Cut one into fourths.

Show one way Luna can cut the cakes.

▶ **Plan It** Answer this question to help you start thinking about a plan.

Look at the sample answer. How can you cut each shape into a different number of pieces?

_____

_____

_____

_____

▶ **Mathematical Discourse**

1 *Explain how you are going to cut your cake(s). How do you know that your parts are halves/thirds/fourths?*

Students should be able to explain how their cuts make equal parts.

2 *How can you tell which shapes can't be cut into square pieces?*

Some students may recognize that the rectangle could be cut into square pieces, but the pieces would not be fourths. Students should recognize that a circle can never make square pieces because of its curved edges.

▶ **Hands-On Activity**

Explore ways to make halves, thirds, and fourths.

Materials: toothpicks, tape, paper, pencils

Have students work in pairs. Have them draw a circle, square, and rectangle. Then guide them to use the toothpicks to show the "cuts" in each shape to make halves, thirds, or fourths. Encourage students to try different ways to "cut" each shape. Students can tape the toothpicks in place to show their "cuts."

▶ **Solve It** Find a different solution for the Cake Shapes problem. Show all your work on a separate sheet of paper.

You may want to use the problem-solving tips to get started.

Problem-Solving Tips

- **Questions**
  - Can I make pieces that are triangles?
  - Can I make pieces that are rectangles?
  - Can I cut a circle into 3 equal parts? 4 equal parts?

Problem-Solving Checklist

Make sure that you . . .
- ☐ tell what you know.
- ☐ tell what you need to do.
- ☐ show all your work.
- ☐ show that the solution works.

- **Word Bank**

equal	a half	halves	square
shape	a third	thirds	rectangle
	a fourth	fourths	circle

- **Sentence Starters**
  - There are _____ equal parts.
  - This shape is cut into _____

▶ **Reflect**

Use Mathematical Practices Talk about this question with a partner.

- **Use Structure** How can you use the name of the fraction to tell how many equal parts it describes?

273

Scoring Rubric

Points	Expectations
4	The student's response is accurate and complete. The shapes are correctly divided and the student has verified that the solution works.
3	The student has attempted all parts of the problem but has made limited minor errors. The shapes are divided into the correct number of pieces, but a few of the pieces may be slightly different in size. The student has verified that the solution works.
2	The student's response contains several mistakes. Some of the shapes are divided into the correct number of pieces, but many of the "equal" pieces vary in size. The solution does not mention equal parts and is only partly verified.
1	The solution is incorrect. At least 2 shapes show an incorrect number of pieces and the pieces do not look equal. The verification is inaccurate and incomplete.

Step By Step

Solve It

- Remind students that the **Problem-Solving Tips** are ideas they may use to explain their thinking when they write their solution.

- Invite students to share ideas about how they might use the **Problem-Solving Tips**. Ask if there are other words that might be useful. Solicit suggestions for how they might complete each of the sentence starters.

- Encourage students to share their ideas with a partner. Have partners discuss the **Reflect** questions about Mathematical Practices.

- Have students use the plan they created to solve the problem. Encourage them to work out their preliminary ideas on scrap paper and try different approaches as necessary. Have them write their complete solution on a copy of Activity Sheet 23 (Solution Sheet 2) or a blank sheet of paper.

- If time permits, students can explain their solutions to the class. Alternatively, you can share the solution below and invite the class to discuss it.

Possible Solution

Halves are 2 equal parts, thirds are 3 equal parts, and fourths are 4 equal parts. I can cut the round cake into fourths, the square cake into thirds, and the rectangle cake into halves.

2 same-size rectangles   4 same-size pieces   3 same-size rectangles
halves   fourths   thirds

One cake is cut into halves. One cake is cut into thirds. One cake is cut into fourths.

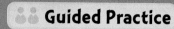
Guided Practice

At A Glance

With **Problem-Solving Tips** as support, students understand, plan, and solve an open-ended, multi-step problem. They choose appropriate models and strategies to solve the problem, checking their thinking with a partner.

Materials Activity Sheet 24 (Cutting Cakes), two copies per student

Step By Step

- Read the problem out loud with students. As you read, encourage students to ask clarifying questions about the shape of the cake and the requirements of the task. [The top face of the cake has a square shape, and they need to cut it into square pieces that are all the same size.]

▶ **Mathematical Discourse 1**

- Show students the diagram they will use (Activity Sheet 24). Do not distribute yet.

- Discuss the task requirements on the next page. Talk about ways to figure out the lengths of the sides of the squares that they will make.

▶ **Mathematical Discourse 2 and 3**

- Distribute a copy of Activity Sheet 24. Ask students to work with a partner to think about solving the problem and discuss possible approaches.

> **SMP TIP Attend to Precision**
> Encourage students to be precise as they communicate their plans. They can use inches to describe the length of the sides of the squares they make. They may discuss the exact number of squares they will make. They can accurately describe the square shape of the cake and the pieces. *(SMP 6)*

Discuss ▶ **Models and Strategies**

Solve the problem on a separate sheet of paper. There are different ways you can solve it.

Cutting Cakes

Luna's friends make cakes in all shapes and sizes. Luna helps them plan ways to cut the cakes into pieces of different sizes. Here is one plan.

> **My Cake Cutting Plan**
> - Draw squares on the top of the cake to show how to cut it into pieces.
> - Each square must be the same size.

Luna has a square cake like this one. Each side is 6 inches long.

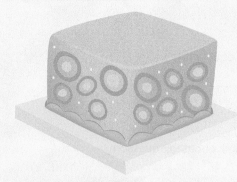

What size squares can Luna cut the cake into?

274

▶ **Mathematical Discourse**

1 *How do you know that this cake is square shaped?*

Some students will say that it looks like a square. Mathematically, the sides of the top face of the cake must be of equal length. If students think it looks like a diamond instead of a square, validate that observation. It's true that they can't tell from the picture that the shape has square corners.

2 *How could you be sure you have made square pieces?*

Possible answers: Use a ruler to make sure the sides of the pieces are the same length. Use square tiles.

3 *Why might you want to cut small pieces? Why might you want to cut big pieces?*

Listen for evidence that students understand what happens when a greater number of equal shares is made. The more pieces they make, the smaller the pieces will be.

▶ **Plan It and Solve It** Find a solution for Luna's Cake Cutting problem.

Use the diagram of Luna's square cake on the Cutting Cakes Activity Sheet.

• Divide the square into same-size smaller squares.
• Then write the length of the sides of your squares.
• Last, tell why the pieces work with Luna's plan.

You may want to use the problem-solving tips to get started.

Problem-Solving Tips

• **Questions**
  • Can I use squares that have 1-inch sides? 2-inch sides? 4-inch sides?

Problem-Solving Checklist

Make sure that you . . .
☐ tell what you know.
☐ tell what you need to do.
☐ show all your work.
☐ show that the solution works.

• **Tools**

• **Word Bank**

square	sides	equal
inches	size	

▶ **Reflect**

Use Mathematical Practices Talk about this question with a partner.

• **Use Tools** How can you put the square tiles together to make different-size squares?

275

Step By Step

Plan It and Solve It

• Discuss the **Problem-Solving Tips** as ideas students may use to explain their thinking when they write their solution.

• Invite students to share ideas about answers to the questions, other words they might use, and how they might complete the sentences. Discuss ways students could label the square on the Activity Sheet to show their thinking.

• Put students in pairs to discuss solution ideas. Ask them to also talk about the **Reflect** question about Mathematical Practices.

• Discuss a variety of approaches as a class. Let students revise their plans and discuss again with a partner. Encourage students to think about solutions beyond cutting the cake into just 4 squares.

• When students are confident that their plans make sense, tell them to write a complete solution on the Activity Sheet.

• If time permits, share and discuss student solutions or the one below.

Possible Solution

I have a square cake with 6-inch sides. I need to mark squares on the top to cut square pieces. All the pieces must be the same size.

I can draw fourths.

To make fourths, I can divide each side in half. The sides of the big square are 6 inches. Since $3 + 3 = 6$, the sides of each small square are 3 inches. I can measure to check.

This fits Luna's plan because the pieces are all squares and are the same size.

Scoring Rubric

Points	Expectations
4	The solution is accurate and complete, and shows understanding of the task. The squares are all the same size and completely cover the cake. The squares' sizes are identified correctly. The explanation accurately verifies the solution.
3	The student has attempted all parts of the problem but has made limited minor errors. The solution shows understanding of the task. The squares are all the same size and cover the cake but their size is not identified correctly. The explanation makes sense.
2	The solution contains several mistakes and is incomplete. The squares may not all be the same size and some squares may be missing. The squares' sizes may not be correctly identified. The explanation is incomplete.
1	The solution is incorrect. The cake is not cut into squares, and/or the entire cake is not covered. The squares' sizes are incorrect. The solution is not explained.

Independent Practice

At A Glance

Students find and share solutions to multi-step, open-ended problems.

Materials Pattern Blocks or Activity Sheet 25 (Pattern Blocks), Activity Sheet 26 (Create a Cake 1), Activity Sheet 27 (Create a Cake 2)

Step By Step

Solve It

- Have students read the problem. Help them with any language issues. Encourage them to come up with some ideas and ask any questions they may have.

- Distribute pattern blocks and Activity Sheet 26. Post spelling for the words *square*, *triangle*, *trapezoid*, *hexagon*, and *rhombus* for students to reference.

- Then put students in pairs to discuss their preliminary solutions. When they are confident that their plan will work, have students independently write their solutions on the Activity Sheet.

- After students complete their solutions, put them in pairs to discuss the **Reflect** question about Mathematical Practices.

- If time permits, invite various students to explain their solutions for the class to discuss, compare, and critique. Alternatively, share the solution below and invite the class to discuss.

Possible Solution

I need to use triangles, squares, and parallelograms to make the fish shape. I have lots of each shape.

I decided to make each of the trapezoids from 3 triangles.

I used 9 triangles. 2 squares, and 2 rhombuses.

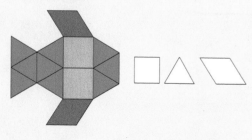

Persevere ▶ **On Your Own**

Solve the problem on a separate sheet of paper.

Create a Cake 1

Luna wants to make a cake that looks like this fish.

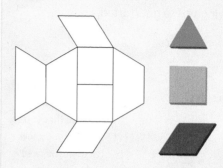

How can Luna make the cake with the shapes shown?

▶ **Solve It** **Help Luna make the cake shown above.**

Use the Create a Cake 1 Activity Sheet and the shapes shown above.
- Find a way to use Luna's pieces to make the fish.
- Draw outlines of the shapes you used.
- Make a list of the shapes that you used.
- Tell how many of each shape you used.

▶ **Reflect**

Use Mathematical Practices Talk about this question with a partner.

- **Make an Argument** How do you know that you named each shape correctly?

276

Scoring Rubric	
Points	**Expectations**
4	The solution is accurate and complete. The diagram shows a correct solution. The student shows the shapes used and accurately lists how many of each shape were used.
3	The student has attempted all parts of the problem but has made limited minor errors. The diagram shows a correct solution, and the shapes are shown. The student has made a few errors in listing how many of each shape were used.
2	The student's response contains several errors. Drawings of some shapes are inaccurate. The list of the number of each shape used does not accurately reflect the diagram.
1	The solution is incorrect. The diagram does not match the given shape. The drawings of some shapes are missing. The list of the number of each shape used does not accurately reflect the diagram and would not make a correct solution.

Create a Cake 2

Luna needs to make a cake in this design.

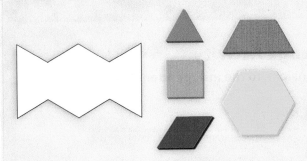

You can use any of the shapes shown above.
You can use any shape more than once.

▶ **Solve It** **Help Luna make the cake shown above.**
Use the Create a Cake 2 Activity Sheet and the shapes shown above.
• Find two different ways to make the design.
• Draw outlines of the shapes you used.
• Make a list of the shapes that you used.
• Tell how many of each shape you used.

▶ **Reflect**
Use Mathematical Practices Talk about this question with a partner.
• **Use Tools** How did you use the pattern block shapes to help you solve this problem?

277

Step By Step

Solve It

• Have students work through this problem entirely on their own. However, help with any reading or language issues.

• Distribute pattern blocks and Activity Sheet 27. Post spelling for the words *square*, *triangle*, *trapezoid*, *hexagon*, and *rhombus* for students to reference.

• Remind students that there are many different ways to solve a problem. Have them write their solution on the Activity Sheet.

• After students complete their solutions, put them in pairs to discuss the **Reflect** question about Mathematical Practices. Students may also describe other Math Practices they used.

• If time permits, invite various students to explain their solutions for the class to discuss, compare, and critique. Alternatively, share the solution below and invite the class to discuss.

Possible Solution

I need to put shapes together in 2 different ways to make the given design. I can use trapezoids, rhombuses, triangles, squares, and hexagons.

First, I can use these shapes so that I could use as few pieces as possible.

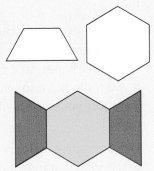

This design uses 1 hexagon and 2 trapezoids.

Next, I can use all triangles.

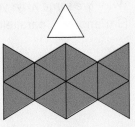

This design uses 12 triangles.

Scoring Rubric	
Points	**Expectations**
4	The solution is accurate and complete. The diagrams show two correct ways to make the cake. The student shows the shapes used and accurately lists how many of each shape were used in each example.
3	The student has attempted all parts of the problem but has made limited minor errors. The solution is substantially complete and accurate. The diagram shows two correct ways to make the cake. But the student has made a few errors in listing how many of each shape were used.
2	The solution contains several mistakes. Each diagram has one or two errors. Drawings of some shapes are inaccurate. The lists of the number of each shape used does not accurately reflect the diagrams.
1	The solution is incorrect. The diagrams do not match the given design. The drawings of many shapes are missing. The list of the number of each shape used does not accurately reflect the diagrams and would not make a correct solution.

Differentiated Instruction

▶ Intervention Activity
Provide support for the Independent Practice.

Create a Cake 1

Materials: Pattern Blocks or Activity Sheet 25 (Pattern Blocks)

Help students approach the problem by working with pattern. Ask, *How can you make the trapezoid shape using these blocks?* Encourage students to lay blocks on top of the trapezoid until they have found a way to cover it completely without gaps. Discuss the shapes they used and how they came to this discovery. Ask, *Are there other shapes you can make out of the triangles?* Students will find that they can make the parallelogram with 2 triangles but that there is no way to use these triangles to make a square. Discuss why this is so. [These triangles do not have "square corners" (right angles).]

Create a Cake 2

Discuss the following questions. Then circulate while students work independently, providing support as needed.

Which of these shapes could you use to make this cake? Why? [The hexagon and trapezoid are shown in the cake plan, so these can be used. The parallelogram and triangle can make a trapezoid or a hexagon, so they can be used.

Which shapes would you not use to make this cake? Why? [The square does not have angles (corners) that fit with the other shapes, so it cannot be used to make this cake. If you try to put a square into the trapezoid or the hexagon, you are left with a shape that you cannot make.]

What are some ways you can make a hexagon? [6 triangles; 2 trapezoids; 3 parallelograms; 2 parallelograms and 2 triangles, 1 trapezoid, 1 parallelogram, and 1 triangle; etc.]

What are some ways you can make a trapezoid? [3 triangles, 1 parallelogram and 1 triangle]

▶ Challenge Activity
Solve extensions to the Independent Practice.

Create a Cake 1

Extension

Luna wants to make another fish cake that looks just like the cake shown. This time she has none of the blue parallelograms but she has many trapezoids. Show two ways she can make the cake.

Possible Solution

One way—Use 2 squares, 3 trapezoids, and 4 triangles.

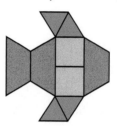

Another way—Use 2 squares and 13 triangles.

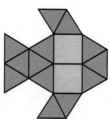

Create a Cake 2

Extension

Luna wants to make this cake using exactly 3 of the blue parallelograms. What are 2 ways she can do this?

Possible Solution

One way—Use 3 parallelograms, 3 triangles, and 1 trapezoid.

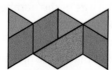

Another way—Use 3 parallelograms and 6 triangles.

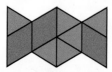

Teacher Notes

Solutions

1 **Solution**

B, C; Add or skip count to find the totals.

$2 + 2 + 2 + 2 + 2 + 2 + 2 + 2 + 2 = 18$

$3 + 3 + 3 + 3 + 3 + 3 = 18$

DOK 2

2 **Solution**

C, D; The shaded rectangle is divided into fourths. The answer choice rectangles are identical wholes, so those with fourths are correct. Answer choices C and D show fourths. Answer choice A shows thirds, and B shows 4 unequal sections.

DOK 2

Solve the problems.

1 Kate has 18 square tiles. How can she arrange them to make a rectangle? Circle all the correct answers.

A 10 rows of 8 squares

Ⓑ 9 rows of 2 squares

Ⓒ 6 rows of 3 squares

D 5 rows of 4 squares

2 Meg drew this rectangle and divided it into four equal parts.

Which rectangle below is divided into parts that are the same size as the parts in Meg's rectangle? Circle all the correct answers.

A   Ⓒ

B   Ⓓ

278

Teacher Notes

3 Dennis drew a hexagon. Circle *True* or *False* for each statement below about the shape Dennis drew.

a. It has 6 angles.   (True)   False

b. It is a quadrilateral.   True   (False)

c. It has more than 5 sides.   (True)   False

d. It has fewer angles than a rectangle.   True   (False)

4 Draw the rest of the squares to fill this rectangle. Make all your squares the same size as the gray square.

Possible answer:

How many squares are there in all?

Answer   8   squares

5 Scott says that one third of this circle is shaded. Do you agree? Explain why or why not.

Possible answer: I don't agree. The circle is divided into 4 equal parts.

So one fourth of the circle is shaded, not one third.

279

Solutions

3 **Solution**

a. **True**

b. **False**

c. **True**

d. **False**

Hexagons have 6 sides and 6 angles. Quadrilaterals and rectangles have only 4 sides and 4 angles.

DOK 2

4 **Solution**

8; A total of 8 squares that are 2 units on each side can fit in the rectangle.

DOK 2

5 **Solution**

I don't agree. Possible explanation: The circle is divided into 4 equal parts. So one fourth of the circle is shaded, not one third.

DOK 3

Teacher Notes

👤 Assessment

Standards: 2.G.A.3

DOK: 3

Materials: (optional) rectangular sheet of paper, scissors

Standards for Mathematical Practice
2, 3, 4, 5, 6

Step By Step

About the Task

For this task, students reason about equal divisions of shapes. They divide rectangles and squares into equal parts and identify the names and shapes of those parts.

Getting Started

Read the problem aloud with students. Have them identify the shapes they will be working with on the page. Guide students to understand that each shape is being used to model a field at the school. **(SMP 4, 5)**

Completing the Task

Students first need to divide the rectangle into 2 equal parts. Encourage students to see that there are multiple ways that the rectangle can be divided into 2 equal parts. Some students might see division using only horizontal or vertical lines, but miss dividing the shape across a diagonal. This could be because they don't recognize the parts as being the same size when a diagonal line is used. You could illustrate the equivalence of the 2 parts formed by a diagonal line by cutting a rectangular sheet of paper diagonally into halves and turning one piece to match the other. After students have divided the rectangle into 2 equal parts, they need to identify the name of each equal part by selecting a word from the box at the right. **(SMP 2, 4, 5)**

Next, students explain how to divide the rectangle into halves that are a different shape. Dividing vertically or horizontally should result in rectangles, and dividing diagonally should result in triangles. **(SMP 6)**

Students will follow a similar process to divide the two squares into fourths. Students will

Performance Task

Answer the questions. Use the shapes on this page. Show the rest of your work on separate paper.

Keeth Elementary School is having Field Day. Each grade plays on a separate field.

- Grade 1 has two classes. Draw a line to divide the rectangular field into 2 equal parts. What shape is each part? What is the name of each equal part? Choose a word from the box at the right.

  Possible drawing:

Checklist
Did You . . .
☐ make the parts equal in size?
☐ check your answers?
☐ explain your answers?

| one half |
| one third |
| one fourth |

- Explain how you could divide the same field into 2 equal parts that are a different shape. What shape is each part?

- There are four Grade 2 classes and four Grade 3 classes. Draw lines to divide each square field into 4 equal parts. Divide the two fields in different ways. What is the name of each equal part? Choose a word from the box above.

  Possible drawings:

  Grade 2   Grade 3

▶ **Reflect**

Use a Tool How could you fold a piece of square paper to show that your squares have 4 equal parts?

280

draw lines to divide each shape into 4 equal parts. If students need help dividing the squares in two different ways, remind them that they can use horizontal, vertical, or diagonal lines. Then students will identify the name of each equal part by selecting a word from the box. **(SMP 4, 5, 6)**

▶ **Extension**

4-Point Solution

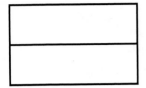

The shape of each part is a rectangle. Each equal part is one half of the rectangle.

The same field could be divided into two equal parts by drawing a line between opposite corners. The shape of each part would be a triangle.

Grade 2

Grade 3

Each equal part is one fourth of the square.

Scoring Rubric

Points	Expectations
4	The student's response is accurate and complete. All divisions and identifications are correct. All explanations are complete and correct.
3	The student divides all the shapes into equal parts, but the two squares are not divided in different ways. The student correctly identifies the names and shapes of the parts, but the explanations are not complete.
2	The student divides all the shapes into parts. However, for one of the shapes, the student does not create the correct number of equal parts or does not correctly identify the names and shapes of the parts. Explanations contain several errors or are mostly incomplete.
1	Two of the three shapes are not divided into the correct number of equal parts. The student misidentifies the names and shapes of parts at least two times. Explanations are incorrect or incomplete.

▶ Extension

Take the performance task further.

The two Grade 4 classes will be playing in a circular area at the school. Explain how to divide the circular area into halves. Can you divide the same area into halves that are a different shape? Why or why not?

Solution

Possible answer: Students may suggest that the circle can be divided along a line that passes through its center. There is only one possible shape for the halves, which is a half-circle. The shape of the parts does not change with different orientations of the dividing line.

Reflect

Possible answer: Folding a shape in half and then in half again makes 4 equal parts. So I could fold a square piece of paper in half to make a line like one of the lines I drew in a square. Then I could fold the paper in half again to make a line like the other line I drew in that square. If I open up the paper and the fold lines match the lines I drew, this shows that my square has 4 equal parts. I would do this with a second piece of square paper for the other square I divided into 4 equal parts.

Glossary

A

AM morning, or the time from midnight until noon.

add to combine, or find the total.

addend a number being added.

4 + 7 = 11

addends

analog clock a clock with an hour hand and a minute hand.

hour hand — minute hand

angle one of the corners of a shape where two sides meet.

angle

array a set of objects grouped in equal rows and equal columns.

B

bar graph a way to show data using bars.

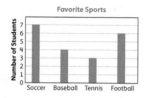

Favorite Sports

Number of Students — Soccer, Baseball, Tennis, Football

C

cent the smallest unit of money in the United States. One penny is one cent.

centimeter a unit of length. Your little finger is about 1 centimeter across.

column a top-to-bottom line of objects in an array.

compare to decide if one number is greater than (>), less than (<), or equal to (=) another number.

D

data a set of collected information.

difference the result of subtraction.

9 – 3 = 6 ← difference

digit a symbol used to write numbers. The digits are 0, 1, 2, 3, 4, 5, 6, 7, 8, and 9.

digital clock a clock that uses digits to show the time.

dime a coin with a value of 10 cents.

dollar a unit of money equal to 100 cents.

E

equal (=) the same value or same amount.

3 + 1 is equal to 4

equation a number sentence that uses an equal sign (=).

3 + 5 = 8 is an addition **equation**.

estimate (noun) a close guess made using math thinking.

estimate (verb) to make a close guess using math thinking.

even number a whole number that has a 0, 2, 4, 6, or 8 in the ones place. Even numbers are the numbers you say when you skip count by 2.

F

fact family a group of math facts that all use the same three numbers.

7 – 3 = 4

7 – 4 = 3

3 + 4 = 7

4 + 3 = 7

foot a unit of length. One foot is equal to 12 inches.

---

fourths the parts you get when you cut a whole into 4 equal parts.

fourths

4 equal parts

G

greater than symbol (>) a symbol used to show that one number is more than another number.

6 is greater than 4.

H

halves the parts you get when you cut a whole into 2 equal parts.

halves

2 equal parts

hexagon a flat shape with exactly six sides and six angles.

hour a unit of time equal to 60 minutes.

hour hand the shorter hand on a clock. It shows hours.

hour hand

I

inch a unit of length. A quarter is about 1 inch across.

L

length how long something is.

---

less than symbol (<) a symbol used to show that one number is not as much as another number.

3 is less than 5.

line plot a graph that uses marks above a number line to show data.

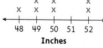

Sea Lion Lengths

48 49 50 51 52

Inches

M

meter a unit of length. One meter is equal to 100 centimeters.

minute a unit of time equal to 60 seconds.

minute hand the longer hand on a clock. It shows minutes.

minute hand

N

nickel a coin with a value of 5 cents.

O

odd number a whole number that has a 1, 3, 5, 7, or 9 in the ones place.

P

PM the time from noon until midnight.

penny a coin with a value of 1 cent.

pentagon a flat shape with exactly five sides.

picture graph a way to show data using pictures.

Favorite Vegetables

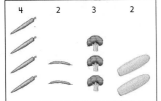

| 4 | 2 | 3 | 2 |

Carrots Beans Broccoli Corn

place value the value of a digit based on its place in a number.

Hundreds	Tens	Ones
4	4	4

400 40 4

 Q

quadrilateral a flat shape with exactly four sides and four angles.

quarter a coin with a value of 25 cents.

 R

rectangle a flat shape with 4 sides and four square corners.

regroup to put together or take apart tens and ones. For example, 12 ones is 1 ten and 2 ones.

Regroup 12 ones as 1 ten and 2 ones

rhombus a flat shape with 4 sides and all sides the same length.

row a side-to-side line of objects in an array.

 S

second a unit of time.

side one of the lines that make a two-dimensional shape.

square a flat shape with four sides all the same length and four square corners.

subtract to take away, or to compare.

sum the result of addition.

$9 + 3 = 12$ ← sum

 T

thirds the parts you get when you cut a whole into three equal parts.

thirds

3 equal parts

triangle a flat shape with three straight sides and three angles.

Y

yard a unit of length. One yard is equal to 3 feet, or 36 inches.

MATHEMATICAL PRACTICES HANDBOOK

We use our math thinking to figure out all kinds of problems. We can even solve hard problems from real life.

There are eight math habits that help make your math thinking grow stronger.

Keep practicing! You'll learn to think like a math pro. Then you'll be ready to take on any problem.

THE 8 MATH HABITS

1 Solve problems.
Keep looking for clues until you solve the problem.

2 Think and reason.
Make sense of the words and the numbers in a problem.

3 Show and explain.
Share your math ideas to help others understand you.

4 Use math in the real world.
Solve problems in real life.

5 Choose a tool.
Decide when to use tools like counters, a pencil, or mental math.

6 Be clear and precise.
Try to be exactly right in what you say and do.

7 Zoom in and zoom out.
Look for what's the same and what's different.

8 Use patterns.
Look for patterns in math to find shortcuts.

Read more about each math habit on the pages that follow.

SMPi

MATH HABIT ❶

SMP 1 Make sense of problems and persevere in solving them.

Solve problems.

Keep looking for clues until you solve the problem.

For some math problems, you may not know where to start. You may have to try more than one way to find the answer. But the answer you get should always make sense.

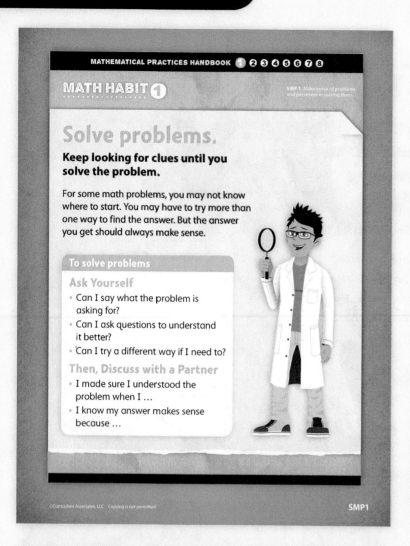

To solve problems

Ask Yourself
- Can I say what the problem is asking for?
- Can I ask questions to understand it better?
- Can I try a different way if I need to?

Then, Discuss with a Partner
- I made sure I understood the problem when I …
- I know my answer makes sense because …

©Curriculum Associates, LLC   Copying is not permitted.

SMP1

MATH HABIT ❷

SMP 2 Reason abstractly and quantitatively.

Think and reason.

Make sense of the words and the numbers in a problem.

Reasoning is thinking about how ideas go together. If you know one thing, then you know another thing. Reasoning is using math rules and common sense together.

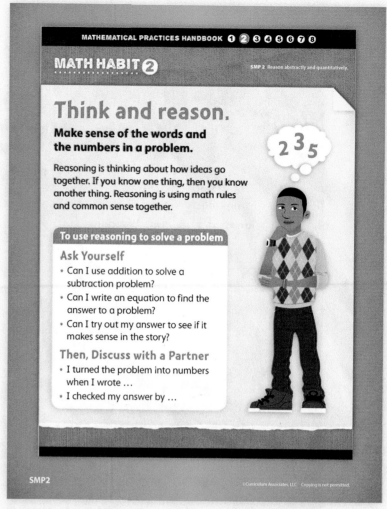

To use reasoning to solve a problem

Ask Yourself
- Can I use addition to solve a subtraction problem?
- Can I write an equation to find the answer to a problem?
- Can I try out my answer to see if it makes sense in the story?

Then, Discuss with a Partner
- I turned the problem into numbers when I wrote …
- I checked my answer by …

©Curriculum Associates, LLC   Copying is not permitted.

SMP2

MATH HABIT ❸

SMP 3 Construct viable arguments and critique the reasoning of others.

Show and explain.

Share your math ideas to help others understand you.

Explaining math ideas to others helps you understand them even better. And that helps you solve other problems later. It also helps to listen to other people. You can get new ideas too!

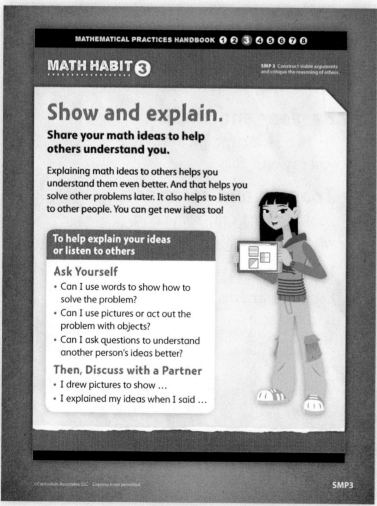

To help explain your ideas or listen to others

Ask Yourself
- Can I use words to show how to solve the problem?
- Can I use pictures or act out the problem with objects?
- Can I ask questions to understand another person's ideas better?

Then, Discuss with a Partner
- I drew pictures to show …
- I explained my ideas when I said …

©Curriculum Associates, LLC   Copying is not permitted.

SMP3

MATH HABIT ❹

SMP 4 Model with mathematics.

Use math in the real world.

Solve problems in real life.

One of the best ways to use your math thinking is to solve real problems. Words tell the story for the problem. Math can turn the words into a model, like a picture or equation.

You can use models to solve problems about shopping, sports, or … almost anything!

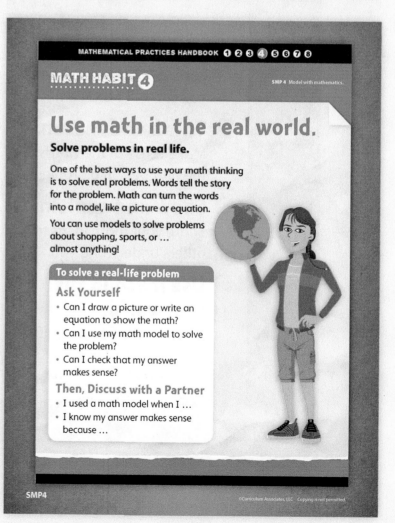

To solve a real-life problem

Ask Yourself
- Can I draw a picture or write an equation to show the math?
- Can I use my math model to solve the problem?
- Can I check that my answer makes sense?

Then, Discuss with a Partner
- I used a math model when I …
- I know my answer makes sense because …

SMP4

©Curriculum Associates, LLC   Copying is not permitted.

MATH HABIT ❺

SMP 5 Use appropriate tools strategically.

Choose a tool.

Decide when to use tools like counters, a pencil, or mental math.

There are many tools to use in math. You can use a pencil to do a lot of math. Sometimes you can use counters or base ten blocks. Often you can just do the math in your head.

To choose the best tools

Ask Yourself
- Can I do any part of the problem in my head?
- Can I write the problem on paper?
- Can I use base ten blocks?

Then, Discuss with a Partner
- The tools I chose for this problem are …
- I chose these tools because …

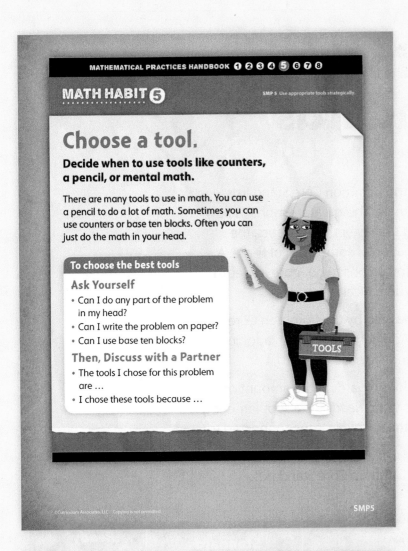

SMP5

MATH HABIT ❻

SMP 6 Attend to precision.

Be clear and precise.

Try to be exactly right in what you say and do.

Everybody likes to be right when they do math. But sometimes people make mistakes. So it's good to check your work. And it's good to say exactly what you mean when you talk about your math ideas.

To be exactly right

Ask Yourself
- Can I use words that will help everyone understand my math ideas?
- Can I find different ways to check my work when I add or subtract?

Then, Discuss with a Partner
- I was careful to use the right words when I …
- I checked my answer by …

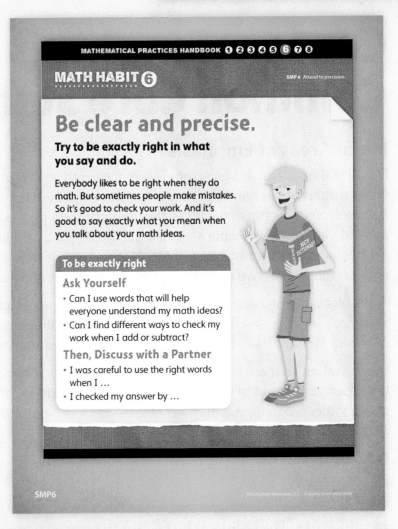

SMP6

MATH HABIT ❼

SMP 7 Look for and make use of structure.

Zoom in and zoom out.

Look for what's the same and what's different.

Math has rules. Look at these problems:

$2 + 0 = 2$
$3 + 0 = 3$

Zoom out to see what's the *same* about problems. Any number plus 0 is that number.

Zoom in to see what's *different* about problems. The numbers added to 0 are different.

To zoom in and zoom out

Ask Yourself
- Can I see how different numbers are made from tens and ones?
- Can I see what happens when I add numbers in any order?

Then, Discuss with a Partner
- I zoomed out and used a math rule when I …
- I zoomed in and found a difference when I looked at …

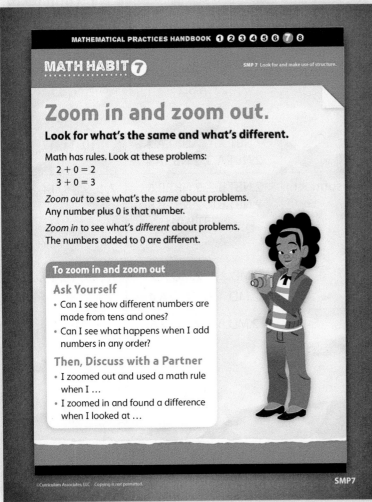

SMP7

MATH HABIT ❽

SMP 8 Look for and express regularity in repeated reasoning.

Use patterns.

Look for patterns in math to find shortcuts.

It's important in math to pay close attention. You might find a pattern or see a math idea.

Think about the pattern you can see when you count by tens:

10, 20, 30, 40, 50 …

You can use the pattern to make a good guess about what comes next.

To use patterns

Ask Yourself
- Can I find a pattern in a math problem?
- Can I use math words to describe my pattern?
- Can I figure out what is next?

Then, Discuss with a Partner
- I saw a pattern in this problem when I looked at …
- I used the pattern to make a good guess when I …

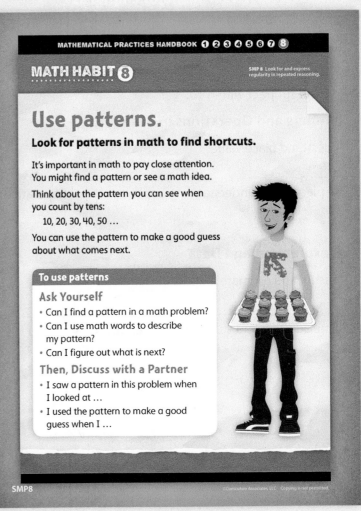

SMP8

Content Emphasis in the Common Core Standards

Major Areas of Emphasis

Not all of the content in a given grade is emphasized equally in the Common Core Standards. Some clusters of the standards require greater emphasis than others. This greater emphasis may be based on the depth of the ideas, the time that students need to master the concepts, the content's importance to future mathematics topics, or a combination of some or all of these. A greater focus on the most critical material at each grade allows for lessons to go more in-depth and for students to have more time to master concepts and mathematical practices.

The tables on these two pages identify the Major Clusters emphasized by the Common Core Standards and assessments and those that are Supporting and Additional Clusters. In addition, the *Ready®* lessons that correspond to these clusters are also identified.

Use the tables on these pages to help inform instructional decisions regarding the amount of time spent on clusters of varying degrees of emphasis. If you are using *Ready®* as a supplement with another program, you may want to spend more time with the *Ready®* lessons connected to clusters with a major emphasis.

The table below indicates the clusters of Major Emphasis in the Common Core Standards.

Standard Clusters with Major Emphasis	Standards	*Ready®* Lesson(s)
Operations and Algebraic Thinking		
Represent and solve problems involving addition and subtraction.	2.OA.A.1	2, 6
Add and subtract within 20.	2.OA.B.2	1, 3
Numbers and Operations in Base Ten		
Understand place value.	2.NBT.A.1, 2.NBT.A.2, 2.NBT.A.3, 2.NBT.A.4	10, 11, 12
Use place value understanding and properties of operations to add and subtract.	2.NBT.B.5, 2.NBT.B.6, 2.NBT.B.7, 2.NBT.B.8, 2.NBT.B.9	7, 8, 9, 13, 14, 15
Measurement and Data		
Measure and estimate lengths in standard units.	2.MD.A.1, 2.MD.A.2, 2.MD.A.3, 2.MD.A.4	16, 17, 18, 19, 20
Relate addition and subtraction to length.	2.MD.B.5, 2.MD.B.6	21, 22

Supporting and Additional Areas of Emphasis

Although some clusters have greater emphasis in the Common Core Standards, this does not mean that standards within the clusters identified as Supporting or Additional can be neglected during instruction. Neglecting material will leave gaps in students' skills and understanding and may leave students unprepared for the challenges of a later grade. Standards for topics that are not major emphases are written in such a way as to support and strengthen the areas of major emphasis. This allows for valuable connections that add coherence to the grade.

In addition, the Supporting and Additional clusters provide students with understanding that is essential for success on the Common Core assessments, though they are not a major focus of the assessments. The Common Core assessments will mirror the emphasis developed by the Common Core and highlighted here. Major clusters will represent the majority of the questions on the Common Core assessments, but it is important to note that items identified as being Supporting or Additional will also be included.

The table below indicates the clusters with Supporting or Additional Emphasis in the Common Core Standards.

Standard Clusters with Supporting or Additional Emphasis	Standards	Ready® Lesson(s)
Operations and Algebraic Thinking		
Work with equal groups of objects to gain foundations for multiplication.	2.OA.C.3, 2.OA.C.4	4, 5
Measurement and Data		
Work with time and money.	2.MD.C.7, 2.MD.C.8	24, 25
Represent and interpret data.	2.MD.C.9, 2.MD.C.10	23
Geometry		
Reason with shapes and their attributes.	2.G.A.1, 2.G.A.2, 2.G.A.3	26, 27, 28

Additional Resources

For more information on Content Emphases, see these helpful resources.

http://www.corestandards.org/other-resources/key-shifts-in-mathematics/

www.parcconline.org/parcc-model-content-frameworks

www.smarterbalanced.org/wordpress/wp-content/uploads/2011/12/Math-Content-Specifications.pdf

engageny.org/resource/math-content-emphases/

Correlation Charts

Common Core State Standards Coverage by *Ready® Instruction*

The table below correlates each Common Core State Standard to the *Ready®* Common Core Instruction lesson(s) that offer(s) comprehensive instruction on that standard. Use this table to determine which lessons your students should complete based on their mastery of each standard.

Common Core State Standards for Grade 2 Mathematical Standards	Content Emphasis	Ready® Lesson(s)
Operations and Algebraic Thinking		
Represent and solve problems involving addition and subtraction.		
2.OA.A.1 Use addition and subtraction within 100 to solve one- and two-step word problems involving situations of adding to, taking from, putting together, taking apart, and comparing, with unknowns in all positions, e.g., by using drawings and equations with a symbol for the unknown number to represent the problem.	Major	2, 6, 9, 21
Add and subtract within 20.		
2.OA.B.2 Fluently add and subtract within 20 using mental strategies. By end of Grade 2, know from memory all sums of two one-digit numbers.	Major	1, 3
Work with equal groups of objects to gain foundations for multiplication.		
2.OA.C.3 Determine whether a group of objects (up to 20) has an odd or even number of members, e.g., by pairing objects or counting them by 2s; write an equation to express an even number as a sum of two equal addends.	Supporting/Additional	4
2.OA.C.4 Use addition to find the total number of objects arranged in rectangular arrays with up to 5 rows and up to 5 columns; write an equation to express the total as a sum of equal addends.	Supporting/Additional	5
Number and Operations in Base Ten		
Understand place value.		
2.NBT.A.1 Understand that the three digits of a three-digit number represent amounts of hundreds, tens, and ones; e.g., 706 equals 7 hundreds, 0 tens, and 6 ones. Understand the following as special cases:	Major	10
2.NBT.A.1a 100 can be thought of as a bundle of ten tens — called a "hundred."	Major	10
2.NBT.A.1b The numbers 100, 200, 300, 400, 500, 600, 700, 800, 900 refer to one, two, three, four, five, six, seven, eight, or nine hundreds (and 0 tens and 0 ones).	Major	10
2.NBT.A.2 Count within 1000; skip-count by 5s, 10s, and 100s.	Major	5, 10, 24, 25
2.NBT.A.3 Read and write numbers to 1000 using base-ten numerals, number names, and expanded form.	Major	11
2.NBT.A.4 Compare two three-digit numbers based on meanings of the hundreds, tens, and ones digits, using $>$, $=$, and $<$ symbols to record the results of comparisons.	Major	12

Common Core State Standards for Grade 2 Mathematical Standards	Content Emphasis	Ready® Lesson(s)

Number and Operations in Base Ten *continued*

Use place value understanding and properties of operations to add and subtract.

2.NBT.B.5 Fluently add and subtract within 100 using strategies based on place value, properties of operations, and/or the relationship between addition and subtraction.	Major	7, 8, 9
2.NBT.B.6 Add up to four two-digit numbers using strategies based on place value and properties of operations.	Major	15
2.NBT.B.7 Add and subtract within 1000, using concrete models or drawings and strategies based on place value, properties of operations, and/or the relationship between addition and subtraction; relate the strategy to a written method. Understand that in adding or subtracting three-digit numbers, one adds or subtracts hundreds and hundreds, tens and tens, ones and ones; and sometimes it is necessary to compose or decompose tens or hundreds.	Major	13, 14
2.NBT.B.8 Mentally add 10 or 100 to a given number 100–900, and mentally subtract 10 or 100 from a given number 100–900.	Major	7, 8
2.NBT.B.9 Explain why addition and subtraction strategies work, using place value and the properties of operations.	Major	13, 14

Measurement and Data

Measure and estimate lengths in standard units.

2.MD.A.1 Measure the length of an object by selecting and using appropriate tools such as rulers, yardsticks, meter sticks, and measuring tapes.	Major	16, 17
2.MD.A.2 Measure the length of an object twice, using length units of different lengths for the two measurements; describe how the two measurements relate to the size of the unit chosen.	Major	18
2.MD.A.3 Estimate lengths using units of inches, feet, centimeters, and meters.	Major	19
2.MD.A.4 Measure to determine how much longer one object is than another, expressing the length difference in terms of a standard length unit.	Major	20

Relate addition and subtraction to length.

2.MD.B.5 Use addition and subtraction within 100 to solve word problems involving lengths that are given in the same units, e.g., by using drawings (such as drawings of rulers) and equations with a symbol for the unknown number to represent the problem.	Major	21
2.MD.B.6 Represent whole numbers as lengths from 0 on a number line diagram with equally spaced points corresponding to the numbers 0, 1, 2, …, and represent whole-number sums and differences within 100 on a number line diagram.	Major	21, 22

Work with time and money.

2.MD.C.7 Tell and write time from analog and digital clocks to the nearest five minutes, using A.M. and P.M.	Supporting/ Additional	24
2.MD.C.8 Solve word problems involving dollar bills, quarters, dimes, nickels, and pennies, using $ and ¢ symbols appropriately. *Example: If you have 2 dimes and 3 pennies, how many cents do you have?*	Supporting/ Additional	25

Common Core State Standards for Grade 2 Mathematical Standards	Content Emphasis	Ready® Lesson(s)
Measurement and Data *continued*		
Represent and interpret data.		
2.MD.D.9 Generate measurement data by measuring lengths of several objects to the nearest whole unit, or by making repeated measurements of the same object. Show the measurements by making a line plot, where the horizontal scale is marked off in whole-number units.	Supporting/ Additional	22
2.MD.D.10 Draw a picture graph and a bar graph (with single-unit scale) to represent a data set with up to four categories. Solve simple put-together, take-apart, and compare problems using information presented in a bar graph.	Supporting/ Additional	23
Geometry		
Reason with shapes and their attributes.		
2.G.A.1 Recognize and draw shapes having specified attributes, such as a given number of angles or a given number of equal faces. Identify triangles, quadrilaterals, pentagons, hexagons, and cubes.	Supporting/ Additional	26
2.G.A.2 Partition a rectangle into rows and columns of same-size squares and count to find the total number of them.	Supporting/ Additional	27
2.G.A.3 Partition circles and rectangles into two, three, or four equal shares, describe the shares using the words *halves, thirds, half of, a third of,* etc., and describe the whole as two halves, three thirds, four fourths. Recognize that equal shares of identical wholes need not have the same shape.	Supporting/ Additional	28

Math in Action Correlations

Grade 2 Math in Action Lessons	Common Core State Standards
Unit 1 Use Equal Groups and Add	2.OA.A.1, 2.OA.B.2, 2.OA.C.3, 2.OA.C.4, 2.NBT.A.2, 2.NBT.B.5
Unit 2 Add, Subtract, and Compare Numbers	2.NBT.A.1, 2.NBT.A.3, 2.NBT.A.4, 2.NBT.B.5, 2.NBT.B.6, 2.NBT.B.7, 2.NBT.B.8, 2.NBT.B.9, 2.OA.A.1
Unit 3 Use Measurement	2.MD.A.1, 2.MD.A.4, 2.MD.B.5, 2.MD.C.8
Unit 4 Recognize and Use Shapes	2.G.A.1, 2.G.A.2, 2.G.A.3

Interim Assessment Correlations

Depth of Knowledge and Standards Coverage by *Ready® Instruction*

The tables below show the depth-of-knowledge (DOK) level for the items in the Interim Assessments, as well as the standard(s) addressed, and the corresponding *Ready® Instruction* lesson(s) being assessed by each item. Use this information to adjust lesson plans and focus remediation.

Question	DOK[1]	Standard(s)	Ready® Lesson(s)
Unit 1: Operations and Algebraic Thinking			
1	1	2.OA.C.4	5
2	2	2.OA.A.1	2
3	2	2.OA.B.2	3
4	1	2.OA.C.3	4
5	3	2.OA.A.1	2
6	3	2.OA.A.1, 2.OA.B.2, 2.NBT.B.5	1–6
Unit 2: Number and Operations in Base Ten			
1	1	2.NBT.A.4	12
2	2	2.NBT.B.7	13
3	2	2.NBT.B.7	14
4	2	2.NBT.B.7	14
5	2	2.NBT.A.1a, 2.NBT.A.1b, 2.NBT.A.2, 2.NBT.A.3	10, 11
6	3	2.NBT.A.1a, 2.NBT.A.1b, 2.NBT.A.3, 2.NBT.B.7	10–15
Unit 3: Measurement and Data			
1	2	2.MD.C.8, 2.NBT.A.2	25
2	2	2.MD.D.10	23
3	2	2.MD.B.5, 2.MD.B.6, 2.OA.A.1	21
4	2	2.MD.A.3	19
5	2	2.MD.C.7, 2.NBT.A.2	24
6	3	2.OA.A.1, 2.MD.A.1, 2.MD.A.2, 2.MD.D.9	16–18, 20–22

[1] Depth of Knowledge levels:

1. The item requires superficial knowledge of the standard.
2. The item requires processing beyond recall and observation.
3. The item requires explanation, generalization, and connection to other ideas.

Interim Assessment Correlations, *continued*

Question	DOK[1]	Standard(s)	*Ready*® Lesson(s)
Unit 4: Geometry			
1	2	2.G.A.2	27
2	2	2.G.A.3	28
3	2	2.G.A.1	26
4	2	2.G.A.2	27
5	3	2.G.A.3	28
6	3	2.G.A.3	28

[1]Depth of Knowledge levels:

1. The item requires superficial knowledge of the standard.
2. The item requires processing beyond recall and observation.
3. The item requires explanation, generalization, and connection to other ideas.

Supporting Research

References

Ball, D. L., Ferrini-Mundy, J., Kilpatrick, J., Milgram, R. J., Schmid, W., & Schaar, R. (2005). Reaching for common ground in K–12 mathematics education. *Notices of the American Mathematical Society, 52(9).*

Beed, P. L., Hawkins, E. M., & Roller, C. M. (1991). Moving learners toward independence: The power of scaffolded instruction. *The Reading Teacher, 44(9)*, 648–655.

Eastburn, J. A. (2011). The effects of a concrete, representational, abstract (CRA) instructional model on tier 2 first-grade math students in a response to intervention model: Educational implications for number sense and computational fluency. Dissertation. *ProQuest Information & Learning,* AAI3408708.

Furner, J. M., Yahya, N., & Duffy, M. L. (2005). 20 Ways to teach mathematics: strategies to reach all students. *Intervention in School and Clinic*, 41(1).

Hall, T., Strangman, N., & Meyer, A. (2003). Differentiated instruction and implications for UDL implementation. National Center on Accessing the General Curriculum. Accessed at: *http://aim.cast.org/learn/historyarchive/backgroundpapers/differentiated*

Hess, K. K., Carlock, D., Jones, B., & Walkup, J. R. (2009). *What exactly do "fewer, clearer, and higher standards" really look like in the classroom? Using a cognitive rigor matrix to analyze curriculum, plan lessons, and implement assessments.* Accessed at: *http://www.nciea.org/cgi-bin/pubspage.cgi?sortby=pub_date.*

National Council of Teachers of Mathematics. (2007). Effective strategies for teaching students with difficulties in mathematics.

———. (2008). Teaching mathematics to English language learners.

National Governors Association Center for Best Practices and Council of Chief State School Officers. (2010). *Common Core State Standards for Mathematics.* Accessed at: *http://www.corestandards.org/the-standards.*

———. (2012). *Publisher's Criteria for the Common Core State Standards in Mathematics, K–8.* Accessed at: *http://www.corestandards.org/resources.*

National Mathematics Advisory Panel. (2008). Foundations for success: The final report of the National Mathematics Advisory Panel. Accessed at: *http://www2.ed.gov/about/bdscomm/list/mathpanel/index.html.*

National Research Council. (2001). *Adding it Up: Helping Children Learn Mathematics.* Mathematics Learning Study Committee: Kilpatrick, J., Swafford, J., & Findell, B. (eds.). Washington, D.C.: National Academy Press.

Partnership for Assessment of Readiness for College and Careers. (2011). *PARCC model content frameworks: English language arts/literacy grades 3–11.* Accessed at: *http://www.parcconline.org/parcc-model-content-frameworks.*

Pashler, H., Bain, P., Bottge, B., Graesser, A., Koedinger, K., McDaniel, M., & Metcalfe, J. (2007). *Organizing instruction and study to improve student learning* (NCER 2007–2004). Washington, D.C.: National Center for Education Research, Institute of Education Sciences, U.S. Department of Education. Retrieved from *http://ies.ed.gov/ncer.*

Robertson, K. (2009). Math instruction for English language learners. *Colorìn Colorado!* Accessed at: *http://www.colorincolorado.org/article/30570/.*

Schmidt, W., Houang, R., & Cogan, L. (2002). A coherent curriculum, *American Educator,* Summer, 2002.

Seethaler, P. M., Fuchs, L. S., Fuchs, D., & Compton, D. L. (2012). Predicting first graders' development of calculation versus word-problem performance: the role of dynamic assessment. *Journal of Educational Psychology* 104(1), 224–234.

Smarter Balanced Assessment Consortium. (2012). *General Item Specifications.* Accessed at: *http://www. smarterbalanced. org/wordpress/wp-content/uploads/2012/05/TaskItemSpecifications/ItemSpecifications/GeneralItemSpecifications.pdf.*

Activity Sheets

These activity sheets are provided for use with a variety of activities in the **Ready**® Student Book and Teacher's Resource Book. These masters may be photocopied for classroom use. Refer to the activity in the lesson for a full list of materials and instructions.

Digit Cards

0	1	2	3
4	5	6	7
8	9	+	−
=	☐	<	>

Name _____

Hundreds Chart

1	2	3	4	5	6	7	8	9	10
11	12	13	14	15	16	17	18	19	20
21	22	23	24	25	26	27	28	29	30
31	32	33	34	35	36	37	38	39	40
41	42	43	44	45	46	47	48	49	50
51	52	53	54	55	56	57	58	59	60
61	62	63	64	65	66	67	68	69	70
71	72	73	74	75	76	77	78	79	80
81	82	83	84	85	86	87	88	89	90
91	92	93	94	95	96	97	98	99	100

1-Inch Grid Paper

1-Centimeter Grid Paper

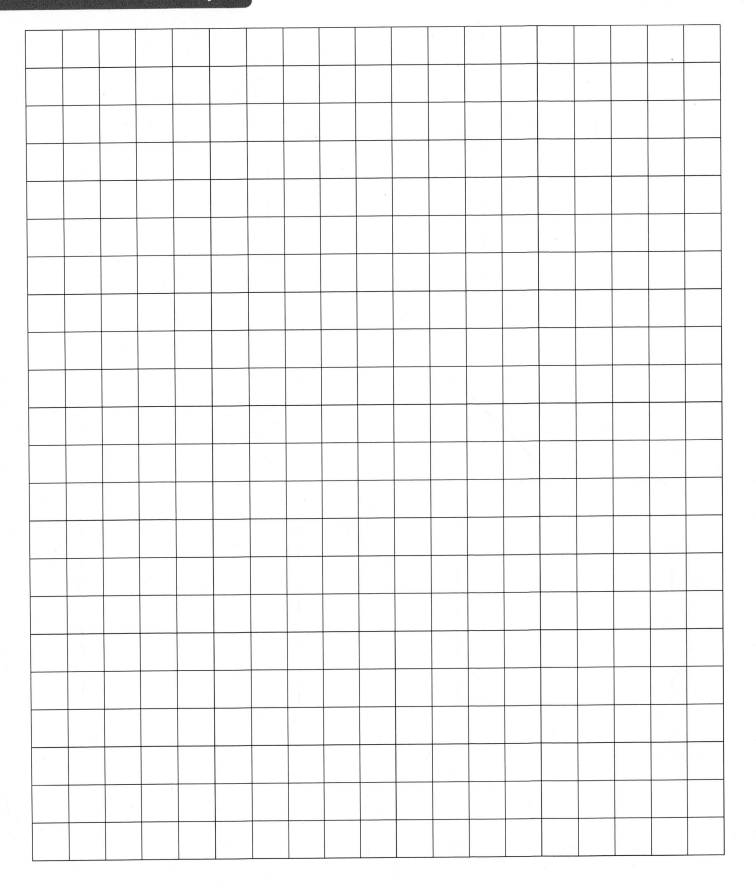

Number-Bond Mat

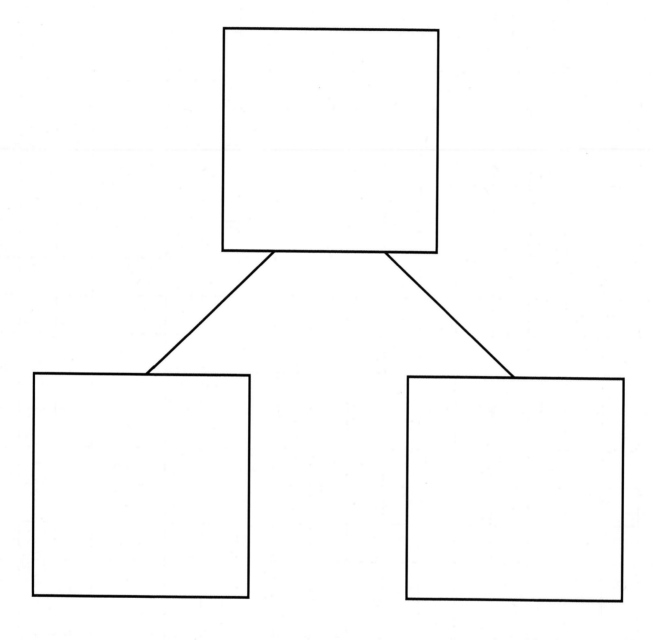

Place-Value Mat

		Hundreds
		Tens
		Ones

Name _____

301	456	729	128
988	506	222	438
793	650	114	269
834	940	175	407

AS8a

20	95	76	44
11	71	53	83
62	39	25	17
41	58	73	50

(continued on next page)

Name _____

99	78	36	26
19	47	68	91
54	12	30	84
32	65	56	24

Name _____

Measuring Worksheet

Measure each object.

1. Measure the stem.

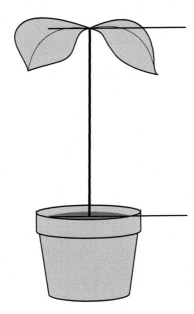

2. Measure the slanted side of the triangle.

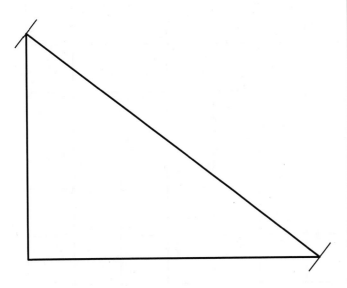

3. Measure the marker.

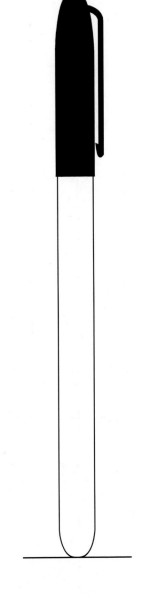

4. Measure the length of the paper clip.

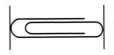

Half-Inch Grid Paper

Name _____

A 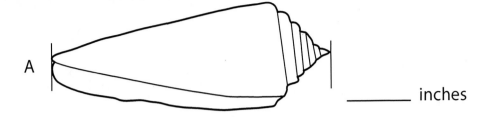 _____ inches

B  _____ inches

C  _____ inches

D  _____ inches

E 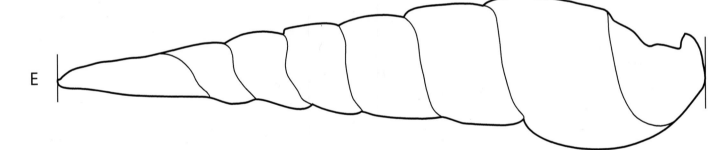 _____ inches

F  _____ inches

G 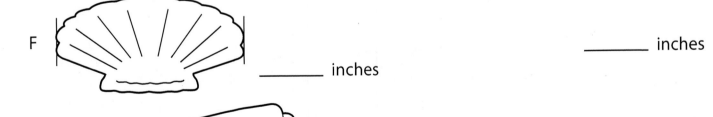 _____ inches

Name _____

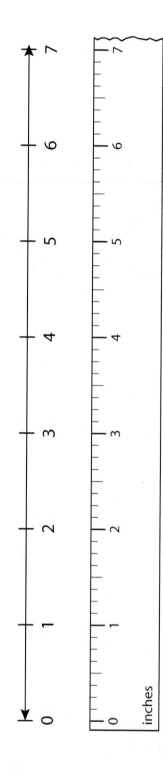

Name _____

Blank Number Lines

1	2	3	4
5	6	7	8
9	10	11	12
:	AM	PM	

(continued on next page)

Name _____

Digital Clock Cards

00	05	10	15
20	25	30	35
40	45	50	55

Name _____

55¢	38¢	4¢	92¢
49¢	7¢	50¢	61¢
70¢	25¢	13¢	84¢
10¢	15¢	98¢	1¢

Name _____

Triangle

Quadrilateral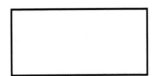

Rectangle

Square

Pentagon

Hexagon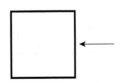

Side

Angle

©Curriculum Associates, LLC   Copying is permitted for classroom use

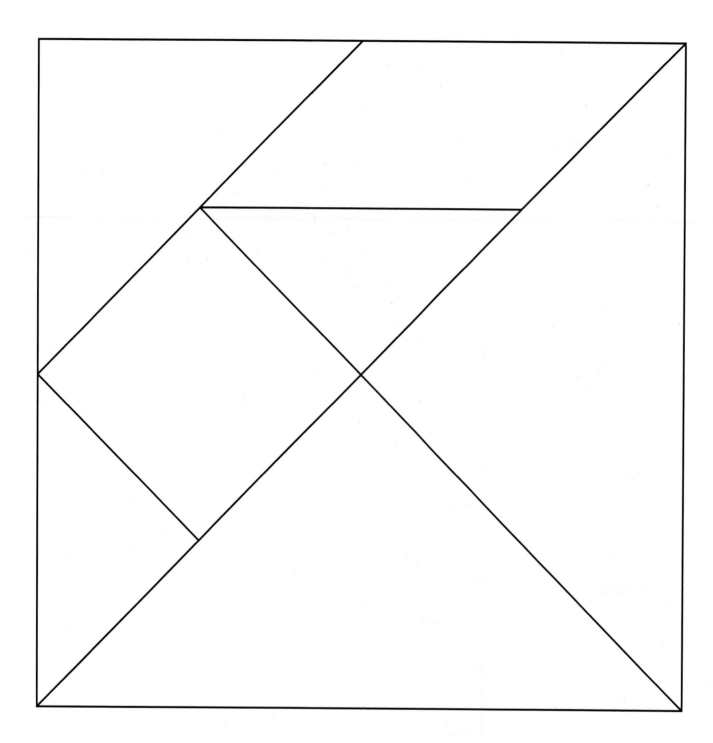

Shapes for Tiling

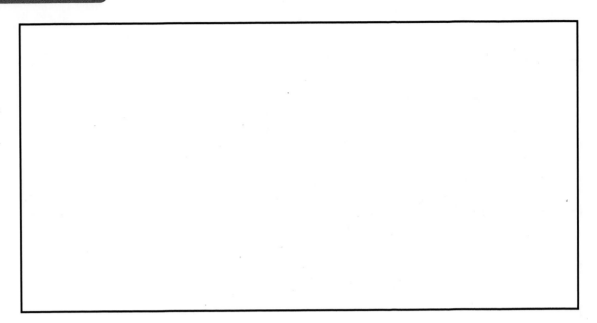

2-Inch Grid Paper

Name _____

Dot Paper

Name _____

Solution Sheet 1

I know . . .

_____

_____

_____

I need to find . . .

_____

_____

_____

I can find the solution by . . .

_____

_____

_____

I know my solution works . . .

_____

_____

_____

Solution Sheet 2

I know . . . _____

_____

I need to find . . . _____

_____

I can find the solution by . . . _____

_____

I know my solution works . . . _____

_____

Cutting Cakes

Name _____

(continued on next page)

Name _____

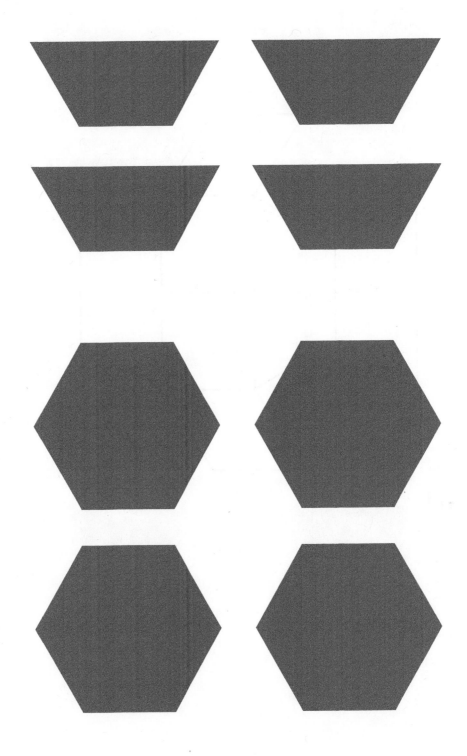

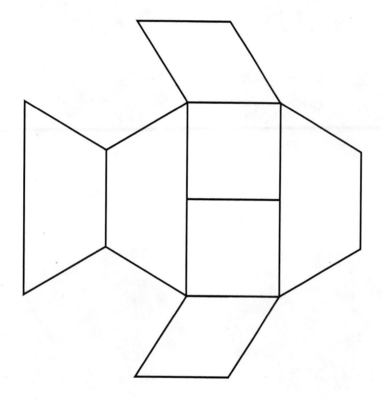

Name _____

Design 1

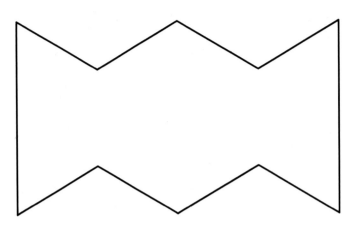

Design 2

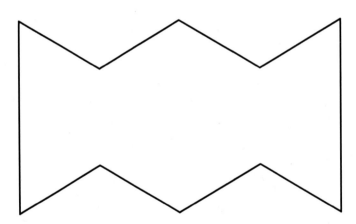

AS27